Windows PowerShell in Action

Windows PowerShell in Action

Bruce Payette

MANNING

Greenwich
(74° w. long.)

For online information and ordering of this and other Manning books, please go to
www.manning.com. The publisher offers discounts on this book when ordered in quantity.
For more information, please contact:

Special Sales Department
Manning Publications
Sound View Court 3B   Fax: (609) 877-8256
Greenwich, CT 06830   email: orders@manning.com

Manning Publications Co.   Copyeditor: Benjamin Berg
Sound View Court 3B   Typesetter: Gordan Salinovic
Greenwich, CT 06830   Cover designer: Leslie Haimes

ISBN 1932394-90-7

Printed in the United States of America
1 2 3 4 5 6 7 8 9 10 – MAL – 11 10 09 08 07

To my wife, Tina, for all her love and support

brief contents

contents

foreword

Windows PowerShell has the widest range of any language I know. You can quickly learn the basic concepts and use it as an interactive command line shell to write simple, ad hoc scripts. Learn a bit more and you can use it to write rich, sophisticated scripts to manage your most important production servers. Learn a bit more still, and you can write .NET programs to access the awesome power of the .NET frameworks.

When we started to develop PowerShell, I was advised to deliver an interactive shell or scripting language and to avoid .NET programming, because C# and VB.NET had that covered. This had been the standard approach of every OS in the last 30 years. I knew that we could do better. A new architecture based upon a deep rethink of the problem to provide our customers with a single solution which would do the following:

- Allow beginners a quick start and the ability to become advanced users over time, enhancing their careers and salary potential.

- Let advanced users use it in lightweight, ad hoc ways for simple problems and in sophisticated, production-oriented ways for complex problems.

- Create a large community of beginners and advanced users to share experiences, approaches, and scripts.

- Create a large ecosystem which would increase the opportunities for job hunters as well as increase the hiring pool for employers.

Designing and implementing a solution that could do all that was challenging. At times, we had to make some difficult choices, but we were on a mission and we stuck to our vision. This is where Bruce Payette comes in. Bruce is a founding member of the PowerShell team and the development leader of the PowerShell language. I paired Bruce with Jim Truher, a Program Manager (PM) and another founding member of the team. As a PM, Jim was the advocate for the user and the voice of sanity. Bruce and Jim worked incredibly well together, producing the PowerShell language and addressing the many problems that came up. Bruce is a walking encyclopedia of every good, bad, solid, and wacky language idea that has been tried in the last few decades. As issues came up, Bruce explained how the different languages addressed similar issues, where and why they worked well, or failed. Bruce was crucial in solving the problems we encountered and in fulfilling our ambitious goals.

Since PowerShell is new, we know that you will have to invest time to learn it. When we added a new concept, technique, or syntax, we did so in a way that allows you to reuse that element everywhere so you can minimize the number of things to learn and maximize the value of each one.

One of my favorite jokes goes like this: Two guys are in the woods when they encounter a bear who decides to eat them for lunch. They are about to run away when one of them stops to put on a pair of running shoes. His buddy informs him that bears can run over 30 mph and that there is no way he can outrun it, even with running shoes. His friend replies, "I don't have to out-run the bear, I just have to outrun you."

It is often difficult to understand something you see or read until you understand what motivated it. One of reasons I love Bruce's book is that, in addition to providing a great language reference, it provides a clear description of the motivations and the thinking behind the language. This is a book that only Bruce could have written.

JEFFREY SNOVER
Windows PowerShell Architect

preface

Wow, I wrote a book! How the heck did that happen? One moment you're a humble programming language designer, and the next you're up until 2 a.m. every night trying to figure out how to say "and in the next example" 500 times without being boring.

So why write it? Because of PowerShell. Although PowerShell draws heavily from existing technologies, it combines them in novel ways. This novelty leads to misunderstandings, which then turn into urban myths, such as, PowerShell does X because its designers are kitten-eating aliens.

Trust me–we're not.

As we showed our work to the world (three public betas and two release candidates), I found that there were a few questions that were being asked over and over again. These questions would arise as a result of an earlier language experience that the user had had. Typically, a simple explanation was all it took to clear up the confusion (we had a very smart group of beta testers). However, we couldn't keep answering these questions one-by-one; that just wouldn't scale. There needed to be a way to gather the information in one place. This book is my attempt to do just that.

The other astonishing thing was just how much power comes out of the synergy of the technologies underlying PowerShell. We saw this in our own internal uses of PowerShell as well as in some of the community examples. The PowerShell team read people's blogs and was astonished by the creativity that was being demonstrated. So the second goal of this book is to foster that creativity by conveying how capable PowerShell is.

Finally, this is the book I had always wanted to *read* myself. I love programming languages and reading about them, and the best programming books I found are the ones that explain not only "what" but also "why." Look at the books that continue to sell year after year, like Kernighan and Ritchie's *The C Programming Language*, Stroustrup's C++ book, and Ousterhout's TCL book. The TCL book is a very good example: it describes an early version of the TCL language, it has never been updated, yet it continues to sell. Why? This book, and others like it, give the reader something more than just technical detail. They convey a sense of the overall design as well as some of the intent of the designer. So please let me know if you think I succeed in doing that with this book, OK?

The very last goal of the book was to help build and maintain momentum around PowerShell. PowerShell was released around the time of Microsoft's biggest product release ever: the revamped operating system Vista together with the new Office suite (with all those wild graphical 3D doo-hickeys added everywhere). But we're just a command line. There is a good rule to follow when planning a product launch: never open a lemonade stand next to a Wal-Mart. But we did, and now…would you care for some lemonade?

Come on in, learn PowerShell, be creative, and, above all, have fun!

acknowledgments

This book is for my wife, Tina. It literally wouldn't exist without her patience, support, and encouragement. She kept me fed, sane, and she even read early drafts of material about which she knows nothing. Now that's support! She also contributed the Gnome picture in chapter 13 and the bird-watching information and pictures in chapter 2.

Thanks to my parents for their love and support over the years. Yes, I am finally done with the book.

Of course there wouldn't be a PowerShell book without a PowerShell product in the first place, and PowerShell wouldn't exist without the vision of its chief architect, Jeffrey Snover. Special thanks to Jeffrey for reviewing the manuscript and for agreeing to write the foreword to the book.

Another other major contributor was Jim Truher, my co-conspirator in the PowerShell language design. Yes, it's our fault.

I'd like to thank the rest of PowerShell language team: George Xie, Marcel Ortiz Soto (test-dude extraordinaire), and Wei Wu, all of whom contributed enormously to the project. Kaushik Pushpavanam, one of the original PowerShell team members, gets major props for introducing a unit test framework into the PowerShell development process early and then getting the developers to use it and write tests. This gave us the freedom and agility to listen to customers and incorporate changes throughout the development process. Thanks to Hilal Al-Hilali for knowing how to ship; he's a mean man with a theme. Thanks to Charlie Chase for winning. PowerShell team members Arul Kumaravel and Abhishek Agrawal contributed significantly to the COM and WMI examples in chapter 12. (Arul wrote the COM support, so who could have been better?)

Thanks also to all of the reviewers of the manuscript in its many stages of development: Jeffrey Copeland, Arul Kumaravel, Rene Gobeyn, Jeffrey Snover, Steve Simmons, Keith Hill, Oliver Sturm, Thomas Restrepro, Anil Radhakrishna, Alex K. Angelopoulos, David McMahon, Curt Christianson, Anderson Patricio, Jon Skeet, and Robert. W. Anderson. A special thanks to Alex Angelopolous who did the final technical review of the book. I'd also like to thank all of the participants in the Manning Early Access Program. You guys rock! Much appreciation to everyone at Manning, starting with my publisher Marjan Bace, my editor Michael Stephens, my development editors Betsey Henkels and Jackie Carter, and all the production staff for their hard work and patience with a new author.

Finally, I want to thank my friend and mentor David Tillbrook for never being satisfied with the merely adequate. He has a lot to teach us all.

about this book

Windows PowerShell is the next-generation shell and scripting environment created by Microsoft. It's intended to fix the weaknesses in existing Windows command-line and scripting solutions. The driving force behind its creation was the need to address the problems in automating Windows system management. Windows lacked the ad hoc management capabilities found in many competing systems. With PowerShell's comprehensive support for .NET, it now has broad application potential beyond the system administration space. PowerShell can be used for text processing, general scripting, build management, creating test frameworks, and so on.

This book is written by one of principal creators of PowerShell. It uses many examples, both small and large, to illustrate the features of the language and its environment and shows how to compose those features into solutions, quickly and effectively.

Because of the broad focus of the PowerShell product, the book has a commensurately broad focus. It was not designed as a cookbook of preconstructed management examples, such as how to deal with Active Directory or how to script Exchange. Instead, it provides information about the core of the PowerShell runtime and how to compose solutions in the "PowerShell Way." After reading this book, the reader should be able to take any example written in other languages, such as C# or Visual Basic, and leverage those examples to build solutions in PowerShell. (To facilitate this, appendix A in the book includes a number of discussions about the differences between PowerShell and other languages.)

The other thing this book doesn't cover is the PowerShell SDK. PowerShell is both a hostable (that is, it can be embedded in other applications) as well as an extensible environment. This book doesn't address these topics. Instead, it focuses on the shell user and scripter. Though we do explain how to load and use .NET assemblies from a PowerShell script in chapter 11.

Who should read this book?

This book is designed for anyone who wants to learn PowerShell *and use it well*. Rather than being a book of recipes, this book tries to give the reader deep knowledge about how PowerShell works and how to apply it. All users of PowerShell will find this book beneficial and useful.

If you're a Windows sysadmin, this book is for you. If you're a developer and you need to get things done in a hurry, if you're interested in .NET, or just if you like to experiment with computers, PowerShell is for you—and this book is for you!

Roadmap

The book is divided into two and a half parts. The two major parts of the book are "Learning PowerShell" and "Using PowerShell," described below. The "half" part is primarily appendix B which contains examples showing how to use PowerShell to solve system administration problems. In appendix A we provide comparisons between PowerShell and other languages. Finally, in appendix C we present the grammar for the PowerShell language.

Part 1 "Learning PowerShell" is a comprehensive tour of the PowerShell language and runtime. The goal is to introduce new PowerShell users to the language as well as to provide experienced users with deep insight into how and why things are the way they are.

In part 1 we look at all aspects of the PowerShell language, including the syntax, the type system, and so on. Along the way, we'll present examples showing how each feature works. Since the goal of the first part of the book is to focus on the individual features of the environment, most of the examples are small and are intended to be entered in an interactive session. The second part of this book focuses on larger examples that bring the individual features together to build larger applications.

Chapter 1 begins with some history and the rationale for why PowerShell was created in the first place, followed by a quick tour of the features of the environment. The remaining chapters in part 1 cover each element of the language, starting with basic PowerShell concepts in chapter 2.

Chapter 3 introduces the PowerShell type system and its relationship to .NET. This chapter also presents the syntax for each of the PowerShell literal data types.

The discussion of operators and expressions (PowerShell has lots of these) begins in chapter 4, which covers the basic arithmetic, comparison, and assignment operators. It also covers the wildcard and regular expression pattern matching operators.

Chapter 5 continues the discussion of operators with the advanced operations for working with arrays (indexing and slicing) and objects (properties and methods). It also covers output redirection and the formatting operator, and introduces PowerShell variables.

Chapter 6 covers the PowerShell language constructs such as `if` statement and loops.

Chapter 7 introduces programming in PowerShell and covers functions and scripts, variable scoping, and other programming-related topics.

Chapter 8 builds on the material in chapter 7 and introduces advanced programming techniques, such as object construction and extensions. It also covers first-class functions (scriptblocks) and shows how to extend the PowerShell language using these features.

Chapter 9 completes part 1, covering the features available in PowerShell for handling errors and debugging scripts.

In part 2 of the book, we shift our focus from individual features toward combining those features into larger examples. This part of the book looks at applying PowerShell in specific technology areas and problem domains.

We begin in chapter 10, looking at how PowerShell can be used to attack the kind of text processing tasks that have been the traditional domain of languages such as Perl. This chapter begins with basic string processing, then introduces file processing (including handling binary files), and finishes up with a section on working with XML documents.

Then, in chapter 11, we look at how we can discover and apply the vast capabilities of the .NET framework from .NET. We cover locating, exploring, and instantiating types in the .NET framework, including generic types. Then we look at a number of applications using these types, including network programming and graphical programming with WinForms.

In chapter 12, we look at how to use and apply other Microsoft object technologies, specifically COM and WMI. This includes using the application automation models to script applications such as Microsoft Word using PowerShell. We look at how to use WMI from the command line and in scripts to inspect, update, and manage a Windows system. We also spend some time looking at how to interact with VBScript, Microsoft's previous-generation scripting tool.

Finally, in chapter 13, we introduce the security features in PowerShell, along with a general discussion of security. This is an important chapter to read. Like all powerful scripting tools (Perl, Python, and so forth), PowerShell can be used to create *malware* such as virus and worm programs. The PowerShell runtime contains features which allow you to deploy it in a manner that minimizes these risks.

That covers two out of the two and a half parts. Since the examples in part 2 of the book, while larger, still focus on particular technology areas, we have appendix B, which presents examples where we solve some common system administration tasks using PowerShell. While it's not a complete management cookbook, it does show what can be done with PowerShell and how to do it.

In appendix A we present comparisons of PowerShell with other programming or scripting languages, including cmd.exe, UNIX shells, and VBScript. This appendix includes tips for experienced users and highlights some potential problems users of other languages may run into with PowerShell. Finally, appendix C contains the annotated grammar and tokenization rules for the PowerShell language along with syntax examples.

Code conventions

Since PowerShell is an interactive environment, we'll show a lot of example commands as the user would type them, followed by the responses the system generates. Before the command text, there will be a prompt string that looks like this: PS (2) >. Following the prompt, the actual command will be displayed in **bold font**. PowerShell's responses will follow on the next few lines. Since PowerShell doesn't display anything in front of the output lines, you can distinguish output from commands by looking for the prompt string. These conventions are illustrated as follows:

```
PS (1) > get-date
```

```
Sunday, October 08, 2006 11:24:42 PM
```

Sometimes commands will span multiple lines. In this case, subsequent lines of user input will be preceded by >> as shown:

```
PS (2) > 1..3 |
>> foreach {"+" * $_}
>>
+
```

```
++
+++
PS (4) >
```

Note that the actual prompt sequence you see in your PowerShell session will be somewhat different than what is shown in the book. The prompt display is user-controllable by redefining the prompt function (see section A.1.8 for more information). For this book, a prompt sequence was chosen that includes command numbers to make it easier to follow the examples.

Source code for all of the examples used in this book can be downloaded from the publisher's website at www.manning.com/payette.

Author Online

Purchase of *Windows PowerShell in Action* includes free access to a private web forum run by Manning Publications where you can make comments about the book, ask technical questions, and receive help from the author and from other users. To access the forum and subscribe to it, point your web browser to www.manning.com/payette. This page provides information on how to get on the forum once you are registered, what kind of help is available, and the rules of conduct on the forum. Manning's commitment to our readers is to provide a venue where a meaningful dialog between individual readers and between readers and the author can take place. It is not a commitment to any specific amount of participation on the part of the author, whose contribution to the AO remains voluntary (and unpaid). We suggest you try asking the author some challenging questions, lest his interest stray! The Author Online forum and the archives of previous discussions will be accessible from the publisher's website as long as the book is in print.

About the author

BRUCE PAYETTE is one of the founding members of the Windows PowerShell team. He is co-designer of the PowerShell language along with Jim Truher, and is the principal author of the language implementation. He joined Microsoft in 2001, working on Interix—the POSIX subsystem for Windows—and then moved to help found the PowerShell project shortly thereafter. Prior to joining Microsoft, he worked at various companies including Softway (the creators of Interix) and MKS (producers of the MKS Toolkit) building UNIX tools for Windows. He lives in Bellevue, Washington, with his wife, many computers, and three extremely over-bonded and very spoiled cats.

About the title

By combining introductions, overviews, and how-to examples, the *In Action* books are designed to help learning *and* remembering. According to research in cognitive science, the things people remember are things they discover during self-motivated exploration.

Although no one at Manning is a cognitive scientist, we are convinced that for learning to become permanent, it must pass through stages of exploration, play, and, interestingly, retelling of what is being learned. People understand and remember new things, which is to say they master them, only after actively exploring them. Humans learn *in action*. An essential part of an *In Action* guide is that it is example-driven. It encourages the reader to try things out, to play with new code, and explore new ideas.

There is another, more mundane, reason for the title of this book: our readers are busy. They use books to do a job or solve a problem. They need books that allow them to jump in and jump out easily and learn just what they want just when they want it. They need books that aid them *in action*. The books in this series are designed for such readers.

About the cover illustration

The figure on the cover of *Windows PowerShell* in Action is a "Mufti, the chief of religion," or the chief scholar who interpreted the religious law and whose pronouncements on matters both large and small were binding to the faithful. The illustration is taken from a collection of costumes of the Ottoman Empire published on January 1, 1802, by William Miller of Old Bond Street, London. The title page is missing from the collection and we have been unable to track it down to date. The book's table of contents identifies the figures in both English and French, and each illustration bears the names of two artists who worked on it, both of whom would no doubt be surprised to find their art gracing the front cover of a computer programming book...two hundred years later.

The collection was purchased by a Manning editor at an antiquarian flea market in the "Garage" on West 26th Street in Manhattan. The seller was an American based in Ankara, Turkey, and the transaction took place just as he was packing up his stand for the day. The Manning editor did not have on his person the substantial amount of cash that was required for the purchase and a credit card and check were both politely turned down. With the seller flying back to Ankara that evening the situation was getting hopeless. What was the solution? It turned out to be nothing more than an old-fashioned verbal agreement sealed with a handshake. The seller simply proposed that the money be transferred to him by wire and the editor walked out with the bank information on a piece of paper and the portfolio of images under his arm. Needless to say, we transferred the funds the next day, and we remain grateful and impressed by this unknown person's trust in one of us. It recalls something that might have happened a long time ago.

The pictures from the Ottoman collection, like the other illustrations that appear on our covers, bring to life the richness and variety of dress customs of two centuries ago. They recall the sense of isolation and distance of that period—and of every other historic period except our own hyperkinetic present.

Dress codes have changed since then and the diversity by region, so
rich at the time, has faded away. It is now often hard to tell the inhabitant of one continent from another. Perhaps, trying to view it optimistically, we have traded a cultural and visual diversity for a more varied personal life. Or a more varied and interesting intellectual and technical life. We at Manning celebrate the inventiveness, the initiative, and, yes, the fun of the computer business with book covers based on the rich diversity of regional life of two centuries ago, brought back to life by the pictures from this collection.

Learning PowerShell

This book is composed of two parts. Part 1 is a comprehensive tour of the Power-Shell language and runtime. The goal is to introduce new PowerShell users to the language as well as provide experienced users with deep insight into how and why things are the way they are. Part 2 focuses on larger examples that bring the individual features together to build larger applications.

In part 1, we'll look at all aspects of the PowerShell language, including the syntax and the type system. Along the way, we'll present examples showing how each feature works. Since the goal of this part of the book is to focus on the individual features of the environment, most examples are quite small and are intended to be entered in an interactive session.

Chapter 1 begins with history and rationale for why PowerShell was created. It then proceeds through a tour of the features of the environment. The remaining chapters in part 1 touch on each element of the language, starting with the basic concepts (chapter 2), then continuing through types (chapter 3), operators and expressions (chapters 4 and 5), language constructs such as flow control statements (chapter 6), and functions and scripts (chapter 7). Chapter 8 covers advanced programming techniques and constructing objects, and chapter 9 covers PowerShell features for handling errors and debugging scripts.

C H A P T E R   1

Welcome to PowerShell

*Space is big. Really big. You just won't believe how vastly hugely
mind-bogglingly big it is. I mean you may think it's a long way down
the road to the chemist, but that's just peanuts compared to space.*
Don't Panic.
> —Douglas Adams, *The Hitchhiker's Guide to the Galaxy*

Welcome to Windows PowerShell, the new command and scripting language from
Microsoft. We begin this chapter with two quotes from *The Hitchhiker's Guide to the
Galaxy*. What do they have to do with a new scripting language? In essence, where a
program solves a particular problem or problems, a programming language can solve
any problem, at least in theory. That's the "big, really big" part. The "Don't Panic" bit
is, well—don't panic. While PowerShell is new and different, it has been designed to
leverage what you already know, making it easy to learn. It's also designed to allow
you to learn it a bit at a time. Starting at the beginning, here's the traditional "Hello
world" program in PowerShell.

```
"Hello world."
```

As you can see, no panic needed. But "Hello world" by itself is not really very interesting. Here's something a bit more complicated:

```
dir $env:windir\*.log | select-string -List error |
format-table path,linenumber -auto
```

Although this is more complex, you can probably still figure out what it does. It searches all the log files in the Windows directory, looking for the string "error", then prints the full name of the matching file and the matching line number. "Useful, but not very special," you might think, because you can easily do this using cmd.exe on Windows or bash on UNIX. So what about the "big, really big" thing? Well, how about this example?

```
([xml](new-object net.webclient).DownloadString(
"http://blogs.msdn.com/powershell/rss.aspx"
)).rss.channel.item | format-table title,link
```

Now we're getting somewhere. This script downloads the RSS feed from the PowerShell team weblog, and then displays the title and a link for each blog entry.

> **NOTE** RSS stands for Really Simple Syndication. This is a mechanism that allows programs to download web logs automatically so they can be read more conveniently than in the browser.

By the way, you weren't really expected to figure this example out yet. If you did, you can move to the head of the class!

Finally, one last example:

```
[void][reflection.assembly]::LoadWithPartialName(
    "System.Windows.Forms")
$form = new-object Windows.Forms.Form
$form.Text = "My First Form"
$button = new-object Windows.Forms.Button
$button.text="Push Me!"
$button.Dock="fill"
$button.add_click({$form.close()})
$form.controls.add($button)
$form.Add_Shown({$form.Activate()})
$form.ShowDialog()
```

This script uses the Windows Forms library (WinForms) to build a graphical user interface (GUI) that has a single button displaying the text "Push Me". The window this script creates is shown in figure 1.1.

When you click the button, it closes the form and exits the script. With this you go from "Hello world" to a GUI application in less than two pages.

Now let's come back down to earth for minute. The intent of chapter 1 is to set the stage for understanding

Figure 1.1 **When you run the code from the example, this window will be displayed. If you don't see it, it may be hidden behind another window.**

PowerShell—what it is, what it isn't and, almost as important—why we made the decisions we made in designing the PowerShell language. Chapter 1 covers the goals of the project along with some of the major issues we faced in trying to achieve those goals. By the end of the chapter you should have a solid base from which to start learning and using PowerShell to solve real-world problems. Of course all theory and no practice is boring, so the chapter concludes with a number of small examples to give you a feel for PowerShell. But first, a philosophical digression: while under development, the code-name for this project was Monad. The name Monad comes from *The Monadology* by Gottfried Wilhelm Leibniz, one of the inventors of calculus. Here is how Leibniz defined the Monad, "The Monad, of which we shall here speak, is nothing but a simple substance, which enters into compounds. By 'simple' is meant 'without parts.'"

In *The Monadology*, Leibniz described a world of irreducible components from which all things could be composed. This captures the spirit of the project: to create a toolkit of simple pieces that you compose to create complex solutions.

1.1 WHAT IS POWERSHELL?

What is PowerShell and why was it created? As we said, PowerShell is the new command-line/scripting environment from Microsoft. The overall goal for this project was to *provide the best shell scripting environment possible for Microsoft Windows*. This statement has two parts, and they are equally important, as the goal was not just to produce a good generic shell environment, but rather to produce one designed specifically for the Windows environment. While drawing heavily from existing command-line shell and scripting languages, the PowerShell language and runtime were designed from scratch to be an optimal environment for the modern Windows operating system.

Historically, the Windows command line has been weak. This is mainly the result of the early focus in Microsoft on computing for the average user, who is neither particularly technical nor particularly interested in computers. Most of the development effort for Windows was put into improving the graphical environment for the non-technical user, rather than creating an environment for the computer professional. Although this was certainly an enormously successful commercial strategy for Microsoft, it has left some segments of the community under-served.

In the next couple of sections, we'll go over some of the other environmental forces that led to the creation of PowerShell. By environmental forces, we mean the various business pressures and practical requirements that needed to be satisfied. But first we'll refine our definitions of *shell* and *scripting*.

1.1.1 Shells, command-lines, and scripting languages

In the previous section, we called PowerShell a command-line shell. You may be asking, what is a shell? And how is that different from a command interpreter? What about scripting languages? If you can script in a shell language, doesn't that make it a scripting language? In answering these questions, let's start with shells.

Defining what a shell is can be a bit tricky, especially at Microsoft, since pretty much everything at Microsoft has something called a shell. Windows Explorer is a shell. Even the Xbox has a shell. Historically, the term *shell* describes the piece of software that sits over an operating system's core functionality. This core functionality is known as the operating system kernel (shell... kernel... get it?). A shell is the piece of software that lets you access the functionality provided by the operating system. Windows Explorer is properly called a shell because it lets you access the functionality of a Windows system. For our purposes, though, we're more interested in the traditional text-based environment where the user types a command and receives a response. In other words, a shell is a command-line interpreter. The two terms can be used for the most part interchangeably.

If this is the case, then what is scripting and why are scripting languages not shells? To some extent, there isn't really a difference. Many scripting languages have a mode in which they take commands from the user and then execute those commands to return results. This mode of operation is called a Read-Evaluate-Print loop or *REP* loop. Not all scripting languages have these interactive loops, but many do. In what way is a scripting language with a REP loop not a shell? The difference is mainly in the user experience. A proper command-line shell is also a proper user interface. As such, a command line has to provide a number of features to make the user's experience pleasant and customizable. The features that improve the user's experience include aliases (shortcuts for hard-to-type commands), wildcard matching so you don't have to type out full names, and the ability to start other programs without having to do anything special such as calling a function to start the program. Finally, command-line shells provide mechanisms for examining, editing, and re-executing previously typed commands. These mechanisms are called *command history*.

If scripting languages can be shells, can shells be scripting languages? The answer is, emphatically, yes. With each generation, the UNIX shell languages have grown more and more powerful. It's entirely possible to write substantial applications in a modern shell language, such as bash or zsh. Scripting languages characteristically have an advantage over shell languages, in that they provide mechanisms to help you develop larger scripts by letting you break a script into components or *modules*. Scripting languages typically provide more sophisticated features for debugging your scripts. Next, scripting language runtimes are implemented in a way that makes their code execution more efficient, so that scripts written in these languages execute more quickly than they would in the corresponding shell script runtime. Finally, scripting language syntax is oriented more toward writing an application than toward interactively issuing commands.

In the end, there really is no hard and fast distinction between a shell language and a scripting language. Some of the features that make a good scripting language result in a poor shell user experience. Conversely, some of the features that make for a good interactive shell experience can interfere with scripting. Since PowerShell's goal is to be both a good scripting language and a good interactive shell, balancing the trade-offs between user-experience and scripting authoring was one of the major language design challenges.

1.1.2 Why a new shell? Why now?

In the early part of this decade, Microsoft commissioned a study to identify areas where it could improve its offerings in the server space. Server management, and particularly command-line management of Windows systems, were called out as areas for improvement. While some might say that this is like discovering that water is wet, the important point is that people cared about the problem. When comparing the command-line manageability of a Windows system to a UNIX system, Windows was found to be limited, and this was a genuine pain point with customers.

There are a number of reasons for the historically weak Windows command line. First, as mentioned previously, limited effort had been put into improving the command line. Since the average desktop user doesn't care about the command line, it wasn't considered important. Secondly, when writing graphical user interfaces, you need to access whatever you're managing through programmer-style interfaces called *Application Programmer Interfaces (APIs)*. APIs are almost universally binary (especially on Windows), and binary interfaces are not command-line friendly.

Another factor is that, as Windows acquired more and more subsystems and features, the number of issues you had to think about when managing a system increased dramatically. To deal with this increase in complexity, the manageable elements were factored into structured data objects. This collection of management objects is known internally at Microsoft as the Windows management surface. While this factoring addressed overall complexity and worked well for graphical interfaces, it made it much harder to work with using a traditional text-based shell environment.

Finally, as the power of the PC increased, Windows began to move off the desktop and into the corporate data center. In the corporate data center, you have a large number of servers to manage, and the graphical point-and-click management approach that worked well for one machine doesn't scale. All these elements combined to make it clear that Microsoft could no longer ignore the command line.

1.1.3 The last mile problem

Why do we care about command-line management and automation? Because it helps to solve the Information Technology professional's version of the last mile problem. The last mile problem is a classical problem that comes from the telecommunications industry. It goes like this: the telecom industry can effectively amortize its infrastructure costs across all its customers until it gets to the *last mile* where the service is finally run to an individual location. Installing service across this last mile can't be amortized because it serves only a single location. Also, what's involved in servicing any particular location can vary significantly. Servicing a rural farmhouse is different and significantly more expensive than running service to a house on a city street.

In the Information Technology (IT) industry, the last mile problem is figuring out how to manage each IT installation effectively and economically. Even a small IT environment has a wide variety of equipment and applications. One approach to solving this is through consulting: IT vendors provide consultants who build custom last-mile solutions for each end-user. This, of course, has problems with recurring costs and scalability (it's great for the vendor, though). A better solution for end-users is to empower them to solve their own last mile problems. We do this by providing a toolkit to enable end-users to build their own custom solutions. This toolkit can't merely be the same tools used to build the overall infrastructure as the level of detail required is too great. Instead, you need a set of tools with a higher level of abstraction. This is where PowerShell comes in—its higher-level abstractions allow you to connect the various bits of your IT environment together more quickly and with less effort.

Now that we understand the environmental forces that led to the creation of PowerShell, the need for command-line automation in a distributed object-based operating environment, let's look at the form the solution took.

1.2   SOUL OF A NEW LANGUAGE

The title of this section was adapted from Tracey Kidder's *Soul of a New Machine*, one of the best non-technical technical books ever written. Kidder's book described how Data General developed a new 32-bit minicomputer, the Eclipse, in a single year. At that time, 32-bit minicomputers were not just new computers; they represented a whole new class of computers. It was a bold, ambitious project; many considered it crazy. Likewise, the PowerShell project is not just about creating a new shell language. We are developing a new class of object-based shell languages. And we've been told more than a few times that we were crazy.

In this section, we're going to cover some of the technological forces that shaped the development of PowerShell. A unique set of customer requirements in tandem with the arrival of the new .NET wave of tools at Microsoft led to this revolution in shell languages.

1.2.1   Learning from history

In section 1.1.2, we described why Microsoft needed to improve the command line. Now let's talk about *how* we decided to improve it. In particular, let's talk about why we created a new language. This is certainly one of the most common questions people ask about PowerShell (right after "What, are you guys nuts?"). People ask "why not just use one of the UNIX shells?" or "why not extend the existing Windows command line?"

In practice, we did start with an existing shell language. We began with the shell grammar for the POSIX standard shell defined in IEEE Specification 1003.2. The POSIX shell is a mature command-line environment available on a huge variety of platforms. including Microsoft Windows. It's based on a subset of the UNIX Korn shell, which is itself a superset of the original Bourne shell. Starting with the POSIX shell gave us a well-specified and stable base. Then we had to consider how to accommodate the differences that properly supporting the Windows environment would entail. We wanted to have a shell optimized for the Windows environment in the same way that the UNIX shells are optimized for this UNIX environment.

To begin with, traditional shells deal only with strings. Even numeric operations work by turning a string into a number, performing the operation, and then turning it back into a string. Given that a core goal for PowerShell was to preserve the structure of the Windows data types, we couldn't simply use the POSIX shell language as is. This factor impacted the language design more than any other. Next, we wanted to support a more conventional scripting experience where, for example, expressions could be used as you would normally use them in a scripting language such as VBScript, Perl, or Python. With a more natural expression syntax, it would be easier to work with the Windows management objects. Now we just had to decide how to make those objects available to the shell.

1.2.2 Leveraging .NET

One of the biggest challenges in developing any computer language is deciding how to represent data in that language. For PowerShell, the key decision was to leverage the .NET object model. .NET is a unifying object representation that is being used across all of the groups at Microsoft. It is a hugely ambitious project that has taken years to come to fruition. By having this common data model, all the components in Windows can share and understand each other's data.

One of .NET's most interesting features for PowerShell is that the .NET object model is *self-describing*. By this, we mean that the object itself contains the information that describes the object's structure. This is important for an interactive environment, as you need to be able to look at an object and see what you can do with it. For example, if PowerShell receives an event object from the system event log, the user can simply inspect the object to see that it has a data stamp indicating when the event was generated.

Traditional text-based shells facilitate inspection because everything is text. Text is great—what you see is what you get. Unfortunately, what you see is *all* you get. You can't pull off many interesting tricks with text until you turn it into something else. For example, if you want to find out the total size of a set of files, you can get a directory listing, which looks something like the following:

```
02/26/2004  10:58 PM              45,452 Q810833.log
02/26/2004  10:59 PM              47,808 Q811493.log
02/26/2004  10:59 PM              48,256 Q811630.log
02/26/2004  11:00 PM              50,681 Q814033.log
```

You can see where the file size is in this text, but it isn't useful as is. You have to extract the sequence of characters starting at column 32 (or is it 33?) until column 39, remove the comma, and then turn those characters into numbers. Even removing the comma might be tricky, because the thousands separator can change depending on the current cultural settings on the computer. In other words, it may not be a comma—it may be a period. Or it may not be present at all.

It would be easier if you could just ask for the size of the files as a number in the first place. This is what .NET brings to PowerShell: self-describing data that can be easily inspected and manipulated without having to convert it to text until you really need to.

Choosing to use the .NET object model also brings an additional benefit, in that it allows PowerShell to directly use the extensive libraries that are part of the .NET framework. This brings to PowerShell a breadth of coverage rarely found in a new language. Here's a simple example that shows the kinds of things .NET brings to the environment. Say we want to find out what day of the week December 13, 1974 was. We can do this in PowerShell as follows:

```
PS (1) > (get-date "12/13/1974").DayOfWeek
Friday
```

In this example, the `get-date` command returns a .NET `DateTime` object, which has a property that will calculate the day of the week corresponding to that date. The PowerShell team didn't need to create a library of date and time manipulation routines for PowerShell—we got them for free by building on top of .NET. And the same `DateTime` objects are used throughout the system. For example, say we want to find out which of two files is newer. In a text-based shell, we'd have to get a string that contains the time each file was updated, covert those strings into numbers somehow, and then compare them. In PowerShell, we can simply do:

```
PS (6) > (dir data.txt).lastwritetime -gt
>> (dir hello.ps1).lastwritetime
>>
True
```

We use the `dir` command to get the file information objects and then simply compare the last write time of each file. No string parsing is needed.

Now that we're all sold on the wonders of objects and .NET (I'm expecting my check from the Microsoft marketing folks real soon), let's make sure we're all talking about the same thing when we use words like object, member, method, and instance. The next section discusses the basics of object-oriented programming.

1.3   BRUSHING UP ON OBJECTS

Since the PowerShell environment uses objects in almost everything it does, it's worth running through a quick refresher on object-oriented programming. If you're comfortable with this material, feel free to skip most of this section, but do please read the section on objects and PowerShell.

There is no shortage of "learned debate" (also known as bitter feuding) about what objects are and what object-oriented programming is all about. For our purposes, we'll use the simplest definition. An object is a package that contains both data and the information on how to use that data. Take a light bulb object as a simple example. This object would contain data describing its state—whether it's off or on. It would also contain the mechanisms or *methods* needed to change the on/off state. Non-object-oriented approaches to programming typically put the data in one place, perhaps a table of numbers where 0 is off and 1 is on, and then provide a separate library of routines to change this state. To change its state, the programmer would have to tell these routines where the value representing a particular light bulb was. This could be complicated and is certainly error prone. With objects, because both the data and the methods are packaged as a whole, the user can work with objects in a more direct and therefore simpler manner, allowing many errors to be avoided.

1.3.1   Reviewing object-oriented programming

That's the basics of what objects are. Now what is object-oriented programming? Well, it deals mainly with how you build objects. Where do the data elements come from? Where do the behaviors come from? Most object systems determine the object's capabilities through its *type*. In the light bulb example, the type of the object is (surprise) LightBulb. The type of the object determines what properties the object has (for example, IsOn) and what methods it has (for example, TurnOn and TurnOff).

Essentially, an object's type is the blueprint or pattern for what an object looks like and how you use it. The type LightBulb would say that that it has one data element—IsOn—and two methods—TurnOn() and TurnOff(). Types are frequently further divided into two subsets:

- Types that have an actual implementation of TurnOn() and TurnOff(). These are typically called *classes*.
- Types that only describe what the members of the type should look like but not how they work. These are called *interfaces*.

The pattern IsOn/TurnOn()/TurnOff() could be an *interface* implemented by a variety of classes such as LightBulb, KitchenSinkTap, or Television. All these objects have the same basic pattern for being turned on and off. From a programmer's perspective, if they all have the same *interface* (that is, the same mechanism for being turned on and off), once you know how to turn one of these objects on or off, you can use any type of object that has that interface.

Types are typically arranged in hierarchies with the idea that they should reflect logical taxonomies of objects. This taxonomy is made up of classes and subclasses. An example taxonomy is shown in figure 1.2.

In this taxonomy, Book is the parent *class*, Fiction and Non-fiction are *subclasses* of Book, and so on. While taxonomies organize data effectively, designing a good taxonomy is hard. Frequently, the best arrangement is not immediately

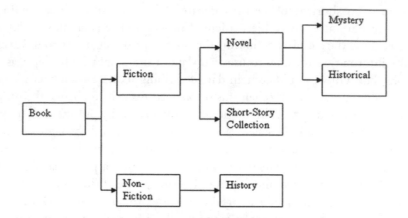

Figure 1.2 This diagram shows how books can be organized in a hierarchy of classes, just as object types can be organized into classes.

obvious. In figure 1.2, it might be better to organize by subject matter first, instead of the `Novel/Short-story Collection` grouping. In the scientific world, people spend entire careers categorizing items. Since it's hard to categorize well, people also arrange instances of objects into collections by containment instead of by type. A library contains books, but it isn't itself a book. A library also contains other things that aren't books, such as chairs and tables. If at some point you decide to re-categorize all of the books in a library, it doesn't affect what building people visit to get a book. It only changes how you find a book once you reach that building. On the other hand, if the library moves to a new location, you have to learn where it is. Once inside the building, however, your method for looking up books hasn't changed. This is usually called a *has-a* relationship—a library *has-a* bunch of books. Now let's see how these concepts are used in the PowerShell environment.

1.3.2 Objects in PowerShell

We've said that PowerShell is an *object-based* shell as opposed to an object-oriented language. What do we mean by object-based? In object-based scripting, you typically use objects somebody else has already defined for you. While it's possible to build your own objects in PowerShell, it isn't something that you need to worry about—at least not for most basic PowerShell tasks.

Returning to the `LightBulb` example, PowerShell would probably use the `LightBulb` class like this:

```
$lb = get-lightbulb -room bedroom
$lb.TurnOff()
```

Don't worry about the details of the syntax for now—we'll cover that later. The key point is that you usually get an object "foo" by saying:

```
get-foo -option1 -option2 bar
```

rather than saying something like:

```
new foo()
```

as you would in an object-oriented language.

PowerShell commands, called *cmdlets*, use verb-noun pairs. The *get-** verb is used universally in the system to get at objects. Note that we didn't have to worry about whether LightBulb is a class or an interface, or care about where in the object hierarchy it comes from. You can get all of the information about the member properties of an object though the get-member command (see the pattern?), which will tell you all about an object's properties.

But enough talk! By far the best way to understand PowerShell is to use it. In the next section, we'll get you up and going with PowerShell, and quickly tour through the basics of the environment.

1.4 DUDE! WHERE'S MY CODE?

In this section, we'll look at the things you need to know to get going with PowerShell as quickly as possible. This is a brief introduction intended to provide a taste of what PowerShell can do and how it works. We begin with how to download and install PowerShell and how to start the interpreter once it's installed. Then we'll cover the basic format of commands, command-line editing, and how to use command completion with the Tab key to speed up command entry. Once you're up and running, we'll look at what you can do with PowerShell. We'll start with basic expressions and then move on to more complex operations.

NOTE The PowerShell documentation package also includes a short Getting Started guide that will include up-to-date installation information and instructions. You may want to take a look at this as well.

1.4.1 Installing and starting PowerShell

First things first—you'll almost certainly have to download and install the PowerShell package on your computer. Go to the PowerShell page on the Microsoft website:

> http://microsoft.com/powershell

This page should contain a link that will take you to the latest installer and any documentation packages or other materials available. Alternatively, you can go to Microsoft Update and search for the installer there. Once you've located the installer, follow the instructions to install the package. After you have it installed, to start an interactive PowerShell session go to:

```
Start -> Programs -> Windows PowerShell
```

When it's started, you'll see a screen like that shown in figure 1.3:

PS C:\Documents and Settings\brucepay
Windows(R) PowerShell
Copyright (C) 2006 Microsoft Corporation. All rights reserved.
PS (1) >

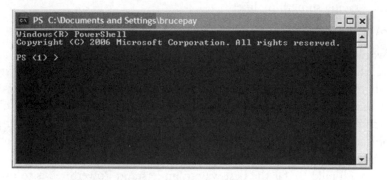

Figure 1.3 When you start an interactive PowerShell session, the first thing you see is the PowerShell logo and then the prompt. As soon as you see the prompt, you can begin entering commands.

Now type the first command most people type: "`dir`". This produces a listing of the files on your system, as shown in figure 1.4.

As you would expect, the `dir` command prints a listing of the current directory to standard output.

NOTE Let's stop for a second and talk about the conventions we're going to use in examples. Since PowerShell is an interactive environment, we'll show a lot of example commands as the user would type them, followed by the responses the system generates. Before the command text, there will be a prompt string that looks like "PS (2) > ". Following the prompt, the actual command will be displayed in bold font. PowerShell's responses will follow on the next few lines. Since PowerShell doesn't display anything in front of the output lines, you can distinguish output from commands by looking for the prompt string. These conventions are illustrated in figure 1.5.

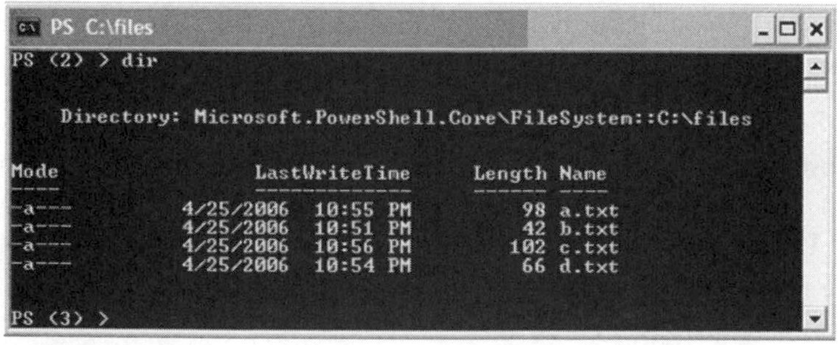

PS C:\files
PS (2) > dir
Directory: Microsoft.PowerShell.Core\FileSystem::C:\files
Mode LastWriteTime Length Name
-a--- 4/25/2006 10:55 PM 98 a.txt
-a--- 4/25/2006 10:51 PM 42 b.txt
-a--- 4/25/2006 10:56 PM 102 c.txt
-a--- 4/25/2006 10:54 PM 66 d.txt
PS (3) >

Figure 1.4 At the prompt, type "`dir`" and press the Enter key. PowerShell will then execute the `dir` command and display a list of files in the current directory.

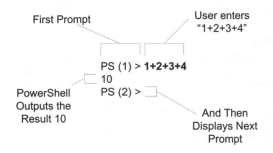

First Prompt

User enters "1+2+3+4"

PS (1) > **1+2+3+4**
10
PS (2) >

PowerShell Outputs the Result 10

And Then Displays Next Prompt

Figure 1.5 This diagram illustrates the conventions we're using for showing examples in this book. The text that the user types is shown in bold. Prompts and other output from the interpreter are shown in normal weight text.

On to the examples. Instead of simply displaying the directory listing, let's save it into a file using output redirection. In the following example, we redirect the output into the file c:\foo.txt and then use the type command to display what was saved:

```
PS (2) > dir c:\config.sys > c:\foo.txt
PS (3) > type c:\foo.txt


    Directory: Microsoft.PowerShell.Core\FileSystem::C:\


Mode                LastWriteTime     Length Name
----                -------------     ------ ----
-a---         11/17/2004   3:32 AM          0 config.sys
PS (4) >
```

As you can see, commands work more or less as you'd expect if you've used other shells. Let's go over some other things that should be familiar to you.

1.4.2 Command editing

Command-line editing works the same way for PowerShell as it does for cmd.exe. The available editing features and keystrokes are listed in table 1.1.

Table 1.1 Command editing features

Keyboard sequence	Editing operation
Left/Right Arrows	Move the editing cursor left and right through the current command line.
Ctrl-Left Arrow, Ctrl-Right Arrow	Holding the control (CTRL) key down while pressing the left and right arrow keys will move the editing cursor through the current command line one word at a time, instead of one character at a time.
Home	Moves the editing cursor to the beginning of the current command line.
End	Moves the editing cursor to the end of the current command line.
Up/Down Arrows	Moves up and down through the command history.
Insert Key	Toggles between character insert and character overwrite modes.
Delete Key	Deletes the character under the cursor.
Backspace Key	Deletes the character behind the cursor.

continued on next page

Table 1.1 Command editing features *(continued)*

Keyboard sequence	Editing operation
F7	Pops up command history in a window on the console. Use the up and down arrows to select a command, then Enter to execute that command.
Tab	Does command line completion. (See the next section for details.)

These key sequences let you create and edit commands effectively at the command line. In fact, they aren't really part of PowerShell at all. These command-line editing features are part of the Windows console subsystem, so they are the same across all console applications. There is one editing feature, however, that is significantly different for PowerShell. This is command completion, also call tab-completion. While cmd.exe does have tab-completion, PowerShell's implementation is significantly more powerful. We'll describe this feature next.

1.4.3 Command completion

An important feature at the command line is tab-completion. This allows you to partially enter a command, then hit the Tab key and have PowerShell try to fill in the rest of the command. By default, PowerShell will do tab completion against the file system, so if you type a partial file name and then hit Tab, the system matches what you've typed against the files in the current directory and returns the first matching file name. Hitting Tab again takes you to the next match, and so on. PowerShell also supplies the powerful capability of tab-completion on wild cards (see chapter 4 for information on PowerShell wild cards). This means that you can type:

```
PS (1) > cd c:\pro*files<tab>
```

and the command is expanded to:

```
PS (2) > cd 'C:\Program Files'
```

PowerShell will also do tab-completion on partial cmdlet names. If you enter a cmdlet name up to the dash and then hit the Tab key, the system will step through the matching cmdlet names.

So far, this isn't much more interesting than what cmd.exe provide. What is significantly different is that PowerShell also does completion on parameter names. If you enter a command followed by a partial parameter name and hit Tab, the system will step through all of the possible parameters for that command.

PowerShell also does tab-completion on variables. If you type a partial variable name and then hit the Tab key, PowerShell will complete the name of the variable.

And finally, PowerShell does completion on properties in variables. If you've used the Microsoft Visual Studio development environment, you've probably seen the Intellisense feature. Property completion is kind of a limited Intellisense capability at the command line. If you type something like:

```
PS (1) > $a="abcde"
PS (2) > $a.len<tab>
```

The system expands the property name to:

```
PS (2) > $a.Length
```

Again, the first Tab returns the first matching property or method. If the match is a method, an open parenthesis is displayed:

```
PS (3) > $a.sub<tab>
```

which produces:

```
PS (3) > $a.Substring(
```

Note that the system corrects the capitalization for the method or property name to match how it was actually defined. This doesn't really impact how things work. PowerShell is case-insensitive by default whenever it has to match against something. (There are operators that allow you to do case-sensitive matching, which are discussed in chapter 3).

AUTHOR'S NOTE The PowerShell tab completion mechanism is user extendable. While the path completion mechanism is built into the executable, features such as parameter and property completion are implemented through a shell function that users can examine and modify. The name of this function is TabExpansion. Chapter 7 describes how to write and manipulate PowerShell functions.

1.4.4 Evaluating basic expressions

In addition to running commands, PowerShell can also evaluate expressions. In effect, it operates as a kind of calculator. Let's evaluate a simple expression:

```
PS (4) > 2+2
4
```

Notice that as soon as you typed the expression, the result was calculated and displayed. It wasn't necessary to use any kind of print statement to display the expression. It is important to remember that whenever an expression is evaluated, the result of the expression is output, not discarded. We'll explore the implications of this in later sections.

Here are few more examples of PowerShell expressions examples:

```
PS (5) > (2+2)*3
12
PS (6) > (2+2)*6/2
12
PS (7) > 22/7
3.14285714285714
```

You can see from these examples that PowerShell supports most of the basic arithmetic operations you'd expect, including floating point.

> **NOTE** PowerShell supports single and double precision floating point, as well as the .NET decimal type. See chapter 3 for more details.

Since we've already shown how to save the output of a command into a file using the redirection operator, let's do the same thing with expressions:

```
PS (8) > (2+2)*3/7
1.71428571428571
PS (9) > (2+2)*3/7 > c:\foo.txt
PS (10) > type c:\foo.txt
1.71428571428571
```

Saving expressions into files is useful; saving them in variables is more useful:

```
PS (11) > $n = (2+2)*3
PS (12) > $n
12
PS (13) > $n / 7
1.71428571428571
```

Variables can also be used to store the output of commands:

```
PS (14) > $files = dir
PS (15) > $files[1]


    Directory: Microsoft.PowerShell.Core\FileSystem::C:\Document
    s and Settings\brucepay


Mode             LastWriteTime      Length Name
----             -------------      ------ ----
d----        4/25/2006  10:32 PM           Desktop
```

In this example, we extracted the second element of the collection of file information objects returned by the dir command.

> **AUTHOR'S** Note that collections in PowerShell start at 0, not at 1. This is a character-
> **NOTE** istic we've inherited from the .NET Common Language Runtime specifi-
> cation. This is why $files[1] is actually extracting the *second* element,
> not the first.

1.4.5 Processing data

As we've seen in the preceding sections, we can run commands to get information and then store it in files and variables. Now let's do some processing on that data. First we'll look at how to sort objects and how to extract properties from those objects. Then we'll look at using the PowerShell flow control statements to write scripts that use conditionals and loops to do more sophisticated processing.

Sorting objects

First let's sort a list of files. Here's the initial list, which by default is sorted by name.

```
PS (16) > cd c:\files
PS (17) > dir


    Directory: Microsoft.PowerShell.Core\FileSystem::C:\files


Mode                LastWriteTime     Length Name
----                -------------     ------ ----
-a---         4/25/2006  10:55 PM         98 a.txt
-a---         4/25/2006  10:51 PM         42 b.txt
-a---         4/25/2006  10:56 PM        102 c.txt
-a---         4/25/2006  10:54 PM         66 d.txt
```

The output of this shows the basic properties on the file system objects sorted by the name of the file. Now, let's run it through the sort utility:

```
PS (18) > dir | sort


    Directory: Microsoft.PowerShell.Core\FileSystem::C:\files


Mode                LastWriteTime     Length Name
----                -------------     ------ ----
-a---         4/25/2006  10:55 PM         98 a.txt
a             4/25/2006  10:51 PM         42 b.txt
-a---         4/25/2006  10:56 PM        102 c.txt
a             4/25/2006  10:54 PM         66 d.txt
```

Granted, it's not very interesting. Sorting an already sorted list by the same property yields you the same result. Let's do something a bit more interesting. Let's sort by name in descending order:

```
PS (19) > dir | sort -descending


    Directory: Microsoft.PowerShell.Core\FileSystem::C:\files


Mode                LastWriteTime     Length Name
----                -------------     ------ ----
-a---         4/25/2006  10:54 PM         66 d.txt
-a---         4/25/2006  10:56 PM        102 c.txt
-a---         4/25/2006  10:51 PM         42 b.txt
-a---         4/25/2006  10:55 PM         98 a.txt
```

So there you have it—files sorted by name in reverse order. Now let's sort by something other than the name of the file. Let's sort by file length. You may remember from an earlier section how hard it would be to sort by file length if the output were just text.

AUTHOR'S NOTE
In fact, on a UNIX system, this `sort` command looks like:

```
ls -l | sort -n -k 5
```

which, while pithy, is pretty opaque. Here's what it's doing. The `-n` option tells the `sort` function that you want to do a numeric sort. `-k` tells you which *field* you want to sort on. (The sort utility considers space-separated bits of text to be fields.) In the output of the `ls -l` command, the field containing the length of the file is at offset 5, as shown in the following:

```
-rw-r--r--    1 brucepay  brucepay  5754 Feb 19   2005 index.html
-rw-r--r--    1 brucepay  brucepay   204 Aug 19  12:50 page1.htm
```

We need to set things up this way because `ls` produces unstructured strings. We have to tell `sort` how to parse those strings before it can sort them.

In PowerShell, when we use the `Sort-Object` cmdlet, we don't have to tell it to sort numerically—it already knows the type of the field, and we can specify the sort key by property name instead of a numeric field offset.

```
PS (20) > dir | sort -property length

    Directory: Microsoft.PowerShell.Core\FileSystem::C:\files


Mode                LastWriteTime     Length Name
----                -------------     ------ ----
-a---         4/25/2006  10:51 PM         42 b.txt
-a---         4/25/2006  10:54 PM         66 d.txt
-a---         4/25/2006  10:55 PM         98 a.txt
-a---         4/25/2006  10:56 PM        102 c.txt
```

In this example, we're working with the output as objects; that is, things having a set of distinct characteristics accessible by name.

Selecting properties from an object

In the meantime, let's introduce a new cmdlet—`Select-Object`. This cmdlet allows you to either select some of the objects piped into it or select some properties of each object piped into it.

Say we want to get the largest file in a directory and put it into a variable:

```
PS (21) > $a = dir | sort -property length -descending |
>> select-object -first 1
>>
PS (22) > $a

    Directory: Microsoft.PowerShell.Core\FileSystem::C:\files


Mode                LastWriteTime     Length Name
----                -------------     ------ ----
-a---         4/25/2006  10:56 PM        102 c.txt
```

From this we can see that the largest file is `c.txt`.

NOTE   Note the secondary prompt ">>" in the previous example. The first line of the command ended in a pipe symbol. The PowerShell interpreter noticed this, saw that the command was incomplete, and prompted for additional text to complete the command. Once the command is complete, you type a second blank line to send the command to the interpreter.

Now say we want only the name of the directory containing the file and not all of the other properties of the object. We can also do this with `Select-Object`. As with the `sort` cmdlet, `Select-Object` also takes a -property parameter (you'll see this frequently in the PowerShell environment—commands are consistent in their use of parameters).

```
PS (23) > $a = dir | sort -property length -descending |
>> select-object -first 1 -property directory
>>
PS (24) > $a


Directory
---------
C:\files
```

We now have an object with a single property.

Processing with the Foreach-Object cmdlet

The final simplification is to get just the value itself. Let's introduce a new cmdlet that lets you do arbitrary processing on each object in a pipeline. The `Foreach-Object` cmdlet executes a block of statements for each object in the pipeline.

```
PS (25) > $a = dir | sort -property length -descending |
>> select-object -first 1 |
>> foreach-object { $_.DirectoryName }
>>
PS (26) > $a
C:\files
```

This shows that we can get an arbitrary property out of an object, and then do arbitrary processing on that information using the `Foreach-Object` command. Combining those features, here's an example that adds up the lengths of all of the objects in a directory.

```
PS (27) > $total = 0
PS (28) > dir | foreach-object {$total += $_.length }
PS (29) > $total
308
```

In this example, we initialize the variable `$total` to 0, then add to it the length of each file returned by the `dir` command and finally display the total.

Processing other kinds of data

One of the great strengths of the PowerShell approach is that once you learn a pattern for solving a problem, you can use this same pattern over and over again. For example, say we want to find the largest three files in a directory. The command line might look like this:

```
PS (1) > dir | sort -desc length | select -first 3

    Directory: Microsoft.PowerShell.Core\FileSystem::C:\files

Mode                LastWriteTime     Length Name
----                -------------     ------ ----
-a---          4/25/2006  10:56 PM       102 c.txt
-a---          4/25/2006  10:55 PM        98 a.txt
-a---          4/25/2006  10:54 PM        66 d.txt
```

We ran the `dir` command to get the list of file information objects, sorted them in descending order by length, and then selected the first three results to get the three largest files.

Now let's tackle a different problem. We want to find the three processes on the system with the largest working set size. Here's what this command line looks like:

```
PS (2) > get-process | sort -desc ws | select -first 3

Handles  NPM(K)    PM(K)      WS(K) VM(M)   CPU(s)     Id ProcessName
-------  ------    -----      ----- -----   ------     -- -----------
   1294      43    51096      81776   367    11.48   3156 OUTLOOK
    893      25    55260      73340   196    79.33   5124 iexplore
   2092      64    42676      54080   214   187.23    988 svchost
```

This time we run `Get-Process` to get the data and sort on the working set instead of the file size. Otherwise the pattern is identical to the previous example. This command pattern can be applied over and over again. For example, to get the three largest mailboxes on an Exchange mailserver, the command might look like:

```
get-mailboxstatistics | sort -desc  TotalItemSize | select -first 3
```

Again the pattern is repeated except for the `Get-MailboxStatistics` command and the property to filter on.

Even when we don't have a specific command for the data we're looking for and have to use other facilities such as WMI (see chapter 12 for more information on WMI), we can continue to apply the pattern. Say we want to find the three drives on the system that have the most free space. To do this we need to get some data from WMI. Not surprisingly, the command for this is `Get-WmiObject`. Here's how we'd use this command:

```
PS (4) > get-wmiobject win32_logicaldisk |
>> sort -desc freespace | select -first 3 |
>> format-table -autosize deviceid, freespace
>>
```

```
deviceid    freespace
--------    ---------
C:          97778954240
T:          31173663232
D:           932118528
```

Once again, the pattern is almost identical. The `Get-WmiObject` command returns a set of objects from WMI. We pipe these objects into `sort` and sort on the `freespace` property, then use `Select-Object` to extract the first three.

> **AUTHOR'S NOTE** Because of this ability to apply a command pattern over and over, most of the examples in this book are deliberately generic. The intent is to highlight the *pattern* of the solution rather than show a specific example. Once you understand the basic patterns, you can effectively adapt them to solve a multitude of other problems.

Flow control statement

Pipelines are great, but sometimes you need more control over the flow of your script. PowerShell has the usual script flow control statements, such as `while` loops and `if` statements:

```
PS (1) > $i=0
PS (2) > while ($i++ -lt 10) { if ($i % 2) {"$i is odd"}}
1 is odd
3 is odd
5 is odd
7 is odd
9 is odd
PS (3) >
```

Here we're using the `while` loop to count from 0 through 9. In the body of the `while` loop, we have an `if` statement that tests to see whether the current number is odd, and then writes out a message if it is. There are a number of additional flow control statements. The complete set of these features is covered in chapter 6.

This is the end of our "Cook's tour" of PowerShell, and we've only breezed over the features and capabilities of the environment. In the subsequent chapters, we'll cover each of the elements discussed here in detail and a whole lot more.

1.5   SUMMARY

This chapter covered what PowerShell is and, just as important, why it is. We also took a whirlwind tour through some simple examples of using PowerShell interactively. Here are the key points that were covered:

- PowerShell is the new command-line and scripting environment from Microsoft Corporation.
- The Microsoft Windows management model is primarily object-based, which required us to take a novel approach to command-line scripting.

- PowerShell uses the .NET object model as the base for its type system.
- We're not crazy. Really! We've written papers and everything!

In the next chapter, we'll look at each of the language features we showed you in much more detail.

CHAPTER 2

The basics

"Begin at the beginning," the king said "and then go on till you come to the end, then stop."

—Lewis Carroll, *Alice in Wonderland*

Vizzini: Inconceivable!
Inigo: You keep on using that word. I do not think it means what you think it means.

—William Goldman, *The Princess Bride*

Having read chapter 1, you have the history and rationale of PowerShell under your belt, and you're ready to move on to the details of the PowerShell language and its environment. This chapter covers language details that are specific to PowerShell and how the PowerShell interpreter parses the commands you type. It also outlines the anatomy of the command line itself. The chapter presents many examples that are not completely explained. If you don't understand everything when you read the examples, don't worry—we'll revisit the material in later. In this chapter, we just want to cover the major concepts, and then focus on the details in subsequent chapters.

Before digging into PowerShell concepts and terminology, let's capture some first impressions of the language: What does the PowerShell language look like? Bird-watchers have to learn how to distinguish hundreds of different species of fast-moving little brown birds (or LBBs as they're known). To understand how they do this, I consulted with my wife (the only bird I can identify is a chicken, preferably stuffed and roasted). Birdwatchers use something called the G.I.S.S. principle. This stands for General Impression, Size, and Shape of the bird. It's the set of characteristics that allow you to determine what you saw from a brief or distant glance. Take a look at the silhouettes shown in figure 2.1. The figure shows the relative sizes of four birds and highlights the characteristic shape of each one. This is more than enough information to recognize each bird.

What does this have to do with computers (other than to prove we aren't the only ones who make up strange acronyms)? In essence, the G.I.S.S. principle also works well with programming languages. The overall G.I.S.S. of the PowerShell syntax is that it's like any of the C programming language descendents with specific differences. Variables are distinguished by a leading dollar ("$") sign.

NOTE PowerShell uses the "at" symbol ("@") in a few places, has $_ as a default variable, and uses "&" as the function call operator. These elements lead people to say that PowerShell looks like Perl. In fact, at one point, we were using Perl as a root language, and these elements stem from the period. Later on, the syntax was changed to align more with C#, but we kept these elements because they worked well. In Perl terminology, they contributed significantly to the "whipupitude quotient" of the language.

In fact, the language that PowerShell looks most like is PHP. (This wasn't deliberate. It's a case of parallel evolution—great minds thinking alike and all that.) But don't let this fool you; semantically, PowerShell and PHP are quite different.

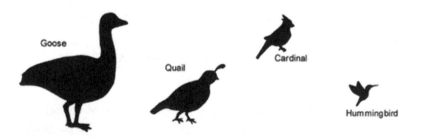

Figure 2.1 This figure illustrates the G.I.S.S. principle—the general impression, size, and shape of some common birds. Even without any detail, the basic shape and size is enough for most people to identify these birds. This same principle can be applied when learning programming languages; a sense of the overall shape of the language allows you to identify common coding patterns in the language.

The core PowerShell language is based on the POSIX 1003.2 grammar for the Korn shell. Originally, Perl idioms were appropriated for some of the more advanced concepts such as hash tables. However, as the project progressed, it became clear that aligning PowerShell syntax with C# was more appropriate. If nothing else, this would facilitate migrating code between PowerShell and C#. The major value this brings is that PowerShell code can be migrated to C# when necessary for performance improvements, and C# examples can be easily converted to PowerShell. This second point is important, since the more examples you have in a new language, the better off you are.

2.1 COMMAND CONCEPTS AND TERMINOLOGY

As with any piece of new technology, PowerShell has its own terminology, although we've tried to stick to existing terms as much as we could. Consequently, much of the terminology used in PowerShell will be familiar if you've used other shells. However, because PowerShell is a new kind of shell, there are a number of terms that are different and a few new terms we just made up. In this section, we'll go over the PowerShell-specific concepts and terminology for command types and command syntax.

2.1.1 Commands and cmdlets

Commands are the fundamental part of any shell language; they're what you type to get things done. As we saw in the previous chapter, a simple command looks like this:

```
command -parameter1 -parameter2 argument1 argument2
```

A more detailed illustration of the anatomy of this command is shown in figure 2.2. This figure calls out all the individual elements of the command.

All commands are broken down into the command name, the parameters specified to the command, and the arguments to those parameters.

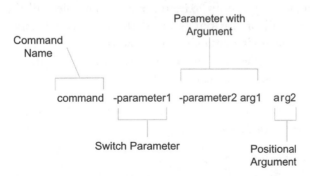

Figure 2.2 This figure shows the anatomy of a basic command. It begins with the name of the command, followed by some number of parameters. These may be switch parameters that take no arguments, regular parameters that do take arguments, or positional parameters where the matching parameter is inferred by the argument's position on the command line.

The distinction between "parameter" and "argument" may seem a bit strange from a programmer's perspective. However, if you're used to languages such as Python or Visual Basic that allow for keyword parameters, PowerShell parameters correspond to the keywords, and arguments correspond to the values.

The first element in the command is the name of the command to be executed. The PowerShell interpreter looks at this name and figures out what actually has to be done. It must figure out not which command to run but which *kind* of command to run. In PowerShell, there are currently four different categories of commands: cmdlets, shell function commands, script commands, and native Windows commands. (We'll cover the different categories in detail in the following sections.) Following the command name comes zero or more parameters and/or arguments. A parameter starts with a dash, followed by the name of the parameter. An argument, on the other hand, is the value that will be associated with or *bound* to a specific parameter. Let's look at an example:

```
PS (1) > write-output -inputobject Hello
Hello
```

In this example, the command is `Write-Output`, the parameter is `-inputobject`, and the argument is `Hello`.

What about the positional parameters mentioned in figure 2.1? When a command is created, the author of the command can provide information that allows PowerShell to determine which parameter to bind an argument to, even if the parameter name itself is missing. For example, the `Write-Output` command has been defined so that the first parameter is `-inputobject`. This lets us write

```
PS (2) > write-output Hello
Hello
```

instead of having to actually specify `-inputobject`. The piece of the PowerShell interpreter that figures all of this out is called the *parameter binder*. In fact, the parameter binder is smart—it doesn't require that you specify the full name of a parameter as long as you specify enough for it to uniquely distinguish what you meant. This means that you can write any of the following:

```
PS (3) > write-output -input Hello
Hello
PS (4) > write-output -IN Hello
Hello
PS (5) > write-output -i Hello
Hello
```

and the parameter binder still does the right thing. (Notice that it doesn't matter whether you use uppercase or lowercase letters, either.) So what else does the parameter binder do? It's in charge of figuring out how to match the types of arguments to the types of parameters. Remember that PowerShell is an object-based shell. Everything in PowerShell has a type. For this to work seamlessly, PowerShell has to use a fairly complex type conversion system to correctly put things together, a subject that is covered in chapter 3. When you type a command at the command line, you're really typing strings. What happens if the command requires a different type of object? The parameter binder uses the type converter to try to convert that string into the correct type for the parameter. Here's a simple example. Let's use the `Get-Process` command to get the process with the process Id 0. Instead of passing it the number 0, we'll put the argument in quotes to force the argument to be a string. This means that the `-id` parameter, which requires a number, will be passed a string instead.

```
PS (7) > get-process -id "0"

Handles  NPM(K)    PM(K)      WS(K) VM(M)   CPU(s)     Id ProcessName
-------  ------    -----      ----- -----   ------     -- -----------
      0       0        0         28     0              0 Idle
```

When trying to run this command, the parameter binder detects that `-id` needs a number, not a string, so it takes the string "0" and tries to convert it into a number. If this succeeds, the command continues as we see in the example. What happens if it can't be converted? Let's try it:

```
PS (8) > get-process -id abc
Get-Process : Cannot bind parameter 'Id'. Cannot convert value "abc"
to type "System.Int32". Error: "Input string was not in a correct fo
rmat."
At line:1 char:16
+ get-process -id  <<<< abc
PS (9) >
```

We get an error message explaining that the type conversion failed. We'll discuss this in more detail in chapter 3 when we talk about types. Since we've introduced the use of quotation marks, let's see one more example. What happens if the argument you want to pass to the command starts with a dash? This is where the quotes come in. Let's use write-output to print out the string `"-inputobject"`.

```
PS (1) > write-output -inputobject "-inputobject"
-inputobject
```

And it works as desired. Alternatively we could simply type:

```
PS (2) > write-output "-inputobject"
-inputobject
```

The quotes keep the parameter binder from treating the quoted string as a parameter.

AUTHOR'S NOTE Another, less frequently used way of doing this is by using the special end-of-parameters parameter which is two hyphens back to back, as in "`--`". Everything after this sequence will be treated as an argument, even if it looks like a parameter. For example, using "`--`" we could also write out the string `-inputobject` without using quotes by doing:

```
PS (3) > write-output -- -inputobject
 -inputobject
```

The "--" sequence tells the parameter binder to treat everything after it as an argument, even if it looks like a parameter. This is a convention adopted from the UNIX shells and is standardized in the POSIX Shell and Utilities specification.

The final element of the basic command is the *switch* parameter. These are parameters that don't require an argument. They're usually either present or absent (so obviously they can't be positional). The best example of this is the `-recurse` parameter on the `dir` command. This switch tells the `dir` command to display files from a specified directory as well as all of its subdirectories.

```
PS (1) > dir -recurse -filter c*d.exe c:\windows

    Directory: Microsoft.PowerShell.Core\FileSystem::C:\windows\
    system32


Mode            LastWriteTime     Length Name
----            -------------     ------ ----
-a---        8/10/2004  12:00 PM   102912 clipbrd.exe
-a---        8/10/2004  12:00 PM   388608 cmd.exe


PS (2) >
```

As you can see, the `-recurse` switch takes no arguments.

AUTHOR'S NOTE While it's almost always the case that switch parameters don't take arguments, it is possible to specify arguments to them. We'll save when and why you might do this for the chapter on scripts (shell functions and scripts are the only time you need this particular feature, so we'll keep you in suspense for the time being).

Now that we've covered the basic anatomy of the command line, let's go over the types of commands that PowerShell supports.

2.1.2 Command categories

As we mentioned earlier, there are four categories of commands in PowerShell: cmdlets, functions, scripts, and native Win32 executables.

The first category of command is a *cmdlet* (pronounced *"command-let"*). Cmdlet is a term that's specific to the PowerShell environment. A cmdlet is implemented by a .NET class that derives from the `Cmdlet` base class in the PowerShell Software Developers Kit (SDK).

NOTE Building cmdlets is a developer task and requires the PowerShell SDK. This SDK is freely available for download from Microsoft and includes extensive documentation along with many code samples. However, since the goal of *Windows PowerShell in Action* is to coach you to effectively use and script in the PowerShell environment, we're not going to do much more than mention the SDK in this book.

This category of command is compiled into a DLL and loaded into the PowerShell process when the shell starts up. Since the compiled code is loaded into the process, it's the most efficient category of command to execute.

Cmdlets always have names of the form Verb-Noun, where the verb specifies the action and the noun specifies the object to operate on. In traditional shells, cmdlets correspond most closely to what is usually called a *built-in* command. In PowerShell, since anybody can add a cmdlet to the runtime, there isn't any special class of built-in commands. Cmdlets have the best support in version 1 of PowerShell: full online help support, localization, and the best parameter binding support.

In listing 2.1, you can see the C# source code for a simple cmdlet. This cmdlet just copies its input to its output. If -Parameter1 is specified then its argument will be used as a prefix on the output string. This example was included to show the basic structure of a cmdlet. There are a couple of important things to note in this listing. The first is the way the parameters are declared using the [Parameter] attribute ❶. This information is used by the PowerShell runtime to automatically determine the parameters for the cmdlet. The cmdlet author doesn't have to write any code to do parameter parsing; the runtime takes care of all of this work. Another thing to note is the ValueFromPipeline=true notation ❷. This indicates that this parameter may be fulfilled by values coming from the pipeline. (We'll discuss what this means when we talk about pipelines later in this chapter.)

> **Listing 2.1   C# source code for a simple cmdlet**

```
[Cmdlet("Write", "InputObject")]
public class MyWriteInputObjectCmdlet : Cmdlet
{
    [Parameter]                          How to mark a para-
    public string Parameter1;        ❶  meter in a cmdlet class

    [Parameter(Mandatory = true, ValueFromPipeline=true)]
    public string InputObject;
                                     Marking a parameter
                                     that takes pipeline input ❷
    protected override void ProcessRecord()
    {
        if (Parameter1 != null)
            WriteObject(Parameter1 +  ":" +  InputObject);
        else
            WriteObject(InputObject);
    }
}
```

The next type of command is a *function*. This is a named piece of PowerShell script code that lives in memory while the interpreter is running, and is discarded on exit. (See chapter 7 for more information on how you can load functions into your environment.) Functions are made up of user-defined code that is parsed once when defined. This parsed representation is preserved so it doesn't have to be reparsed every time it is used. Functions can have named parameters like cmdlets, but don't have the full parameter specification capabilities of cmdlets in the first version of PowerShell. Notice, though, that the same basic structure is followed. The section in the script that begins with the process keyword (line 4 of listing 2.2) corresponds to the ProcessRecord method shown in listing 2.1. This allows functions and cmdlets to have the same streaming behavior. (See section 2.3.1 for more information on streaming.)

Listing 2.2   Source code for a simple shell function command

```
function Write-InputObject
{
    param($Parameter1)
    process {
        if ($Parameter1)
        {
            "$Parameter1:$_"
        } else {
            "$_"
        }
}
}
```

A *script command* is a piece of PowerShell code that lives in a file with a .ps1 extension. In version 1.0 of PowerShell, these script files are loaded and parsed every time they are run, making them somewhat slower than functions to start (although once started, they run at the same speed). In terms of parameter capabilities, shell function commands and script commands are identical.

Listing 2.3   Source code for the simple shell script command "my-script.ps1"

```
param($Parameter1)
process {
    if ($Parameter1)
    {
        "$Parameter1:$_"
    } else {
        "$_"
    }
}
```

The last type of command is called a *native command*. These are external programs (typically executables) that can be executed by the operating system.

Choosing names for things is always difficult, and the term *native command* does sound a bit strange. We had originally called external executables "legacy commands", but the feedback was that "legacy" was perceived as being a negative term. On the other hand, simply calling them executables wasn't really suitable, because this class of command also includes cmd.exe batch files. In the end, we settled on "native command" as being sufficiently distinctive.

Since running a native command means creating a whole new process for the command, native commands are the slowest of the command types. Also, native commands do their own parameter processing and so don't necessarily match the syntax of the other types of commands.

Of course, since native commands cover anything that can be run on a Windows computer, you get a wide variety of behaviors. One of the biggest issues is when PowerShell waits for a command to finish but it just keeps on going. For example, if you're staring a text document, at the command line

```
PS (1) > .\foo.txt
PS (2) >
```

You get the prompt back more or less immediately, and your default text editor will pop up (probably notepad.exe since that's the default). The program to launch is determined by the file associations that are defined as part of the Windows environment.

NOTE In PowerShell, unlike in cmd.exe, you have to prefix a command with ./ or .\ if you want to run it out of the current directory. This is part of PowerShell's "Secure By Design" philosophy. This particular security feature was adopted to prevent "Trojan horse" attacks where the user is lured into a directory and then told to run an innocuous command such as notepad.exe. Instead of running the system notepad.exe, they end up running a hostile program that the attacker has placed in that directory and named notepad.exe. Chapter 13 covers the security features of the PowerShell environment in detail.

So what about when you specify the editor explicitly?

```
PS (2) > notepad foo.txt
PS (3) >
```

The same thing happens—the command returns immediately. But what about when you run the command in the middle of a pipeline?

```
PS (3) > notepad foo.txt | sort
<exit notepad>
PS (4) >
```

Now PowerShell waits for the command to exit before giving you back the prompt. This can be handy when you want to insert something such as a graphical form editor in the middle of a script to do some processing.

Finally, let's run the `edit.com` program. This is the old console-based full screen editor that has come with Windows since about DOS 4.0. (Of course this also works with other console editors—vi, emacs, and so forth.)

```
PS (6) > edit.com ./foo.txt
PS (7) >
```

As you would expect, the editor starts up, taking over the console window. You can edit the file and then exit the editor and return to PowerShell, all as one would expect. As you can see, the behavior of native commands depends on the type of native command, as well as where it appears in the pipeline.

Now that we've covered all four PowerShell command types, let's get back to looking at the PowerShell syntax.

2.1.3 Aliases and elastic syntax

We haven't really talked about aliases yet or how they're used to achieve an elastic syntax in PowerShell. Since this concept is important in the PowerShell environment, we need to spend some time on it.

The cmdlet verb-noun syntax, while regular, is also verbose. Also you may have noticed that in most of our examples we're using commands such as `dir` and `type`. The trick behind all this is *aliases*. The `dir` command is really `Get-ChildItem` and the `type` command is really `Get-Content`. In fact, you can see this by using the `Get-Command` command:

```
PS (1) > get-command dir

CommandType     Name            Definition
-----------     ----            ----------
Alias           dir             Get-ChildItem
```

This tells you that the command is an alias for `Get-ChildItem`. To get information about the `Get-ChildItem` command, you then do:

```
PS (2) > get-command get-childitem

CommandType     Name            Definition
-----------     ----            ----------
Cmdlet          Get-ChildItem   Get-ChildItem [[-P...
```

which truncates the information at the width of the console window. To see all of the information, pipe the output of get-command into `fl`:

```
PS (3) > get-command get-childitem | fl

Name            : Get-ChildItem
CommandType     : Cmdlet
Definition      : Get-ChildItem [[-Path] <String[]>] [[-Filter]
                     <String>] [-Include <String[]>] [-Exclude <S
                     tring[]>] [-Recurse] [-Force] [-Name] [-Verbo
                     se] [-Debug] [-ErrorAction <ActionPreference>
                     ] [-ErrorVariable <String>] [-OutVariable <St
                     ring>] [-OutBuffer <Int32>]
                     Get-ChildItem [-LiteralPath] <String[]> [[-Fi
                     lter] <String>] [-Include <String[]>] [-Exclu
                     de <String[]>] [-Recurse] [-Force] [-Name] [-
                     Verbose] [-Debug] [-ErrorAction <ActionPrefer
                     ence>] [-ErrorVariable <String>] [-OutVariabl
                     e <String>] [-OutBuffer <Int32>]

Path            :
AssemblyInfo    :
DLL             : C:\WINDOWS\assembly\GAC_MSIL\Microsoft.PowerS
                     hell.Commands.Management\1.0.0.0__31bf3856ad3
                     64e35\Microsoft.PowerShell.Commands.Managemen
                     t.dll
HelpFile        : Microsoft.PowerShell.Commands.Management.dll-
                     Help.xml
ParameterSets   : {Items, LiteralItems}
ImplementingType : Microsoft.PowerShell.Commands.GetChildItemCom
                     mand
Verb            : Get
Noun            : ChildItem
```

This shows you the full detailed information about this cmdlet. But wait—what's the fl command? Again we can use Get-Command to find out:

```
PS (4) > get-command fl

CommandType     Name            Definition
-----------     ----            ----------
Alias           fl              Format-List
```

PowerShell comes with a large set of predefined aliases. There are two basic categories of aliases—*transitional* aliases and convenience aliases. By transitional aliases, we mean a set of aliases that map PowerShell commands to commands that people are used to using in other shells, specifically cmd.exe and the UNIX shells. For the cmd.exe user, PowerShell defines dir, type, copy, and so on. For the UNIX user, PowerShell defines ls, cat, cp, and so forth. These aliases allow some basic level of functionality for new users right away.

The other set of aliases are the convenience aliases. These aliases are derived from the names of the cmdlets they map to. So Get-Command becomes gcm, Get-ChildItem becomes gci, Invoke-Item becomes ii, and so on. For a list of the defined aliases, just type Get-Alias at the command line. You can use the Set-Alias command (whose alias is sal by the way) to define your own aliases.

AUTHOR'S NOTE Aliases in the first version of PowerShell are limited to aliasing the command name only. Unlike other systems such as ksh, bash, or zsh, Power-Shell aliases cannot take parameters. The plan is to fix this in later releases. In the first version, if you need to do something more sophisticated than simple command name translations, you'll have to use shell functions or scripts.

This is all well and good, but what does it have to do with elastics? Glad you asked! The idea is that PowerShell can be terse when needed and descriptive when appropriate. The syntax is concise for simple cases and can be stretched like an elastic band for larger problems. This is important in a language that is both a command-line tool and a scripting language. The vast majority of "scripts" that you will write in Power-Shell will be no more than a few lines long. In other words, they'll be a string of commands that you'll type on the command line and then never use again. To be effective in this environment, the syntax needs to be very concise. This is where aliases like `fl` come in—they allow you to write concise command lines. When you're scripting, however, it is best to use the long name of the command. This is because sooner or later, you'll have to read the script you wrote (or—worse—someone else will). Would you rather read something that looks like this?

```
gcm|?{$_.parametersets.Count -gt 3}|fl name
```

or this?

```
get-command |
where-object {$_.parametersets.count -gt 3} |
format-list name
```

I'd certainly rather read the latter. (As always—we'll cover the details of these examples later on.)

AUTHOR'S NOTE PowerShell has two (or more) names for many of the same commands. Some people find this unsettling—they prefer having only one way of doing things. In fact this "only one way to do it" principle is also true for Power-Shell, but with a significant variation: we want to have *one best way* of doing something for each particular scenario or situation. Fundamentally this is what computers are all about; at their simplest, everything is just a bunch of bits. To be practical, you start from the simple bits and build out solutions that are more appropriate for the problem you're trying to solve. Along the way, you create an intermediate-sized component that may be reused to solve other problems. This is the approach that PowerShell uses: a series of components at different levels of complexity intended to address a wide range of problem classes. Not every problem is a nail, so having more tools than a hammer is a good idea even if requires a bit more learning.

Now that we've covered the core concepts of how commands are processed, let's step back a bit and look at PowerShell language processing overall.

2.2 PARSING AND POWERSHELL

In this section, we'll cover the details of how PowerShell scripts are parsed. Before the PowerShell interpreter can execute the commands you type, it first has to parse the command text and turn it into something the computer can execute. More formally, parsing is the process of turning human-readable source code into a form the computer understands. This is one area of computer science that actually deserves both of these the words—computer and science. Science in this case means formal language theory, which is a branch of mathematics. And since it's mathematics, discussing it usually requires a collection of Greek letters. We'll keep things a bit simpler here.

A piece of script text is broken up into tokens by the *tokenizer* (or *lexical analyzer* if you want to be more technical). A token is a particular type of symbol in the programming language, for example a number, a keyword, or variable. Once the raw text has been broken into a stream of tokens, these tokens are processed into structures in the language through *syntactic analysis*. In syntactic analysis, the stream of tokens is processed according to the grammatical rules of the language. In normal languages, this process is straightforward—a token always has the same meaning. A sequence of digits is always a number; an expression is always an expression, and so on. For example the sequence

```
2+2
```

would always be an addition expression, and `"Hello world"` would always be a constant string. Unfortunately, this isn't the case in shell languages. Sometimes you can't tell what a token is except through its context. In the next section, we go into more detail on why this is and how the PowerShell interpreter parses a script.

2.2.1 How PowerShell parses

For PowerShell to be successful as a shell, it cannot require that everything be quoted. PowerShell would fail if it required that people to continually type

```
cd ".."
```

or

```
copy "foo.txt" "bar.txt"
```

On the other hand, people have a strong idea of how expressions should work:

```
2
```

is the number 2, not a string "2". Consequently, PowerShell has some rather complicated parsing rules. The next three sections will cover these rules. We'll cover how quoting is handled, the two major parsing modes, and the special rules around newlines and statement termination.

2.2.2 Quoting

Quoting is the mechanism used to turn a token that has special meaning to the PowerShell interpreter into a simple string value. For example, the `Write-Output` cmdlet has a parameter `-InputObject`. But what if we want to actually use the string *–InputObject* as an argument, as mentioned earlier? To do this, we have to quote it; that is, we surround it in single or double quotes. The result looks like this:

```
PS (2) > write-output '-inputobject'
-inputobject
```

What would happen if we hadn't put the argument in quotes? Let's find out:

```
PS (3) > write-output -inputobject
Write-Output : Missing an argument for parameter 'InputObject'.
Specify a parameter of type 'System.Management.Automation.PSObje
ct[]' and try again.
At line:1 char:25
+ write-output -inputobject <<<<
PS (4) >
```

As you can see, this produces an error message indicating that an argument to the parameter `-InputObject` is required.

PowerShell supports several forms of quoting, each with somewhat different meanings (or semantics). Putting single quotes around an entire sequence of characters causes them to be treated like a single string. This is how you deal with file paths that have spaces in them. For example, if you want to `cd` into a directory whose path contains spaces, you would do

```
PS (4) > cd 'c:\program files'
PS (5) > pwd
Path
----
C:\Program Files
```

What happens if we don't use the quotes? Again, let's try it and find out:

```
PS (6) > cd c:\program files
Set-Location : A parameter cannot be found that matches paramete
r name 'files'.
At line:1 char:3
+ cd  <<<< c:\program files
```

When we don't use the quotes, we receive an error complaining about an unexpected parameter in the command because `"c:\program"` and `"files"` are treated as two separate tokens.

> **NOTE** Notice that the error message reports the name of the cmdlet, not the alias that was used. This way you know what is actually being executed. The "position message" on the other hand shows you the text that was entered so you can see that an alias was used.

One problem with using matching quotes as we did in the previous examples is that you have to remember to start the token with an opening quote. This raises an issue when you want to quote a single character. You can use the backquote (`) character to do this (the backquote is usually the upper leftmost key, below escape):

```
PS (6) > cd c:\program` files
PS (7) > pwd
Path
----
C:\Program Files
```

The backquote, or backtick, as it tends to be called, has other uses that we'll explore later in this section. Now let's look at the other form of matching quote: double quotes. Once again, here's our favorite example.

```
PS (8) > cd "c:\program files"
PS (9) > pwd

Path
----
C:\Program Files
```

It looks pretty much like the example with single quotes, so what's the difference? In double quotes, variables are *expanded*. In other words, if the string contains a variable reference starting with a "$", it will be replaced by the string representation of the value stored in the variable. Let's look at an example of this. First assign the string "files" to the variable $v.

```
PS (10) > $v = "files"
```

Now let's reference that variable in a string with double quotes:

```
PS (11) > cd "c:\program $v"
PS (12) > pwd
Path
----
C:\Program Files
```

The cd succeeded and the current directory was set as we expected. So what happens if we try it with single quotes? Here you go:

```
PS (13) > cd 'c:\program $v'
set-location : Cannot find path 'C:\program $v' because it does
not exist.
At line:1 char:3
+ cd  <<<< 'c:\program $v'
PS (14) >
```

Since expansion is performed only in double quotes and not in single quotes, you get an error because the unexpanded path doesn't exist.

Take a look at the next example:

```
PS (14) > '$v is $v'
$v is $v
PS (15) > "$v is $v"
files is files
```

In the single-quoted case, $v is never expanded and in the double-quoted case, it's always expanded. But what if we really want to show what the value of $v is? To do this, we need to have expansion in one place but not in the other. This is one of those other uses we had for the backtick. It can be used to quote or *escape* the dollar sign in a double-quoted string to suppress expansion. Let's try it out:

```
PS (16) > write-output "`$v is $v"
$v is files
```

Here's one final tweak to this example—if $v contained spaces, we'd want to make clear what part of the output was the value. Since single-quotes can contain double-quotes and double quotes can contain single quotes, this is straightforward:

```
PS (17) > write-output "`$v is '$v'"
$v is 'files'
PS (18) >
```

Now suppose we wanted to display the value of the $v on another line instead of in quotes. Here is another situation where we can use the backtick as an escape character. The sequence `n in a string, either single-quoted or double-quoted, will be replaced by a newline character. We can write the example with value of $v on a separate line as follows:

```
PS (19) > "The value of `$v is:`n$v"
The value of $v is:
Files
```

Table 2.1 lists the special characters that can be generated using backtick (also called *escape*) sequences.

Table 2.1 Backtick escape sequences

Escape Sequence	Corresponding Special Character
`n	Newline
`r	Carriage return
`t	Horizontal tab
`a	Alert
`b	Backspace
`'	Single quote
`"	Double quote
`0	Null
``	A single backtick

Note that escape sequence processing, like variable expansion, is only done in double-quoted strings. In single quoted strings, what you see is what you get. This is particularly important when writing a string to pass to a subsystem that does additional levels of quote processing.

If you've used other languages such as C, C#, or Perl, you'll be used to using backslash instead of backtick for escaping characters. Because PowerShell is a shell and has to deal with Windows's historical use of backslash as a path separator, it isn't practical to use backslash as the escape character. Too many applications expect backslash-separated paths, and that would have required every path to be typed with the slashes doubled. Choosing a different escape character was a difficult decision that we had to make, but there really wasn't any choice. It's one of the biggest cognitive bumps that experienced shell and script language users run into with PowerShell, but in the end, most people adapt without too much difficulty.

2.2.3 Expression mode and command mode parsing

As mentioned previously, because PowerShell is a shell, it has to deal with some parsing issues not found in other languages. In practice, most shell languages are collections of mini-languages with many different parsing modes. For PowerShell, we simplified this and trimmed the number of modes down to two: *expression mode* and *command mode*.

In expression mode, the parsing is conventional: strings must be quoted, numbers are always numbers, and so on. In command mode, numbers are treated as numbers but all other arguments are treated as strings unless they start with a $, @, ', ", or (. When an argument begins with one of these special characters, the rest of the argument is parsed as a value expression. (There is also special treatment for leading variable references in a string, which we'll discuss later on.) Table 2.2 shows some examples that illustrate how items are parsed in each mode.

Table 2.2 Parsing mode examples

Example command line	Parsing mode and explanation
2+2	Expression mode; results in 4
write-output 2+2	Command mode; results in "2+2"
$a=2+2	Expression mode; the variable $a is assigned the value 4
write-output (2+2)	Expression mode; because of the parentheses, 2+2 is evaluated as an expression producing 4. This result is then passed as an argument to the write-output cmdlet.
write-output $a	Expression mode; produces 4. This is actually ambiguous—evaluating it in either mode produces the same result. The next example shows why we default to expression mode in this case instead of command mode.

continued on next page

Table 2.2 Parsing mode examples *(continued)*

Example command line	Parsing mode and explanation
write-output $a.Equals(4)	Expression mode; $a.Equals(4) evaluates to true so write-output writes the Boolean value true. This is why a variable is evaluated in expression mode by default. We want simple method and property expressions to work without parentheses.
write-output $a/foo.txt	Command mode; $a/foo.txt expands to 4/foo.txt. This is the opposite of the previous example. Here we want it to be evaluated as a string in command mode. The interpreter first parses in expression mode and sees that it's not a valid property expression, so it backs up and rescans the argument in command mode. As a result it is treated as an expandable string.

Notice that in the `write-output (2+2)` case, the open parenthesis causes the interpreter to enter a new level of interpretation where the parsing mode is once again established by the first token. This means that the sequence 2+2 is actually parsed in expression mode, not command mode, so the result of the expression (4) is emitted. Also, the last example in the table illustrates the exception mentioned previously for a leading variable reference in a string. A variable itself is treated as an expression, but a variable followed by arbitrary text is treated as though the whole thing were in double quotes. This is so you can write

```
cd $HOME/scripts
```

instead of

```
cd "$HOME/scripts"
```

As mentioned earlier, quoted and unquoted strings are recognized as different tokens by the parser. This is why

```
my-cmdlet -parm arg
```

treats `-parm` as a parameter and

```
my-cmdlet "-parm" arg
```

treats `"-parm"` as an argument. There is an additional wrinkle in the parameter binding. If an unquoted parameter like `-notAparameter` is not actually a parameter on `my-cmdlet`, it will be treated as an argument. This lets you say

```
write-host  -this -is -a parameter
```

without requiring quoting.

This finishes our coverage of the basics of parsing modes, quoting, and commands. However, since commands can take arbitrary lists of arguments, knowing when the statement ends is important. We'll cover this in the next section.

2.2.4 Statement termination

In PowerShell, there are two statement terminator characters: the semicolon (;) and (sometimes) the newline. Why is newline a statement separator only sometimes? The rule is that if the previous text is a syntactically complete statement, a newline is considered to be a statement termination. If it isn't complete, the newline is simply treated like any other whitespace. This is how the interpreter can determine when a command or expression crosses multiple lines. For example, in the following:

```
PS (1) > 2 +
>> 2
>>
4
PS (2) >
```

the sequence "2 +" is incomplete so the interpreter prompts you to enter more text. (This is indicated by the nest prompt characters >>.) On the other hand, in the next sequence

```
PS (2) > 2
2
PS (3) > + 2
2
PS (4) >
```

The number 2 by itself is a complete expression, so the interpreter goes ahead and evaluates it. Likewise, "+ 2" is a complete expression and is also evaluated (+ in this case is treated as the unary plus operator). From this, you can see that if the newline comes *after* the plus operator, the interpreter will treat the two lines as a single expression. If the newline comes *before* the plus operator, it will treat the two lines as two individual expressions.

Most of the time, this mechanism works the way you expect, but sometimes you can receive some unanticipated results. Take a look at the following example:

```
PS (22) > $b = ( 2
>> + 2 )
>>
Missing closing ')' in expression.
At line:2 char:1
+ + <<<<  2 )
PS (23) >
```

This was a question raised by one of our beta testers. They were surprised by this result and thought there was something wrong with the interpreter, but in fact, this is not a bug. Here's what's happening:

Consider the following text:

```
> $b = (2 +
> 2)
```

It is parsed as $b = (2 + 2) because a trailing "+" operator is only valid as part of a binary operator expression. Since the sequence $b = (2 + can't be a syntactically complete statement, the newline is treated as whitespace. On the other hand, consider the text

```
> $b = (2
> + 2)
```

In this case, 2 is a syntactically complete statement, so the newline is now treated as a line terminator. In effect, the sequence is parsed like $b = (2 ; +2); that is, two complete statements. Since the syntax for a parenthetical expression is

```
( <expr> )
```

you get a syntax error—the interpreter is looking for a closing parenthesis as soon as it has a complete expression. Contrast this with using a *subexpression* instead of just the parentheses:

```
>> $b = $(
>> 2
>> +2
>> )
>>
PS (24) > $b
2
2
```

Here the expression is valid because the syntax for subexpressions is

```
$( <statementList> )
```

But how do you deal with the case when you do need to extend a line that isn't extensible by itself? This is another place where you can use the backtick escape character. If the last character in the line is a backtick then the newline will be treated as simple breaking space instead of as a new line:

```
PS (1) > write-output `
>> -inputobject `
>> "Hello world"
>>
Hello world
PS (2) >
```

Finally, one thing that surprises some people is that strings are not terminated by a newline character. Strings can carry over multiple lines until a matching, closing quote is encountered:

```
PS (1) > write-output "Hello
>> there
>> how are
>> you?"
>>
```

```
Hello
there
how are
you?
PS (2) >
```

In this example, you could see a string that extended across multiple lines. When that string was displayed, the newlines were preserved in the string.

The handling of end-of-line characters in PowerShell is another of the tradeoffs we had to make for PowerShell to be useful as a shell. Although the handling of end-of-line characters is a bit strange compared to non-shell languages, the overall result is easy for most people to get used to.

2.3   PIPELINES AND COMMANDS

At long last we get to the details of pipelines. We've been talking about them throughout this chapter, but here we discuss them in detail. A pipeline is a series of commands separated by the pipe operator "|" as shown in figure 2.3. In some ways, the term *production line* better describes pipelines in PowerShell. Each command in the pipeline receives an object from the previous command, performs some operation on it, and then passes it along to the next command in the pipeline.

AUTHOR'S NOTE   This, by the way, is the great PowerShell Heresy. All (for some definition of all) previous shells passed strings only through the pipeline. Many people had difficulty with the notion of doing anything else. Like the character in *The Princess Bride*, they would cry "inconceivable!" And we would respond, "I do not think that word means what you think it means."

All of the command categories take parameters and arguments. To review, a parameter is a special token that starts with a hyphen ("-") and is used to control the behavior of the command. An argument is a data value consumed by the command. In the following example:

```
get-childitem –filter *.dll –path c:\windows -recurse
```

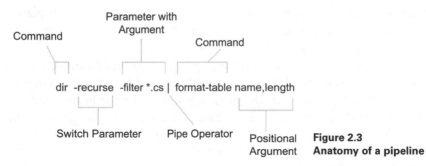

Figure 2.3
Anatomy of a pipeline

-filter is a parameter that takes one argument *.dll. The string c:\windows is the argument to the positional parameter -path.

Next we'll discuss the signature characteristic of pipelines—streaming behavior.

2.3.1 Pipelines and streaming behavior

Streaming behavior occurs when objects are processed one at a time in a pipeline. As mentioned, this is one of the characteristic behaviors of shell languages. In stream processing, objects are output from the pipeline as soon as they become available. In more traditional programming environments, the results are returned only when the entire result set has been generated—the first result and the last result are returned at the same time. In a pipelined shell, the first result is returned as soon as it is available and subsequent results return as they also become available.

This aspect of streaming is important in an interactive shell environment, since you want to see objects as soon as they are available. The next example shows a simple pipeline that traverses through C:\WINDOWS looking for all of the DLLs that have the word "system" in their names:

```
PS (1) > dir -rec -fil *.dll | where {$_.name -match "system.*dll"}


    Directory:
Microsoft.Management.Automation.Core\FileSystem::C:\WINDOWS\assembly
\GAC\System\1.0.3300.0__b77a5c561934e089


Mode                LastWriteTime     Length Name
----                -------------     ------ ----
-a---         2/26/2004   6:29 PM    1167360 System.dll


    Directory:
Microsoft.Management.Automation.Core\FileSystem::C:\WINDOWS\assembly
\GAC\System\1.0.5000.0__b77a5c561934e089


Mode                LastWriteTime     Length Name
----                -------------     ------ ----
-a---         2/26/2004   6:36 PM    1216512 System.dll
```

With streaming behavior, as soon as the first file is found, it's displayed. Without streaming, you would have to wait until the entire directory structure has been searched before you'd start to see any results.

In most shell environments, streaming is accomplished by using separate processes for each element in the pipeline. In PowerShell, which only uses a single process (and a single thread as well), streaming is accomplished by splitting cmdlets into three clauses: begin-processing, process-object, and end-processing. In a pipeline, the begin-processing clause is run for all cmdlets in the pipeline. Then the process-object clause is run for the first cmdlet. If this clause produces an object, that object is passed to the process-object clause of the next cmdlet in the pipeline, and so on. Finally the end-processing clauses are all run. (We cover this sequencing again in more detail in chapter 7, which is about scripts and functions, since they can also have these clauses.)

2.3.2 Parameters and parameter binding

Now let's talk about more of the details involved in binding parameters to commands. *Parameter binding* is the process in which values are bound to the parameters on a command. These values can come from either the command line or the pipeline. Here is an example of a parameter argument being bound from the command line:

```
PS (1) > write-output -inputobject 123
123
```

and here is the same example where the parameter is taken from the input object stream:

```
PS (2) > 123 | write-output
123
```

The binding process is controlled by declaration information on the command itself. Parameters can have the following characteristics: they are either mandatory or optional; they have a type to which the formal argument must be convertible; and they can have attributes that allow the parameters to be bound from the pipeline. Table 2.3 describes the actual steps in the binding process:

Table 2.3 Steps in the parameter binding process

Binding Step	Description
1. Bind all named parameters	Find all unquoted tokens on the command line that start with a dash. If the token ends with a ":" then an argument is required. If there is no ":" then look at the type of the parameter and see if an argument is required. Convert the type of actual argument to the type required by the parameter and bind the parameter.
2. Bind all positional parameters	If there are any arguments on the command line that haven't been used, look for unbound parameters that take positional parameters and try to bind them.
3. Bind from the pipeline by value with exact match	If the command is not the first command in the pipeline and there are still unbound parameters that take pipeline input, try to bind to a parameter that matches the type exactly.
4. If not bound, then bind from the pipe by value with conversion	If the previous step failed, then try to bind using a type conversion.
5. If not bound, then bind from the pipeline by name with exact match	If the previous step failed, then look for a property on the input object that matches the name of the parameter. If the types exactly match, then bind the parameter.
6. If not bound, then bind from the pipeline by name with conversion	If the input object has a property whose name matches the name of a parameters and the type of the parameter is convertible to the type of the parameter, then bind the parameter.

As you can see, this binding process is quite involved. In practice, the parameter binder almost always does what you want—that's why a sophisticated algorithm is used; however, there are times when you'll need to understand the binding algorithm to get a particular behavior. PowerShell has built-in facilities for debugging the parameter binding process that can be accessed through the `Trace-Command` cmdlet. (`Trace-Command` is covered in detail in chapter 9.) Here is an example showing how to use this cmdlet:

```
trace-command -name ParameterBinding  -Option All `
-Expression { 123 | write-output } -PSHost
```

In this example, we are tracing the expression in the braces—that is the expression:

```
123 | write-output
```

This expression pipes the number 123 to the cmdlet `Write-Output`. The `Write-Output` cmdlet takes a single mandatory parameter `-InputObject`, which allows pipeline input by value. (The tracing output is long but fairly self-explanatory, so I haven't included it here. This is something that you should experiment with to see how it can help you figure out what's going on in the parameter binding process.)

And now for the final topic in this chapter: formatting and output. The formatting and output subsystem is the magic that lets PowerShell figure out how to display the output of the commands you type.

2.4 FORMATTING AND OUTPUT

We've reached this point without actually discussing how PowerShell figures out how to display output. In general, we've just run commands and depended on the system to figure out how to display the results. Occasionally we've used commands such as `Format-Table` and `Format-List` to give general guidance on the shape of the display, but no specific details. Let's dig in now and see how this all works.

As always, since PowerShell is a type-based system, types are used to determine how things are displayed. However, normal objects don't usually know how to display themselves. PowerShell deals with this by including a database of formatting information for different types of objects. This is part of the *extended type system*, which is an important component of the overall system. This extended type system allows PowerShell to add new behaviors to existing .NET objects. The default formatting database is stored in the PowerShell install directory, which you can get to by using the `$PSHOME` shell variable. Here's a list of the files that were included at the time this book was written:

```
PS (1) > dir $PSHOME/*format* | ft name

Name
----
Certificate.Format.ps1xml
DotNetTypes.Format.ps1xml
FileSystem.Format.ps1xml
Help.Format.ps1xml
PowerShellCore.Format.ps1xml
PowerShellTrace.Format.ps1xml
Registry.format.ps1xml
```

You can more or less figure out what types of things each of these files contains descriptions for. (The others should become clear after reading the rest of this book.) These files are XML documents that contain descriptions of how each type of object should be displayed. In fact, these descriptions are fairly complex and somewhat difficult to write. It is possible for end-users to add their own type descriptions, but that's beyond the scope of this chapter. The important thing to understand is how the formatting and outputting commands work together.

2.4.1 The formatting cmdlets

Display of information is controlled by the type of the objects being displayed, but the user can choose the *shape* of the object by using the "format-*" commands:

```
PS (5) > get-command format-* | ft name

Name
----
Format-Custom
Format-List
Format-Table
Format-Wide
```

By shape, we mean things such as a table or a list. Here's how they work. The Format-Table cmdlet formats output as a series of columns displayed across your screen:

```
PS (1) > get-item c:\ | format-table

    Directory:

Mode             LastWriteTime     Length Name
----             -------------     ------ ----
d--hs       4/9/2006  10:04 PM            C:\
```

By default, it tries to use the maximum width of the display and guesses at how wide a particular field should be. This allows you to start seeing data as quickly as possible (streaming behavior), but doesn't always produce optimal results. You can achieve a better display by using the -autosize switch, but this requires the formatter to process every element before displaying any of them. It has to do this to figure out the best width to use for each field. The result in this example looks like:

```
PS (3) > get-item c:\ | format-table -autosize

    Directory:

Mode          LastWriteTime Length Name
----          ------------- ------ ----
d--hs    4/9/2006  10:04 PM        C:\
```

Okay—so it doesn't look much different: things are more compressed with less whitespace. In practice, the streaming default layout is pretty good and you don't need to use -autosize, but sometimes it can help make things more readable.

The Format-List command, on the other hand, displays the elements of the objects as a list, one after the other:

```
PS (2) > get-item c:\ | format-list

    Directory:

Name           : C:\
CreationTime   : 2/26/2001 3:38:39 PM
LastWriteTime  : 4/9/2006 10:04:38 PM
LastAccessTime : 4/11/2006 9:33:51 PM
```

If there is more than one object to display, they will appear as a series of lists. Let's try this:

```
PS (3) > get-item c:\,d:\ | fl

    Directory:

Name           : C:\
CreationTime   : 2/26/2001 3:38:39 PM
LastWriteTime  : 6/21/2006 1:20:06 PM
LastAccessTime : 6/21/2006 9:14:46 PM

Name           : D:\
CreationTime   : 12/31/1979 11:00:00 PM
LastWriteTime  : 12/31/1979 11:00:00 PM
LastAccessTime : 12/31/1979 11:00:00 PM
```

This is usually the best way to display a large collection of fields that won't fit well across the screen. (Obviously the idea of an -autosize switch makes no sense for this type of formatter.)

The Format-Wide cmdlet is used when you want to display a single object property in a concise way. It will treat the screen as a series of columns for displaying the same information. Here's an example:

```
PS (1) > gps s* | format-wide -Column 8 id

1372      640      516      1328     400      532      560      828
876       984      1060     1124     4
```

In this example, we want to display the process ids of all processes whose names start with "s" in eight columns. This formatter allows for dense display of information.

The final formatter is `Format-Custom`. This displays objects while preserving the basic structure of the object. Since most objects have a structure that contains other objects which, in turn, contain other objects, this can produce extremely verbose output. Here's a small part of the output from the `Get-Item` cmdlet, displayed using `Format-Custom`:

```
PS (10) > get-item c:\ | format-custom -depth 1

class DirectoryInfo
{
  PSPath = Microsoft.PowerShell.Core\FileSystem::C:\
  PSParentPath =
  PSChildName = C:\
  PSDrive =
    class PSDriveInfo
    {
      CurrentLocation =
      Name = C
      Provider = Microsoft.PowerShell.Core\FileSystem
      Root = C:\
      Description = C_Drive
      Credential = System.Management.Automation.PSCredential
    }
```

The full output is considerably longer, and notice that we've told it to stop walking the object structure at a depth of 1. You can imagine just how verbose this output can be! So why have this cmdlet? Because it's a useful debugging tool, either when you're creating your own objects or just for exploring the existing objects in the .NET class libraries. You can see that this is a tool to keep in your back pocket for when you're getting down and dirty with objects, but not something that you'll typically use on a day-to-day basis.

2.4.2 The outputter cmdlets

Now that we know how to format something, how do we output it? You don't have to worry because, by default, things are automatically sent to (can you guess?) `Out-Default`.

> **AUTHOR'S NOTE**
> Note that all of the following three examples do exactly the same thing.
>
> dir | out-default
> dir | format-table
> dir | format-table | out-default
>
> This is because the formatter knows how to get the default outputter, the default outputter knows how to find the default formatter, and the system in general knows how to find the defaults for both. The Möbius strip of subsystems!

As with the formatters, there are several outputter cmdlets available in PowerShell out of the box. You can use the Get-Command command to find them:

```
PS (1) > get-command out-* | ft name

Name
----
Out-Default
Out-File
Out-Host
Out-Null
Out-Printer
Out-String
```

Here we have a somewhat broader range of choices. We've already talked about Out-Default. The next one we'll talk about is Out-Null. This is a simple outputter; anything sent to Out-Null is simply discarded. This is useful when you don't care about the output for a command; you want the side effect of running the command. For example, the mkdir command outputs a listing of the directory it just created.

```
PS (1) > mkdir foo


    Directory: Microsoft.PowerShell.Core\FileSystem::C:\Temp


Mode                LastWriteTime     Length Name
----                -------------     ------ ----
d----          6/25/2006   8:50 PM           foo
```

If you don't want to see this output, pipe it to Out-Null. First remove the directory we created, then create the directory.

```
PS (2) > rmdir foo
PS (3) > mkdir foo | out-null
PS (4) > get-item foo


    Directory: Microsoft.PowerShell.Core\FileSystem::C:\Temp


Mode                LastWriteTime     Length Name
----                -------------     ------ ----
d----          6/25/2006   8:50 PM           foo
```

And finally, since we didn't get the message, we verify that the directory was actually created.

AUTHOR'S NOTE   For the I/O redirection fans in the audience; piping to Out-Null is essentially equivalent to doing redirecting to $null. So

```
mkdir foo | out-null
```

is equivalent to

```
mkdir foo > $null
```

Next we have `Out-File`. Instead of sending the output to the screen, this sends it to a file. (This command is also used by I/O redirection when doing output to a file.) In addition to writing the formatted output, `Out-File` has several flags that control how this output is written. These flags include the ability to append to a file instead of replacing it, to force writing to read-only files, and to choose the output encodings for the file. This last item is the trickiest one. You can choose from a number of the text encodings supported by Windows. Since I can never remember what they all are, here's a trick: enter the command with an encoding that you know doesn't exist:

```
PS (9) > out-file -encoding blah
Out-File : Cannot validate argument "blah" because it does
not belong to the set "unicode, utf7, utf8, utf32, ascii, b
igendianunicode, default, oem".
At line:1 char:19
+ out-file -encoding  <<<< blah
PS (10) >
```

You can see in the error message that all of the valid encoding names are displayed. Now, if you don't understand what these encodings are, don't worry about it and just let the system use its default value.

> **AUTHOR'S NOTE** Where you are likely to run into problems with output encoding (or input encoding for that matter) is when you are creating files that are going to be read by another program. These programs may have limitations on what encodings they can handle, especially older programs. To find out more about file encodings, search for "file encodings" on http://msdn.microsoft.com. MSDN contains a wealth of information on this topic. Chapter 10 also contains additional information about working with file encodings in PowerShell.

The `Out-Printer` cmdlet doesn't need much additional explanation; it simply routes its output to the printer instead of to a file or to the screen.

The `Out-Host` cmdlet is a bit more interesting—it sends its output back to the *host*. This has to do with the separation in PowerShell between the interpreter or engine and the application that *hosts* that engine. In theory, the host could be any application. It could be Visual Studio, it could one of the Microsoft Office applications, or it could be a custom third-party application. In each of those cases, the host application would have to implement a special set of interfaces so that `Out-Host` could render its output properly. In practice, since the only host that's shipped with version 1 of PowerShell is a console host, this means that `Out-Host` renders its output on the screen.

> **AUTHOR'S NOTE** `Out-Default` delegates the actual work of outputting to the screen to `Out-Host`.

The last output cmdlet to discuss is `Out-String`. This one's a bit different. All of the other cmdlets sent the output off somewhere else and didn't write anything to the pipeline. The Out-String cmdlet formats its input and sends it as a string to the next cmdlet in the pipeline. Note that I said *string*, not *strings*. By default, it sends the entire output as a single string. This is not always the most desirable behavior—a collection of lines is usually more useful—but at least once you have the string, you can manipulate it into the form you want. Now, if you do want the output as a series of strings, use the -stream switch parameter. When this parameter is specified, the output will be broken into lines and streamed one at a time.

Note that this cmdlet runs somewhat counter to the philosophy of PowerShell; once you've rendered the object to a string, you've lost its structure. The main reason for including this cmdlet is for interoperation with existing APIs and external commands that expect to deal with strings. So, if you find yourself using Out-String a lot in your scripts, stop and think if it's really the best way to be attacking the problem.

That's it for the basics: commands, parameters, pipelines, parsing, and presentation. You should now have a sufficient foundation to start moving on to some of the more advanced topics in PowerShell.

2.5   SUMMARY

Chapter 2 covered the basic structure of PowerShell commands, pipelines, and syntax:

- We discussed the basic command and pipeline syntax and command parameter binding.
- PowerShell has four types of commands: cmdlets, functions, script commands, and native commands, each with slightly different characteristics.
- We discussed the notion of elastic syntax—concise on the command line and complete in scripts.
- The fact that PowerShell is a command language as well as a scripting language impacts how it parses text in a number of ways:
- PowerShell parses scripts in two modes: expression mode and command mode, which is a critical point to appreciate when using PowerShell.
- The PowerShell escape character is backtick (`), not backslash.
- PowerShell supports both double-quotes and single-quotes; variable and expression expansion is done in double quotes but not in single quotes.
- Line termination is handled specially in PowerShell because it is a command language.
- PowerShell uses a sophisticated formatting and outputting system to determine how to render objects without requiring detailed input from the user.

Working with types

*"When I use a word," Humpty Dumpty said, in rather a scornful
tone, "it means just what I choose it to mean—neither more nor less."*

—Lewis Carroll, *Through the Looking Glass*

As we've discussed previously, the use of objects in PowerShell makes PowerShell unlike most shell environments, which can only deal with strings. And where you have objects, you also have object *types*. In fact much of the power in PowerShell comes from the innovative way we use types. In this chapter, we'll look at the PowerShell type system and how to take advantage of it, and examine some of the things you can accomplish with types in PowerShell.

3.1   TYPE MANAGEMENT IN THE WILD, WILD WEST

Shell languages are frequently called *typeless* languages. This is not really accurate since, fundamentally, programming is all about working with different types of objects. The more interesting question is how much implicit work the system does in handling types and how much work is required of you. This spectrum of effort is conventionally split into static and dynamic typing. In statically typed systems, much work is done for you as long as you stay within the domain of the types you're working on. Once you move outside that domain, it's up to the user to figure out how to move objects between those domains. The other cost of static typing is that you are required to declare the type of every variable, even when the compiler can figure it out for itself. Take the following C# statement for example:

```
string myString = "hello world";
```

The variable myString is declared to be a string, even though it's obvious that it has to be a string. You're assigning a string to it, so what else could it be? It's this kind of redundancy that dynamic languages try to avoid. In dynamically typed languages, the user is rarely required to specify the type of a variable. Typically you don't even have to declare the variable at all.

3.1.1 PowerShell: a type-promiscuous language

The tendency is to characterize PowerShell as a dynamically typed language, but a better description is that PowerShell is a *type-promiscuous* language (sounds salacious doesn't it?). By *type-promiscuous*, we mean that PowerShell will expend a tremendous amount of effort trying to turn what you have into what you need with as little work on your part as it can manage. When you ask for a property Y, PowerShell doesn't care if the object foo is a member of class X. It only cares whether foo has a property Y.

People who are used to strongly typed environments find this approach disturbing. It sounds too much like "Wild Wild West" type management. In practice, the interpreter is very careful about making sure its transformations are reasonable and that no information is unexpectedly lost. This is particularly important when dealing with numeric calculations. In PowerShell, you can freely mix and match different types of numbers in expressions. You can even include strings in this mix. PowerShell converts everything as needed *as long as there is no loss in precision without specific guidance from the user.* We'll use the remainder of this section to present a number of examples that illustrate this point. We'll look at operations where the conversions succeed and the type of the result of the operation. (For convenience, we'll use the .NET GetType() method to look at the base type of the results of the various expressions.) We'll also look at some examples where there is an error because the conversion causes some significant loss of information.

In our first example, let's add an integer, a floating point number, and a string that contains only digits.

```
PS (1) > 2 + 3.0 + "4"
9
PS (2) > (2 + 3.0 + "4").GetType().FullName
System.Double
```

As you can see from the result, everything was *widened* to a double-precision floating point number. (*Widening* means converting to a representation that can handle larger or wider numbers: a [long] is wider than an [int], and so forth.) Now let's be a bit trickier. Let's put the floating point number into quotes this time.

```
PS (3) > 2 + "3.0" + 4
9
PS (4) > (2 + "3.0" + 4).GetType().FullName
System.Double
```

Once again the system determines that the expression has to be done in floating point.

NOTE   The .NET single-precision floating point representation isn't typically used unless you request it. In PowerShell, there usually isn't a performance benefit for using single precision, so there is no reason to use this less precise representation.

Now let's look at some simple examples that involve only integers. As you would expect, all these operations result in integers as long as the result can be represented as an integer.

```
PS (5) > (3 + 4)
7
PS (6) > (3 + 4).GetType().FullName
System.Int32
PS (7) > (3 * 4).GetType().FullName
System.Int32
```

Let's try an example using the division operator:

```
PS (8) > 6/3
2
PS (9) > (6/3).GetType().FullName
System.Int32
```

Since 6 is divisible by 3, the result of this division is also an integer. But what happens if the divisor isn't a factor? Let's try it and see.

```
PS (10) > 6/4
1.5
PS (11) > (6/4).GetType().FullName
System.Double
```

The result is now a double. The system noticed that there would be a loss of information if the operation were performed with integers, so it's executed using doubles instead.

Finally, let's try some examples using scientific notation. Let's add an integer to a large decimal.

```
PS (10) > 1e300
1E+300
PS (11) > 1e300 + 12
1E+300
```

The operation executed with the result being a double. In effect, adding an integer to a number of this magnitude means that the integer is ignored. This sort of loss is considered "OK" by the system. But there is another numeric type that is designed to be precise: System.Decimal. Normally you only use this type when you really care about the precision of the result. Let's try the previous example, adding a decimal instead of an integer.

```
PS (12) > 1e300 + 12d
Cannot convert "1E+300" to "System.Decimal". Error: "Value was
either too large or too small for a
Decimal."
At line:1 char:8
+ 1e300 +  <<<< 12d
PS (13) >
```

This results in an error because when one of the operands involved is a [decimal] value, all operands are converted to decimal first and then the operation is performed. Since 1e300 is too large to be represented as a decimal, the operation will fail with an exception rather than lose precision.

From these examples, you can see that while the PowerShell type conversion system is aggressive in the types of conversions it performs, it is also careful about how it does things.

Now that you have a sense of the importance of types in PowerShell, let's look at how it all works.

3.1.2 The type system and type adaptation

Since everything in PowerShell involves types in one way or another, it's important to understand how the PowerShell type system works. That's what we're going to cover in this section. At the core of the PowerShell type system is the .NET type system. Little by little, .NET is expanding to encapsulate everything in the Windows world, but it hasn't swallowed everything yet. There are still several other object representations that Windows users, especially Windows system administrators, have to deal with. There's COM (essentially the precursor to .NET); WMI, which uses MOF (Management Object Format) definitions; ADO database objects; ADSI directory services; and so on (welcome to Object Alphabet Soup). There's even everyone's favorite old/new (as in "everything old is new" again) object representation: XML. And finally the .NET libraries, as well-designed as they are, aren't always quite what you want them to be.

In an effort to bring harmony to this object soup and fix some of the shortcomings of the various object representations, PowerShell uses a *type-adaptation system* that masks all of the details of these different objects' representations. A PowerShell script never directly accesses an object. It always goes through the type adaptation layer—the *PSObject* layer—that rationalizes the interfaces presented to the user. The PSObject layer allows for a uniquely consistent user experience when working with the different types of objects. This architecture is shown in figure 3.1.

When you see an expression like

```
$x.Count
```

you don't have to know or care about the type of object stored in $x. You only care that it has a property named Count. PowerShell never generates code to directly access the Count property on a particular type of object. Instead it makes an indirect call through

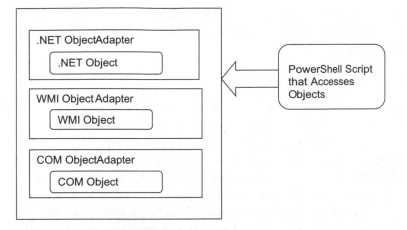

Figure 3.1 This diagram shows the architecture of the PowerShell type adaptation system. For each kind of data that PowerShell works with, there is a corresponding adapter. An instance of a particular data object is subsequently wrapped in an instance of the associated type adapter. This type adapter instance acts as an intermediary between the object and PowerShell, proxying all accesses.

the PSObject layer, which figures out how a Count property for the object can be accessed. If $x contains a .NET object, it will return that object's Length property. If $x contains an XML document, the XML adapter will look for a node called "count" on the top level of that XML document. The object in the variable might not even contain a Count property at all. With PowerShell, you can have a type system with a synthetic property (called a PSMember) defined by the type system itself, instead of on the object. Table 3.1 lists the available set of PowerShell object adapters.

Let's recap. The adapter mechanism lets you work with objects in PowerShell. Commands produce objects for you to manipulate through the adapters. But what about

Table 3.1 The basic set of object adapters available in PowerShell

Adapted Object Type	Description
.NET Adapter	This is the basic adapter for all .NET types. This adapter directly maps the properties on the .NET object and adds several new ones that start with a PS prefix.
COM Object Adapter	This adapter provides access to COM objects. Supported objects include the Windows Script Host classes and scriptable applications such as Microsoft Word or Internet Explorer.
WMI Adapter	This adapts objects returned from a WMI provider.
ADO Adapter	This adapter allows you to treat the columns in ADO data tables as though they were properties.
Custom Object Adapter	This adapter manages objects for which there is no actual underlying object, only synthetic properties.
ADSI Object Adapter	This adapts objects returned from the Active Directory Service Interfaces.

data contained or embedded in the script itself? In other words, how are objects stored inline in the scripts? This is accomplished through the various types of *object literals* that we address in the next section.

3.2   BASIC TYPES AND LITERALS

All programming languages have a set of basic or primitive types from which everything else is built up. These primitive types usually have some form of corresponding syntactic *literal*. Literal tokens in the language are used to represent literal data objects in the program. In PowerShell there are the usual literals—strings, numbers, and arrays—but there are some other literals that aren't typically found outside of dynamic languages, namely dictionaries or hashtables. PowerShell also makes heavy use of *type literals* that correspond to type objects in the system. In this section, we'll go through each of the literals, how they are represented in script text, and the details of how they are implemented in the PowerShell runtime.

3.2.1   Strings

There are actually four different kinds of string literals in PowerShell—single-quoted strings, double-quoted strings, single-quoted here-strings, and double-quoted here-strings. The underlying representation for all of these strings is the same, however.

String representation in PowerShell

In PowerShell, a *string* is a sequence of 16-bit Unicode characters and is directly implemented using the .NET System.String type. Since PowerShell strings use Unicode, they can effectively contain characters from every language in the world.

> **AUTHOR'S NOTE**   The encoding used in strings is obviously important in international environments. If you are interested in the nitty-gritty details of the encoding used in System.String, here's what the Microsoft Developer's Network documentation has to say:
>
> "Each Unicode character in a string is defined by a Unicode scalar value, also called a Unicode code point or the ordinal (numeric) value of the Unicode character. Each code point is encoded using UTF-16 encoding, and the numeric value of each element of the encoding is represented by a Char. The resulting collection of Char objects constitutes the String.
>
> "A single Char usually represents a single code point; that is, the numeric value of the Char equals the code point. However, a code point might require more than one encoded element. For example, a Unicode supplementary code point (a surrogate pair) is encoded with two Char objects."
>
> Refer to the MSDN documentation for additional details.

There are a couple of other characteristics that strings in PowerShell inherit from the underlying .NET strings. They can also be arbitrarily long and they are *immutable*—the contents of a string can be copied but can't be changed.

Single and double-quoted strings

Because of the expression-mode/command-mode parsing dichotomy described in chapter 2, there are several ways strings can be represented. In expression mode, a string is denoted by a sequence of characters surrounded by matching quotes, as shown in the following example:

```
PS (1) > "This is a string in double quotes"
This is a string in double quotes
PS (2) > 'This is a string in single quotes'
This is a string in single quotes
PS (3) >
```

Literal strings can contain any character including newlines, with the exception of an unquoted closing quote character. In double-quoted strings, to embed the closing quote character, you have to either quote it with the *backtick* character or double it up. In other words, two adjacent quotes become a single literal quote in the string. In single-quoted strings, doubling up the quote is the only way to embed a literal quote in the string. This is one area where there is an important difference between single- and double-quoted strings. In single-quote strings, the backtick is not special. This means that it can't be used for embedding special characters such as newlines or escaping quotes.

Like the UNIX shells, PowerShell supports variable substitutions. These variable substitutions or *expansions* are only done in double-quoted strings (which is why these are sometimes called *expandable* strings).

AUTHOR'S NOTE Arguments to commands are treated as though they were in double quotes, so variables will be expanded in that situation as well. We'll see examples of this later on.

Let's look at an example of string expansion:

```
PS (1) > $foo = "FOO"
PS (2) > "This is a string in double quotes: $foo"
This is a string in double quotes: FOO
PS (3) > 'This is a string in single quotes: $foo'
This is a string in single quotes: $foo
PS (4) >
```

In the preceding lines, you can see that $foo in the double-quoted string was replaced by the contents of the variable "FOO", but not in the single-quoted case.

Subexpression expansion in strings

Expandable strings can also include arbitrary expressions by using the *subexpression* notation. A subexpression is a fragment of PowerShell script code that is replaced by the value resulting from the evaluation of that code. Here are some examples of sub-expression expansion in strings.

```
PS (1) > "2+2 is $(2+2)"
2+2 is 4
PS (2) > $x=3
```

```
PS (3) > "$x * 2 is $($x * 2)"
3 * 2 is 6
PS (4) >
```

The expression in the $ (...) sequence in the string is replaced by the result of evaluating the expression. $(2+2) is replaced by 4 and so on.

Using complex subexpressions in strings

So far, these examples show only simple embedded expression. In fact, subexpressions allow statement lists—a series of PowerShell statements separated by semicolons—to be embedded. Here's an example where the subexpression contains three simple statements. First let's just execute the three simple statements:

```
PS (1) > 1;2;3    # three statements
1
2
3
```

Now let's execute the same set of statements in a subexpression expansion:

```
PS (2) > "Expanding three statements in a string: $(1; 2; 3)"
Expanding three statements in a string: 1 2 3
PS (3) >
```

The result shows the output of the three statements concatenated together, space-separated, and inserted into the result string. Here's another example of using a for statement in a subexpression expansion.

```
PS (1) > "Numbers 1 thru 10: $(for ($i=1; $i -le 10; $i++) { $i })."
Numbers 1 thru 10: 1 2 3 4 5 6 7 8 9 10.
PS (2) >
```

The output of all the iterations for the loop are gathered up, turned into a string with one value separated from the next by a space, and then substituted into overall string. As you can see, this can be quite powerful. Using a subexpression in a string is one way to quickly generate formatted results when presenting data.

String expansion considerations

PowerShell expands strings when an assignment is executed. It doesn't re-evaluate those strings when the variable is used later on. This is an important point. Let's look at two examples that will make this clear. In these examples, we'll use the post-increment operator ++, which adds one to a variable, and the range operator, which expands to a sequence of numbers. Let's take a look. In the first example, we initialize $x to 0 and then assign a string with an expansion that increments $x to a variable $a. Next we'll output $a three times to see what happens to the value of $x.

```
PS (1) > $x=0
PS (2) > $a = "x is $($x++; $x)"
PS (4) > 1..3 | foreach {$a}
```

```
x is 1
x is 1
x is 1
```

As you can see, $x was incremented once when $a was assigned, but didn't change on subsequent references. Now let's inline the string literal into the body of the loop and see what happens.

```
PS (5) > 1..3 | foreach {"x is $($x++; $x)"}
x is 2
x is 3
x is 4
```

This time around, we can see that $x is being incremented each time. To reiterate, string literal expansion is done only when the literal is assigned.

AUTHOR'S
NOTEThere actually is a way to force a string to be re-expanded if you really need to do it. You can do this by calling $ExecutionContext.InvokeCommand.ExpandString('a is $a'). This method will return a new string with all of the variables expanded.

Here-string literals

Getting back to the discussion of literal string notation, there is one more form of string literal, called a *here-string*. A here-string is used to embed large chunks of text inline in a script. This can be powerful when you're generating output for another program. Here's an example that assigns a here-string to the variable $a.

```
PS (1) > $a = @"
>> Line one
>> Line two
>> Line three
>> "@
>>
PS (2) > $a
Line one
Line two
Line three
```

NOTE TO C# USERS There is a lexical element in C# that looks a lot like PowerShell here-strings. In practice, the C# feature is most like PowerShell's single-quoted strings. In PowerShell, a here-string begins at the end of the line and the terminating sequence must be at the beginning of the line that terminates the here-string. In C#, the string terminates at the first closing quote that isn't doubled up.

When $a is displayed, it contains all of the lines that were entered. Now you're probably saying, "Wait a minute—you told me I can do the same thing with a regular string. What makes here-strings so special?" It has to do with how quoting is handled. Here-strings have special quoting rules.

BASIC TYPES AND LITERALS

63

Here-strings start with @<quote><newline> and end with <newline><quote>@. The <newlines> are important because the here-string quote sequences won't be treated as quotes without the newlines. The content of the here-string is all of the lines between the beginning and ending quotes, but not the lines the quotes are on. Because of the fancy opening and closing quote sequences, other special characters such as quotes that would cause problems in regular strings are fine here. This makes it easy to generate string data without having quoting errors. Here is a more elaborate example

```
PS (1) > $a = @"
>> One is "1"
>> Two is '2'
>> Three is $(2+1)
>> The date is "$(get-date)"
>> "@ + "A trailing line"
>>
PS (2) > $a
One is "1"
Two is '2'
Three is 3
The date is "1/8/2006 9:59:16 PM"A trailing line
PS (3) >
```

On line 1, the here-string is assigned to the variable $a. The contents of the here-string start on line 2. which has a string containing double quotes. Line 3 has a string with single quotes. Line 4 has an embedded expression, and line 5 calls the Get-Date cmdlet in a subexpression to embed the current date into the string. Finally, line 6 appends some trailing text to the whole string. When you look at the output of the variable shown in lines 9-12, you see that the quotes are all preserved and the expansions are shown in place.

That should be enough about strings. We can move on to numbers and numeric literals.

3.2.2 Numbers and numeric literals

As mentioned earlier, PowerShell supports all the basic .NET numeric types and performs conversions to and from the different types as needed. Table 3.2 lists these numeric types.

Table 3.2 Numeric literals

Example Numeric Literal	.NET Full Type Name	Short Type Name
1	System.Int32	[int]
10000000000	System.Int64	[long]
1.1	System.Double	[double]
1d	System.Decimal	[decimal]

Now that we know the basic numeric types, we need to understand how are literals of each type are specified.

Specifying numeric literals

In general, you don't specify a literal having a particular type; the system will figure out the best way to represent the number. By default, an integer will be used. If the literal is too large for a 32-bit integer, a 64-bit integer will be used instead. If it's still too big or if it contains a decimal point, a System.Double will be used. (System.Single is usually skipped, but it offers no advantages and just complicates the process.) The one case where you do want to tell the system that you're requesting a specific type is with the System.Decimal type. These are specified by placing a "d" at the end of the number with no intervening space, as shown:

```
PS (1) > ( 123 ).gettype().fullname
System.Int32
PS (2) > ( 123d ).gettype().fullname
System.Decimal
PS (3) > ( 123.456 ).gettype().fullname
System.Double
PS (4) > ( 123.456d ).gettype().fullname
System.Decimal
```

You can see that in each case where there is a trailing "d", the literal results in a [decimal] value being created. (If there is a space between the number and the "d", you'll just get an error.)

The multiplier suffixes

Of course, plain numbers are fine for most applications, but in the system administration world, there are many special values that you want to be able to conveniently represent, namely those powers of two—kilobytes, megabytes, and gigabytes. PowerShell provides a set of multiplier suffixes for common sizes to help with this, as listed in table 3.3.

Table 3.3 The numeric multiplier suffixes

Multiplier Suffix	Multiplication Factor	Example	Equivalent Value	.NET Type
kb or KB	1024	1KB	1024	System.Int32
kb or KB	1024	2.2kb	2252.8	System.Double
mb or MB	1024*1024	1Mb	1048576	System.Int32
mb or MB	1024*1024	2.2mb	2306867.2	System.Double
gb or GB	1024*1024*1024	1Gb	1073741824	System.Int32
gb or GB	1024*1024*1024	2.14gb	3371549327.36	System.Double

Yes, the PowerShell team is aware that these notations are not consistent with the IEC recommendations (kibabyte, and so on). Since the point of this notation is convenience and most people in the IT space are more comfortable with Kb than with Ki, we choose to err on the side of comfort over conformance in this one case. Sorry. This particular issue generated easily the second most heated debate on the PowerShell internal and external beta tester lists. We'll cover the most heated debate later when we get to the comparison operators.

Hexadecimal literals

The last item we cover in this section is hexadecimal literals. When working with computers, it's obviously useful to be able to specify hex literals. PowerShell uses the same notation as C, C#, and so on; namely preceding the number with the sequence "0x" and allowing the letters A-F as the extra digits. As always, the notation is case-insensitive as shown in the following examples.

```
PS (1) > 0x10
16
PS (2) > 0x55
85
PS (3) > 0x123456789abcdef
81985529216486895
PS (4) > 0xDeadBeef
-559038737
```

Now that we've covered the "basic" literals, string and numbers, let's move on to the more interesting and less common ones.

3.2.3 Collections: dictionaries and hashtables

One of the most flexible datatypes supported in PowerShell is the hashtable. This datatype lets you map a set of keys to a set of values. For example, we may have a hashtable that maps "red" to 1, "green" to 2, and "yellow" to 4.

A dictionary is the general term for a data structure that maps keys to values. In the .NET world, this takes the form of an interface (IDictionary) that describes how a collection should do this mapping. A hashtable is a specific implementation of that interface. While the PowerShell hashtable literal syntax only creates instances of `System.Collections.Hashtable`, scripts that you write will work properly with any object that implements IDictionary.

Creating and inspecting hashtables

In PowerShell, you use hash literals to create a hashtable inline in a script. Here is a simple example:

```
PS (26) > $user = @{ FirstName = "John"; LastName = "Smith";
>> PhoneNumber = "555-1212" }
PS (27) > $user

Key                           Value
---                           -----
LastName                      Smith
FirstName                     John
PhoneNumber                   555-1212
```

This example created a hashtable that contained three key-value pairs. The hashtable starts with the token "@{" and ends with "}". Inside the delimiters, you define a set of key-value pairs where the key and value are separated by an equals sign "=". Formally, the syntax for a hash literal is

```
<hashLiteral> = '@{' <keyExpression> '='  <pipeline> [ <separator>
<keyExpression> '=' <pipeline> ] * '}'

<separator> = ';' | <newline>
```

Now that we've created a hashtable, let's see how we can use it. PowerShell allows you to access members in a hashtable in two ways—through property notation and through array notation. Here's what the property notation looks like:

```
PS (3) > $user.firstname
John
PS (4) > $user.lastname
Smith
```

This notation lets you treat a hashtable like an object. This access method is intended to facilitate the use of hashtables as a kind of lightweight data record. Now let's look at using the array notation.

```
PS (5) > $user["firstname"]
John
PS (6) > $user["firstname","lastname"]
John
Smith
```

Property notation works pretty much the way you'd expect; you specify a property name and get the corresponding value back. Array notation, on the other hand, is more interesting. In the second command in the example, we provided two keys and got two values back.

Here's an example that shows some additional features of the underlying hashtable object. The underlying object for PowerShell hashtables is the .NET type System.Collections.Hashtable. This type has a number of properties and methods that you can use. One of these properties is the keys property. This property will give you a list of all of the keys in the hashtable.

```
PS (7) > $user.keys
LastName
FirstName
PhoneNumber
```

In the array access notation, you can use keys to get a list of all of the values in the table.

```
PS (8) > $user[$user.keys]
Smith
John
555-1212
```

A more efficient way to get all of the values from a hashtable is to use the Values property. The point of this example is to demonstrate how you can use multiple indexes to retrieve the values based on a subset of the keys.

You might have noticed that the keys property didn't return the keys in alphabetical order. This is because of the way hashtables work; i.e., keys are randomly distributed in the table to speed up access. If you do need to get the values in alphabetical order, here's how you can do it:

```
PS (10) > $user.keys | sort-object
FirstName
LastName
PhoneNumber
```

The Sort-Object (or just sort) cmdlet sorts the keys into alphabetical order and returns a list. Let's use this list to index the table.

```
PS (11) > $user[[string[]] ($user.keys | sort)]
John
Smith
555-1212
```

You'll notice something funny about the last example: we had to *cast* or convert the sorted list into an array of strings. This is because the hashtable keys mechanism expects strings, not objects, as keys. There's much more on casts later in this chapter.

Modifying and manipulating hashtables

Now let's look at adding, changing, and removing elements from the hashtable. First let's add the date and the city where the user lives to the $user table.

```
PS (1) > $user.date = get-date
PS (2) > $user
Key                     Value
---                     -----
LastName                Smith
date                    1/15/2006 12:01:10 PM
FirstName               John
PhoneNumber             555-1212
```

```
PS (3) > $user["city"] = "Seattle"
PS (4) > $user
Key                        Value
---                        -----
city                       Seattle
LastName                   Smith
date                       1/15/2006 12:01:10 PM
FirstName                  John
PhoneNumber                555-1212
```

A simple assignment using either the property or array accessor notation allows you to add an element to a hashtable. Now let's say we got the city wrong—Bob really lives in Detroit. Let's fix that.

```
PS (5) > $user.city = "Detroit"
PS (6) > $user
Key                        Value
---                        -----
city                       Detroit
LastName                   Smith
date                       1/15/2006 12:01:10 PM
FirstName                  John
PhoneNumber                555-1212
```

As this example shows, simple assignment is the way to update an element. Finally, we don't really want this element, so let's remove it from the table with the remove() method.

```
PS (7) > $user.remove("city")
PS (8) > $user
Key                        Value
---                        -----
LastName                   Smith
date                       1/15/2006 12:01:10 PM
FirstName                  John
PhoneNumber                555-1212
```

The hashtable no longer contains the element.

If you want to create an empty hashtable, use @{ } with no member specifications between the braces. This creates an empty table that you can then add members to incrementally.

```
PS (1) > $newHashTable = @{}
PS (2) > $newHashTable
PS (3) > $newHashTable.one =1
PS (4) > $newHashTable.two = 2
PS (5) > $newHashTable

Key                        Value
---                        -----
two                        2
one                        1
```

In the example, there were no members initially; we added two by making assignments. The members are created on assignment.

Hashtables as reference types

Hashtables are *reference types*, so if you create a hashtable, assign it to a variable $foo, and assign $foo to another variable $bar, you will have two variables that point to or *reference* the same object. Consequently, any changes that are made to one variable will affect the other, because they're pointing to the same object. Let's try this out. Create a new hashtable and assign it to $foo.

```
PS (2) > $foo = @{
>> a = 1
>> b = 2
>> c = 3
>> }
>>
PS (3) > $foo
Key                     Value
---                     -----
a                       1
b                       2
c                       3
```

Now assign $foo to $bar and verify that it matches $foo as we expect.

```
PS (4) > $bar = $foo
PS (5) > $bar
Key                     Value
---                     -----
a                       1
b                       2
c                       3
```

Next assign a new value to the element "a" in $foo.

```
PS (6) > $foo.a = "Hi there"
PS (7) > $foo.a
Hi there
```

And let's look at what happened to $bar:

```
PS (8) > $bar.a
Hi there
PS (9) > $bar
Key                     Value
---                     -----
a                       Hi there
b                       2
c                       3
```

The change that was made to $foo has been reflected in $bar.

There is still more to know about hashtables and how they work with operators, but we'll cover that in chapters 4 and 5. For now, we'll move on to the next data type.

3.2.4 Collections: arrays and sequences

In the previous section, we talked about hashtables and hash literals. Now let's talk about the PowerShell syntax for arrays and array literals. Most programming languages have some kind of array literal notation similar to the PowerShell hash literal notation, where there is a beginning character sequence followed by a list of values, followed by a closing character sequence. Here's how array literals are defined in PowerShell:

They're not. There is no array literal notation in PowerShell.

Yes, you read that correctly. There is no array literal notation in PowerShell. So how exactly does this work? How do you define an inline array in a PowerShell script? Here's how to do it: instead of having array literals, there is a set of operations that create collections as needed. In fact, collections of objects are created and discarded transparently throughout PowerShell. If you need an array, one will be created for you. If you need a singleton (or *scalar*) value, the collection will be unwrapped as needed.

Collecting pipeline output as an array

The most common operation resulting in an array in PowerShell is collecting the output from a pipeline. When you run a pipeline that emits a sequence of objects and assign that output to a variable, it automatically collects the elements into an array, specifically into a .NET object of type [object[]].

But what about building a simple array in an expression? The simplest way to do this is to use the comma operator (","). For example, at the command line, type

```
1,2,3
```

and you'll have created a sequence of numbers. (See chapter 5 for more information about using the comma operator.) When you assign that sequence to a variable, it is stored as an array. Let's assign these three numbers to a variable $a and look at the type of the result.

```
PS (1) > $a = 1,2,3
PS (2) > $a.gettype().fullname
System.Object[]
```

As in the pipeline case, the result is stored in an array of type [object[]].

Array indexing

Let's explore some of the operations that can be performed on arrays. As is commonly the case, getting and setting elements of the array (*array indexing*) is done with square brackets. The length of an array can be retrieved with the Length property.

```
PS (3) > $a.length
3
PS (4) > $a[0]
1
```

Note that arrays in PowerShell are *origin-zero*; that is, the first element in the array is at index 0, not index 1. As the example showed, the first element of $a is in $a[0].

As with hashtables, changes are made to an array by assigning new values to indexes in the array. In the following example, we'll assign new values to the first and third elements in $a.

```
PS (5) > $a[0] = 3.1415
PS (6) > $a
3.1415
2
3
PS (7) > $a[2] = "Hi there"
PS (8) > $a
3.1415
2
Hi there
PS (9) >
```

Looking at the output, we can see that elements of the array have been changed. Simple assignment updates the element at the specified index.

Polymorphism in arrays

Another important thing to note from the previous example is that arrays are *polymorphic* by default. By polymorphic we mean that you can store *any* type of object in an array. (A VBScript user would call these *variant* arrays). When we created the array, we assigned only integers to it. In the subsequent assignments, we assigned a floating-point number and a string. The original array was capable of storing any kind of object. In formal terms, PowerShell arrays are *polymorphic* by default (though it is possible to create type-constrained arrays).

Earlier we saw how to get the length of an array. What happens when we try to assign to an element past the end of the array? The next example illustrates this.

```
PS (9) > $a.length
3
PS (10) > $a[4] = 22
Array assignment failed because index '4' was out of range.
At line:1 char:4
+ $a[4 <<<< ] = 22
PS (11) >
```

Attempts to assign outside the bounds of an array will result in a range error. This is because PowerShell arrays are based on .NET arrays and they are of fixed size. So how can I add more elements to a PowerShell array if the underlying objects are fixed in size? In fact, this is easily done through array concatenation using the plus ("+") or plus-equals ("+=") operators. Let's add two more elements to the array from the previous example.

```
PS (11) > $a += 22,33
PS (12) > $a.length
5
PS (13) > $a[4]
33
PS (14) >
```

So the length of the array in $a is now five. The addition operation did add elements. Here's how this works:

- First PowerShell creates a new array large enough to hold the total number of elements.
- Then it copies the contents of the original array into the new one.
- Finally it copies the new elements into the end of the array.

We didn't add any elements to the original array after all. Instead we created a new, larger one.

Arrays as reference types

This copying behavior has some interesting consequences. Let's explore this further. First create a simple array and look at the value. We'll use string expansion here so that the values in the variable are all displayed on one line.

```
PS (1) > $a=1,2,3
PS (2) > "$a"
1 2 3
```

Now assign $a to a new variable $b and check that $a and $b have the same elements.

```
PS (3) > $b = $a
PS (4) > "$b"
1 2 3
```

Next change the first element in $a.

```
PS (5) > $a[0] = "Changed"
PS (6) > "$a"
Changed 2 3
```

Yes, the first element in $a was changed. But what about $b? Let's examine it now.

```
PS (7) > "$b"
Changed 2 3
```

It was also changed. As with hashtables, array assignment is done *by reference*. When we assigned $a to $b, $b we got a copy of the reference to the array instead of a copy of contents of the array. Let's add a new element to $b.

```
PS (8) > $b += 4
PS (9) > "$b"
Changed 2 3 4
```

$b is now four elements long. As we've just discussed, due to the way array catenation works, $b contains a copy of the contents of the array instead of a reference. If we change $a now, it won't affect $b. Let's verify that:

```
PS (10) > $a[0] = "Changed again"
PS (11) > "$a"
Changed again 2 3
PS (12) > "$b"
Changed 2 3 4
```

We see that $b was in fact not changed. Conversely, changing $b should have no effect on $a.

```
PS (13) > $b[0] = 1
PS (14) > "$a"; "$b"
Changed again 2 3
1 2 3 4
PS (15) >
```

Again, there was no change.

To reiterate, arrays in PowerShell, like arrays in other .NET languages, are reference types, not value types. When you assign them to a variable, you get another reference to the array, not another copy of the array.

Singleton arrays and empty arrays

Returning to array literals, we saw how to use the comma operator to build up an array containing more than one element. You also use the comma operator as a prefix operator to create an array containing only one element. The next example shows this:

```
PS (1) > , 1
1
PS (2) > (, 1).length
1
PS (3) >
```

In the example we made an array containing a single element "1".

How about empty arrays? The comma operator always takes an argument to work on. Even using $null as an argument to the comma operator will result in a one-element array containing the $null reference. Empty arrays are created through a special form of sub-expression notation that uses the "@" symbol instead of the "$" sign to start the expression. Here's what it looks like:

```
PS (3) > @()
PS (4) > @().length
0
PS (5) >
```

In the preceding example, we created an array of length 0. In fact, this notation is more general. It takes the result of the expression it encloses and ensures that it is always returned as an array. If the expression returns $null or a scalar value, it will be wrapped in a one-element array. Given this behavior, the other solution to creating an array with one element is:

```
PS (1) > @(1)
1
PS (2) > @(1).length
1
PS (3) > @(1)[0]
1
PS (4) >
```

That is, you place the value you want in the array in @(. . .) and you get an array back.

This notation is used when you don't know if the command you're calling is going to return an array or not. By executing the command in this way, you are guaranteed to get an array back. Note that if what you're returning is already an array, it won't be wrapped in a new array. Compare this to the use of the comma operator.

```
PS (1) > 1,2,3
1
2
3
PS (2) > (1,2,3).Length
3
PS (3) > ( , (1,2,3) ).Length
1
PS (4) > ( @( 1,2,3 ) ).Length
3
```

On line 1 of the example, we created a regular array. On line 5, we get the length and we see that it's 3. Next on line 7, we apply the prefix operator to the array and then get the length. The result now is only 1. This is because the unary comma operator always wraps its arguments in a new array. Finally, on line 9, we use the @(. . .) notation and then get the length. This time it remains three. The @(. . .) sequence doesn't wrap unless the object is not an array.

3.2.5 Type literals

In earlier sections, we showed a number of things that looked like [type]. These are type literals. In PowerShell, you use type literals to specify a particular type. They can be used as operators in a *cast*, as part of a variable declaration, or as an object itself. Here's an example of a cast using a type literal:

```
$i = [int] "123"
```

In this example, we are *casting* a string into a number, specifically an instance of primitive .NET type System.Int32. In fact, we could use the longer .NET type name to accomplish this:

```
$i = [System.Int32] "123"
```

It would be useful to try something more sophisticated. If we wanted to make this into an array of integers, we would do

```
$i = [int[]][object[]] "123"
```

In this example, we're not just casting the base type, we're also changing it from a scalar object to an array. Notice that we had to do this in two steps. In the first step, we converted it into a collection but without changing the element type. In the second step, we convert the types of the individual elements. This follows the general type converter rule that no more than one conversion will be performed in a single step. This rule makes it much easier to predict what any given conversion will do.

Type name aliases

Obviously, the shorter type name (or type alias as it's known) is more convenient. Table 3.4 lists all of the type aliases defined in PowerShell and the .NET types they correspond to. Anything in the `System.Management.Automation` namespace is specific to PowerShell and will be covered in later chapters in this book. The other types are core .NET types and are covered in the Microsoft Developers Network documentation.

Table 3.4 PowerShell type aliases and their corresponding .NET types

PowerShell Type Alias	Corresponding .NET Type
[int]	System.Int32
[int[]]	System.Int32[]
[long]	System.Int64
[long[]]	System.Int64[]
[string]	System.String
[string[]]	System.String[]
[char]	System.Char
[char[]]	System.Char[]
[bool]	System.Boolean
[bool[]]	System.Boolean[]
[byte]	System.Byte
[byte[]]	System.Byte[]
[double]	System.Double
[double[]]	System.Double[]
[decimal]	System.Decimal
[decimal[]]	System.Decimal[]
[float]	System.Single

continued on next page

Table 3.4   PowerShell type aliases and their corresponding .NET types *(continued)*

PowerShell Type Alias	Corresponding .NET Type
[single]	System.Single
[regex]	System.Text.RegularExpressions.Regex
[array]	System.Array
[xml]	System.Xml.XmlDocument
[scriptblock]	System.Management.Automation.ScriptBlock
[switch]	System.Management.Automation.SwitchParameter
[hashtable]	System.Collections.Hashtable
[psobject]	System.Management.Automation.PSObject
[type]	System.Type
[type[]]	System.Type[]

The primary use of type literals is in performing type conversions. We'll look at the type conversion process in detail in the next section.

Accessing static members with type literals

The other operation type literals get used for is getting at static methods in .NET classes. This will also be covered later on in detail, but here's a quick taste.

You can use the Get-Member cmdlet to look at the members on an object. To look at the static members, use the -static flag as shown:

```
PS (1) > [string] | get-member -static


    TypeName: System.String


Name           MemberType Definition
----           ---------- ----------
Compare        Method     static System.Int32 Compare(String...
CompareOrdinal Method     static System.Int32 CompareOrdinal...
Concat         Method     static System.String Concat(Object...
Copy           Method     static System.String Copy(String str)
Equals         Method     static System.Boolean Equals(Strin...
Format         Method     static System.String Format(String...
Intern         Method     static System.String Intern(String...
IsInterned     Method     static System.String IsInterned(St...
IsNullOrEmpty  Method     static System.Boolean IsNullOrEmpt...
Join           Method     static System.String Join(String s...
op_Equality    Method     static System.Boolean op_Equality(...
op_Inequality  Method     static System.Boolean op_Inequalit...
ReferenceEquals Method    static System.Boolean ReferenceEqu...
Empty          Property   static System.String Empty {get;set;}
```

This will dump out all of the static members on the .NET System.String class. If you want to call one of these methods, you need to use the ":" operator. Let's use the join method to join an array of string. First create the array:

```
PS (2) > $s = "one","two","three"
```

Then use the join method to join all of the pieces into a single string with plus signs in between:

```
PS (3) > [string]::join(' + ', $s)
one + two + three
PS (4) >
```

Example: using advanced math functions

Another interesting use of static methods is with the math class. This class—[System.Math]—is a pure static class. You can't actually create an instance of it—you can only use the static methods on it. Again, let's use the Get-Member cmdlet to look at the methods. Here's a truncated listing of the output you would see:

```
PS (1) > [math] | get-member -static


    TypeName: System.Math

Name            MemberType  Definition
----            ----------  ----------
Abs             Method      static System.Single Abs(Single va...
Acos            Method      static System.Double Acos(Double d)
Asin            Method      static System.Double Asin(Double d)
Atan            Method      static System.Double Atan(Double d)
Atan2           Method      static System.Double Atan2(Double ...
        :
        :
Sqrt            Method      static System.Double Sqrt(Double d)
Tan             Method      static System.Double Tan(Double a)
Tanh            Method      static System.Double Tanh(Double v...
Truncate        Method      static System.Decimal Truncate(Dec...
E               Property    static System.Double E {get;}
PI              Property    static System.Double PI {get;}
```

As you can see, it contains a lot of useful methods and properties. For example, it contains useful constants like Pi and e:

```
PS (2) > [math]::Pi
3.14159265358979
PS (3) > [math]::e
2.71828182845905
PS (4) >
```

There are also all of the trigonometric functions:

```
PS (4) > [math]::sin(22)
-0.00885130929040388
PS (5) > [math]::cos(22)
-0.999960826394637
PS (6) >
```

As we've said, types in PowerShell provide tremendous power and breadth of capabilities. In many cases, before rolling your own solution, it's worth browsing the Microsoft Developers Network documentation on the .NET libraries to see if there is something you can use to solve your problems. Now that we've seen the types, let's look at how PowerShell does type conversions.

3.3   TYPE CONVERSIONS

In the previous section, we introduced type literals and the major datatypes used in PowerShell. But how do all of these types work together? This is a critical question we had to address in designing PowerShell. In shell languages, there is usually only string data, so you never have to worry about things being of the wrong type. So how could we achieve this "typeless" behavior in PowerShell? The answer was a comprehensive system for handling type conversions automatically.

Automatic type conversion is the "secret sauce" that allows a strongly typed language like PowerShell to behave like a typeless command-line shell. Without a comprehensive type conversion system to map the output of one command to the input type required by another command, PowerShell would be nearly impossible to use as a shell.

In the next few sections, we'll go through an overview of how the type conversion system works, then look at the conversion algorithm in detail. Finally we'll look at some of the special conversion rules that only apply when binding cmdlet parameters.

3.3.1   How type conversion works

Type conversions are used any time an attempt is made to use an object of one type in a context that requires another type (such as adding a string to a number). Here's a good example: in the previous chapter, we talked about how parameters are bound to cmdlets. The parameter binder uses the type conversion system heavily when trying to bind incoming objects to a particular parameter. If the user has supplied a string and the cmdlet requires a number, the system will quietly convert the source object to the destination type as long as it's not a destructive conversion. A destructive conversion is one where the sense of the original object has been lost or distorted in some significant way. With numbers, this typically means a loss of precision.

The type conversion facility is also surfaced directly to the shell user through cast operations in the PowerShell language, as we mentioned in the previous section. In PowerShell, you use types to accomplish many things that you'd do with methods or functions in other languages. You use type literals as operators to convert (or cast) one type of object to another. Here's a simple example:

```
PS (1) > [int] "0x25"
37
PS (2) >
```

In this example, a string representing a hexadecimal number is converted into a number by using a cast operation. A token specifying the name of a type in square brackets can be used as a unary operator that will try to convert its argument into the desired type. These type cast operations can be *composed*—that is—several casts can be chained together. Here's an example of that type of composition. To get the ordinal value for a char, you can do:

```
PS (2) > [int] [char]"a"
97
```

Notice that we first cast the string into a char and then into an int. This is necessary because the simple conversion would try to parse the entire string as a number. This only works for a string containing exactly one character, however. If you want to convert an entire string, you need to use array types. Here's what that looks like:

```
PS (3) > [int[]] [char[]] "Hello world"
72
101
108
108
111
32
119
111
114
108
100
```

The string was split into an array of characters, then that array of characters was converted into an array of integers, and finally displayed as a list of decimal numbers. If you wanted to see those numbers in hex, you'd have to use the –f format operator and a format specifier string:

```
PS (4) > "0x{0:x}" -f [int] [char] "a"
0x61
```

And next, if you want to make a round trip, string to char to int to char to string you can do:

```
PS (6) > [string][char][int] ("0x{0:x}" -f [int] [char] "a")
a
```

Finally, here's a somewhat extreme example (for *2001* fans). We'll take the string "HAL" and increment each of the characters in the string by one. Let's try it out.

```
PS (7) > $s = "HAL"
PS (8) > $OFS=""; [string] [char[]] ( [int[]] [char[]] $s |
>> foreach {$_+1} )
>>
IBM
```

Creepy, but cool (or just weird if you're not a *2001* fan)! Moving closer to home, we know that the Windows NT kernel was designed by the same person who designed the VMS operating system. Let's prove that Windows NT (WNT) is just VMS plus one. Here we go:

```
PS (9) > $s = "VMS"
PS (10) > $OFS=""; [string] [char[]] ( [int[]] [char[]] $s |
>> foreach {$_+1} )
>>
WNT
```

One final issue you may be wondering about: what is the $OFS (Output Field Separator) variable doing in the example? When PowerShell converts arrays to strings, it takes each array element, converts that element into a string, and then concatenates all the pieces together. Since this would be an unreadable mess, it inserts a separator between each element. That separator is specified using the $OFS variable. It can be set to anything you want, even the empty string. Here's an interesting example. Say we want to add the numbers from 1 to 10. Let's put the numbers into an array:

```
PS (1) > $data = 1,2,3,4,5,6,7,8,9,10
```

Now convert them to a string:

```
PS (2) > [string] $data
1 2 3 4 5 6 7 8 9 10
```

As an aside, variable expansion in strings goes through the same mechanism as the type converter, so you'll get the same result:

```
PS (3) > "$data"
1 2 3 4 5 6 7 8 9 10
```

Now change $OFS to be the plus operator ("+"), and then display the data.

```
PS (4) > $OFS='+'
PS (5) > "$data"
1+2+3+4+5+6+7+8+9+10
```

Previously, the fields had been separated by spaces. Now they're separated by plus operators. This is almost what we need. We just have to find a way to execute this string. PowerShell provides ability through the Invoke-Expression cmdlet. Here's how it works.

```
PS (6) > invoke-expression "$data"
55
PS (7) >
```

Ta-da! Note that this is not an efficient way to add a bunch of numbers. The looping language constructs are a much better way of doing this.

Now let's take a quick trip into the "too-much-information" zone and look in detail at the process PowerShell uses to perform all of these type conversions.

3.3.2   PowerShell's type-conversion algorithm

In this section, we'll cover the steps in the conversion process in painful detail—much more than you'll generally need to know in your day-to-day work. However, if you really want to be an expert on PowerShell, this stuff's for you.

> **NOTE**   Type conversion is one of the areas of the PowerShell project that grew "organically". In other words, we sat down, wrote a slew of specifications, threw them out, and ended up doing something completely different. This is one of the joys of this type of work. Nice clean theory falls apart when you put it in front of real people. The type conversion algorithm as it exists today is the result of feedback from many of the early adopters both inside Microsoft as well as outside. The betaplace community helped us tremendously in this area.

In general, the PowerShell type conversions are separated into two major buckets:

- *PowerShell Language Standard Conversions*   These are built-in conversions performed by the engine itself. They are always processed first and consequently cannot be overridden. This set of conversions is largely guided by the historical behavior of shell and scripting languages, and is not part of the normal .NET type conversion system.
- *.NET-based custom converters*   This class of converters uses (and abuses in some cases) existing .NET mechanisms for doing type conversion.

Table 3.5 lists the set of built-in language conversions that PowerShell uses. The conversion process always starts with an object of a particular type and tries to produce a representation of that object in the requested target type. The conversions are applied in the order shown in table 3.5. Only one conversion is applied at a time. The PowerShell engine does not automatically chain conversions.

Table 3.5   PowerShell language standard conversions

Converting From	To Target Type	Result Description
$null	[string]	" " (empty string)
	[char]	"0' (string containing a single character 0)
	Any kind of number	The object corresponding to 0 for the corresponding numeric type.
	[bool]	$false
	[PSObject]	$null
	Any other type of object	$null

continued on next page

Table 3.5 PowerShell language standard conversions *(continued)*

Converting From	To Target Type	Result Description
Derived Class	Base Class	The original object is returned unchanged.
Anything	[void]	The object is discarded.
Anything	[string]	The PowerShell internal string converter is used.
Anything	[xml]	The original object is first converted into a string and then into an XML Document object.
Array of type [X]	Array of type [Y]	PowerShell creates a new array of the target type, then copies and converts each element in the source array into an instance for the target array type.
Non-array (singleton) object	Array of type [Y]	Creates an array containing one element and then places the singleton object into the array, converting if necessary.
IDictionary	[Hashtable]	A new instance of `System.Collections.Hash-Table` is created, and then the members of the source IDictionary are copied into the new object.
[string]	[char[]]	Converts the string to an array of characters.
[string]	[regex]	Constructs a new instance of a .NET regular expression object.
[string]	Number	Converts the string into a number using the smallest representation available that can accurately represent that number. If the string is not purely convertible (i.e., only contains numeric information) then an error is raised.
[int]	System.Enum	Converts the integer to the corresponding enumeration member if it exists. If it doesn't, a conversion error is generated.

If none of the built-in PowerShell language-specific conversions could be applied successfully then the .NET custom converters are tried. Again, these converters are tried in order until a candidate is found that will produce the required target type. This candidate conversion is applied. If the candidate conversion throws an exception (that is, a matching converter is found but it fails during the conversion process) then no further attempt to convert this object will be made and the overall conversion process will be considered to have failed.

> **NOTE** Understanding these conversions depend upon a fair knowledge of the .NET type conversion mechanisms. You'll need to refer to additional documentation if you want to understand everything in table 3.6. On the other hand, with the .NET docs, you can see exactly what steps are being applied in the type conversion process.

Custom converters are executed in the order described in table 3.6.

Table 3.6 Custom Type Conversions

Converter type	Description
PSTypeConverter	A `PSTypeConverter` can be associated with a particular type using the `TypeConverterAttribute` or the `<TypeConverter>` tag in the `types.ps1xml` file. If the value to convert has a `PSTypeConverter` that can convert to the target type, then it is called. If the target type has a `PSTypeConverter` that can convert from values to convert, then it is called. The `PSTypeConverter` allows a single type converter to work for N different classes. For example, an `enum` type converter can convert a string to any `enum` (there doesn't need to be separate type to convert each `enum`). Refer to the PowerShell SDK documentation for complete details on this converter.
TypeConverter	This is a CLR defined type that can be associated with a particular type using the `TypeConverterAttribute` or the `<TypeConverter>` tag in the types file. If the value to convert has a `TypeConverter` that can convert to the target type then it is called. If the target type has a `TypeConverter` that can convert from the source value, then it is called. Note: The CLR `TypeConverter` does not allow a single type converter to work for N different classes. Refer to the PowerShell SDK documents and the Microsoft .NET framework documentation for details on the `TypeConverter` class.
Parse Method	If the value to convert is a string, and the target type has a `Parse()` method, then that `Parse()` method is called. `Parse()` is a well-known method name in the CLR world and is commonly implemented to allow conversion of strings to other types.
Constructors	If the target type has a constructor that takes a single parameter matching the type of the value to convert, then this constructor is used to create a new object of the desired type.
Implicit Cast Operator	If the value to convert has an *implicit cast operator* that converts to the target type, then it is called. Conversely, if the target type has an implicit cast operator that converts from value to convert's type, then that is called.
Explicit Cast Operator	If the value to covert has an *explicit cast operator* that converts to the target type then it is called. Alternatively, if the target type has an explicit cast operator that converts from value to convert's type then that is called.
IConvertable	`System.Convert.ChangeType` is then called.

This section covered the set of type conversions that PowerShell will apply in expressions. In the parameter binder, however, are a few extra steps that are applied first.

3.3.3 Special type conversions in parameter binding

In this final section, we'll go over the extra type conversion rules that are used in parameter binding that haven't already been covered. If these steps are tried and are not successful, the parameter binder goes on to call the normal PowerShell type converter code.

> **NOTE** If at any time there is a failure doing the type conversion, an exception will be thrown.

Here are the extra steps:

- If there is no argument for the parameter, then the parameter type must be either a [bool] or the special PowerShell type SwitchParameter; otherwise a parameter binding exception is thrown. If the parameter type is a [bool], it is set to true. If the parameter type is a SwitchParameter, it is set to SwitchParameter.Present.

- If the argument value is null and the parameter type is [bool], it is set to false. If the argument value is null and the parameter type is SwitchParameter, it is set to SwitchParameter.Present. Null can be bound to any other type, so it just passes through.

- If the argument type is the same as the parameter type, the argument value is used without any type conversion.

- If the parameter type is [object], the current argument value is used without any coercion.

- If the parameter type is a [bool], then we use the PowerShell Boolean IsTrue() method to determine whether the argument value should set the parameter to true or false.

- If the parameter type is a collection, then the argument type must be encoded into the appropriate collection type. Note, we will encode a scalar argument type or a collection argument type to a target collection parameter type. We will not encode a collection argument type into a scalar parameter type (unless that type is System.Object or PSObject).

- If the argument type is a scalar, then we create a collection of the parameter type (currently only arrays and IList are supported) of length 1 and set the argument value as the only value in the collection. If needed, the argument type is converted to the element type for the collection using the same type coercion process this section describes

- If the argument type is a collection, we create a collection of the parameter type with length equal to the number of values contained in the argument value. Each value is then coerced to the appropriate element type for the new collection using the recursive application of this algorithm.

- If none of these steps worked, use the conversion in table 3.6. If those fail, then the overall parameter binding attempt fails.

Once again, this is a level of detail that you don't usually need to consider, but it's useful to know it's available when you need it.

You now know everything you need to know about how types work on PowerShell. Well, not quite everything. In the next two chapters, we'll discuss how the PowerShell operators build on this basic type foundation. But for now, we're through!

3.4   SUMMARY

A solid understanding of the PowerShell type system will allow you to use PowerShell most effectively. By taking advantage of the built-in type system and conversions, you can accomplish startlingly complex tasks with little code. In this chapter, we covered the following topics:

- The PowerShell type system, how it works, and how you can use it.

- The basic PowerShell types and how they are represented in PowerShell script (*literals*).

- Some of the more advanced types—hashtables and arrays.

- The use of type literals in type *casts* and as a way to call static methods.

- The type conversion process for language conversions, the pre-conversion steps that are used by the parameter binder, and the relationship between the PowerShell types and the underlying .NET types.

CHAPTER 4

Operators and expressions

Operators, Mr. Rico! Millions of them!

—Robert A. Heinlein, *Starship Troopers*, paraphrased

This chapter covers two of the basic elements of the PowerShell language: operators and expressions. PowerShell has operators. Lots of operators—the full complement you would expect in a conventional programming language and several more. In addition, PowerShell operators are typically more powerful than the corresponding operators in conventional languages such as C or C++. So, if you invest the time to learn what the PowerShell operators are and how they work, in a single line of code you will be able to accomplish tasks that would normally take a significant amount of programming.

Here's an example of the kind of thing that can be done using just the PowerShell operators. Say we have a file `old.txt` with the following text in it:

```
Hello there.
My car is red.  Your car is blue.
His car is orange and hers is gray.
Bob's car is blue too.
Goodbye.
```

Our task is to copy this content to a new file, making certain changes. In the new file, the word "is" should be replaced with "was", but only when it's in front of the words "red" or "blue". In most languages, this would require a fairly complex program. In PowerShell, it takes exactly one line. Here's the "script". It uses the `-replace` operator along with *output redirection* and *variable namespaces*. The `-replace` operator is decribed later in this chapter. Redirection and variable namespaces are features for working with files that are covered in chapter 5.

> **AUTHOR'S NOTE**   For the impatient reader, the notation `${c:old.txt}` says: return the contents of the file "old.txt" from the *current working directory* on the C: drive. In contrast, `${c:\old.txt}` says get the file "old.txt" from the *root* of the C: drive.

```
${c:old.txt} -replace 'is (red|blue)','was $1' > new.txt
```

After running this script, the content of `new.txt` looks like:

```
Hello there.
My car was red.  Your car was blue.
His car is orange and hers is gray.
Bob's car was blue too.
Goodbye.
```

As you can see, only the second and fourth lines have been changed as desired. The phrases "is red" and "is blue" have been changed to "was red" and "was blue". The "is orange" and "is gray" phrases weren't changed. From this example, you can also see that it's possible to do quite a bit of work just with the operators.

> **AUTHOR'S NOTE**   In this example we used the `-replace` operator to do a regular expression substitution on the strings in the file. In the replacement string after the comma, the "$1" refers to the text matched by the part of the pattern in parentheses. This notation is described in more detail in chapter 10, where regular expressions are discussed at length.

One of the characteristics that makes PowerShell operators powerful is the fact that they are *polymorphic*. In other words, they work on many types of objects. While this is generally true in other object-based languages, in those languages the type of the object defines the behavior of the operator. For example, the `Integer` class would define an operator for adding a number to a class.

> **AUTHOR'S NOTE**   If you're a C# or Visual Basic user, here's something you might want to know. In "conventional" NET languages, the operator symbols are mapped to a specific method name on a class called *op_<operatorName>*. For example, in C#, the plus operator "+" maps to the method `op_Addition()`. While PowerShell is a .NET language, it takes a different approach that is more consistent with dynamic scripting languages as we'll see in the following sections.

In PowerShell, the interpreter primarily defines the behavior of the operators, at least for common datatypes. Type-based polymorphic methods are only used as a backup. By common types, we mean strings, numbers, hashtables, and arrays. This allows PowerShell to provide more consistent behavior over this range of common objects and also to provide higher-level behaviors than are provided by the objects themselves, especially when dealing with collections. We'll cover these special behaviors in the sections for each class of operator. (The following sections have many examples, but the best way to learn this is to try the examples in PowerShell yourself.) Now let's get going and start looking at the operators.

4.1   ARITHMETIC OPERATORS

First we'll cover the basic arithmetic operators. The polymorphic behavior of these operators was touched on briefly in chapter 3, where the various type conversions were covered. The operators themselves are listed in table 4.1.

Table 4.1   The basic arithmetic operators In PowerShell

Operator	Description	Example	Result
+	Add two values together.	2+4	6
		"Hi " + "there"	"Hi There"
		1,2,3 + 4,5,6	1,2,3,4,5,6
*	Multiply 2 values.	2 * 4	8
		"a" * 3	"aaa"
		1,2 * 2	1,2,1,2
-	Subtract one value from another.	6-2	4
/	Divide two values.	6/2	3
		7/4	1.75
%	Return the remainder from a division operation.	7%4	3

In terms of behavior, the most interesting operators are + and *. We'll cover these operators in detail in the next two sections.

4.1.1   The addition operator

As mentioned previously, PowerShell itself defines the behavior of the + and * operators for numbers, strings, arrays, and hashtables. Adding or multiplying two numbers produces a numeric result following the numeric widening rules. Adding two strings performs string concatenation, resulting in a new string, and adding two arrays joins the two arrays (*array catenation*), producing a new array. The interesting part occurs when you mix operand types. In this situation, the type of the left operand determines how the operation will proceed. We'll look at how this works with addition first.

The "left-hand" rule for arithmetic operators: The type of the left-hand operand determines the type of the overall operation. This is an important
rule to remember.

If the left operand is a number, PowerShell will try to convert the right operand to a
number. Here's an example. In the following expression, the operand on the left is a
number and the operand on the right is the string "123".

```
PS (1) > 2 + "123"
125
```

Since the operand on the left is a number, according to the conversion rule, the oper-
and "123" must be converted into a number. Once the conversion is complete, the
numeric addition operation proceeds and produces the result 125 as shown. Conversely, in the next example, when a string is on the left side:

```
PS (2) > "2" + 123
2123
```

the operand on the right (the number 123) is converted to a string and appended to "2"
to produce a new string "2123".

If the right operand can't be converted into the type of the left operand then a
type conversion error will be raised, as we see in the next example:

```
PS (3) > 2 + "abc"
Cannot convert "abc" to "System.Int32". Error: "Input string was not
 in a correct format."
At line:1 char:4
+ 2 +  <<<< "abc"
```

Since "abc" can't be converted into a number, you receive a type conversion error. If
this had been done using the hex notation as discussed in section 3.3.2, everything
would fine:

```
PS (4) > 2 + "0xabc"
2750
```

Since "a", "b", and "c" are valid hex digits, the string "0xabc" converts into the number 2748 and is then added to 2, giving 2750.

The next PowerShell-defined polymorphic behavior for + involves arrays or collections. If the operand on the left is an array or collection, the operand on the right
will be appended to that collection. If the right operand is a scalar value, it will be
added to the array as-is. If it's already an array (or any type of enumerable collection),
it will be appended to the collection.

At this point, it's probably a good idea to reiterate how array catenation is done
in PowerShell. Because the underlying .NET array objects are of fixed size (as discussed in section 3.3.4), catenation is accomplished by creating a new array of type
[object[]] and copying the elements from the operands into this new array. In
the process of creating the new array, any type constraint on the original arrays will

be lost. For example, if the left operand is `[int[]]`, that is, an array of type `[int]`, and you add a non-numeric string to it, a new array will be created that will be of type `[object[]]`, which can hold any type of object. Let's look at an example. First create an integer array.

```
PS (1) > $a = [int[]] (1,2,3,4)
PS (2) > $a.gettype().fullname
System.Int32[]
```

Now let's do some assignments. First assign an integer.

```
PS (3) > $a[0] = 10
```

This works without error. Next try it with a string that can be converted into an integer. We'll use the hex string mentioned earlier.

```
PS (4) > $a[0] = "0xabc"
```

This also works fine. Finally, let's try assigning a non-numeric string to the array element.

```
PS (5) > $a[0] = "hello"
Array assignment to [0] failed: Cannot convert "hello" to
"System.Int32". Error: "Input string was not in a correct format.".
At line:1 char:4
+ $a[0 <<<< ] = "hello"
```

This fails, as you might expect. An array of type `[int[]]` can only hold integers. Since "hello" can't be converted into an integer, we get the type conversion error shown. So far, so good. Now let's do an array catenation.

```
PS (6) > $a = $a + "hello"
```

And now try the assignment that failed previously.

```
PS (7) > $a[0] = "hello"
PS (8) > $a
hello
2
3
4
hello
```

This time the assignment succeeds without error. What happened here? Let's look at the type of the array now.

```
PS (9) > $a.gettype().fullname
System.Object[]
```

When the new, larger array was created to hold the combined elements, it was created as type `[object[]]`, which is not type-constrained. Since it can hold any type of object, the assignment proceeded without error.

Finally, let's look at how addition works with hashtables. Similar to arrays, addition of hashtables creates a new hashtable and copies the elements of the original tables into the new one. The left elements are copied first, then the elements from the right operand are copied. (This only works if both operands are hashtables.) If there are any collisions, that is, if the keys of any of the elements in the right operand match the keys of any element in the left operand, then an error will occur saying that the key already exists in the hashtable. (This was an implementation decision, by the way; we could have had the new element overwrite the old one, but the consensus was that generating an error message is usually the better thing to do.)

```
PS (1) > $left=@{a=1;b=2;c=3}
PS (2) > $right=@{d=4;e=5}
PS (3) > $new = $left + $right
PS (4) > $new

Key                         Value
---                         -----
d                           4
a                           1
b                           2
e                           5
c                           3
```

The new hashtable is of type System.Collections.Hashtable:

```
PS (5) > $new.GetType().FullName
System.Collections.Hashtable
```

The table is created in such a way that the strings that are used as keys are compared in a case-insensitive way.

This completes our discussion of the behavior of the addition operator. We covered how it works with numbers, strings, hashtables, and arrays. Now that we're finished with addition, let's move on to the multiplication operator.

4.1.2 The multiplication operator

As with addition, PowerShell defines multiplication behavior for numbers, strings, and arrays. (We don't do anything special for hashtables for multiplication.) Multiplying numbers works as expected and follows the widening rules discussed in chapter 3. In fact, the only legal right-hand operand for multiplication is a number. If the operand on the left is a string then that string is *repeated* the number of times specified in the left operand. Let's try this out. We'll multiply the string "abc" by 1, 2, then 3:

```
PS (1) > "abc" * 1
abc
PS (2) > "abc" * 2
abcabc
PS (3) > "abc" * 3
abcabcabc
```

The results are "abc", "abcabc", and "abcabcabc", respectively. What about multiplying by zero?

```
PS (4) > "abc" * 0

PS (5) >
```

The result appears to be nothing—but which "nothing"—spaces, empty string, or null? The way things are displayed, you can't tell by looking. Here's how to check. First check the type of the result:

```
PS (5) > ("abc" * 0).gettype().fullname
System.String
```

We see that it's a string, not $null. But it could still be spaces, so we need to check the length:

```
PS (6) > ("abc" * 0).length
0
```

And, since the length is zero, we can tell that it is in fact an empty string.

Now let's look at how multiplication works with arrays. Since multiplication applied to strings repeats the string, logically you would expect that multiplication applied to arrays should repeat the array, which is exactly what it does. Let's look at some examples of this. First create an array with three elements:

```
PS (1) > $a=1,2,3
PS (2) > $a.length
3
```

Now multiply it by 2:

```
PS (3) > $a = $a * 2
PS (4) > $a.length
6
```

The length of the new array is 6. Looking at the contents of the array (using variable expansion in strings to save space) we see that it is "1 2 3 1 2 3"—the original array doubled.

```
PS (5) > "$a"
1 2 3 1 2 3
```

Now multiply the new array by three:

```
PS (6) > $a = $a * 3
```

And check that the length is now 18.

```
PS (7) > $a.length
18
```

It is, so looking at the contents:

```
PS (8) > "$a"
1 2 3 1 2 3 1 2 3 1 2 3 1 2 3 1 2 3
```

we see that it is six repetitions of the original three elements.

As with addition, first a new larger array is created during multiplication, then the component elements are copied into it. This has the same issue that addition had, where the new array is created without type constraints. Even if the original array could only hold numbers, the new array can hold any type of object.

4.1.3 Subtraction, division, and the modulus operator

Addition and multiplication are the most interesting of the arithmetic operators in terms of polymorphic behavior, but let's go over the remaining operators. Subtraction, division, and the modulus (%) operators are only defined for numbers by PowerShell. (Modulus returns the remainder from a division operation.) Again, as with all numeric computations, the widening rules for numbers are obeyed. Since, for the basic types (string, number), these operations are only defined for numbers, if either operand is a number (not just the left-hand operand) then an attempt will be made to convert the other operand into a number as well, as shown in the following:

```
PS (1) > "123" / 4
30.75
PS (2) > 123 / "4"
30.75
PS (3) >
```

In the first example, the string "123" is converted into a number. In the second example, the string "4" will be converted into a number.

AUTHOR'S NOTE
Here is an important characteristic about how division works in PowerShell that you should keep in mind. Integer division *underflows* into floating point (technically System.Double). This means that 5 divided by 4 in PowerShell results in 1.25 instead of 1 as it would in C#. If you want to round the decimal part to the nearest integer, simply cast the result into [int]. You also need to be aware that PowerShell uses what's called "Banker's Rounding" when converting floating point numbers into integers. Banker's rounding rounds .5 up sometimes, and down sometimes. The convention is to round to the nearest even number, so that both 1.5 and 2.5 round to 2, and 3.5 and 4.5 both round to 4.

If neither operand is a number, the operation is undefined and you'll get an error as shown:

```
PS (3) > "123" / "4"
Method invocation failed because [System.String] doesn't contain
a method named 'op_Division'.
At line:1 char:8
+ "123" /  <<<< "4"
PS (4) >
```

Take note of this particular error message, though. PowerShell has no built-in definition for this operation, so as a last step it looks to see whether the type of the left operand defines a method for performing the operation. In fact, PowerShell looks for the op_<operation> methods on the left operand if the operation is not one of those defined by PowerShell itself. This allows the operators to work on types such as System.Datetime (the .NET representation of dates) even though there is no special support for these types in PowerShell.

Here's an example. In the following, we want to find the total number of days between January 1, 2006, and February 1, 2006. We can create objects representing these dates by casting strings into DateTime objects. Once we have these objects, we can convert them:

```
PS (1) > ([datetime] "2006-2-1" - [datetime]"2006-1-1").TotalDays
31
```

For those of you with children, here's a more useful example. Jeffrey Snover, the architect of PowerShell tells a story about his daughter:

> My daughter loves Christmas. She often asks me, "How long is it till Christmas?" The problem with that is that I'm one of those people that can barely remember what year it is, much less the date. Well, it is one thing to be a flawed person and it's another thing to disappoint your daughter. PowerShell to the rescue! Here is a little date math routine I wrote to help me out:
>
> ```
> function tillXmas ()
> {
>     $now = [DateTime]::Now
>     [Datetime]( [string] $now.Year + "-12-25") - $Now
> }
>
> PS> tillxmas
>
> Days              : 321
> Hours             : 18
> Minutes           : 8
> Seconds           : 26
> Milliseconds      : 171
> Ticks             : 277997061718750
> TotalDays         : 321.755858470775
> TotalHours        : 7722.14060329861
> TotalMinutes      : 463328.436197917
> TotalSeconds      : 27799706.171875
> TotalMilliseconds : 27799706171.875
> ```
>
> Thanks to PowerShell, I can tell my daughter how many seconds to go till Xmas! Now if I can only get her to stop asking me in the car.

To take a look at the operator methods defined for System.DateTime, we can use the Getmembers() method. Here's a partial listing of the operator methods defined. We're using the PowerShell Select-String cmdlet to limit what gets displayed to only those methods whose names contain the string "op_":

```
PS (5) > [datetime].getmembers()| foreach{"$_"}| select-string op_
System.DateTime op_Addition(System.DateTime, System.TimeSpan)
System.DateTime op_Subtraction(System.DateTime, System.TimeSpan)
System.TimeSpan op_Subtraction(System.DateTime, System.DateTime)
```

As you can see, not all of the arithmetic operator methods are defined. In fact, there are no methods defined for any operations other than addition and subtraction. If you try to divide a DateTime object by a number, you'll get the same error we saw when we tried to divide two strings:

```
PS (4) > [datetime] "1/1/2006" / 22
Method invocation failed because [System.DateTime] doesn't contain
a method named 'op_Division'.
At line:1 char:24
+ [datetime] "1/1/2006" / <<<< 22
PS (5) >
```

The error occurred because PowerShell was looking for an op_Division() on the object on the left. Since it didn't find one, the operation failed.

That's it for the arithmetic operations. However, now that we know how to do arithmetic, it's not very interesting if we can't save the results. Next we need to talk about the assignment operators.

4.2   THE ASSIGNMENT OPERATORS

In this section we'll cover the assignment operators, which are listed in table 4.2. As you can see, along with simple assignment, PowerShell supports the compound operators that are found in C-based languages. These compound operators retrieve, update, and reassign a variable.

In table 4.2, for each of the compound assignment operators, the third column shows the equivalent decomposed operation. Of course, the arithmetic parts of the compound arithmetic/assignment operators follow all of the rules for the arithmetic

Table 4.2   PowerShell assignment operators

Operator	Example	Equivalent	Description
=	$a= 3		Sets the variable to the specified value.
+=	$a += 2	$a = $a + 2	Performs the addition operation in the existing value, then assigns the result back to the variable.
-=	$a -= 13	$a = $a – 13	Performs the subtraction operation in the existing value, then assigns the result back to the variable.
*=	$a *= 3	$a = $a * 3	Multiplies the value of a variable by the specified value or appends to the existing value.
/=	$a /= 3	$a = $a / 3	Divides the value of a variable by the specified value.
%=	$a %= 3	$a = $a % 3	Divides the value of a variable by the specified value and assigns the remainder (modulus) to the variable.

operators described in the previous section. The formal syntax for an assignment expression is:

```
<lvalueList> <assignmentOperator> <pipeline>
<lvalueList> := <lvalue> [ , <lvalue> ] *
<lvalue> := <variable> | <propertyReference> | <arrayReference>
```

One interesting thing to note from this syntax is that multiple assignments are allowed. For example, the expression

```
$a,$b,$c = 1,2,3,4
```

is a perfectly legal statement. It says "assign 1 to $a, assign 2 to $b, and assign the remaining elements 3 and 4 of the list to $c. Multiple assignments can be used to greatly simplify certain types of operators as we'll see in the next section.

4.2.1 Multiple assignments

Multiple assignment works only with the basic assignment operator. You can't use it with any of the compound operators. It can, however, be used with any type of assignable expression such as an array element or property reference. Here's a quick example where multiple assignment is particularly useful. The canonical pattern for swapping two variables is conventional languages is

```
$temp = $a
$a = $b
$b = $temp
```

This takes three lines of code and requires you to use a temporary variable. Here's how to do it using multiple assignments in PowerShell:

```
$a,$b = $b,$a
```

It's simple, straightforward, and clean—only one line of code with no temporary variable to worry about. Here's a more interesting example. The Fibonacci sequence is a sequence of numbers where each element is defined as the sum of the previous two numbers in the sequence. It looks like:

```
1 1 2 3 5 8 13 21 …
```

AUTHOR'S NOTE   The Fibonacci sequence is an oddly popular bit of mathematics. It shows up in books, movies, and seashells. In the West, it was first studied by Leonardo of Pisa a.k.a. Fibonacci. He used this sequence to describe how rabbits multiply. Rabbits are not good at math, so it wasn't very accurate. The sequence also describes the progression of the spiral found in some shells. Mollusks are better at math than rabbits, apparently.

Here's how to generate this sequence in PowerShell using multiple assignments:

```
PS (53) > $c=$p=1; while ($c -lt 100) { $c; $c,$p = ($c+$p),$c }
1
2
3
5
8
13
21
34
55
89
```

In this example, we begin by initializing the two variables $c (current) and $p (previous) to 1. Then we loop while $c is less than 100. $c contains the current value in the sequence, so we emit that value. Next we have the double assignment, where $c becomes the next element in the sequence and $p becomes the current (now previous) value in the sequence. So far, we've seen that using multiple assignments can simplify basic operations such as swapping values. However, when combined with some of PowerShell's other features, you can do much more interesting things than that. We'll see this in the next section.

4.2.2 Multiple assignments with type qualifiers

This is all interesting, but let's look at a more practical example. Say we are given a text file containing some data that we want to parse into a form we can work with. First let's look at the data file:

```
quiet 0 25
normal 26 50
loud 51 75
noisy 75 100
```

This file contains a set of sound level descriptions. The format is a string describing the level, followed by two numbers describing the upper and lower bounds for these levels out of a possible 100. We want to read this information into a data structure so we can use it to categorize a list of sounds later on. Here's the fragment of PowerShell code needed to do this:

```
PS (2) > $data = get-content data.txt | foreach {
>>      $e=@{}
>>      $e.level, [int] $e.lower, [int] $e.upper = $_.split()
>>      $e
>> }
>>
```

We start by using the Get-Content cmdlet to write the data into a pipeline. Each line of the file is sent to the Foreach-Object cmdlet to be processed. The first thing we do in the body of the foreach cmdlet is initialize a hashtable in $e to hold the result. We take each line stored in the $_ variable and call the string split()

method on it. This splits the string into an array at each space character in the string. For example, the string

```
"quiet 0 25"
```

becomes an array of three strings

```
"quiet","0","25"
```

Then we assign the split string to three elements of the hashtable: $e.level, $e.lower, and $e.upper. But there's one more thing we want to do. The array being assigned is all strings. For the upper and lower bounds, we want numbers, not strings. To do this, we add a cast before the assignable element. This causes the value being assigned to first be converted to the target type. The end result is that the upper and lower fields in the hashtable are assigned numbers instead of strings. Finally, note that the result of the pipeline is being assigned to the variable $data, so we can use it later on.

Let's look at the result of this execution. Since there were four lines in the file, there should be four elements in the target array.

```
PS (3) > $data.length
4
```

We see that there are. Now let's see if the value stored in the first element of the array is what we expect. It should be the "quiet" level.

```
PS (4) > $data[0]
Key                           Value
---                           -----
upper                         25
level                         quiet
lower                         0
```

It is. Finally, let's verify that the types were properly converted.

```
PS (5) > $data[0].level
quiet
PS (6) > $data[0].lower
0
PS (7) > $data[0].upper
25
PS (8) > $data[0].level.gettype().fullname
System.String
PS (9) > $data[0].lower.GetType().fullname
System.Int32
PS (10) > $data[0].upper.GetType().fullname
System.Int32
```

Again we use the GetType() method to look at the types, and we can see that the level description field is a string and that the two bounds fields are integers, as expected.

In this last example, we've seen how array assignment can be used to perform sophisticated tasks in only a few lines of code. By now, you should have a good sense of the utility of assignments in processing data in PowerShell. There's just one last point to cover about assignment expressions, which we'll cover in the next section.

4.2.3 Assignment operations as value expressions

The last thing you need to know about assignment expressions is that they are, in fact, expressions. This means that you can use them anywhere you'd use any other kind of expression. This lets you initialize multiple variables at once. Let's initialize $a, $b, and $c to the number 3.

```
PS (1) > $a = $b = $c = 3
```

Now verify that the assignments worked:

```
PS (2) > $a, $b, $c
3
3
3
```

Yes, they did. So what exactly happened? Well, it's the equivalent of the following expression:

```
PS (3) > $a = ( $b = ( $c = 3 ) )
```

That is, $c is assigned 3. The expression ($c = 3) returns the value 3, which is in turn assigned to $b, and the result of that assignment (also 3) is finally assigned to $a so once again, all three variables end up with the same value:

```
PS (4) > $a, $b, $c
3
3
3
```

Now, since we can "intercept" the expressions with parentheses, we can perform additional operations on the values returned from the assignment statements before this value is bound in the outer assignment. Here's an example that does this:

```
PS (5) > $a = ( $b = ( $c = 3 ) + 1 ) + 1
```

In this expression, $c gets the value 3. The result of this assignment is returned, and 1 is added to that value, giving 4, which is then assigned to $b. The result of this second assignment also has 1 added to it, so $a is finally assigned 5, as shown in the output:

```
PS (6) > $a, $b, $c
5
4
3
```

Now we have assignment and arithmetic operators covered, but a language isn't much good if you can't compare things, so let's move on to the comparison operators.

4.3 COMPARISON OPERATORS

In this section, we'll cover what the comparison operators are in PowerShell and how they work. We'll cover how case sensitivity factors into comparisons and how the operators work for scalar values and for collections of values.

PowerShell has a sizeable number of comparison operators, in large part because there are case-sensitive and case-insensitive versions of all of the operators. These are listed in table 4.3.

Table 4.3 PowerShell comparison operators

Operator	Description	Example	Result
-eq –ceq –ieq	Equals	5 –eq 5	$true
-ne –cne –ine	Not equals	5 –ne 5	$false
-gt –cgt –igt	Greater than	5 –gt 3	$true
-ge –cge –ige	Greater than or equal	5 –ge 3	$true
-lt –clt –ilt	Less than	5 –lt 3	$false
-le –cle -ile	Less than or equals	5 –le 3	$false
-contains -ccontains -icontains	The collection on the left side contains the value specified on the right side.	1,2,3 –contains 2	$true
-notcontains onotcontains -inotcontains	The collection on the left side does not contain the value on the right side.	1,2,3 notcontains 2	$false

In table 4.3, you can see that for each operator there is a base or *unqualified* operator form, like -eq and its two variants -ceq and -ieq. The "c" variant is case-sensitive and the "i" variant is case-insensitive. This raises the obvious question, what is the behavior for the base operators with respect to case? The answer is that the unqualified operators are case-insensitive. All three variants are provided to allow script authors to make their intention clear—that they really meant a particular behavior rather than accepting the default.

AUTHOR'S NOTE   Let's talk about the most contentious design decision in the PowerShell language. And the winner is: why the heck did we not use the conventional symbols for comparison like ">", ">=", "<", "<=", "==", and "!=" ? My, this was a touchy issue. The answer is that the ">" and "<" characters are used for output redirection. Since PowerShell is a shell and all shell languages in the last 30 years have used ">" and "<" for I/O redirection, people expected that PowerShell should do the same. During the first public beta of PowerShell, this topic generated discussions that went on for months. We looked at a variety of alternatives, such as modal parsing where sometimes ">" meant greater-than and sometimes it meant redirection. We looked at alternative character sequences for the operators like ":>" or "->", either for redirection or comparison. We did usability tests and held focus groups, and in the end, settled on what we had started with. The redirection operators are ">" and "<", and the comparison operators are taken from the UNIX test(1) command. We expect that, since these operators have a 30-year pedigree, they are adequate and appropriate to use in PowerShell. (We also expect that people will continue to complain about this decision, though hopefully not for 30 more years.)

Now that we're clear on the case-sensitivity issue, let's move on to discuss the semantics of the comparison operators. We begin in the next section by describing their operation on scalar datatypes, then in the subsequent section, we'll describe how they work with collections of objects.

4.3.1 Scalar comparisons

In this section, we'll cover how the comparison operators work with scalar objects. In particular, we'll cover their polymorphic behavior with the scalar data types.

Basic comparison rules

As with the assignment operators, the behavior of the comparison operators is significantly affected by the type of the left operand. If you are comparing a number and a string, the string will be converted into a number and a numerical comparison will be done. If the left operand is a string, the right operand will be converted to a string, and the results compared as strings. Let's look through some examples. First a simple numeric comparison:

```
PS (26) > 01 -eq 001
True
```

Because we're doing a numeric comparison, the leading zeros don't matter and the numbers compare as equal. Now let's try it when the right operand is a string.

```
PS (28) > 01 -eq "001"
True
```

Following the rule, the right operand is converted from a string into a number, then the two are compared and are found to be equal. Finally, try the comparison when the left operand is a string.

```
PS (27) > "01" -eq 001
False
```

In this example, the right operand is converted to a string, and consequently they no longer compare as equal. Of course you can always use casts to force a particular behavior. In the next example, let's force the left operand to be a number:

```
PS (29) > [int] "01" -eq 001
True
```

And, because we forced a numeric comparison, once again they are equal.

Type conversions and comparisons

As with any PowerShell operator that involves numbers, when comparisons are done in a numeric context, the widening rules are applied. This can produce somewhat unexpected results. Here's an example that illustrates this. In the first part of the example, we use a cast to convert the string "123" into a number. Once we're doing the conversion in a numeric context, the numbers get widened to double since the right operand is a double; and since 123.4 is larger than 123.0, the -lt operator returns true.

```
PS (37) > [int] "123" -lt 123.4
True
```

Now try it using a string as the right operand. The cast forces the left operand to be numeric; however, the right operand is not yet numeric. It is converted to the numeric type of the left operand, which is [int], not [double]. This means that the value is truncated and the comparison now returns false.

```
PS (38) > [int] "123" -lt "123.4"
False
```

Finally, if we force the context to be [double] explicitly, the comparison again returns true.

```
PS (39) > [double] "123" -lt "123.4"
True
```

While all these rules seem complicated (and, speaking as the guy who implemented them, they are), the results are generally what you would intuitively expect. This satisfies the principle of least astonishment. So most of the time you don't need to worry about the specifics and can just let the system take care of the conversions. It's only when things don't work as expected that you really need to understand the details of the conversion process. To help you debug cases where this happens, PowerShell provides a type conversion tracing mechanism to help you track down the problems. How to use this debugging feature is described in chapter 7. Finally, you can always apply a set of casts to override the implicit behavior and force the results you want.

Comparisons and case-sensitivity

Next let's look at the "i" and "c" versions of the comparison operators—the case-sensitive and case-insensitive versions. Obviously, case sensitivity only applies to strings. All of the comparison operators have both versions. For example, the -eq operator has the following variants:

```
PS (1) > "abc" -eq "ABC"
True
PS (2) > "abc" -ieq "ABC"
True
PS (3) > "abc" -ceq "ABC"
False
```

The default case -eq is case-insensitive, as is the explicitly case-insensitive operator -ieq, so in the example, "abc" and "ABC" compare as equal. The -ceq operator is case-sensitive, so with this operator, "abc" and "ABC" compare as not equal.

The final item to discuss with scalar comparisons is how things that aren't strings and numbers are compared. In this case, the .NET comparison mechanisms are used. If the object implements the .NET IComparable interface, then that will be used. If not, and if the object on the left side has a .Equals() method that can take an object of the type of the right operand, this is used. If there is no direct mechanism for comparing the two an attempt will be made to convert the right operand into an instance of the type of the left operand, then PowerShell will try to compare the resulting objects. This lets you compare things such as [datetime] objects as shown in the next example:

```
PS (4) > [datetime] "1/1/2006" -gt [datetime] "1/1/2005"
True
PS (5) > [datetime] "1/1/2006" -gt [datetime] "2/1/2006"
False
PS (6) >
```

Of course, not all objects are directly comparable. For example, there is no direct way to compare a System.DateTime object to a System.Diagnostics.Process object.

```
PS (6) > [datetime] "1/1/2006" -gt (get-process)[0]
The '-gt' operator failed: Cannot convert
"System.Diagnostics.Process (ALCXMNTR)" to "System.DateTime"..
At line:1 char:26
+ [datetime] "1/1/2006" -gt  <<<< (get-process)[0]
PS (7) >
```

In the example, since there is no direct way to compare a DateTime object to a Process object, the next step is to try to convert the Process object into an instance of DateTime. This also failed; and, as this is the last step in the comparison algorithm, an error message is produced explaining what happened. This is where a human has to intervene. The obvious field on a Process object to compare is the StartTime of the process. We'll use the property notation to do this.

```
PS (7) > [datetime] "1/1/2006" -gt (get-process)[0].StartTime
False
PS (8) > [datetime] "1/1/2007" -gt (get-process)[0].StartTime
True
```

In this expression, we're looking to see whether the first element in the list of Process objects had a start time greater than the beginning of this year (no) and whether it had a start time from before the beginning of next year (obviously true). You can use this approach to find all the processes on a computer that started today, as shown:

```
get-process | where {$_.starttime -ge [datetime]::today}
```

The Get-Process cmdlet returns a list of all of the processes on this computer, and the where cmdlet selects those processes where the StartTime property of the process is greater than or equal to today.

AUTHOR'S NOTE The where used in the previous example is an alias for the Where-Object cmdlet, which is described in chapter 6.

This completes our discussion of the behavior of the comparison operators with scalar data. We paid a lot of attention to the role types play in comparisons, but so far we've avoided discussing collection types—lists, arrays and so on. We'll get to that in the next section.

4.3.2   Using comparison operators with collections

In this section, we focus on the behavior of the comparison operators when they are used with collections of objects.

Basic comparison operations involving collections

Here is the basic behavior. If the left operand is an array or collection, then the comparison operation will return the elements of that collection which match the right operand. Let's illustrate the rule with an example:

```
PS (1) > 1,2,3,1,2,3,4 -eq 2
2
2
```

This expression searches the list of numbers on the left side and returns those that match—the two "2"s. And of course this works with strings as well:

```
PS (2) > "one","two","three","two","one" -eq "two"
two
two
```

When processing the array, the scalar comparison rules are used to compare each element. In the next example, the left operand is an array containing a mix of numbers and strings, and the right operand is the string "2".

```
PS (3) > 1,"2",3,2,"1" -eq "2"
2
2
```

Again, it returns the two "2"s. Let's look at some more examples where we have leading zeros in the operands. In the first example:

```
PS (4) > 1,"02",3,02,"1" -eq "2"
2
```

we only return the number 2 because 2 and "02" compare equally in a numeric context; however "2" and "02" are different in a string context. The same thing happens in the next example.

```
PS (5) > 1,"02",3,02,"1" -eq 2
2
```

When the elements are compared as numbers, they match. When compared as strings, they don't match because of the leading zero. Now one final example:

```
PS (6) > 1,"02",3,02,"1" -eq "02"
02
2
```

Now they both match. In a numeric context, the leading zeros don't matter and in the string context, the strings match.

The containment operators

All of the comparison operators we've discussed so far return the matching elements from the collection. While this is extremely useful, there are times when you just want to find out whether an element is there or not. This is what the -contains and -notcontains operators are for. They return true if the set contains the element you're looking for instead of returning the matching elements. Let's redo the last example, but with -contains this time.

```
PS (1) > 1,"02",3,02,"1" -contains "02"
True
PS (2) > 1,"02",3,02,"1" -notcontains "02"
False
```

Now, instead of returning 02 and 2, we just return a single Boolean value. Since all values in PowerShell can be converted into a Boolean value, this doesn't seem as if it would particularly matter, and usually it doesn't. The one case where it does matter is if the matching set of elements is something that is false. This even includes Booleans. This is easiest to understand with an example:

```
PS (3) > $false,$true -eq $false
False
PS (4) > $false,$true -contains $false
True
```

In the first command, -eq searches the list for $false, finds it, then returns the matching value. However, since the matching value was literally $false, a successful match looks as if it failed. When we use the -contains operator in the expression, we get the result we'd expect, which is $true. The other way to work around this issue is to use the @(..) construction and the Count property. This looks like:

```
PS (5) > @($false,$true -eq $false).count
1
```

The @(...) sequence forces the result to be an array and then takes the count of the results. If there are no matches the count will be zero, which is equivalent to $false. If there are matches the count will be nonzero, equivalent to true. There can also be some performance advantages to -contains, since it stops looking on the first match instead of checking every element in the list.

> **NOTE**   The @ (..) construction is described in detail in chapter 5.

In this section, we covered all of the basic comparison operators. We addressed the issue of case-sensitivity in comparisons, and we covered the polymorphic behavior of these operations, first for scalar data types. then for collections. Now let's move on to some of the more advanced operators.

One of the hallmark features of dynamic languages is good support for pattern matching. In the next section, we'll cover how PowerShell incorporates pattern matching operators into the language.

4.4   THE PATTERN MATCHING OPERATORS

In this section, we cover the pattern matching operators in PowerShell. Along with the basic comparison operators, PowerShell has a number of pattern matching operators. These operators work on strings, matching and manipulating them using two types of patterns—*wildcard expressions* and *regular expressions*.

4.4.1   Wildcard patterns

You usually find wildcard patterns in a shell for matching file names. For example, the following command

```
dir *.txt
```

finds all of the files ending in .txt. Similarly,

```
cp *.txt c:\backup
```

will copy all the text files into the directory c:\backup. In these examples, the "*" matches any sequence of characters. Wildcard patterns also allow you to specify character ranges. In the next example, the pattern

```
dir [st]*.txt
```

will return all of the files that start with either the letters "s" or "t" that have a ".txt" extension. Finally, you can use the question mark (?) to match any single character.

The wildcard pattern matching operators are listed in table 4.4. This table lists the operators and includes some simple examples of how each one works.

Table 4.4   PowerShell wildcard pattern matching operators

Operator	Description	Example	Result
-like –clike –ilike	Do a wildcard pattern match.	"one" –like "o*"	$true
-notlike –cnotlin -inotlike	Do a wildcard pattern match; true if the pattern doesn't match.	"one" –notlike "o*"	$false

You can see from the table that there are several variations on the basic -like operator. These variations include case-sensitive and case-insensitive versions of the operator, as well as variants that return true if the target doesn't match the pattern. Table 4.5 summarizes the special characters that can be used in PowerShell wildcard patterns.

Table 4.5 Special characters in PowerShell wildcard patterns

Wildcard	Description	Example	Matches	Doesn't Match
*	Matches zero or more characters anywhere in the string.	a*	a aa abc ab	bc babc
?	Matches any single character	a?b	abc aXc	a, ab
[*<char>-*<char>*]	Matches a sequential range of characters	a[b-d]c	abc acc adc	aac aec afc abbc
[*<char><char>*...*]	Matches any one character from a set of characters	a[bc]c	abc acc	a ab Ac adc

While wildcard patterns are very simple, their matching capabilities are limited, so PowerShell also provides a set of operators that use *regular expressions*.

4.4.2 Regular expressions

Regular expressions are conceptually (if not syntactically) a superset of wildcard expressions. By this, we mean that you can express the same patterns in regular expressions that you could in wildcard expression, but with slightly different syntax.

AUTHOR'S NOTE In fact, in version 1 of PowerShell, wildcard patterns are translated internally into the corresponding regular expressions under the covers.

With regular expressions, instead of using "*" to match any sequence of characters as you would in wildcard patterns, you use ".*". And, instead of using "?" to match any single character, you use the dot "." instead.

ACADEMIC ALERT The name "regular expressions" comes from theoretical computer science, specifically the branches of automata theory (state machines) and formal languages. Ken Thompson, one of the creators of the UNIX operating system, saw an opportunity to apply this theoretical aspect of computer science to solve a real-world problem—namely finding patterns in text in an editor—and the rest is history. Most modern languages and environments that work with text now allow you to use regular expressions. This includes languages such as Perl, Python, and VBScript, and environments such as EMACS and

Microsoft Visual Studio. The regular expressions in PowerShell are implemented using the .NET regular expression classes. The pattern language implemented by these classes is very powerful; however, it's also very large, so we can't completely cover it in this book. On the other hand, since PowerShell directly uses the .NET regular expression classes, any source of documentation for .NET regular expressions is also applicable to PowerShell. For example, the Microsoft Developer Network has extensive (if rather fragmented) online documentation on .NET regular expressions.

The operators that work with regular expressions are -match and -replace. These operators are shown in table 4.6 along with a description and some examples.

Table 4.6 PowerShell regular expression matching operators

Operator	Description	Example	Result
-match -cmatch -imatch	Do a pattern match using regular expressions.	"Hello" –match "[jkl]"	$true
-notmatch -cnotmath -inotmatch	Do a regex pattern match; return true if the pattern doesn't match.	"Hello" –notmatch "[jkl]"	$false
-replace -creplace -ireplace	Do a regular expression substitution on the string on the right side and return the modified string.	"Hello" –replace "ello","i"	"Hi"
	Delete the portion of the string matching the regular expression.	"abcde" –replace "bcd"	"ae"

Using the $matches variable

The -match operator is similar to the -like operator in that it matches a pattern and returns a result. However, along with that result, it also sets the $matches variable. This variable contains the portions of the string that are matched by individual parts of the regular expressions. The only way to clearly explain this is with an example. Here we go:

```
PS (1) > "abc" -match "(a)(b)(c)"
True
```

In this example, the string on the left side of the -match operator is matched against the pattern on the right side. In the pattern string, you can see three sets of parentheses. Figure 4.1 shows this expression in more detail. You can see on the right side of the match operator that each of the components in parentheses is a "submatch". We'll get to why this is important in the next section.

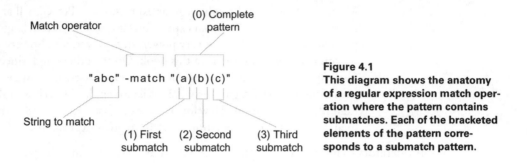

Figure 4.1
This diagram shows the anatomy of a regular expression match operation where the pattern contains submatches. Each of the bracketed elements of the pattern corresponds to a submatch pattern.

The result of this expression was true, which means that the match succeeded. It also means that $matched should be set, so let's look at what it contains:

```
PS (2) > $matches

Key                     Value
---                     -----
3                       c
2                       b
1                       a
0                       abc
```

$matches contains a hashtable where the keys of the hashtable are indexes that correspond to parts of the pattern that matched. The values are the substrings of the target string that matched. Note that even though we only specified three subpatterns, the hashtable contains four elements. This is because there is always a default element that represents the entire string that matched. Here's a more complex example that shows multiple nested matches.

```
PS (4) > "abcdef" -match "(a)(((b)(c))de)f"
True
PS (5) > $matches

Key                     Value
---                     -----
5                       c
4                       b
3                       bc
2                       bcde
1                       a
0                       abcdef
```

Now we have the outermost match in index 0, which matches the whole string. Next we have a top-level match at the beginning of the pattern that matches "a" at index 1. At index 2, we have the complete string matched by the next top-level part, which is "bcde". Index 3 is the first nested match in that top-level match, which is "bc". This match also has two nested matches: b at element 4 and c at element 5.

Matching using named captures

Of course, calculating these indexes is fine if the pattern is simple. If it's complex as in the previous example, it's hard to figure out what goes where; and even if you do, when you look at what you've written a month later, you'll have to figure it out all over again. The .NET regular expression library provides a way to solve this problem by using *named captures*. You specify a named capture by placing the sequence "?<*name*>" immediately inside the parentheses that indicate the match group. This allows you to reference the capture by name instead of by number, making complex expressions easier to deal with. This looks like:

```
PS (10) > "abcdef" -match "(?<o1>a)(?<o2>((?<e3>b)(?<e4>c))de)f"
True
PS (11) > $matches

Key                           Value
---                           -----
o1                            a
e3                            b
e4                            c
o2                            bcde
1                             bc
0                             abcdef
```

Now let's look at a more realistic example.

Parsing command output using regular expressions

Existing utilities for Windows produce text output, so you have to parse the text to extract information. (As you may remember, avoiding this kind of parsing was one of the reasons PowerShell was created. However, we still need to interoperate with the rest of the world.) For example, the net.exe utility can return some information about your computer configuration. The second line of this output contains the name of the computer. Our task is to extract the name and domain for this computer from that string. One way to do this is to calculate the offsets and then extract substrings from the output. This is tedious and error prone (since the offsets might change). Here's how to do it using the $matches variable. First let's look at the form of this string.

```
PS (1) > (net config workstation)[1]
Full Computer name           brucepay64.redmond.corp.microsoft.com
```

It begins with a well-known pattern "Full Computer name", so we start by matching against that to make sure there are no errors. Then we see that there is a space before the name, and the name itself is separated by a period. We're pretty safe in ignoring the intervening characters, so here's the pattern we'll use:

```
PS (2) > $p='^Full Computer.* (?<computer>[^.]+)\.(?<domain>[^.]+)'
```

Figure 4.2 shows this pattern in more detail.

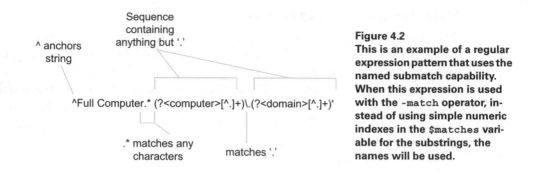

Figure 4.2
This is an example of a regular expression pattern that uses the named submatch capability. When this expression is used with the -match operator, instead of using simple numeric indexes in the $matches variable for the substrings, the names will be used.

We check the string at the beginning, then allow any sequence of characters that ends with a space, followed by two fields that are terminated by a dot. Notice that we don't say that the fields can contain any character. Instead we say that they can contain anything but a period. This is because regular expressions are greedy—that is, they match the longest possible pattern, and since the period is any character, the match will not stop at the period. Now let's apply this pattern.

```
PS (3) > (net config workstation)[1] -match $p
True
```

It matches, so we know that the output string was well formed. Now let's look at what we captured from the string.

```
PS (4) > $matches.computer
brucepay64
PS (5) > $matches.domain
redmond
```

We see that we've extracted the computer name and domain as desired. This approach is significantly more robust than using exact indexing for the following reasons. First, we checked with a guard string instead of assuming that the string at index 1 was correct. In fact, we could have written a loop that went through all of the strings and stopped when the match succeeded. In that case, it wouldn't matter which line contained the information; we would find it anyway. We also didn't care about where in the line the data actually appeared, only that it followed a basic well-formed pattern. With a pattern-based approach, output format can vary significantly, and this pattern would still retrieve the correct data. By using techniques like this, you can write more change-tolerant scripts than you would otherwise

Whew! So that's it for the pattern matching operators. In this section, we covered the two types of pattern matching operators—wildcard patterns and regular expressions. Wildcard patterns are pretty simple, but learning to use regular expressions effectively requires more work. On the other hand, you'll find that the power of regular expressions is more than worth the effort invested to learn them. We'll come back to these patterns again in chapter 6 when we discuss the switch statement. For now, though, let's come back down to earth and cover the last of the basic operators in the PowerShell language. These are the logical operators (-and, -or, -not) and the bitwise equivalents (-band, -bor, -bnot).

4.5   LOGICAL AND BITWISE OPERATORS

Along with the comparison operators, PowerShell also has the logical operators -and, -or, -xor, and -not for combining simpler comparisons into more complex expressions. The logical operators convert their operands into Boolean values and then perform the logical operation. Table 4.7 lists these operators.

Table 4.7   Logical and bitwise operators

Operator	Description	Example	Result
-and	Do a logical and of the left and right values.	0xff -and $false	$false
-or	Do a logical or of the left and right values.	$false -or 0x55	$true
-xor	Do a logical exclusive-or of the left and right values.	$false -xor $true $true -xor $true	$true $false
-not	Do the logical complement of the left and right values.	-not $true	$false
-band	Do a binary and of the bits in the values on the left and right side.	0xff -band 0x55	85 (0x55)
-bor	Do a binary or of the bits in the values on the left and right side.	0x55 -bor 0xaa	255 (0xff)
-bxor	Do a binary exclusive-or of the left and right values.	0x55 -bxor 0xaa 0xbb -bxor 0xa5	255 (0xff) 240 (0xf0)
-bnot	Do the bitwise complement of the argument value.	-bnot 0xff	-256 (0x ffffff00)

> **AUTHOR'S NOTE** The PowerShell logical operators are short-circuit operators—they only do as much work as they need to. With the -and operator, if the left operand evaluates to $false then the right operand expression is not executed. With the -or operator, if the left operand evaluates to $true then the right operand is not evaluated.

PowerShell also provides equivalent bitwise operators for doing binary operations on integer values. These operators can be used to test and mask bit fields, as shown in the examples in table 4.6. In the first version of PowerShell, the bitwise operators are limited in that they only support [int].

4.6   SUMMARY

This concludes our tour of the basic PowerShell operators. We covered a lot of information, much of it in great detail. We covered the basic PowerShell operators and expressions with semantics and applications of those operators. The important points to remember are:

- PowerShell operators are polymorphic with special behaviors defined by PowerShell for the basic types: numbers, strings, arrays, and hashtables.

- The behavior of most of the binary operators is determined by the type of the operand on the left.

- There are two types of pattern matching operations in PowerShell—wildcard patterns (usually used for matching filenames) and regular expressions.

- Because the comparison and pattern matching operators work on collections, in many cases you don't need a looping statement to search through collections.

- Regular expressions are powerful and can be used to do complex text manipulations with very little code. PowerShell uses the .NET regular expression classes to implement the regular expression operators in the language.

But we're not done yet! Join us in the next chapter for "Operators: The Sequel" or "Son of Operators". In that chapter, we'll finish off operators and expressions and also go over how variables are used. Please stay tuned.

CHAPTER 5

Advanced operators and variables

The greatest challenge to any thinker is stating the problem in a way
that will allow a solution.

—Bertrand Russell

The previous chapter covered the basic operators in PowerShell, and in this chapter we're going to continue the discussion of operators by covering the more advanced ones, which include things that some people don't think of as operators at all. We're also going to cover how to build complex data structures using these operators. The chapter concludes with a detailed discussion of how variables work in PowerShell, and how you can use them with operators to accomplish significant tasks.

5.1 OPERATORS FOR WORKING WITH TYPES

The type of an object is fundamental to determining the sorts of operations we can perform on that object. Up until now, we've been allowing the type of the object to *implicitly* determine the operations that are performed. But sometimes we want to do this *explicitly*. So that we may do this, PowerShell provides a set of operators that can work with types, as listed in table 5.1. These operators let us test whether an object is of a particular type or enable us to convert an object to a new type. The -is operator returns true if the object on the left side is of the type specified on the right side. By "is", we mean that the left operator is either of the type specified on the right side or is derived from that type. (See the section "Brushing up on objects" in chapter 1 for an explanation of derivation.)

The -isnot operator returns true if the left side is not of the type specified on the right side. The right side of the operator must be represented as a type or a string that names a type. This means that you can either use a type literal such as [int] or the literal string "int". The -as operator will try to convert the left operand into the type specified by the right operand. Again, either a type literal can be used or you can use a string naming a type.

AUTHOR'S NOTE The PowerShell -is and -as operators are directly modeled on the corresponding operators in C#. However, PowerShell's version of -as uses PowerShell's more aggressive approach to casting. For example, the C# as will not cast the string "123" into the number 123, whereas the PowerShell operator will do so. The PowerShell -as operator will also work on any type and the C# operator is restricted to reference types.

You may be wondering why we need the -as operator when we can just use a cast. The reason is that the -as operator allows you to use a runtime expression to specify the type, whereas the cast is fixed at parse time. Here's an example showing how you can use this runtime behavior.

```
PS (1) > foreach ($t in [float],[int],[string]) {"0123.45" -as $t}
123.45
123
0123.45
```

In this example, we looped over a list of type literals and converted the string into each of the types. This isn't possible when types are used as operators.

Finally, there is one additional difference between a regular cast and using the -as operator. In a cast, if the conversion doesn't succeed, an error is generated. With the -as operator, if the cast fails then the expression returns $null instead of generating an error.

```
PS (2) > [int] "abc" -eq $null
Cannot convert "abc" to "System.Int32". Error: "Input string was not
in a correct format."
At line:1 char:6
+ [int]  <<<< "abc" -eq $null
PS (3) > ("abc" -as [int]) -eq $null
True
PS (4) >
```

We see this in the example. Casting "abc" to [int] generated an error, but the -as operator just returned $null instead. Table 5.1 provides several more examples of how to use the type operators PowerShell provides.

Table 5.1 PowerShell operators for working with types

Operator	Example	Results	Description
-is	$true –is [bool]	$true	True if the type of the left side matches the type of the right side.
	$true -is [object]	$true	This is always true—everything is an object except $null.
	$true -is [ValueType]	$true	The left side is an instance of a .NET value type.
	"hi" -is [ValueType]	$false	A string is not a value type; it's a reference type.
	"hi" –is [object]	$true	But a string is still an object.
	12 –is [int]	$true	12 is an integer.
	12 –is "int"	$true	The right side of the operator can be either a type literal or a string naming a type.
-isnot	$true –isnot [string]	$true	The object on the left side is not of the same type as the right side.
	$true –isnot [object]	$true	The null value is the only thing that isn't an object.
-as	"123" -as [int]	123	Takes the left side and converts it to the type specified on the right side.
	123 –as "string"	"123"	Turns the left side into an instance of the type named by the string on the right.

In practice, most of the time the automatic type conversion mechanism will be all you need, and explicit casts will take care of the majority of the remaining cases. So why have these operators? They're mostly used in scripting. For example, if you want to have a script that behaves differently based on whether it's passed a string or a number, you'll need to use the -is operator to select which operation to perform. Obvious examples of this kind of functionality are the binary operators described in the previous chapter. The addition operator has different behavior depending on the type of its left argument. To write a script that did the same thing, you'd have to use -is to select the type of the operation to perform and -as to convert the right operand to the correct type. We'll look at examples of this in the chapter on scripting.

5.2   THE UNARY OPERATORS

Now let's take a detailed look at the unary operators. These operators are listed in table 5.2. We've actually seen most of these operators already in previous sections. The unary + and - operators do what you'd expect for numbers. Applying them to any other type results in an error. The use of the type casts as unary operators was discussed at length in chapter 3, so we won't go into it again. The interesting operators in this section are the increment and decrement operators. They match the behavior of the equivalent operators in C with both the prefix and postfix forms of the operators.

Again, these operators are defined only for variables containing numbers. Applying them to a variable containing anything other than a number results in an error. The prefix form of the ++ operator increments the variable by 1 and returns the new value. The postfix form increments the variable by 1 but returns the original value stored in the variable. The -- operator does the same thing, except that it subtracts 1 instead of adding it.

Table 5.2   PowerShell unary operators

Operator	Example	Results	Description
-	- (2+2)	-4	Negation. Tries to convert its argument to a number, then negates the result.
+	+ " "	123	Unary plus. Tries to convert its argument to a number and returns the result. This is effectively a cast to a number.
--	--$a ; $a--	Depends on the current value of the variable.	Pre and post decrement operator. Converts the content of the variable to a number, then tries to subtract one from it. The prefix version returns the new value; the postfix version returns the original value.
++	++$a; $a++	Depends on the current value of the variable.	Pre and post increment. Converts the variable to a number, then adds 1 to the result. The prefix version returns the new value; the postfix version returns the original value.
[<type>]	[int] "0x123"	291	Type cast. Converts the argument into an instance of the type specified by the cast
,	, (1+2)	1-element array containing the value of the expression.	Unary comma operator. Creates a new one-element array of type [object[]] and stores the operand in it.

The increment and decrement operators were almost not included in PowerShell because they introduced a problem. In languages such as C and C#, when you use one of these operators as a statement:

```
$a++
```

nothing is displayed. This is because statements in C and C# don't return values. In PowerShell, however, all statements return a value. This led to confusion. People would write scripts like this:

```
$sum=0
$i=0
while ($i -lt 10) { $sum += $i; $i++ }
$sum
```

       CHAPTER 5   ADVANCED OPERATORS AND VARIABLES

and be surprised to see the numbers 1 through 10 displayed. This was because $a++ returned a value and PowerShell was displaying the results of every statement. This was so confusing that we almost removed these operators from the language. Then we hit on the idea of a *voidable* statement. Basically, this means that certain types of expressions, when used as statements, are not displayed. Voidable statements include assignments and the increment/decrement operators. When they are used in an expression, they return a value, but when they're used as a standalone statement, they return no value. Again, this is one of those details that won't affect how you use PowerShell other than to make it work as you expect.

<table>
<tr><td>**AUTHOR'S NOTE**</td><td>Sometimes you want to explicitly discard the output of a statement. In effect, you want to turn a regular statement into a voidable one. The way to do this through an explicit cast is to [void] as in [void] (write-object "discard me"). The statement whose value you want to discard is enclosed in parentheses and the whole thing is cast to void. We'll see another way to accomplish the same effect using the redirection operators later in this chapter.</td></tr>
</table>

One area where voidable statements are particularly interesting is in the use of subexpressions for grouping sets of statements. We'll cover these expressions next.

5.3 GROUPING, SUBEXPRESSIONS, AND ARRAY SUBEXPRESSIONS

So far we've seen a variety of situations where collections of expressions or statements have been grouped together. We've even used these grouping constructs in string expansions back in chapter 3. Now we'll look at them in more detail. In fact, there are three ways of grouping expressions in PowerShell, as shown in table 5.3.

Table 5.3 Expression and statement grouping operators

Operator	Example	Results	Description
(...)	(2 + 2) * 3 (get-date).dayofweek	12 Returns the current week day.	Parentheses group expression operations and may contain either a simple expression or a simple pipeline.
$(...)	$($p = "a*"; get-process $p)	Returns the process objects for all processes starting with the letter a.	Subexpressions group collections of statements as opposed to being limited to a single expression. If the contained statements return a single value, it will be retuned as a scalar. If the statements return more than one value, they will be accumulated in an array.
@(...)	@(dir c:\; dir d:\)	Returns an array containing the FileInfo objects in the root of the C:\ and D:\ drives.	The array subexpression operator groups collections of statements in the same manner as the regular subexpression operator, but with the additional behavior that the result will always be returned as an array.

The first grouping notation is the simple parenthetical notation. As in most languages, the conventional use for this notation is to control the order of operations, as shown by the following example:

```
PS (1) > 2+3*4
14
PS (2) > (2+3)*4
20
```

The parentheses in the second expression cause the addition operation to be performed first. In PowerShell, parentheses also have another use. Looking at the syntax specification for parenthetical expressions illustrates this:

```
( <pipeline> )
```

From the syntax, we can see that pipelines are allowed between simple parentheses. This allows us to use a command or pipeline as a value in an expression. For example, to obtain a count of the number of files in a directory, we can use the dir command in parentheses, then use the count property to get the number of objects returned.

```
PS (1) > (dir).count
46
```

Using a pipeline in the parentheses lets us get a count of the number of files matching the wildcard pattern "*.doc".

```
PS (2) > (dir | where {$_.name -like '*.doc'}).count
32
```

AUTHOR'S NOTE People familiar with other languages tend to assume that the expression (1,2,3,4) is an array literal in PowerShell. In fact, as was discussed at length in chapter 3, this is not the case. The comma operator, discussed in the next section, allows you to easily construct arrays in PowerShell, but there are no array literals as such in the language. All that the parentheses do is control the order of operations. Otherwise, there is nothing special about them. In fact, the precedence of the comma operator is such that you typically never need parentheses for this purpose. More on that later.

Now let's move on to the next set of grouping constructs—the subexpressions. There are two forms of the subexpression construct, as shown in the following:

$(*<statementList>*)
@(*<statementList>*)

The syntactic difference between a subexpression (either form) and a simple parenthetical expression is that you can have any list of statements in a subexpression instead of being restricted to a single pipeline. This means that you can have any PowerShell language element in these grouping constructs, including loop statements. It also means that you can have several statements in the group. Let's look at an example. Earlier in this chapter, we looked at a short piece of PowerShell code that calculates the numbers in the Fibonacci sequence below 100. At the time, we didn't count the number of elements in that sequence. We can do this easily using the subexpression grouping construct.

```
PS (1) > $($c=$p=1; while ($c -lt 100) {$c; $c,$p=($c+$p),$c}).count
10
```

By enclosing the statements in $ (...), we can retrieve the result of the enclosed collection of statements as an array.

<table>
<tr><td>AUTHOR'S
NOTE</td><td>Many languages have a special notation for generating collections of objects. For example, Python and functional languages such as Haskell have a feature called list comprehensions for doing this. PowerShell (and shell languages in general) don't need special syntax for this kind of operation. Collections occur naturally as a consequence of the shell pipeline model. If a set of statements used as a value returns multiple objects, they will automatically be collected into an array.</td></tr>
</table>

Another difference between the subexpression construct and simple parentheses is how voidable expressions are treated. We mentioned this concept earlier with the increment and decrement operators. A voidable expression is one whose result is discarded when used directly as a statement. Here's an example that illustrates this. First we initialize $a to 0 and then use a post-increment expression in parentheses and assign it to the variable $x.

```
PS (1) > $a=0
PS (2) > $x=($a++)
```

And checking the value of $x, we see that it is zero, as expected, and that $a is now 1.

```
PS (3) > $x
0
PS (4) > $a
1
```

Now do a second assignment, this time with the expression in $ (...).

```
PS (5) > $x=$($a++)
```

Checking the value, we see that it's actually $null.

```
PS (6) > $x
PS (7) > $x -eq $null
True
```

This is because the result of the post-increment operation was discarded, so the expression returned nothing. Now try a more complex statement in the subexpression:

```
PS (8) > $x=$($a++;$a;$a++;$a)
PS (9) > $x
3
4
```

Notice that even though there are four statements in the subexpression, $x only received two values. Again, the results of the post-increment statements were discarded so they don't appear in the output.

Now let's take a look at the difference between the array subexpression @(...) and the regular subexpression. The difference is that in the case of the array subexpression, the result is always returned as an array; this is a fairly small but very useful difference. In effect, it's shorthand for:

```
[object[]] $( ... )
```

This shorthand exists because in many cases you don't know if a pipeline operation is going to return a single element or a collection. Rather than writing complex checks, you can use this construction and be assured that the result will always be a collection. If the pipeline returns an array, no new array is created. If, however, the pipeline returns a scalar value, that value will be wrapped in a single element. (Note that this is not the same as the comma operator, which always wraps its argument value in a new one-element array.)

> **NOTE** What the pipeline returns is the single hardest thing to explain in the PowerShell language. As one of the designers of the language, this more than anything kept me up at night. The problem is that people get confused; they see that @(12) returns a one-element array containing the number 12. Because of prior experience with other languages, they expect that @(@(12)) should therefore produce a nested array, an array of one element containing an array of one element which is the integer 12. This is not the case. @(@(12)) returns exactly the same thing as @(12). If you think of rewriting this expression as [object[]] $([object[]] $(12)), then it is clear why this is the case—casting an array into an array of the same type has no effect; it's already the correct type, so you just get the original array.

Here's an example of where this feature is useful. We'll write a pipeline expression that sorts some strings, then returns the first element in the sorted collection. We'll start by sorting an array of three elements:

```
PS (1) > $("bbb","aaa","ccc" | sort )[0]
aaa
```

This returns "aaa" as we expect. Now do it with two elements:

```
PS (2) > $("bbb","aaa" | sort )[0]
aaa
```

Still "aaa", so everything makes sense. Now try it with one element:

```
PS (3) > $("aaa" | sort )[0]
a
```

Wait a minute—what happened here? We sorted one element. In a pipeline, you can't tell if the commands in the pipeline mean to return a single object (a *scalar*) or an array containing a single object. The default behavior in PowerShell is to assume that if you return one element, you intended to return a scalar. In this case, the scalar is the string "aaa" and index 0 of this array is the letter "a", which is what the example returns. This is where you use the array subexpression notation. You know what you want the pipeline to return, and by using this notation, you can enforce the correct behavior. Here are the same three examples again, but this time using the array subexpression:

```
PS (4) > @("bbb","aaa","ccc" | sort )[0]
aaa
PS (5) > @("bbb","aaa" | sort )[0]
aaa
PS (6) > @("aaa" | sort )[0]
aaa
PS (7) >
```

This time, all three commands return "aaa" as intended. So why have this notation? Why not just use the casts? Well, here's what it looks like using the case notation:

```
PS (7) > ( [object[]] ("aaa" | sort ))[0]
aaa
```

Because of the way precedence works, you need an extra set of parentheses to get the ordering right, which makes the whole expression harder to write. In the end, the array subexpression notation is easy to use, but it is a bit difficult to learn and understand. As we discussed in chapter 1, on the whole, we'd rather be both—easy to use and easy to learn—but we'll take easy to use over easy to learn. You only have to learn something once, but you have to use it over and over again.

In any case, since we're discussing arrays, this is a great time to move on to the other operations PowerShell provides for dealing with arrays.

5.4   ARRAY OPERATORS

Arrays or collections of objects occur naturally in many of the operations that you undertake. Getting a directory listing in the file system results in a collection of objects. Getting the set of processes running on a machine or a list of services configured on a server both result in collections of objects. Not surprisingly, PowerShell has a set of operators and operations for dealing with arrays and collections that are described in the following sections.

5.4.1   The comma operator ","

We've already seen many examples using the comma operator to build arrays. This was covered in some detail in chapter 3, but there are a couple of things we still need to cover. In terms of precedence, the comma operator has the highest precedence of any operator except for casts and property or array references. This means that when you're building up an array with expressions, you need to wrap those expressions in parentheses. In the next example, we're trying to build up an array containing the values 1, 2, and 3. We're using addition to calculate the final value. Because "," binds more strongly than plus, we won't get what we wanted.

```
PS (1) > 1,2,1+2
1
2
1
2
```

The result was an array of four elements `1,2,1,2` instead of `1,2,3`. This is because the expression was parsed as `(1,2,1)+2`, building an array of three elements and then appending a fourth. You have to use parentheses to get the desired effect:

```
PS (2) > 1,2,(1+2)
1
2
3
```

Now you get the result you wanted.

> **AUTHOR'S NOTE** The comma operator has higher precedence than any other operator except casts and property and array references. This is worth calling out again because it's important to keep in mind when writing expressions. If you don't remember this, you will produce some strange results.

The next thing to look at is nested arrays. Since a PowerShell array can hold any type of object, obviously it can also hold another array. We've already mentioned that using the array subexpression operation was not the way to build a nested array. Now let's talk about how we actually do it using assignments and the comma operator. First, you can build nested arrays one piece at a time using assignments. Alternatively, you can just nest the comma operator within parentheses. Starting with last things first, here's how to build up a nested array structure using commas and parentheses. The result is concise:

```
PS (1) > $a = (((1,2),(3,4)),((5,6),(7,8)))
```

> **AUTHOR'S NOTE** LISP users should feel fairly comfortable with this expression if they ignore the commas. Everybody else is probably shuddering.

And here's the same construction using intermediate variables and assignments. It's rather less concise but perhaps more easily understood.

```
$t1 = 1,2
$t2 = 3,4
$t3 = 5,6
$t4 = 7,8
$t1_1 = $t1,$t2
$t1_2 = $t3,$t4
$a = $t1_1, $t2_2
```

In either case, what we've done is built up a data structure that looks like the tree shown in figure 5.1:

CHAPTER 5   ADVANCED OPERATORS AND VARIABLES

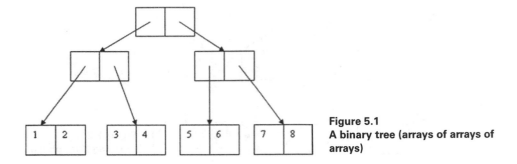

Figure 5.1
A binary tree (arrays of arrays of arrays)

The data structure in figure 5.1 is an array of two elements that are both arrays of two elements, which in turn contain arrays of two numbers.

AUTHOR'S NOTE For Perl and PHP users: in those languages, you have to do something special to get reference semantics with arrays. In PowerShell, arrays are always reference types, so there is no special notation needed.

Let's verify the shape of this data structure. First, use the length property to verify that `$a` does hold an array of two elements.

```
PS (2) > $a.length
2
```

Next, check the length of the of the array stored in the first element of that array:

```
PS (3) > $a[0].length
2
```

It's also two elements long, as is the array stored in the second element.

```
PS (4) > $a[1].length
2
```

Now let's look two levels down. This is done by indexing the result of an index as shown:

```
PS (5) > $a[1][0].length
2
```

Note that `$a[0][0]` is not the same as `$a[0,0]`, which is either a subset of the elements in the array called a *slice* if `$a` is one-dimensional, or a single index if the array is two dimensional (see the section on Array slices for more information on slices). You can compose index operations as deeply as you need to. Here we're retrieving the second element of the first element of the second element stored in `$a`.

```
PS (6) > $a[1][0][1]
6
```

To see exactly what's going on here, take a look at figure 5.2. In this figure, the heavily dashed lines show the path we followed in this last example that led us to get to the value 6.

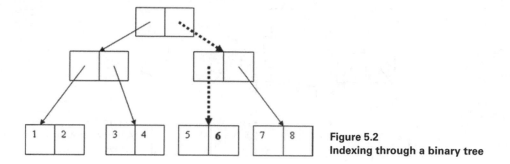

Figure 5.2
Indexing through a binary tree

These examples show how you can construct arbitrarily complex data structures in PowerShell. While this is not something you'll need to use frequently, the capability is there if you need it. In the section on array slices, we'll see an example where we use nested arrays to index multi-dimensional arrays.

5.4.2 The range operator

The next operator to discuss is the range operator ".". This operator is effectively a shortcut for generating a sequential array of numbers. For example, the expression:

```
1..5
```

is equivalent to

```
1,2,3,4,5
```

although it's somewhat more efficient than using the commas. The syntax for the range operator is:

```
<valueExpression> .. <valueExpression>
```

It has higher precedence than all the binary operators except for the comma operator. This means that expressions like:

```
PS (1) > 1..3+4..6
1
2
3
4
5
6
```

work, but the following gives you a syntax error:

```
PS (2) > 1+3..4+6
Cannot convert "System.Object[]" to "System.Int32".
At line:1 char:3
+ 1+3 <<<< ..4+6
```

It's an error because the expression is being parsed like:

```
1 + (3..4) + 6
```

This is because the range operator has higher precedence than the addition operator.

In a range operator expression, the left and right operands represent bounds; however, either the left or the right can be the upper bound. If the left operand is greater that the right operand, a descending sequence is generated:

```
PS (3) > 5..1
5
4
3
2
1
```

The boundaries can also be negative:

```
PS (4) > -5..-1
-5
-4
-3
-2
-1
```

Finally, the upper and lower bounds must be integer values with the usual type conversions applied so a string that looks like a number will automatically be converted into a number and a floating point value will automatically be converted to an integer using the banker's rounding algorithm described in chapter 4:

```
PS (5) > "1.1" .. 2.6
1
2
3
```

The range operator is most commonly used in the `foreach` loop, described in the next chapter, and in array slices, which are covered in the next section.

5.4.3 Array indexing

Most people don't think of indexing into an array as involving operators or that "[ ]" is an operator, but in fact, that's exactly what it is. It has a left operand and a right operand (the "right" operand is inside the square brackets). The syntax for an array indexing expression is

```
<valueExpression> [ <valueExpression> ]
```

There are a couple of things to note here. First, this is one of the few areas where you can't directly use a pipeline. That's because square brackets don't (and can't) delimit a pipeline. Square brackets are used in pipeline arguments as wildcard patterns, as shown in the following command:

```
dir [abc]*.txt | sort length
```

This pipeline returns all the text files in the current directory that start with a, b, or c, sorted by length. Now, if the square bracket ended the pipeline, you'd have to type this instead:

```
dir "[abc]*.txt" | sort length
```

So, if you do want to use a pipeline as an index expression, you have to use the subexpression notation.

The second thing to note is that spaces are not allowed between the last character of the expression being indexed and the opening square bracket. This is necessary to distinguish array expressions on the command line from wildcard patterns. Here's an example to illustrate why this is a problem. First assign an array of three elements to $a:

```
PS (14) > $a=1,2,3
```

Now write out the entire array along with the string "[0]" (remember, on the command line, strings don't need to be quoted).

```
PS (15) > write-host $a [0]
1 2 3 [0]
```

Next, let's just write out the first element of the array:

```
PS (16) > write-host $a[0]
1
```

You can see that the only difference between the first and second command lines is the presence of a space between the array variable and the opening square bracket. This is why spaces are not permitted in array indexing operations. The square bracket is used for wildcard expressions, and we don't want those confused with array indexing on the command line.

From the syntax (and from previous examples), you can see that array indexing works on more than just variables. In fact, it can be applied to any expression that returns a value. Of course, because the precedence of the square brackets is high, you usually have to put the expression in parentheses. If you don't, you'll get an error, as in the following example.

```
PS (1) > 1,2,3[0]
Unable to index into an object of type System.Int32.
At line:1 char:7
+ 1,2,3[0 <<<< ]
```

The error occurred because, due to precedence rules, we were in effect trying to index into the scalar quantity "3", which is not indexable. If we put the left value expression in parentheses, it works as desired.

```
PS (2) > (1,2,3)[0]
1
PS (3) >
```

We retrieved the first element (indexes start at zero) in the array, which is 1. Power-Shell also supports negative indexes, which index from the end of the array. Let's try it out.

```
PS (3) > (1,2,3)[-1]
3
PS (4) > (1,2,3)[-2]
2
PS (5) > (1,2,3)[-3]
1
```

Specifying -1 retrieves the last element in the array, -2 retrieves the second-to-last element, and so on. In fact, negative indexes are exactly equivalent to taking the length of the array and subtracting the index from the array:

```
PS (7) > $a[$a.length - 1]
3
PS (8) > $a[$a.length - 2]
2
PS (9) > $a[$a.length - 3]
1
```

In the example, $a.Length - 1 retrieves the last element of the array just like -1 did. In effect, negative indexing is just a shorthand for $array.Length - $index.

Array slices

We've seen how to get individual elements out of the array. We can also get sequences of elements out of arrays as well. This is done by specifying an array of indexes to the array:

```
PS (1) > $a = 1,2,3,4,5,6,7
PS (2) > $a[2,3,4,5]
3
4
5
6
PS (3) >
```

In this example, we used the array 2,3,4,5 to get the corresponding elements out of the array in $a. This is called *slicing* an array. Here's a variation on this example:

```
PS (3) > $indexes = 2,3,4,5
PS (4) > $a[$indexes]
3
4
5
6
```

This time we stored the list of indexes in a variable, then used the variable to do the indexing. The effect was the same. Now let's process the values that are stored in the

$indexes variable. We'll use the Foreach-Object cmdlet to process each element of the array and assign the results back to the array.

```
PS (5) > $indexes = 2,3,4,5 | foreach {$_-1}
```

We want to adjust for the fact that arrays start at index 0, so we subtract one from each index element. Now when we do the indexing:

```
PS (6) > $a[$indexes]
2
3
4
5
```

we get the elements that correspond to the original index value—2 returns 2, and so on. But do we need to use the intermediate variable? Let's try it:

```
PS (7) > $a[2,3,4,5 | foreach {$_-1}]
Missing ']' after array index expression.
At line:1 char:12
+ $a[2,3,4,5 | <<<<  foreach {$_-1}]
```

So we got a parsing error. This doesn't mean that we can't do it. It just means that we have to wrap the expression in brackets so it will be treated as a single value. We do this in the following:

```
PS (8) > $a[(2,3,4,5 | foreach {$_-1})]
2
3
4
5
PS (9) >
```

This time there was no error and we get the values we expected.

Using the range operator with arrays

There is one other tool in the indexing toolkit, and that is the range operator discussed in the previous section. This operator is a convenient way to get slices of arrays. Say we have an array of 10 elements 0 through 9. To get the first four elements of an array, you can use the range operator as follows:

```
PS (2) > $a[0..3]
0
1
2
3
```

By taking advantage of the way negative indexing works, you can get the last four elements of the array by doing:

```
PS (3) > $a[-4..-1]
6
```

```
7
8
9
```

You can even use ranges to reverse an array. To do this, you need to know the length of the array, which you can get through the length property. The following example shows this. (We're casting the result of the expression to string so it will be displayed on one line.)

```
PS (6) > [string] $a[ ($a.length-1) .. 0]
9 8 7 6 5 4 3 2 1 0
```

AUTHOR'S NOTE This isn't an efficient way of reversing the array. Using the Reverse static member on the [array] class is more efficient. See section 5.4.4 for more information on how to use .NET methods in PowerShell.

In PowerShell, slicing works for retrieving elements of an array, but you can't use it for assignments. You get an error if you try. For example, let's try to replace the slice [2,3,4] with a single value 12.

```
PS (1) > $a = 1,2,3,4,5,6,7,8
PS (2) > $a[2,3,4] = 12
Array assignment to [2,3,4] failed because assignment to slices is
not supported.
At line:1 char:4
+ $a[2 <<<< ,3,4] = 12
```

As you can see, you get an error telling you that assignment to slices is not supported. Here's what you have to do get the desired transformation:

```
PS (3) > $a = $a[0,1] + 12 + $a[5 .. 7]
PS (4) > $a
1
2
12
6
7
8
```

Basically, you have to take the array slices before and after the desired values and then concatenate all three pieces together to produce a new array,

Working with multi-dimensional arrays

So far we've covered one-dimensional arrays, but .NET allows for arrays to be n-dimensional. PowerShell supports this by looking at the type of the array and mapping the set of indexes onto the number of dimensions the array has. If you specify two indexes and the array is one-dimensional, you'll get two elements back. If the array is two dimensional, you'll get one element back. Let's try this. First we need to construct a multi-dimensional array using the New-Object cmdlet.

```
PS (1) > $2d = new-object 'object[,]' 2,2
```

This statement created a 2 by 2 array of objects. Now let's set the value in the array to particular values. We do this by indexing into the array.

```
PS (2) > $2d[0,0] = "a"
PS (3) > $2d[1,0] = 'b'
PS (4) > $2d[0,1] = 'c'
PS (5) > $2d[1,1] = 'd'
PS (6) > $2d[1,1]
d
```

This appears to imply that slices don't work in multi-dimensional arrays, but in fact they do when you use nested arrays of indexes and wrap the expression by using the comma operator in parentheses.

```
PS (7) > $2d[ (0,0) , (1,0) ]
a
b
```

Here we retrieved the elements of the array at indexes (0,0) and (1,0). And, as in the case of one-dimensional arrays, we can use variables for indexing:

```
PS (8) > $one=0,0 ; $two=1,0
PS (9) > $2d [ $one, $two ]
Unexpected token ' $one, $two ' in expression or statement.
At line:1 char:18
+ $2d [ $one, $two ] <<<<
PS (10) > $2d[ $one, $two ]
a
b
```

And you can even use a variable containing a pair of index arrays.

```
PS (11) > $pair = $one,$two
PS (12) > $2d[ $pair ]
a
b
```

This covers pretty much everything we need to say about arrays. Now let's move on to properties and methods.

5.5   PROPERTY AND METHOD OPERATORS

As we've seen in many examples so far, the property dereference operator in Power-Shell is the dot ".". As was the case with array indexing, this is properly considered an operator in PowerShell with left and right operand expressions. We'll get to what that means in a second.

> **AUTHOR'S NOTE**   When we say property here, we're talking about any kind of data member on an object, regardless of the underlying Common Language Runtime representation (or implementation) of the member.

First let's look back at the basics. Everything in PowerShell is an object (even scripts and functions as we'll see later on). As discussed in chapter 1, objects have properties (data) and methods (code). To get at both, you use the dot "." operator. To get the length of a string, you use the `length` property:

```
PS (1) > "Hello world!".length
12
```

In a similar fashion, we can get the length of an array:

```
PS (3) > (1,2,3,4,5).length
5
```

As was the case with the left square bracket in array indexing, spaces are not permitted between the left operand and the dot.

```
PS (4) > (1,2,3,4,5) .count
Unexpected token '.count' in expression or statement.
At line:1 char:18
+ (1,2,3,4,5) .count <<<<
```

This is necessary to make sure that arguments to cmdlets are not mistaken for property reference operations:

```
PS (5) > write-output (1,2,3,4,5) .count
1
2
3
4
5
.count
```

5.5.1 The "." operator

So much for the basics—now let's get back to this statement about "." being an operator. What's special about that? Well, just as the left operand can be an expression, so can the right operand. The right operand is evaluated, which results in a value. That value is then used as the name of the property on the left operand to retrieve. Let's look at an example of how this can be used. First we define a variable to hold the name of a property.

```
PS (6) > $prop = "length"
```

Now we can use that variable to retrieve the property:

```
PS (7) > "Hello world".$prop
11
```

This mechanism gives you that magic "one more level of indirection" computer science people are so very fond of. Let's expand on this. To get a list of all of the properties on an object, we can use the `Get-Members` (or `gm`) cmdlet. Let's use this on an object. We'll use dir to get a `FileInfo` object to work with.

```
PS (1) > @(dir c:\windows\*.dll)[0] | gm -type property

    TypeName: System.IO.FileInfo

Name                 MemberType  Definition
----                 ----------  ----------
Attributes           Property    System.IO.FileAttributes Attributes …
CreationTime         Property    System.DateTime CreationTime {get;s …
CreationTimeUtc      Property    System.DateTime CreationTimeUtc {ge …
Directory            Property    System.IO.DirectoryInfo Directory   …
DirectoryName        Property    System.String DirectoryName {get;}
Exists               Property    System.Boolean Exists {get;}
Extension            Property    System.String Extension {get;}
FullName             Property    System.String FullName {get;}
IsReadOnly           Property    System.Boolean IsReadOnly {get;set;}
LastAccessTime       Property    System.DateTime LastAccessTime {get;s …
LastAccessTimeUtc    Property    System.DateTime LastAccessTimeUtc {ge …
LastWriteTime        Property    System.DateTime LastWriteTime {get;se …
LastWriteTimeUtc     Property    System.DateTime LastWriteTimeUtc {get …
Length               Property    System.Int64 Length {get;}
Name                 Property    System.String Name {get;}
```

This gives us a list of all of the properties. Of course, we only need the name, so we can use the Name property on these objects.

```
PS (2) > @(dir c:\windows\*.dll)[0] | gm -type property |
>>> foreach {$_.name}
Attributes
CreationTime
CreationTimeUtc
Directory
DirectoryName
Exists
Extension
FullName
IsReadOnly
LastAccessTime
LastAccessTimeUtc
LastWriteTime
LastWriteTimeUtc
Length
Name
```

Now we'll use this list of names to get the corresponding values from the original object. First get the object into a variable:

```
PS (1) > $obj = @(dir c:\windows\*.dll)[0]
```

And get list of names; for brevity's sake, we'll just get the properties that start with "l".

```
PS (2) > $names = $obj | gm -type property l* | foreach {$_.name}
```

Finally use the list of names to print out the value:

```
PS (3) > $names | foreach { "$_ = $($obj.$_)" }
LastAccessTime = 3/25/2006 2:18:50 AM
LastAccessTimeUtc = 3/25/2006 10:18:50 AM
LastWriteTime = 8/10/2004 12:00:00 PM
LastWriteTimeUtc = 8/10/2004 7:00:00 PM
Length = 94784
PS (4) >
```

Next let's look at using methods. The method call syntax is:

```
<valueExpression> . <methodName> ( <argument> , <argument> , … )
```

As always, spaces are not allowed before or after the dot or before the opening parenthesis for the reasons discussed previously. Here's a basic example:

```
PS (1) > "Hello world!".substring(0,5)
Hello
```

In this example, we used the substring method to extract the first five characters from the left operand string. As you can see, the syntax for method invocations in PowerShell matches what you see in pretty much every other language that has methods. Contrast this with how commands are called. In method calls, arguments in the argument list are separated by commas and the whole list is enclosed in parentheses. With commands, the arguments are separated with spaces and the command ends at the end of line or at a command terminator, such as the semicolon or the pipe symbol.

This is another area where we experimented with alternate syntaxes. One of the experiments we conducted resulted in a command-like method invocation syntax that looked something like:

```
"Hello world!".(substring 0 5)
```

We chose not to use this syntax for two reasons (which, by the way, means that you'll get an error if you try using it). First, it collided with the ability to perform indirect property name retrievals. The second (and more important) reason was that people also found it uncomfortably strange. Empirically, a programmer-style syntax for method invocations and a shell-style syntax for command invocation seems to work best. Of course, this is also not without some small issues. First, if you want to pass an expression to a method, you have to wrap that array in parentheses so the array comma operator is not confused with the argument separator commas. Next, if you want to use the output of a command as an argument, you have to wrap the command in parentheses. Here's an example:

```
PS (1) > [string]::join('+',(1,2,3))
1+2+3
```

We're using the [string]::join method to create a string out of the array 1,2,3 with a plus sign between each one. Now let's do the same thing with the output of a command. Here's a command that returns the handle count for the rundll processes.

```
PS (1) > get-process rundll* | foreach{$_.handles}
58
109
```

Now let's join that output into a string, again separated with the plus sign (with spaces on either side this time).

```
PS (2) > [string]::join(" + ", (get-process rundll* |
>>> foreach{$_.handles}))
58 + 109
```

5.5.2   Static methods and the "::" operator

Of course, the observant reader will have noticed the use of the :: operator, which we briefly discussed in chapter 3. To reiterate, this is the static member accessor. Where the "." operator retrieved instance members, the double-colon operator accesses static members on a class, as is the case with the join method. Its left operand is required to be a type—either a type literal or an expression returning a type as we see here:

```
PS (1) > $t = [string]
PS (2) > $t::join('+',(1,2,3))
1+2+3
PS (3) >
```

We chose to use a separate operator for accessing static methods because of the way static methods are accessed. Here's the problem. If we had a type MyModule with a static property called Module, then the expression

```
[MyModule].Module
```

is ambiguous. This is because there is also an instance member Module on the System.Type instance representing the type MyModule. Now we can't tell if the "Module" instance member on System.Type or the "Module" static member on MyModule should be retrieved. By using the double-colon operator, this ambiguity is removed.

> **AUTHOR'S NOTE** Other languages get around this ambiguity by using the typeof() operator. Using typeof() in this example, typeof(MyModule).Module retrieves the instance property on the Type object and MyModule.Module retrieves the static property implemented by the MyModule class.

This finishes our discussion of properties and methods. You may have noticed that in some of the examples so far, we've gone to some lengths in taking expressions apart to present them. Clearly, on occasion you'll need a better way to present output, and that's what the format operator, covered in the next section, is for.

5.6   THE POWERSHELL FORMAT OPERATOR -F

Most of the time, PowerShell's built-in formatting and output system will take care of presenting your results, but sometimes you need more explicit control over the formatting of your output. You may also want to format text strings in a specific way. PowerShell allows you to do these things with the format operator. The format operator -f is a binary operator that takes a format string as its left operand and an array of values to format as its right operand. Here's an example:

```
PS (1) > '{2} {1} {0}' -f 1,2,3
3 2 1
```

In the format string, the values enclosed in braces correspond to the index of the element in the right operand array. The element is converted into a string and then displayed. Along with reordering, when the elements are displayed, you can also control how they are laid out.

> **AUTHOR'S NOTE**   For people familiar with the Python language, the PowerShell format operator is modeled on the Python % operator. However, since PowerShell doesn't use the % character as part of its formatting directives, it didn't make mnemonic sense for the format operator in PowerShell to be %. Instead we chose -f.

Here are some more examples:

```
PS (3) > '|{0,10}| 0x{1:x}|{2,-10}|' -f 10,20,30
|        10| 0x14|30        |
```

Here, the first format specifier element ",10" tells the system to pad the text out to 10 characters. The next element is printed with the specifier ":x" telling the system to display the number as a hexadecimal value. The final display specification has a field width specifier, but this time it's a negative value, indicating that the field should be padded to the right instead of to the left.

The -f operator is, in fact, shorthand for calling the .NET Format method on the System.String class. The previous example can be rewritten as

```
PS (4) > [string]::Format('|{0,10}| 0x{1:x}|{2,-10}|',10,20,30)
|        10| 0x14|30        |
```

and you'll get exactly the same results. The key benefit of the -f operator is that it's a lot shorter to type. This is useful when you're typing on the command line. The underlying Format() method has a rich set of specifiers. The basic syntax of these specifiers is

```
{<index>[,<alignment>][:<formatString>]}
```

Some examples using format specifiers are shown in table 5.4.

Table 5.4 Expression and statement grouping operators

Formant Specifier	Description	Example	Output
{0}	Display a particular element.	"{0} {1}" –f "a","b"	a b
{0:x}	Display a number in Hexadecimal.	"0x{0:x}" -f 181342	0x2c45e
{0:X}	Display a number in Hexadecimal with the letters in uppercase.	"0x{0:X}" -f 181342	0x2C45E
{0:dn}	Display a decimal number left-justified, padded with zeros.	"{0:d8}" -f 3	00000003
{0:p}	Display a number as a percentage.	"{0:p}" -f .123	"{0:p}" -f .123
{0:C}	Display a number as currency.	"{0:c}" -f 12.34	$12.34
{0,n}	Display with field width n, left aligned.	"|{0,5}|" –f "hi"	| hi|
{0,-n}	Display with field width n, right aligned.	"|{0,-5}|" –f "hi"	|hi |
{0:hh} {0:mm}	Displays the hours and minutes from a DateTime value.	"{0:hh}:{0:mm}" –f (get-date)	01:34
{0:C}	Display using the currency symbol for the current culture.	"|{0,10:C}|" -f 12.4	| $12.40|

Of course, there are many more things you can do with formatting than we can cover here. Refer to the Microsoft MSDN documentation for the full details of all of the various options.

5.7 REDIRECTION AND THE REDIRECTION OPERATORS

All modern shell languages have input/output redirection operators, and PowerShell is no different. The redirection operators supported in version 1 of PowerShell are shown in table 5.5.

Table 5.5 Expression and statement grouping operators

Operator	Example	Results	Description
>	dir > out.txt	Contents of out.txt are replaced.	Redirect pipeline output to a file, overwriting the current contents.
>>	dir >> out.txt	Contents of out.txt are appended to.	Redirect pipeline output to a file, appending to the existing content.
2>	dir nosuchfile.txt 2> err.txt	Contents of err.txt are replaced by the error messages.	Redirect error output to a file, overwriting the current contents.
2>>	dir nosuchfile.txt 2>> err.txt	Contents of err.txt are appended with the error messages.	Redirect error output to a file, appending to the current contents.

continued on next page

CHAPTER 5   ADVANCED OPERATORS AND VARIABLES

Table 5.5 Expression and statement grouping operators *(continued)*

Operator	Example	Results	Description
2>&1	dir nosuchfile.txt 2>&1	The error message is written to the output.	The error messages are written to the output pipe instead of the error pipe.
<	Not implemented in PowerShell V1.0		This operator is reserved for input redirection which is not implemented in version 1.0 of PowerShell. Using this operator in an expression will result in a syntax error.

The redirection operators allow you to control where output and error objects are written (including discarding them if that's what you want to do). In the following example, we're saving the output of the Get-Date cmdlet to a file called out.txt.

```
PS (1) > get-date > out.txt
```

Now let's display the contents of this file:

```
PS (2) > type out.txt

Tuesday, January 31, 2006 9:56:25 PM
```

You can see that the object has been rendered to text using the same mechanism as would be used when displaying on the console. Now let's see what happens when we redirect the error output from a cmdlet. We'll let the output be displayed normally.

```
PS (3) > dir out.txt,nosuchfile 2> err.txt


    Directory: Microsoft.Management.Automation.Core\FileSystem::C:\
    working


Mode                LastWriteTime     Length Name
----                -------------     ------ ----
-a---         1/31/2006   9:56 PM         40 out.txt
```

Obviously no error was displayed on the console. Let's see what was written to the error file.

```
PS (4) > type err.txt
get-childitem : Cannot find path 'C:\working\nosuchfile' because it
 does not exist.
At line:1 char:4
+ dir  <<<< out.txt,nosuchfile 2> err.txt
```

We see the full error message that would have been displayed on the console. Now let's try the append operator. We'll add another line to the output file we created earlier, and display the contents of the file.

```
PS (5) > get-date >> out.txt
PS (6) > type out.txt

Tuesday, January 31, 2006 9:56:25 PM

Tuesday, January 31, 2006 9:57:33 PM
```

We see that there are now two records containing the current date. You can also append error records to a file using the 2>> operator.

The next operator to discuss is the stream combiner 2>&1. This operator causes error objects to be routed into the output stream instead of going to the error stream. This allows you to capture error records along with your output. For example, if you want to get all of the output and error records from a script to go to the same file, you would just do

```
myScript > output.txt 2>&1
```

or

```
myScript 2>&1 > output.txt
```

The order doesn't matter. Now all of the error records will appear inline with the output records in the file. This also works with assignment.

```
$a = myScript  2>&1
```

This causes all the output and error objects from myScript to be placed in $a. You could then separate the errors by checking for their type with the -is operator, but it would be easier to separate them up front. This is another place where you can use the grouping constructs. The following construction allows you to capture the output objects in $output and the error objects in $error.

```
$error = $( $output = myScript ) 2>&1
```

You would use this idiom when you wanted to take some additional action on the error objects. For example, you might be deleting a set of files in a directory. Some of the deletions might fail. These will be recorded in $error, allowing you to take additional actions after the deletion operation has completed.

Sometimes you want to discard output or errors. In PowerShell, you do this by redirecting to $null. For example, if you don't care about the output from myScript then you would write:

```
myScript > $null
```

and to discard the errors, you would write:

```
myScript 2> $null
```

The last thing to mention for I/O redirection is that, under the covers, redirection is done using the Out-File cmdlet. If fact,

```
myScript > file.txt
```

is just *syntactic sugar* for

```
myScript | out-file -path file.txt
```

In some cases, you'll want to use Out-File directly because it gives you more control over the way the output is written. The synopsis for Out-File is

```
Out-File [-FilePath] <String> [[-Encoding] <String>]
[-Append] [-Force] [-NoClobber] [-Width <Int32>]
[-InputObject <PSObject>]
[-Verbose] [-Debug] [-ErrorAction <ActionPreference>]
[-ErrorVariable <String>] [-OutVariable <String>]
[-OutBuffer <Int32>] [-WhatIf] [-Confirm]]
```

The interesting parameters are -encoding, which lets you specify the encoding (such as ASCII, Unicode, UTF8, and so on); -append, which appends to an existing file instead of overwriting it; -noclobber, which prevents you from overwriting (clobbering) an existing file; and -width, which tells the cmdlet how wide you want the output formatted. The full details for this cmdlet are available by running the command:

```
get-help out-file
```

at the PowerShell command line.

Earlier in this section, we talked about assignment as being a kind of output redirection. In fact, this analogy is even more significant than we alluded to there. We'll go into details in the next section, when we finally cover variables themselves.

5.8   VARIABLES

In many of the examples we've seen so far, we've used variables. Now let's look at the actual details of PowerShell variables. First off, PowerShell variables aren't declared; they're just created as needed on first assignment. There also isn't really any such thing as an uninitialized variable. If you reference a variable that does not exist yet, the system will return the value $null (although it won't actually create a variable).

```
PS (1) > $NoSuchVariable
PS (2) > $NoSuchVariable -eq $null
True
```

In the example, we looked at a variable that doesn't exist and see that it returns $null.

> **AUTHOR'S NOTE** $null, like $true and $false, is a special constant variable that is defined by the system. You can't change the value of these variables.

You can tell whether a variable exists or not by using the Test-Path cmdlet as shown:

```
PS (3) > test-path variable:NoSuchVariable
False
```

This works because variables are part of the PowerShell unified namespaces. Just as files and the registry are available through virtual drives, so are PowerShell variables. You can get a list of all of the variables that currently exist by doing

```
dir variable:/
```

So how do we create a variable? First off, there are a number of variables that are defined by the system: `$true`, `$false`, and `$null` are the ones we've seen so far (we'll mention the others as we come to them). User variables are created on first assignment, as we see in the next example.

```
PS (3) > $var = 1
PS (4) > $var
1
PS (5) > $var = "Hi there"
PS (6) > $var
Hi there
PS (7) > $var = get-date
PS (8) > $var

Sunday, January 29, 2006 7:23:29 PM
```

In this example, first we assigned a number, then a string, then a `DateTime` object. This illustrates that PowerShell variables can hold any type of object. If you do want to add a *type attribute* to a variable, you use the cast notation on the left of the variable. Let's add a type attribute to the variable `$val`.

```
PS (1) > [int] $var = 2
```

Looking at the result, we see the number 2.

```
PS (2) > $var
2
```

That's fine. What happens if we try to assign a string to the variable? Let's try it.

```
PS (3) > $var = "0123"
PS (4) > $var
123
```

First, there was no error. Second, by looking at the output of the variable, you can see that the string "0123" was converted into the number 123. This is why we say that the variable has a *type attribute*. Unlike strongly typed languages where a variable can only be assigned an object of the correct type, PowerShell will allow you to assign any object as long as it is convertible to the target type using the rules described in chapter 3. If the type is not convertible then you'll get a runtime type conversion error (as opposed to a "compile-time" error.)

```
PS (5) > $var = "abc"
Cannot convert "abc" to "System.Int32". Error: "Input string was no
t in a correct format."
At line:1 char:5
+ $var  <<<< = "abc"
```

In this example, we tried to assign "abc" to a variable with the type attribute [int]. Since "abc" can't be can't be converted to a number, you see a type conversion error.

Now what about variable names? What characters are allowed in a variable name? The answer is: any character you want, with some caveats. There are two notations for variables. The simple notation starts with a dollar sign followed by a sequence of characters, which can include letters, numbers, the underscore, and the colon. The colon has a special meaning that we'll get to in a minute. The second notation allows you to use any character in a variable name. It looks like this:

```
${This is a variable name}
```

You can use any character you want in the braces. You can even use a close brace if you escape it, as we see in the next example.

```
PS (7) > ${this is a variable name with a `} in it}
PS (8) > ${this is a variable name with a `} in it} = 13
PS (9) > ${this is a variable name with a `} in it}
13
```

Earlier, we said that the colon character was special in a variable name. This is used to delimit the *namespace* that the system uses to locate the variable. For example, to access PowerShell global variables, you use the global namespace:

```
PS (1) > $qlobal:var = 13
PS (2) > $global:var
13
```

This example set the variable "var" in the global context to the value 13. You can also use the namespace notation to access variables at other scopes. This is called a *scope modifier*. Scopes will be covered in chapter 6, so we won't say anything more about that here.

Along with the scope modifiers, the namespace notation lets you get at any of the resources surfaced in PowerShell as drives. For example, to get at the environment variables, you use the env namespace as shown:

```
PS (1) > $env:SystemRoot
C:\WINDOWS
```

In this example, we retrieved the contents of the SystemRoot environment variable. You can use these variables directly in paths. For example:

```
PS (3) > dir $env:systemroot\explorer.exe


    Directory: Microsoft.Management.Automation.Core\FileSystem::C:\
    WINDOWS


Mode             LastWriteTime       Length Name
----             -------------       ------ ----
-a---        8/10/2004  12:00 PM     1032192 explorer.exe
```

This retrieved the filesystem information for explorer.exe.

AUTHOR'S NOTE	For cmd.exe or command.com users, the equivalent syntax would be %systemroot%\explorer.exe. There, the percent signs delimit the variable. In PowerShell, this is done with braces.

Many of the namespace providers are also available through the variable notation (but you usually have to wrap the path in braces). Let's look back at an example we saw at the beginning of chapter 4:

```
${c:old.txt} -replace 'is (red|blue)','was $1' > new.txt
```

The initial construct should now start to make sense. The sequence `${c:old.txt}` is a variable that references the filesystem provider through the C: drive and retrieves the contexts of the file named "old.txt". With this simple notation, we read the contents of a file. No open/read/close—we treat the file itself as an atomic value.

AUTHOR'S NOTE	Using variable notation to access a file can be startling at first, but it's a logical consequence of the unified data model in PowerShell. Since things like variables and functions are available as drives, things such as drives are also available using the variable notation. In effect, this is an application of the Model-View Controller (MVC) pattern. Each type of data store (filesystem, variables, registry, and so forth) is a "model". The PowerShell provider infrastructure acts as the controller and there are (by default) two views: the "filesystem" navigation view and the variable view. The user is free to choose and use the view most suitable to the task at hand.

You can also write to a file using the namespace variable notation. Here's that example rewritten to use variable assignment instead of a redirection operator (remember, earlier we said that assignment can be considered a form of redirection in PowerShell.)

```
${c:new.txt} = ${c:old.txt} -replace 'is (red|blue)','was $1'
```

In fact, you can even do an in-place update of a file by using the same variable on both sides of the assignment operator. To update the file "old.txt" instead of making a copy, do

```
${c:old.txt} = ${c:old.txt} -replace 'is (red|blue)','was $1'
```

All we did was change the name in the variable reference from "new.txt" to "old.txt". This won't work if you use the redirection operator, because the output file is opened before the input file is read. This would have the unfortunate effect of truncating the previous contents of the output file. In the assignment case, the file is read atomically; that is, all at once, processed, then written atomically. This allows for "in-place" edits because the file is actually buffered entirely in memory instead of in a temporary file. To do this with redirection, you'd have to save the output to a temporary file and then rename the temporary file so it replaces the original. Now let's leverage this feature along with multiple assignments to swap two files "f1.txt" and "f2.txt". Earlier in this chapter we showed how to swap two variables. We can use the same technique to swap two files. Here we go:

```
${c:f1.txt},${c:f2.txt} = ${c:f2.txt},${c:f1.txt}
```

AUTHOR'S NOTE All of these examples using variables to read and write files cause the entire contents of files to be loaded into memory as a collection of strings. On modern computers it's possible to handle moderately large files this way, but doing it with very large files is memory-intensive, inefficient, and might even fail under some conditions. Keep this in mind when using these techniques.

When the filesystem provider reads the file, it returns the file as an array of strings.

AUTHOR'S NOTE When accessing a file using the variable namespace notation, PowerShell assumes that it's working with a text file. Since the notation doesn't provide a mechanism for specifying the encoding, you can't use this technique on binary files. You'll have to use the `Get-Content` and `Set-Content` cmdlets instead.

This provides a simple way to get the length of a file:

```
${c:file.txt}.length
```

The downside of this simple construct is that it requires reading the entire file into memory and then counting the result. It works fine for small files (a few megabytes) but it won't work on files that are gigabytes in size.

This is all we're going to cover about variables here. In chapter 7, we'll return to variables and talk about how variables are scoped in the PowerShell language.

5.9 SUMMARY

In this chapter, we finished our coverage of PowerShell operators and expressions. We covered how to build complex data structures in PowerShell and how to use the redirection operators to write output to files. We covered arrays, properties, and methods. Finally, we covered the basics of PowerShell variable semantics and variable namespaces. The important points to remember are:

- The type operators allow you to write scripts that have polymorphic behavior. By using these operators to examine the types of objects, you can decide how to process those objects.

- The prefix and postfix operators `++` and `--` are a convenient way of incrementing and decrementing variables.

- The subexpression operator `$( ... )` allows you to use arbitrary PowerShell script code anywhere that you can use a value expression. The array subexpression operator `@( ... )` allows you to guarantee that the result of an expression is always an array.

- PowerShell arrays support both *jagged arrays*—that is, arrays that contain or *reference* other arrays and multi-dimensional arrays. Array *slicing* is also supported.

- Use the comma operator to build arrays and complex nested data structures.

- Use the dot operator "." for accessing instance members and the double-colon "::" for accessing static members.
- The PowerShell redirection operators allow you to control where the output and error objects are written. They also allow you to easily discard these objects if so desired.
- The format operator -f can be used to do complex formatting tasks when the default formatting doesn't produce the desired results.
- PowerShell variable namespaces let you access a variety of Windows "data stores", including environment variables and the filesystem, not just PowerShell variables.

C H A P T E R   6

Flow control in scripts

I may not have gone where I intended to go, but I think I have ended up where I needed to be.

—Douglas Adams, *The Long Dark Teatime of the Soul*

Previous chapters showed you how to solve remarkably complex problems in Power-Shell using only commands and operators. You can select, sort, edit, and present all manner of data by composing these elements into pipelines and expressions. In fact, commands and operators were the only elements available in the earliest prototypes of PowerShell. Sooner or later, however, if you want to write significant programs or scripts, you need to add some sort of custom looping or branch logic to your solution. This is what we're going to cover in this chapter: PowerShell's take on the traditional programming constructs that all languages possess.

PowerShell has the usual flow control statements for branching and loops; however, there are some behavioral differences that even experienced shell users should be aware of. The most obvious difference is that *PowerShell typically allows the use of pipelines* in places where other programming languages only allow simple expressions. An interesting implication of this pipeline usage is that the PowerShell `switch` statement is both a looping construct and a conditional statement, as you'll see in this chapter.

This is also the first time we've really dealt with *keywords* in PowerShell. Keywords are part of the core PowerShell language. This means that, unlike cmdlets, keywords cannot be redefined or aliased. Keywords are also case insensitive so you can write `foreach`, `ForEach`, or `FOREACH` and they will all be accepted by the interpreter. (By convention, however, keywords in PowerShell scripts are usually written in lowercase.)

With these basics out of the way, let's look at the PowerShell flow control statements themselves.

6.1 USING THE IF/ELSEIF/ELSE STATEMENT

The first statement we'll look at is the `if` statement. This is the basic conditional statement found in all languages. Figure 6.1 shows the structure of this statement.

The statement shown in figure 6.1 is somewhat hard to read, so here's an example to clarify how the `if` statement works

```
if ($x -gt 100)
{
    "It's greater than one hundred"
} elseif ($x -gt 50)
{
    "It's greater than 50"
} else
{
    "It's not very big."
}
```

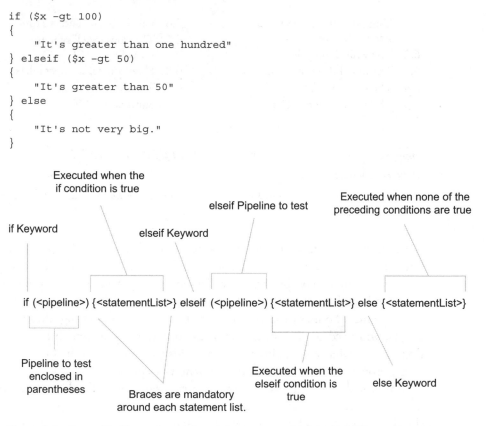

Figure 6.1   PowerShell's version of the `if` Statement, which is the basic conditional statement found in all software languages.

In this example, if the variable $x holds a value greater than 100, the string "It's greater than one hundred" will be emitted. If $x is greater than 50 but less than 100, it will emit "It's greater than 50"; otherwise you'll get "It's not very big". Of course, you can have zero or more elseif clauses to test different things.

As you might have noticed, the PowerShell if statement is modeled on the if statement found in C-derived languages such as C#, but there are a couple of exceptions. First, elseif is a single keyword with no spaces allowed between the words. Next, the braces are mandatory around the statement lists, even if you only have a single statement in the list (or no statements for that matter, in which case you would have to type "{ }"). If you try to write something like

```
if ($x -gt 100) "It's greater than one hundred"
```

you'll get a syntax error:

```
PS (1) > if ($x -gt 100) "It's greater than one hundred"
Missing statement block after if ( condition ).
At line:1 char:17
+ if ($x -gt 100) " <<<< It's greater than one hundred"
PS (2) >
```

AUTHOR'S NOTE The PowerShell grammar technically could support the construction shown in the preceding code segment. In fact, I did enable this construct at one point, but when we tried it out, the result was a lot of errors. The problem is that a newline or a semicolon is required to terminate a command. This leads to the situation where you write something like:

```
if ($x -gt 3) write x is $x while ($x--) $x
```

and discover that, because you've missed the semicolon before the while statement, it writes out the while statement instead of executing it. In the end, the cost of typing a couple of additional characters was more than offset by a decreased error rate. For this reason, we made the braces mandatory.

In general, the syntax of the if statement (and all of the PowerShell flow control statements) is freeform with respect to white space. In other words, you can lay out your code pretty much any way you want. You can write an if statement that looks like this:

```
if($true){"true"}else{"false"}
```

with no white space whatsoever. Alternatively, you could also write it like this:

```
if
(
$true
)
{
"true"
}
```

```
else
{
"false"
}
```

where each token is on a separate line.

There is, however, one constraint on how you can format an `if` statement. When PowerShell is being used interactively, the `else` or `elseif` keywords have to be on the same line as the previous closing brace; otherwise the interpreter will consider the statement complete and execute it immediately.

It's important to note that the PowerShell `if` statement allows a *pipeline* in the condition clause, not just a simple expression. This means that it's possible to do the following:

```
if ( dir telly*.txt | select-string penguin )
{
    "There's a penguin on the telly."
}
```

In this example, the pipeline in the condition part of the `if` statement will scan all of the text files whose names start with "telly" to see whether they contain the word "penguin". If at least one of the files contains this word, the statement block will be executed, printing out:

```
There's a penguin on the telly.
```

Here's another example:

```
if (( dir *.txt | select-string spam ).Length -eq 3)
{
    "Spam! Spam! Spam!"
}
```

In this case, we search all the text files in the current directory looking for the word "spam". If exactly three files contain this word then we print out

```
Spam! Spam! Spam!
```

AUTHOR'S NOTE   Yes, these are, in fact, Monty Python references. Think of it as a respectful tip of the hat to the Python language community. If you're familiar with Python or Perl, you'll occasionally recognize cultural references from those languages in PowerShell examples here and elsewhere. Many of the PowerShell development team members had their first scripting experiences with those languages.

Because you can use pipelines and subexpressions in the conditional part of an `if` statement, you can write quite complex conditional expressions in PowerShell. With subexpressions, you can even use an `if` statement inside the condition part of another `if` statement. Here's what this looks like:

```
PS (2) > $x = 10
PS (3) > if ( $( if ($x -lt 5) { $false } else { $x } ) -gt
>>> 20) { $false } else {$true}
True
PS (4) > $x = 25
PS (5) > if ( $( if ($x -lt 5) { $false } else { $x } ) -gt
>>> 20) { $false } else {$true}
False
PS (6) > $x = 4
PS (7) > if ( $( if ($x -lt 5) { $false } else { $x } ) -gt
>>> 20) { $false } else {$true}
True
PS (8) >
```

If looking at this makes your head hurt, welcome to the club—it made mine hurt to write it. Let's dissect this statement and see what it's doing. Let's take the inner `if` statement first.

```
if ($x -lt 5) { $false } else { $x }
```

You can see that this statement is straightforward. If $x is less than the number 5, it returns false; otherwise it returns the value of $x. Based on this, let's split this into two separate statements.

```
$temp = $( if ($x -lt 5) { $false } else { $x } )
if ($temp -gt 20) { $false } else {$true}
```

Now what the outer `if` statement is doing is also pretty obvious: if the results of the first (formally inner) statement is greater than 20, return `$false`; otherwise return `$true`.

6.2   THE WHILE LOOP

In this section, we'll cover the basic iteration or looping statements in PowerShell. The `while` statement (also known as a `while` loop) is the basic PowerShell language construct for creating a loop. It executes the commands in the statement list as long as a conditional test evaluates to true. Figure 6.2 shows the `while` statement syntax:

When you execute a `while` statement, PowerShell evaluates the *<pipeline>* section of the statement before entering the *<statementList>* section. The output from the pipeline is then converted to either true or false, following the rules for the Boolean interpretation of values described in chapter 3. As long as this result converts to true, PowerShell reruns the *<statementList>* section, executing each statement in the list.

For example, the following `while` statement displays the numbers 1 through 3.

```
$val = 0
while($val -ne 3)
{
    $val++
    write-host "The number is $val"
}
```

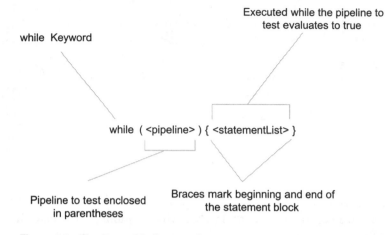

Executed while the pipeline to
test evaluates to true

while Keyword

while (<pipeline>) { <statementList> }

Pipeline to test enclosed
in parentheses

Braces mark beginning and end of
the statement block

Figure 6.2   The PowerShell `while` loop statement syntax

In this example, the condition ($val is not equal to 3) is true while $val is 0, 1, and 2. Each time through the loop, $val is incremented by one using the ++ unary increment operator ($val++). The last time through the loop, $val is 3. When $val equals 3, the condition statement evaluates to false and the loop exits.

To more conveniently enter this command at the PowerShell command-prompt, you can simply enter it all on one line as shown:

```
$val=0; while ($val -ne 3){$val++; write-host "The number is $val"}
```

Notice that the semicolon separates the first command that adds one to $val from the second command, which writes the value of $val to the console.

You can accomplish all of the basic iterative patterns just using the `while` loop, but PowerShell provides several other looping statements for common cases. Let's look at those now.

6.3   THE DO/WHILE LOOP

The other `while` loop variant in PowerShell is the `do-while` loop. This is a bottom-tested variant of the `while` loop. In other words, it always executes the statement list at once before checking the condition. The syntax of the `do-while` loop is shown in figure 6.3.

The `do-while` loop is effectively equivalent to:

```
<statementList>
while ( <pipeLine> )
{
        <statementList>
}
```

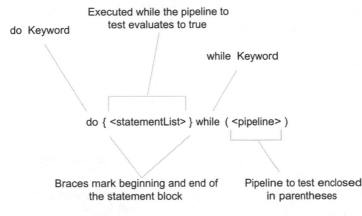

Figure 6.3   The PowerShell `do-while` loop statement syntax

where the two statement lists are identical. Having covered the two types of `while` loop, we'll look at the `for` and `foreach` loops next.

6.4   THE FOR LOOP

The `for` loop is the basic counting loop in PowerShell. It's typically used to step though a collection of objects. It's not used as often in PowerShell as in other languages because there are frequently better ways of processing a collection, as we'll see with the `foreach` statement in the next section. However, the `for` loop is useful when you need to know explicitly which element in the collection you're working with. Figure 6.4 shows the `for` loop syntax.:

Notice that the three pipelines in the parentheses are just general pipelines. Conventionally, the initialization pipeline initializes the loop counter variable; the test

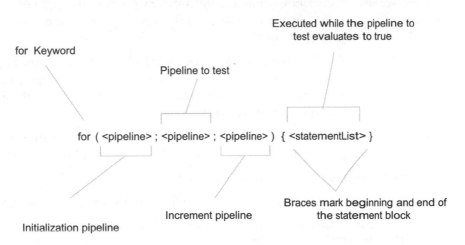

Figure 6.4   The PowerShell `for` loop statement syntax

pipeline tests this variable against some condition; and the increment pipeline increments the loop counter. The canonical example is:

```
PS (1) > for ($i=0; $i -lt 5; $i++) { $i }
0
1
2
3
4
PS (2) >
```

However, since these are arbitrary pipelines, they can do anything. (Note: if these pipelines produce output, it is simply discarded by the interpreter.) Here's an example where the condition test is used to generate a side-effect that is then used in the statement list body:

```
PS (2) > for ($i=0; $($y = $i*2; $i -lt 5); $i++) { $y }
0
2
4
6
8
PS (3) >
```

In this example, the pipeline to be tested is actually a subexpression that first sets $y to be twice the current value of $i, and then compares $i to 5. In the loop body, we use the value in $y to emit the current loop counter times 2. A more practical example would be initializing two values in the initialization pipeline:

```
PS (3) > for ($($result=@(); $i=0); $i -lt 5; $i++) {$result += $i }
PS (4) > "$result"
0 1 2 3 4
```

Here we use a subexpression in the initialization pipeline to set $result to the empty array and the counter variable $i to 0. Then the loop counts up to 5, adding each value to the result array.

> **NOTE** It's a little funny to talk about the initialization and increment pipelines. One usually thinks of pipelines as producing some output. In the for statement, the output from these pipelines is discarded and the side-effects of their execution are the interesting part.

Now let's look at one last example of the for loop. Here we'll use it to sum up the number of handles used by the "svchost" processes. First we'll get a list of these processes:

```
PS (1) > $svchosts = get-process svchost
```

We'll loop through this list and add the handle count for the process to $total:

```
PS (2) > for ($($total=0;$i=0); $i -lt $svchosts.count; $i++)
>> {$total+=$svchosts[$i].handles}
>>
```

and finally print out the total:

```
PS (3) > $total
3457
```

So using the `for` loop is straightforward, but it's kind of annoying to have to manage the loop counter. Wouldn't it be nice if we could just let the loop counter count take care of itself? That is exactly what the `foreach` loop does for you, and we'll discuss it next.

6.5 THE FOREACH LOOP

Collections are important in any shell environment. In fact, the whole point of using a scripting language for automation is that you can operate on collections. As we've seen in chapters 3 and 4, PowerShell provides many ways of operating on collections. Perhaps the most straightforward of these mechanisms is the `foreach` loop.

> **AUTHOR'S NOTE**
> Astute readers will remember that there is also an alias "foreach" for the `Foreach-Object` cmdlet that we've discussed a number of times earlier on. To clarify, when the word "foreach" is used at the beginning of a statement, it is recognized as the `foreach` keyword. When it appears in the middle of a pipeline, it's treated as the name of a cmdlet.

This statement is syntactically identical to the C# `foreach` loop with the exception that you don't have to declare the type of the loop variable (in fact you can't actually do this). Figure 6.5 shows you the syntax for the `foreach` statement.

Here's an example. This example loops over all of the text files in the current directory, calculating the total size of all of the files.

```
$l = 0; foreach ($f in dir *.txt) { $l += $f.length }
```

First we set the variable that will hold the total length to zero. Then in the `foreach` loop, we use the `dir` command to get a list of the text files in the current directory (that is, files with the .txt extension). The `foreach` statement assigns elements from

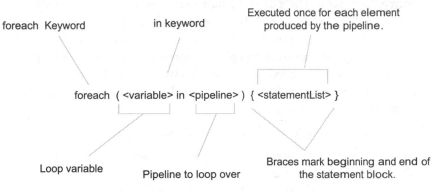

Figure 6.5   The PowerShell `foreach` loop statement syntax

this list one at a time to the loop variable $f and then executes the statement list with this variable set. At the end of the statement, $f will retain the last value that was assigned to it, which is the last value in the list. Compare this example to the `for` loop example at the end of the previous section. Because we don't have to manually deal with the loop counter and explicit indexing, this example is significantly simpler.

AUTHOR'S NOTE   In C#, the `foreach` loop variable is local to the body of the loop and is undefined outside of the loop. This is not the case in PowerShell. In PowerShell, the loop variable is simply another variable in the current scope. After the loop has finished executing, the variable is still visible and accessible outside of the loop and will be set to the last element in the list.

Now let's use a variation of a previous example. Here we want to find out the number of text files in the current directory and the total length of those files. First we'll initialize two variables: $c to hold the count of the files, and $l to hold the total length.

```
PS (1) > $c=0
PS (2) > $l=0
```

Next we run the `foreach` statement.

```
PS (3) > foreach ($f in dir *.txt) {$c += 1; $l += $f.length }
```

Finally we display the results accumulated in the variables.

```
PS (4) > $c
5
PS (5) > $l
105
PS (6) >
```

Let's look at the actual `foreach` statement in detail now. The *<pipeline>* part in this example is

```
dir *.txt
```

This produces a collection of `FileInformation` objects representing the files in the current directory. The `foreach` statement loops over this collection, binding each object to the variable $f and then executing the loop body.

It is important to note that this statement doesn't stream the results of the pipeline. The pipeline is run to completion and only then does the loop body begin executing. Let's take a second to contrast this behavior with the way the aforementioned `Foreach-Object` cmdlet works. Using the `Foreach-Object` cmdlet, this statement would look like:

```
dir *.txt | foreach-object { $c += 1; $l += $_.length }
```

In the case of the `Foreach-Object`, the statement body is executed as soon as each object is produced. In the `foreach` statement, all the objects are collected before the loop body begins to execute. This has two implications.

First, because in the foreach statement case all the objects are gathered at once, you need to have enough memory to hold all these objects. In the Foreach-Object case, only one object is read at a time so less storage is required. From this, you would think that Foreach-Object should always be preferred. In the bulk-read case, however, there are some optimizations that the foreach statement does that allow it to perform significantly faster than the Foreach-Object cmdlet. The result is a classic speed versus space tradeoff. In practice, though, you rarely need to consider these issues, so use whichever seems most appropriate to the solution at hand.

The second difference is that in the Foreach-Object case, the execution of the pipeline element generating the object is interleaved with the execution of the Foreach-Object cmdlet. In other words, the command generates one object at a time and then passes it to foreach for processing before generating the next element. This means that the statement list can affect how subsequent pipeline input objects are generated.

Executing the foreach statement also defines a special variable for the duration of the loop. This is the $foreach variable and it's bound to the loop enumerator. (The foreach statement keeps track of where it is in the collection through the loop enumerator.) By manipulating the loop enumerator, you can skip forward in the loop. Here's an example:

```
PS (1) > foreach ($i in 1..10)
>> { [void] $foreach.MoveNext(); $i + $foreach.current }
>>
3
7
11
15
19
PS (2) >
```

In this example, the foreach loop iterates over the collection of numbers from 1 to 10. In the body of the loop, the enumerator is used to advance the loop to the next element. It does this by calling the $foreach.MoveNext() method and then retrieving the next value using $foreach.current. This lets you sum up each pair of numbers—(1,2), (3,4) and so on as the loop iterates.

AUTHOR'S NOTE The foreach statement can be used to iterate over anything PowerShell considers enumerable. This typically includes anything that implements the .NET IEnumerable interface; however, we adapt that slightly. In particular, there are some classes that implement IEnumerable that PowerShell does not consider enumerable. This includes strings and dictionaries or hashtables. Because PowerShell unravels collections freely, we don't want a string to suddenly be turned into a stream of characters or a hashtable to be shredded into a sequence of key/value pairs. Hashtables in particular are commonly used as lightweight (that is. typeless) objects in the PowerShell environment, so we need to preserve their scalar nature.

The value stored in $foreach is an instance of an object that implements [System.Collection.IEnumerator]. Here's a quick example that shows you how to look at the members that are available on this object:

```
PS (1) > [System.Collections.IEnumerator].Getmembers()|foreach{"$_"}
Boolean MoveNext()
System.Object get_Current()
Void Reset()
System.Object Current
PS (2) >
```

In the output of this statement, you can see the Current and MoveNext() members we've used. There is also a Reset() member that will reset the enumerator back to the start of the collection.

One final thing you need to know about the foreach statement is how it treats scalar objects. Because of the way pipelines work, you don't know ahead of time if the pipeline will return a collection or a single scalar object. In particular, if the pipeline returns a single object, you can't tell if it is returning a scalar or a collection consisting of one object. You can use the @(...) construction described in the advanced operators chapter to force an array interpretation, but this ambiguity is common enough that the foreach statement takes care of this by itself. A scalar object in the foreach statement is automatically treated as a one-element collection:

```
PS (2) > foreach ($i in "hi") {$i }
hi
```

In this example, the value to iterate over is the scalar string "hi". The loop executes exactly once, printing hi. Now here's the example that really surprises people. What happens if the value to iterate over is $null? Let's find out:

```
PS (3) > foreach ($i in $null) { "executing" }
Executing
```

So the loop executes. This illustrates that we treat $null as a scalar value. Compare this with the empty array:

```
PS (4) > foreach ($i in @()) { "executing" }
PS (5) >
```

This time it didn't execute. The empty array is unambiguously a collection with no members, which is quite different from a collection having one member whose value is $null. At this point, you're thinking "do I really need to know this?" Probably not. This is not a situation you're likely to encounter. (I think the only person who's ever actually noticed this is our attentive and extremely patient lead language tester Marcel.) Still, it always helps to have a complete understanding of the way systems operate.

On that note, let's move on to a slightly different topic and talk about break, continue, and using labeled loops to exit out of nested loop statements.

6.6   LABELS, BREAK, AND CONTINUE

In this section, we discuss how to do nonstructured exits from the various looping statements using the break and continue statements as well as labeled loops.

In the dawn of computer languages, there was only one flow control statement: goto. While this was simple, it also resulted in programs that were hard to understand and maintain. Then along came structured programming. Structured programming introduced the idea of loops with single entry and exit points. This made programs much easier to understand and therefore maintain. Constructs such as while loops and if/then/else statements made it simpler to write programs that are easy to follow.

> **AUTHOR'S NOTE**   For the academically inclined reader, Wikipedia.org has a nice discussion on the topic of structured programming.

So structured programming is great; that is, until you have to exit from a set of deeply nested while loops. That's when pure structured programming leads to pathologically convoluted logic because you have to litter your program with Boolean variables and conditionals to achieve the flow of control you need. This is when being a little "impure" and allowing the use of unstructured flow control elements (including the infamous goto statement) is useful. Now, PowerShell doesn't actually have a goto statement. Instead, it has break and continue statements and labeled loops.

Let's look at some simple examples. Here's a while loop that stops counting at 5.

```
PS (1) > $i=0; while ($true) { if ($i++ -ge 5) { break } $i }
1
2
3
4
5
PS (2) >
```

Notice in this example that the while loop condition is simply $true. Obviously, this loop would run forever were it not for the break statement. As soon as $i hits 5, the break statement is executed and the loop terminates. Now let's look at the continue statement. In this example, we have a foreach loop that loops over the numbers from 1 to 10.

```
PS (1) > foreach ($i in 1..10)
>> {
>>     if ($i % 2)
>>     {
>>         continue
>>     }
>>     $i
>> }
>>
2
4
6
8
10
PS (2) >
```

If the number is not evenly divisible by two then the continue statement is executed. Where the break statement immediately terminates the loop, the continue
statement causes the flow of execution to jump back to the beginning of the loop and
move on to the next iteration. The end result is that only even numbers are emitted.
The continue statement skips the line that would have printed the odd numbers.

So the basic break and continue statements can handle flow control in a single
loop. But what about nested loops, which was the real problem we wanted to address?
This is where labels come in. Before the initial keyword on any of PowerShell's loop
statements, you can add a label naming that statement. Then you can use the break
and continue keywords to jump to that statement. Here's a simple example:

```
:outer while (1)
{
    while(1)
    {
        break outer;
    }
}
```

In this example, without the break statement, the loop would repeat forever.
Instead, the break will take you out of both the inner and outer loops.

AUTHOR'S NOTE   In PowerShell, the break and continue statements have one rather
strange but useful characteristic. They will continue to search up the calling
stack until a matching label is found. This search will even cross script and
function call boundaries. This means that a break inside a function inside
a script can transfer control to an enclosing loop in the calling script. This
allows for wide-ranging transfer of control. This will make more sense
when we get to the chapter on scripts and functions.

One last thing to know about the break and continue statements—the name of the
loop to jump to is actually an expression, not a constant value. You could, for example,

CHAPTER 6 FLOW CONTROL IN SCRIPTS

use a variable to name the target of the statement. Let's try this out. First we set up a variable to hold the target name:

```
PS (1) > $target = "foo"
```

Now we'll use it in a loop. In this loop, if the least significant bit in the value stored in $i is 1 (yet another way to test for odd numbers), we skip to the next iteration of the loop named by $target as we see in the following:

```
PS (2) > :foo foreach ($i in 1..10) {
>> if ($i -band 1) { continue $target } $i
>> }
>>
2
4
6
8
10
PS (3) >
```

At this point, we've covered all of the basic PowerShell flow control statements, as well as using labels and break/continue to do non-local flow control transfers. Now let's move on to the switch statement, which, as you will see, is extremely useful.

6.7   THE POWERSHELL SWITCH STATEMENT

The switch statement is the most powerful statement in the PowerShell language. This statement combines pattern matching, branching, and iteration all into a single control structure. The switch statement in PowerShell is similar to the switch statement in many other languages—it's a way of selecting an action based on a particular value. But the PowerShell switch statement has a number of additional capabilities. It can be used as a looping construct where it processes a collection of objects instead of a just a single object. It supports the advanced pattern matching features that we've seen with the -match and -like operators. (How the pattern is matched depends on the flags specified to the switch statement.) Finally, it can be used to efficiently process an entire file in a single statement.

6.7.1   Basic use of the PowerShell switch statement

Before exploring the basic functions of the switch statement, you need to understand its syntax. Figure 6.6 illustrates this basic syntax.

This is a pretty complex construct, so let's start by looking at the simplest form of the statement. Here's the basic example:

```
PS (1) > switch (1) { 1 { "One" } 2 { "two" } }
One
```

The value to switch on is in the parentheses after the switch keyword. In this example, it's the number 1. That value is matched against the pattern in each clause and *all*

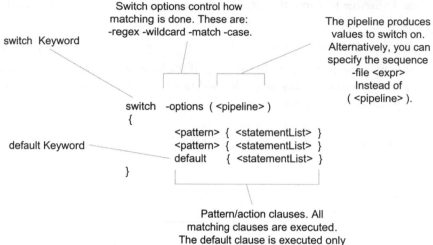

Figure 6.6   The PowerShell `switch` statement syntax

matching actions are taken. In this example, the switch value matches "1" so that clause emits the string "one". Of course, if we change the value to switch to 2, we get:

```
PS (2) > switch (2) { 1 { "One" } 2 { "two" } }
two
```

Now try a somewhat different example. In this case, we have two clauses that match the switch value:

```
PS (4) > switch (2) { 1 { "One" } 2 { "two" } 2 {"another 2"} }
two
another 2
```

You can see that both of these actions are executed. As we stated earlier, the `switch` statement executes all clauses that match the switch value. If you want to stop at the first match, then you use the `break` statement:

```
PS (5) > switch (2) {1 {"One"} 2 {"two"; break} 2 {"another 2"}}
two
```

This causes the matching process to stop after the first matching statement was executed. But what happens if no statements match? Well, the statement quietly returns nothing:

```
PS (6) > switch (3) { 1 { "One" } 2 { "two"; break } 2 {"another 2"} }
PS (7) >
```

To specify a default action, you can use the `default` clause:

```
PS (7) > switch (3) { 1 { "One" } 2 { "two" } default {"default"} }
default
```

```
PS (8) > switch (2) { 1 { "One" } 2 { "two" } default {"default"} }
Two
```

In this example, when the switch value is 3, no clause matches and the default clause is run. However, when there is a match, the default is not run, as it's not really considered a match. This covers the basic mode of operation. Now let's move on to more advanced features.

6.7.2 Using wildcard patterns with the switch statement

By default, the matching clauses make a direct comparison against the object in the clause. If the matching object is a string, then the check is done in a case-insensitive way, as we see in the next example.

```
PS (1) > switch ('abc') {'abc' {"one"} 'ABC' {"two"}}
one
two
```

The switch value "abc" in this example was matched by both "abc" and "ABC". You can change this behavior by specifying the -casesensitive option:

```
PS (2) > switch -case ('abc') {'abc' {"one"} 'ABC' {"two"}}
one
```

Now the match occurs only when the case of the elements match.

> **AUTHOR'S NOTE** In this example, we only used the prefix "-case" instead of the full option string. In PowerShell version 1, only the first letter of the option is actually checked. In later versions, prefixes will still be supported, but the entire string will be validated instead of just the first character.

Now let's discuss the next switch option, the -wildcard option. When this flag is specified, the switch value is converted into a string and the tests are conducted using the wildcard pattern. (Wildcard patterns were discussed in chapter 4 with the -like operator.) This is shown in the next example:

```
PS (4) > switch -wildcard ('abc') {a* {"astar"} *c {"starc"}}
astar
starc
```

In this example, the pattern a* matches anything that begins with the letter "a" and the pattern *c matches anything that ends with the letter "c". Again, all matching clauses are executed.

There is one more element to mention at this point. When a clause is matched, the element that matched is assigned to the variable $_ before running the clause. This is always done, even in the simple examples we discussed earlier, but there it wasn't interesting because we were doing exact comparisons so we already knew what matched. Once you introduce patterns, it's much more useful to be able to get at the object that matched. For example, if you're matching against filename extensions, you'd want to be able to get at the full filename to do any processing on that file.

We'll look at some more practical uses for this feature in later sections. For now, here's a basic example that shows how this match works:

```
PS (5) > switch -wildcard ('abc') {a* {"a*: $_"} *c {"*c: $_"}}
a*: abc
*c: abc
```

In the result strings, you can see that $_ was replaced by the full string of the actual switch value.

6.7.3 Using regular expressions with the switch statement

As we discussed in chapter 4, the wildcard patterns, while useful, have limited functions. For more sophisticated pattern matching, we used regular expressions. Regular expressions are available in the switch statement through the -regex flag. Let's rewrite the previous example using regular expressions instead of wildcards. It looks like this:

```
PS (6) > switch -regex ('abc') {^a {"a*: $_"} 'c$' {"*c: $_"}}
a*: abc
*c: abc
```

As we see, $_ is still bound to the entire matching key. But one of the most powerful features of regular expressions is submatches. A submatch is a portion of the regular expression that is enclosed in parentheses, as discussed in chapter 4 with the -match operator. With the -match operator, the submatches are made available through the $matches variable. This same variable is also used in the switch statement. The next example shows how this works.

```
PS (8) > switch -regex ('abc') {'(^a)(.*$)' {$matches}}

Key                     Value
---                     -----
2                       bc
1                       a
0                       abc
```

In the result shown here, $matches[0] is the overall key, $matches[1] is the first submatch, in this case the leading "a", and $matches[2] is the remainder of the string. As always, matching is case-insensitive by default, but you can specify the -case option to make it case-sensitive. This is demonstrated in the next example.

```
PS (9) > switch -regex ('abc') {'(^A)(.*$)' {$matches}}

Key                     Value
---                     -----
2                       bc
1                       a
0                       abc

PS (10) > switch -regex -case  ('abc') {'(^A)(.*$)' {$matches}}
```

In the first command, we changed the match pattern from a to A and the match still succeeded—case was ignored. In the second command, we added the -case flag and this time the match did not succeed.

So far we've discussed three ways to control how matching against the switch value works; in other words, three matching modes. (Actually six, since the -case flag can be used with any of the previous three.) But what if you need something a bit more sophisticated than a simple pattern match? The switch statement lets you handle this by specifying an expression in braces instead of a pattern. In the next example, we specify two expressions that check against the switch value. Again the switch value is made available through the variable $_.

```
PS (11) > switch (5) {
>> {$_ -gt 3} {"greater than three"}
>> {$_ -gt 7} {"greater than 7"}}
>>
greater than three
PS (12) > switch (8) {
>> {$_ -gt 3} {"greater than three"}
>> {$_ -gt 7} {"greater than 7"}}
>>
greater than three
greater than 7
PS (13) >
```

In the first statement, only the first clause was triggered because 5 is greater than 3 but less than 7. In the second statement, both clauses fired.

You can use these matching clauses with any of the other three matching modes, as we see in the following:

```
PS (13) > switch (8) {
>> {$_ -gt 3} {"greater than three"}
>> 8 {"Was $_"}}
>>
greater than three
Was 8
```

The first expression {$_ -gt 3} evaluated to true so "greater than three" was printed, and the switch value matched 8 so "Was 8" also printed (where $_ was replaced by the matching value).

Now we have exact matches, pattern matches, conditional matches, and the default clause. But what about the switch value itself? So far, all of the examples have been simple scalar values. What happens if you specify a collection of values? This is where the switch statement acts like a form of loop.

AUTHOR'S NOTE   switch works like the other looping statement in that the expression in the parentheses is fully evaluated before it starts iterating over the individual values.

Let's look at another example where we specify an array of values.

```
PS (2) > switch(1,2,3,4,5,6) {
>> {$_ % 2} {"Odd $_"; continue}
>> 4 {"FOUR"}
>> default {"Even $_"}
>> }
>>
Odd 1
Even 2
Odd 3
FOUR
Odd 5
Even 6
```

In this example, the switch value was 1,2,3,4,5,6. The switch statement iterates over the collection, testing each element against all of the clauses. The first clause returns "Odd $_" if the current switch element is not evenly divisible by two. The next clause prints out "FOUR" if the value is 4. The default clause prints out "Even $_" if the number is even. Note the use of continue in the first clause. This tells the switch statement to stop matching any further clauses and move on to the next element in the collection. In this instance, the switch statement is working in the same way that the continue statement works in the other loops. It skips the remainder of the body of the loop and continues on with the next loop iteration. What happens if we'd used break instead of continue? Let's try it:

```
PS (3) > switch(1,2,3,4,5,6) {
>> {$_ % 2} {"Odd $_"; break}
>> 4 {"FOUR"}
>> default {"Even $_"}
>> }
>>
Odd 1
```

As with the other loops, break doesn't just skip the remainder of the current iteration; it terminates the overall loop processing. (If you want to continue iterating, use continue instead. More on that later.)

Of course, iterating over a fixed collection is not very interesting. In fact, you can use a pipeline in the switch value, as the next example shows. In this example, we want to count the number of DLLs, text files, and log files in the directory c:\windows. First we initialize the counter variables:

```
PS (1) > $dll=$txt=$log=0
```

Now we run the actual switch statement. This switch statement uses wildcard patterns to match the extensions on the filenames. The associated actions increment a variable for each extension type:

```
PS (2) > switch -wildcard (dir c:\windows)
>> {*.dll {$dll++} *.txt {$txt++} *.log {$log++}}
```

Once we have the totals, let's display them:

```
PS (3) > "dlls: $dll text files: $txt log files: $log"
dlls: 6 text files: 9 log files: 120
```

Note that in this example the pipeline element is being matched against every clause. Since a file can't have more than one extension, this doesn't affect the output, but it does affect performance somewhat. It's faster to include a `continue` statement after each clause so the matching process stops as soon as the first match succeeds.

Here's something else we glossed over earlier in our discussion of $_ —it always contains the object that was matched against. This is important to understand when you're using the pattern matching modes of the `switch` statement. The pattern matches create a string representation of the object to match against, but $_ is still bound to the original object. Here's an example that illustrates this point. This is basically the same as the last example, but this time, instead of counting the number of files, we want to calculate the total size of all of the files having a particular extension. Here are the revised commands:

```
PS (1) > $dll=$txt=$log=0
PS (2) > switch -wildcard (dir) {
>> *.dll {$dll+= $_.length; continue}
>> *.txt {$txt+=$_.length; continue}
>> *.log {$log+=$_.length; continue}
>> }
>>
PS (3) > "dlls: $dll text files: $txt log files: $log"
dlls: 166913 text files: 1866711 log files: 6669437
PS (4) >
```

Notice how we're using $_.length to get the length of the matching file object. If $_ were bound to the matching string, we would be counting the length of the file names instead of the lengths of the actual files.

6.7.4   Processing files with the switch statement

There is one last mode of operation for the `switch` statement to discuss: the `-file` option. Instead of specifying an expression to iterate over as the switch value, the `-file` option allows you to name a file to process. Here's an example where we're processing the Windows update log file. Again we start by initializing the counter variables:

```
PS (1) > $au=$du=$su=0
```

Next we use the `-regex` and `-file` options to access and scan the file WindowsUpdate.log, looking update requests from automatic updater, Windows Defender, and SMS triggered updates.

```
PS (2) > switch -regex -file c:\windows\windowsupdate.log {
>> 'START.*Finding updates.*AutomaticUpdates' {$au++}
>> 'START.*Finding updates.*Defender' {$du++}
```

```
>> 'START.*Finding updates.*SMS' {$su++}
>> }
>>
```

Finally we print out the results.

```
PS (3) > "Automatic:$au Defender:$du SMS:$su"
Automatic:195 Defender:10 SMS:34
```

Now it's possible to do basically the same thing by using Get-Content or even the filesystem name trick we looked at in chapter 4:

```
PS (4) > $au=$du=$su=0
PS (5) > switch -regex (${c:windowsupdate.log}) {
>> 'START.*Finding updates.*AutomaticUpdates' {$au++}
>> 'START.*Finding updates.*Defender' {$du++}
>> 'START.*Finding updates.*SMS' {$su++}
>> }
>>
PS (6) > "Automatic:$au Defender:$du SMS:$su"
Automatic:195 Defender:10 SMS:34
```

Here we used ${c:windowsupdate.log} to access the file content instead of -file. So why have the -file option? There are two reasons.

The -file operation reads one line at a time, so it uses less memory than Get-Content, which has to read the entire file into memory before processing. Also, because -file is part of the PowerShell language, the interpreter can do some optimizations, which gives -file some performance advantages.

So overall, the -file option can potentially give you both speed and space advantages in some cases (the space advantage typically being the more significant, and therefore more important of the two).

6.7.5 Using the $switch loop enumerator in the switch statement

One more point: just as the foreach loop used $foreach to hold the loop enumerator, the switch statement uses $switch to hold the switch loop enumerator. This is useful in a common pattern—processing a list of options. Say we have a list of options where the option -b takes an argument and -a, -c, and -d don't. Let's write a switch statement to process a list of these arguments. First let's set up a list of test options. For convenience, we'll start with a string and then use the string split() method to break it into an array of elements:

```
PS (1) > $options="-a -b Hello -c".split()
```

Next let's initialize the set of variables that will correspond to the flags:

```
PS (2) > $a=$c=$d=$false
PS (3) > $b=$null
```

Now we can write our switch statement. The interesting clause is the one that handles -b. This clause uses the enumerator stored in $switch to advance the item being processed to the next element in the list. We use a cast to [void] to discard the return value from the call to $switch.movenext() (more on that later). Then we use $switch.current to retrieve the next value and store it in $b. Then the loop continues processing the remaining arguments in the list.

```
PS (4) > switch ($options)
>> {
>> '-a' { $a=$true }
>> '-b' { [void] $switch.movenext(); $b= $switch.current }
>> '-c' { $c=$true }
>> '-d' { $d=$true }
>> }
>>
```

The last step in this example is to print out the arguments in the list to make sure they were all set properly.

```
PS (5) > "a=$a b=$b c=$c d=$d"
a=True b=Hello c=True d=False
PS (6) >
```

We see that $a and $c are true, $b contains the argument "Hello", and $d is still false since it wasn't in our list of test options. The option list has been processed correctly.

AUTHOR'S NOTE This isn't a robust example because it's missing all error handing. In a complete example, you would have a default clause that generated errors for unexpected options. Also, in the clause that processes the argument for -b , rather than discarding the result of MoveNext() it should check the result and generate an error if it returns false. This would indicate that there are no more elements in the collection, so -b would be missing its mandatory argument.

This finishes the last of the flow-control *statements* in the PowerShell language, but there is another way to do selection and iteration in PowerShell—by using cmdlets. In the next section, we'll go over a couple of the cmdlets that are a standard part of the PowerShell distribution. These cmdlets let you control the flow of your script in a manner similar to the flow control statements. (In later sections, we'll describe how you can add your own specialized flow control elements to PowerShell.)

AUTHOR'S NOTE For a more pragmatic example of using the switch statement, take a look at listing 10.5 in chapter 10. This is a function that illustrates the use of nested switch statements in processing XML documents using the .NET XmlReader class.

6.8 FLOW CONTROL USING CMDLETS

While PowerShell's control statements are part of the language proper, there are also some cmdlets that can be used to accomplish the same kinds of things. These cmdlets use blocks of PowerShell script enclosed in braces to provide the "body" of the control statement. These pieces of script are called *ScriptBlocks* and are described in detail in chapter 7 as part of the discussion on functions and scripts. The two most frequent flow-control cmdlets that you'll encounter are `Foreach-Object` and `Where-Object`.

6.8.1 The Foreach-Object cmdlet

The `Foreach-Object` cmdlet operates on each object in a pipeline in much the same way that the `foreach` statement operates on the set of values that are provided to it. For example, here's a `foreach` statement that prints out the size of each text file in the current directory:

```
PS (1) > foreach ($f in dir *.txt) { $f.length }
48
889
23723
328
279164
```

Using the `Foreach-Object` cmdlet, the same task can be accomplished this way:

```
PS (2) > dir *.txt | foreach-object {$_.length}
48
889
23723
328
279164
```

The results are the same, so what's the difference? One obvious difference is that you didn't have to create a new variable name to hold the loop value. The automatic variable `$_` is used as the loop variable.

AUTHOR'S NOTE   Automatic variables are common in scripting languages. These variables aren't directly assigned to in scripts. Instead, they are set as the side-effect of an operation. One of the earlier examples of this is in AWK. When a line is read in AWK, the text of the line is automatically assigned to `$0`. The line is also split into fields. The first field is placed in `$1`, the second is in `$2`, and so on. The Perl language is probably the most significant user of automatic variables. In fact, as mentioned previously, Perl inspired the use of `$_` in PowerShell. Things are, however, not all skittles and beer. Automatic variables can help reduce the size of a script, but they can also make a script hard to read and difficult to reuse because your use of automatics may collide with mine. From a design perspective, our approach with automatic variables follows the salt curve. A little salt makes everything taste better. Too much salt makes food inedible. We've tried to keep the use of automatics in PowerShell at the "just right" level. Of course, this is always a subjective judgment. Some people really like salt.

A more subtle difference, as discussed previously, is that the loop is processed one object at a time. In a normal `foreach` loop, the entire list of values is generated before a single value is processed. In the `Foreach-Object` pipeline, each object is generated and then passed to the cmdlet for processing.

The `Foreach-Object` cmdlet has an advantage over the `foreach` loop in the amount of space being used at a particular time. For example, if you are processing a large file, the `foreach` loop would have to load the entire file into memory before processing. When using the `Foreach-Object` cmdlet, the file will be processed one line at a time. This significantly reduces the amount of memory needed to accomplish a task.

You'll end up using the `Foreach-Object` cmdlet a lot in command lines to perform simple transformations on objects (we've already used it in many examples so far). Given the frequency of use, there are two standard aliases for this cmdlet. The first one is (obviously) `foreach`. But wait a second—didn't we say earlier in this chapter that `foreach` is a keyword, and keywords can't be aliased? This is true, but keywords are only special when they are the *first unquoted word in a statement.* If they appear anywhere else (for example as an argument or in the middle of a pipeline), they're just another token with no special meaning. Here's another way to think about this: the first word in a statement is the key that the PowerShell interpreter uses to decide what kind of statement it is processing, hence the term "keyword".

This positional constraint is how the interpreter can distinguish between the keyword "foreach":

```
foreach ($i in 1..10) { $i }
```

and the aliased cmdlet "foreach":

```
1..10 | foreach ($_}
```

When `foreach` is the first word in a statement, it's a keyword; otherwise it's the name of a command.

Now let's look at the second alias. Even though `foreach` is significantly shorter than `Foreach-Object`, there have still been times when users wanted it to be even shorter.

AUTHOR'S NOTE Actually users wanted to get rid of this notation entirely and have "foreach" be implied by an open brace following the pipe symbol. This would have made about half of our users very happy. Unfortunately, the other half were adamant that the implied operation be `Where-Object` instead of `Foreach-Object`.

Where extreme brevity is required, there is a second alias that is simply the percent sign (%). Oh ho—now people are really upset! You told us the percent sign is an operator! Well that's true *but only when it's used as a binary operator.* If it appears as the first symbol in a statement, it has no special meaning, so we can use it as an alias for `Foreach-Object`. This lets you write concise (but somewhat hard to read) statements such as the following, which prints out the numbers from 1 to 5, times two:

```
PS (1) > 1..5|%{$_*2}
2
4
6
8
10
PS (2) >
```

Clearly this construction is great for interactive use where brevity is very important, but it probably shouldn't be used when writing scripts. The issue is that Foreach-Object is so useful that a single-character symbol for it, one that is easy to distinguish, is invaluable for experienced PowerShell users. However, unlike the word "foreach", "%" is not immediately meaningful to new users. So this notation is great for "conversational" PowerShell, but generally terrible for broad formal use.

The last thing to know about the Foreach-Object cmdlet is that it can take multiple scriptblocks. If three scriptblocks are specified, the first one is run before any objects are processed, the second is run once for each object, and the last is run after all objects have been processed. This is good for conducting accumulation-type operations. Here's another variation, where we sum up the number of handles used by the service host "svchost" processes:

```
PS (3) > gps svchost |%{$t=0}{$t+=$_.handles}{$t}
3238
```

The standard alias for Get-Process is gps. This is used to get a list of processes where the process name matches "svchost". These process objects are then piped into Foreach-Object, where the handle counts are summed up in $t and then emitted in the last scriptblock. We used the % alias here to show how concise these expressions can be. In an interactive environment, brevity is important.

And now here's something to keep in mind when using Foreach-Object. The Foreach-Object cmdlet works like all cmdlets: if the output object is a collection, it gets unraveled. One way to suppress this behavior is to use the unary comma operator. For example, in the following, we assign $a an array of two elements, the second of which is a nested array.

```
PS (1) > $a =  1,(2,3)
```

Now when we check the length, we see that it is two as expected:

```
PS (2) > $a.length
2
```

and the second element is still an array.

```
PS (3) > $a[1]
2
3
```

However, if we simply run it through Foreach-Object, we'll find that the length of the result is now three, and the second element in the result is simply the number "2".

```
PS (4) > $b = $a | foreach { $_ }
PS (5) > $b.length
3
PS (6) > $b[2]
2
```

In effect, the result has been "flattened". However, if we use the unary comma operator before the $_ variable, the result has the same structure as the original array.

```
PS (7) > $b = $a | foreach { , $_ }
PS (8) > $b.length
2
PS (9) > $b[1]
2
3
```

When chaining foreach cmdlets, we need to repeat the pattern at each stage:

```
PS (7) > $b = $a | foreach { , $_ } | foreach { , $_ }
PS (8) > $b.length
2
PS (9) > $b[1]
2
3
```

Why did we do this? Why didn't we just preserve the structure as we pass the elements through instead of unraveling by default? Well, both behaviors are, in fact, useful. Consider the follow example, which returns a list of loaded module names:

```
get-process | %{$_.modules} | sort -u modulename
```

Here the unraveling is exactly what we want. When we were designing PowerShell, we considered both cases; and in applications, on average, unraveling by default was usually what we needed. Unfortunately, it does present something of a cognitive bump that surprises users learning to use PowerShell.

6.8.2   The Where-Object cmdlet

The other flow control cmdlet that is used a lot is Where-Object. This cmdlet is used to select objects from a list, kind of a simple switch cmdlet. It takes each element it receives as input, executes its scriptblock argument, passing in the current pipeline element as $_ and then, if the scriptblock evaluates to true, the element is written to the pipeline. We'll show this with an example that selects the even numbers from a sequence of integers:

```
PS (4) > 1..10 | where {! ($_ -band 1)}
2
4
6
8
10
```

The scriptblock enclosed in the braces receives each pipeline element, one after another. If the least significant bit in the element is 1 then the scriptblock returns the logical complement of that value ($false) and that element is discarded. If the least significant bit is zero then the logical complement of that is $true and the element is written to the output pipeline. Notice that the common alias for Where-Object is simply where. And, as with Foreach-Object, because this construction is so commonly used interactively, there is an additional alias, which is simply the question mark (?). This allows the previous example to be written as:

```
PS (5) > 1..10|?{!($_-band 1)}
2
4
6
8
10
```

Again—this is brief, but it looks like the cat walked across the keyboard (trust me on this one). So while this is fine for interactive use, it is not recommended in scripts because it's hard to understand and maintain. As another, more compelling example of "Software by Cats", here's a pathological example that combines elements from the last few chapters—type casts, operators, and the flow control cmdlets to generate a list of strings of even-numbered letters in the alphabet, where the length of the string matches the ordinal number in the alphabet ("A" is 1, "B" is 2, and so on).

```
PS (1) > 1..26|?{!($_-band 1)}|%{[string][char](
>> [int][char]'A'+$_-1)*$_}
>>
BB
DDDD
FFFFFF
HHHHHHHH
JJJJJJJJJJ
LLLLLLLLLLLL
NNNNNNNNNNNNNN
PPPPPPPPPPPPPPPP
RRRRRRRRRRRRRRRRRR
TTTTTTTTTTTTTTTTTTTT
VVVVVVVVVVVVVVVVVVVVVV
XXXXXXXXXXXXXXXXXXXXXXXX
ZZZZZZZZZZZZZZZZZZZZZZZZZZ
PS (2) >
```

The output is fairly self-explanatory, but the code is not. Figuring out how this works is left as an exercise to the reader and as a cautionary tale not to foist this sort of rubbish on unsuspecting coworkers.

6.9 THE VALUE OF STATEMENTS

For the final topic in this chapter, let's return to something we discussed a bit previously in the advanced operators chapter—namely the difference between statements and expressions. In general, statements don't return values, but if they're used as part of a subexpression (or a function or script as we'll see later on), they do return a result. This is best illustrated with an example. Assume that we didn't have the range operator and wanted to generate an array of numbers from 1 to 10. Here's the traditional approach we might use in a language such as C#.

```
PS (1) > $result = new-object System.Collections.ArrayList
PS (2) > for ($i=1; $i -le 10; $i++) { $result.Append($i) }
PS (3) > "$($result.ToArray())"
1 2 3 4 5 6 7 8 9 10
```

First we create an `ArrayList` to hold the result. Then we use a `for` loop to step through the numbers, adding each number to the result `ArrayList`. Finally we convert the `ArrayList` to an array and display the result. This is a straightforward approach to creating the array, but requires several steps. Using loops in subexpressions, we can simplify it quite a bit. Here's the rewritten example:

```
PS (4) > $result = $(for ($i=1; $i -le 10; $i++) {$i})
PS (5) > "$result"
1 2 3 4 5 6 7 8 9 10
```

Here we don't have to initialize the result or do explicit adds to the result collection. The output of the loop is captured and automatically saved as a collection by the interpreter. In fact, this is more efficient than the previous example, because the interpreter can optimize the management of the collection internally. This approach applies to any kind of statement. Let's look at an example where we want to conditionally assign a value to a variable if it doesn't currently have a value. First verify that the variable has no value:

```
PS (1) > $var
```

Now do the conditional assignment. This uses an `if` statement in a subexpression:

```
PS (2) > $var = $(if (! $var) { 12 } else {$var})
PS (3) > $var
12
```

From the output, we can see that the variable has been set. Now change the variable and rerun the conditional assignment:

```
PS (4) > $var="Hello there"
PS (5) > $var = $(if (! $var) { 12 } else {$var})
PS (6) > $var
Hello there
```

This time the variable is not changed.

Used judiciously, the fact that statements can be used as value expressions can be used to simplify your code in many circumstances. By eliminating temporary variables and extra initializations, creating collections is greatly simplified, as we saw with the for loop. On the other hand, it's entirely possible to use this statement-as-expression capability to produce scripts that are hard to read. (Remember the nested if statement example we looked at earlier in this chapter?) You should always keep that in mind when using these features in scripts.

6.10 SUMMARY

In chapter 6, we formally covered the branching and looping statements in the Power-Shell language as summarized in the following list.

- PowerShell allows you to use pipelines where other languages only allow expressions. This means that, while the PowerShell flow control statements appear to be similar to the corresponding statements in other languages, there are enough differences to make it useful for you to spend time experimenting with them.

- There are two ways of handling flow control in PowerShell. The first way is to use the language flow control statements such as while and foreach. However, when performing pipelined operations, the alternative mechanism—the flow control cmdlets Foreach-Object and Where-Object—can be more natural and efficient.

- When iterating over collections, you should keep in mind the tradeoffs between the foreach statement and the Foreach-Object cmdlet.

- Any statement can be used as a value expression when nested in a subexpression. For example, you could use a while loop in a subexpression to generate a collection of values. This can be a concise way of generating a collection, but keep in mind the potential complexity that this kind of nested statement can introduce.

- The PowerShell switch statement is a powerful tool. On the surface it looks like the switch statement in C# or the select statement in VB, but with powerful pattern matching capabilities, it goes well beyond what the statements in the other languages can do. And, along with the pattern matching, it can also be used as a looping construct for selecting and processing objects from a collection or lines read from a file.

CHAPTER 7

Functions and scripts

And now for something completely different…

—Monty Python

Porcupine quills. We've always done it with porcupine quills

—Dilbert

Seven chapters in and no scripts? Okay—fine—here you go:

```
"Hello, world"
```

As you will have astutely observed from the title, in this chapter we finally get into writing PowerShell scripts in all their myriad forms. As mentioned in chapter 2, functions and scripts are two of the four types of PowerShell commands (the others are cmdlets and external commands). Prior programming experience is both a blessing and a curse when using functions and scripts. Most of the time, what you already know makes it easier to program in PowerShell. The syntax and most of the concepts will be familiar. Unfortunately, similar is not identical, and this is where prior experience can trip you up. You'll expect PowerShell to work like your favorite language,

177

and it won't work quite the same way. In particular, you need to be aware of a number of issues concerning the way that PowerShell scripts and functions return values. For example, in the preceding example script, the string "Hello, world" did not have a print statement. The string was simply returned from the script. This is true of all expressions in a script: if the value isn't consumed (for example, by assigning it to a variable) then it will be returned. If you have multiple statements in your script, then your script will return multiple values. Considerations like this will be called out as we discuss the scripting features in PowerShell. So, put away your porcupine quills and let's move on to something not quite so completely different.

7.1   FUNCTION BASICS

The beginning is always the best place to start. In this section we'll cover the most basic features of PowerShell functions and supply you with a number of examples that show you how to use these features.

The following example is obviously a function. And, equally obvious, this function prints out the string `hello world` as shown:

```
PS (1) > function hello { "Hello world" }
PS (2) > hello; hello; hello
Hello world
Hello world
Hello world
```

But a function that writes only "hello world" isn't very useful. Let's personalize this a bit and add a parameter to the function. In fact, we don't have to do anything at all, because there is a default argument array that contains all of the arguments to the function. This default array is available in the variable `$args`. Here's a basic example:

```
PS (3) > function hello { "Hello there $args, how are you?" }
PS (4) > hello Bob
Hello there Bob, how are you?
```

This example uses string expansion to insert the value stored in `$args` into the string that is emitted from the `hello` function. Now let's see what happens with multiple arguments:

```
PS (5) > hello Bob Alice Ted Carol
Hello there Bob Alice Ted Carol, how are you?
```

Following the string expansion rules described in chapter 3, the values stored in `$args` get interpolated into the output string with each value separated by a space. Or, more specifically, separated by whatever is stored in the `$OFS` variable. So let's take one last variation on this example. We'll set `$OFS` in the function body with the aim of producing a more palatable output. We'll take advantage of the interactive nature of the PowerShell environment to enter this function over several lines:

```
PS (6) > function hello
>> {
>> $ofs=","
>> "Hello there $args and how are you?"
>> }
>>
PS (7) > hello Bob Carol Ted Alice
Hello there Bob,Carol,Ted,Alice and how are you?
```

That's better. Now at least we have commas between the names. Let's try it again, with commas between the arguments:

```
PS (8) > hello Bob,Carol,Ted,Alice
Hello there System.Object[] and how are you?
```

Yuck! So what happened? Let's define a new function to clear up what happened.

```
PS (1) > function count-args {
>> "`$args.count=" + $args.count
>> "`$args[0].count=" + $args[0].count
>> }
>>
```

This function will display the number of arguments passed to it as well as the number of elements in the first argument. First we use it with three scalar arguments:

```
PS (2) > count-args 1 2 3
$args.count=3
$args[0].count=
```

As expected, it shows that we passed three arguments. It doesn't show anything for the Count property on $args[0] because $args[0] is a scalar (the number 1) and consequently doesn't have a Count property. Now let's try it with a comma between each of the arguments:

```
PS (3) > Count-Args 1,2,3
$args.count=1
$args[0].count=3
```

Now we see that the function received one argument, which is an array of three elements. And finally, let's try it with two sets of comma-separated numbers:

```
PS (4) > count-args 1,2,3 4,5,6,7
$args.count=2
$args[0].count=3
```

The results show that the function received two arguments, both of which are arrays. The first argument is an array of three elements and the second is an array with four elements. Hmm, you should be saying to yourself—this sounds familiar. And it is— the comma here works like the binary comma operator in expressions, as discussed in chapter 5.

Two values on the command line with a comma between them will be passed to the command as a single argument. The value of that argument is an array of those elements. This applies to any command, not just functions. If you want to copy three files f1.txt, f2.txt, and f3.txt to a directory, the command would be

```
copy-item f1.txt,f2.txt,f3.txt target
```

The Copy-Item cmdlet receives two arguments: the first is an array of three file names, and the second is a scalar element naming the target directory.

This is pretty simple and straightforward, but these characteristics allow you to write some pretty slick commands. Here are two that aren't in the PowerShell base installation (although they maybe in the future).

```
function ql { $args }
function qs { "$args" }
```

They may not look like much, but they can streamline operations. The first function is ql. which stands for "quote list". This is a Perl-ism. Here's what you can do with it. Say you want to build up a list of the color names. To do this with the normal comma operator, you'd do the following:

```
$col = "black","brown","red","orange","yellow","green",
    "blue","violet","gray","white"
```

which requires lots of quotes and commas. With the ql function, you could write it this way:

```
$col = ql black brown red orange yellow green blue violet gray white
```

This is much shorter and requires less typing. Does it let you do anything you couldn't do before? No, but it lets you do something more efficiently when you have to. Remember that elastic syntax concept? When you're trying to fit a complex expression onto one line, things like ql can help. What about the other function qs? It does approximately the same thing, but uses string catenation to return the arguments as a single string.

```
PS (1) > $string = qs This is a      string
PS (2) > $string
This is a string
PS (3) >
```

Note that the arguments are concatenated with a single space between them. The original spacing on the command line has been lost, but that usually doesn't matter.

Now let's write a function that takes two arguments and adds them together:

```
PS (1) > function Add-Two { $args[0] + $args[1] }
PS (2) > add-two 2 3
5
```

Notice that most of the work in this function is getting the arguments out of the array. One way we could make this a bit simpler is by using PowerShell's multiple assignment feature:

```
PS (3) > function Add-Two {
>> $x,$y=$args
>> $x+$y
>> }
>>
PS (4) > add-two 1 2
3
```

In this example, the first statement in the function assigns the values passed in $args to the local variables $x and $y. Perl users will be familiar with this approach for dealing with function arguments, and, while it's a reasonable way to handle the problem, it isn't the way most languages deal with function parameters.

> **AUTHOR'S NOTE** The $args approach will be familiar to Perl 5 or earlier users. Perl 6 has a solution to the problem that is similar to what PowerShell does. I'd claim great minds think alike, but it's really just the most obvious way to solve the problem.

For this reason, PowerShell provides other ways to declare the formal parameters. We'll cover those approaches in the next couple of sections.

7.2 FORMAL PARAMETERS AND THE PARAM STATEMENT

With the basics out of the way, we'll take a look at the more sophisticated features PowerShell provides for declaring function parameters. We'll cover untyped and typed parameters and the advantages of each. We'll cover how to handle variable numbers of arguments and, finally, how to initialize parameters.

While the $args variable is a simple and automatic way of getting at the arguments to functions, it takes a fair amount of work to do anything with a level of sophistication. PowerShell provides a much more convenient (and probably more familiar) way to declare parameters, which is shown in Figure 7.1.

Here's a simple example of what this looks like:

```
function subtract ($from, $count) { $from - $count }
```

In this example, there are two formal parameters to the function: $from and $count. When the function is called, each actual parameter will be bound to the corresponding formal parameter, either by position or by name. What does that mean? Well, binding by position is obvious, as we can see:

```
PS (1) > subtract 5 3
2
```

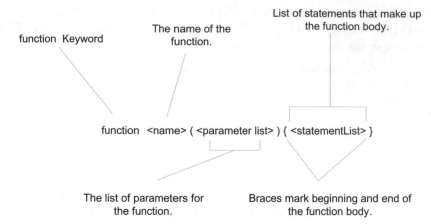

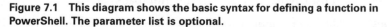

function <name> (<parameter list>) { <statementList> }

The list of parameters for the function.

Braces mark beginning and end of the function body.

Figure 7.1   This diagram shows the basic syntax for defining a function in PowerShell. The parameter list is optional.

In this example, the first argument 5 is bound to the first formal parameter $x, and the second argument is bound to the second parameter $y. Now let's look at using the parameter names as keywords:

```
PS (2) > subtract -from 5 -count 2
3
PS (3) > subtract -from 4 -count 7
3
```

What happens if you try and use the same parameter twice? You'll receive an error message that looks like this:

```
PS (4) > subtract -count 4 -count 7
subtract : Cannot bind parameter because parameter 'count' is  spec
ified more than once. To provide multiple values to parameters tha
t can accept multiple values,  use the array syntax.  For example,
 "-parameter value1,value2,value3".
At line:1 char:25
+ subtract -count 4 -count  <<<< 7
```

As the message says, you can't specify a named parameter more than once. So we now know that there are two ways to match format parameters with actual arguments. Can we mix and match? Let's try it.

```
PS (5) > subtract -from 5 6
-1
```

We see that it did work as one would expect. $from is set to 5, $count is set to 6, and we know that 5 minus 6 is -1. Now let's change which parameter is named.

```
PS (6) > subtract -count 5 6
1
```

Now $count is set to 5 and $from is set to 6. This may seem bit odd. Here's how it works. Any named parameters are bound and then removed from the list of parameters that still need to be bound. These remaining parameters are then bound positionally. If no named parameters are specified in this example then $from is position 0 and $count is position 1. If we specify -from then $from is bound by name and removed from the list of things that need to be bound positionally. This means that $count, which is normally in position 2, is now in position 1. Got all that? Probably not, as I have a hard time following it myself. All you really need to think about is whether you're using named parameters or positional ones. Try to avoid mixing and matching if possible. If you do want to mix and match, always put the parameters that you want to specify by name at the end of the parameter list. In other words, put them at the end of the param statement or the function argument list. That way they don't affect the order of the parameters you want to bind by position.

AUTHOR'S NOTE Gotcha #1: Calling functions in PowerShell. A lot of people with previous programming experience see the word function and will try to call a function like subtract by doing

```
subtract(1,2)
```

PowerShell will happily accept this since there's nothing syntactically wrong with it. The problem is that the statement is totally wrong semantically. Functions (as opposed to *methods* on objects) in PowerShell are commands like any other command. Arguments to commands are separated by spaces. If you want to provide multi-valued argument for a single command then you separate those multiple values with commas (more on this later). Also, parentheses are only needed if you want the argument to be evaluated as an expression (see chapter 2 on parsing modes). So—what this "function call" is actually doing is passing a single argument, which is an array of two values. And that is just wrong. Consider yourself warned. Really. This has tripped up some *very* smart people. If you remember this discussion, then someday, somewhere, you'll be able to lord this bit of trivia over your coworkers, crushing their spirits like—oh—wait—sorry—it's that darned inner-voice leaking out again…

So far, all our work has been with typeless parameters, and this has its advantages. It means that our functions can typically work with a wider variety of data types. But sometimes you want to make sure that the parameters are of a particular type (or at least convertible to that type). While you could do this the hard way and write a bunch of type-checking code, PowerShell is all about making life easier for the user, so let's talk about a better way to do this by specifying typed parameters.

7.2.1 Specifying parameter types

Scripting languages don't usually type the parameters to functions and, by default, you don't have to specify the types of parameters in PowerShell. But sometimes it can be quite useful. Adding these type constraints is what we'll cover in this section. In order to type-constrain a parameter, you provide a type literal before the variable name in the parameter list. Here's an example. Let's define a function nadd that takes two parameters that we want to be integers.

```
PS (1) > function nadd ([int] $x, [int] $y) {$x + $y}
```

Now we'll use this function to add two numbers.

```
PS (2) > nadd 1 2
3
```

Adding 1 and 2 gives 3. No surprise there. Now let's add two strings.

```
PS (3) > nadd "1" "2"
3
```

The answer is still 3. Because of the type constraints on the parameters, numeric addition is performed even though we passed in two strings. Now let's see what happens when we pass in something that can't be converted to a number:

```
PS (4) > nadd @{a=1;b=2}  "2"
nadd : Cannot convert "System.Collections.Hashtable" to "System.
Int32".
At line:1 char:5
+ nadd  <<<< @{a=1;b=2}  "2"
```

We get an error message mentioning where the function was used and why it failed. Let's define another function that doesn't have the type constraints.

```
PS (5) > function add ($x, $y) {$x + $y}
```

Now we'll call this function with a hashtable argument.

```
PS (6) > add @{a=1;b=2}  "2"
You can add another hash table only to a hash table.
At line:1 char:28
+ function add ($x, $y) {$x +  <<<< $y}
```

We still get an error, but notice where the error message is reported. Because it happened in the body of the function, the error message is reported in the function itself, not where the function was called as it was in the previous function. It's much more useful for the user of the function to know where the call that failed was rather than knowing where in the function it failed.

Now let's look at the other two examples with the unconstrained function, first with strings and then with numbers.

```
PS (7) > add "1"  "2"
12
PS (8) > add 1 2
3
```

CHAPTER 7   FUNCTIONS AND SCRIPTS

This function has the normal polymorphic behavior we expect from PowerShell. The type-constrained version only worked on numbers. Of course, if the arguments can be safely converted to numbers then the operation will proceed. Let's try the type-constrained function with strings.

```
PS (9) > nadd "4" "2"
6
```

Because the strings "2" and "4" can be safely converted into numbers, they are, and the operation proceeds. If not, as in the following example:

```
PS (10) > nadd "4a" "222"
nadd : Cannot convert value "4a" to type "System.Int32". Error:
"Input string was not in a correct format."
At line:1 char:5
+ nadd  <<<< "4a" "222"
```

You'll get a type conversion error. In effect, the type constraints on function parameters are really casts, and follow the type conversion rules described in chapter 3.

> **AUTHOR'S NOTE**   If you are used to traditional object-oriented languages, you might expect to be able to create overloads for a particular function name by specifying different signatures. Overloading is not supported in version 1 of Power-Shell. If you define a
>
> ```
> function a ([int] $b) { }
> ```
>
> and later define
>
> ```
> function a ([string] $b) { }
> ```
>
> the new definition will replace the old definition rather than adding a new overload.

When we started our discussion of parameters, we used $args, which was a bit awkward, but it let us specify a variable number of arguments to a function. In the next section, we'll see how we can do this even when we have a formal parameter list.

7.2.2 Handling variable numbers of arguments

Now that you know how to create explicit argument specifications, you're probably wondering if you can still handle variable numbers of arguments. The answer is yes. Any remaining arguments that don't match formal arguments will be captured in $args. Here's an example function that illustrates this.

```
PS (11) > function a ($x, $y) {
>> "x is $x"
>> "y is $y"
>> "args is $args"
>> }
>>
```

Now let's use it with a single argument.

```
PS (12) > a 1
x is 1
y is
args is
```

The single argument is bound to $x. $y is initialized to $null and $args has zero elements in it. Now try it with two arguments.

```
PS (13) > a 1 2
x is 1
y is 2
args is
```

This time $x and $y are bound, but $args is still empty. Next try it with three arguments, and then with five.

```
PS (14) > a 1 2 3
x is 1
y is 2
args is 3
PS (15) > a 1 2 3 4 5
x is 1
y is 2
args is 3 4 5
```

Now you can see that the extra arguments end up in $args.

AUTHOR'S NOTE Here's a tip: if you want to make sure that no extra arguments are passed to your function, check whether the length of the $args.length is zero in the function body. If it's not zero then some arguments were passed.

Earlier we mentioned that formal arguments that didn't have corresponding actual arguments were initialized to $null. While this is a handy default, it would be more useful to have a way to initialize the arguments. We'll look at that next.

7.2.3   Initializing function parameters

In this section, we'll show you how to initialize the values of function parameters. The syntax for this is shown in figure 7.2.

Let's move right into an example:

```
PS (14) > function add ($x=1, $y=2) { $x + $y }
```

This function initializes the formal parameters $x to 1 and $y to 2 if no actual parameters are specified. So when we use it with no arguments:

```
PS (15) > add
3
```

it returns 3. With one argument:

```
PS (16) > add 5
7
```

it returns the argument plus 2, which in this case is 7. And finally with two actual arguments

```
PS (17) > add 5 5
10
```

it returns the result of adding them. From this example, it's obvious that you can initialize the variable to a constant value. What about something more complex? The initialization sequence as shown in figure 7.2 says that an initializer can be an expression. If you remember from chapter 5, an expression can be a subexpression and a subexpression can contain any PowerShell construct. In other words, an initializer can do anything: calculate a value, execute a pipeline, reformat your hard-drive (not recommended), or send out for snacks from Tahiti by carrier pigeon (I've not had much luck with this one).

Let's try this out. We'll define a function that returns the day of the week for a particular date.

```
PS (28) > function dow ([datetime] $d = $(get-date))
>> {
>> $d.dayofweek
>> }
>>
```

This function takes one argument $d that is constrained to be something that matches a date or time. If no argument is specified then it is initialized to the result of executing the Get-Date cmdlet (which returns today's date). Now let's try it out. First run it with no arguments:

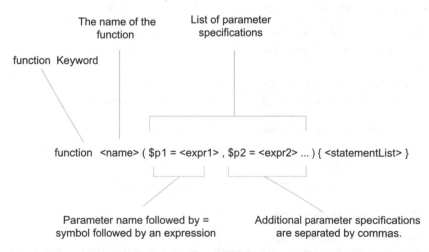

Figure 7.2 This figure shows the more complex function definition syntax where initializer expressions are provided for each variable. Note that the initializers are constrained to be expressions, but using the subexpression notation, you can actually put anything here.

```
PS (29) > dow
Tuesday
```

And it prints out what today is. Then run it with a specific date:

```
PS (30) > dow "jun 2, 2001"
Saturday
```

and we see that June 2, 2001 was a Saturday. This is a simple example of using a subexpression to initialize a variable.

There is one interesting scenario that we should still talk about. What happens if we don't want a default value? In other words, how can we require the user to specify this value? This is another place where you can use initializer expressions. Since the expression is can do anything, it can also generate an error. Here's how you can use the throw statement to generate an error (we'll cover the throw statement in detail in chapter 9). First we define the function.

```
PS (31) > function zed ($x=$(throw "need x")) { "x is $x" }
```

Notice how the throw statement is used in the initializer subexpression for $x. Now run the function—first with a value to see whether it works properly

```
PS (32) > zed 123
x is 123
```

and then without an argument

```
PS (33) > zed
need x
At line:1 char:25
+ function zed ($x=$(throw  <<<< "need x")) { "x is $x" }
```

Without the argument, the initializer statement is executed and this results in an exception being thrown. This is how you make arguments mandatory in PowerShell version 1.

Finally, there is one other thing we need to discuss with function parameters: how to define what are traditionally called flags or switches on commands.

7.2.4 Using switch parameters to define flags

In this section, we're going to cover how to specify switch parameters, but before we do that, let's talk a bit more about parameter processing in general. In all shell environments, commands typically have three kinds of parameters, as shown in table 7.1.

Table 7.1 Types of parameters found in all shells

Parameter type	Description
Switches	Switches are present or absent, such as Get-ChildItem –Recurse
Options	Options take an argument value, such as Get-ChildItem -Filter *.cs
Arguments	These are positional and don't really have a name associated with them

This pattern holds true for almost all shells, including cmd.exe, the Korn Shell, and so on, although the specific details of the syntax may vary. In PowerShell we've canonicalized things a bit more. In other words, we've used formal terms for each of these, as shown in table 7.2.

Table 7.2 Formal names for parameter types in PowerShell

Parameter Type	Formal name in PowerShell
Switches	Switch parameters
Options	Parameters
Arguments	Positional parameters

Arguments are called positional parameters because they are always associated with a parameter name. However, it's permitted to leave the name out and the interpreter will figure out what parameter it is from its position on the command line. For example, in the `dir` command, the `-path` parameter is a positional parameter whose position is zero. Therefore the command

```
dir c:\
```

is equivalent to

```
dir -path c:\
```

and the system infers that "c:\" should be associated with `-path`.

Switch parameters are just the opposite; you specify the parameter but the argument is left out. The interpreter assigns the parameter a value based on whether the parameter is present or absent. The `-recurse` parameter for `dir` is a good example. If it's present then you will get a recursive directory listing starting at the current directory.

```
dir -recurse
```

So how do you indicate that something should be a switch parameter? Since PowerShell characteristically uses types to control behavior, it makes sense to indicate that a parameter is a switch parameter by marking it with the type `SwitchParameter`. For convenience in scripts, this is written as `[switch]`. (In early versions of PowerShell, we used the Boolean type for this, but co-opting a primitive type caused too many problems.)

Now, since the value of a switch is highly constrained, initializing switches is not necessary or recommended. Here's an example using a switch:

```
PS (1) > function get-soup (
>>      [switch] $please,
>>      [string] $soup= "chicken noodle"
>> )
>> {
>>      if ($please) {
>>          "Here's your $soup soup"
>>      }
```

```
>>    else
>>    {
>>        "No soup for you!"
>>    }
>> }
>>
```

Trying this function out:

```
PS (2) > get-soup
No soup for you!
PS (3) > get-soup -please
Here's your chicken noodle soup
PS (4) > get-soup -please tomato
Here's your tomato soup
PS (5) >
```

So if you say "please", you get soup. If not, no soup for you!

AUTHOR'S NOTE You should *never* have a function, script, or cmdlet with a switch parameter that you initialize to true, because this makes commands hard to use. Switch parameters on a command should be designed such that they need only be present to get the desired effect.

In all this discussion of parameters, we haven't really discussed the lifetime of function variables or when they are visible to other functions. This is called *variable scoping*. If I have a function that uses a variable $x and it calls another function that also uses $x, what happens? And if I set a variable in a function, can I still use that function after the script has exited? All of these questions are answered in the next section.

7.2.5 Variables and scoping rules

In this section we're going to cover the lifetime of variables, including when they come into existence and where they are visible. The rules that cover these things are called the *scoping rules* of the language. These scoping rules cover the lifetime and visibility of a variable.

In programming languages, there are two general types for scoping—lexical and dynamic. Most programming languages and many scripting languages are lexically scoped. In a lexically scoped language, names are visible in the module they are defined in and in any nested modules, but are not visible outside the enclosing module unless they are explicitly exported in some way. Since *where* they are defined controls the visibility for the variable, this is determined at "compile" time and is therefore called lexical (or sometimes static) scoping.

On the other hand, dynamic scoping involves *when* the variable is defined. In other words, the visibility of the variable is controlled by the runtime behavior of the program, not the compile-time behavior (hence the term "dynamic"). PowerShell has no declaration statement like the `Dim` statement in Visual Basic; a variable is simply defined on first assignment. We discussed this in chapter 5, but it's more important now. Let's look at an example. First we'll define two simple functions, "one" and "two".

```
PS (1) > function one { "x is $x" }
PS (2) > function two { $x = 22; one }
```

Function one prints out a string displaying the value of $x. Function two sets the variable $x to a particular variable, and then calls function one. Now let's try them out. Before we work with the functions, we will set $x to 7 interactively, to help illustrate how scoping works.

```
PS (3) > $x=7
```

Now we'll call function one.

```
PS (4) > one
x is 7
```

As expected, it prints out "x is 7". Now let's call function two.

```
PS (5) > two
x is 22
```

Not surprisingly, since two sets $x to 22 before calling one, we see "x is 22" being returned. So what happened to $x? Let's check:

```
PS (6) > $x
7
```

It's still 7! Let's call one again.

```
PS (7) > one
x is 7
```

It prints out "x is 7". So what exactly happened here? When we first assigned 7 to $x, we created a new global variable $x. When we called function one the first time, it looked for a variable $x, found the global definition, and used that to print out the message. When we called function two, it defined a new local variable called $x before calling one. This variable is local; i.e., it didn't change the value of the global $x, but it did put a new $x on the scope stack. When it called one, this function searched up the scope stack looking for $x, found the new variable created by function two, and used that to print out "x is 22". On return from function two, the scope containing its definition of $x was discarded. The next time we called function one, it found the top-level definition of $x. Now let's compare this to a language that is lexically scoped. I happen to have Python installed on my computer, so from PowerShell, I'll start the Python interpreter.

```
PS (1) > python
Python 2.2.3 (#42, May 30 2003, 18:12:08) [MSC 32 bit (Intel)] on
 win32
Type "help", "copyright", "credits" or "license" for more informa
tion.
```

Now let's set the global variable x to 7. (Note—even if you aren't familiar with Python, these examples are very simple, so you shouldn't have a problem following them.)

```
>>> x=7
```

Now print out x to make sure it was properly set.

```
>>> print x
7
```

We see that it is, in fact, 7. Now let's define a Python function one.

```
>>> def one():
...     print "x is " + str(x)
...
```

And now define another function two that sets x to 22 and then calls one.

```
>>> def two():
...     x=22
...     one()
...
```

As with the PowerShell example, we call one and it prints out "x is 7".

```
>>> one()
x is 7
```

Now call two.

```
>>> two()
x is 7
```

Even though two defines x to be 22, when it calls one, one still prints out 7. This is because the local variable x is not lexically visible to one—it will always use the value of the global x, which we can see hasn't changed.

```
>>> print x
7
>>>
```

So now, hopefully, you have a basic understanding of how variables are looked up in PowerShell. Sometimes, though, you want to be able to override the default lookup behavior. We'll discuss this in the next section.

AUTHOR'S NOTE UNIX shells used dynamic scoping because they didn't really have a choice. Each script is executed in its own process and receives a copy of the parent's environment. Any environment variables that a script defines will then be inherited by any child scripts it, in turn, calls. The process-based nature of the UNIX shells predetermines how scoping can work. The interesting thing is that these semantics are pretty much what PowerShell uses, even though we weren't limited by the process boundary. We tried a number of different schemes and the only one that was really satisfactory was the one that most closely mimicked traditional shell semantics. I suppose this shouldn't be a surprise, since it's worked pretty well for several decades now.

7.2.6 Using variable scope modifiers

We've now arrived at the subject of variable scope modifiers. In the previous section we discussed scope and the default PowerShell lookup algorithm. Now you'll see that you can override the default lookup by using a scope modifier. These modifiers look like the namespace qualifiers mentioned in chapter 6. To access a global variable $var, you would write:

```
$global:var
```

Let's revisit the functions from the previous section.

```
PS (1) > function one { "x is $global:x" }
```

This time, in the function one, we'll use the scope modifier to explicitly reference the global $x.

```
PS (2) > function two { $x = 22; one }
```

The definition of function two is unchanged. Now set the global $x to 7 (commands at the top level always set global variables, so you don't need to use the global modifier).

```
PS (3) > $x=7
```

Now run the functions.

```
PS (4) > one
x is 7
PS (5) > two
x is 7
```

This time, because we told one to bypass searching the scope change for $x and go directly to the global variable, calls to both one and two return the same result, "x is 7".

But enough about putting stuff into functions, how about getting results out? Let's switch our focus to achieving returns for all our hard efforts. This is the topic of the next section.

7.3 RETURNING VALUES FROM FUNCTIONS

Now it's time to talk about returning values from functions. We've been doing this all along of course, but there is something we need to highlight. Because PowerShell is a shell, it doesn't really return results—it writes output. As we've seen, the result of any expression or pipeline is to emit the result. At the command line, if you type three expressions separated by semicolons, the results of all three statements are output:

```
PS (1) > 2+2; 9/3; [math]::sqrt(27)
4
3
5.19615242270663
```

In this example, there were three statements in the list, so three numbers were displayed. Now let's put this into a function.

```
PS (2) > function numbers { 2+2; 9/3; [math]::sqrt(27) }
```

Now run that function.

```
PS (3) > numbers
4
3
5.19615242270663
```

Just as when we typed it on the command line, three numbers are output. Now let's run it and assign the results to a variable.

```
PS (4) > $result = numbers
```

Then check the content of that variable.

```
PS (5) > $result.length
3
PS (6) > $result[0]
4
PS (7) > $result[1]
3
PS (8) > $result[2]
5.19615242270663
```

From the output, we can see that $result contains an array with three values in it. Here's what happened. As each of the statements in the function was executed, the result of that statement was captured in an array, and then that array was stored in $result. The easiest way to understand this is to imagine variable assignments working like redirection, except the result is stored in a variable instead of in a file.

Let's try something more complex. The goal here is twofold. First, we want to increase our understanding of how function output works. Second, we want to see how to take advantage of this feature to simplify our scripts and improve performance.

Let's redefine the function numbers to use a while loop that generates the numbers 1 to 10:

```
PS (11) > function numbers
>> {
>> $i=1
>> while ($i -le 10)
>> {
>> $i
>> $i++
>> }
>> }
>>
```

Now run it.

```
PS (12) > numbers
1
2
```

```
3
4
5
6
7
8
9
10
```

And capture the results in a variable.

```
PS (13) > $result = numbers
```

What actually ended up in the variable? First let's check the type:

```
PS (14) > $result.gettype().fullname
System.Object[]
```

And the length:

```
PS (15) > $result.length
10
```

The output of the function ended up in an array of elements, even though we never mentioned an array anywhere. This should look familiar by now, because we talked about it extensively in chapter 4 in our discussion of arrays. The PowerShell runtime will spontaneously create a collection when needed. Compare this to the way you'd write this function in a traditional language. Let's rewrite this as a new function tradnum. In the traditional approach, you have to initialize a result variable $result to hold the array being produced, add each element to the array, then *emit* the array.

```
PS (16) > function tradnum
>> {
>> $result = @()
>> $i=1
>> while ($i -le 10)
>> {
>>     $result += $i
>>     $i++
>> }
>> $result
>> }
>>
```

This is significantly more complex, in that you have to manage two variables in the function now instead of one. If you were writing in a language that didn't automatically extend the size of the array, it would be even more complicated, as you would have to add code to resize the array manually. And even though PowerShell will automatically resize the array, it's not very efficient compared to capturing the streamed output. The point is to make you think about how you can use the facilities that

PowerShell offers to improve your code. If you find yourself writing code that explicitly constructs arrays, you should consider looking at it to see if it can be rewritten to take advantage of streaming instead.

Of course, every silver lining has a cloud. As wonderful as all of this is, there are some potential pitfalls. We'll cover what these are and how to go about debugging them in the next section.

7.3.1 Debugging function output

When writing a function, there's something you need to keep in mind. The result of *all statements executed* will appear in the output of the function. This means that if you add debug statements that write to the output stream, this debug output will be mixed into the actual output of the function.

> **AUTHOR'S NOTE** In text-based shells, the usual way to work around mixing debug information with output is to write the debug messages to the error stream (stderr). This works fine when the error stream is simple text; however, in Power-Shell, the error stream is composed of error objects. All of the extra information in these objects, while great for errors, makes them unpalatable for writing simple debug messages. There are better ways of handling this, as we'll see in chapter 9 when we talk about debugging.

Here's an example function where we've added a couple of debug statements:

```
PS (1) > function my-func ($x) {
>>      "Getting the date"
>>      $x = get-date
>>      "Date was $x, now getting the day"
>>      $day = $x.day
>>      "Returning the day"
>>      $day
>> }
>>
```

Let's run the function.

```
PS (2) > my-func
Getting the date
Date was 5/17/2006 10:39:39 PM, now getting the day
Returning the day
17
```

We see the debug output as well as the result. Now let's capture the output of the function into a variable.

```
PS (3) > $x = my-func
```

We see no output, but neither do we see the debugging messages. Now look at what's in $x.

```
PS (4) > $x
Getting the date
Date was 5/17/2006 10:39:39 PM, now getting the day
Returning the day
17
```

We see that everything is there. This is a trivial example and I'm sure it feels like we're beating it to death, but this is the kind of thing that leads to those head-slapping how-could-I-be-so dumb moments in which you'll be writing a complex script and wonder why the output looks funny. Then you'll remember that debugging statement you forgot to take out. "Doh!" you cry, "How could I be so dumb!?"

AUTHOR'S
NOTE

This, of course, is not exclusive to PowerShell. Back before the advent of good debuggers, people would do "printf-debugging" (named after the printf output function in C). It wasn't uncommon to see stray output in programs because of this. Now with good debuggers, this is pretty infrequent. PowerShell provides debugging features that you can use instead of "printf-debugging", which we'll cover in chapter 9.

Be careful also about doing something that emits objects when you didn't expect them. This usually happens when you're using .NET methods. The problem is that in .NET languages such as C#, the default behavior is to discard the result of an expression.

PowerShell always emits the result of expressions, so they unexpectedly appear in your output. Most of the time this is fine, but there are some .NET framework methods that return values that are mostly never used. The best example is the System.Collections.ArrayList class. The Add() method on this class helpfully returns the index of the object that was added by the call to Add() (I'm aware of no actual use for this feature—it probably seemed like a good idea at the time). This behavior looks like:

```
PS (1) > $al = new-object system.collections.arraylist
PS (2) > $al.count
0
PS (3) > $al.add(1)
0
PS (4) > $al.add(2)
1
PS (5) > $al.add(3)
2
```

Every time we call Add(), a number displaying the index of the added element is emitted. Now say we write a function that copies its arguments into an ArrayList. This might look like:

```
PS (6) > function addArgsToArrayList {
>> $al = new-object System.Collections.ArrayList
>> $args | foreach { $al.add($_) }
>> }
>>
```

It's a pretty simple function, but what happens when we run it? Take a look:

```
PS (7) > addArgsToArrayList a b c d
0
1
2
3
```

As you can see, every time we call Add(), a number gets returned. This isn't very helpful. To make it work properly, we need to discard this undesired output. Let's fix this. Here is the revised function definition.

```
PS (8) > function addArgsToArrayList {
>> $al = new-object System.Collections.ArrayList
>> $args | foreach { [void] $al.add($_) }
>> }
>>
```

It looks exactly like the previous one except for the cast to void in the third line. Now let's try it out.

```
PS (9) > addArgsToArrayList a b c d
PS (10) >
```

This time we don't see any output, as desired. This is a tip to keep in mind when working with .NET classes in functions.

7.3.2 The return statement

Now let's talk about the return statement. So far we've talked about how functions in PowerShell are best described as writing output rather than returning results. So why do we need a return statement? Because sometimes you want to exit a function early instead of writing the conditional statements you need to get the flow of control to reach the end. In effect, the return statement is like the break statement we covered in chapter 6—it breaks to the end of the function.

It is possible to "return" a value from a function using the return statement. This looks like

```
return 2+2
```

This is effectively shorthand for

```
write-object (2+2) ; return
```

We included the return statement in PowerShell because it's a common pattern that programmers expect to have. Unfortunately, it can sometimes lead to confusion for new users and non-programmers. They forget that, because PowerShell is a shell, every statement emits values into the output stream. Using the return statement can make this somewhat less obvious. Because of this potential for confusion, you should generally avoid using the return statement unless you really need it to make your logic simpler. Even then, you should probably avoid using it to return a value. The one circumstance where it makes sense is in a "pure" function where you're only returning a single value. For example, look at this recursive definition of the factorial function:

```
PS (5) > function fact ($x) {
>> if ($x -lt 2) {return 1}
>> $x * (fact ($x-1))
>> }
>>
PS (6) > fact 3
6
```

This is a simple function that returns a single value with no side-effects. In this case, it makes sense to use the `return` statement with value.

> **AUTHOR'S GEEK NOTE**
>
> The *factorial* of a number x is the product of all positive numbers less than or equal to x. Therefore the factorial of 6 is
>
> $$6 * 5 * 4 * 3 * 2 * 1$$
>
> which is really
>
> $$6 * (fact 5)$$
>
> which, in turn, is
>
> $$6 * 5 * (fact 4)$$
>
> and so on down to 1.
>
> Factorials are useful in calculating permutations. Understanding permutations is useful if you're playing poker. This should not be construed as an endorsement for poker—it's just kind of cool. Bill Gates plays bridge.

7.4 USING FUNCTIONS IN A PIPELINE

So far we've only talked about using functions as standalone statements. But what about using functions in pipelines? After all, PowerShell is all about pipelines, so shouldn't you be able to use functions in pipelines? Of course, the answer is yes with some considerations that need to be taken into account. The nature of a function is to take a set of inputs, process it, and produce a result. So how do we make the stream of objects from the pipeline available in a function? This is accomplished through the `$input` variable. When a function is used in a pipeline, a special variable `$input` is available that contains an *enumerator* that allows you to process through the input collection. Let's see how this works:

```
PS (1) > function sum {
>> $total=0;
>> foreach ($n in $input) { $total += $n }
>> $total
>> }
>>
```

Here we've defined a function `sum` that takes no arguments but has one implied argument, which is `$input`. It will add each of the elements in `$input` to `$total` and then return $total. In other words, it will return the sum of all the input objects. Let's try this on a collection of numbers:

```
PS (2) > 1..5 | sum
15
```

Clearly it works as intended.

We said that $input is an enumerator. You may remember our discussion of enumerators from chapter 6 when we talked about the $foreach and $switch variables. The same principles apply here. You move the enumerator to the next element using the MoveNext() method and get the current element using the Current property. Here's the sum function rewritten using the enumerator members directly.

```
PS (3) > function sum2 {
>> $total=0
>> while ($input.movenext())
>> {
>> $total += $input.Current
>> }
>> $total
>> }
>>
```

Of course, it produces the same result.

```
PS (4) > 1..5 | sum2
15
```

Let's write a variation of this that works with something other than numbers. This time we'll write a function that has a formal parameter and also processes input. The parameter will be the name of the property on the input object to sum up. Here's the function definition:

```
PS (7) > function sum3 ($p)
>> {
>> $total=0
>> while ($input.MoveNext())
>> {
>> $total += $input.current.$p
>> }
>> $total
>> }
>>
```

In line 6 of the function, you can see the expression $input.current.$p. This expression returns the value of the property named by $p on the current object in the enumeration. Let's use this function to sum up the lengths of the files in the current directory.

```
PS (8) > dir | sum3 length
9111
```

We invoke the function passing in the string "length" as the name of the property to sum. The result is the total of the lengths of all of the files in the current directory.

This shows that it's pretty easy to write functions that you can use in a pipeline, but there's one thing we haven't touched on. Because functions run all at once, they can't do streaming processing. In the previous example, where we piped the output of dir into the function, what actually happened was that the dir cmdlet ran to completion and the accumulated results from that were passed as a collection to the function. So how can we use functions more effectively in a pipeline? That's what we'll cover next when we talk about the concept of filters.

7.4.1 Filters and functions

In this section, we'll talk about filters: a variation on the general concept of functions. Where a function in a pipeline runs once, a filter is run for each input object coming from the pipeline. The general form of a filter is shown in figure 7.3.

As you can see from the diagram, the only syntactic difference between a function and a filter is the keyword. The significant differences are all semantic. A function runs once and runs to completion. When used in a pipeline, it halts streaming—the previous element in the pipeline runs to completion; only then does the function begin to run. It also has a special variable $input defined when used as anything other than the first element of the pipeline. By contrast, a filter is run once and to completion *for each element* in the pipeline. Instead of the variable $input, it has a special variable $_ that contains the current pipeline object.

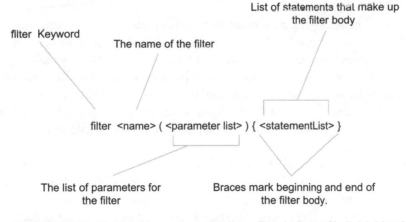

Figure 7.3 This diagram shows how to define a filter in PowerShell. It's identical to the basic function definition except that it uses the `filter` keyword instead of the `function` keyword.

At this point, we should look at an example to see what all this means. Let's write a filter to double the value of all of the input objects.

```
PS (1) > filter double {$_*2}
PS (2) > 1..5 | double
2
4
6
8
10
```

You should now be feeling a nagging sense of déjà vu. A little voice should be telling you, "I've seen this before." Remember the Foreach-Object cmdlet from chapter 6?

```
PS (3) > 1..5 | foreach {$_*2}
2
4
6
8
10
```

The Foreach-Object cmdlet is, in effect, a way of running an *anonymous* filter. By anonymous, we mean that you don't have to give it a name or predefine it. You just use it when you need it. The ability to create named filters is also very useful.

Functions in a pipeline run when all of the input has been gathered. Filters run once for each element in the pipeline. In the next section, we'll talk about generalizing the role of a function so that it can be a first class participant in a pipeline.

7.4.2 Functions as cmdlets

We've seen how to write a function that sums up values in a pipeline but can't stream results. And we've seen how to write a filter to calculate the sum of values in a pipeline, but filters have problems with setting up initial values for variables or conducting processing after all of the objects have been received. It would be nice if we could write user-defined cmdlets that can initialize some state at the beginning of the pipeline, process each object as it's received, then do clean-up work at the end of the pipeline. And of course we can. The full structure of a function cmdlet is shown in figure 7.4.

In the figure you see that you can define a clause for each phase of the cmdlet processing. This is exactly like the phases used in a compiled cmdlet, as mentioned in chapter 2. The begin keyword specifies the clause to run before the first pipeline object is available. The process clause is executed once for each object in the pipeline, and the end clause is run once all of the objects have been processed.

As with filters, the current pipeline object is available in the process clause in the special variable $_. As always, an example is the best way to illustrate this.

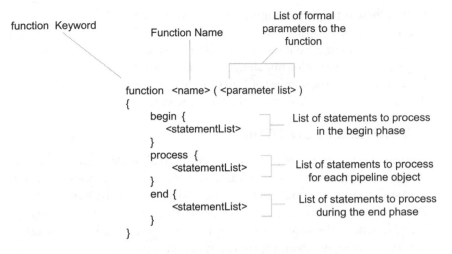

Figure 7.4 This shows the complete function definition syntax for a function in PowerShell that will have cmdlet-like behavior.

```
PS (1) > function my-cmdlet ($x) {
>> begin {$c=0; "In Begin, c is $c, x is $x"}
>> process {$c++; "In Process, c is $c, x is $x, `$_ is $_"}
>> end {"In End, c is $c, x is $x"}
>> }
>>
```

We defined all three clauses in this function. Each clause reports what it is and then prints out the values of some variables. The variable $x comes from the command line; the variable $c is defined in the begin clause, incremented in the process clauses, and displayed again in the end clause. The process clause also displays the value of the current pipeline object. Now let's run it. We'll pass the numbers 1 through 3 in through the pipeline and give it an argument "22" to use for $x. Here's what the output looks like:

```
PS (2) > 1,2,3 | my-cmdlet 22
In Begin, c is 0, x is 22
In Process, c is 1, x is 22, $_ is 1
In Process, c is 2, x is 22, $_ is 2
In Process, c is 3, x is 22, $_ is 3
In End, c is 3, x is 22
```

As you can see, the argument 22 is available in all three clauses and the value of $c is also maintained across all three clauses. What happens if there is no pipeline input? Let's try it.

```
PS (3) > my-cmdlet 33
In Begin, c is 0, x is 33
In Process, c is 1, x is 33, $_ is
In End, c is 1, x is 33
```

Even if there is no pipeline input, the process clause is still run exactly once. Of course, you don't have to specify all three of the clauses. If you only specify the `process` clause, you might as well just use the filter keyword, because the two are identical.

If you've been following along with the examples in this chapter, by now you'll have created quite a number of functions. Care to guess how to find out what you've defined? We'll cover how to do this in the next section.

7.5 MANAGING FUNCTIONS

Because it's easy to create functions in PowerShell, it also needs to be easy to manage those functions. Rather than provide a custom set of commands (or worse yet, a set of keywords) to manage functions, we take advantage of the namespace capabilities in PowerShell and provide a `function` drive. Since it's mapped as a drive, you can get a list of functions the same way you get a listing of the contents of any other drive. Let's use `dir` to find out about the `mkdir` function.

```
PS (7) > dir function:/mkdir


CommandType     Name                    Definition
-----------     ----                    ----------
Function        mkdir                   param([string[]]$pat...
```

By doing a dir of the path `function:/mkdir`, you can see the `mkdir` exists and is a function. And of course wild cards can be used, so we could have just written "mk*" as shown.

```
PS (8) > dir function:/mk*


CommandType     Name                    Definition
-----------     ----                    ----------
Function        mkdir                   param([string[]]$pat...
```

And, if you just do `dir` on the function drive, you'll get a complete listing of all functions. Let's do this but just get a count of the number of functions.

```
PS (9) > (dir function:/).count
78
```

In my environment, I have 78 functions defined. Now let's create a new one.

```
PS (10) > function clippy { "I see you're writing a function." }
```

And check the count again.

```
PS (11) > (dir function:/).count
79
```

Yes—there's one more function than was there previously. Now check for the function itself.

```
PS (12) > dir function:clippy

CommandType     Name            Definition
-----------     ----            ----------
Function        clippy                          "I see you're writin...
```

Running `dir` on `function:clippy` gives us the function definition entry for this function. Now let's remove it.

```
PS (13) > rm function:/clippy
```

And make sure that it's gone.

```
PS (14) > (dir function:/).count
78
PS (15) > dir function:clippy
Get-ChildItem : Cannot find path 'clippy' because it does not ex
ist.
At line:1 char:4
+ dir  <<<< function:clippie
```

Yes! We've removed `clippy` from the system.

<table>
<tr><td>AUTHOR'S
NOTE</td><td>Long-time Microsoft Office users will no doubt be feeling an intense burst of satisfaction with this last example. We've all longed to eradicate that annoying paperclip "assistant", and at last we have the pleasure, if in name only. And, even more amusing: Microsoft Word doesn't even recognize "clippy"—it keeps trying to autocorrect to "clippie". Some unresolved issues perhaps?</td></tr>
</table>

The techniques we've covered in this section allow you to manipulate the functions defined in your current session. As with any drive, you can list the functions, create new ones, delete them, and rename them. But regardless, all these functions will disappear when the session ends and you exit PowerShell. What about permanent functions? How do you define those? This is where scripts come in, and we'll cover that topic next.

7.6   SCRIPTS AT LONG LAST

All of the discussions up to this point have covered the basics of programming in PowerShell. These same principles and features also apply to writing scripts. In fact, a script is simply a piece of PowerShell code stored in a file. If you'll remember, back in chapter 1 we talked about how PowerShell has the world's shortest "Hello world" program, which is

```
PS (1) > "Hello world"
Hello world
```

Now let's make this into a script. We'll use redirection to write this command to a file in the current directory called hello.ps1.

```
PS (2) > '"Hello world"' > hello.ps1
```

Note the double quoting in the example. We want the script to contain

```
"Hello world"
```

with the quotes intact, not

```
Hello world
```

Now let's execute the script:

```
PS (3) > ./hello.ps1
Hello world
```

We see that the file executed and returned the expected phrase.

AUTHOR'S NOTE   In this example, even though hello.ps1 is in the current directory, we had to put "./" in front of it to run it. This is because PowerShell doesn't execute commands out of the current directory by default. This prevents accidental execution of the wrong command. See chapter 13 on security for more information.

Now there's a possibility that instead of achieving the output you expected, you received a nasty error message instead. This error message would look something like:

```
PS (5) > ./hello.ps1
The file C:\Documents and Settings\brucepay\hello.ps1 cannot be
loaded. The file C:\Documents and Settings\brucepay\hello.ps1 is
 not digitally signed. The script will not execute on the system
. Please see "get-help about_signing" for more details..
At line:1 char:11
+ ./hello.ps1 <<<<
```

This is another security feature in PowerShell. When the system is installed, by default you can't run scripts. This is controlled by the *execution policy*. The Execution Policy setting controls what kind of scripts can be run and is intended to prevent virus attacks like the I-love-you virus from a few years back. Users were being tricked into accidentally executing code mailed to them. The default execution policy for PowerShell prevents this type of attack.

Of course, a scripting tool is no good if you can't script. There is a command Set-Executionpolicy that can be used to change the default execution policy. If you see that error on your system, you should run the following command:

```
PS (6) > Set-ExecutionPolicy remotesigned
PS (7) > ./hello.ps1
Hello world
PS (8) >
```

This will change the execution policy so that you can execute scripts that you create yourself. It still won't execute scripts that come from remote sources such as email or are downloaded from a website. However, this is a generally safe policy to use with PowerShell. Chapter 9 covers all of these security topics in detail.

The RemoteSigned check depends on the mail tool or the web browser used
to do the download to set the Zone Identifier Stream to indicate where the
file came from. Internet Explorer and Microsoft Outlook do set this properly.

Now let's look at scripts in detail. (Spoiler alert—scripts are almost exactly like functions except that they live on disk instead of in memory.)

7.6.1 Passing arguments to scripts

Now that we know how to create and run scripts, how can we pass arguments to a
script? The answer is the same way we did it for basic functions—through the $args
variable. Let's look at a modified version of the previous script. Again, we'll use redirection to create the script. In fact we'll overwrite the old version of the script:

```
PS (8) > '"Hello $args"' > hello.ps1
```

and run it with an argument:

```
PS (9) > ./hello Bruce
Hello Bruce
```

Great—hello PowerShell! But if we don't supply an argument:

```
PS (10) > ./hello
Hello
```

we get a very impersonal greeting. So let's fix this up and change the script again. This
time we'll take advantage of a here-string to generate a longer script.

```
PS (11) > @'
>> if ($args) { $name = "$args" } else { $name = "world" }
>> "Hello $name!"
>> '@ > hello.ps1
>>
```

This script has two lines. The first sets a local variable $name to the value of $args if
it's defined. If it's not defined then it sets $name to "world". If we run the script with
no arguments, we get:

```
PS (12) > ./hello
Hello world!
```

the generic greeting. If we run it with an argument, we get a specific greeting:

```
PS (13) > ./hello Bruce
Hello Bruce!
PS (14) >
```

These are the same basic things we did with functions, and, as was the case with functions, they have limitations. It would be much more useful to have named, typed
parameters as we did with functions. We could do the same multivariable assignment
trick again, but we really want actual language support for formal argument to
scripts. There's a problem, though. The formal arguments to a function are defined

outside the body of the function. This isn't possible to do with scripts since there's no "declaration". The way we get around this is to introduce a new keyword in the PowerShell language—param—which we cover in the next section,

7.6.2 The param statement

As mentioned in the previous section, if we want to specify formal parameters for a script, we need a new keyword to do this. This is the purpose of the param statement. Note that the param statement must be the first executable line in the script. Only comments and empty lines may precede it. Let's visit our hello example one more time. Again we'll use a here-string and redirection to create the script.

```
PS (14) > @'
>> param($name="world")
>> "Hello $name!"
>> '@ > hello.ps1
>>
```

It's still two lines, but this time we explicitly name the variable, making the script clearer and simpler. Of course, when we run it, we find the expected results.

```
PS (15) > ./hello
Hello world!
PS (16) > ./hello Bruce
Hello Bruce!
PS (17) >
```

For amusement purposes, here's the script being generated all on one line.

```
PS (17) > 'param($name="world") "Hello $name"' > hello.ps1
PS (18) > ./hello
Hello world
PS (19) > ./hello Bruce
Hello Bruce
```

This example illustrates that there is no need for any kind of separator after the param statement for the script to be valid. Now let's talk about some more of the ways that functions and scripts aren't quite the same.

7.6.3 Scopes and scripts

In section 7.3, we talked about the scoping rules for functions. These same general rules also apply to scripts. Variables are created when they are first assigned. They are always created in the current scope, so a variable with the same name in an outer (or global) scope is not affected. In both scripts and functions, you can use the $global:name scope modifier to explicitly modify a global variable.

Scripts do introduce one extra named scope, however, called the script scope. This scope modifier is intended to allow functions defined in a script to affect the "global" state of the script without affecting the overall global state of the interpreter. Let's look at an example. First, define a global $x to be 1.

```
PS (1) > $x = 1
```

Then create a script called `my-script`. In this script, we'll create a function called `lfunc`. This `lfunc` function will define a function-scoped variable $x to be 100 and a script-scoped variable $x to be 10. The script itself will run this function and then print out the script-scoped variable x. We'll use a here-string and redirection to create the script interactively.

```
PS (2) > @'
>> function lfunc { $x = 100; $script:x = 10 ; "lfunc: x = $x"}
>> lfunc
>> "my-script:x = $x"
>> '@ > my-script.ps1
>>
```

Now let's run the script.

```
PS (3) > ./my-script.ps1
lfunc: x = 100
my-script:x = 10
```

We see that the function scoped variable $x was 100; the script scoped $x was 10

```
PS (4) > "global: x = $x"
global: x = 1
```

while the global $x is still 1.

7.6.4   Exiting scripts and the exit statement

So far we've seen that we can exit scripts or functions simply by getting to the end of the script or function. We've also seen the `return` statement, which will let you exit from a function. In fact, what it does is let you exit from the current scope, whether that scope is a function or script. But what happens when you want to cause a script to exit from within a function defined in that script? One way to do this would be to use a script-scoped variable and conditionals, but that would be pretty awkward. To make this easier, PowerShell has the `exit` keyword. (You've probably already been using this to exit from PowerShell.) When `exit` is used in a script, it exits that script. This is true even when called from a function in that script. Here's what that looks like:

```
PS (1) > @'
>> function callExit { "calling exit from callExit"; exit}
>> CallExit
>> "Done my-script"
>> '@ > my-script.ps1
>>
```

The function `CallExit` defined in this script calls `exit`. Since the function is called before the line that emits

```
    "Done my-script"
```

we shouldn't see this line emitted. Let's run it:

```
PS (2) > ./my-script.ps1
calling exit from CallExit
```

We see that the script was correctly terminated by the call to exit in the function CallExit.

The exit statement is also how we set the exit code for the PowerShell process when calling PowerShell.exe from another program. Here's an example that shows how this works. From within cmd.exe, we'll run PowerShell.exe, passing it a string to execute. This "script" will emit the message "Hi there" and then call exit with an exit code of 17.

```
C:\>powershell "'Hi there'; exit 17"
Hi there
```

And now we're back at the cmd.exe prompt. Cmd.exe makes the exit code of a program it's run available in the variable ERRORLEVEL, so we'll check that variable:

```
C:\>echo %ERRORLEVEL%
17
```

We see that it is 17 as expected. This shows how a script executed by PowerShell can return an exit code to the calling process.

Before we move on, let's look at one more thing that can trip people up. Take a second look at what we actually ran in this example. The arguments to Power-Shell.exe are actually accumulated and then treated as a script to exit. This is important to remember when we try to run a script using PowerShell from cmd.exe. Here's the problem people run into: because the arguments to the PowerShell.exe are a script to execute, not the name of a file to run, if the path to that script has a space in it, then, since PowerShell treats the spaces as delimiters, we'll get an error. Consider a script called "my script.ps1". When we try to run this by doing:

```
PowerShell "./my script.ps1"
```

PowerShell will complain about "my" being an unrecognized command. It treated "my" as a command name and "script.ps1" as an argument to that command. To execute a script with a space in the name, we need to do the same thing we'd do at the PowerShell command prompt: put the name in quotes and use the call (&) operator:

```
PowerShell.exe "& './my script.ps1'"
```

Now the script will be run properly. This is one of the areas where having two types of quotes comes in handy. Also note that we still have to use the relative path to find the script if it's in the current directory.

7.6.5 Dotting scripts and functions

There's one last topic that we need to cover with respect to functions, scripts, and scoping, and this is something called "dotting" a script or function.

AUTHOR'S NOTE The terminology used here comes from UNIX shells. Depending on your regional background, you may consider the "correct" term to be, variously, "dotting", "sourcing", or "dot sourcing". It's entertaining to see regional terminology even within a single technology community. In fact, this is very reminiscent of "The Great Pop vs. Soda Controversy". In the United States, people refer to soft drinks as "pop", "soda", or "soda pop", depending on what part of the country they come from. This latter phenomenon is (startlingly) well documented at http://www.popvssoda.com.

As we've discussed, we usually only care about the results of a function and want all of the intermediate variables and so on discarded when the script or function exits. This is why scripts and functions get their own scope. But sometimes you do care about all of the intermediate by-products. This is typically the case when you want to create a library of functions or variable definitions. In this situation, you want the script to run in the current scope.

AUTHOR'S NOTE This is how cmd.exe works by default, as this example shows. We have a cmd file foo.cmd

```
C:\files>type foo.cmd
set a=4
```

now set a variable a to 1 and display it:

```
C:\files>set a=1
C:\files>echo %a%
1
```

Next run the cmd file

```
C:\files>foo
C:\files>set a=4
```

and we see that the variable has been changed.

```
C:\files>echo %a%
4
```

As a consequence of this behavior, it's common to have cmd files that do nothing but set a bunch of variables. To do this in PowerShell, you would dot the script.

So how do you "dot" a script? By putting a dot or period in front of the name when you execute it. Note that there has to be a space between the dot and the name, otherwise it will be considered part of the name. Let's look at an example. First we create a script that sets $x to 22.

```
PS (5) > @'
>> "Setting x to 22"
>> $x = 22
>> '@ > my-script.ps1
>>
```

and we'll test it. First set $x to a known value

```
PS (6) > $x=3
PS (7) > $x
3
```

then run the script as we would normally:

```
PS (8) > ./my-script
Setting x to 22
```

Checking $x, we see that it is (correctly) unchanged.

```
PS (9) > $x
3
```

Now we'll dot the script.

```
PS (10) > . ./my-script
Setting x to 22
PS (11) > $x
22
```

This time $x is changed. What follows the . isn't limited to a simple file name. It could be a variable or expression, as was the case with "&":

```
PS (12) > $name = "./my-script"
PS (13) > . $name
Setting x to 22
```

The last thing to note is that dotting works for both scripts and functions. Let's define a function to show this:

```
PS (17) > function set-x ($x) {$x = $x}
PS (18) > . set-x 3
PS (19) > $x
3
```

In this example, we define the function set-x and dot it, passing in the value 3. The result is that the global variable $x is set to 3.

7.7   SUMMARY

This chapter finally introduced scripting and programming in general in PowerShell. While there was a lot of material, the following are the key points:

- PowerShell programming can be done either with functions or scripts. Functions are created using the function keyword, whereas scripts are simply pieces of PowerShell script text stored in a file.

- In PowerShell, scripts and functions are closely related. The same principles and techniques apply to both.

- Parameters can be specified for functions either immediately after the `function` keyword or in the body of the function using the `param` keyword. In scripts, only the `param` keyword can be used.
- PowerShell uses dynamic scoping for variables. You can modify how a variable name is resolved by using the scope modifiers in the variable names.
- Functions and scripts stream their output. In other words, they return the results of every statement executed as though it were written to the output stream. This feature means that you almost never have to write your own code to accumulate results.
- Because of the differences between how functions work in PowerShell and how they work in more conventional languages, you may receive some unexpected results when creating your functions, so you picked up some tips on debugging these problems.
- Functions can be used as simple functions, filters, or as full-fledged cmdlets.
- The `function` drive is used to manage the functions defined in your session. This means that you use the same commands you use for managing files to manage functions.

Even though we covered a lot of material in this chapter, we've really only covered the surface aspects of programming with PowerShell. In chapter 8, we'll cover *scriptblocks*, which are the objects underlying the infrastructure for scripts and functions. We'll talk about how you can use these scriptblocks to extend the PowerShell language, extend existing objects, and even create your own objects

CHAPTER 8

Scriptblocks and objects

Philosophy have I digested,
The whole of Law and Medicine,
From each its secrets I have wrested,
Theology, alas, thrown in.
Poor fool, with all this sweated lore,
I stand no wiser than I was before.

—Johann Wolfgang Goethe, *Faust*

Greek letters are cool...

—Not actually a quote from Beavis and Butthead

Chapter 7 covered the basic elements of programming in PowerShell: functions and scripts. In this chapter, we'll take things to the next level and talk about *metaprogramming*. Metaprogramming is the term used to describe the activity of writing programs that write or manipulate other programs. If you're not already familiar with this concept, you may be asking why you should care. In chapter 1, we talked about designing classes and how hard it is to get those designs right. In most environments, if the designer makes a mistake then the user is stuck with the result. This is not true in PowerShell. Metaprogramming lets us delve into the heart of the system and make things work the way we need them to. Here's an analogy that should give you the full picture.

Imagine buying a computer that was welded shut. There is still a lot you can do with it—run all the existing programs and even install new programs. But there are some things you can't do. If it doesn't have any USB ports then you can't add them. If it doesn't have any way to capture video, you can't add that either without opening the case. And even though most people buy a computer with the basic features they need and never add new hardware, a case that's welded shut allows for no hardware tinkering.

Traditional programming languages are much like the welded computer. They have a basic set of features, and while you can extend what they do by adding libraries, you can't really extend the core capabilities of the language. For example, you can't add a new type of looping statement. On the other hand, in a language that supports metaprogramming, you can undertake such activities as adding new control structures. This is how the `Where-Object` and `Foreach-Object` cmdlets are implemented. They use the metaprogramming features in PowerShell to add new language elements. You can even create your own versions of these commands. Metaprogramming is one of the features that make dynamic languages such as PowerShell extremely powerful. That power translates into dramatic improvements in conceptual and code simplicity. Investing the time to learn how to use PowerShell's metaprogramming capabilities can significantly increase your productivity with PowerShell. Now let's get started with cracking open the case on PowerShell.

We'll begin with a discussion of a feature in the PowerShell language called *scriptblocks*. This discussion takes up the first part of this chapter and lays the groundwork for the rest of what we'll discuss. With the basic material out of the way, we'll look at how and where this scriptblock feature is used in PowerShell. We'll look at the role scriptblocks play in the creation of custom objects and types, and how they can be used to extend the PowerShell language. We'll go through an example that uses less than a hundred lines of PowerShell script to add a new "keyword" that allows you to define your own classes in PowerShell. We'll also cover several cmdlets that make use of these objects, and we'll wrap up with a look at some programming *patterns* that take advantage of scriptblocks. (Programming patterns are common approaches to solving a particular class of problems—in other words, common sense with a fancy name.) But first we need to understand scriptblocks themselves.

8.1   SCRIPTBLOCK BASICS

In this section we'll talk about how to create and use scriptblocks. We'll begin by looking at how commands are invoked so we can understand all the ways to invoke scriptblocks. Next we'll cover the syntax for scriptblock literals and the various types of scriptblocks you can create. This includes using scriptblocks as functions, as filters, and as cmdlets. Finally we'll look at how we can use scriptblocks to define new functions at runtime. Let's dive into the topic by starting with definitions.

In PowerShell, the key to metaprogramming (writing programs that write or manipulate other programs) is something called the *scriptblock*. This is a block of script code that exists as an object reference, but does not require a name. The `Where-Object` and `Foreach-Object` cmdlets rely on scriptblocks for their implementation. In the example

```
1..10 | foreach { $_ * 2 }
```

the expression in braces "{ $_ * 2 }" is actually a scriptblock. It's a piece of code that is passed to the `Foreach-Object` cmdlet and is called by the cmdlet as needed.

So that's all a scriptblock is—a piece of script in braces—but it's the key to all of the advanced programming features in PowerShell.

<table>
<tr><td>AUTHOR'S NOTE</td><td>What we call scriptblocks in PowerShell are called anonymous functions or sometimes lambda expressions in other languages. The term lambda comes from the lambda calculus developed by Alonzo Church and Stephen Cole Kleene in the 1930s. A number of languages, including Python and dialects of LISP, still use lambda as a language keyword. In designing the PowerShell language, we felt that calling a spade and spade (and a scriptblock a scriptblock) was more straightforward (the coolness of using Greek letters aside).</td></tr>
</table>

We've said that scriptblocks are anonymous functions, and of course functions are one of the four types of commands. But wait! You invoke a command by specifying its name. If scriptblocks are anonymous, they have no name—so how can you invoke them? This necessitates one more diversion before we really dig into scriptblocks. Let's talk about how commands can be executed.

8.1.1 Invoking commands

The way to execute a command is just to type its name followed by a set of arguments, but sometimes you can't type the command name as is. For example, you might have a command with a space in the name. You can't simply type the command because the space would cause part of the command name to be treated as an argument. And you can't put it in quotes, as this turns it into a string value. So you have to use the call operator "&". If, for instance, you have a command called "my command", you would invoke this command by typing the following:

```
& "my command"
```

The interpreter sees the call operator and uses the value of the next argument to look up the command to run. This process of looking up the command is called *command discovery*. The result of this command discovery operation is an object of type `System.Management.Automation.CommandInfo`, which tells the interpreter what command to execute. There are different subtypes of `CommandInfo` for each of the types of PowerShell commands. In the next section, we'll look at how to obtain these objects and how to use them.

8.1.2 Getting CommandInfo objects

We've mentioned the `Get-Command` cmdlet before as a way to attain information about a command. For example, to get information about the `Get-ChildItem` cmdlet, you'd do the following:

```
PS (1) > get-command get-childitem

CommandType     Name              Definition
-----------     ----              ----------
Cmdlet          Get-ChildItem     Get-ChildItem [[-Pat...
```

This shows you the information about a command: the name of the command, the type of command, and so on.

> **AUTHOR'S NOTE** In the previous `Get-Command` example, the command's defintion was truncated to fit the book-formatting requirements. You can control how this information is described by using the `Format-List` and `Format-Table` commands.

This is useful as a kind of lightweight help, but in addition to displaying information, the object returned by `Get-Command` can be used with the call operator to invoke that command. This is pretty significant. This extra degree of flexibility, invoking a command indirectly, is the first step on the road to metaprogramming.

Let's try this out—we'll get the `CommandInfo` object for the `Get-Date` command.

```
PS (1) > $d = get-command get-date
PS (2) > $d.CommandType
Cmdlet
PS (3) > $d.Name
Get-Date
```

As we can see from this example, the name "get-date" resolves to a cmdlet with the name "get-date". Now let's run this command using the `CommandInfo` object with the call operator:

```
PS (4) > & $d

Sunday, May 21, 2006 7:29:47 PM
```

It's as simple as that. So why do we care about this? Because it's a way of getting a handle to a specific command in the environment. Say we defined a function "get-date".

```
PS (1) > function get-date {"Hi there"}
PS (2) > get-date
Hi there
```

Our new `get-date` command outputs a string. Because PowerShell looks for functions before it looks for cmdlets, this new function definition hides the `Get-Date` cmdlet. Even using "&" with the string "get-date" still runs the function:

```
PS (3) > & "get-date"
Hi there
```

Since we created a second definition for `get-date` (the function), now if you use `Get-Command` you will see two definitions. So how do we unambiguously select the cmdlet `Get-Date`?

```
PS (4) > get-command get-date

CommandType     Name                    Definition
-----------     ----                    ----------
Cmdlet          Get-Date                Get-Date [[-Date] <D...
Function        get-date                "Hi there"
```

One way is to select the `CommandInfo` object based on the type of the command:

```
PS (5) > get-command -commandtype cmdlet get-date

CommandType     Name                    Definition
-----------     ----                    ----------
Cmdlet          Get-Date                Get-Date [[-Date] <D...
```

Let's put the result of this command into a variable.

```
PS (6) > $ci = get-command -commandtype cmdlet get-date
```

and then run it using the call operator.

```
PS (7) > &$ci

Sunday, May 21, 2006 7:34:33 PM
```

The `Get-Date` cmdlet was run as expected. Another way to select which command to run, since `Get-Command` returns a collection of objects, is to index into the collection to get the right object:

```
PS (8) > &(get-command get-date)[0]

Sunday, May 21, 2006 7:41:28 PM
```

Here we used the result of the index operation directly with the call operator to run the desired command.

This is all interesting, but what does it have to do with scriptblocks? We've demonstrated that you can invoke a command through an object reference instead of by name. This was the problem we set out to work around. Scriptblocks are functions that don't have names; so, as you might expect, the way to call a scriptblock is to use the call operator. Here's what that looks like:

```
PS (1) > & {param($x,$y) $x+$y} 2 5
7
```

In this example, the scriptblock is

```
{param($x,$y) $x+$y}
```

We called it with two arguments, 2 and 5, so the result of executing the scriptblock is 7.

8.1.3 The ScriptBlock literal

Now we'll take a detailed look at the syntax for creating a scriptblock. We'll cover how to define a scriptblock that acts as a function, how to define one that acts like a filter, and finally how to define a scriptblock cmdlet.

What we've been writing to create scriptblocks is called a *scriptblock literal*—in other words, a chunk of legitimate PowerShell script surrounded by braces. The syntax for this literal is shown in figure 8.1.

The definition of a scriptblock looks more or less like the definition of a function, except the function keyword and function name are missing. If the param statement is not present then the scriptblock will get its arguments through $args, exactly as a function would.

AUTHOR'S NOTE The param statement in PowerShell corresponds to the *lambda* keyword in other languages. For example, the PowerShell expression

```
& {param($x,$y) $x+$y} 2 5
```

is equivalent to the LISP expression

```
(lambda (x y) (+ x y)) 2 5
```

or the Python expression

```
(lambda x,y: x+y)(2,5)
```

Also note that, unlike Python lambdas, PowerShell scriptblocks can contain any collection of legal PowerShell statements.

Scriptblocks, like regular functions or scripts, can also behave like cmdlets. In other words, they can have one or all of the begin, process, or end clauses that you can

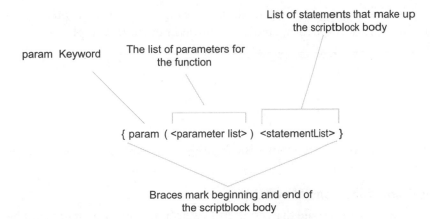

Figure 8.1 This shows how to define a simple scriptblock. Note that the param statement is optional, so a minimal scriptblock only has the braces.

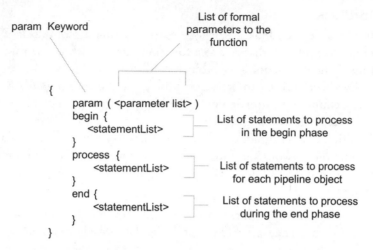

Figure 8.2 How to define a scriptblock that works like a cmdlet.

have in a function or script. Figure 8.2 shows the most general form of the script-block syntax, showing all three clauses.

As was the case with a function cmdlet, you don't have to define all the clauses. Here's an example that uses only the process clause.

```
PS (1) > 1..5 |&{process{$_ * 2}}
2
4
6
8
10
```

A scriptblock written this way works like the filters we saw in chapter 7. It also works like the Foreach-Object cmdlet, as shown in the next example:

```
PS (2) > 1..5 |foreach {$_ * 2}
2
4
6
8
10
```

The Foreach-Object cmdlet is effectively a shortcut for the more complex script-block construction.

8.1.4 Defining functions at runtime

In earlier sections, we said that scriptblocks were functions without names. The converse is also true—functions are scriptblocks with names. So how are the two related? In chapter 7, we showed you how to manage the functions in your PowerShell session using the function: drive. To get a list of functions, you could do a dir of that drive:

```
dir function:/
```

You could also delete or rename functions. But we didn't cover the whole story. In fact, the function: drive is, in effect, a set of variables containing scriptblocks. Let's explore this further. We'll define our favorite function foo:

```
PS (1) > function foo {"2+2"}
PS (2) > foo
4
```

We can use the dir cmdlet to get the command information from the function provider:

```
PS (3) > dir function:foo

CommandType     Name                          Definition
-----------     ----                          ----------
Function        foo                           2+2
```

Let's use Get-Member to get more information about the object that was returned:

```
PS (4) > dir function:foo | gm sc*

   TypeName: System.Management.Automation.FunctionInfo

Name        MemberType Definition
----        ---------- ----------
ScriptBlock Property   System.Management.Automation.ScriptBlo...
```

The object that came back to us was a FunctionInfo object. This is the subclass of CommandInfo that is used to represent a function. As we see, one of the properties on the object is the scriptblock that makes up the body of the function. Let's retrieve that member:

```
PS (5) > (dir function:foo).ScriptBlock
2+2
```

The scriptblock, when displayed as a string, shows the source code for the scriptblock. Another, simpler way to get back the scriptblock that defines a function is to use the variable syntax:

```
PS (6) > $function:foo
2+2
PS (7) > $function:foo.gettype().Fullname
System.Management.Automation.ScriptBlock
```

Now here's the interesting part. Let's change the definition of this function. We can do this simply by assigning a new scriptblock to the function:

```
PS (8) > $function:foo = {"Bye!"}
```

When we run the function again,

```
PS (9) > foo
Bye!
```

we see that it's changed. The `function` keyword is, in effect, shorthand for assigning to a name in the function provider.

Now that we know how to manipulate scriptblocks and functions, let's take this one step further. As we discussed in chapter 1, objects encapsulate data and code. Now that we have a way of manipulating code, we can take the next step and look into building objects.

8.2 BUILDING AND MANIPULATING OBJECTS

Let's switch gears here. Up to this point in the chapter we've been talking about scriptblocks. Now it's time to start talking about objects. Here's why: at their core, as we discussed in chapter 1, objects are a *binding* of data and behaviors. These behaviors are implemented by blocks of code. We needed to know how to build the blocks of code, scriptblocks, before we could talk about building objects. With a good understanding of scriptblocks, we may now discuss manipulating and building objects in PowerShell.

In chapter 2, we talked extensively about types. Now we're concerned with objects; that is, instances of types. A *type* is the pattern or template that describes an object, and an object is an instance of that pattern. In statically typed languages such as C#, once an object is instantiated, its interfaces can't be changed. With dynamic languages such as PowerShell (or Ruby or Python), this isn't true. Dynamic languages allow you to alter the set of members available at runtime. In the rest of this section, we'll cover how to do this in PowerShell. We start with a discussion of how to examine existing members, followed by a look at the types of members available on an object. Then we'll cover the various ways to add members to an object, and finally we'll take a look at the plumbing of the PowerShell type system to give you a sense of the flexibility of the overall system.

8.2.1 Looking at members

An object's interface is defined by the set of public members it exposes. Public members are the public fields, properties, and methods of the class. As always, the easiest way to look at those members is with the `Get-Member` cmdlet. For example, here are the members defined on an integer:

```
PS (1) > 12 | get-member


    TypeName: System.Int32

Name        MemberType Definition
----        ---------- ----------
CompareTo   Method     System.Int32 CompareTo(Int32 value), S...
Equals      Method     System.Boolean Equals(Object obj), Sys...
GetHashCode Method     System.Int32 GetHashCode()
GetType     Method     System.Type GetType()
GetTypeCode Method     System.TypeCode GetTypeCode()
ToString    Method     System.String ToString(), System.Strin...
```

Note that this doesn't show you all of the members on an `[int]`. It only shows you the instance members. You can also use `Get-Member` to look at the static members:

```
PS (2) > 12 | get-member -static

    TypeName: System.Int32

Name            MemberType Definition
----            ---------- ----------
Equals          Method     static System.Boolean Equals(Objec...
Parse           Method     static System.Int32 Parse(String s...
ReferenceEquals Method     static System.Boolean ReferenceEqu...
TryParse        Method     static System.Boolean TryParse(Str...
MaxValue        Property   static System.Int32 MaxValue {get;}
MinValue        Property   static System.Int32 MinValue {get;}
```

We'll use this mechanism to look at the members we'll be adding to objects in the next couple of sections.

8.2.2 Synthetic members

One of the most powerful features in the PowerShell environment is the ability to extend existing object types and instances. This allows PowerShell to perform adaptation across a wide variety of different types of data. By *adaptation*, we mean overlaying a common set of interfaces onto existing data sources. This may be as simple as unifying the name of the property that counts a collection to be the string "count" across all countable objects, or as complex as taking a string containing some XML data and being able to treat that string as an object with a set of properties and attributes.

This isn't the same as subclassing or creating derived types as you would in traditional object-oriented programming languages. In those languages, if you want to extend a new type, you can only do it by creating an entirely new type. In dynamic languages such as PowerShell, you can add members to existing types and objects. This sounds odd from the point of view of a conventional object-oriented language, since types and member definitions are so tightly tied together. In languages such as PowerShell, it's possible to have objects that don't really have any type at all.

AUTHOR'S NOTE If you're a JavaScript user, this won't be surprising. The object-oriented mechanisms in JavaScript use a mechanism called "Prototypes". Prototype-based systems don't have types as discrete objects. Instead you use an object that has the set of members you want to use and use it as the prototype for your new object. While PowerShell is not strictly a prototype-based language, its type extension mechanisms can be used in much the same way.

Since the members we'll be adding to objects aren't natively part of the object's definition, we call them *synthetic members*. Synthetic members are used extensively throughout PowerShell for adaptation and extension. Let's take a look at an example. First we'll examine the synthetic properties on an object returned by `dir` from the filesystem:

```
PS (6) > dir $profile | get-member ps*


    TypeName: System.IO.FileInfo

Name            MemberType   Definition
----            ----------   ----------
PSChildName     NoteProperty System.String PSChildName=Microsof...
PSDrive         NoteProperty System.Management.Automation.PSDri...
PSIsContainer   NoteProperty System.Boolean PSIsContainer=False
PSParentPath    NoteProperty System.String PSParentPath=Microso...
PSPath          NoteProperty System.String PSPath=Microsoft.Pow...
PSProvider      NoteProperty System.Management.Automation.Provi...
```

Now let's get the same information from the registry:

```
PS (8) > dir hklm:\software | get-member ps*


    TypeName: Microsoft.Win32.RegistryKey

Name            MemberType   Definition
----            ----------   ----------
PSChildName     NoteProperty System.String PSChildName=Adobe
PSDrive         NoteProperty System.Management.Automation.PSDri...
PSIsContainer   NoteProperty System.Boolean PSIsContainer=True
PSParentPath    NoteProperty System.String PSParentPath=Microso...
PSPath          NoteProperty System.String PSPath=Microsoft.Pow...
PSProvider      NoteProperty System.Management.Automation.Provi...
```

You can see the same set of PS* properties with the PowerShell (PS) prefix on the object, even though they are completely different types. Take a look at these properties. They allow you to work with these two different objects in the same way. This means that you can always tell if an object might have children by looking at the PSIsContainer property, regardless of the type of the underlying object. And you can always get the path to the object through the PSPath property. We call this type of adaptation *object normalization*. By adding this set of synthetic properties to all objects returned from the provider infrastructure, it becomes possible to write scripts that are independent of the type of object that the provider surfaces. This makes the scripts both simpler and more reusable.

8.2.3   Using Add-Member to extend objects

The Add-Member cmdlet is the easiest way to add a new member to an object instance, either an existing object or a synthetic object. It can be used to add any type of member supported by the PowerShell type system. The list of possible member types that can be added with Add-Member is shown in table 8.1.

We'll work through some examples showing how to use these members. We'll use an instance of the string "Hi there" to do this. For convenience, we'll store it in a variable $s as shown:

```
PS (1) > $s = "Hi there"
```

Table 8.1 Member types that can be added with `Add-Member`

Member Type	Description
AliasProperty	An alias property provides an alternate name for an existing property. For example, if there is an existing Length property then you might alias this to Count.
CodeProperty	A property that maps to a static method on a .NET class.
Property	A *native* property on the object. In other words, a property that exists on the underlying object that is surfaced directly to the user. For example, there might be a native property Length that we choose to also make available through an extended alias member.
NoteProperty	A data-only member on the object (equivalent to a .NET field).
ScriptProperty	A property whose value is determined by a piece of PowerShell script.
Properties	The collection of properties exposed by this object.
PropertySet	A named group of properties.
Method	A native method on the underlying object. For example, the Sub-String() method on the class System.String shows up as a method.
CodeMethod	A method that is mapped to a static method on a .NET class.
ScriptMethod	A method implemented in PowerShell script.
ParameterizedProperty	A property that takes both arguments and a value to assign. This is typically used for things lino indexers and might look like: `$collection.item(?.3) = "hello"` This sets the element at 2,3 in the collection to the value "hello".

Now let's go over each of the interesting member types.

Adding AliasProperty members

The first type of synthetic member we'll add is called an *alias property*. This property allows you to provide a new name for an existing property. Let's work with the length property on a string.

```
PS (2) > $s.length
8
```

As we can see, this string has a length of 8. Let's say that we want to add an alias "size" for length because we'll be working with a set of objects that all have a `size` property.

```
PS (3) > $s = add-member -passthru -in $s aliasproperty size length
```

There are a couple things to note in this example. First (and most important) is that when you first add a synthetic member to an object, you're really creating a new object (but not a new type). This new object wraps the original object in an instance of `System.Management.Automation.PSObject`. Just as `System.Object` is the root of the type system in .NET, `PSObject` is the root of the synthetic type system in PowerShell. For this reason, we assign the result of the `Add-Member` call back to the original variable. To do this, we have to add the -passthru parameter to the command since, by default, the Add-Member cmdlet doesn't emit anything.

Now let's look at the new member we've added using gm (the alias for Get-Member).

```
PS (4) > $s | gm size


    TypeName: System.String

Name MemberType    Definition
---- ----------    ----------
size AliasProperty size = length
```

Again, there are a couple things to note. We can see that the size member is there and is an alias property that maps size to length. Also we need to note that the object's type is still System.String. The fact that it's wrapped in a PSObject is pretty much invisible from the script user's view, though you can test for it as shown in the next example. Using the -is operator, you can test to see whether the object you're dealing with is wrapped in a PSObject or not.

```
PS (5) > $s -is [PSObject]
True
PS (6) > "abc" -is [PSObject]
False
PS (7) > $s -is [string]
True
```

The result of the first command in the example shows that $s does contain a PSObject. The second command shows that the raw string doesn't, and the last line shows that the object in $s is still considered a string, even though it's also a PSObject.

The question now is, after all that explanation, did we actually create this aliased member? The answer is yes:

```
PS (8) > $s.size
8
PS (9) > $s.length
8
```

Both the size and length members return the value 8.

Adding NoteProperty members

Now let's add a note property. A note property is simply a way of attaching a new piece of data (a note) to an existing object, rather like putting a sticky note on your monitor. Again we'll use the same string in $s. Let's add a note property called description. In this example, since we know that $s is already wrapped in a PSObject, we don't need to use -passthru and do the assignment—we simply add the property to the existing object.

```
PS (10) > add-member -in $s noteproperty description "A string"
PS (11) > $s.description
A string
```

We see that we've added a "description" property to the object with the value "A string". And, to prove that this property isn't present on all strings, we do

```
PS (12) > "Hi there".description
PS (13) >
```

and see that the property returned nothing.

Of course, the note property is a settable property, so we can change it with an assignment like any other settable property.

```
PS (14) > $s.description = "A greeting"
PS (15) > $s.description
A greeting
```

In this example, we changed the value in the note property to "A greeting". Note properties allow you to attach arbitrary data to an object. They aren't type constrained, so they can hold any type. Let's set the description property to a [datetime] object:

```
PS (16) > $s.description = get-date
PS (17) > $s.description

Sunday, May 28, 2006 4:24:50 PM
```

But the value stored in the object is still a [datetime] object, not a string. As such, we can get the dayofweek property out of the description property.

```
PS (18) > $s.description.dayofweek
Sunday
PS (19) > $s.description.gettype().fullname
System.DateTime
```

Adding ScriptMethod members

Both of the synthetic members we've added so far have been pure data properties; no code was involved. Now we'll look at adding members that execute code. We'll start with ScriptMethods, since they're easiest. Let's add a method that returns the string that it's associated with, reversed. First let's find an easy way to reverse a string. If we examine [string], we'll see that there is (unfortunately) no reverse method on the string class. There is, however, a static reverse method on [array] that we can use.

```
PS (1) > [array] | gm -static reverse

   TypeName: System.Array

Name     MemberType Definition
----     ---------- ----------
Reverse  Method     static System.Void Reverse(Array array), s...
```

This method takes an array and, since it's void, it must obviously reverse the array in place. This tells us two things: we need to turn the string into an array (of characters) and then save it in a variable so it can be reversed in place. Converting the string to an array of characters is simple—we can just use a cast.

```
PS (19) > $s
Hi there
PS (20) > $a = [char[]] $s
```

Casting a string into the type [char[]] (array of characters) produces a new object that is the array of individual characters in the original string; and just to verify this:

```
PS (21) > $a.gettype().fullname
System.Char[]
PS (22) > "$a"
H i   t h e r e
```

We see that the type of the new object is [char[]] and it does contain the expected characters. Now let's reverse it using the [array]::reverse() static method.

```
PS (23) > [array]::reverse($a)
PS (24) > "$a"
e r e h t   i H
```

When we look at the contents of the array, we see that it has been reversed. But it's still an array of characters. The final step is to turn this back into a string. We could simply cast it or use string interpolation (expansion), but that means that we have to set $OFS to get rid of the extra spaces this would introduce (see chapter 3 for an explanation of this). Instead, we're going to use the static join() method available on the string class.

```
PS (25) > $ns = [string]::join("", $a)
PS (26) > $ns
ereht iH
PS (27) > $ns.gettype().fullname
System.String
```

At this point we have the reversed string in $ns. But the goal of this effort was to attach this as a method to the string object itself. To do so, we need to construct a scriptblock to use as the body of the ScriptMethod. This definition looks like:

```
PS (28) > $sb = {
>>     $a = [char[]] $this
>>     [array]::reverse($a)
>>     [string]::join('',$a)
>> }
>>
```

This example introduces a new "magic" variable which is only defined for script-blocks that are used as methods or properties: the $this variable. $this holds the reference to the object that the scriptmethod member was called from. Now let's bind this scriptblock to the object as a scriptmethod using Add-Member:

```
PS (29) > add-member -in $s scriptmethod Reverse $sb
```

Finally let's try it out:

```
PS (30) > $s.reverse()
ereht iH
```

We get the reversed string as desired.

Adding ScriptProperties members

The next type of member we'll look at is the ScriptProperty. A ScriptProperty has up to two methods associated with it—a getter and (optionally) a setter, just like a .NET property. These methods are expressed using two scriptblocks. As was the case with the ScriptMethod, the referenced object is available in the $this member. And, in the case of the setter, the value being assigned is available in $args[0]. Here's an example. We're going to add a ScriptProperty member "desc" to $s that will provide an alternate way to get at the description NoteProperty we added earlier, with one difference. We're only going to allow values to be assigned that are already strings. An attempt to assign something that isn't a string will result in an error.

Here is the definition of this property:

```
PS (31) > Add-Member -in $s scriptproperty desc `
>>    {$this.description} `
>>    {
>>      $t = $args[0]
>>      if ($t -isnot [string]) {
>>        throw "this property only takes strings"
>>      }
>>      $this.description = $t
>>    }
>>
```

The first scriptblock:

```
{$this.description}
```

is the code that will be executed when getting the property's value. All it does is return the value stored in the description NoteProperty. Since the setter needs to do some additional work, its scriptblock is more complex:

```
{
    $t = $args[0]
    if ($t -isnot [string])
    {
        throw "this property only takes strings"
    }
    $this.description = $t
}
```

First it saves the value to be assigned into a local variable $t. Next it checks whether this variable is of the correct type. If not, it throws an exception, failing the assignment.

Let's try out this property. First let's directly set the note property to the string "Old description".

```
PS (32) > $s.description = "Old description"
```

Now we'll use the ScriptProperty getter to retrieve this value.

```
PS (33) > $s.desc
```

We see that it's changed as expected. Next we'll use the ScriptProperty to change the description.

```
PS (34) > $s.desc = "New description"
```

Verify the change by checking both the NoteProperty directly and the Script-Property.

```
PS (35) > $s.description
New description
PS (36) > $s.desc
New description
PS (37) >
```

Yes, it's been changed. Now let's try assigning a [datetime] object to the property as we did with the description NoteProperty previously.

```
PS (37) > $s.desc = get-date
Exception setting "desc": "this property only takes strings"
At line:1 char:4
+ $s.d <<<< esc = get-date
```

The assignment failed. Using ScriptProperty members is a way to do validation and transformation in properties on objects.

AUTHOR'S NOTE The idea of adding properties to synthetic objects may seem like an academic exercise, but it turns out to be very useful. In particular, it's incredibly useful when we need to adapt existing utilities so that they work effectively in the PowerShell environment. For example, section B.7 shows how to adapt the output of the task scheduler utility "schtasks.exe" so that it can work effectively in the PowerShell environment. Another useful scenario for this technique is joining two collections of data properties into a single object, as illustrated in appendix B.9.

8.2.4 Using the select-object cmdlet

Now that we know all about synthetic members, let's look at some more ways they are used. The Select-Object cmdlet, which is used to select a subset of properties on an object, uses synthetic members to hold these properties.

The Select-Object cmdlet is a way to select elements from a stream of objects. You can select a range of objects:

```
PS (1) > 1..10 | select-object -first 3
1
2
3
```

Here we've selected the first three elements. But much more interesting for this discussion, it's a way to select fields from an object.

```
PS (1) > dir | select-object name,length
```

```
Name                                                    Length
----                                                    ------
a.txt                                                       98
b.txt                                                       42
c.txt                                                      102
d.txt                                                       66
```

At first this looks a lot like Format-Table. Let's use Get-Member to see how different it is:

```
PS (2) > dir | select-object name,length | gm
```

```
    TypeName: System.Management.Automation.PSCustomObject

Name          MemberType    Definition
----          ----------    ----------
Equals        Method        System.Boolean Equals(Object obj)
GetHashCode   Method        System.Int32 GetHashCode()
GetType       Method        System.Type GetType()
ToString      Method        System.String ToString()
Length        NoteProperty  System.Int64 Length=98
Name          NoteProperty  System.String Name=a.txt
```

The first thing we see is that the type of the object is System.Management.Automation.PSCustomObject, which is not a type we've seen before. This is a PowerShell-specific type that is used as the base for pure synthetic objects. We already talked about synthetic members in the previous section. An object whose base is PSCustomObject only has synthetic members and is therefore a synthetic object.

Even though it's a synthetic object, it is still a "first-class" citizen in the Power-Shell environment. We can sort these objects:

```
PS (3) > dir | select-object name,length | sort length
```

```
Name                                                    Length
----                                                    ------
b.txt                                                       42
d.txt                                                       66
a.txt                                                       98
c.txt                                                      102
```

or do anything else that we can do with a regular object. But there's more to this than simply selecting from the existing set of members. For example, say we want to add a new field "minute" to these objects. This will be a calculated field as follows:

```
PS (9) > dir | %{$_.lastwritetime.minute}
55
51
56
54
```

In other words, it will be the minute at which the file was last written. We attach this field by passing a specially constructed hashtable describing the member to Select-Object. This hashtable has to have two members: name and expression (which can be shortened to "n" and "e" for brevity). The name is the name to call the property, and the expression is the scriptblock used to calculate the value of the field. This definition will look like:

```
@{n="minute";e={$_.lastwritetime.minute}}
```

Let's use it in the pipeline:

```
PS (11) > dir | select-object  name,length,
>>  @{n="minute";e={$_.lastwritetime.minute}}
>>

Name                                    Length              minute
----                                    ------              ------
a.txt                                       98                  55
b.txt                                       42                  51
c.txt                                      102                  56
d.txt                                       66                  54
```

As intended, the result has three fields, including the synthetic "minute" property we specified with the hashtable. Using Get-Member to see what the object looks like:

```
PS (12) > dir | select-object  name,length,
>>  @{n="minute";e={$_.lastwritetime.minute}} | gm
>>

    TypeName: System.Management.Automation.PSCustomObject

Name           MemberType   Definition
----           ----------   ----------
Equals         Method       System.Boolean Equals(Object obj)
GetHashCode    Method       System.Int32 GetHashCode()
GetType        Method       System.Type GetType()
ToString       Method       System.String ToString()
Length         NoteProperty System.Int64 Length=98
minute         NoteProperty System.Management.Automation.PSObjec...
Name           NoteProperty System.String Name=a.txt
```

we see that there are now three NoteProperty members on the objects that were output.

Having looked at the "nice" way to add members to objects and build synthetic objects, let's dig into the actual plumbing of the PowerShell type system. In the next section, we'll look at what's happening under the covers.

8.3 A CLOSER LOOK AT THE TYPE-SYSTEM PLUMBING

Earlier in this chapter, we said that the core of the PowerShell type system was the PSObject type. This type is used to wrap other objects, providing adaptation and inspection capabilities, as well as a place to attach synthetic members. We've used Get-Member to explore objects and used the Add-Member and Select-Object cmdlets to extend and create objects. In fact, you can do all of this directly by using the PSObject class itself. And there's one thing you can't do without understanding PSObject: wrapping or shadowing an existing property. In this technique, the synthetic property calls the base property that it's hiding. (Don't worry; this is less esoteric than it sounds. A simple example will clarify what we're talking about here.)

> **AUTHOR'S NOTE**   If you've done much object-oriented programming, this concept is similar to creating an override to a virtual method that calls the overridden method on the base class. The difference here is that it's all instance-based; there is no new type involved.

Let's look at PSObject in more detail. First, let's look at the properties on this object:

```
PS (1) > [psobject].getproperties() | %{$_.name}
Members
Properties
Methods
ImmediateBaseObject
BaseObject
TypeNames
```

From the list, we see some obvious candidates of interest. But how does one get at these members, given that the whole point of PSObject is to be invisible? The answer is that there's a special property attached to all objects in PowerShell called (surprise) PSObject. Let's look at this. First we need a test object to work on. We'll use get-item to retrieve the DirectoryInfo object for the C: drive.

```
PS (2) > $f = get-item c:\
PS (3) > $f


    Directory:


Mode                LastWriteTime     Length Name
----                -------------     ------ ----
d--hs         5/29/2006   3:11 PM            C:\
```

Now let's look at the PSObject member attached to this object.

```
PS (4) > $f.psobject
```

```
Members              : {PSPath, PSParentPath, PSChildName, PSDriv
                        e...}
Properties           : {PSPath, PSParentPath, PSChildName, PSDriv
                        e...}
Methods              : {get_Name, get_Parent, CreateSubdirectory,
                         Create...}
ImmediateBaseObject  : C:\
BaseObject           : C:\
TypeNames            : {System.IO.DirectoryInfo, System.IO.FileSy
                        stemInfo, System.MarshalByRefObject, Syste
                        m.Object}
```

Right away you see a wealth of information: all of the properties we saw on the PSObject type, populated with all kinds of interesting data. First let's look at the TypeNames member:

```
PS (6) > $f.psobject.typenames
System.IO.DirectoryInfo
System.IO.FileSystemInfo
System.MarshalByRefObject
System.Object
```

This member contains the names of all of the types in the inheritance hierarchy for a DirectoryInfo object. (These types are all documented in the .NET class library documentation that is part of the Microsoft Developers Network [MSDN] collection. See http://msdn.microsoft.com for more information.)

We'll look at the Properties member next. This is a collection that contains all of the properties defined by this type. Let's get information about all of the properties that contain the pattern "name":

```
PS (7) > $f.psobject.properties | ?{$_.name -match "name"}
```

```
MemberType      : NoteProperty
IsSettable      : True
IsGettable      : True
Value           : C:\
TypeNameOfValue : System.String
Name            : PSChildName
IsInstance      : True

MemberType      : Property
Value           : C:\
IsSettable      : False
IsGettable      : True
TypeNameOfValue : System.String
Name            : Name
IsInstance      : True
```

```
MemberType       : Property
Value            : C:\
IsSettable       : False
IsGettable       : True
TypeNameOfValue  : System.String
Name             : FullName
IsInstance       : True
```

This returned information on three properties, one NoteProperty PSPath and two base object properties, Name and FullName. Of course, we've seen these properties before; this is the same information that would be returned from Get-Member. In fact, this is exactly what Get-Member does—it uses the PSObject properties to get this information.

8.3.1 Adding a property

Now let's add a new member to this object. We could use Add-Member (and typically we would), but we're talking about the plumbing here so we'll do it the hard way. First we need to create the NoteProperty object that we want to add. We'll do this with the New-Object cmdlet.

```
PS (8) > $np = new-object           `
>> system.management.automation.PSnoteProperty `
>> hi,"Hello there"
>>
```

Next we'll add it to the member collection

```
PS (9) > $f.psobject.members.add($np)
```

and we're done (so it wasn't really that hard after all). The hi member has been added to this object, so let's try it out:

```
PS (10) > $f.hi
Hello there
```

Of course, all of the normal members are still there.

```
PS (11) > $f.name
C:\
```

Let's look at the member in the member collection:

```
PS (12) > $f.psobject.members | ?{$_.name -match "^hi"}

MemberType       : NoteProperty
IsSettable       : True
IsGettable       : True
Value            : Hello there
TypeNameOfValue  : System.String
Name             : hi
IsInstance       : True
```

Notice the `Value` member on the object. Since we can get at the member, we can also set the member:

```
PS (13) > ($f.psobject.members | ?{
>> $_.name -match "^hi"}).value = "Goodbye!"
>>
PS (14) > $f.hi
Goodbye!
```

which is equivalent to setting the property directly on $f:

```
PS (15) > $f.hi = "Hello again!"
PS (16) > $f.psobject.members | ?{$_.name -match "^hi"}
```

```
MemberType      : NoteProperty
IsSettable      : True
IsGettable      : True
Value           : Hello again!
TypeNameOfValue : System.String
Name            : hi
IsInstance      : True
```

Now the `Value` member on the note property is "Hello again!".

8.3.2 Shadowing an existing property

There's one last item we want to cover in our discussion of the plumbing: the mechanism that allows you to bypass the adapted members and lets you get at the raw object underneath. This is accomplished through another special member on PSObject called PSBase. This member allows you to get at the object directly, bypassing all of the synthetic member lookup. It also makes it possible to create a synthetic member to adapt an existing member. We can clarify this with an example. Say I want to change the "Name" property on a `DirectoryInfo` object to always return the name in uppercase. Here's what it looks like unadapted:

```
PS (18) > $f = get-item c:\windows
PS (19) > $f.name
windows
```

To do this I'll create a new `PSProperty` object called `Name` that will "shadow" the existing property.

```
PS (20) > $n=new-object Management.Automation.PSScriptProperty `
>>     name,{$this.psbase.name.ToUpper()}
>>
```

In the body of the scriptblock for this `PSProperty`, we'll use `$this.psbase` to get at the `name` property on the base object (if we just accessed the `name` property directly, we'd be calling ourselves). We apply the `ToUpper()` method on the string returned by name to acquire the desired result. Now add the member to the object's `Members` collection

```
PS (21) > $f.psobject.members.add($n)
```

and try it out.

```
PS (22) > $f.name
WINDOWS
```

When we access the name property on this object, the synthetic member we created gets called instead of the base member, so the name is returned in uppercase. The base object's name property is, of course, unchanged and can be retrieved through psbase.name:

```
PS (23) > $f.psbase.name
windows
PS (24) >
```

While this isn't a technique that you'll typically use on a regular basis, it allows you to do some pretty sophisticated work. You could use it to add validation logic, for example, and prevent a property from being set to an undesired value. You could also use it to log accesses to a property to gather information about how your script or application is being used.

With a solid understanding of the plumbing, let's take the pieces and look at how they can be used to extend the PowerShell language.

8.4   EXTENDING THE POWERSHELL LANGUAGE

In the previous section, we learned how to add members to existing objects one at a time, but sometimes you'll want to construct new types rather than extend the existing types. In this section, we'll cover how to do that and also how to use scripting techniques to "add" the ability to create objects to the PowerShell language.

8.4.1   Little languages

The idea of "little languages", i.e., small domain-specific languages, has been around for a long time. This was one of the powerful ideas that made the UNIX environment so attractive. Many of the tools that were the roots for today's dynamic languages came from this environment.

Of course, in effect, all programs are essentially an exercise in building their own languages. You create the nouns (objects) and verbs (methods or functions) in this language. These patterns are true for all languages that support data abstraction. Dynamic languages go further because they allow you to extend how the nouns, verbs, and modifiers are composed in the language. For example, in a language such as C#, it would be difficult to add a new looping construct. In PowerShell, this is minor. To illustrate how easy it is, let's define a new looping keyword called loop. This construct will repeat the body of the loop for the number of times the first argument specifies. We can add this keyword by defining a function that takes a number and scriptblock. Here's the definition:

```
PS (1) > function loop ([int] $i, [scriptblock] $b) {
>> while ($i-- -gt 0) { . $b }
>> }
>>
```

Here we try it out:

```
PS (2) > loop 3 { "Hello world" }
Hello world
Hello world
Hello world
PS (3) >
```

In a few lines of code, we've added a new flow control statement to the PowerShell language that looks pretty much like any of the existing flow control statements.

We can apply this technique to creating language elements that allow you to define your own custom types. Let's add some "class" to PowerShell!

8.4.2 Adding a CustomClass keyword to PowerShell

We shall use the technique from the previous section to extend the PowerShell language to allow us to define our own custom classes. First we'll gather our requirements. We want the syntax for defining a class to look fairly natural (at least for PowerShell). Here's what we want a class definition to look like:

```
CustomClass point {
    note x 0
    note y 0
    method ToString { "($($this.x), $($this.y))"}
    method scale {
        $this.x *= $args[0]
        $this.y *= $args[0]
    }
}
```

Once we've defined this custom class, we want to be able to use it as follows. First we can create a new instance of the point class:

```
$p = new point
```

then set the x and y members on this class to particular values:

```
$p.x=2
$p.y=3
```

and finally call the ToString() method to display the class.

```
$p.tostring()
```

This would give us a natural way to define a class in PowerShell. Now let's look at how to implement these requirements.

We'll put the code for this script in a file called class.ps1. Let's go over the contents of that script a piece at a time.

First we need a place to store the types we're defining. We need to use a global variable for this, since we want it to persist for the duration of the session. We'll give it a name that is unlikely to collide with other variables (we'll put two underscores at each end to help ensure this) and initialize it to an empty hashtable.

```
$global:__ClassTable__ = @{}
```

Next, we define the function needed to create an instance of one of the classes we'll create. This function will take only one argument: the scriptblock that creates an instance of this class. This function will invoke the scriptblock provided to it. This scriptblock is expected to return a collection of synthetic member objects. The function will then take these members and attach them to the object being created. This is a helper function that also has to be global, so again we'll give it a name that is unlikely to collide with other global functions.

```
function global:__new_instance ([scriptblock] $definition)
{
```

At this point we define some local functions to use in the body of the __new_instance function. First we'll define a helper method for generating error messages.

```
function elementSyntax ($msg)
{
    throw "class element syntax: $msg"
}
```

In the example, we had "keywords" for each of the member types we could add. We'll implement this by defining functions that implement these keywords. Because of the way dynamic scoping works (see chapter 7), these functions will be visible to the scriptblock when it's invoked, because they're defined in the enclosing dynamic scope.

First, let's define the function for creating a note element in the class. This implements the note keyword in the class definition. It takes the name of the note and the value to assign to it and returns a PSNoteProperty object to the caller.

```
function note ([string]$name, $value)
{
    if (! $name) {
        elementSyntax "note name <value>"
    }
    new-object management.automation.PSNoteProperty `
        $name,$value
}
```

Next, define the function that implements the method keyword. This function takes the method name and scriptblock that will be the body of the method and returns a PSScriptMethod object.

```
function method ([string]$name, [scriptblock] $script)
{
    if (! $name) {
        elementSyntax "method name <value>"
    }
    new-object management.automation.PSScriptMethod `
        $name,$script
}
```

We could continue to define keyword functions for all of the other member types, but to keep it simple, we'll stick with just these two.

Having defined our keyword functions, we can look at the code that actually builds the object. First we need to create an empty PSObject with no methods or properties.

```
$object = new-object Management.Automation.PSObject
```

Next, execute the scriptblock that defines the body of this class. As mentioned previously, the result of that execution will be the set of members to attach to the new object we're creating.

```
$members = &$definition
```

Finally, attach the members to the object:

```
foreach ($member in $properties) {
    if (! $member) {
        write-error "bad member $member"
    } else {
            $object.psobject.members.Add($member)
    }

}
```

The last thing to do is return the constructed object.

```
    $object
}
```

As mentioned, the __new_instance function was a worker function; the user never calls it directly. Now we'll define the function that the user employs to define a new class. Again, this has to be a global function; but this time, since the user calls it, we'll give it a conventional name.

```
function global:CustomClass
{
```

This function takes the name of the class and the scriptblock to execute to produce the members that will be attached to that class.

```
    param ([string] $type, [scriptblock] $definition)
```

If there is already a class defined by the name that the user passed, throw an error.

```
    if ($global:__ClassTable__[$type]) {
        throw "type $type is already defined"
    }
```

At this point, we'll execute the scriptblock to build an instance of the type that will be discarded. We do this to catch any errors in the definition at the time the class is defined, instead of the first time the class is used. It's not strictly necessary to do this, but it will help you catch any errors sooner rather than later.

```
    __new_instance $definition > $null
```

Finally, add the class to the hashtable of class definitions:

```
    $global:__ClassTable__[$type] = $definition
}
```

and we're finished implementing the class keyword. Next we have to define the new keyword. This turns out to be a simple function. The new keyword takes the name of the class you want to create an instance of, looks up the scriptblock to execute, and calls __new_instance to build the object.

```
function global:new ([string] $type)
{
    $definition = $__ClassTable__[$type]
    if (! $definition) {
        throw "$type is undefined"
    }
    __new_instance $definition

}
```

Finally, we'll add one last helper function that will allow us to remove a class definition from the hashtable.

```
function remove-class ([string] $type)
{
    $__ClassTable__.remove($type)
}
```

This then is the end of the class.ps1 script.

We should try it out with the point example we looked at at the beginning of this section. First we have to run the script containing the code to set up all of the definitions. (Since we explicitly defined things to be global in the script, there's no need to "dot" this script.)

```
PS (1) > ./class
```

Now define the point class

```
PS (2) > CustomClass point {
>>      note x 0
>>      note y 0
>>      method ToString { "($($this.x), $($this.y))"}
```

```
>>      method scale {
>>          $this.x *= $args[0]
>>          $this.y *= $args[0]
>>      }
>> }
>>
```

Next create an instance of this class:

```
PS (3) > $p = new point
```

Use Get-Member to look at the members on the object that was created:

```
PS (4) > $p | gm


    TypeName: System.Management.Automation.PSCustomObject

Name         MemberType   Definition
----         ----------   ----------
Equals       Method       System.Boolean Equals(Object obj)
GetHashCode  Method       System.Int32 GetHashCode()
GetType      Method       System.Type GetType()
x            NoteProperty System.Int32 x=0
y            NoteProperty System.Int32 y=0
scale        ScriptMethod System.Object scale();
ToString     ScriptMethod System.Object ToString();
```

We see the actual type of the object is PSCustomType—the type that PowerShell uses for pure synthetic objects. You can also see the members we defined in the class definition: the two NoteProperties x and y and the two methods scale() and ToString(). To try them out, we'll first call ToString():

```
PS (5) > $p.tostring()
(0, 0)
```

We see the default values for the note members, formatted as intended. Next, set the note members to new values:

```
PS (6) > $p.x=2
PS (7) > $p.y=3
```

Verify that they've been set:

```
PS (8) > $p.tostring()
(2, 3)
```

Now call the scale() method to multiply each note member by a scale value.

```
PS (9) > $p.scale(3)
```

And again, verify the values of the note members with ToString().

```
PS (10) > $p.tostring()
(6, 9)
```

The values have been scaled.

Finally, to see how well this all works, let's use this object with the format operator and we see that our `ToString()` method is properly called.

```
PS (11) > "The point p is {0}" -f $p
The point p is (6, 9)
```

So, in less than a hundred lines of PowerShell script, we've added a new "keyword" that lets you define you own classes in PowerShell. Obviously, this isn't a full-featured type definition system; it doesn't have any form of inheritance, for example. But it does illustrate how you can use scriptblocks along with dynamic scoping to build new language features in PowerShell in a sophisticated way.

Now let's change gears a bit to talk about types.

8.5   TYPE EXTENSION

You might have noticed that all of the examples we've shown so far involve adding members to *instances*. But what about adding members to types? Having to explicitly add members to every object we encounter would be pretty tedious, no matter how clever we were. We really need some way to extend types. Of course, PowerShell also let's you do this. In this section, we'll introduce the mechanisms that PowerShell provides which let you extend types.

Type extension is performed in PowerShell through a set of XML configuration files. These files are usually loaded at startup time; however, they can be extended after the shell has started. In this section, we'll show you how you can take advantage of these features.

Let's look at an example. Consider an array of numbers. It's fairly common to sum up a collection of numbers; unfortunately, there's no `Sum()` method on the `Array` class.

```
PS (1) > (1,2,3,4).sum()
Method invocation failed because [System.Object[]] doesn't conta
in a method named 'sum'.
At line:1 char:14
+ (1,2,3,4).sum( <<<< )
```

Using the techniques we've discussed previously, we could add such a method to this array:

```
PS (3) > $a = add-member -pass -in $a scriptmethod sum {
>> $r=0
>> foreach ($e in $this) {$r += $e}
>> $r
>> }
>>
```

and finally use it:

```
PS (4) > $a.sum()
10
```

But this would be painful to do for every instance of an array. What we really need is a way to attach new members to a type, rather than through an instance. PowerShell does this through type configuration files. These configuration files are stored in the installation directory for PowerShell and loaded at startup. The installation directory path for PowerShell is stored in the $PSHome variable, so it's easy to find these files. They have the word "type" in their names and have an extension .ps1xml:

```
PS (5) > dir $pshome/*type*.ps1xml


    Directory: Microsoft.PowerShell.Core\FileSystem::C:\Program
    Files\Windows PowerShell\v1.0


Mode                LastWriteTime     Length Name
----                -------------     ------ ----
-a---        4/19/2006   4:12 PM       50998 DotNetTypes.Format.
                                             ps1xml
-a---        4/19/2006   4:12 PM      117064 types.ps1xml
```

We don't want to update the default installed types files because when we install updates for PowerShell, they will likely be overwritten and our changes will be lost. What we want to do here is create our own custom types file containing the specification of the new member for System.Array. Once we've created the file, we can use the Update-TypeData cmdlet to load it.

Here's the definition for the Sum() method extension we want to add to System.Array.

```
<Types>
  <Type>
      <Name>System.Array</Name>
      <Members>
          <ScriptMethod>
              <Name>Sum</Name>
              <Script>
                  $r=$null
                  foreach ($e in $this) {$r += $e}
                  $r
              </Script>
          </ScriptMethod>
      </Members>
  </Type>
</Types>
```

This definition is saved to a file called SumMethod.ps1xml. Now let's load the file and update the type system definitions:

```
PS (9) > update-typedata SumMethod.ps1xml
```

If the file loaded successfully, you won't see any output. We can now try out the sum() function:

```
PS (10) > (1,2,3,4,5).sum()
15
```

It worked. And, because of the way the script was written, it will work on any type that can be added. So let's add some strings:

```
PS (11) > ("abc","def","ghi").sum()
abcdefghi
```

You can even use it to add hashtables:

```
PS (12) > (@{a=1},@{b=2},@{c=3}).sum()

Name                           Value
----                           -----
a                              1
b                              2
c                              3
```

We can see that the result is the composition of all three of the original hashtables. We can even use it to put a string back together. Here's the "hal" to "ibm" example from chapter 3, this time using the Sum() method:

```
PS (13) > ([char[]] "hal" | %{[char]([int]$_+1)}).sum()
ibm
```

Here we break the original string into an array of characters, add 1 to each character, and then use the Sum() method to add them all back into a string.

You should take some time to examine the set of type configuration files that are part of the default PowerShell installation. Examining these files is a good way to see what that can be accomplished using these tools. In the meantime, let's move on to the final section in this chapter—building code at runtime.

8.6   BUILDING CODE AT RUNTIME

Scriptblocks can be passed around, invoked, and assigned at runtime, but the body of these blocks is still defined at compile time. This final section covers how PowerShell provides for compiling scriptblocks and executing code at runtime. Compiling may seem like a funny word, but that's essentially what creating a scriptblock is: a piece of script is compiled into an executable object. In addition, PowerShell provides a mechanism for directly executing a string without first building a scriptblock. This is done with the Invoke-Expression cmdlet—the first thing we'll talk about.

8.6.1   The Invoke-Expression cmdlet

The Invoke-Expression cmdet is a way to execute an arbitrary string as a piece of code. It takes the string, compiles it, and then immediately executes it in the current scope. Here's an example:

```
PS (1) > invoke-expression '$a=2+2; $a'
4
```

In this example, the script passed to the cmdlet assigned the result of 2+2 to $a, and wrote $a to the output stream. Since this expression was evaluated in the current context, it should also have affected the value of $a in the global scope.

```
PS (2) > $a
4
```

We see that it did. Let's invoke another expression.

```
PS (3) > invoke-expression '$a++'
PS (4) > $a
5
```

Evaluating this expression changes the value of $a to 5.

There are no real limits on what you can evaluate with Invoke-Expression. It can take any arbitrary piece of script code. Here's an example where we build up a string with several statements in it and execute it:

```
PS (5) > $expr = '$a=10;'
PS (6) > $expr += 'while ($a--) { $a }'
PS (7) > $expr += '"A is now $a"'
PS (8) > [string](invoke-expression $expr)
9 8 7 6 5 4 3 2 1 0 A is now -1
```

The first three commands in this example build up a string to execute. The first line initializes the variable $a, the second adds a while loop that decrements and outputs $a, and the final line outputs a string telling us the final value of $a. Note the double quoting in the last script fragment. Without the nested double quotes, it would try to execute the first word in the string instead of emitting the whole string.

8.6.2 The ExecutionContext variable

One of the predefined variables (also called *automatic variables*) provided by the PowerShell engine is $ExecutionContext. This variable is another way to get at various facilities provided by the PowerShell engine. It's intended to mimic the interfaces available to the cmdlet author. The services that matter most to us in this chapter are those provided through the InvokeCommand member. Let's look at the methods this member surfaces:

```
PS (1) > $ExecutionContext.InvokeCommand | gm

   TypeName: System.Management.Automation.CommandInvocationIntri
nsics

Name          MemberType Definition
----          ---------- ----------
Equals        Method     System.Boolean Equals(Object obj)
ExpandString  Method     System.String ExpandString(String s...
GetHashCode   Method     System.Int32 GetHashCode()
GetType       Method     System.Type GetType()
```

```
InvokeScript    Method      System.Collections.ObjectModel.Coll...
NewScriptBlock  Method      System.Management.Automation.Script...
ToString        Method      System.String ToString()
```

The interesting methods in this list are `ExpandString()`, `InvokeScript()`, and `NewScriptBlock()`. These methods are covered in the next few sections.

The ExpandString() method

The `ExpandString()` method lets you perform the same kind of variable interpolation that the PowerShell runtime does in scripts. Here's an example. First we set $a to a known quantity:

```
PS (2) > $a = 13
```

Next we create a variable $str that will display the value of $a.

```
PS (3) > $str='a is $a'
```

Since the variable was assigned using single-quotes, no string expansion took place. We verify this by displaying the string:

```
PS (4) > $str
a is $a
```

Now call the `ExpandString()` method, passing in $str:

```
PS (5) > $ExecutionContext.InvokeCommand.ExpandString($str)
a is 13
```

and it returns the string with the variable expanded into its value.

The InvokeScript() method

The next method to look at is `InvokeScript()`. This method does the same thing that the `Invoke-Expression` cmdlet does. It takes its argument and evaluates it like a script. Call this method passing in the string "2+2"

```
PS (7) > $ExecutionContext.InvokeCommand.InvokeScript("2+2")
4
```

and it will return 4.

The NewScriptBlock() method

The final method to look at is the `NewScriptBlock()` method. Like `Invoke-Script()`, this method takes a string, but instead of executing it, it returns a script-block object that represents the compiled script. Let's use this method to turn the string `'1..4 | foreach {$_ * 2}'` into a scriptblock.

```
PS (8) > $sb = $ExecutionContext.InvokeCommand.NewScriptBlock(
>> '1..4 | foreach {$_ * 2}')
>>
```

We saved this scriptblock into a variable, so let's look at it. Since the `ToString()` on a scriptblock is the code of the scriptblock, we just see the code that makes up the body of the scriptblock.

```
PS (9) > $sb
1..4 | foreach {$_ * 2}
```

Now let's execute the scriptblock using the "&" call operator.

```
PS (10) > & $sb
2
4
6
8
```

The scriptblock executed, printing out the even numbers from 4 to 8.

AUTHOR'S NOTE   Many people have asked why we (the PowerShell team) don't allow you to simply cast a string to a scriptblock. The reason is that we want to make the system resilient against code injection attacks. We want to minimize the number of places where executable code can be injected into the system, and we particularly want code creation to be an explicit act. Casts are more easily hidden, leading to accidental code injections, especially when the system may prompt for a string. We don't want those user-provided strings to be converted into code without some kind of check. See chapter 13 for more extensive discussions about security.

8.6.3   Creating functions using the function: drive

The final way to create a scriptblock is actually a side-effect of creating elements in the function drive. Earlier we saw that you can create a named function by assigning a scriptbock to a name in the function drive:

```
PS (1) > $function:foo = {"Hello there"}
PS (2) > foo
Hello there
```

You could also use the `New-Item` cmdlet to do this:

```
PS (3) > new-item function:foo -value {"Hi!"}
New-Item : The item at path 'foo' already exists.
At line:1 char:9
+ new-item <<<< function:foo -value {"Hi!"}
```

We received an error because the function already exists, so let's use the `-force` parameter to overwrite the existing definition:

```
PS (4) > new-item function:foo -value {"Hi!"} -force

CommandType     Name                    Definition
-----------     ----                    ----------
Function        foo                     "Hi!"
```

New-Item returns the item created, so we can see that the function has been changed. But that's using scriptblocks. What happens if we pass in strings? The interpreter will compile these strings into scriptblocks and then assign the scriptblock to the name. Here's an example where the body of the function is determined by the expanded string.

```
PS (5) > $x=5
PS (6) > $y=6
PS (7) > $function:foo = "$x*$y"
PS (8) > foo
30
PS (9) > $function:foo
5*6
```

The variables $x and $y expanded into the numbers 5 and 6 in the string, so the resulting scriptblock was

```
{5*6}
```

Now let's define another function using foo, but adding some more text to the function.

```
PS (10) > new-item function:bar -value "$function:foo*3"
```

```
CommandType     Name                   Definition
-----------     ----                   ----------
Function        bar                    5*6*3
```

```
PS (11) > bar
90
```

In the expanded string, $function:foo expanded into "5*6" so the new function bar was assigned a scriptblock

```
{5*6*3}
```

This concludes our survey of ways to build new code at runtime in PowerShell. There are even more ways to build code using .NET's Reflection.Emit classes. We'll cover those techniques in chapter 11. For now, though, we've covered everything about metaprogramming in PowerShell.

8.7   SUMMARY

In chapter 8, we covered advanced topics in programming and metaprogramming with PowerShell. Although many of the techniques covered in the chapter are quite advanced, used appropriately they can significantly improve your productivity as a scripter. We'll also see in later chapters how language elements such as scriptblocks make graphical programming in PowerShell easy and elegant. In this chapter you learned to:

- To use powerful metaprogramming techniques to essentially "crack open" the PowerShell runtime. This allows you to extend the runtime with new keywords and control structures. You can directly add properties and methods to objects in PowerShell; this is useful because you can adapt or extend objects logically in specific problem domains.

- Units of PowerShell code, including the content of scripts and functions and the code you type in a PowerShell session, are actually scriptblocks. Properties and methods are added to objects as script property/method blocks. Scriptblocks don't necessarily need to be named, and can be used in many situations, including as the content of variables. But in all cases, they have the same set of features.

- While scriptblocks are the key to all of the metaprogramming features in Power-Shell, they're also an "everyday" feature that users work with all the time when they use the `Foreach-Object` and `Where-Object` cmdlets.

- To use the call operator `&` to invoke commands indirectly; that is, by reference rather than by name (since a scriptblock is just a reference). This also works with the `CommandInfo` objects returned from `Get-Command`.

- To use scriptblocks along with the `PSObject` and `PSCustomObject` classes to build new objects and extend existing object instances.

- When using the `Update-TypeData` cmdlet, you can load type configuration files which allow you to extend a type instead of a single instance of that type.

- To use the "little language" technique to extend the PowerShell language to add new language elements such as keywords and control structures.

- To employ a variety of techniques for compiling and executing code at runtime. You can use the `Invoke-Expression` cmdlet or engine invocation intrinsics on the `$ExecutionContext` variable.

CHAPTER 9

Errors, exceptions, and script debugging

Progress, far from consisting in change, depends on retentiveness.
Those who cannot remember the past are condemned to repeat it.

—George Santayana, *The Life of Reason*

Big Julie: I had the numbers taken off for luck, but I remember where
the spots formerly were.

—*Guys and Dolls*, words and music by Frank Loesser

It's important to keep in mind that PowerShell is not "just" a shell or scripting language. Its primary purpose is to be an automation tool for managing Microsoft Windows. And when you're depending on a script to perform some critical management task on a server, such as to send software updates, inspect log files for intrusion attempts, or provision user accounts, you want to be sure that either the task is completed properly or the reason for failure is appropriately recorded.

In this chapter, we're going to focus on the latter topic: how PowerShell reports, records, and manages error conditions. This is one of the areas that really makes PowerShell stand out from other scripting tools. The support for diagnostic tracing and logging is practically unprecedented in traditional scripting languages. Unfortunately, these features don't come entirely free—there are costs in terms of complexity and execution overhead that just aren't there in other languages. All these capabilities are very much a part of PowerShell as a management tool; we've set a higher bar for PowerShell than has been set for most other language environments.

We'll begin with the error objects themselves. Errors in PowerShell are not simply error codes, strings, or even exceptions as found in languages such as C# and VB.Net. They are *rich* objects that include just about everything we could think of that might be useful in debugging a problem.

<table>
<tr><td>AUTHOR'S
NOTE</td><td>Some people dislike (okay, despise) the use of the word "rich" in this context. However, given the wealth of information that PowerShell error objects contain, rich really is the right word. So I'm going to use it several more times. So there.</td></tr>
</table>

In this chapter, we're going to examine these `ErrorRecord` objects in detail, along with how they're used by the various PowerShell mechanisms to manage error conditions. We're also going to look at the other mechanisms that are available for solving script execution problems, including tracing and script debugging. Even though this is a long chapter with a good deal of information, it can't cover everything. The main goal is to cover in detail the features that are most likely to affect the day-to-day user and make you aware of the other resources that exist.

9.1   ERROR HANDLING

Error handling in PowerShell is very structured. As we said previously, errors are not simply bits of text written to the screen. PowerShell errors are rich objects that contain a wealth of information about where the error occurred and why. There is one aspect to error handling in PowerShell that is unique: the notion of terminating and non-terminating errors. This aspect is a consequence of the streaming model PowerShell uses in processing objects. Here's a simple example that will help you understand this concept. Think about how removing a list of files from your system should work. You stream this list of files to the cmdlet that will delete the files. Imagine that you can't delete all the files on the list for various reasons. Do you want the command to stop processing as soon as it hits the first element in the list? The answer is probably "No." You'd like the cmdlet to do as much work as it can, but capture any errors so that you can look at them later. This is the concept of a *non-terminating error*—the error is recorded and the operation continues. On the other hand, there are times when you do want an operation to stop on the first error. These are called *terminating errors*. Of course, sometimes you want an error to be terminating in one situation and non-terminating in another. PowerShell provides mechanisms to allow you to do this.

Since the architecture supports multiple non-terminating errors being generated by a pipeline, it can't just throw or return an error. This is where streaming comes into play; non-terminating errors are simply written to the error stream. By default, these errors are displayed, but there are a number of other ways of working with them. In the next few sections, we'll look at those mechanisms. But first we need to take at look at the error records themselves.

9.1.1 ErrorRecords and the error stream

As we delve into the topic of error handling, we'll first take a look at capturing error records in a file using redirection, and then learn how to capture error messages in a variable. Let's start with getting hold of an error record. Error records are written to the output stream, which by default is simply displayed.

```
PS (1) > dir nosuchfile
Get-ChildItem : Cannot find path 'C:\files\nosuchfile' because i
t does not exist.
At line:1 char:4
+ dir  <<<< nosuchfile
```

Using the redirection operators we talked about in chapter 5, we can change this. We could redirect the error messages to a file:

```
PS (2) > dir nosuchfile 2> err.txt
```

but this has the downside that the error message is rendered to displayable text before writing it to the file. When that happens, we lose all that extra richness in the objects. Take a look at what was saved to the file.

```
PS (3) > Get-Content err.txt
Get-ChildItem : Cannot find path 'C:\files\nosuchfile' because i
t does not exist.
At line:1 char:4
+ dir  <<<< nosuchfile 2> err.txt
```

The error text is there as it would have been displayed on the console, but we've lost all of the elements of the object that haven't been displayed. And this lost information may be critical to diagnosing the problem. We need a better way to capture this information. The first mechanism we'll look at is capturing the error record by using the stream merge operator 2>&1, and then assigning the result to a variable.

```
PS (4) > $err = dir nosuchfile 2>&1
```

Now use Get-Member to display the properties on the object. We'll use the -type parameter on Get-Member to filter the display and only show the properties. (In order to be concise, we'll use the gm alias instead of the full cmdlet name.)

```
PS (5) > $err | gm -type property


    TypeName: System.Management.Automation.ErrorRecord

Name                     MemberType Definition
----                     ---------- ----------
CategoryInfo             Property   System.Management.Automation...
ErrorDetails             Property   System.Management.Automation...
Exception                Property   System.Exception Exception {...
FullyQualifiedErrorId    Property   System.String FullyQualified...
InvocationInfo           Property   System.Management.Automation...
TargetObject             Property   System.Object TargetObject {...
```

Although this shows you all of the properties and their definitions, some of the property names are a little tricky to figure out, so further explanation is in order. Table 9.1 lists all of the properties, their types, and a description of what the property is.

Table 9.1 `ErrorRecord` **properties and their descriptions**

Name	Type	Description
CategoryInfo	ErrorCategoryInfo	This string breaks errors into a number of broad categories.
ErrorDetails	ErrorDetails	This may be null. If present, ErrorDetails can specify additional information, most importantly ErrorDetails.Message, which (if present) is a more exact description and should be displayed instead of Exception.Message.
Exception	System.Exception	This is the underlying .NET exception corresponding to the error that occurred.
FullyQualifiedErrorId	System.String	This identifies the error condition more specifically than either the ErrorCategory or the Exception. Use FullyQualifiedErrorId to filter highly specific error conditions.
InvocationInfo	System.Management.Automation.InvocationInfo	This is an object that contains information about where the error occurred—typically the script name and line number.
TargetObject	System.Object	This is the object that was being operated on when the error occurred. It may be null, as not all errors will set this field.

Let's look at the content of the properties for this error:

```
PS (10) > $err | fl * -force

Exception                : System.Management.Automation.ItemNotFoun
                           dException: Cannot find path 'C:\files\n
                           osuchfile' because it does not exist.
                               at System.Management.Automation.Sessi
                           onStateInternal.GetChildItems(String pat
```

```
                        h, Boolean recurse, CmdletProviderContex
                        t context)
                           at System.Management.Automation.Child
                        ItemCmdletProviderIntrinsics.Get(String
                        path, Boolean recurse, CmdletProviderCon
                        text context)
                           at Microsoft.PowerShell.Commands.GetC
                        hildItemCommand.ProcessRecord()
TargetObject            : C:\files\nosuchfile
CategoryInfo            : ObjectNotFound: (C:\files\nosuchfile:Str
                        ing) [Get-ChildItem], ItemNotFoundExcept
                        ion
FullyQualifiedErrorId   : PathNotFound,Microsoft.PowerShell.Comman
                        ds.GetChildItemCommand
ErrorDetails            :
InvocationInfo          : System.Management.Automation.InvocationI
                        Nfo
```

In this output, you can see the exception that caused the error was `ItemNotFound-Exception`. The `TargetObject` member contains the full path the cmdlet used to locate the item. This overall error is placed in the broader category of `ObjectNotFound`. There are no additional error details for this object.

Let's take a closer look at the `InvocationInfo` member. This member provides information about where the error occurred. Here's what it looks like:

```
PS (6) > $err.InvocationInfo

MyCommand          : Get-ChildItem
ScriptLineNumber   : 1
OffsetInLine       : 11
ScriptName         :
Line               : $err = dir nosuchfile 2>&1
PositionMessage    :
                     At line:1 char:11
                     + $err = dir  <<<< nosuchfile 2>&1
InvocationName     : dir
PipelineLength     : 1
PipelinePosition   : 1
```

Since we entered this command on the command line, the script name is empty and the script line is 1. The offset is the offset in the script line where the error occurred. There is also other information available, such as the number of commands in the pipeline that caused an error, as well as the index of this command in the pipeline. This message also includes the line of script text where the error occurred. Finally, there is the `PositionMessage` member. This member takes all of the other information and formats it into what you see in PowerShell errors.

Clearly, there is a lot of information in these objects that can help you figure out where and why an error occurred. The trick is to make sure that we have the right error objects available at the right time. It simply isn't possible to record every error that occurs as it would take up too much space and be impossible to manage. If we limit the set of error objects that are preserved, we want to make sure that we keep those we care about. Obviously, having the wrong error objects doesn't help. Sometimes we're interested only in certain types of errors or only in errors from specific parts of a script. To address these requirements, PowerShell provides a rich set of tools for capturing and managing errors. The next few sections cover these tools and the techniques for using them.

9.1.2 The $error variable and –ErrorVariable parameter

The point of rich error objects is that you can examine them after the error has occurred and possibly take remedial action. Of course, to do this, you have to capture them first. In the previous section, we looked at how we can do this by redirecting the error stream, but the problem with doing so is that you have to think of it beforehand. Since you don't know when errors occur, in practice you'd have to do it all the time. Fortunately, PowerShell performs some of this work for you. There is a special variable $error that contains a collection of the errors that occurred. This is maintained as a circular bounded buffer. As new errors occur, old ones are discarded. The number of errors that are retained is controlled by the $MaximumErrorCount variable. The collection in $error is an array (technically an instance of System.Collections.ArrayList) that buffers errors as they occur. The most recent error is always stored in $error[0].

> **AUTHOR'S NOTE** While it's tempting to think that you could just set $MaximumErrorCount to some very large value and never have to worry about capturing errors, in practice this is not a good idea. Rich error objects also imply fairly large error objects. If you set $MaximumErrorCount to too large a value, you won't have any memory left. In practice, there usually is no reason to set it to anything larger than the default, though you may want to set it to something smaller if you want to make more space available for other things.

Let's explore using the $error variable. We'll start with the same error as before.

```
PS (1) > dir nosuchfile
Get-ChildItem : Cannot find path 'C:\working\book\nosuchfile' be
cause it does not exist.
At line:1 char:4
+ dir  <<<< nosuchfile
```

We didn't explicitly capture it, but it is available in $error[0]

```
PS (2) > $error[0]
Get-ChildItem : Cannot find path 'C:\working\book\nosuchfile' be
cause it does not exist.
At line:1 char:4
+ dir  <<<< nosuchfile
```

with all of the error properties. For example, here is the exception object:

```
PS (3) > $error[0].exception
Cannot find path 'C:\working\book\nosuchfile' because it does no
t exist.
```

and here's the target object that caused the error:

```
PS (4) > $error[0].targetobject
C:\working\book\nosuchfile
```

Now let's do something that will cause a second error.

```
PS (5) > 1/$null
Attempted to divide by zero.
At line:1 char:3
+ 1/$ <<<< null
```

Here we have a division by zero error.

<table>
<tr><td>AUTHOR'S
NOTE</td><td>The example here uses 1/$null. The reason for doing this instead of simply 1/0 is because the PowerShell interpreter does something called constant expression folding. It looks at expressions that contain only constant values. When it sees one, it evaluates that expression once at compile time so it doesn't have to waste time doing it again at runtime. This means that impossible expressions, such as division by zero, are caught and treated as parsing errors. Parsing errors can't be caught and don't get logged when they're entered interactively, so they don't make for a good example. (If one script calls another script and that script has one of these errors, the calling script can catch it, but the script being parsed cannot.)</td></tr>
</table>

Let's verify that the second error is in $error[0]. We'll do so by looking at the exception member

```
PS (6) > $error[0].exception
Attempted to divide by zero.
```

Yes, it is. We'll also verify that the previous error, the file not found error, is now in position 1.

```
PS (7) > $error[1].exception
Cannot find path 'C:\working\book\nosuchfile' because it does no
t exist.
```

Again, yes it is. As you can see, each new error shuffles the previous error down one element in the array. The key lesson to take away from this is that when you are going to try to diagnose an error, you should copy it to a "working" variable so it doesn't get accidentally shifted out from under you because you made a mistake in one of the commands you're using to examine the error.

The $error variable is a convenient way to capture errors automatically, but there are two problems with it. First, as we discussed earlier, it only captures a limited number of errors. The second problem is that it mixes all of the errors from all commands together in one collection. The first problem can be worked around using redirection to capture all the errors, but that still doesn't address mixing all the errors together. To deal with this second issue when you want to capture all the errors from a specific command, you use a standard parameter on all commands called -ErrorVariable. This parameter names a variable to use for capturing all the errors that the command generates. Here's an example. This command generates three error objects, since the files "nofuss", "nomuss", and "nobother" don't exist.

```
PS (1) > dir nofuss,nomuss,nobother -ErrorVariable errs
Get-ChildItem : Cannot find path 'C:\Documents and Settings\bruc
epay\nofuss' because it does not exist.
At line:1 char:4
+ dir  <<<< nofuss,nomuss,nobother -ErrorVariable errs
Get-ChildItem : Cannot find path 'C:\Documents and Settings\bruc
epay\nomuss' because it does not exist.
At line:1 char:4
+ dir  <<<< nofuss,nomuss,nobother -ErrorVariable errs
Get-ChildItem : Cannot find path 'C:\Documents and Settings\bruc
epay\nobother' because it does not exist.
At line:1 char:4
+ dir  <<<< nofuss,nomuss,nobother -ErrorVariable errs
```

In the command, we specified the name of the error variable to place these records into: "errs".

<table>
<tr><td>**AUTHOR'S NOTE**</td><td>In this example, the argument to -ErrorVariable is specified as a string with no leading $. If it had instead been written as $errs then the errors would have been stored in the variable *named* by the value in $errs, not $errs itself. Also note that the -ErrorVariable parameter works like a *tee*; i.e., the objects are captured in the variable, but they are also streamed to the error output. In a later section, we'll look at ways to suppress the output of error objects altogether.</td></tr>
</table>

Let's verify that the errors were actually captured. First, the number of elements in $err should be three.

```
PS (2) > $errs.count
3
```

It is. Now let's dump the errors themselves.

```
PS (3) > $errs
Get-ChildItem : Cannot find path 'C:\Documents and Settings\bruc
epay\nofuss' because it does not exist.
At line:1 char:4
+ dir  <<<< nofuss,nomuss,nobother -ErrorVariable errs
Get-ChildItem : Cannot find path 'C:\Documents and Settings\bruc
epay\nomuss' because it does not exist.
At line:1 char:4
+ dir  <<<< nofuss,nomuss,nobother -ErrorVariable errs
Get-ChildItem : Cannot find path 'C:\Documents and Settings\bruc
epay\nobother' because it does not exist.
At line:1 char:4
+ dir  <<<< nofuss,nomuss,nobother -ErrorVariable errs
```

They do, in fact, match the original error output.

They should match the original output because they are actually the same error objects. The -ev parameter captures references to each object written to the error stream. In effect, the same object is in two places at once. Well, three if you count the default $error variable.

Since there is no need to actually see the object twice, you can use redirection to discard the written objects and save only the references stored in the specified variable. Let's rerun the example this way.

```
PS (4) > dir nofuss,nomuss,nobother -ErrorVariable errs 2>$null
```

This time nothing was displayed; let's verify the error count:

```
PS (5) > $errs.count
3
```

It's three again, as intended. Let's just check the TargetObject member of the last error object to verify that it's the file name "nobother".

```
PS (6) > $errs[0].TargetObject
C:\Documents and Settings\brucepay\nofuss
PS (7) >
```

Yes, it is. This example illustrates a more sophisticated way of capturing error objects than merely displaying them. In section 9.1.5, we'll see an even more flexible way to control how errors are redirected.

All of these mechanisms provide useful tools for handling collections of error objects, but sometimes all you care about is that an error occurred at all. A couple of additional status variables, $? and $LASTEXITCODE, enable you to determine whether an error occurred.

9.1.3 The $? and $LASTEXITCODE variables

Displaying errors is very useful; it lets the user know what happened. But scripts also need to know when an error has occurred. To do this, a script can check the status of the variable $?. This is a Boolean variable that holds the execution status of the last variable.

The use of the $? variable is borrowed from the UNIX shells (but we promised to return it folded and pressed, so try not to get it dirty).

The $? variable will be true if the entire operation succeeded, and false otherwise. If any of the operations generated an error object, then $? will be set to false. This is an important point. It means that a script can determine whether an error occurred even if the error is not displayed. Here are some examples showing the use of $?. We'll call Get-Item, passing in two item names that we know exist and one we know doesn't exist.

```
PS (1) > get-item c:,nosuchfile,c:


    Directory:


Mode                LastWriteTime     Length Name
----                -------------     ------ ----
d--hs         6/13/2006  10:12 PM            C:\
Get-Item : Cannot find path 'C:\nosuchfile' because it does not
exist.
At line:1 char:9
+ get-item <<<< c:,nosuchfile,c:
d--hs         6/13/2006  10:12 PM            C:\
```

We got the expected error.

```
PS (2) > $?
False
```

And $? is false. Now let's try the same command, but this time specify only the names of items that exist.

```
PS (3) > get-item c:,c:


    Directory:


Mode                LastWriteTime     Length Name
----                -------------     ------ ----
d--hs         6/13/2006  10:12 PM            C:\
d--hs         6/13/2006  10:12 PM            C:\


PS (4) > $?
True
```

This time, there are no errors and $? is true.

Where the $? variable only indicates success or failure, $LASTEXITCODE contains the exit code of the last command run. This, however, only applies to two types of commands: native or external commands and PowerShell scripts.

On Windows, when a process exits, it can return a single integer as its exit code. This integer is used to encode a variety of different conditions, but the only one we're interested in is whether it's zero or non-zero. This is a convention that is used by almost all programs. If they were successful then their exit code is zero. If they encountered an error then the exit code will be non-zero. PowerShell captures this exit code in $LASTEXITCODE, and if that value is non-zero then it sets $? to false. Let's use cmd.exe to demonstrate this. You can tell cmd.exe to execute a single command by passing it the /c option along with the text of the command. In this example, the command we want to run is exit, which takes a value to use as the exit code for the command:

```
PS (1) > cmd /c exit 0
```

We told cmd.exe to exit with code 0. Verify this by checking the values of $LAST-EXITCODE and $?, respectively.

```
PS (2) > $LASTEXITCODE
0
PS (3) > $?
True
```

As expected, the exit code was zero, and consequently $? is true. Next try it with a non-zero value.

```
PS (4) > cmd /c exit 1
PS (5) > $LASTEXITCODE
1
PS (6) > $?
False
```

This time, the exit code is 1, so $? is set to false. We can do the same exercises with scripts. First create a script that exits with a zero exit code.

```
PS (7) > "exit 0" > invoke-exit.ps1
PS (8) > ./invoke-exit
PS (9) > $LASTEXITCODE
0
PS (10) > $?
True
```

$LASTEXITCODE is 0 and $? is true. Now try it with a non-zero value.

```
PS (11) > "exit 25" > invoke-exit.ps1
PS (12) > ./invoke-exit
PS (13) > $LASTEXITCODE
25
PS (14) > $?
False
```

Now $LASTEXITCODE contains the value the script exited with, which is 25, and $? is set to false.

So far, we've looked at how to capture errors and how to detect when they occurred. Next we'll look at some of the methods PowerShell provides to control what actually happens when an error is generated.

9.1.4 $ErrorActionPreference and the -ErrorAction parameter

Earlier, we talked about the differences between terminating and non-terminating errors. Sometimes you want to be able to turn non-terminating errors into terminating ones because the operation you're performing is too critical to tolerate non-terminating errors. For example, imagine you're setting up a website for a user. You want to reuse a directory that had been previously used for someone else. First you want to remove all the old files and then install the new user's files. Obviously, you can't start installing the new files until all the old ones are deleted. In this situation, the failure to delete a file, which is normally a non-terminating error, must now be treated as a terminating error. The next step in the process can't begin until the current step is 100 percent complete.

The way to control whether errors are terminating or non-terminating is by setting the *error action preference*. This is a mechanism that allows you to control the behavior of the system when an error occurs. There are three possible settings for this preference: `continue`, `silentlycontinue`, and `stop`. These preferences are described in table 9.2.

Table 9.2   The supported values for `ErrorActionPreference`

Preference	Identifier	Description
Continue	"continue"	This is the default preference setting. The error object is written to the output pipe and added to $error, and $? is set to false. Execution then continues at the next script line.
Silently Continue	"silentlycontinue"	When this action preference is set, the error message is not written to the output pipe before continuing execution. Note that it is still added to $error and $? is still set to false. Again, execution continues at the next line.
Stop	"stop"	This error action preference changes an error from a non-terminating error to a terminating error. The error object is thrown as an exception instead of being written to the output pipe. $error and $? are still updated. Execution does not continue.

There are two ways to set the error action preference: by setting the variable `$Error-ActionPreference` as in

```
$ErrorActionPreference = "silentlycontinue"
```

or by using the `-erroraction` (or `-ea`) parameter that is available on all cmdlets.

Let's see some examples of these preferences in action. Here's a simple one. First we'll run a command that has some non-terminating errors. We'll use the `Get-Item` cmdlet to get two items that exist and two items that don't exist.

```
PS (1) > get-item c:\,nosuchfile,c:\,nosuchfile

    Directory:


Mode                LastWriteTime     Length Name
----                -------------     ------ ----
d--hs          6/13/2006   10:12 PM          C:\
Get-Item : Cannot find path 'C:\Documents and Settings\brucepay\
nosuchfile' because it does not exist.
At line:1 char:9
+ get-item  <<<< c:\,nosuchfile,c:\,nosuchfile
d--hs          6/13/2006   10:12 PM          C:\
Get-Item : Cannot find path 'C:\Documents and Settings\brucepay\
nosuchfile' because it does not exist.
At line:1 char:9
+ get-item  <<<< c:\,nosuchfile,c:\,nosuchfile
```

CHAPTER 9   *ERRORS, EXCEPTIONS, AND SCRIPT DEBUGGING*

If you look at the output, you can see that there are two output objects and two error messages. We can use redirection to discard the error messages, making the code easier to read.

```
PS (2) > get-item c:\,nosuchfile,c:\,nosuchfile 2> $null


    Directory:


Mode                LastWriteTime     Length Name
----                -------------     ------ ----
d--hs         6/13/2006  10:12 PM            C:\
d--hs         6/13/2006  10:12 PM            C:\
```

Now we just see the output objects because we've sent the error objects to $null. We can use the -erroraction parameter to do the same.

```
PS (3) > get-item c:\,nosuchfile,c:\,nosuchfile `
>> -ea silentlycontinue
>>

    Directory:


Mode                LastWriteTime     Length Name
----                -------------     ------ ----
d--hs         6/13/2006  10:12 PM            C:\
d--hs         6/13/2006  10:12 PM            C:\
```

Again, the error messages aren't displayed, but this time it's because they aren't being written at all instead of written and discarded. Finally, let's try the "stop" preference.

```
PS (4) > get-item c:\,nosuchfile,c:\,nosuchfile `
>> -ea stop
>>

    Directory:


Mode                LastWriteTime     Length Name
----                -------------     ------ ----
d--hs         6/13/2006  10:12 PM            C:\
Get-Item : Command execution stopped because the shell variable
"ErrorActionPreference" is set to Stop: Cannot find path 'C:\Doc
uments and Settings\brucepay\nosuchfile' because it does not exi
st.
At line:1 char:9
+ get-item  <<<< c:\,nosuchfile,c:\,nosuchfile `
```

This time, you only see one output message and one error message—the first one. This is because the error is treated as a terminating error and execution stops. Note that the error message contains additional text explaining that execution stopped because of the error action preference setting.

Of course, the -erroraction parameter controls the error behavior for exactly one cmdlet. If you want to change the behavior for an entire script or even a whole session, you do this by setting the $ErrorActionPreference variable. Let's redo the last example, but use the variable instead of the parameter.

```
PS (5) > & {
>> $ErrorActionPreference="stop"
>> get-item c:\,nosuchfile,c:\,nosuchfile
>> }
>>

    Directory:

Mode              LastWriteTime     Length Name
----              -------------     ------ ----
d--hs         6/13/2006  10:12 PM          C:\
Get-Item : Command execution stopped because the shell variable
"ErrorActionPreference" is set to Stop: Cannot find path 'C:\Doc
uments and Settings\brucepay\nosuchfile' because it does not exi
st.
At line:3 char:9
+ get-item  <<<< c:\,nosuchfile,c:\,nosuchfile
```

Again, the cmdlet stops at the first error instead of continuing.

AUTHOR'S NOTE In this example, note the use of the call operator '&' with a scriptblock containing the scope for the preference setting. Using the pattern

```
& {
        ... script code...
}
```

you can execute fragments of script code so that any variables set in the script are discarded at the end of the scriptblock. Because setting $Error-ActionPreference has such a profound effect on the execution of the script, we're using this technique to isolate the preference setting.

Through the -erroractionpreference parameter and the $ErrorAction-Preference variable, the script author has fine control over when errors are written and when they are terminating. Non-terminating errors can be displayed or discarded at will. But what about terminating errors? How does the script author deal with them? Sometimes you only want an error to terminate part of an operation. For example, you might have a script move a set of files using a series of steps for each move. If one of the steps fails, you want the overall move operation to terminate for that file, but you want to continue processing the rest of the files. To do this, you need a way to trap these terminating errors or exceptions, and that's what we'll discuss next.

9.2 DEALING WITH ERRORS THAT TERMINATE EXECUTION

This section will deal with the way that PowerShell deals with errors that terminate the current flow of execution, also called *terminating errors*. Here we'll cover the language elements for dealing with terminating errors and how you can apply these features. You're probably familiar with terminating errors when they are called by their more conventional name—*exceptions*. So call them what you will; we're going to delve into catching these terminating errors. In other words, how can you grab these errors and take corrective or remedial actions instead of simply giving up and quitting?

9.2.1 The trap statement

Exceptions are caught using the `trap` statement. This is a statement that can appear anywhere in a block of code. When an exception (terminating error) occurs that is not otherwise handled, control will be transferred to the body of the `trap` statement. The body of the `trap` statement is then executed. The `trap` statement syntax is shown in figure 9.1.

You can optionally specify the type of exception to catch; for example, division by zero. If no exception is specified then it will trap all exceptions.

Here's an example:

```
PS (1) > trap { "Got it!" } 1/$null
Got it!
Attempted to divide by zero.
At line:1 char:30
+ trap { "Got it!" ; break } 1/$ <<<< zero
```

In this example, the statement

```
1/$null
```

was executed. `$null` is treated like zero in integer expressions, causing a division-by-zero exception to occur. When this happens, control transfers to the statement list in the body of the `trap` statement. In this case, it just writes "Got it!" which we see in the output. We also see that the error message is still displayed, even though we

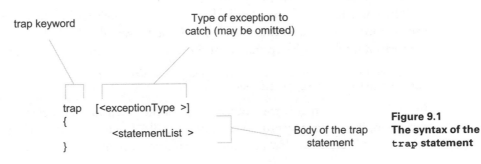

Figure 9.1
The syntax of the
`trap` statement

trapped this exception. This is a significant point. What happens after a trap handler is complete depends on how the statement terminates. If the body of the statement simply exits normally then an error object will be written to the error stream, and, depending on the setting of $ErrorActionPreference, either the exception will be rethrown or execution will continue at the statement after the statement that caused the exception. This is what we saw in the previous example. To make this point clearer, let's add another statement after the one that caused the error:

```
PS (2) > trap { "Got it!" } 1/$zero; "LAST"
Got it!
Attempted to divide by zero.
At line:1 char:22
+ trap { "Got it!" } 1/$ <<<< zero; "LAST"
LAST
```

We see the error message; but following it, we see output from the last statement. The interpreter's behavior after you leave the trap handler can be controlled by the break and continue keywords. (See chapter 6 for other uses of these keywords.) Let's look at break first. Here's the example again, but this time we'll terminate the trap block with break.

```
PS (3) > trap { "Got it!"; break  } 1/$zero; "LAST"
Got it!
Attempted to divide by zero.
At line:1 char:30
+ trap { "Got it!"; break  } 1/$ <<<< zero; "LAST"
```

We see the error record, but we don't see the output "LAST" because after the trap block exited, the error was rethrown as a terminating error instead of resuming execution. The other modification to the trap flow control is to use the continue statement.

```
PS (4) > trap { "Got it!"; continue  } 1/$zero; "LAST"
Got it!
LAST
```

This time, we see the see the output from the trap block and from the "LAST" statement, but no error record. Exiting a trap block is approximately equivalent to the error action preference "silently continue".

There is one other feature available in the trap block itself. The exception that was trapped is available in the trap block in the $_ variable. Here's the example, but with the output of the trap statement showing the value in $_ as a string.

```
PS (5) > trap { "Got it: $_"; continue  } 1/$zero;
Got it: Attempted to divide by zero.
```

In this case, the output is the ToString() of the exception. However, $_ is not an exception; it's an error record, so the trap handler has full access to all of the information in the error handler. Let's verify the type of this object.

```
PS (6) > trap { "Got it: " + $_.gettype(); continue  } 1/$zero;
Got it: System.Management.Automation.ErrorRecord
```

In the `trap` block in this example, we're displaying the type of the value in $_.

Let's look at a somewhat more complex example. We said earlier that control transfers to the next statement after the one that caused the exception. That's not quite true. It transfers to the next statement in the same scope as the `trap` statement. In this example, we'll use scriptblocks to create the two scopes.

```
PS (7) > &{
>> trap {"TRAP"}
```

Here's the trap block in the outer scope.

```
>> &{
```

Now create an inner scope that will emit a number of strings.

```
>> "one"
>> "two"
>> 1/$null
```

Part of the way through, throw an exception.

```
>> "three"
>> "four"
>> }
>> "OUTERBLOCK"
```

Back in the output block, write out the string "OUTERBLOCK" so we'll see what's happening.

```
>> }
>>
one
two
TRAP
Attempted to divide by zero.
At line:6 char:3
+ 1/$ <<<< null
OUTERBLOCK
```

Look at the output that was produced. You can see the first couple of numbers printed and then the exception, but look where execution resumed—at the first statement outside the block. This pattern allows you to skip entire sections of code instead of a single line. It essentially mimics the try/catch pattern found in other languages such as C#.

Having mastered catching exceptions, let's look at how to throw our own.

9.2.2 The throw statement

To complete the error-handing story, we need a way to generate terminating errors or exceptions. This is accomplished by using the throw statement.

AUTHOR'S NOTE   In the original design, "throw" was supposed to be a cmdlet rather than a keyword in the language. This was less successful than we would have liked. Having a cmdlet throw the exception meant that the thrown exception was subject to the cmdlet's error action policy, and the whole point of throw was to bypass this policy and always generate an exception. It wasn't so much a case of the tail wagging the dog as it was staple-gunning the poor beast to the floor. And so, learning from our mistakes, we made it into a keyword.

The syntax of the throw statement is shown in figure 9.2.

The simplest example is to throw nothing:

```
PS (8) > throw
ScriptHalted
At line:1 char:5
+ throw <<<<
```

This is convenient for casual scripting. We didn't need to create an error object or exception object—the throw statement takes care of all of this. Unfortunately, the message you get isn't very informative. If you want to include a meaningful message, you can easily provide your own:

```
PS (9) > throw "My Message!"
My Message!
At line:1 char:6
+ throw  <<<< "My Message!"
```

We see the message in the output. It's also possible to use throw to throw Error-Record objects or .NET exceptions if you want to use more detailed error handling. Instead of passing a string, you pass these objects instead.

Now let's revisit the multi-scope catch and use throw this time instead of dividing by $null.

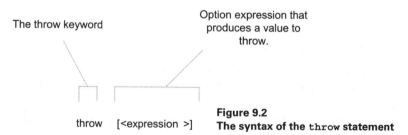

The throw keyword

Option expression that produces a value to throw.

throw   [<expression >]

Figure 9.2
The syntax of the throw statement

```
PS (10) > &{
>> trap { "$_" ; continue}
>> &{
>> "one"
>> "two"
>> throw "CATCH"
>> "three"
>> }
>> "ALL DONE"
>> }
>>
one
two
CATCH
ALL DONE
```

The pattern is the same as in the previous case, except that now we throw a specific message that appears in the output. This is then followed by the output from the next statement in the outer scope.

There are other important applications of the trap statement in function definitions. For instance, times when you want to make a function parameter mandatory. The throw statement provides an efficient way to do this. Take a look at the following function definition.

```
PS (11) > function hi ($name=$(throw '$name is required'))
>> { "Hi $name" }
>>
```

In this example, we're using the throw statement in a subexpression as the initializer for $name. As you will remember from chapter 7, the initializer expression is executed if no value was provided on the command line. Let's try this function out, first with a value for name:

```
PS (12) > hi Bob
Hi Bob
```

We receive the expected greeting. Next try it without a value.

```
PS (13) > hi
$name is required
At line:1 char:27
+ function hi ($name=$(throw  <<<< '$name is required'))
PS (14) >
```

We get a terminating error telling us we need to provide a value for $name. This is a simple pattern that can be used to enforce mandatory parameters on functions and scripts. And speaking of functions and scripts, while all these error features are great for letting us know something is wrong, how do we go about fixing the problem? This is our cue to segue into our next section: debugging.

9.3   SCRIPT DEBUGGING

This section covers the various tools and techniques for debugging PowerShell scripts. We'll cover ways you can add a debugging message to your script, the built-in debugging capabilities in the interpreter, and the novel low-level tracing capabilities that are available through the `Trace-Command` cmdlet.

9.3.1   Debugging with the host APIs

The most basic form of debugging a script is simply to put statements in your script that display information about the execution of the script. Since you don't want your debugging output mixed into the rest of the output, you need mechanisms to display output directly on the console. You do this either by using the `Write-Host` cmdlet or by using what are called the *host APIs*. These APIs are available through the `$host` variable. This object has the following members:

```
PS (1) > $host

Name            : ConsoleHost
Version         : 1.0.10568.0
InstanceId      : 5c685c70-c950-4ce5-9aae-78331e4091a7
UI              : System.Management.Automation.Internal.Host.In
                  ternalHostUserInterface
CurrentCulture  : en-US
CurrentUICulture : en-US
PrivateData     :
```

The information available from `$host` includes the name of the host, its version, and so forth. The member that we're most interested in is the `UI` member. This member surfaces a number of methods that can be used to write messages directly to the host instead of the error stream. The ones we're most interested in are the read and write methods:

```
PS (2) > $host.ui | gm [rw]*line*


   TypeName: System.Management.Automation.Internal.Host.Internal
HostUserInterface

Name                     MemberType Definition
----                     ---------- ----------
ReadLine                 Method     System.String ReadLine()
ReadLineAsSecureString   Method     System.Security.SecureStrin...
WriteDebugLine           Method     System.Void WriteDebugLine(...
WriteErrorLine           Method     System.Void WriteErrorLine(...
WriteLine                Method     System.Void WriteLine(), Sy...
WriteVerboseLine         Method     System.Void WriteVerboseLin...
WriteWarningLine         Method     System.Void WriteWarningLin...
```

For example, if you want to write out a text message, you can do:

```
PS (3) > $host.ui.writeline("Hi there")
Hi there
```

to print out a simple string. Or you can use a more complex form of this method

```
PS (4) > $host.ui.writeline("red","green", "Hi there")
Hi there
```

to print out a string in color. You can also get input from the user. To read a line from the console, use the `ReadLine()` method:

```
PS (6) > $host.ui.readline()
Hi
Hi
```

There is a second level of host UI available called RawUI. This provides even more low-level functions for accessing the console. For example, to read a single key from the console, you can do

```
PS (7) > $host.ui.rawui.readkey()
g
  VirtualKeyCode      Character ControlKeyState         KeyDown
  --------------      --------- ---------------         -------
            71              g                 0            True
```

This returns information about the key code and other attributes of the key press instead of simply the character.

The other way to access the host interfaces is through the `Read-Host` and `Write-Host` cmdlets. These cmdlets do approximately the same thing as the host methods, but can be a bit easier to use. In particular, the `Read-Host` cmdlet allows you to specify a prompt when reading:

```
PS (8) > read-host "Enter some text"
Enter some text: some text
some text
```

It even inserts a colon after your text when prompting.

Using the features described in this section, you can instrument your scripts in order to debug their behavior. While this is a tried and true way of debugging, PowerShell provides some tools that are a bit more, shall we say, modern? It's worth it to take a look at these features.

9.3.2 The Set-PSDebug cmdlet

PowerShell provides some built-in debugging capabilities. These are available through the `Set-PSDebug` cmdlet. This cmdlet allows you to turn on tracing and stepping, and also enable a form of "strict-mode". The syntax for this command is shown in figure 9.3.

The details of each of these features are covered in the following sections.

9.3.3 Tracing statement execution

Basic script tracing is turned on by setting as follows:

```
PS (1) > Set-PSDebug -trace 1
```

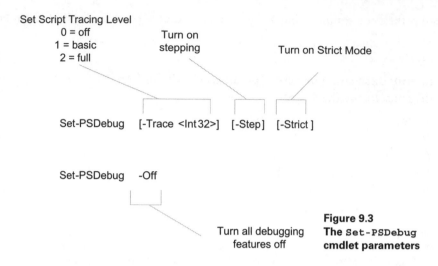

Set Script Tracing Level
0 = off
1 = basic
2 = full

Turn on stepping

Turn on Strict Mode

Set-PSDebug [-Trace <Int32>] [-Step] [-Strict]

Set-PSDebug -Off

Turn all debugging features off

**Figure 9.3
The** Set-PSDebug **cmdlet parameters**

In this trace mode, each statement executed by the interpreter will be displayed on the console as shown.

```
PS (2) > 2+2
DEBUG:    1+ 2+2
4
PS (3) > $a=3
DEBUG:    1+ $a=3
PS (4) > pwd
DEBUG:    1+ pwd

Path
----
C:\files
```

The debugging output is prefixed with the DEBUG: tag and is typically shown in a different color than normal text. Note that the entire script line is displayed. This means that if you have a loop all on one line, you'll see the line repeated:

```
PS (5) > foreach ($i in 1..3) {"i is $i"}
DEBUG:    1+ foreach ($i in 1..3) {"i is $i"}
DEBUG:    1+ foreach ($i in 1..3) {"i is $i"}
i is 1
DEBUG:    1+ foreach ($i in 1..3) {"i is $i"}
i is 2
DEBUG:    1+ foreach ($i in 1..3) {"i is $i"}
i is 3
```

In this example, you'll see the line repeated four times: once for evaluating the expression 1..3 in the foreach loop and then once for each iteration of the loop, for a total of four times. This is a good reason, even though PowerShell doesn't require it, to write scripts with one statement per line. It can help with debugging.

Basic tracing doesn't show you any function calls or scripts you're executing. First, define a function foo:

```
PS (6) > function foo {"`$args is " + $args}
DEBUG:    1+ function foo {"`$args is " + $args}
```

And run it in a loop:

```
PS (7) > foreach ($i in 1..3) {foo $i}
DEBUG:    1+ foreach ($i in 1..3) {foo $i}
DEBUG:    1+ foreach ($i in 1..3) {foo $i}
DEBUG:    1+ function foo {"`$args is " + $args}
$args is 1
DEBUG:    1+ foreach ($i in 1..3) {foo $i}
DEBUG:    1+ function foo {"`$args is " + $args}
$args is 2
DEBUG:    1+ foreach ($i in 1..3) {foo $i}
DEBUG:    1+ function foo {"`$args is " + $args}
$args is 3
```

You can see the line that's being executed, but you can't see the actual function call. Here we'll turn on full tracing.

```
PS (8) > Set-PSDebug -trace 2
DEBUG:    1+ Set-PSDebug -trace 2
```

In this mode, you will see the function calls:

```
PS (9) > foreach ($i in 1..3) {foo $i}
DEBUG:    1+ foreach ($i in 1..3) {foo $i}
DEBUG:    1+ foreach ($i in 1..3) {foo $i}
DEBUG:     ! CALL function 'foo'
DEBUG:    1+ function foo {"`$args is " + $args}
$args is 1
DEBUG:    1+ foreach ($i in 1..3) {foo $i}
DEBUG:     ! CALL function 'foo'
DEBUG:    1+ function foo {"`$args is " + $args}
$args is 2
DEBUG:    1+ foreach ($i in 1..3) {foo $i}
DEBUG:     ! CALL function 'foo'
DEBUG:    1+ function foo {"`$args is " + $args}
$args is 3
```

In addition to this, full tracing adds to the display by showing you variable assignments. Let's redefine our function so that it performs a variable assignment. We'll split it across multiple lines so the trace is a bit clearer:

```
PS (10) > function foo {
>> $x = $args[0]
>> "x is $x"
>> }
>>
DEBUG:    1+ function foo {
```

And run it again.

```
PS (11) > foreach ($i in 1..3) {foo $i}
DEBUG:    1+ foreach ($i in 1..3) {foo $i}
DEBUG:    1+ foreach ($i in 1..3) {foo $i}
DEBUG:     ! CALL function 'foo'
DEBUG:    2+ $x = $args[0]
DEBUG:     ! SET $x = '1'.
DEBUG:    3+ "x is $x"
}
x is 1
DEBUG:    1+ foreach ($i in 1..3) {foo $i}
DEBUG:     ! CALL function 'foo'
DEBUG:    2+ $x = $args[0]
DEBUG:     ! SET $x = '2'.
DEBUG:    3+ "x is $x"
}
x is 2
DEBUG:    1+ foreach ($i in 1..3) {foo $i}
DEBUG:     ! CALL function 'foo'
DEBUG:    2+ $x = $args[0]
DEBUG:     ! SET $x = '3'.
DEBUG:    3+ "x is $x"
}
x is 3
```

You can see that for each iteration in the loop, tracing shows the

- Loop iteration
- Function call
- Statement doing the assignment
- Actual assignment to $x including the value assigned
- Statement that emits the value

The value displayed is the string representation of the object being assigned, truncated to fit in the display. It depends on the ToString() method defined for that object to decide what to display. This isn't always as useful as one would like. For example, with the hashtable:

```
PS (12) > $a = @{x=1; y=2}
DEBUG:    1+ $a = @{x=1; y=2}
DEBUG:     ! SET $a = 'System.Collections.Hashtable'.
```

It shows you the type of the object, but nothing about its actual value. For arrays and other collections, it shows you a truncated representation of the elements of the list. So, for an array of one hundred numbers, you see:

```
PS (13) > $a = 1..100
DEBUG:    1+ $a = 1..100
DEBUG:     ! SET $a = '1 2 3 4 5 6 7 8 9 10 11 12 13 14 15 16 17
 18 19 20 21 22 23...'.
```

Overall, script tracing is pretty effective, but sometimes you still need to add calls to Write-Host to your script to help with debugging.

9.3.4 Stepping through statement execution

The next debugging feature we'll look at is the mechanism that PowerShell provides for stepping through a script. You turn stepping on by calling the Set-PSDebug cmdlet with the -step parameter.

```
PS (14) > Set-PSDebug -step
DEBUG:    1+ Set-PSDebug -step
```

Rerun the foreach loop and take a look at the prompt that's displayed:

```
PS (15) > foreach ($i in 1..3) {foo $i}

Continue with this operation?
   1+ foreach ($i in 1..3) {foo $i}
[Y] Yes  [A] Yes to All  [N] No  [L] No to All  [S] Suspend
[?] Help(default is "Y"): y
DEBUG:    1+ foreach ($i in 1..3) {foo $i}

Continue with this operation?
   1+ foreach ($i in 1..3) {foo $i}
[Y] Yes  [A] Yes to All  [N] No  [L] No to All  [S] Suspend
[?] Help(default is "Y"): y
DEBUG:    1+ foreach ($i in 1..3) {foo $i}
DEBUG:     ! CALL function 'foo'

Continue with this operation?
```

The interpreter displays the line to be executed, then asks the user to select one of Yes, Yes to All, No, or No to All. The default is "Yes".

If you answer "Yes", then that line will be executed and you will be prompted as to whether you want to execute the next line. If you answer "Yes to All", then step mode will be turned off and execution will continue normally. If you answer either "No" or "No to All", the current execution will be stopped and you will be returned to the command prompt. There is no difference in the behavior between "No" and "No to All". The following shows the message you will see if you enter "No".

```
Continue with this operation?
   2+ $x = $args[0]
[Y] Yes  [A] Yes to All  [N] No  [L] No to All  [S] Suspend
[?] Help(default is "Y"): y
DEBUG:    2+ $x = $args[0]
DEBUG:     ! SET $x = '2'.

Continue with this operation?
   3+ "x is $x"
}
[Y] Yes  [A] Yes to All  [N] No  [L] No to All  [S] Suspend
```

```
[?] Help(default is "Y"): 1
WriteDebug stopped because the DebugPreference was 'Stop'.
At line:1 char:23
+ foreach ($i in 1..3) {f <<<< oo $i}
PS (16) >
```

AUTHOR'S NOTE As you can see, this is a pretty limited feature. Full debugging was cut from version one of PowerShell. We were only able to provide the most basic features. This will be corrected in future releases. We didn't even get a chance to make what's there pretty. It is, however, still useful.

There is one more option in the stepping list that we haven't talked about yet, and that is "Suspend". This option is interesting enough to merit its own section, and is discussed in section 9.4. In the meantime, let's finish our discussion of the Set-PSDebug debugging features.

9.3.5 Catching undefined variables with strict mode

The last debugging feature accessible through Set-PSDebug is "strict mode".

AUTHOR'S NOTE This feature is conceptually similar to "Option Explicit" in Visual Basic or strict mode in PERL, and is named after the PERL feature, though it's not as rigorous as either the VB or PERL features. Still, it can make it easier to write a robust script.

Normally in PowerShell, if a variable is undefined, it's treated as though it has the value $null. We can try this in an expression.

```
PS (1) > 2 * $nosuchvariable
0
```

In this expression, $nosuchvariable is not defined. This means that it is treated as though it were $null. And $null in a numeric expression is treated as zero, so the whole expression evaluates to zero. It is important to note that the variable is treated as though it were null. This doesn't mean that there is now a variable called $nosuchvariable. We can verify this with the dir command:

```
PS (2) > dir variable:\nosuchvariable
Get-ChildItem : Cannot find path 'nosuchvariable' because it doe
s not exist.
At line:1 char:4
+ dir  <<<< variable:\nosuchvariable
```

Now turn on strict mode

```
PS (3) > Set-PSDebug -strict
```

and try the expression again:

```
PS (4) > 2 * $nosuchvariable
The variable $nosuchvariable cannot be retrieved because it has
not been set yet.
At line:1 char:19
+ 2 * $nosuchvariable <<<<
```

This time, you are sent an error telling you that the variable has not been defined. So let's define it.

```
PS (5) > $nosuchvariable=13
```

Run the expression again:

```
PS (6) > 2 * $nosuchvariable
26
```

We get the expected result. Delete the variable:

```
PS (7) > del variable:\nosuchvariable
```

and run the expression for a third time.

```
PS (8) > 2 * $nosuchvariable
The variable $nosuchvariable cannot be retrieved because it has
not been set yet.
At line:1 char:19
+ 2 * $nosuchvariable <<<<
```

We're back to the error message.

9.4 NESTED PROMPTS AND BREAKPOINTS

One of the more interesting aspects of dynamic language environments is that a script can recursively call the interpreter. We've already seen this with the Invoke-Expression cmdlet in chapter 8. A variation of this is to call the interpreter in interactive mode. This means that you essentially suspend the current session and start a new session. In other words, you can suspend the currently executing Power-Shell code and interact with PowerShell at what is called a *nested prompt*. Why is this interesting? Because now you can type commands that can examine and modify the state of the suspended session. And instead of creating a language just for debugger operations, you use the same language you're debugging. There are a couple ways to enter a nested prompt session, as we'll see in the next couple sections.

9.4.1 Suspending a script while in step-mode

Creating a nested interactive session is what the "Suspend" operation does. Let's try it out. First turn on stepping:

```
PS (1) > Set-PSDebug -step
```

then run a statement that should loop 10 times, printing out the numbers from 1 to 10:

```
PS (2) > $i=0; while ($i++ -lt 10) { $i }

Continue with this operation?
   1+ $i=0; while ($i++ -lt 10) { $i }
[Y] Yes  [A] Yes to All  [N] No  [L] No to All  [S] Suspend
[?] Help(default is "Y"):
DEBUG:    1+ $i=0; while ($i++ -lt 10) { $i }
```

We'll see all of the intermediate blather. Keep stepping until you see the first number displayed.

```
Continue with this operation?
   1+ $i=0; while ($i++ -lt 10) { $i }
[Y] Yes   [A] Yes to All   [N] No   [L] No to All   [S] Suspend
[?] Help(default is "Y"):
DEBUG:     1+ $i=0; while ($i++ -lt 10) { $i }

Continue with this operation?
   1+ $i=0; while ($i++ -lt 10) { $i }
[Y] Yes   [A] Yes to All   [N] No   [L] No to All   [S] Suspend
[?] Help(default is "Y"):
DEBUG:     1+ $i=0; while ($i++ -lt 10) { $i }
1
```

At this point, use the suspend operation, and when you see the prompt, respond with "s<enter>" instead of hitting enter.

```
Continue with this operation?
   1+ $i=0; while ($i++ -lt 10) { $i }
[Y] Yes   [A] Yes to All   [N] No   [L] No to All   [S] Suspend
[?] Help(default is "Y"): y
DEBUG:     1+ $i=0; while ($i++ -lt 10) { $i }
1

Continue with this operation?
   1+ $i=0; while ($i++ -lt 10) { $i }
[Y] Yes   [A] Yes to All   [N] No   [L] No to All   [S] Suspend
[?] Help(default is "Y"): s
1>> PS (3) >
```

You immediately receive a new prompt. Notice that the prompt has changed to indicate that you are in a subshell.

AUTHOR'S NOTE   The way to tell this is by checking the variable $NestedPromptLevel. If you are in a nested prompt, this variable will be greater than zero.

In this nested prompt, we can do anything we would normally do in PowerShell. In this case, we want to inspect the state of the system. For example, we'll check to see what the variable $i is set to. Since the last statement executed was $i++ and the printed value for $i was 1, the value should be 2

```
1>> PS (4) > $i
2
```

In fact, it is. But we're not limited to inspecting the state of the system. We can actually change it. In this case, let's make the loop end early by setting the value to something larger than the terminating condition. We'll set it to 100.

```
1>> PS (5) > $i=100
1>> PS (6) > $i
100
```

Now exit the nested prompt session with the normal `exit` statement. This returns you to the previous level in the interpreter where, since we're stepping, you're prompted to continue. Respond with "a<enter>" for "[A] Yes to All" to get out of stepping mode.

```
1>> PS (7) > exit

Continue with this operation?
   1+ $i=0; while ($i++ -lt 10) { $i }
[Y] Yes  [A] Yes to All  [N] No  [L] No to All  [S] Suspend
[?] Help(default is "Y"): a
DEBUG:    1+ $i=0; while ($i++ -lt 10) { $i }
100
```

There are two things to notice here: the loop terminates, printing only one number, and that value is the value we set $i to, which is 100. We'll check one more time to verify that $i is actually 100.

```
PS (8) > $i
100
```

Using this suspend feature, you stop a script at any point and examine or modify the state of the interpreter. You could even redefine functions in the middle of execution (although you can't change the function that is currently executing). This makes for a powerful debugging technique, but it can be annoying to use stepping all the time, so there's another way to invoke this. That's the topic of the next section.

9.4.2 Creating a breakpoint command

In section 9.3.1, we introduced the $host variable and talked about using it to write our debugging messages. The $host variable has another method that can be used for debugging called `EnterNestedPrompt()`. This is the other way to start a nested session, and can be used approximately like a breakpoint. You can insert a call to this method in your script code, and when it's hit, a new interactive session starts, just like hitting a breakpoint in a debugger. Let's try it out. We'll execute a loop that counts from 0 to 9. In this loop, when the loop counted is equal to 4, we'll call `EnterNestedPrompt()`.

```
PS (1) > for ($i=0; $i -lt 10; $i++)
>> {
>>     "i is $i"
>>     if ($i -eq 4) {
```

When execution gets to this point, we'll output the string "*break*" and then enter a nested prompt level.

```
>>         "*break*"
>>         $host.EnterNestedPrompt()
>>     }
>> }
```

```
>>
i is 0
i is 1
i is 2
i is 3
i is 4
```

Now $i is equal to four, so we hit the "breakpoint" code. As in the stepping case, we can examine and change the state of the interpreter,

```
*break*
1>> PS (2) > $i
4
1>> PS (3) > $i=8
```

and use exit to resume the top-level execution thread.

```
1>> PS (4) > exit
i is 9
PS (6) >
```

Now let's look at how we can use this feature to create a breakpoint command. Once again, we'll take advantage of scriptblocks to add a way to trigger the breakpoint based on a particular condition.

```
PS (1) > function bp ([scriptblock] $condition)
>> {
>>     if ($condition)
>>     {
>>         if (. $condition)
>>         {
```

If the $condition parameter to bp is not null, evaluate it. If it evaluates to $true, then execute the breakpoint and enter a nested shell level.

```
>>             $host.UI.WriteLine("*break*")
>>             $host.EnterNestedPrompt()
>>         }
>>     } else {
>>         $host.UI.WriteLine("*break*")
>>         $host.EnterNestedPrompt()
>>     }
>> }
>>
PS (2) > for ($i=0; $i -lt 10; $i++)
>> {
>>     . bp {$i -eq 5}
```

Here we're inserting a breakpoint that will cause execution to break when $i is equal to 5. Note that we're dotting the bp function. This is because we want it to be executed in the current scope, allowing us to change the state of the loop variable.

```
>>      "`$i is $i"
>> }
>>
$i is 0
$i is 1
$i is 2
$i is 3
$i is 4
*break*
```

We hit the breakpoint. Increment the loop variable so that 5 is never displayed, and exit the nested prompt level and resume execution.

```
1>> PS (3) > $i++
1>> PS (4) > exit
$i is 6
$i is 7
$i is 8
$i is 9
PS (5) >
```

The loop exits, never having printed 5.

This bp function is a handy tool to keep in your script debugging toolbox. You must modify your scripts to use the bp function, but it can really help when debugging complex scripts.

9.4.3   The script call stack, or "How did I get here?"

The bp function is a handy little debugging tool. From within a nested prompt, you can examine and change the state of interpreter. Another tool that would be nice would be one that tells you where you are and how you got there. In other words, we need a way to dump the script call stack. How to do this in PowerShell is not obvious, but it is possible. The key is to use the $MyInvocation variable. This variable is set to a new value every time you call a function or script. It provides you with a lot of information about what kind of command is running, where it was defined, and where it was called from. We can write a short script to illustrate this. We'll use redirection to save it into a file myinfo.ps1.

```
PS (1) > @'
>> function showit
>> {
>>      "Called from:" + $myinvocation.scriptname + ":" +
>>          $myinvocation.scriptlinenumber
>> }
>>
>> showit
>> '@ > myinfo.ps1
>>
```

This script defines a function that prints out the information about where it was called from, and then calls the function it defined:

```
PS (2) > ./myinfo
Called from:C:\Temp\myinfo.ps1:6
PS (3) >
```

We can see that the function faithfully reported where it was called from.

<table>
<tr><td>AUTHOR'S
NOTE</td><td>There are a number of interesting properties on the <code>InvocationInfo</code> object in <code>$MyInvocation</code>. We won't be covering them here, so take some time to explore it using <code>Get-Member</code>. The PowerShell software developer's kit also documents this object.</td></tr>
</table>

We can figure out where the current function was called from. The trick is to find out where its parent was called from. This requires looking up the call stack and seeing what $MyInvocation was set to for the parent. The way to do that is to use the Get-Variable cmdlet. This cmdlet has a parameter that's used to specify what scope you want to get the variable from. If you specify scope 0, it looks the variable up in the current scope. If you specify 1 then the parent scope is searched, and so on.

We'll take these two features and combine them in a function called gcs that will display the script call stack. Here's what that function looks like:

```
function gcs
{
  trap { continue }
  0..100 | % {
    (gv -scope $_ myinvocation).value.positionmessage -replace "`n"
  }
}
```

This is a pretty simple function. It walks up the call stack, starting at 0 (current scope), until an error occurs. At that point, the trap statement catches the error and uses the continue statement to quietly exit the function. For each scope level, we print out a message displaying where it was called from. At this point we create a test script with a grouping of functions that call each other:

```
PS (1) > @'
>> function a { b }
>> function b { c }
>> function c { d }
>> function d { e }
>> function e { gcs }
>> a
>> '@ > showstack.ps1
>>
```

In this function, a calls b, which calls c, and so on until finally e calls our gcs function. Let's run it:

```
PS (2) > ./showstack
At C:\Temp\showstack.ps1:5 char:17+ function e { gss  <<<< }
At C:\Temp\showstack.ps1:4 char:15+ function d { e  <<<< }
At C:\Temp\showstack.ps1:3 char:15+ function c { d  <<<< }
```

```
At C:\Temp\showstack.ps1:2 char:15+ function b { c  <<<< }
At C:\Temp\showstack.ps1:1 char:15+ function a { b  <<<< }
At C:\Temp\showstack.ps1:6 char:2+ a <<<<
At line:1 char:11+ ./showstack <<<<
```

We can see that the output starts with the innermost call and works its way back out
until it reaches the line that called the script in the first place. Each line of output
shows the file and line number where the function was called and what the line looks
like. To make it even clearer, we'll modify the myinfo.ps1 script from earlier to call
gcs and then call myinfo from showstack instead. (The actual modifications are
left as an exercise for the reader.) Here's what the output of the revised set of scripts
looks like:

```
PS (3) > C:\Temp\showstack.ps1
Called from:C:\Temp\myinfo.ps1:7
At C:\Temp\myinfo.ps1:5 char:8+      gcs <<<< }
At C:\Temp\myinfo.ps1:7 char:7+ showit <<<<
At C:\Temp\showstack.ps1:19 char:13+     ./myinfo <<<< }
At C:\Temp\showstack.ps1:15 char:6+     e <<<< }
At C:\Temp\showstack.ps1:11 char:6+     d <<<< }
At C:\Temp\showstack.ps1:7 char:6+     c <<<< }
At C:\Temp\showstack.ps1:3 char:6+     b <<<< }
At C:\Temp\showstack.ps1:21 char:2+ a <<<<
At line:1 char:21+ C:\Temp\showstack.ps1 <<<<
```

First we see the line of output explicitly written by the myinfo script and then we see
call stack displayed, starting at gcs and ending at the command typed on the command line. Notice that transition between the two files in the output. This makes it
easy to see the call order of the functions in different scripts.

The gcs function is another simple tool you can use to help debug your scripts.
In the next section we'll look at a more detailed tracing mechanism that lets you see
into the operation of the PowerShell interpreter itself.

9.5   LOW-LEVEL TRACING

The next type of tracing we're going to cover is the internal expression tracing facility.
This is a much lower-level tracing mechanism than script tracing. In fact, it's implemented using a tracing mechanism in the .NET framework that is designed for use by
application developers, not end-users. It was originally intended to allow Microsoft to
debug PowerShell applications deployed in the field, but it turns out to be quite useful for script developers. It is, however, not for the faint of heart. It traces the execution of the engine at the level of object constructor and method calls. As such, it can
be very "noisy" with a lot of detail that most users would prefer to avoid.

9.5.1   The Trace-Command cmdlet

Low-level expression tracing is controlled by the Trace-Command cmdlet.

AUTHOR'S NOTE It is an unfortunate accident of timing that this cmdlet ended up being called `Trace-Command` instead of `Trace-Expression`. Two separate cleanup activities were undertaken at the same time, with the result that this cmdlet ended up with a strange name. It is, however, fully functional.

This cmdlet has a complex set of parameters. A subset of those parameters is shown in figure 9.4.

As you can see from the names of the parameters, it is very developer-focused. A "listener" is a mechanism for capturing the trace events and routing them to a particular location. There are three listeners that you can specify using this cmdlet. These are described in table 9.3.

Table 9.3   The various trace listener options you can specify

Trace listener option	Description
-PSHost	When this option is specified, the trace events will be written to the console.
-Debugger	If a debugger is attached to the PowerShell process, the debugger will receive the trace events.
-FilePath <string>	Writes the trace records to a file for later examination.

You can specify any or all of these listeners, and the trace records will be written to all that were specified.

The `-ListenerOption` parameter allows you to control the information that appears in each trace record. The type of information includes things such as the date and time, as well as more complex information such as the process and thread identifiers and the call stack.

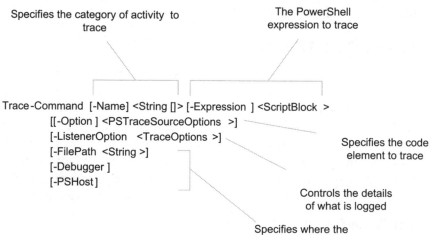

Figure 9.4   The `Trace-Command` cmdlet parameters

CHAPTER 9   ERRORS, EXCEPTIONS, AND SCRIPT DEBUGGING

The -Option parameter controls the type of operation to call. Types of operations include specific .NET activities such as object construction, method calls, and property references as well as more general categories such as "WriteLine", "Verbose", and so on. A list of these options can be specified, and all of the categories mentioned will be displayed. Alternatively, if you specify the category "All", everything will be shown (this is what is usually used).

The last parameter to discuss is -Name. This parameter selects the category of the trace events to display. Although there are a large number of trace categories, there are really only two that are of interest to the script author: typeconversion and parameterbinding. We'll cover these in the next two sections.

9.5.2 Tracing type conversions

First, we'll talk about tracing type conversions. Because automatic type conversion is so important in PowerShell, having a way of seeing exactly what's going on is very useful. Let's look at an example. We'll trace a simple conversion, from a string to a number:

```
[int] "123"
```

We're going to trace all of the activities, so we'll specify -Option all, and we want the output to go to the console, so we'll also specify -PShost. Here's what it looks like (this is all the output from one command, by the way!):

```
PS (1) > trace-command -opt all typeconversion {[int] "123"} `
>> -pshost
>>
DEBUG: TypeConversion Information: 0 : Converting "int" to
"System.Type".
```

This is the first conversion—taking the type literal [int] and resolving it to the instance of System.Type that represents an integer.

```
DEBUG: TypeConversion Information: 0 :     Original type before
getting BaseObject: "System.String".
DEBUG: TypeConversion Information: 0 :     Original type after
getting BaseObject: "System.String".
DEBUG: TypeConversion Information: 0 :     Standard type
conversion.
DEBUG: TypeConversion Information: 0 :       Converting
integer to System.Enum.
DEBUG: TypeConversion Information: 0 :       Type conversion
from string.
DEBUG: TypeConversion Information: 0 :         Conversion to
  System.Type
```

And we're done with step 1; we now have the type we need.

```
DEBUG: TypeConversion Information: 0 :      The conversion is a
standard conversion. No custom type conversion will be
attempted.
DEBUG: TypeConversion Information: 0 : Converting "123" to
"System.Int32".
```

The next step is to figure out how to convert the string "123" into an integer.

```
DEBUG: TypeConversion Information: 0 :        Original type before
getting BaseObject: "System.String".
DEBUG: TypeConversion Information: 0 :        Original type after
getting BaseObject: "System.String".
DEBUG: TypeConversion Information: 0 :        Standard type
conversion.
DEBUG: TypeConversion Information: 0 :            Converting
integer to System.Enum.
DEBUG: TypeConversion Information: 0 :             Type conversion
from string.
DEBUG: TypeConversion Information: 0 :                 Converting to
 integer.
DEBUG: TypeConversion Information: 0 :      The conversion is a
standard conversion. No custom type conversion will be
attempted.
```

This is a standard .NET type conversion, so no special steps are needed. The conversion is performed and finally we get the result as a number.

```
123
PS (2) >
```

Did you follow all that? Remember what I said about this type of tracing being verbose? I wasn't kidding. Let's look at a second example. Again, we'll trace everything and output to the console. This time, we'll trace casting a string into an [xml]. We'll also use the -ListenerOption parameter to say that we want to include the timestamp in the option. Here we go:

```
PS (6) > trace-command -opt all typeconversion -pshost `
>> -listen timestamp `
>> { [xml] '<h>Hi</h>' }
>>
DEBUG: TypeConversion Information: 0 : Converting "xml" to
"System.Type".
DEBUG: Timestamp=5536598202692
```

Again, the first step is to resolve the type literal. Note that timestamp information is now being output as we requested.

```
DEBUG: TypeConversion Information: 0 :        Original type before
getting BaseObject: "System.String".
DEBUG: Timestamp=5536598216733
DEBUG: TypeConversion Information: 0 :        Original type after
getting BaseObject: "System.String".
DEBUG: Timestamp=5536598230212
DEBUG: TypeConversion Information: 0 :        Standard type
conversion.
DEBUG: Timestamp=5536598243271
DEBUG: TypeConversion Information: 0 :            Converting
integer to System.Enum.
DEBUG: Timestamp=5536598255383
DEBUG: TypeConversion Information: 0 :             Type conversion
```

```
from string.
DEBUG: Timestamp=5536598267714
DEBUG: TypeConversion Information: 0 :                Conversion to
 System.Type
DEBUG: Timestamp=5536598279950
DEBUG: TypeConversion Information: 0 :     The conversion is a
standard conversion. No custom type conversion will be
attempted.
DEBUG: Timestamp=5536598292383
DEBUG: TypeConversion Information: 0 : Converting "<h>Hi</h>" to
 "System.Xml.XmlDocument".
```

This tells us what the final type of the object will be.

```
DEBUG: Timestamp=5536598308660
DEBUG: TypeConversion Information: 0 :        Original type before
getting BaseObject: "System.String".
DEBUG: Timestamp=5536598321106
DEBUG: TypeConversion Information: 0 :        Original type after
getting BaseObject: "System.String".
DEBUG: Timestamp=5536598334410
DEBUG: TypeConversion Information: 0 :        Standard type
conversion.
DEBUG: Timestamp=5536598347058
DEBUG: TypeConversion Information: 0 :           Converting to
XmlDocument.
DEBUG: Timestamp=5536598382014
DEBUG: TypeConversion Information: 0 :           Standard type
conversion to XmlDocument.
DEBUG: Timestamp=5536598396299
DEBUG: TypeConversion Information: 0 :     The conversion is a
standard conversion. No custom type conversion will be
attempted.
DEBUG: Timestamp=5536598409092

h
-
Hi
```

Finally, the XML object is displayed. Now let's look at tracing parameter binding.

9.5.3 Tracing parameter binding

The other category of trace information that is interesting to the script user is parameter binding. This allows you to see just how the parameters are being bound to a cmdlet. The example we'll use is the simple command:

```
"c:\" | get-item
```

In this example, Get-Item will take its mandatory parameter -path from pipeline. When we run the command we see that the set of parameters is mostly the same as in the previous section, except that we're now using the parameterbinding trace category.

```
PS (7) > trace-command -opt all parameterbinding -pshost `
>> { "c:\" | get-item }
>>
```

The first step is to go through each of the command-line parameter binding steps—named parameters, positional parameters, and finally dynamic parameters (see chapter 2 for more information for each of these steps).

```
DEBUG: ParameterBinding Information: 0 : BIND NAMED cmd line
args [Get-Item]
DEBUG: ParameterBinding Information: 0 : BIND POSITIONAL cmd
line args [Get-Item]
DEBUG: ParameterBinding Information: 0 : BIND cmd line args to
DYNAMIC parameters.
DEBUG: ParameterBinding Information: 0 : MANDATORY PARAMETER
CHECK on cmdlet [Get-Item]
```

At this point, the parameter binder is checking to see if there are any unbound mandatory parameters that can't be bound to input from the pipeline. If this were the case, a terminating error would occur here. Since this is not the case in this example, the binding process continues.

```
DEBUG: ParameterBinding Information: 0 : CALLING BeginProcessing
DEBUG: ParameterBinding Information: 0 : BIND PIPELINE object to
 parameters: [Get-Item]
DEBUG: ParameterBinding Information: 0 :      PIPELINE object
TYPE = [System.String]
```

We have an object from the pipeline to bind.

```
DEBUG: ParameterBinding Information: 0 :      RESTORING pipeline
parameter's original values
```

First, restore all of the parameters that can take pipeline input to their default state, since not all of them may be bound from this object.

```
DEBUG: ParameterBinding Information: 0 :      Parameter [Path]
PIPELINE INPUT ValueFromPipeline NO COERCION
```

This is the first step in matching the parameter; if the parameter type exactly matches, then binding proceeds immediately.

```
DEBUG: ParameterBinding Information: 0 :      BIND arg [c:\] to
parameter [Path]
DEBUG: ParameterBinding Information: 0 :            Binding
collection parameter Path: argument type [String], parameter
type [System.String[]], collection type Array, element type
[System.String], no coerceElementType
```

In this case, the target type is a collection, but the element type of the collection matches the pipeline object, so the interpreter will wrap the pipeline object in an array so the binding can succeed.

```
DEBUG: ParameterBinding Information: 0 :         Creating array
with element type [System.String] and 1 elements
DEBUG: ParameterBinding Information: 0 :         Argument type
String is not IList, treating this as scalar
DEBUG: ParameterBinding Information: 0 :         Adding scalar
element of type String to array position 0
DEBUG: ParameterBinding Information: 0 :         BIND arg
[System.String[]] to param [Path] SUCCESSFUL
```

At this point, we've bound the -path parameter. Let's check the remaining parameters that can take their values from the pipeline.

```
DEBUG: ParameterBinding Information: 0 :      Parameter
[Credential] PIPELINE INPUT ValueFromPipelineByPropertyName NO
COERCION
DEBUG: ParameterBinding Information: 0 :      Parameter
[Credential] PIPELINE INPUT ValueFromPipelineByPropertyName WITH
 COERCION
```

Nothing was bound at this point, so the last thing to do is check to make sure that all mandatory parameters for this cmdlet are now bound. If there were an unbound mandatory parameter, a non-fatal error would be generated and an error record would be written to the output pipe. Note how this is different from the command-line parameters. In that case, it's a fatal error; there's no way to continue. For the pipeline parameter, even if the current object doesn't result in all parameters being bound successfully, the next pipeline object may succeed. This is why pipeline binding failures are non-terminating and command line binding failures are terminating.

```
DEBUG: ParameterBinding Information: 0 : MANDATORY PARAMETER
CHECK on cmdlet [Get-Item]
```

Finally, now that all parameters are bound, the cmdlet's ProcessRecord and End-Processing clauses are executed.

```
DEBUG: ParameterBinding Information: 0 : CALLING ProcessRecord
DEBUG: ParameterBinding Information: 0 : CALLING EndProcessing


    Directory:


Mode           LastWriteTime     Length Name
----           -------------     ------ ----
d--hs       6/9/2006    2:30 AM           C:\
```

Again, this is a verbose tracing mechanism, but it shows you the binding algorithm in great detail. If you are having a problem understanding why a pipeline is exhibiting some unexpected behavior, this is the way to see what's happening. You can also combine the two tracing mechanisms to see even more detail of what's going on. We can try this with a user-defined function just to see that this mechanism works with functions as well as cmdlets. First we'll define a function:

```
PS (8) > function foo ([int] $x) {$x}
```

Now let's trace its execution.

```
PS (9) > trace-command -opt all parameterbinding,
>> typeconversion -pshost {foo "123"}
>>
DEBUG: ParameterBinding Information: 0 : POSITIONAL parameter
[x] found for arg []
```

We see the parameter binding trace messages for positional parameter binding.

```
DEBUG: ParameterBinding Information: 0 : BIND arg [123] to
parameter [x]
DEBUG: ParameterBinding Information: 0 :     Executing DATA
GENERATION metadata:
[System.Management.Automation.ArgumentTypeConverterAttribute]
DEBUG: TypeConversion Information: 0 :         Converting "123"
to "System.Int32".
```

And now we see the type conversion messages.

```
DEBUG: TypeConversion Information: 0 :             Original type
 before getting BaseObject: "System.String".
DEBUG: TypeConversion Information: 0 :             Original type
 after getting BaseObject: "System.String".
DEBUG: TypeConversion Information: 0 :             Standard type
 conversion.
DEBUG: TypeConversion Information: 0 :
Converting integer to System.Enum.
DEBUG: TypeConversion Information: 0 :                 Type
conversion from string.
DEBUG: TypeConversion Information: 0 :
Converting to integer.
DEBUG: TypeConversion Information: 0 :             The
conversion is a standard conversion. No custom type conversion
will be attempted.
DEBUG: ParameterBinding Information: 0 :         result returned
 from DATA GENERATION: 123
DEBUG: ParameterBinding Information: 0 :     COERCE arg type
[System.Int32] to [System.Int32]
DEBUG: ParameterBinding Information: 0 :         Parameter and
arg types the same.
DEBUG: TypeConversion Information: 0 :     Converting "123" to
"System.Int32".
DEBUG: TypeConversion Information: 0 :         Result type is
assignable from value to convert's type
```

Finally, the binding process is complete and the script is executed.

```
DEBUG: ParameterBinding Information: 0 :     BIND arg [123] to
param [x] SUCCESSFUL
123
PS (10) >
```

In summary, the Trace-Command cmdlet provides a mechanism for tracing the execution of command in PowerShell in a very low-level and detailed way. Sometimes this mechanism can be the only way to debug the behavior of a script. It is not, however, a tool intended for the casual user; it requires considerable sophistication to interpret the output of these trace logs. For the casual user, the most effective way to go about it is to use the `-FileLog` parameter to create a trace log that can then be analyzed by a developer.

9.6 THE POWERSHELL EVENT LOG

And now, the final topic in this chapter: the last diagnostic tool available in Power-Shell is the Windows event log. Note that we're only going to touch on the basics of this feature area. The point of this section is to make you aware that this feature exists, and to discuss when and where you might want to use it. For more detailed information, refer to the PowerShell product documentation.

9.6.1 Examining the event log

When PowerShell is installed, it creates a new event log called "PowerShell". As PowerShell executes, it writes a variety of information to this log. You can view this information using the standard graphical Event Viewer tool provided with Windows, or you can use the PowerShell `Get-EventLog` cmdlet. Let's use the cmdlet to get the last few records from the PowerShell event log. As always, we can use the tools PowerShell provides to filter and scope the data we want to look at. We'll use an array slice to get the last five records from the log.

```
PS (13) > (get-eventlog powershell)[-5..-1]

Index Time            Type Source                EventID Message
----- ----            ---- ------                ------- -------
    5 Apr 26 19:20    Info PowerShell                600 Provid...
    4 Apr 26 19:20    Info PowerShell                600 Provid...
    3 Apr 26 19:20    Info PowerShell                600 Provid...
    2 Apr 26 19:20    Info PowerShell                600 Provid...
    1 Apr 26 19:20    Info PowerShell                600 Provid...
```

The default presentation of the event records doesn't show much information. Let's look at one event in detail and see what it contains.

```
PS (12) > (get-eventlog powershell)[0] | fl *

EventID           : 400
MachineName       : BRUCEPAY64H
Data              : {}
Index             : 428
```

First, we get some basic event log elements common to all event log entries.

```
Category          : Engine Lifecycle
CategoryNumber    : 4
```

Next, we see the event category. This is not the same as the error category discussed earlier. PowerShell event log entries are grouped into several large categories.

```
EntryType          : Information
Message            : Engine state is changed from None to Available.
```

Next is the entry type and a message describing the entry. This is followed by a collection of detail elements, which include things such as the state transition for the engine, as well as some of the versioning information we saw on the $host object earlier. This is included in case you have multiple hosts for a particular engine.

```
            Details:
                NewEngineState=Available
                PreviousEngineState=None

                SequenceNumber=8

                HostName=ConsoleHost
                HostVersion=1.0.10568.0
                HostId=8ac4a201-5d34-4fa7-9d68-bdcc5cb1
            9f45
                EngineVersion=1.0.10568.0
                RunspaceId=ec811562-43da-48d8-9136-7383
            171fbccf
```

The following fields are only populated when detailed logging is turned on for a PowerShell snap-in (a collection of commands).

```
                PipelineId=
                CommandName=
                CommandType=
                ScriptName=
                CommandPath=
                CommandLine=
Source             : PowerShell
```

The flowing fields specify the replacement strings that are available. These strings are substituted into the log message text.

```
ReplacementStrings : {Available, None,      NewEngineState=Availa
                   ble
                       PreviousEngineState=None

                       SequenceNumber=8

                       HostName=ConsoleHost
                       HostVersion=1.0.10568.0
                       HostId=8ac4a201-5d34-4fa7-9d68-bdcc5cb1
                   9f45
                       EngineVersion=1.0.10568.0
                       RunspaceId=ec811562-43da-48d8-9136-7383
                   171fbccf
```

```
                    PipelineId=
                    CommandName=
                    CommandType=
                    ScriptName=
                    CommandPath=
                    CommandLine=}
```

Finally, some additional information for identifying the event log record and when it occurred.

```
InstanceId          : 400
TimeGenerated       : 6/9/2006 10:05:07 PM
TimeWritten         : 6/9/2006 10:05:07 PM
UserName            :
Site                :
Container           :
```

Granted, that was long and boring. As you can see, there isn't a lot of interesting information from a user's perspective. However, from a system administrator's perspective, being able to see when the PowerShell interpreter was started or stopped can be very useful when you're using it to automate your system. There are also certain types of errors that may cause a PowerShell session to terminate. These errors will be logged in the PowerShell event log.

9.6.2   Exchange 2007 and the PowerShell event log

This chapter concludes by briefly describing the possibility of turning on extended logging for all the commands present in a PowerShell snap-in. This is useful when using PowerShell to manage server applications. This feature was added at the request of the Exchange team for the Microsoft Exchange 2007 mail server product. In Exchange 2007, all management activities are performed using PowerShell. Even the Exchange Management console, a graphical user interface for managing Exchange, uses PowerShell commands for all activities. When extended logging is turned on for the Exchange snap-in, all Exchange commands (and therefore all management activities) for an Exchange server are logged.

That's all we're going to cover on event logs. For day-to-day user activities, the event log doesn't provide a lot of value, but when using PowerShell to perform system administration, this log can be invaluable for debugging how and when a system has been modified.

9.7   SUMMARY

This chapter focused on the diagnostic features of PowerShell: the error handling mechanisms and the various debugging, tracing, and logging features. And, despite over 40 pages of text, this was not an exhaustive discussion of all these features (see Manning's *Windows PowerShell in Practice* by Jim Truher for additional information on this topic). Let's summarize the areas that we did cover. We started with basic error handling covering:

- The types of errors in PowerShell: terminating and non-terminating
- The `ErrorRecord` object and the error stream
- The `$error` variable and `-ErrorVariable` parameter
- The `$?` and `$LASTEXITCODE` variables
- `$ErrorActionPreference` and the `-ErrorAction` parameter

Next, we covered how to work with terminating errors or exceptions:

- The `trap` statement and how to use it
- Using the `throw` statement to generate your own terminating exceptions

And then we covered the tools and techniques available for script debugging:

- Old-fashioned "printf-style" debugging using the host APIs
- The debugging features available using the `Set-PSdebug` cmdlet
- Script tracing
- Strict mode
- Using the nested prompt feature while stepping through a script and also using it to create "breakpoints"

Finally, we covered the low-level tracing features and logging features.

- Using the `Trace-Command` cmdlet
- Two types of activities you can trace with this cmdlet
- Getting and examining PowerShell event log entries

A final note: the diagnostic capabilities in PowerShell are rich and deep. This makes it difficult to get a handle on all of them and how they can be used. The key take-away from this chapter is to be aware that these capabilities exist, so that when you do encounter a situation where you need to debug your scripts, you'll know where to look for the tools that can help you solve your problem.

P A R T   2

Using PowerShell

Part 1 covered the PowerShell language and runtime features in great detail; however, those features were discussed mostly in isolation. In part 2, we shift our focus to combine the features we learned about in part 1 into larger examples. Now we'll look at applying PowerShell in specific technology areas and problem domains.

We begin in chapter 10, looking at how PowerShell can be used to attack the kind of text processing tasks that have been the traditional domain of languages such as Perl. In chapter 11, we look at how we can discover and apply the vast capabilities of the .NET framework from PowerShell. In chapter 12, we'll look at how to use and apply other Microsoft object technologies, specifically COM and WMI. We'll also look at how to interact with VBScript, Microsoft's previous-generation scripting tool.

In chapter 13, we'll introduce the security features in PowerShell along with a general discussion of security. This is a very important chapter to read. Like all powerful scripting tools (Perl, Python, and so forth), PowerShell can be used to create malware such as virus and worm programs. The PowerShell runtime contains numerous features to allow you to deploy it in a manner that minimizes these risks.

The examples in part 2, while larger, are still focused on particular technology areas, so appendix B includes additional examples of performing system administration tasks using PowerShell. While it's by no means a management cookbook, it does show what can be done with PowerShell and how to do it.

The PowerShell language is the focus of appendix A and appendix C. In appendix A we compare PowerShell to other languages, looking at issues that Perl, VBScript, and C# programmers may encounter. Appendix C explains the grammar of the PowerShell language.

C H A P T E R   1 0

Processing text, files, and XML

Where is human nature so weak as in the bookstore?

—Henry Ward Beecher

Outside of a dog, a book is man's best friend. Inside of a dog, it's too dark to read.

—Groucho Marx

One of the most common applications for scripting languages is processing text and text files. In this chapter, we're going to cover PowerShell's features for this kind of processing. We'll revisit regular expressions and take another look at the language features and cmdlets that are provided for dealing with text. This chapter also covers the features that PowerShell offers for dealing with a special kind of text—XML—as strings and in files. In the process, we'll see how to use the .NET classes to accomplish tasks when the native PowerShell language features may not be sufficient.

10.1 PROCESSING UNSTRUCTURED TEXT

While PowerShell is an object-based shell, it still has to deal with text. In chapter 4, we covered the operators (-match, -replace, -like) that PowerShell provides for working with text. We showed how to concatenate two strings together using the plus operator. In this section, we'll cover some of the more advanced string processing operations. We'll discuss techniques for splitting and joining strings using the [string] and [regex] members, and using filters to extract statistical information from a body of text.

10.1.1 Using System.String to work with text

One common scenario for scripting is processing log files. This requires breaking the log strings into pieces to extract relevant bits of information. Unfortunately, Power-Shell has no split operator, so there is no way to split a string into pieces in the language itself. This is where our support for .NET is very important. If you want to split a string into pieces, you use the Split() method on the [string] class.

```
PS (1) > "Hello there world".Split()
Hello
there
world
```

The Split() method with no arguments splits on spaces. In this example, it produces an array of three elements.

```
PS (2) > "Hello there world".Split().length
3
```

We can verify this with the length property. In fact, it splits on any of the characters that fall into the WhiteSpace character class. This includes tabs, so it works properly on a string containing both tabs and spaces.

```
PS (3) > "Hello`tthere world".Split()
Hello
there
world
```

In the revised example, we still get three fields, even though space is used in one place and tab in another.

And while the default is to split on a whitespace character, you can specify a string of characters to use split fields.

```
PS (4) > "First,Second;Third".Split(',;')
First
Second
Third
```

Here we specified the comma and the semicolon as valid characters to split the field.

There is, however, an issue; the default behavior for "split this" isn't necessarily what you want. The reason why is that it splits on each separator character. This means that if you have multiple spaces between words in a string, you'll get multiple empty elements in the result array. For example:

```
PS (5) > "Hello there   world".Split().length
6
```

In this example, we end up with six elements in the array because there are three spaces between "there" and "world". Let's find out if there's a better way to do this.

Using SplitStringOptions

The string method we've been using has worked well so far, but we've gotten to the point where we need to add some cmdlets to help us out. In this case, we'll use the Get-Member cmdlet to look at the signature of the Split() method:

```
PS (6) > ("hello" | gm split).definition
System.String[] Split(Params Char[] separator), System.String[]
Split(Char[] separator, Int32 count), System.String[] Split(Char
[] separator, StringSplitOptions options), System.String[] Split
(Char[] separator, Int32 count, StringSplitOptions options), Sys
tem.String[] Split(String[] separator, StringSplitOptions option
s), System.String[] Split(String[] separator, Int32 count, Strin
gSplitOptions options)
```

The default display of the definition is a little hard to read. Fortunately, we now know how to split a string.

```
PS (7) > ("hello" | gm split).definition.split(',')
System.String[] Split(Params Char[] separator)
 System.String[] Split(Char[] separator
 Int32 count)
 System.String[] Split(Char[] separator
 StringSplitOptions options)
 System.String[] Split(Char[] separator
 Int32 count
 StringSplitOptions options)
 System.String[] Split(String[] separator
 StringSplitOptions options)
 System.String[] Split(String[] separator
 Int32 count
 StringSplitOptions options)
```

It's not perfect as it split on the method argument commas as well; but we can still read it. The methods that take the options argument look promising. Let's see what the SplitStringOptions are. We'll do this by trying to cast a string into these options.

```
PS (8) > [StringSplitOptions] "abc"
Cannot convert value "abc" to type "System.StringSplitOptions" d
ue to invalid enumeration values. Specify one of the following e
```

```
numeration values and try again. The possible enumeration values
 are "None, RemoveEmptyEntries".
At line:1 char:21
+ [StringSplitOptions]  <<<< "abc"
```

The error message tells us the legitimate values for the enumeration. If we look this class up in the online documentation on MSDN, we'll see that this option tells the Split() method to discard empty array elements. This sounds just like what we need, so let's try it:

```
PS (9) > "Hello there     world".split(" ",
>> [StringSplitOptions]::RemoveEmptyEntries)
>>
Hello
there
world
```

It works as desired. Now we can apply this to a larger problem.

Analyzing word use in a document

Given a body of text, we want to find the number of words in the text as well as the number of unique words, and then display the 10 most common words in the text. For our purposes, we'll use one of the PowerShell help text files: about_Assignment_operators.help.txt. This is not a particularly large file (it's around 17 kilobytes) so we can just load it into memory using the Get-Content (gc) cmdlet.

```
PS (10) > $s = gc $PSHOME/about_Assignment_operators`.help.txt
PS (11) > $s.length
434
```

The variable $s now contains the text of the file as a collection of lines (434 lines, to be exact.) This is usually what we want, since it lets us process a file one line at time. But, in this example, we actually want to process this file as a single string. To do so we'll use the String.Join() method and join all of the lines, adding an additional space between each line.

```
PS (12) > $s = [string]::join(" ", $s)
PS (13) > $s.length
17308
```

Now $s contains a single string containing the whole text of the file. We verified this by checking the length rather than displaying it. Next we'll split it into an array of words.

```
PS (14) > $words = $s.split(" `t",
>> [stringsplitoptions]::RemoveEmptyEntries)
>>
PS (15) > $words.length
2696
```

So the text of the file has 2,696 words in it. We need to find out how many unique words there are. There are a couple ways of doing this. The easiest way is to use the `Sort-Object` cmdlet with the `-unique` parameter. This will sort the list of words and then remove all of the duplicates.

```
PS (16) > $uniq = $words | sort -uniq
PS (17) > $uniq.count
533
```

This help topic contains 533 unique words. Using the `Sort` cmdlet is fast and simple, but it doesn't cover everything we said we wanted to do, because it doesn't give the frequency of use. Let's look at another approach: using the `Foreach-Object` cmdlet and a hashtable.

Using hashtables to count unique words

In the previous example, we used the `-unique` parameter to `Sort-Object` to generate a list of unique words. Now we'll take advantage of the *set-like* behavior of hashtables to do the same thing, but in addition we will be able to count the number of occurrences of each word.

> **AUTHOR'S NOTE** In mathematics, a set is simply a collection of unique elements. This is how the keys work in a hashtable. Each key in a hashtable occurs exactly once. Attempting to add a key more than once will result in an error. In Power-Shell, assigning a new value to an existing key simply replaces the old value associated with that key. The key itself remains unique. This turns out to be a powerful technique, because it's a way of building index tables for collections of objects based on arbitrary property values. These index tables let us run database-like operations on object collections. See section B.9 for an example of how you can use this technique to implement a SQL-like "join" operation on two collections of objects.

Once again, we split the document into a stream of words. Each word in the stream will be used as the hashtable key, and we'll keep the count of the words in the value. Here's the script:

```
PS (18) > $words | % {$h=@{}} {$h[$_] += 1}
```

It's not really much longer than the previous example. We're using the `%` alias for `Foreach-Object` to keep it short. In the `begin` clause in `Foreach-Object`, we're initializing the variable `$h` to hold the resulting hashtable. Then, in the `process` scriptblock, we increment the hashtable entry indexed by the word. We're taking advantage of the way arithmetic works in PowerShell. If the key doesn't exist yet, the hashtable returns `$null`. When `$null` is added to a number, it is treated as zero. This allows the expression

```
$h[$_] += 1
```

to work. Initially, the hashtable member for a given key doesn't exist. The += operator retrieves $null from the table, converts it to 0, adds one, then assigns the value back to the hashtable entry.

Let's verify that the script produces the same answer for the number of words as we found with the Sort -Unique solution.

```
PS (19) > $h.psbase.keys.count
533
```

We have 533, the same as before.

AUTHOR'S NOTE Notice that we used $h.psbase.keys.count. This is because there is a member in the hashtable that hides the keys property. In order to access the base keys member, we need to use the PSBase property to get at the base member on the hashtable.

Now we have a hashtable containing the unique words and the number of times each word is used. But hashtables aren't stored in any particular order, so we need to sort it. We'll use a scriptblock parameter to specify the sorting criteria. We'll tell it to sort the list of keys based on the frequency stored in the hashtable entry for that key.

```
PS (20) > $frequency = $h.psbase.keys | sort {$h[$_]}
```

The words in the sorted list are ordered from least frequent to most frequent. This means that $frequency[0] contains the least frequently used word.

```
PS (21) > $frequency[0]
avoid
```

And the last entry in frequency contains the most commonly used word. If you remember from chapter 3, we can use negative indexing to get the last element of the list.

```
PS (22) > $frequency[-1]
the
```

It comes as no surprise that the most frequent word is "the" and it's used 300 times.

```
PS (23) > $h["The"]
300
```

The next most frequent word is "and", which is used 126 times.

```
PS (24) > $h[$frequency[-2]]
126
PS (25) > $frequency[-2]
to
```

Here are the top 10 most frequently used words the about_Assignment_operators help text:

```
PS (26) > -1..-10 | %{ $frequency[$_]+" "+$h[$frequency[$_]]}
the 300
to 126
```

CHAPTER 10   PROCESSING TEXT, FILES, AND XML

```
value 88
a 86
you 68
variable 64
of 55
$varA 41
For 41
following 37
```

PowerShell includes a cmdlet that is also useful for this kind of task: the Group-Object cmdlet. This cmdlet groups its input objects by into collections sorted by the specified property. This means that we can achieve the same type of ordering by the following:

```
PS (27) > $grouped = $words | group | sort count
```

Once again, we see that the most frequently used word is "the":

```
PS (28) > $grouped[-1]

Count Name                    Group
----- ----                    -----
  300 the                     {the, the, the, the...}
```

And we can display the 10 most frequent words by doing:

```
PS (29) > $grouped[-1..-10]

Count Name                    Group
----- ----                    -----
  300 the                     {the, the, the, the...}
  126 to                      {to, to, to, to...}
   88 value                   {value, value, value, value...}
   86 a                       {a, a, a, a...}
   68 you                     {you, You, you, you...}
   64 variable                {variable, variable, variable...
   55 of                      {of, of, of, of...}
   41 $varA                   {$varA, $varA, $varA, $varA...}
   41 For                     {For, for, For, For...}
   37 following               {following, following, follow...
```

We create a nicely formatted display courtesy of the formatting and output subsystem built into PowerShell.

In this section, we saw how to split strings using the methods on the string class. We even saw how to split strings on a sequence of characters. But in the world of unstructured text, you'll quickly run into examples where the methods on [string] are not enough. As is so often the case, regular expressions come to the rescue. In the next couple of sections, we'll see how we can do more sophisticated string processing using the [regex] class.

10.1.2   Using regular expressions to manipulate text

In the previous section, we looked at basic string processing using members on the [string] class. While there's a lot of potential with this class, there are times when you need to use more powerful tools. This is where regular expressions come in. As we discussed in chapter 4, regular expressions are a mini-language for matching and manipulating text. We covered a number of examples using regular expressions with the -match and -replace operators. This time, we're going to work with the regular expression class itself.

Splitting strings with regular expressions

As mentioned in chapter 3, there is a shortcut [regex] for the regular expression type. The [regex] type also has a Split() method, but it's much more powerful because it uses a regular expression to decide where to split strings instead of a single character.

```
PS (1) > $s = "Hello-1-there-22-World!"
PS (2) > [regex]::split($s,'-[0-9]+-')
Hello
there
World!
PS (3) > [regex]::split($s,'-[0-9]+-').count
3
```

In this example, the fields are separated by a sequence of digits bound on either side by a dash. This is a pattern that couldn't be specified with String.Split().

When working with the .NET regular expression library, the [regex] class isn't the only class that you'll run into. We'll see this in the next example, when we take a look at using regular expressions to tokenize a string.

Tokenizing text with regular expressions

Tokenization, or the process of breaking a body of text into a stream of individual symbols, is a common activity in text processing. In chapter 2 we talked a lot about how the PowerShell interpreter has to tokenize a script before it can be executed. In the next example, we're going to look at how we might write a simple tokenizer for basic arithmetic expressions in a programming language. First we need to define the valid tokens in these expressions. We want to allow numbers made up of one or more digits; any of the operators +,-,*, /; and we'll also allow sequences of spaces. Here's what the regular expression to match these elements looks like:

```
PS (4) > $pat = [regex] "[0-9]+|\+|\-|\*|/| +"
```

This is a pretty simple pattern using only the alternation operator "|" and the quantifier "+", which matches one or more instances. Since we used the [regex] cast in the assignment, $pat contains a regular expression object. We can use this object directly against an input string by calling its Match() operator.

```
PS (5) > $m = $pat.match("11+2 * 35 -4")
```

The Match() operator returns a Match object (full name System.Text.Regular-Expressions.Match). We can use the Get-Member cmdlet to explore the full set of members on this object at our leisure, but for now we're interested in only three members. The first member is the Success property. This will be true if the pattern matched. The second interesting member is the Value member, which will contain the matched value. The final member we're interested in is the NextMatch() method. Calling this method will step the regular expression engine to the next match in the string, and is the key to tokenizing an entire expression. We can use this method in a while loop to extract the tokens from the source string one at a time. In the example, we keep looping as long the Match object's Success property is true. Then we display the Value property and call NextMatch() to step to the next token:

```
PS (6) > while ($m.Success)
>> {
>>     $m.value
>>     $m = $m.NextMatch()
>> }
>>
11
+
2

*

35

-
4
```

In the output, we see each token, one per line in the order they appeared in the original string.

We now have a powerful collection of techniques for processing strings. The next step is to apply these techniques to processing files. Of course, we also need to spend some time finding, reading, writing, and copying files. In the next section, we'll review the basic file abstractions in PowerShell and then look at file processing.

10.2   FILE PROCESSING

Let's step back for a minute and talk about files, drives and navigation. PowerShell has a *provider abstraction* that allows the user to work with system data stores as though they were drives. A provider is a piece of installable software that surfaces a data store in the form that can be mounted as a "drive".

AUTHOR'S NOTE
By *installable*, we mean that the end user can install new providers or even write their own providers. This activity is outside the scope of this book, however. Refer to the PowerShell user documentation for information on how to install additional providers. The PowerShell Software Developer's Kit includes documentation and examples that can help you write your own providers.

These drives are a PowerShell "fiction"; that is, they only have meaning to PowerShell as opposed to system drives that have meaning everywhere. Also, unlike the system drives, PowerShell drive names can be longer than one character.

We've already seen some examples of non-filesystem providers in earlier chapters, where we worked with the `variable:` and `function:` drives. These providers let you use the `New-Item` and `Remove-Item` cmdlets to add and remove variables or functions just as if they were files.

A key piece to making this provider abstraction is the set of core cmdlets listed in table 10.1. These cmdlets are the "core" set of commands for manipulating the system and correspond to commands found in other shell environments. Because these commands are used so frequently, short aliases—the canonical aliases—are provided for the commands. By *canonical*, we mean that they follow a standard form: usually the first letter or two of the verb followed by the first letter or two of the noun. Two additional sets of "user migration" aliases are provided to help new users work with the system. There is one set for cmd.exe users and one set for UNIX shell users. Note that these aliases only map the name; they don't provide exact functional correspondence to either the cmd.exe or UNIX commands.

Table 10.1 The core cmdlets for working with files and directories

Cmdlet name	Canonical alias	cmd command	UNIX sh command	Description
Get-Location	gl	pwd	pwd	Get the current directory.
Set-Location	sl	cd, chdir	cd, chdir	Change the current directory.
Copy-Item	cpi	copy	cp	Copy files.
Remove-Item	ri	del rd	rm rmdir	Remove a file or directory. PowerShell has no separate command for removing directories as opposed to files.
Move-Item	mi	move	mv	Move a file.
Rename-Item	rni	Rn	ren	Rename a file.
Set-Item	si			Set the contents of a file.
Clear-Item	cli			Clear the contents of a file.
New-Item	ni			Create a new empty file or directory. The type of object is controlled by the -type parameter.

continued on next page

Table 10.1 The core cmdlets for working with files and directories *(continued)*

Cmdlet name	Canonical alias	cmd command	UNIX sh command	Description
Mkdir		md	mkdir	Mkdir is implemented as a function in Power-Shell so that users can create directories without having to specify -type directory.
Get-Content	gc	type	cat	Send the contents of a file to the output stream.
Set-Content	sc			Set the contents of a file. UNIX and cmd.exe have no equivalent. Redirection is used instead. The difference between Set-Content and Out-File is discussed later in this chapter.

On-line help is available for all of these commands; simply type

```
help cmdlet-name
```

and you'll receive detailed help on the cmdlets, their parameters, and some simple examples of how to use them. In the next few sections, we'll look at some more sophisticated applications of these cmdlets, including how to deal with binary data. In traditional shell environments, binary data either required specialized commands or forced us to create new executables in a language such as C, because the basic shell model couldn't cope with binary data. We'll see how PowerShell can work directly with binary data. But first, let's take a minute to look at the PowerShell drive abstraction to simplify working with paths.

10.2.1 Working with PSDrives

One useful aspect of the PowerShell provider feature is the ability to create your own drives. To keep people from mixing up the PowerShell drives with the system drives, we call these *PSDrives*. A common reason for creating a PSDrive is to create a short path for getting at a system resource. For example, it might be convenient to have a "docs:" drive that points to our document directory. We can create this using the New-PSDrive cmdlet:

```
PS (1) > new-psdrive -name docs -PSProvider filesystem `
>>   -Root (resolve-path ~/*documents)
>>

Name       Provider      Root                                    Current
                                                                 Location
----       --------      ----                                    --------
docs       FileSystem    C:\Documents and Settings\brucep
```

Now we can cd into this drive

```
PS (2) > cd docs:
```

then use pwd (an alias for Get-Location) to see where we are:

```
PS (3) > pwd

Path
----
docs:\
```

We are, at least according to PowerShell, in the docs: drive. Let's create a file here:

```
PS (4) > "Hello there!" > junk.txt
```

Next, try to use cmd.exe to display it (we'll get to why we're doing this in a second):

```
PS (5) > cmd /c type junk.txt
Hello there!
```

Well, that works fine. Display it using Get-Content with the fully qualified path, including the docs: drive.

```
PS (6) > get-content docs:/junk.txt
Hello there!
```

This works as expected. But when we try this with cmd.exe

```
PS (7) > cmd /c type docs:/junk.txt
The syntax of the command is incorrect.
```

it fails! This is because non-PowerShell applications don't understand the PowerShell drive fiction.

Do you remember the earlier example, where we did a "cd" to the location first, that it did work? This is because when we're "in" that drive, the system automatically sets the current directory properly to the physical path for the child process. This is why using relative paths from cmd.exe works. However, when we pass in a Power-Shell path, it fails. There is another workaround for this besides doing a cd. You can use the Resolve-Path cmdlet to get the ProviderPath. This cmdlet takes the PowerShell "logical" path and translates it into the provider's native physical path. This means that it's the "real" file system path that non-PowerShell utilities can understand. We'll use this to pass the real path to cmd.exe:

```
PS (7) > cmd /c type (resolve-path docs:/junk.txt).ProviderPath
Hello there!
```

This time, it works. This is an area where we need to be careful and think about how things should work with non-PowerShell applications. If we wanted to open a file with notepad.exe in the doc: directory, we'd have to do the same thing we did for cmd.exe and resolve the path first:

```
notepad (resolve-path docs:/junk.txt).ProviderPath
```

If you frequently use `notepad` then you can create a function in your profile:

```
function notepad {
    $args | %{ notepad.exe (resolve-path $_)/ProviderPath
}
```

You could even create a function to launch an arbitrary executable:

```
function run-exe
{
    $cmd, $files = $args
    $cmd =  (resolve-path $path).ProviderPath
    $file | %{ & $cmd  (resolve-path $_).ProviderPath }
}
```

This function resolves both the file to edit and the command to run. This means that you can use a PowerShell drive to map a command path to execute.

10.2.2 Working with paths that contain wildcards

Another great feature of the PowerShell provider infrastructure is universal support for wildcards (see chapter 4 for details on wildcard patterns). We can use wildcards any place we can navigate to, even in places such as the `alias:` drive. For example, say you want to find all of the aliases that begin with "gc". You can do this with wildcards in the alias provider.

```
PS (1) > dir alias:gc*
```

CommandType	Name	Definition
Alias	gc	Get-Content
Alias	gci	Get-ChildItem
Alias	gcm	Get-Command

We see that there are three of them.

We might all agree that this is a great feature, but there is a downside. What happens when you want to access a path that contains one of the wildcard meta-characters: "?", "*", "[" and "]". In the Windows filesystem, "*" and "?" aren't a problem because we can't use these characters in a file or directory name. But we can use "[" and "]". In fact, they are used quite a bit for temporary Internet files. Working with files whose names contain "[" or "]" can be quite a challenge because of the way wildcards and quoting (see chapter 3) work. Square brackets are used a lot in filenames in browser caches to avoid collisions by numbering the files. Let's run some experiments on some of the files in the IE cache.

AUTHOR'S NOTE Here's another tip. By default, the Get-ChildItem cmdlet (and its alias dir) will not show hidden files. To see the hidden files, use the -Force parameter. For example, to find the "Application Data" directory in our home directory, we try

```
PS (1) > dir ~/app*
```

but nothing is returned. This is because this directory is hidden. To see the directory, we use -Force as in:

```
PS (2) > dir ~/app* -Force


    Directory:Microsoft.PowerShell.Core\FileSystem::C:\Docum
    ents and Settings\brucepay


Mode                LastWriteTime     Length Name
----                -------------     ------ ----
d-rh-          12/14/2006   9:13 PM          Application Data
```

and now the directory is visible. We'll need to use -force to get into the directory containing the temporary Internet files.

Suppressing wildcard processing in paths

In one of the directories used to cache temporary Internet files, we want to find all of the files that begin with "thumb*". This is easy enough:

```
PS (2) > dir thumb*


    Directory: Microsoft.PowerShell.Core\FileSystem::C:\Doc
    uments and Settings\brucepay\Local Settings\Temporary I
    nternet Files\Content.IE5\MYNBM9OJ


Mode              LastWriteTime       Length Name
----              -------------       ------ ----
-a---        9/7/2006   10:34 PM        4201 ThumbnailServe
                                             r[1].jpg
-a---        9/7/2006   10:35 PM        3223 ThumbnailServe
                                             r[2].jpg
-a---        7/8/2006    7:58 PM        2066 thumb[1].jpg
-a---        9/11/2006   2:48 PM       12476 thumb[2].txt
-a---        9/11/2006   2:48 PM       11933 thumb[3].txt
```

We get five files. Now we want to limit the set of files to things that match "thumb[". We try this directly using a wildcard pattern:

```
PS (3) > dir thumb[*
Get-ChildItem : Cannot retrieve the dynamic parameters for
the cmdlet. The specified wildcard pattern is not valid: th
umb[*
At line:1 char:3
+ ls  <<<< thumb[*
```

Of course, it fails because the "[" is being treated as part of a wildcard pattern. Clearly we need to suppress treating "[" as a wildcard by escaping it. The obvious first step, per chapter 4, is to try a single backtick

```
PS (4) > dir thumb`[*
Get-ChildItem : Cannot retrieve the dynamic parameters for
the cmdlet. The specified wildcard pattern is not valid: th
```

```
umb\[*
At line:1 char:3
+ ls <<<< thumb`[*
```

This fails because the single backtick is discarded in the parsing process. In fact, it takes four backticks to cause the square bracket to be treated as a regular character.

```
PS (5) > dir thumb````[*


    Directory: Microsoft.PowerShell.Core\FileSystem::C:\Doc
    uments and Settings\brucepay\Local Settings\Temporary I
    nternet Files\Content.IE5\MYNBM9OJ


Mode                LastWriteTime     Length Name
----                -------------     ------ ----
-a---         7/8/2006    7:58 PM       2066 thumb[1].jpg
-a---        9/11/2006    2:48 PM      12476 thumb[2].txt
-a---        9/11/2006    2:48 PM      11933 thumb[3].txt
```

This is because one set of backticks is removed by the interpreter and a second set is removed by the provider itself. (This second round of backtick removal is so we can use escaping to represent filenames that contain literal quotes.) Putting single quotes around the pattern keeps the interpreter from doing escape processing in the string, simplifying this to only needing two backticks:

```
PS (8) > ls 'thumb``[*'


    Directory: Microsoft.PowerShell.Core\FileSystem::C:\Doc
    uments and Settings\brucepay\Local Settings\Temporary I
    nternet Files\Content.IE5\MYNBM9OJ


Mode                LastWriteTime     Length Name
----                -------------     ------ ----
-a---         7/8/2006    7:58 PM       2066 thumb[1].jpg
-a---        9/11/2006    2:48 PM      12476 thumb[2].txt
-a---        9/11/2006    2:48 PM      11933 thumb[3].txt
```

In this particular example, much of the complication arises because we want some of the meta-characters to be treated as literal characters, while the rest still do pattern matching. Trial and error is usually the only way to get this right.

AUTHOR'S NOTE   As we've said previously, this stuff is hard. It's hard to understand and it's hard to get right. But this problem exists in every language that does pattern matching. Patience, practice, and experimentation are the only ways to figure it out.

The –LiteralPath parameter

We don't want trial and error when we know the name of the file and want to suppress all pattern matching behavior. This is accomplished by using the -LiteralPath parameter available on most core cmdlets. Say we want to copy a file from the previous example. If we use the regular path mechanism in Copy-Item:

```
PS (11) > copy thumb[1].jpg c:\temp\junk.jpg
PS (12) > dir c:\temp\junk.jpg
Get-ChildItem : Cannot find path 'C:\temp\junk.jpg' because
 it does not exist.
At line:1 char:4
+ dir  <<<< c:\temp\junk.jpg
```

the copy fails because the square brackets were treated as metacharacters. Now try it using -LiteralPath.

```
PS (13) > copy -literalpath thumb[1].jpg c:\temp\junk.jpg
PS (14) > dir c:\temp\junk.jpg


    Directory: Microsoft.PowerShell.Core\FileSystem::C:\temp


Mode                LastWriteTime     Length Name
----                -------------     ------ ----
-a---       7/8/2006   7:58 PM         2066 junk.jpg
```

This time it works properly. When you pipe the output of a cmdlet such as dir into another cmdlet like Remove-Item, the -LiteralPath parameter is used to couple the cmdlets so that metacharacters in the paths returned by dir do not cause problems for Remove-Item. If we want to delete the files we were looking at earlier, we can use dir to see them:

```
PS (16) > dir thumb````[*


    Directory: Microsoft.PowerShell.Core\FileSystem::C:\Doc
    uments and Settings\brucepay\Local Settings\Temporary I
    nternet Files\Content.IE5\MYNBM9OJ


Mode                LastWriteTime     Length Name
----                -------------     ------ ----
-a---       7/8/2006   7:58 PM         2066 thumb[1].jpg
-a---       9/11/2006  2:48 PM        12476 thumb[2].txt
-a---       9/11/2006  2:48 PM        11933 thumb[3].txt
```

Now pipe the output of dir into del:

```
PS (17) > dir thumb````[* | del
```

and verify that they have been deleted.

```
PS (18) > dir thumb````[*
```

No files are found, so the deletion was successful.

This essentially covers the issues around working with file paths. From here we can move on to working with the file contents instead.

10.2.3 Reading and writing files

In PowerShell, files are read using the Get-Content cmdlet. This cmdlet allows you to work with text files using a variety of character encodings. It also lets you work efficiently with binary files, as we'll see in a minute. Writing files is a bit more complex, because you have to choose between Set-Content and Out-File. The difference here is whether or not the output goes through the formatting subsystem. We'll also explain this later on in this section. One thing to note is that there are no separate open/read/close or open/write/close steps to working with files. The pipeline model allows you to process data and never have to worry about closing file handles—the system takes care of this for you.

Reading files with the Get-Content cmdlet

The Get-Content cmdlet is the primary way to read files in PowerShell. Actually, it's the primary way to read any content available through PowerShell drives. Figure 10.1 shows a subset of the parameters available on the cmdlet.
Reading text files is simple. The command

```
Get-Content myfile.txt
```

will send the contents of "myfile.txt" to the output stream. Notice that the command signature for -path allows for an array of path names. This is how you concatenate a collection of files together. Let's try this. First we'll create a bunch of files:

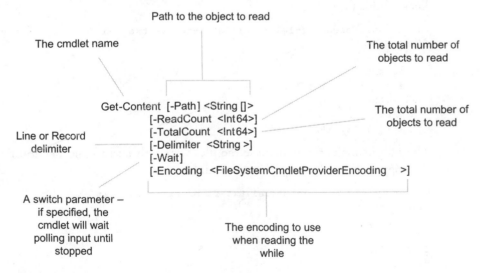

Figure 10.1   The Get-Content **cmdlet parameters**

```
PS (1) > 1..3 | %{ "This is file $_" > "file$_.txt"}
PS (2) > dir


    Directory: Microsoft.PowerShell.Core\FileSystem::C:\Temp\fil
    es


Mode                LastWriteTime     Length Name
----                -------------     ------ ----
-a---         7/6/2006     8:33 PM        34 file1.txt
-a---         7/6/2006     8:33 PM        34 file2.txt
-a---         7/6/2006     8:33 PM        34 file3.txt
```

And now display their contents:

```
PS (3) > cat file1.txt,file2.txt,file3txt
This is file 1
This is file 2
This is file 3
```

or simply

```
PS (4) > cat *.txt
This is file 1
This is file 2
This is file 3
```

In this example, the contents of file1.txt, file2.txt, and file3.txt are sent to the output stream in order. For cmd.exe users, this is equivalent to

```
copy file1.txt+file2.txt+file3.txt con
```

Let's try this in cmd.exe:

```
C:\Temp\files>copy file1.txt+file2.txt+file3txt con
file1.txt
 T h i s   i s   f i l e   1
file2.txt
 h i s   i s   f i l e   2
file2.txt
 h i s   i s   f i l e   3
        1 file(s) copied.
```

The output looks funny because the files were written in Unicode. You need to tell the copy command to write in ASCII, and try it again:

```
C:\Temp\files>copy /a  file1.txt+file2.txt+file3.txt con
file1.txt
This is file 1
file2.txt
This is file 2
file2.txt
This is file 3
        1 file(s) copied.
```

By default, PowerShell uses Unicode for text, but you can override this. We'll see how to do this in the section on writing files. In the meantime, let's look at how to work with binary files.

Example: The Get-HexDump function

Let's look at an example that uses some of these features to deal with non-text files. We're going to write a function that can be used to dump out a binary file. We'll call this function Get-HexDump. It takes the name of the file to display, the number of bytes to display per line, and the total number of bytes as parameters. We want the output of this function to look like the following:

```
PS (130) > Get-HexDump "$env:windir/Soap Bubbles.bmp" -w 12 -t 100
42 4d ba 01 01 00 00 00 00 00 ba 01 BM°.......°.
00 00 28 00 00 00 00 01 00 00 00 01 ............
00 00 01 00 08 00 00 00 00 00 00 00 ............
01 00 12 0b 00 00 12 0b 00 00 61 00 ..........a.
00 00 61 00 00 00 6b 10 10 00 73 10 ..a...k...s.
10 00 73 18 18 00 7b 21 21 00 84 29 ..s.........
29 00 84 31 31 00 6b 08 08 00 8c 39 ...11.k....9
31 00 84 31 29 00 8c 31 31 00 7b 18 1..1...11...
18 00 8c 39 ...9
```

In this example, we're using Get-HexDump to dump out the contents of one of the bit-map files in the Windows installation directory. We've specified that it display 12 bytes per line and stop after the first 100 bytes. The first part of the display is the value of the byte in hexadecimal, and the portion on the right side is the character equivalent. Only values that correspond to letters or numbers are displayed. Nonprintable characters are shown as dots. The code for this function is shown in listing 10.1.

Listing 10.1 Get-HexDump

```
function Get-HexDump ($path = $(throw "path must be specified"),
        $width=10, $total=-1)
{
    $OFS=""                                        ←──┐  ❶ Set $OFS
    Get-Content -Encoding byte $path -ReadCount $width `   to empty
        -totalcount $total | %{                    ◄────  ❷ Read the file
        $record = $_
        if (($record -eq 0).count -ne $width)      ◄──┐  Skip record if
        {                                           ❸ length is zero
            $hex = $record | %{
                " " + ("{0:x}" -f $_).PadLeft(2,"0")}    ❹ Format data
            $char = $record | %{
                if ([char]::IsLetterOrDigit($_))
                    { [char] $_ } else { "." }}
            "$hex $char"   ◄──┐  Emit formatted
        }                   ❺ output
    }
}
```

As required, the function takes a mandatory path parameter and optional parameters for the number of bytes per line and the total number of bytes to display. We're going to be converting arrays to strings and we don't want any spaces added, so we'll set the output field separator character ❶ to be empty.

The Get-Content cmdlet ❷ does all of the hard work. It reads the file in binary mode (indicated by setting encoding to byte), reads up to a maximum of -TotalCount bytes, and writes them into the pipeline in records of length specified by -ReadCount. The first thing we do in the foreach scriptblock is save the record that was passed in, because we'll be using nested pipelines that will cause $_ to be overwritten.

If the record is all zeros ❸, we're not going to bother displaying it. It might be a better design to make this optional, but we'll leave it as is for this example. For display purposes, we're converting the record of bytes ❹ into two-digit hexadecimal numbers. We use the format operator to format the string in hexadecimal and then the PadLeft() method on strings to pad it out to two characters. Finally, we prefix the whole thing with a space. The variable $hex ends up with a collection of these formatted strings.

Now we need to build the character equivalent of the record. We'll use the methods on the [char] class to decide whether we should display the character or a ".". Notice that even when we're displaying the character, we're still casting it into a [char]. This is needed because the record contains a byte value which, if directly converted into a string, will be a formatted as a number instead of as a character. Finally, we'll output the completed record, taking advantage of string expansion to build the output string ❺ (which is why we set $OFS to "").

This example illustrates the basic technique for getting at the binary data in a file. The technique has a variety of applications beyond simply displaying binary data, of course. Once you reach the data, you can determine a variety of characteristics about the content of that file. In the next section, we'll take a look at an example and examine the content of a binary file to double-check on the type of that file.

Example: The Get-MagicNumber function

If you looked closely at the output from the .BMP file earlier, you might have noticed that the first two characters in the file were BP. In fact, the first few bytes in a file are often used as a "magic number" that identifies the type of the file. We'll write a short function Get-MagicNumber that displays the first four bytes of a file so we can investigate these magic numbers. Here's what we want the output to look like. First we'll try this on a .BMP file

```
PS (1) > get-magicnumber $env:windir/Zapotec.bmp
424d 3225 'BM2.'
```

and then on an .EXE.

```
PS (2) > get-magicnumber $env:windir/explorer.exe
4d5a 9000 'MZ..'
PS (3) >
```

This utility dumps the header bytes of the executable. The first two bytes identify this file as an MS-DOS executable.

AUTHOR'S NOTE Trivia time: As you can see, the ASCII representation of the header bytes (0x5A4D) is MZ. These are the initials of Mark Zbikowski, one of the original architects of MS-DOS.

The code for `Get-MagicNumber` is shown in listing 10.2.

Listing 10.2   Get-MagicNumber

```
function Get-MagicNumber ($path)
{                                          ➊  Set $OFS to
    $OFS=""                                   empty string
    $mn = Get-Content -encoding byte $path -read 4 -total 4    ➋ Format
    $hex1 = ("{0:x}" -f ($mn[0]*256+$mn[1])).PadLeft(4, "0")      as hex
    $hex2 = ("{0:x}" -f ($mn[2]*256+$mn[3])).PadLeft(4, "0")
    [string] $chars = $mn| %{ if ([char]::IsLetterOrDigit($_))    ➌ Format
            { [char] $_ } else { "." }}                             as char
    "{0} {1} '{2}'" -f  $hex1, $hex2, $chars    ➍ Emit
}                                                  output
```

There's not much that's new in this function. Again, we set the output field separator string to be empty ➊. We extract the first four bytes as two pairs of numbers formatted in hex ➋ and also as characters ➌ if they correspond to printable characters. Finally, we format the output ➍ as desired.

From these examples, we see that `Get-Content` allows us to explore any type of file on a system, not just text files. For now, though, let's return to text files and look at another parameter on `Get-Content`: `Delimiter`. When reading a text file, the default line delimiter is the newline character.

AUTHOR'S NOTE Actually, the end-of-line sequence on Windows is generally a two-character sequence: carriage return followed by newline. The .NET I/O routines hide this detail and let us just pretend it's a newline. In fact, the runtime will treat newline by itself, carriage return by itself, and the carriage return/newline sequence all as end-of-line sequences.

This parameter lets you change that. With this new knowledge, let's return to the word-counting problem we had earlier. If we set the delimiter to be the space character instead of a newline, we can split the file as we read it. Let's use this in an example.

```
get-content about_Assignment_operators.help.txt `
    -delimiter " " |
    foreach { $_ -replace "[^\w]+"} |
    where { $_ -notmatch "^[ `t]*`$"} |
    group |
    sort -descending count |
    select -first 10 |
    ft -auto name, count
```

In this example, the -delimiter parameter is used to split the file on space boundaries instead of newlines. We're using the same group, sort, and format operations as before; however, this time we're sorting in descending order so we can use the Select-Object cmdlet instead of array indexing to extract the top 10 words. We're also doing more sophisticated filtering. We're using a foreach filter to get rid of the characters that aren't legal in a word. This is accomplished with the -replace operator and the regular expression "[^\w]+". The \w pattern is a meta-character that matches any legal character in a word. Putting it in the square brackets prefixed with the caret says it should match any character that isn't valid in a word. The where filter is used to discard any empty lines that may be in the text or may have been created by the foreach filter.

At this point, we have a pretty good handle on reading files and processing their contents. It's time to look at the various ways to write files.

Writing files

There are two major ways to write files in PowerShell—by setting file content with the Set-Content cmdlet and by writing files using the Out-File cmdlet. The big difference is that Out-File, like all of the output cmdlets, will try to format the output. Set-Content, on the other hand, will simply write the output. If its input objects aren't already strings, it will convert them to strings by calling the .ToString() method. This is not usually what you want for objects, but it's exactly what you want if your data is already formatted or if you're working with binary data.

The other thing you need to be concerned with is how the files are encoded when they're written. In an earlier example, we saw that, by default, text files are written in Unicode. Let's rerun this example, changing the encoding to ASCII instead.

```
PS (48) > 1..3 | %{ "This is file $_" |
>> set-content -encoding ascii file$_.txt }
>>
```

The -encoding parameter is used to set how the files will be written. In this example, the files are written using ASCII encoding. Now let's rerun the cmd.exe copy example that didn't work earlier.

```
PS (49) > cmd /c copy file1.txt+file2.txt+file3.txt con
file1.txt
This is file 1
file2.txt
This is file 2
file3.txt
This is file 3
        1 file(s) copied.
```

This time it works fine, because the encoding matches what cmd.exe expected. In the next section, we'll look at using -encoding to write binary files.

All together now—Reading and writing

Our next topic of interest is combining reading and writing binary files. First we'll set up paths to two files: a source bitmap file:

```
$src = "$env:windir/Soap Bubbles.bmp"
```

and a destination in a temporary file.

```
$dest = "$env:temp/new_bitmap.bmp"
```

Now we'll copy the contents from one file to the other:

```
get-content -encoding byte -read 10kb $src |
    set-content -encoding byte $dest
```

Now let's define a (not very good) checksum function that simply adds up all of the bytes in the file.

```
function Get-CheckSum ($path)
{
    $sum=0
    get-content -encoding byte -read 10kb $path | %{
        foreach ($byte in $_) { $sum += $byte }
    }
    $sum
}
```

We'll use this function to verify that the file we copied is the same as the original file (note that this is a fairly slow function and takes a while to run).

```
PS (5) > Get-CheckSum $src
268589
PS (6) > Get-CheckSum $dest
268589
```

The numbers come out the same, so we have some confidence that the copied file matches the original.

10.2.4 Searching files with the Select-String cmdlet

Another place where regular expressions are used is in the Select-String cmdlet. This cmdlet allows you to search through collections of strings or collections of files. It's similar to the grep command on UNIX-derived systems and the findstr command on Windows. Figure 10.2 shows a subset of the parameters on this cmdlet.

We might ask why this cmdlet is needed—doesn't the base language do everything it does? The answer is yes, but searching through files is such a common operation that having a cmdlet optimized for this purpose makes sense. Let's look at some examples. First, we're going to search through all of the "about_*" topics in the PowerShell installation directory to see if the phrase "wildcard description" is there.

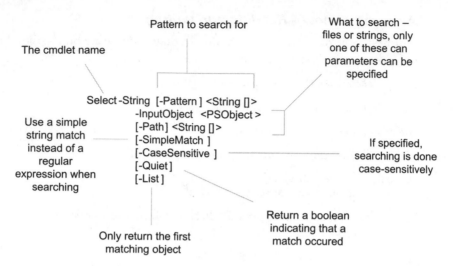

The cmdlet name

Pattern to search for

What to search –
files or strings, only
one of these can
parameters can be
specified

```
Select -String  [-Pattern ] <String []>
            -InputObject  <PSObject >
            [-Path] <String []>
            [-SimpleMatch ]
            [-CaseSensitive ]
            [-Quiet]
            [-List ]
```

Use a simple
string match
instead of a
regular
expression when
searching

If specified,
searching is done
case-sensitively

Only return the first
matching object

Return a boolean
indicating that a
match occured

Figure 10.2 The `Select-String` cmdlet parameters

```
PS (1) > select-string "wildcard description" $pshome/about*.txt

about_Wildcard.help.txt:36:      Wildcard Description          Examp
le  Match                No match
```

We see that there is exactly one match, but notice the uppercase letters in the matching string. Let's rerun the search using the -CaseSensitive parameter.

```
PS (2) > select-string -case "wildcard description" `
>> $pshome/about*.txt
>>
```

This time nothing was found. If we alter the case in the pattern then it works again.

```
PS (3) > select-string -case "Wildcard Description" `
>>  $pshome/about*.txt
>>

about_Wildcard.help.txt:36:      Wildcard Description          Examp
le  Match                No match
```

Now let's try out the -list parameter. Normally Select-String will find all matches in a file. The -list switch limits the search to only the first match in a file:

```
PS (4) > select-string -list wildcard $pshome/about*.txt

about_Comparison_operators.help.txt:28:    -like          wildcard
 comparison    "one" -like "o*"           true
about_Filter.help.txt:60:      -like       A comparison operator t
hat supports wildcard matching
about_Globbing.help.txt:5:     See Wildcard
about_operator.help.txt:71:       -like          Wildcard comp
arison (case insensitive)
```

```
about_Parameter.help.txt:62:        Wildcards are allowed but th
ey must resolve to a single name.
about_switch.help.txt:63:        switch [-regex|-wildcard|-exact
][-casesensitive] ( pipeline )
about_where.help.txt:55:    -like        compare strings using w
ildcard rules
about_Wildcard.help.txt:2:    Wildcards
```

In the result, we see exactly one match per file. Now let's try using the -quiet switch.

```
PS (5) > select-string -quiet wildcard $pshome/about*.txt
True
```

This switch returns true if any of the files contained a match and false if none of them did. We can also combine the two switches so that the cmdlet returns the first match in the set of files.

```
PS (6) > select-string -quiet -list wildcard $pshome/about*.txt

about_Comparison_operators.help.txt:28:    -like        wildcard
 comparison    "one" -like "o*"        true
```

If you want to search a more complex set of files, you can pipe the output of Get-Childitem (dir) into the cmdlet and it will search all of these files. Let's search all of the log files in system32 subdirectory.

```
PS (7) > dir -rec -filter *.log $env:windir\system32 |
>> select-string -list fail | ft path
>>

Path
----
C:\WINDOWS\system32\CCM\Logs\ScanWrapper.LOG
C:\WINDOWS\system32\CCM\Logs\UpdateScan.log
C:\WINDOWS\system32\CCM\Logs\packages\RMSSP1_Client_RTW.log
C:\WINDOWS\system32\CCM\Logs\packages\RMSSP1_Client_RTW_BC_In...
C:\WINDOWS\system32\wbem\Logs\wbemcore.log
C:\WINDOWS\system32\wbem\Logs\wbemess.log
C:\WINDOWS\system32\wbem\Logs\wmiadap.log
C:\WINDOWS\system32\wbem\Logs\wmiprov.log
```

Notice that we're only displaying the path. The output of Select-String is objects, as shown:

```
PS (8) > select-string wildcard $pshome/about*.txt |
>> gm -type property
>>

    TypeName: Microsoft.PowerShell.Commands.MatchInfo

Name        MemberType Definition
----        ---------- ----------
Filename    Property   System.String Filename {get;}
IgnoreCase  Property   System.Boolean IgnoreCase {get;set;}
```

```
Line         Property    System.String Line {get;set;}
LineNumber   Property    System.Int32 LineNumber {get;set;}
Path         Property    System.String Path {get;set;}
Pattern      Property    System.String Pattern {get;set;}
```

You can select as much or as little information from these objects as you want.

All of the text we've been working with so far has been unstructured text where there is no rigorously defined layout for that text. As a consequence, we've had to work fairly hard to extract the information we want out of this text. There are, however, large bodies of structured text, where the format is well-defined in the form of XML documents. In the next section, we'll look at how to work with XML in PowerShell.

10.3   XML PROCESSING

XML (Extensible Markup Language) is becoming more and more important in the computing world. XML is being used for everything from configuration files to log files to databases. PowerShell itself uses XML for its type and configuration files as well as for the help files. Clearly, for PowerShell to be effective, it has to be able to process XML documents effectively. Let's take a look at how XML is used and supported in PowerShell.

> **AUTHOR'S NOTE**   This section assumes some basic knowledge of XML markup.

We'll look at the XML object type, as well as the mechanism that .NET provides for searching XML documents.

10.3.1   Using XML as objects

PowerShell supports XML documents as a primitive data type. This means that you can access the elements of an XML document as though they were properties on an object. For example, we create a simple XML object. We'll start with a string that defines a top-level node called "top". This node contains three descendants "a", "b", and "c", each of which has a value. Let's turn this string into an object:

```
PS (1) > $d = [xml] "<top><a>one</a><b>two</b><c>3</c></top>"
```

The [xml] cast takes the string and converts it into an XML object of type System.XML.XmlDocument. This object is then adapted by PowerShell so you can treat it like a regular object. Let's try this out. First we'll display the object:

```
PS (2) > $d

top
---
top
```

As we expect, the object displays one top-level property corresponding to the top-level node in the document. Now let's see what properties this node contains:

```
PS (3) > $d.a
PS (4) > $d.top
```

a	b	c
-	-	-
one	two	3

There are three properties that correspond to the descendents of top. We can use conventional property notation to look at the value of an individual member:

```
PS (5) > $d.top.a
One
```

We can then change the value of this node. It's as simple as assigning a new value to the node. Let's assign the string "Four" to the node "a":

```
PS (6) > $d.top.a = "Four"
PS (7) > $d.top.a
Four
```

We can see that it's been changed. But there is a limitation: we can only use an actual string as the node value. The XML object adapter won't automatically convert non-string objects to strings in an assignment, so we get an error when we try it, as seen in the following:

```
PS (8) > $d.top.a = 4
Cannot set "a" because only strings can be used as values to
set XmlNode properties.
At line:1 char:8
+ $d.top.a <<<<  = 4
```

All of the normal type conversions apply, of course. The node c contains a string value that is a number.

```
PS (8) > $d.top.c.gettype().FullName
System.String
```

We can add this field to an integer, which will cause it to be converted into an integer.

```
PS (9) > 2 + $d.top.c
5
```

Since we can't simply assign to elements in an XML document, we'll dig a little deeper into the [xml] object and see how we can add elements.

Adding elements to an XML object

Let's add an element "d" to this document. To do this, we need to use the methods on the XML document object. First we have to create the new element:

```
PS (10) > $el= $d.CreateElement("d")
```

In text, what we've created looks like "<d></d>". The tags are there, but they're empty. Let's set the element text, the "inner text":

```
PS (11) > $el.set_InnerText("Hello")

#text
-----
Hello
```

Notice that we're using the property setter method here. This is because the XML adapter hides the basic properties on the XmlNode object. The other way to set this would be to use the PSBase member like we did with the hashtable example earlier in this chapter.

```
PS (12) > $ne = $d.CreateElement("e")
PS (13) > $ne.psbase.InnerText = "World"
PS (14) > $d.top.AppendChild($ne)

#text
-----
World
```

Take a look at the revised object.

```
PS (15) > $d.top

a : one
b : two
c : 3
d : Hello
e : World
```

We see that the document now has five members instead of the original three. But what does the string look like now? It would be great if we could simply cast the document back to a string and see what it looks like:

```
PS (16) > [string] $d
System.Xml.XmlDocument
```

Unfortunately, as you can see, it isn't that simple. Instead, we'll save the document as a file and display it:

```
PS (17) > $d.save("c:\temp\new.xml")
PS (18) > type c:\temp\new.xml
<top>
  <a>one</a>
  <b>two</b>
  <c>3</c>
  <d>Hello</d>
  <e>World</e>
</top>
```

The result is a nicely readable text file. Now that we know how to add children to a node, how can we add attributes? The pattern is basically the same as with elements. First we create an attribute object.

```
PS (19) > $attr = $d.CreateAttribute("BuiltBy")
```

Next we set the value of the text for that object. Again we use the PSBase member to bypass the adaptation layer.

```
PS (20) > $attr.psbase.Value = "Windows PowerShell"
```

And finally we add it to the top-level document.

```
PS (21) > $d.psbase.DocumentElement.SetAttributeNode($attr)

#text
-----
Windows PowerShell
```

Let's look at the top node once again.

```
PS (22) > $d.top

BuiltBy : Windows PowerShell
a       : one
b       : two
c       : 3
d       : Hello
e       : World
```

We see that the attribute has been added.

AUTHOR'S NOTE While PowerShell's XML support is good, there are some issues. The first release of PowerShell has a bug, where trying to display an XML node that has multiple children with the same name causes an error to be generated by the formatter. For example, the statement

```
[xml]$x = "<root><item>1</item><item>2</item></root>"
$x.root
```

will result in an error. This can be disconcerting when you are trying to explore a document. By doing

```
[xml]$x = "<root><item>1</item><item>2</item></root>" ;
$x.root.item
```

instead, you'll be able to see the elements without error. Also, for experienced .NET XML and XPath users, there are times when the XML adapter hides properties on an XmlDocument or XmlNode object that the .NET programmer expects to find. In these scenarios, the .PSBase property is the workaround that lets you access the raw .NET object. Finally, some XPath users may get confused by PowerShell's use of the property operator "." to navigate an XML document. XPath uses / instead. Despite these issues, for the nonexpert user or for "quick and dirty" scenarios, the XML adapter provides significant benefit in terms of reducing the complexity of working with XML.

It's time to save the document:

```
PS (23) > $d.save("c:\temp\new.xml")
```

Then retrieve the file. You can see how the attribute has been added to the top node in the document.

```
PS (24) > type c:\temp\new.xml
<top BuiltBy="Windows PowerShell">
  <a>one</a>
  <b>two</b>
  <c>3</c>
  <d>Hello</d>
</top>
PS (25) >
```

We constructed, edited, and saved XML documents, but we haven't loaded an existing document yet, so that's the next step.

10.3.2   Loading and saving XML files.

At the end of the previous section, we saved an XML document to a file. If we read it back:

```
PS (1) > $nd = [xml] [string]::join("`n",
>> (gc -read 10kb c:\temp\new.xml))
>>
```

Here's what we're doing. We use the Get-Content cmdlet to read the file; however, it comes back as a collection of strings when what we really want is one single string. To do this, we use the [string]::Join() method. Once we have the single string, we cast the whole thing into an XML document.

> **AUTHOR'S NOTE**   Here's a performance tip. By default, Get-Content reads one record at a time. This can be quite slow. When processing large files, you should use the -ReadCount parameter to specify a block size of -1. This will cause the entire file to be loaded and processed at once, which is much faster. Alternatively, here's another way to load an XML document using the .NET methods:
>
> ```
> ($nd = [xml]"<root></root>" ).Load("C:\temp\new.xml")
> ```
>
> Note that this does require that the full path to the file be specified..

Let's verify that the document was read properly by dumping out the top-level node and then the child nodes.

```
PS (2) > $nd

top
---
top
```

```
PS (3) > $nd.top

BuiltBy : Windows PowerShell
a       : one
b       : two
c       : 3
d       : Hello
```

All is as it should be. Even the attribute is there.

While this is a simple approach and the one we'll use most often, it's not necessarily the most efficient approach because it requires loading the entire document into memory. For very large documents or collections of many documents, this may become a problem. In the next section, we'll look at some alternative approaches that, while more complex, are more memory-efficient.

Example: The dump-doc function

The previous method we looked at for loading an XML file is very simple, but not very efficient. It requires that you load the file into memory, make a copy of the file while turning it into a single string, and create an XML document representing the entire file but with all of the overhead of the XML DOM format. A much more space-efficient way to process XML documents is to use the XML reader class. This class streams through the document one element at a time instead of loading the whole thing into memory. We're going to write a function that will use the XML reader to stream through a document and output it properly indented. An XML pretty-printer, if you will. Here's what we want the output of this function to look like when it dumps its built-in default document:

```
PS (1) > dump-doc
<top BuiltBy = "Windows PowerShell">
    <a>
        one
    </a>
    <b>
        two
    </b>
    <c>
        3
    </c>
    <d>
        Hello
    </d>
</top>
```

Now let's test our function on a more complex document where there are more attributes and more nesting. Listing 10.3 shows how to create this document.

Listing 10.3 Creating the text XML document

```
@'
<top BuiltBy = "Windows PowerShell">
    <a pronounced="eh">
        one
    </a>
    <b pronounced="bee">
        two
    </b>
    <c one="1" two="2" three="3">
        <one>
            1
        </one>
        <two>
            2
        </two>
        <three>
            3
        </three>
    </c>
    <d>
        Hello there world
    </d>
</top>
'@ > c:\temp\fancy.xml
```

When we run the function, we see

```
PS (2) > dump-doc c:\temp\fancy.xml
<top BuiltBy = "Windows PowerShell">
    <a pronounced = "eh">
        one
    </a>
    <b pronounced = "bee">
        two
    </b>
    <c one = "1"two = "2"three = "3">
        <one>
            1
        </one>
        <two>
            2
        </two>
        <three>
            3
        </three>
    </c>
    <d>
        Hello there world
    </d>
</top>
```

which is pretty close to the original document. The code for the Dump-Doc function is shown in listing 10.4.

Listing 10.4   Dump-Doc

```
function Dump-Doc ($doc="c:\temp\new.xml")
{                                                          ❶ Create the
    $settings = new-object System.Xml.XmlReaderSettings <—    settings object
    $doc = (resolve-path $doc).ProviderPath             ❷ Create the
    $reader = [xml.xmlreader]::create($doc, $settings) <—   XML reader
    $indent=0
    function indent ($s) { "      "*$indent+$s }
    while ($reader.Read())            Define format-   ❹ Process
    {                                 ting function ❸     element
        if ($reader.NodeType -eq [Xml.XmlNodeType]::Element) <—  nodes
        {
            $close = $(if ($reader.IsEmptyElement) { "/>" } else { ">" })
            if ($reader.HasAttributes)              <—
            {                                         ❺ Process
                $s = indent "<$($reader.Name) "         attributes
                [void] $reader.MoveToFirstAttribute()
                do                                    Move through ❻
                {                                       attributes
                    $s += "$($reader.Name) = `"$($reader.Value)`""
                }
                while ($reader.MoveToNextAttribute())
                "$s$close"            }
            else
            {
                indent "<$($reader.Name)$close"
            }                                    ❼ Increase
            if ($close -ne '/>') {$indent++} <—    indent level
        }
        elseif ($reader.NodeType -eq [Xml.XmlNodeType]::EndElement )
        {
            $indent--                          ❽ Decrease
            indent "</$($reader.Name)>" <—        indent level
        }
        elseif ($reader.NodeType -eq [Xml.XmlNodeType]::Text)
        {
            indent $reader.Value      <—
        }                        ❿ Close reader ❾  Format text
    }                              object            element
    $reader.close() <—
}
```

This is a complex function, so it's worthwhile to take it one piece at a time. We start with the basic function declaration, where it takes an optional argument that names a file. Next we'll create the settings object ❶ we need to pass in when we create the XML reader object. We also need to resolve the path to the document, because the

XML reader object requires an absolute path (see chapter 11 for an explanation of why this is). Now we can create the `XmlReader` object ❷ itself. The XML reader will stream through the document, reading only as much as it needs, as opposed to reading the entire document into memory.

We want to display the levels of the document indented, so we'll initialize an indent level counter and a local function ❸ to display the indented string. Now we'll read through all of the nodes in the document. We'll choose different behavior based on the type of the node. An element node ❹ is the beginning of an XML element. If the element has attributes ❺ then we'll add them to the string to display. We'll use the `MoveToFirstAttribute()`/`MoveToNextAttribute()` methods ❻ to move through the attributes. (Note that this pattern parallels the enumerator pattern we saw in chapter 5 with the `$foreach` and `$switch` enumerators.) If there are no attributes, just display the element name. At each new element, increase ❼ the indent level if it's not an empty element tag. If it's the end of an element, decrease the indent level and display the closing tag ❽. If it's a text element, just display the value of the element ❾. Finally, close the reader ❿. We always want to close a handle received from a .NET method. It will eventually be discarded during garbage collection, but it's possible to run out of handles before you run out of memory.

This example illustrates the basic techniques for using an XML reader object to walk through an arbitrary document. In the next section, we'll look at a more specialized application.

Example: The Select-Help function

Now let's work with something a little more useful. The PowerShell help files are stored as XML documents. We want to write a function that scans through the command file, searching for a particular word in either the command name or the short help description. Here's what we want the output to look like:

```
PS (1) > select-help property
Clear-ItemProperty: Removes the property value from a property.
Copy-ItemProperty: Copies a property between locations or namesp
aces.
Get-ItemProperty: Retrieves the properties of an object.
Move-ItemProperty: Moves a property from one location to another
.
New-ItemProperty: Sets a new property of an item at a location.
Remove-ItemProperty: Removes a property and its value from the l
ocation.
Rename-ItemProperty: Renames a property of an item.
Set-ItemProperty: Sets a property at the specified location to a
 specified value.
PS (2) >
```

In the example, we're searching for the word *property* and we find a list of all of the cmdlets that work with properties. The output is a string containing the property name and a description string. Next let's look at a fragment of document we're going to process:

```
<command:details>
    <command:name>
                Add-Content
    </command:name>
    <maml:description>
        <maml:para>
            Adds to the content(s) of the specified item(s)
        </maml:para>
    </maml:description>
    <maml:copyright>
        <maml:para></maml:para>
    </maml:copyright>
    <command:verb>add</command:verb>
    <command:noun>content</command:noun>
    <dev:version></dev:version>
</command:details>
```

PowerShell help text is stored in MAML (Microsoft Assistance Markup Language) format. From simple examination of the fragment, we can see that the name of a command is stored in the `command:name` element and the description is stored in a `maml:description` element inside a `maml:para` element. The basic approach we'll use is to look for the command tag, extract and save the command name, and then capture the description in the description element that immediately follows the command name element. This means that we'll use a state-machine pattern to process the document. A state machine usually implies using the `switch` statement, so this example is also a good opportunity to use the control structures in the PowerShell language a bit more. The function is shown in listing 10.5.

Listing 10.5 Select-Help

```
function Select-Help ($pat = ".")        ←——❶  Declare function
{
    $cmdHlp="Microsoft.PowerShell.Commands.Management.dll-Help.xml"
    $doc = "$PSHOME\$cmdHlp"             ←——❷  Set up
                                                  paths

    $settings = new-object System.Xml.XmlReaderSettings
    $settings.ProhibitDTD = $false
    $reader = [xml.xmlreader]::create($doc, $settings)   ←——❸  Set up XML
                                                                reader

    $name = $null
    $capture_name = $false           ❹  Initialize
    $capture_description = $false        variables
    $finish_line = $false

    while ($reader.Read())
    {
        switch ($reader.NodeType)
```

```
            {
                ([Xml.XmlNodeType]::Element) {
                    switch ($reader.Name)
                    {
                        "command:name" {
                            $capture_name = $true
                            break
                        }
                        "maml:description" {
                            $capture_description = $true
                            break
                        }
                        "maml:para" {
                            if ($capture_description)
                            {
                                $finish_line = $true;
                            }
                        }
                    }
                    break
                }
                ([Xml.XmlNodeType]::EndElement) {
                    if ($capture_name) { $capture_name = $false }
                    if ($finish_description)
                    {
                        $finish_line = $false
                        $capture_description = $false
                    }
                    break
                }
                ([Xml.XmlNodeType]::Text) {
                    if ($capture_name)
                    {
                        $name = $reader.Value.Trim()
                    }
                    elseif ($finish_line -and $name)
                    {
                        $msg = $name + ": " + $reader.Value.Trim()
                        if ($msg -match $pat)
                        {
                            $msg
                        }
                        $name = $null
                    }
                    break
                }
            }
        }
    }
    $reader.close()
}
```

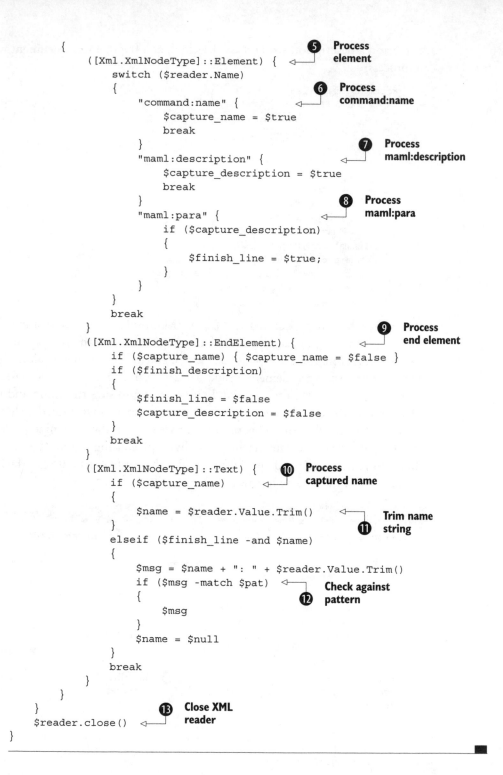

5 Process element

6 Process command:name

7 Process maml:description

8 Process maml:para

9 Process end element

10 Process captured name

11 Trim name string

12 Check against pattern

13 Close XML reader

Once again, this is a long piece of code, so we'll walk through it a piece at a time. The $pat parameter ❶ will contain the pattern to search for. If no argument is supplied then the default argument will match everything. Next, we set up the name of the document ❷ to search in the PowerShell installation directory. Then we create the XmlReader object ❸ as in the previous examples.

Since we're using a state machine, we need to set up ❹ some state variables. The $name variable will be used to hold the name of the cmdlet and the others will hold the state of the processing. We'll read through the document one node at a time and switch on the node type. Unrecognized node types are just ignored.

First, we'll process the Element ❺ nodes. We'll use a nested switch statement to perform different actions based on the type of element. Finding a command:name element ❻ starts the matching process. When we see a maml:description element ❼, we're capturing the beginning of a MAML description field, so we indicate that we want to capture the description. When we see the maml:para ❽ element, we need to handle the embedded paragraph in the description element. In the end tag ❾ of an element, we'll reset some of the state variables if they've been set. And finally, we need to extract the information ❿ we're interested in out of the element. We've captured the cmdlet name of the element, but we want to remove ⓫ any leading and trailing spaces, so we'll use the [string] Trim() method. Now we have both the cmdlet name and the description string. If it matches the pattern the caller specified ⓬, output it. Again, the last thing to do is to close the XML reader ⓭ so we don't waste resources.

But where are the pipelines, we ask? Neither of these last two examples has taken advantage of PowerShell's pipelining capability. In the next section, we'll remedy this omission.

10.3.3 Processing XML documents in a pipeline

Pipelining is one of the signature characteristics of shell environments in general, and PowerShell in particular. Since the previous examples did not take advantage of this feature, we'll look at how it can be applied now. We're going to write a function that scans all of the PowerShell help files, both the text about topics and the XML files. For example, let's search for all of the help topics that mention the word "scriptblock".

```
PS (1) > search-help scriptblock
about_Display
about_Types
Get-Process
Group-Object
Measure-Command
Select-Object
Trace-Command
ForEach-Object
Where-Object
```

This tool provides a simple, fast way to search for all of the help topics that contain a particular pattern. The source for the function is shown in listing 10.6.

Listing 10.6   Search-Help

```
function Search-Help
{
    param ($pattern = $(throw "you must specify a pattern"))

    select-string -list $pattern $PSHome\about*.txt |      ❶ Declare function
        %{$_.filename -replace '\..*$'}                        parameters

    dir $PShome\*dll-help.*xml |                            ❷ Scan the
        %{ [xml] (get-content -read -1 $_) } |                 about files
        %{$_.helpitems.command} |                          ❸ Select the
        ? {$_.get_Innertext() -match $pattern} |              matching files
        %{$_.details.name.trim()}
}
```

This function takes one parameter to use as the pattern for which we are searching. We're using the throw keyword described in chapter 9 to generate an error if the parameter was not provided.

First, we search all of the text files in the PowerShell installation directory and return one line for each matching file ❶. Then we pipe this line into Foreach-Object (or its alias % in this case) to extract the base name of the file using the replace operator and a regular expression. This will list the file names in the form that you type back into Get-Help.

Then get a list of the XML help files ❷ and turn each file into an XML object. We specify a read count of -1 so the whole file is read at once. We extract the command elements from the XML document ❸ and then see if the text of the command contains the pattern we're looking for. If so then emit the name of the command, trimming off unnecessary spaces.

As well as being a handy way to search help, this function is a nice illustration of using the divide-and-conquer strategy when writing scripts in PowerShell. Each step in the pipeline brings you incrementally closer to the final solution.

Now that we know how to manually navigate through an XML document, let's look at some of the .NET framework's features that make this a bit easier and more efficient.

10.3.4   Using XPath

The support for XML in the .NET framework is comprehensive. We can't cover all of it in this book, but we will cover one other thing. XML is actually a set of standards. One of these standards defines a path mechanism for searching through a document. This mechanism is called (not surprisingly) XPath. By using the .NET frameworks XPath supports, we can more quickly retrieve data from a document.

Setting up the test document

We'll work through a couple of examples using XPath, but first we need something to process. The following fragment is a string we'll use for our examples. It's a fragment of a bookstore inventory database. Each record in the database has the name of the author, the book title, and the number of books in stock. We'll save this string in a variable called $inventory as shown in listing 10.7.

Listing 10.7   Creating the bookstore inventory

```
$inventory = @"
  <bookstore>
    <book genre="Autobiography">
      <title>The Autobiography of Benjamin Franklin</title>
      <author>
        <first-name>Benjamin</first-name>
        <last-name>Franklin</last-name>
      </author>
      <price>8.99</price>
      <stock>3</stock>
    </book>
    <book genre="Novel">
      <title>Moby Dick</title>
      <author>
        <first-name>Herman</first-name>
        <last-name>Melville</last-name>
      </author>
      <price>11.99</price>
      <stock>10</stock>
    </book>
    <book genre="Philosophy">
      <title>Discourse on Method</title>
      <author>
        <first-name>Rene</first-name>
        <last-name>Descartes</last-name>
      </author>
      <price>9.99</price>
      <stock>1</stock>
    </book>
    <book genre="Computers">
      <title>Windows PowerShell in Action</title>
      <author>
        <first-name>Bruce</first-name>
        <last-name>Payette</last-name>
      </author>
      <price>39.99</price>
      <stock>5</stock>
    </book>
  </bookstore>
"@
```

Now that we have our test document created, let's look at what we can do with it.

The Get-XPathNavigator helper function

To navigate through an XML document and extract information, we're going to need an XML document navigator. Here is the definition of a function that will create the object we need.

```
function Get-XPathNavigator ($text)
{
    $rdr = [System.IO.StringReader] $text
    $trdr = [system.io.textreader]$rdr
    $xpdoc = [System.XML.XPath.XPathDocument] $trdr
    $xpdoc.CreateNavigator()
}
```

Unfortunately, we can't just convert a string directly into an XPath document. There is a constructor on this type that takes a string, but it uses that string as the name of a file to open. Consequently, the `Get-XPathNavigator` function has to wrap the argument string in a `StringReader` object and then in a `TextReader` object that can finally be used to create the `XPathDocument`. Once we have an instance of `XPathDocument`, we can use the `CreateNavigator()` method to get an instance of a navigator object.

```
$xb = get-XPathNavigator $inventory
```

Now we're ready to go. We can use this navigator instance to get information out of a document. First, let's get a list of all of the books that cost more than $9.

```
PS (1) > $expensive = "/bookstore/book/title[../price>9.00]"
```

We'll store the XPath query in the variable $expensive. Let's look at the actual query string for a minute. As you might expect from the name XPath, this query starts with a path into the document:

```
/bookstore/book/title
```

This path will select all of the title nodes in the document. But, since we only want some of the titles, we extend the path with a qualification. In this case:

```
[../price>9.00]
```

This only matches paths where the price element is greater than 9.00. Note that a path is used to access the price element. Since price is a sibling (that is, at the same level) as the title element, we need to specify this as:

```
../price
```

This should provide a basic idea of what the query is expressing, so we won't go into any more detail. Now let's run the query using the `Select()` method on the XPath navigator.

```
PS (2) > $xb.Select($expensive) | ft value
```

```
Value
-----
Moby Dick
Discourse on Method
Windows PowerShell in Action
```

We're running the result of the query into Format-Table because we're only interested in the value of the element. (Remember that what we're extracting here is only
the title element.) So this is pretty simple; we can search through the database and
find the titles pretty easily. What if we want to print both the title and price? Here's
one way we can do it.

Extracting multiple elements

To extract multiple elements from the document, first we'll have to create a new
query string. This time we need to get the whole book element, not just the title element, so we can also extract the price element. Here's the new query string:

```
PS (3) > $titleAndPrice = "/bookstore/book[price>9.00]"
```

Notice that this time, since we're getting the book instead of the title, we can just filter on the price element without having to use the ".." to go up a path. The problem
now is: how do we get the pieces of data we want—the title and price? The result of
the query has a property called OuterXml. This property contains the XML fragment
that represents the entire book element. We can take this element and cast it into an
XML document as we saw earlier in this section. Once we have it in this form, we can
use the normal property notation to extract the information. Here's what it looks like:

```
PS (4) > $xb.Select($titleAndPrice) | %{[xml] $_.OuterXml} |
>>      ft -auto {$_.book.price},{$_.book.title}
>>

$_.book.price $_.book.title
------------- -------------
11.99         Moby Dick
9.99          Discourse on Method
39.99         Windows PowerShell in Action
```

The call to Select() is similar to what we saw earlier. Now we take each object and
process it using the Foreach-Object cmdlet. First we take the current pipeline
object, extract the OuterXml string, then cast that string into an XML document and
pass that object through to the Format-Table cmdlet. We use scriptblocks in the
field specification to extract the information we want to display.

Performing calculations on elements

Let's look at one final example. We want a total price of all of the books in the inventory. This time, we'll use a slightly different query.

```
descendant::book
```

This query selects all of the elements that have a descendent element titled `book`. This is a more general way to select elements in the document. We'll pipe these documents into `Foreach-Object`. Here we'll specify scriptblocks for each of the begin, process, and end steps in the pipeline. In the begin scriptblock, we'll initialize `$t` to zero to hold the result. In the `foreach` scriptblock, we convert the current pipeline object into an `[xml]` object as we saw in the previous example. Then we get the price member, convert it into a `[decimal]` number, multiply it by the number of books in stock, and add the result to the total. The final step is to display the total in the end scriptblock. Here's what it looks like when it's run:

```
PS (5) > $xb.Select("descendant::book") | % {$t=0} `
>>      {
>>          $book = ([xml] $_.OuterXml).book
>>          $t += [decimal] $book.price * $book.stock
>>      } `
>>      {
>>          "Total price is: `$$t"
>>      }
>>
Total price is: $356.81
```

Having looked at building an XML path navigator on a stream, can we use XPath on an XML document itself? The answer is yes. In fact, it can be much easier than what we've seen previously. First, let's convert our inventory into an XML document.

```
PS (6) > $xi = [xml] $inventory
```

The variable `$xi` now holds an XML document representation of the bookstore inventory. Let's select the genre attribute from each book:

```
PS (7) > $xi.SelectNodes("descendant::book/@genre")

#text
-----
Autobiography
Novel
Philosophy
Computers
```

This query says "select the genre attribute (indicated by the @) from all of the descendant elements book". Now let's revisit another example from earlier in this section and display the books and prices again.

```
PS (8) > $xi.SelectNodes("descendant::book") |
>> ft -auto price, title
>>

price title
----- -----
8.99  The Autobiography of Benjamin Franklin
11.99 Moby Dick
9.99  Discourse on Method
39.99 Windows PowerShell in Action
```

This is quite a bit simpler than the earlier example, because SelectNodes() on an XmlDocument returns XmlElement objects that PowerShell adapts and presents as regular objects. With the XPathNavigator.Select() method, we're returning XPathNavigator nodes, which aren't adapted automatically. As we can see, working with the XmlDocument object is the easiest way to work with XML in PowerShell, but there may be times when you need to use the other mechanisms, either for efficiency reasons (XmlDocument loads the entire document into memory) or because you're adapting example code from another language.

In this section, we've demonstrated how you can use the XML facilities in the .NET framework to create and process XML documents. As the XML format is used more and more in the computer industry, these features will be come critical. We've only scratched the surface of what is available in the .NET framework. We've only covered some of the XML classes and a little of the XPath query language. We haven't discussed how to use XSLT, the eXtensible Stylesheet Language Transformation language that is part of the System.Xml.Xsl namespace. All of these tools are directly available from within the PowerShell environment. In fact, the interactive nature of the PowerShell environment makes it an ideal place to explore, experiment, and learn about XML.

10.3.5 The Import-Clixml and Export-Clixml cmdlets

The last topic we're going to cover on XML is the cmdlets for importing and exporting objects from PowerShell. These cmdlets provide a way to save and restore collections of objects from the PowerShell environment. Let's take a look at how they are serialized.

> **AUTHOR'S NOTE** Serialization is the process of saving an object or objects to a file or a network stream. The components of the objects are stored as a series of pieces, hence the name *serialization*. PowerShell uses a special type of "lossy" serialization, where the basic shape of the objects is preserved but not all of the details. More on this in a minute.

First we'll create a collection of objects.

```
PS (1) > $data = @{a=1;b=2;c=3},"Hi there", 3.5
```

Now serialize them to a file using the Export-CliXml cmdlet:

```
PS (2) > $data | export-clixml out.xml
```

Let's see what the file looks like:

```
PS (3) > type out.xml
<Objs Version="1.1" xmlns="http://schemas.microsoft.com/powershe
ll/2004/04"><Obj RefId="RefId-0"><TN RefId="RefId-0"><T>System.C
ollections.Hashtable</T><T>System.Object</T></TN><DCT><En><S N="
Key">a</S><I32 N="Value">1</I32></En><En><S N="Key">b</S><I32 N=
"Value">2</I32></En><En><S N="Key">c</S><I32 N="Value">3</I32></
En></DCT></Obj><S>Hi there</S><Db>3.5</Db></Objs>
```

It's not very readable, so we'll use the dump-doc function from earlier in the chapter to display it:

```
PS (4) > dump-doc out.xml
<Objs Version = "1.1"xmlns = "http://schemas.microsoft.com/power
shell/2004/04">
```

This first part identifies the schema for the CLIXML object representation.

```
<Obj RefId = "RefId-0">
    <TN RefId = "RefId-0">
        <T>
            System.Collections.Hashtable
        </T>
        <T>
            System.Object
        </T>
    </TN>
    <DCT>
        <En>
```

Here are the key/value pair encodings.

```
            <S N = "Key">
                a
            </S>
            <I32 N = "Value">
                1
            </I32>
        </En>
        <En>
            <S N = "Key">
                b
            </S>
            <I32 N = "Value">
                2
            </I32>
        </En>
        <En>
            <S N = "Key">
                c
            </S>
```

```
            <I32 N = "Value">
                3
            </I32>
        </En>
    </DCT>
</Obj>
```

Now encode the string element

```
<S>
    Hi there
</S>
```

and the double-precision number.

```
<Db>
    3.5
</Db>
</Objs>
```

Import these objects it back into the session

```
PS (5) > $new_data = Import-Clixml out.xml
```

and compare the old and new collections.

```
PS (6) > $new_data

Name                          Value
----                          -----
a                             1
b                             2
c                             3
Hi there
3.5


PS (7) > $data

Name                          Value
----                          -----
a                             1
b                             2
c                             3
Hi there
3.5
```

They match.

These cmdlets provide a simple way to save and restore collections of objects, but they have limitations. They can only load and save a fixed number of primitive types. Any other type is "shredded", that is, broken apart into a property bag composed of these primitive types. This allows any type to be serialized, but with some loss of fidelity. In other words, objects can't be restored to exactly the same type they were originally. This approach is necessary because there can be an infinite number of object types, not all of which may be available when the file is read back. Sometimes you don't have the original type definition. Other times, there's no way to re-create the original object, even with the type information because the type does not support this operation. By restricting the set of types that are serialized with fidelity, the CLIXML format can always recover objects regardless of the availability of the original type information.

There is also another limitation on how objects are serialized. An object has properties. Those properties are also objects which have their own properties, and so on. This chain of properties that have properties is called the serialization depth. For some of the complex objects in the system, such as the Process object, serializing through all of the levels of the object results in a huge XML file. To constrain this, the serializer only traverses to a certain depth. The default depth is two. This default can be overridden either on the command line using the -depth parameter or by placing a <SerializationDepth> element in the type's description file. If you look at $PSHome/types.ps1xml, you can see some examples of where this has been done.

10.4 SUMMARY

In this chapter, we covered the kind of tasks that are the traditional domain of scripting languages. We looked at:

- Basic text processing—how to split and join strings using the [string]::-Split() and [string]::Join() methods.

- More advanced text processing with the [regex] class. We saw how we can use this class to conduct more advanced text operations such as tokenizing a string.

- The core cmdlets and how they correspond to the commands in other shell environments.

- How to set up shortcuts to long or specialized paths in the filesystem using New-PSDrive; for example, New-PSDrive AppData FileSystem "$Home\Application Data" creates a drive named AppData mapped to the root of the current user's Application Data directory.

- How to read and write files in PowerShell using Get-Content and Set-Content, and how to deal with character encodings in text files.

- How to work with binary files. We wrote a couple handy utility functions in the process.

- Using the Select-String cmdlet to efficiently search through collections of files.

- The basic support in PowerShell for XML documents in the form of the XML object adapter. PowerShell provides a shortcut for creating an XML document with the [xml] type accelerator; for example: [$xml]"<docroot>...</docroot>".

- How to construct XML documents by adding elements to an existing document using the `CreateElement()` method.
- Using the `XMLReader` class to search XML documents without loading the whole document into memory.
- Building utility functions for searching and formatting XML documents.
- Examples of processing XML documents using PowerShell pipelines.
- How to save and restore collections of objects using `Import-CLIXml` and `Export-CLIXml`.

CHAPTER 11

Getting fancy—
.NET and WinForms

I love it when a plan comes together!

—Col. John "Hannibal" Smith, *The A-Team* TV Show

When we began designing PowerShell, our focus was almost exclusively on cmdlets. The plan was to have lots of cmdlets and everything would be done through them. Unfortunately, as Robert Burns observed, "the best laid plans of mice and men often go awry" and we found that we didn't have the resources to get all of the planned cmdlets completed in time. Without the cmdlets, we wouldn't have adequate coverage for all of our core scenarios. How to solve this we asked? "Let's just depend on .NET" was the answer. We decided to make it easier to work directly with the .NET framework. That way, while it might not be as easy to do everything as we had wanted, at least it would be possible. (We looked at some of this in chapter 10 where we used the `[string]` and `[regex]` types to do things not directly supported by cmdlets or the language.)

In retrospect, this may have been one of the best things to happen to the project. Not only did we backfill our original scenarios, but the set of problem domains (e.g., graphical user interface [GUI] programming) in which we found PowerShell to be applicable exceeded our wildest expectations. In this chapter, we'll look at some of those scenarios. We'll also look at considerations in PowerShell's support for .NET and how lack of awareness of those considerations might lead to problems.

11.1 USING .NET FROM POWERSHELL

Everything in .NET has a type, whether it's a class, interface, structure, or primitive type such as an integer (see chapter 1). To work with .NET, we need to find the types necessary to get the job done. We've covered many of the most commonly used types in previous chapters, but there are many more available in PowerShell. In this section, we'll look at how to find and inspect those types. We'll also look at how to make additional types available by loading .NET libraries called *assemblies*. For example, loading additional assemblies will be necessary to do things such as the GUI programming we talked about earlier. In the process, we'll build handy tools to help with these tasks. We'll also look at how to create instances of these types, Finally, we'll address some of the potentially problematic areas mentioned previously.

11.1.1 .NET basics

Let's start with an overview of the .NET type system. The basic arrangement of elements on types in .NET is as follows: members (properties, methods, and so on) are contained in classes, structs, and interfaces. Version 2 of .NET also introduced the support of *generic* types. These elements are in turn grouped into namespaces.

> **AUTHOR'S NOTE**
> Keep in mind that the .NET type system was designed to allow you to construct arbitrarily sophisticated applications. As a consequence, it is itself fairly complex. However, the designers of this system did an excellent job of not requiring you to know everything in order to do anything. It, like PowerShell, was designed to support progressive development where what you need to know scales with the complexity of what you're trying to do. Simple things remain simple and the level of complexity scales reasonably with the complexity of the application. PowerShell is an excellent way to learn and explore .NET.

Let's look at `System.Collections.ArrayList.Add()` as an example of this. The `Add()` method exists on the class `ArrayList` that lives in the namespace `System.Collections`. Another example is the `IEnumerable` interface, which is also in `System.Collections`. This interface has a single method, `GetEnumerator()`.

This arrangement of types is called *logical type containment*. We also need to understand *physical type containment*. In other words, where do these collections of types live on a computer? This arranging is done through the assemblies we mentioned earlier. An assembly contains the definitions for one or more types. Since a set of types is contained in an assembly, clearly the set of assemblies that are loaded determines the complete set of types available to us. PowerShell loads most of the assemblies we need for day-to-day work by default when it starts, but sometimes (like when we want to do GUI programming) we'll have to load additional assemblies. In other words, we tell PowerShell the well-known name or path to an assembly and PowerShell inserts the assembly code into its environment. We'll cover how to do this in detail in the next section.

11.1.2 Working with assemblies

As we mentioned, the physical partitioning of the .NET framework is based on the assembly. Assemblies are a refinement of the dynamic link library (DLL) facility that has been part of Microsoft Windows from the beginning. (In UNIX, the equivalent concept is called *shared libraries*.) Let's review the benefits and liabilities of dynamic linking.

The DLL mechanism allows a program to dynamically load code at runtime. The traditional purpose of this feature was simply to cut down on the size of programs—instead of statically linking a library to an executable; all executables could share one copy of that code. This makes the executables smaller and also allows them to be serviced. By *serviced*, we mean that a bug in the DLL could be fixed for all programs that used that DLL by simply replacing one file. But all is not sweetness and light, as they say. Just as you could fix all users of a DLL, you could just as easily break them all. A fix that may be intended to fix a specific executable could unintentionally cause another executable to fail. Another problem is versioning. How can you change things over time? If you add new things to a DLL, you may break existing programs. And so you introduce a new version of the DLL. But now the developer has to decide which version of the DLL to use. Should they use the latest version? What if it isn't on all machines yet? And what if someone installs a malicious copy of the DLL to introduce a virus?

With .NET, Microsoft tried to solve some of these problems. An assembly is a DLL with additional data in the form of a *manifest*. This manifest lists the contents of the DLL as well as the name of the DLL. Assembly names are particularly interesting. .NET introduced the idea of a *strong name*. A strong name uses public key cryptography to verify the author of the DLL. When a .NET program is linked against a strong-named assembly, it will run only if exactly the same assembly it was linked against is present. Simply replacing the file won't work, because the strong name will be wrong. Included in the strong name is the version number. This means that when the DLL is loaded, the correct version will always be loaded even if later versions are available.

Loading and exploring assemblies

All that stuff we just talked about? Well, forget it. Linking and strong naming only apply to compiled .NET programs and PowerShell is an interpreter.

The interpreter itself is a compiled .NET program, so all of the assemblies it's linked against are loaded by default. This is why most of the types we need are already available and we don't have to do anything extra to get at them.

Since PowerShell is an interpreter and has no "link" phase, in order for it to use additional assemblies, we have to explicitly load them. Unfortunately, version 1 of PowerShell doesn't have any cmdlets that do this, so we have to use .NET methods. Remember that whole "not easy but possible" discussion from the start of the chapter? This is where it starts.

To load new assemblies, we need to use the type `System.Reflection.Assembly`. Here's an example:

```
PS (2) > [system.reflection.assembly]::LoadWithPartialName(
>> "System.Windows.Forms") | fl
>>

CodeBase                 : file:///C:/WINDOWS/assembly/GAC_MSIL/Sy
                           stem.Windows.Forms/2.0.0.0__b77a5c56193
                           4e089/System.Windows.Forms.dll
EntryPoint               :
EscapedCodeBase          : file:///C:/WINDOWS/assembly/GAC_MSIL/Sy
                           stem.Windows.Forms/2.0.0.0__b77a5c56193
                           4e089/System.Windows.Forms.dll
FullName                 : System.Windows.Forms, Version=2.0.0.0,
                           Culture=neutral, PublicKeyToken=b77a5c5
                           61934e089
GlobalAssemblyCache      : True
HostContext              : 0
ImageFileMachine         :
ImageRuntimeVersion      : v2.0.50727
Location                 : C:\WINDOWS\assembly\GAC_MSIL\System.Win
                           dows.Forms\2.0.0.0__b77a5c561934e089\Sy
                           stem.Windows.Forms.dll
ManifestModule           : System.Windows.Forms.dll
MetadataToken            :
PortableExecutableKind   :
ReflectionOnly           : False
```

This not only loaded the assembly, it also returned an instance of `System.Reflection.Assembly` that has a lot of information about the assembly. Take a look at the `FullName` field. We loaded the assembly using its *partial name*. The full name is the strong name we talked about previously:

```
System.Windows.Forms, Version=2.0.0.0, Culture=neutral,
PublicKeyToken=b77a5c561934e089
```

It's actually too long to fit on one line. It includes the namespace of the assembly, the version number, the culture for this assembly, and the public key used to sign the assembly. You can load a specific version of an assembly with the full name:

```
PS (5) > [reflection.assembly]::Load(
>> "System.Windows.Forms, Version=2.0.0.0, Culture=neutral," +
>> "PublicKeyToken=b77a5c561934e089")
>>

GAC     Version      Location
---     -------      --------
True    v2.0.50727   C:\WINDOWS\assembly\GAC_MSIL\System.Win...
```

Keep in mind is that we didn't really load the assembly again. Once an assembly has been loaded into a process, it can't be unloaded, so all this really did was verify that the assembly was loaded.

There is something else to note. Even when we specify the full name of the assembly, we didn't have to tell the system were to find the file. This is because the assembly has been "GACed"; that is, it has been added to the Global Assembly Cache (GAC). The GAC is a location defined by the system for where it should look up assemblies by default. Sometimes, however, the assembly that you're loading hasn't been GAC'ed. In this case, we can load it by specifying the path to the file. If you look at the output, we can see where this file is stored. Let's "load" it one more time using the file name:

```
PS (6) > $name = "C:\WINDOWS\assembly\GAC_MSIL\" +
>> "System.Windows.Forms\2.0.0.0__b77a5c561934e089\" +
>> "System.Windows.Forms.dll"
>>
PS (7) > [reflection.assembly]::LoadFrom($name)

GAC     Version      Location
---     -------      --------
True    v2.0.50727   C:\WINDOWS\assembly\GAC_MSIL\System.Win...
```

At this point, we've covered the most important parts of loading assemblies that we need to know to work with PowerShell. This is another "tip of the iceberg" topics where we've only covered the minimum necessary. For more details read the Microsoft Developer Network documentation at http://msdn.microsoft.com.

We've mastered the arcane incantations needed to load assemblies. So what's next? Obviously, now that we have the assembly loaded, we need to be able to find out what types it contains.

11.1.3 Finding types

There are a lot of types with a lot of members loaded into the PowerShell process. To get the list of what's available, we simply ask the system to tell us. To start, we need to get a list of the assemblies that are loaded. A handy function that returns that list is shown in listing 11.1.

```
function Get-Assemblies
{
    [AppDomain]::CurrentDomain.GetAssemblies()
}
```

Once we have the list of assemblies, we can use the GetTypes() method on the assembly object to get all of the types in the assembly. We'll wrap this in a function as well, as shown in listing 11.2.

```
function Get-Types ($Pattern=".")
{
    Get-Assemblies | %{ $_.GetExportedTypes() } |
        where {$_ -match $Pattern}
}
```

This function will get the full names of all of the types in each assembly and match them against the pattern provided in the function argument (which defaults to match everything). Let's use this function to find all of the types that have the namespace prefix System.Timers.

```
PS (1) > Get-Types ^system\.timers | %{ $_.FullName }
System.Timers.ElapsedEventArgs
System.Timers.ElapsedEventHandler
System.Timers.Timer
System.Timers.TimersDescriptionAttribute
```

In this example, we searched through all of the assemblies and found the five types that matched the regular expression we specified. (There are enough types loaded in PowerShell that this can take a while to run.)

Once we know how to get all of the types, let's explore the members of those types. We want to see all of the methods defined on all of the types in the System.Timers namespace that have the word "begin" in their name. To make this task easier, we'll define a couple of filters to help us with it. Here's what we want the output to look like:

```
PS (1) > Get-Types ^system\.timers | Select-Members begin |
>> Show-Members -method
>>
[System.Timers.ElapsedEventHandler]:: System.IAsyncResult BeginI
nvoke(System.Object, System.Timers.ElapsedEventArgs, System.Asyn
cCallback, System.Object)
[System.Timers.Timer]:: Void BeginInit()
```

In the output, we see that two methods match our requirements—the `BeginInvoke()` method on `System.Timers.ElapsedEventHandler` and `BeginInit()` on `System.Timers.Timer`.

Now let's look at the filters we used in this example. The first is a filter that will dump all of the members whose names match a regular expression. The code for this filter is shown in listing 11.3.

Listing 11.3 Select-Members filter

```
filter Select-Members ($Pattern = ".")
{
    $_.getmembers() | ? {$_ -match $Pattern }
}
```

By now, the operation of this filter should be obvious, so we won't bother explaining it. The second filter deals with the presentation of the results, since the default presentation for the member information is not all that it might be. This filter is shown in listing 11.4.

Listing 11.4 Show-Members filter

```
filter Show-Members ([switch] $Method)
{
    if (!$Method -or $_.MemberType -match "method")
    {
        "[{0}]:: {1}" -f $_.declaringtype, $_
    }
}
```

The operation of the filter is very straightforward. If -method is specified, only methods will be displayed. The member to be displayed will be formatted into a string displaying the type containing the method and the name of the method.

Now that we've covered finding types pretty thoroughly, we can move to the next step and create instances of the types we've found.

11.1.4 Creating instances of types

Now that we can find types, we need to know how to create instances of these types, since most of the work is done by instances (although there are some types such as [math] that only have static members). For example, before we can search using the [regex] type, we need to create an instance of that type from a pattern string.

> **AUTHOR'S NOTE**   Yes, [regex] has static members too—we saw that in chapter 10—but secretly the static members are creating instances under the covers. Sneaky critters aren't they?

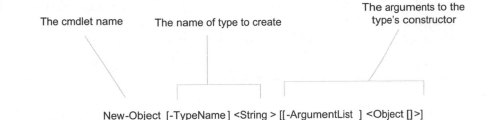

The cmdlet name   The name of type to create   The arguments to the type's constructor

New-Object [-TypeName] <String > [[-ArgumentList] <Object []>]

Figure 11.1   The New-Object cmdlet parameters

The New-Object cmdlet is the preferred way to do it. Figure 11.1 shows the signature for this cmdlet.

Be careful. While the signature for the cmdlet is pretty simple, it can be more difficult to use than you might think. People who are used to programming in languages such as C# have a tendency to use this cmdlet like the new operator in those languages. As a consequence, they tend to write expressions like:

```
New-Object String($x,1,3)
```

Unfortunately, writing it this way obscures the fact that it's a cmdlet, making things confusing. It will work fine, but it looks too much like a function call in other programming languages, and that leads people to misinterpret what's actually happening. As we saw in figure 11.1, the syntax for New-Object is

```
New-Object [-TypeName] <String> [[-ArgumentList] <Object [] >]
```

so the previous example could be written like:

```
New-Object -TypeName string -ArgumentList $x,1,3
```

The comma notation indicates an argument that is passed as an array. This is equivalent to

```
$constructor_arguments= $x,1,3
New-Object string $constructor_arguments
```

Note that we're not wrapping $constructor_arguments in yet another array. If you want to pass an array as a single value, you need to do it yourself and write it in parentheses with the unary comma operator, as discussed in chapter 3.

Let's look at some actual examples using New-Object. In the first example, we want to construct a new string object from a char array, giving a specific offset into the source array and also specify the number of characters to copy:

```
PS (1) > New-Object string ([char[]] "Hello"),1,4
ello
```

In the example command, the object to create was a string and we passed three arguments to the string constructor: the character array, the start index, and the length to copy. This created a string starting from the second character (remember, origin 0 for array indexing) and copied four characters. This example is straightforward. If we put the char array into a variable first, the command is even simpler:

```
PS (2) > $str = [char[]] "Hello"
PS (3) > New-Object string $str,1,4
ello
```

A much trickier example is one where we want to pass the char array as the only argument to the constructor. Now we need to wrap it in a nested array using the unary comma operator:

```
PS (4) > New-Object string (,$str)
Hello
```

In this example, we've created a string by copying all of the characters from the char array, starting from the beginning.

It would have been a better design for New-Object to have taken a variable number of arguments instead of passing them all as a single array; however, the current design matches the underlying *activator* APIs. The activator APIs are the methods .NET provides for dynamically constructing instances of types. In fact, this is what New-Object eventually calls.

```
PS (5) > [activator]::CreateInstance([string],[char[]] "Hello")
Hello
PS (6) > [activator]::CreateInstance([string],
>>> ([char[]] "Hello",1,3))
ell
```

AUTHOR'S NOTE Remember we said earlier that New-Object is the preferred way to create objects? Well, this is the other way to do it. It's somewhat more complex than using the cmdlet, which is why using New-Object is the recommended approach.

Of course, this is PowerShell, and we can fix it if we want to. Here's an example of how we could work around some of these deficiencies by defining a function:

```
PS (7) > function newobj
>> {
>>     param ($type, [switch] $com, [switch] $strict)
>>     if ($com)
>>     {
>>     New-Object -com -strict:$strict $type $args
>>     }
>>     else
>>     {
>>     New-Object $type $args
>>     }
>> }
>>
```

Now we can use this function with the constructor arguments separated by spaces.

```
PS (8) > newobj string ([char[]] "Hello")
Hello
PS (9) > newobj string ([char[]] "Hello") 2 3
llo
PS (10) >
```

In the longer term, we (the PowerShell team) are planning to build the ability to create objects into the PowerShell language itself, making object creation easier and more consistent. For the first version of PowerShell, however, New-Object is the tool of choice out of the box.

While we're on the subject of pitfalls, let's cover a couple other areas where we may run into difficulty.

11.1.5 PowerShell is not C#—A cautionary tale

Experienced .NET developers sometimes have problems learning PowerShell because it doesn't work in quite the same way as they're used to. C# programmers in particular have problems because PowerShell is syntactically similar to C#, resulting in an even stronger expectation that it should behave like C#. In this section, we're going to cover a couple of the areas that cause the most cognitive dissonance. In other words, this is where expected behavior based on prior experience and the actual behavior are most surprisingly different.

Automatic unraveling of enumerators

One problem that people run into with .NET methods that return enumerators is that PowerShell will unravel the enumerator. This behavior is correct and by design for PowerShell, but can be confusing for .NET programmers. Common practice in C# is to use the Open() method to get an enumerator, process that enumerator, and then call Close(). PowerShell will see the enumerator returned from the Open() call and process it immediately. This is especially confusing when people try to use the return keyword. They expect return to return a single value; however:

```
return 1,2,3,4
```

is equivalent to

```
1,2,3,4
return
```

To return an enumerable object, we have to wrap it in another array using the unary comma operator like

```
return ,(1,2,3,4)
```

or

```
,(1,2,3,4)
return
```

One might think that using the array subexpression operator @ (...)
would work here; however, as described in chapter 5, all this operator does
is guarantee that the result is an array. What we really need to do is construct a new one-element array containing the array we want to return. This
new array will be discarded in the unraveling process, but its presence ensures that the contained array is returned as a single element.

As an example, say we're writing a function that executes a query against a database. It
calls Open() to return a database reader object. But this $reader object is an enu-
merator, so instead of being returned as a single element, it's streamed out of the
function. For the function to return it atomically, it should look like listing 11.5.

Listing 11.5   Get-DataBaseReader function

```
function Get-DataBaseReader ($query , $connection)
{
    $SqlCmd = New-Object  System.Data.SqlClient.SqlCommand `
        $query,$connection
    if ( "Open" -ne $connection.state ) { $connection.Open() }
    $reader = $SqlCmd.ExecuteReader()

    , $reader
}
```

We've executed the query and $reader is an enumerator for the results of that query.
To return the enumerator instead of the results, we use the unary comma.

By doing this, we made the example work like the C# equivalent. But we're not
writing C#. To make this more PowerShell-like, consider following the model that
commands such as Get-Content use. These commands hide the details of opening
and closing the stream so the user never has to worry about forgetting to close a handle.
The command pushes objects into the pipeline instead of requiring the user to pull
them out with a read call. Listing 11.6 is the revised, more PowerShell-like function.

Listing 11.6   Get-FromDatabase function

```
function get-fromdatabase ($cmd, $connection)
{
    If ($connection is [string])
    {
        $conn = New-Object -Typename System.Data.SqlClient.SqlConnection
        $conn.ConnectionString = $string
        $conn.open()
    }
    elseif ($connection is [System.Data.SqlClient.SqlConnection])
    {
            $conn = $connection
        if ( "Open" -ne $conn.state ) { $conn.Open() }
```

```
   }
   else {
      throw `
         '$connection must be either a database connection or a string'
   }
   $SqlCmd = New-Object  System.Data.SqlClient.SqlCommand  $cmd,$conn
   # run the query stream the data to output pipe
   $SqlCmd.ExecuteReader()
   # now close the query…
   $connection.close()
}
```

In the revised function, all of the open/read/close details are hidden and we simply stream the results into the `Foreach-Object` cmdlet. Using this revised function to process a query looks like:

```
get-fromdatabase $query, $connection | % { process-data… }
```

The other advantage this approach provides, besides usability, is that when we write PowerShell functions and scripts, we avoid any problems with the enumerators. In fact, the code becomes simpler overall because we don't have to write an explicit loop. PowerShell takes care of all of the details.

In summary, if we write PowerShell like PowerShell, it all works. If we write PowerShell like C#, we run into problems because PowerShell is not C#.

Using methods that take path names

Another thing to keep in mind is that when using any .NET method that takes path names, *we must always use full path names*. This requirement stems from the fact that PowerShell maintains its own idea of what the current working directory is and this may not be the same as the process current working directory. .NET methods that take paths, on the other hand, always use the process current directory when resolving nonabsolute paths.

Let's clarify the current directory question by looking at an example. We'll start PowerShell, and then use the command pwd (which is an alias for `Get-Location`) to see where we are.

```
PS (1) > pwd

Path
----
C:\Documents and Settings\brucepay
```

Now we'll use the `CurrentDirectory` static method on the .NET class `System.Environment` to check the process working directory.

```
PS (2) > [System.Environment]::CurrentDirectory
C:\Documents and Settings\brucepay
```

So far they match. Now use the PowerShell cd command to set the PowerShell current working directory to the root of the C: drive, and then verify the path with pwd.

```
PS (3) > cd c:\
PS (4) > pwd

Path
----
C:\
```

Fine—everything is as we would expect. But now we check the process current working directory.

```
PS (5) > [Environment]::CurrentDirectory
C:\Documents and Settings\brucepay
```

It still points to the original location. Clearly, using cd in PowerShell doesn't affect the process current working directory.

Now let's look at the another reason for always using full path names. Let's cd into the root of the registry.

```
PS (6) > cd hklm:\
PS (7) > pwd

Path
----
HKLM:\
```

The PowerShell current directory is now in the registry. This is something that the process current directory just can't handle. It can only ever point to some place in the filesystem. Clearly, the PowerShell and process notions of current directory have to be different.

> **AUTHOR'S NOTE** There can be more than one PowerShell session (called a *runspace*) in a process at the same time. Each of these runspaces can have its own current directory. The process only has a single current directory value. This is covered in the PowerShell SDK documents and in Jim Truher's book *Windows PowerShell in Practice*, also from Manning Publications.

Let's reiterate why this behavior is a problem when using .NET methods: any .NET method that is passed a relative pathname will use the process current working directory to resolve the path instead of the PowerShell current working directory. Let's check this out. We'll cd back into the root of the C: drive again and create a text file "hello.txt".

```
PS (8) > cd c:\
PS (9) > "Hello there" > hello.txt
```

We can get this file from PowerShell using `Get-Content` and specifying a relative path:

```
PS (10) > get-content  hello.txt
Hello there
```

It works. But now when we try using a .NET method and specify a relative path:

```
PS (11) > [io.file]::ReadAllText("hello.txt")
Exception calling "ReadAllText" with "1" argument(s): "Could not
 find file 'C:\Documents and Settings\brucepay\hello.txt'."
At line:1 char:23
+ [io.file]::ReadAllText( <<<< "hello.txt")
```

it fails. This is because it's using the process current directory to resolve the relative path, and that's still pointing to the directory where PowerShell was started.

```
PS (12) > [environment]::currentdirectory
C:\Documents and Settings\brucepay
```

The PowerShell environment includes a cmdlet `Resolve-Path`, which is intended to make this scenario easy to work around. When the output of this command is converted into a string, it will be the full provider path to the target object—in this case the file. Let's try this:

```
PS (13) > [io.file]::ReadAllText((resolve-path "hello.txt"))
Hello there
```

There is another, even easier way to do this, although it is not strictly speaking per the guidelines. Instead of `Resolve-Path`, we can use the `$PWD` shell variable along with string expansion to prefix the path.

```
PS (13) > [io.file]::ReadAllText("$pwd\hello.txt")
Hello there
```

Not only is this easier, it also has the advantage that it will work to produce paths that don't exist yet. If you're creating a file, `Resolve-Path` will fail because it can only resolve existing paths. With the string expansion approach, this problem doesn't exist. String expansion doesn't know anything about paths—it's just giving us a new string.

This is an important rule to keep in mind. If you look at the examples in chapter 10 where we were using the .NET XML APIs to process files, we always made sure to pass in absolute paths. If we are consistent and always use absolute file paths with methods that take paths, there won't be any problems. (Though it's usually easiest to use the `Get-Content` cmdlet instead. If we do, everything will work and we won't have to remember this extra step or close the handle when we're done with it.)

Working with *generic types*, the next topic, has less to do with prior expectations and more to do with features that were cut from version 1.0 of PowerShell.

11.1.6   Working with generic types

In version 2.0 of .NET, a new feature was introduced called generic types (or simply generics). Do you need to know how to create generic types in your day-to-day work with PowerShell? For the most part, the answer is no. However, you may eventually encounter a situation where you do need to do it, at which point you can come back and reread this section.

Generics introduce the idea of a *type parameter*. Instead of simply passing a bunch of arguments when you create an instance of a object, you can also pass in type parameters that determine the final types of some part of the object. This is rather confusing if you haven't encountered the concept before. As usual, an example should make things clearer. Generics are easiest to understand when we talk about creating collections. Prior to the introduction of generics, if we wanted to create a collection class we had to either write a new version of the class for each type of object we wanted it to store or we had to allow it to hold any type of object, which meant that we had to do our own error checking. With generics, we can write a collection that can be constrained to only containing integers or strings or hashtables.

Again, if you aren't a programmer, you're probably thinking—wow, this is so geeky I can't imagine caring about this. The reason that we, as PowerShell users, need to care is that some of the classes we may want to work with will use generic types. (PowerShell itself uses them a lot.)

The first version of PowerShell makes this moderately easy if we're working with an existing instance of an object where the type parameterization has already been done. The type converter makes it all work. The problem arises if we have to create a generic instance. This is, well, hard. Let's look at an example.

Creating an instance of a generic type

To create an instance of a generic type, we need to have the full name of the generic type. This is made up of the name of the type, followed by a backtick and the number of type parameters. As this is hard to get right when typing it, we'll create a helper function to do the tricky bits for us. This function is shown in the next example:

```
PS (1) > function New-GenericList ([type] $type)
>> {
>>     $base = [System.Collections.Generic.List``1]
>>     $qt = $base.MakeGenericType(@($type))
>>     , (new-object $qt)
>> }
>>
```

We start with the base name of the collection's type, `System.Collec-tions.Generic.List`. This type takes one type parameter, so we have to include `` ``1 `` in the name. This gives us an *open* generic type. It's called "open" because we haven't bound the type parameters yet.

Now we need to create a *closed* type where the type parameters are bound. We do this with the `MakeGenericType()` method on the open generic type object. Once we have the closed type, we can use the `New-Object` cmdlet to create an instance of this type. Note the comma operator in front of the call to `New-Object`. This is necessary because we're creating a list inside a function and the default behavior in PowerShell is to stream the contents of a list rather than returning the list as an atomic object.

Now let's use this function. We'll create a list with the type parameter `[int]`.

```
PS (2) > $intList = New-GenericList int
```

Next we add numbers to the list, then display it.

```
PS (3) > $intList.Add(123)
PS (4) > $intList.Add(456)
PS (5) > $intList
123
456
PS (6) > $intList.count
2
```

When we try to add something that isn't a number, we get an error.

```
PS (7) > $intList.Add("abc")
Cannot convert argument "0", with value: "abc", for "Add" t
o type "System.Int32": "Cannot convert value "abc" to type
"System.Int32". Error: "Input string was not in a correct f
ormat.""
At line:1 char:13
| $intList.Add( <<<< "abc")
```

If we add something that isn't a number but might be, the PowerShell type converter will conveniently convert it for us.

```
PS (8) > $intList.add("789")
PS (9) > $intList[2]
789
```

When we check the target type, it's an integer. This gives us an expandable list like an `ArrayList`, but constrained to only holding integers.

```
PS (10) > $intList[2].gettype().FullName
System.Int32
```

Now let's look at another example. This time we'll build a generic dictionary.

Instantiating a generic dictionary

A generic dictionary is like a hashtable; it's made up of key/value pairs, but we want to limit the keys to strings and the values to integers. Once again, we'll write a convenience function to handle the heavy lifting. Here's the function to do this:

```
PS (11) > function New-GenericDictionary ([type] $keyType,
>> [type] $valueType)
>> {
>>     $base = [System.Collections.Generic.Dictionary``2]
>>     $ct = $base.MakeGenericType(($keyType, $valueType))
>>     , (New-Object $ct)
>> }
>>
```

Again, start with the base type of the collection, followed by `2 because we have two type parameters this time. We pass the two type parameters to the function into the call to MakeGenericType() as an array. This will give us the closed type for the generic dictionary. Finally, we return an instance of the closed type.

We'll use this function to build a dictionary that is constrained to permit only strings for keys and integers for the values.

```
PS (12) > $gd = New-GenericDictionary string int
```

Let's enter values and display the result:

```
PS (13) > $gd["red"] = 1
PS (14) > $gd["blue"] = 2
PS (15) > $gd

Key                                                   Value
---                                                   -----
red                                                       1
blue                                                      2
```

Next try to assign a nonstring key. This would work with a regular hashtable, but fails with the generic dictionary instance.

```
PS (16) > $gd[13] = 3
Array assignment to [13] failed: The value "13" is not of type "
System.String" and cannot be used in this generic collection.
Parameter name: key.
At line:1 char:5
+ $gd[1 <<<< 3] = 3
```

Also note that this time, the PowerShell type converter didn't try to convert to the target type. The type signature is too complex for it to figure out, so we'll have to explicitly cast the arguments.

Finally, let's look at the full name of the type of object stored in $gd.

```
PS (17) > $gd.gettype().FullName
System.Collections.Generic.Dictionary`2[[System.String, mscorlib
, Version=2.0.0.0, Culture=neutral, PublicKeyToken=b77a5c561934e
089],[System.Int32, mscorlib, Version=2.0.0.0, Culture=neutral,
PublicKeyToken=b77a5c561934e089]]
PS (18) >
```

To reiterate the comment from the beginning of this section, very rarely will you need some of these esoteric capabilities, but when you do need them, they can be incredibly valuable.

Enough with the .NET trivia challenge. In the remainder of this chapter, we'll look at how we can apply some of the things we've learned to build more interesting applications.

> **AUTHOR'S NOTE** These examples are designed to demonstrate the range of tasks that can be addressed with PowerShell rather than be strictly practical. For some more purely practical examples using .NET in admin scenarios, take a look at appendix B.

11.2 POWERSHELL AND THE INTERNET

In this section, we're going to put the network back into .NET. As one would expect from a modern programming environment, .NET (and consequently PowerShell) has a pretty comprehensive set of types for doing network programming.

> **AUTHOR'S NOTE** The .NET framework has good networking capabilities, but I suspect that the name came out of the marketing frenzy during the first Internet bubble: .NET 1.0 was released in 2001. At that time, people with calling everything dot-something. I'm surprised we didn't end up with .Coke or Pepsi.NET or some other silliness.

In this section, we'll look at a couple useful examples of doing network programming with the .NET networking types.

11.2.1 Example: Retrieving a web page

The most common networking task in the Internet age is to download a web page. Here's how to do that in PowerShell using the `[system.net.webclient]` type. This is a type that provides common methods for sending data to and receiving data from websites (or anything else that can be addressed with a URL). In this example, we'll use this type to download data from the MSDN blog home page. First we need to create an instance of `System.Net.WebClient`:

```
PS (1) > $wc = New-Object net.webclient
```

And we're ready to go. Let's take a look at what's happening on the MSDN blog site. Let's download the page into a variable:

```
PS (2) > $page = $wc.DownloadString("http://blogs.msdn.com")
PS (3) > $page.length
28778
```

Checking the length, it's a bit long to look at as text. Let's simplify things a bit and get rid of the HTML tags.

```
PS (4) > $page = $page -replace "\<[^<]*\>"
PS (5) > $page.length
11419
```

We used regular expressions to remove anything enclosed in "<" and ">". This has shortened things a lot, but it's still a bit long. Let's get rid of unnecessary spaces.

```
PS (6) > $page = $page -replace " +", " "
PS (7) > $page.length
10999
```

Now let's split it into a collection of lines.

```
PS (8) > $lines = $page.split("`n")
PS (9) > $lines.count
520
```

And get rid of the empty lines.

```
PS (10) > $lines = $lines | ?{$_ -match '[a-z]'}
PS (11) > $lines.count
192
```

And now we have something pretty short. Let's see what we've got. We'll skip ahead in the collection of lines, since there's still some preamble in the document.

```
PS (13) > $lines[20..30]
        RSS
        OPML
        Blogs By Category
Front Page News
        Sydney Only Free WPF Hands On Training 21st July
               Microsoft and Dimension Data would like to invite
 you to a com
plementary half day hands on training covering Windows Presentat
ion Foundation.  The Microsoft Windows Presentation Foundat
ion (formerly code named "Avalon") provides the foundation for..
        .

                posted @
                17 minutes ago
                by
                Ozzie Rules Blogging
        Windows CE 6 and Windows Mobile Virtual Labs
```

In the text, we can see a fragment of a blog posting . Most of this has just been string manipulation, which we've seen before. The only new thing was using the WebClient API. Now let's see what else we can do.

11.2.2   Example: Processing an RSS feed

Let's explore RSS feeds. These are feeds that let us see the most recent postings in a blog formatted in XML. As we saw in the previous chapter, XML is easy to work with in PowerShell. Listing 11.7 shows a function to download an RSS feed and print out the feed titles and links.

Listing 11.7   Get-RSS function

```
function Get-RSS ($url)
{
    $wc = New-Object net.webclient
    $xml = [xml](New-Object net.webclient).DownloadString($url)
    $xml.rss.channel.item| select-object title,link
}
```

Now let's run it:

```
PS (3) > get-rss http://blogs.msdn.com/powershell/rss.aspx |
>> select-object -first 3
>>

title                          link
-----                          ----
Are ScriptBlock parameters im... http://blogs.msdn.com/powers...
Revisiting: Listing all the C... http://blogs.msdn.com/powers...
How can a script tell what di... http://blogs.msdn.com/powers...
```

Now let's use this function in something a bit more useful. Listing 11.8 shows a function that will display a menu of the most recent articles in an RSS feed. You can select an item and it will be displayed in Internet Explorer.

Listing 11.8   Get-RSSMenu function

```
function Get-RSSMenu (
    $url="http://blogs.msdn.com/powershell/rss.aspx",
    $number=3
)
{
    $entries = get-rss $url | select-object -first $number
    $links = @()
    $entries | % {$i=0} {
        "$i - " + $_.title
        $links += $_.link
        $i++
    }
    while (1)
    {
        $val = read-host "Enter a number [0-$($i-1)] or q to quit"
        if ($val -eq "q") { return }
        $val = [int] $val
        if ($val -ge 0 -and $val -le $i)
        {
            $link = $links[$val]
            "Opening $link`n"
            explorer.exe $link
        }
    }
}
```

By default, it downloads the RSS feed for the PowerShell blog and shows the three most recent entries. (Of course, you can override both the blog and the number of items to show.) Here's what it looks like when we run it:

```
PS (1) > Get-RSSMenu
0 - Are ScriptBlock parameters implemented for functions?
1 - Revisiting: Listing all the COM automation PROGIDs
2 - How can a script tell what directory it was run from?
Enter a number from 0 to 2 or q to quit: 0
Opening http://blogs.msdn.com/powershell/archive/2006/07/08/6596
60.aspx

Enter a number [0-2] or q to quit: q
PS (2) >
```

It displays the three most recent items from the blog. We select item 0 and hit Enter. The function displays the URL and then invokes `explorer.exe` on the URL. This will cause a browser window to pop up (or a new tab might open in an existing browser window if your default browser supports tabs like IE7 or Firefox).

Now that we know how to download web pages, what about serving pages? In the next section, we'll look at writing a web server in PowerShell.

11.2.3 Example: Writing a web server in PowerShell

In this example, we'll build a small special-purpose web server in PowerShell. This example is a good illustration of mixing and matching object and string processing. It will also highlight some limitations in PowerShell because of the way the processing has to be done.

Reviewing how a web server works

Let's review how a web server (or any kind of network server for that matter) works. From a web browser's perspective, a network service is identified by a combination of the host and port number. The host identifies the computer to connect to and the port identifies the service on that computer. (We're obviously leaving out a lot of detail here.) A web server, on the other hand, needs to know only the port to "listen" on. It listens for a request to connect to the service, sets up a connection to the requesting client, performs some service on behalf of the client (typically returning some information), and then closes the connection. The server decides what to do based on either the URL of the requested service or the content of the request. In our example, we're going to look only at the URL.

The goal of this web server script is to process the URL it receives and evaluate it as a simple expression. A successful evaluation will be displayed as a table in the web page. Figure 11.2 shows what this will look like.

The expressions supported are limited to adding, subtracting, multiplying, or dividing two numbers. If the expression isn't valid, a "help" page will be displayed, including a valid example URL as a link in the page. We'll give our PowerShell web

Figure 11.2 The Results from evaluating an expression in the Power-Shell web server. The expression "3*5" was extracted, evaluated, and displayed in a table along with the date and time it was evaluated.

server script a proper marketing-approved name: `Invoke-Webserver.ps1`. Here's what it looks like when we run the script:

```
PS (1) > Invoke-Webserver
Press any key to stop Web Server...
Connection at 7/16/2006 6:11:40 PM from 127.0.0.1:1260.
Expression: 3*5
Expression result: 15
Sent 105 bytes to 127.0.0.1:1260
Header sent
Sent 621 bytes to 127.0.0.1:1260
Stopping server...
Server stopped...
PS (2) >
```

We've included lots of status messages in the server to let the user know what's going on. On a "real" web server, these messages are typically written to a log file instead of to the host.

The web server script

Listing 11.9 shows the script `Invoke-Webserver.ps1`, which consists of three functions: one to generate an HTML document, one to send the response back to the client, and one that describes that content of the response.

Listing 11.9   The script code for `Invoke-WebServer.ps1`

```
param($port=80)        ←——❶  Set the port


[void][reflection.Assembly]::LoadWithPartialName(  ←
    "System.Net.Sockets")                              ❷  Load socket
                                                          library
                                ❸  HTML
function html ($content,   ←       generator
    $title = " Example PowerShell Web Server Page")
{
```

```
        @"
        <html>
            <head>
                <title>$title</title>
            </head>
            <body>
            $content
            </body>
        </html>
"@
}


function SendResponse($sock, $string)    ◄─●4  SendResponse function
{
    if ($sock.Connected)
    {
        $bytesSent = $sock.Send(
[text.Encoding]::Ascii.GetBytes($string))
        if ( $bytesSent -eq -1 )
        {
            Write-Host ("Send failed to " + $sock.RemoteEndPoint)
        }
        else
        {
            Write-Host ("Sent $bytesSent bytes to " +
                $sock.RemoteEndPoint)
        }
    }
}


function SendHeader(    ◄─●5  SendHeader function
    [net.sockets.socket] $sock,
    $length,
    $statusCode = "200 OK",
    $mimeHeader="text/html",
    $httpVersion="HTTP/1.1"
)
{

    $response = "HTTP/1.1 $statusCode`r`nServer: " +
        "Localhost`r`nContent-Type: $mimeHeader`r`n" +
        "Accept-Ranges:bytes`r`nContent-Length: $length`r`n`r`n"
    SendResponse $sock $response
    write-host "Header sent"
}


$server = [System.Net.Sockets.TcpListener]$port    ◄─●6  Start server
$server.Start()


$buffer = New-Object byte[] 1024    ◄─┐
                                   ●7  Allocate
                                       receive buffer


write-host "Press any key to stop Web Server..."
```

```
while($true)     ◄────⑧ Start request loop
{

    if ($host.ui.rawui.KeyAvailable)  ◄────⑨ Check for stop key
    {
        write-host "Stopping server..."
        break
    }

    if($server.Pending())  ◄────⑩ Check request
    {
        $socket = $server.AcceptSocket()
    }

    if ( $socket.Connected )
    {
        write-host ("Connection at {0} from {1}." -f
            (get-date), $socket.RemoteEndPoint )

        [void] $socket.Receive($buffer, $buffer.Length, '0')  ◄──⑪ Get
        $received = [Text.Encoding]::Ascii.getString($buffer)      data

        $received = [regex]::split($received, "`r`n")  ◄──┐ Split
        $received = @($received -match "GET")[0]       ⑫ strings

        if ($received)                              Extract ⑬
        {                                           expression
            $expression = $received -replace "GET */" -replace  ◄──
                'HTTP.*$' -replace '%20',' '

            if ($expression -match '[0-9.]+ *[-+*/%] *[0-9.]+')
            {
                write-host "Expression: $expression"
                $expressionResult = . {             Evaluate ⑭
                    invoke-expression $expression    expression
                    trap {
                        write-host "Expression failed: $_"
                        "error"
                        Continue
                    }
                }
                write-host "Expression result: $expressionResult"

                $result = html @"
                    <table border="2">
                    <tr>                        ⑮ Format
                    <td>Expression</td>            result text
                    <td>$expression</td>
                    </tr>
                    <tr>
                    <td>Result</td>
```

```
                    <td>$expressionResult</td>
                    </tr>
                    <tr>
                    <td>Date</td>
                    <td>$(get-date)</td>
                    </tr>
                    </table>
"@
            }
            else
            {
                $message = 'Type expression to evaluate like:'
                $link = '<a href="http://localhost/3*5">' +
                    'http://localhost/3*5</a>'
                $result = html @"
                    <table border="2">
                    <tr>
                    <td>$message</td>
                    <td>$link</td>
                    </tr>
                    <tr>
                    <td>Date</td>
                    <td>$(get-date)</td>
                    </tr>
                    </table>
"@
            }


            SendHeader $socket $result.Length
            SendResponse $socket $result
        }
        $socket.Close()
    }
    else
    {
        start-sleep -milli 100
    }
}

$server.Stop()
write-host "Server stopped..."
```

⓯ Format result text

⓰ Format error text

⓱ Send response

⓲ Close request

⓳ Sleep 100ms

⓴ Stop listener

We begin by setting the port ❶ that the server listens on. The default is the default port for a web server—port 80. If you want to run this script on a machine that's already running a web server such as IIS or Apache, you'll have to choose another port.

The socket library ❷ that we'll need is not part of the default PowerShell environment, so we have to load it.

Next we'll define a function to generate an HTML document ❸. We need more control over the document than we'd get with ConvertTo-Html so we can't just use the cmdlet.

Serving web pages is a request/response protocol. SendResponse ❹ is a function we'll use to send the response back to the client. Note that these are byte-oriented APIs, so we need to convert the response string to an array of bytes before we can send it.

Part of any response is the header that describes the content of the response. The header includes things such as the version of the HTTP protocol being used, the length of the content being sent, the status code of the request, and so on. We'll wrap all of this up into a function called SendHeader ❺.

Now create the listener object and start the web server ❻. We'll need a buffer ❼ to hold the data the comes from the client, so allocate the buffer and save it in $buffer.

Then we begin the request loop ❽. This is where the first version of PowerShell is limited. Ideally, we'd like to wait for events and launch a scriptblock to service each request on its own thread (up to some limit). Unfortunately, that can't be done in version 1 of PowerShell. Instead, we use a simple loop that polls to see if there is anything that needs to be done.

<table>
<tr><td>AUTHOR'S
NOTE</td><td>Asynchronous event handling is not supported in the first version of PowerShell. In fact, if you try to use it, the PowerShell runtime will detect it and generate a fatal exception, killing your shell session. Yes, this is extreme. The rationale is that it's better to fail early and in an obvious way than allow the program to continue in a corrupt state. We tried simply generating a message, but people would miss it, and wonder why their script wasn't working. People don't miss killing the session. They aren't very happy about it, but they notice.

So why prevent asynchronous events? PowerShell has no mechanism for synchronizing access to objects. This means that there is no way to do reliable multithreaded programming. We expect to address this in a future version of the interpreter. In the meantime, there are lots of things that use synchronous events, and fortunately WinForms is one of them. We'll look at how this works in WinForms later on.</td></tr>
</table>

While polling, first we check to see whether there is a key available ❾ and stop if there is. We want to do it this way instead of using Ctrl-C to interrupt the script, because we want to be able to properly close the listener.

On each poll, we check to see whether there are any pending requests and service them if there are ❿. We get the data from the request into the buffer we created earlier ⓫. Since we want to work with strings instead of bytes, we'll convert the contents of the buffer into a string.

Now get the HTTP request out of the text we received. This will look something like "GET /3*5 HTTP/1.1". The first part is the type of operation requested, which is called the HTTP method. The next part is the URL, which is what we want to work with, and finally the version of the HTTP protocol. We want to extract this text, but first we need to split the request string into lines. In the HTTP protocol, lines are separated with the <carriage return><newline> sequence. We'll use the [regex]::Split() ❶❷ method to do this. If we got a valid request then extract the expression out of the URL with regular expressions ❶❸.

Notice that we're very carefully validating the expression ❶❹. This is because we're going to pass it to Invoke-Expression. And since Invoke-Expression can do anything (like format your hard drive), we need to be really, really, really careful about validating data from an untrusted source such as a web browser. Really careful!

Now let's do something a bit tricky ❶❹. We'll call Invoke-Expression to do the evaluation, but we're doing it in a scriptblock. In that scriptblock, we're defining a trap handler. If there is a problem with the expression (such as division by zero) the trap statement will catch the exception, record the error, and return a default value. This useful pattern is a simple way to guarantee a valid value is returned.

We'll format the HTML table that used to display the result by using string expansion ❶❺ in a here-string. This makes constructing the HTML fairly simple and direct.

And likewise in the invalid expression case, we'll format a table to display the hint and the example link ❶❻. Notice that we're hard-coding the example host to be localhost. We're assuming that you're running the server and the client on the same computer.

Finally, send the response header and content ❶❼. Most of the default values for SendHeader are fine, so the call is pretty simple. When we're done servicing this request, we close the connection to this client ❶❽.

Something to keep in mind is that we're polling for activity. If we poll as fast as we can, we'll waste a lot of CPU and interfere with other activities on this computer. To avoid this, we'll sleep for 100 milliseconds on each pooling loop ❶❾.

Eventually we'll exit the service loop because the user pressed a key requesting that the server be stopped. We'll stop the listener, and we're done ❷⓪.

That's the end of our web server script. We've written a complete web server that serves dynamically created pages in less than 200 lines of PowerShell script. And, while it's not by any means a production-worthy application, it illustrates that PowerShell can be used in scenarios that are normally considered outside the range of a shell language. This is largely possible because of the power of the .NET framework.

AUTHOR'S NOTE The corollary to this is that because PowerShell is part of the .NET ecosystem, as Microsoft (and third parties) add new capabilities to the .NET ecosystem, PowerShell benefits directly.

This example also illustrates a number of useful techniques for converting between data formats, generating HTML, and so on.

So far we've written scripts that act as web clients and then a script that acts as a web server. At this point, the next logical step is to write a script that acts as an operating system kernel. In the next section, we'll look at replacing portions of the Windows kernel with PowerShell scripts. Okay—I am totally lying to you. Sorry. What we're really going to talk about is writing graphical client applications. Not as exotic as an operating system kernel, but a great deal more practical.

11.3 POWERSHELL AND GRAPHICAL USER INTERFACES

The full name of the PowerShell package is Windows PowerShell. In this section, we'll look at the "Windows" part of the name. (The name is actually because PowerShell is part of the Windows product group. But we can do GUI programming with PowerShell, as we'll see in ths section.)

One of the earliest successful scripting environments was something called TCL/TK. TCL stands for *Tool Command Language*. It was intended to be a standard scripting language that could be used to automate systems. (Hmm. This sounds familiar!) Its biggest success, however, was TK, which was (and still is) a toolkit for building graphical applications with scripts. The ability to write a basic graphical application in a few dozen lines of code was wildly popular. This same kind of thing can be done in PowerShell using the .NET Windows Forms (WinForms) library. WinForms is a framework and collection of utility classes for building forms-based graphical applications. Let's review the basic structure of a WinForms application and then see how we can build one using PowerShell.

11.3.1 WinForms basics

The core concepts in WinForms are controls, containers, properties, and events. A control is an element in a user interface—buttons, list boxes, and so on. Most controls, like buttons, are visible controls that you interact with directly, but there are some controls, such as timers, that aren't visible but still play a part in the overall user experience. Controls have to be laid out and organized to present a GUI. This is where containers come in. Containers include things such as top-level forms, panels, splitter panels, tabbed panels, and so on. Within a container, you can also specify a layout manager. The layout manager determines how the controls are laid out within the panel. (In TCL/TK, these were called geometry managers.) Properties are just regular properties, except that they are used to set the visual appearance of a control. You use them to set things such as the foreground and background colors or the font of a control.

The final piece in the WinForms architecture is the event. Events are used to specify the behavior of a control both for specific actions, such as when a user clicks on the "Do It" button, as well as when the container is moved or resized and the control has to take some action. In PowerShell, an event corresponds to a scriptblock. If you want a particular event to occur when a button is clicked, you attach a scriptblock to the button click event.

AUTHOR'S NOTE	When an EventHandler is invoked or *fired*, it's passed at least two arguments: the object that fired the event and any arguments that are specific to that event. The signature of the method that is used to invoke an event handler looks like:

```
Void Invoke(System.Object, System.EventArgs)
```

Writing event handlers in WinForms is such a common pattern that PowerShell doesn't require you to explicitly define these arguments for scriptblocks used as event handlers. Instead, we use the automatic variables $this and $_ to pass the System.EventHandler arguments: $this contains a reference to the object that generated the event and $_ holds any event arguments that might have been passed. Note that these arguments get used a lot in PowerShell; as we'll see in the examples, dynamic scoping frequently makes using these variable unnecessary (but they have to be defined anyway to match the EventHandler signature).

These concepts are best illustrated through an example.

11.3.2 Example: "My first form"

We'll now look at the simplest WinForms example. This is the example we saw in chapter 1. The code is shown in listing 11.10:

Listing 11.10 The script code for WinForms example

```
[void] [reflection.assembly]::LoadWithPartialName(
    "System.Windows.Forms")
$form = New-Object Windows.Forms.Form
$form.Text = "My First Form"
$button = New-Object Windows.Forms.Button
$button.text="Push Me!"
$button.Dock="fill"
$button.add_click({$form.close()})
$form.controls.add($button)
$form.Add_Shown({$form.Activate()})
$form.ShowDialog()
```

Since it's short enough to type at the command line, let's go through the code interactively. First we have to load the WinForms assembly, since it's not loaded into PowerShell by default.

```
PS (1) > [void][reflection.assembly]::LoadWithPartialName(
>>     "System.Windows.Forms")
>>
```

All applications have to have a top-level form, so we'll create one and save it in the variable $form.

```
PS (2) > $form = New-Object Windows.Forms.Form
```

We'll set the Text property on the form so that the title bar will display "My First Form".

```
PS (3) > $form.Text = "My First Form"
```

Next we create a button and set the text to display in the button to "Push Me!".

```
PS (4) > $button = New-Object Windows.Forms.Button
PS (5) > $button.text="Push Me!"
```

We'll use the Dock property on the button control to tell the form layout manager that we want the button to fill the entire form.

```
PS (6) > $button.Dock="fill"
```

Now we need to add a behavior to the button. When we click the button, we want the form to close. We add this behavior by binding a scriptblock to the Click event on the button. Events are bound using special methods that take the form *add_<eventName>*.

```
PS (7) > $button.add_Click({$form.close()})
```

Be careful getting all of the parentheses and braces matched up. In the scriptblock we're adding, we'll call the Close() method on the form, which will "end" the application.

AUTHOR'S NOTE If you've programmed with WinForms in other languages such as C# or Visual Basic, you may be curious about how this works. (If not, feel free to skip this note.) The add_Click() function corresponds to the Click event described in the MSDN documentation. PowerShell doesn't support the "+=" notation for adding events so we have to use the corresponding add_Click() method. Now in general, events require an instance of System.Delegate. The Click event in particular requires a subclass of System.Delegate called System.EventHandler. While scriptblocks are not derived from that type, PowerShell knows how to automatically convert a scriptblock into an EventHandler object so it all works seamlessly. Unfortunately, the only subclass of delegate we support is System.EventHandler, and there are a lot of other types that derive from System.Delegate. This means that, in version 1 of PowerShell, you can't use scriptblocks with those other event types. Well, that's not quite true: It is possible to generate arbitrary delegate code for scriptblocks, but it requires some pathologically advanced scripting. However, for most scenarios you're likely to encounter, support for System.EventHandler is sufficient.

Now we need to add our button to the form. This is done by calling the Add() method on the Controls member of the form.

```
PS (8) > $form.Controls.add($button)
```

When the form is first displayed, we want to make it the active form. That's what the next line does. It sets up an event handler that will activate the form when it's first shown.

```
PS (9) > $form.Add_Shown({$form.Activate()})
```

And now we want to show the form we've built. There are two methods we could call. The first—Show()—displays the form and returns immediately. Unfortunately, this also means that the form closes immediately as well. This is because the form is running on the same thread as the command. When the command ends, so does the form. The way to get around this is to use the ShowDialog() method. This shows the form and then waits until the form is closed. This is what we want to do here. We call this method and PowerShell will seem to freeze.

```
PS (9) > $form.ShowDialog()
```

Somewhere on the desktop, a form that looks like figure 11.3 will appear.

Once we locate the window, we can resize it and move it around and everything works fine. Finally, we'll click the "Push Me!" button, causing the form to disappear, and control will return to the PowerShell session. We'll see something like:

```
Cancel
PS (10) >
```

The word "Cancel" is the return value from the Show-Dialog() methods. Dialogs usually return a result such as Cancel or OK. Since we called ShowDialog(), we get a dialog reply.

Figure 11.3 This is what the "my first form" Windows Form looks like. It consists of a single button control that fills the form when it is resized.

11.3.3 Example: Simple dialog

Now let's look at something a bit more sophisticated. Since we're displaying the form like a dialog, let's make it look more like a normal Windows dialog box. We'll build a form with three elements this time—a label and two buttons, "OK" and "Cancel". This form will look the image in figure 11.4:

Figure 11.4
This is what the dialog created by the Get-OKCancel script looks like. It displays a simple message and two buttons, "OK" and "Cancel".

CHAPTER 11 GETTING FANCY— .NET AND WINFORMS

The code for this function is shown in listing 11.11.

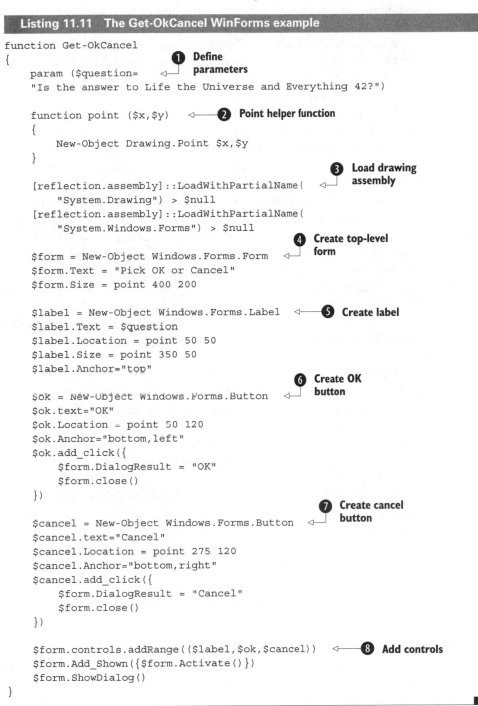

Listing 11.11   The Get-OkCancel WinForms example

```
function Get-OkCancel
{
    param ($question=                        ➊ Define
    "Is the answer to Life the Universe and Everything 42?")    parameters

    function point ($x,$y)     ➋ Point helper function
    {
        New-Object Drawing.Point $x,$y
    }
                                                    ➌ Load drawing
                                                      assembly
    [reflection.assembly]::LoadWithPartialName(
        "System.Drawing") > $null
    [reflection.assembly]::LoadWithPartialName(
        "System.Windows.Forms") > $null
                                        ➍ Create top-level
                                          form
    $form = New-Object Windows.Forms.Form
    $form.Text = "Pick OK or Cancel"
    $form.Size = point 400 200

    $label = New-Object Windows.Forms.Label     ➎ Create label
    $label.Text = $question
    $label.Location = point 50 50
    $label.Size = point 350 50
    $label.Anchor="top"
                                        ➏ Create OK
                                          button
    $ok = New-Object Windows.Forms.Button
    $ok.text="OK"
    $ok.Location = point 50 120
    $ok.Anchor="bottom,left"
    $ok.add_click({
        $form.DialogResult = "OK"
        $form.close()
    })
                                        ➐ Create cancel
                                          button
    $cancel = New-Object Windows.Forms.Button
    $cancel.text="Cancel"
    $cancel.Location = point 275 120
    $cancel.Anchor="bottom,right"
    $cancel.add_click({
        $form.DialogResult = "Cancel"
        $form.close()
    })

    $form.controls.addRange(($label,$ok,$cancel))    ➑ Add controls
    $form.Add_Shown({$form.Activate()})
    $form.ShowDialog()
}
```

This function takes one parameter ❶—the question to ask—with a default. When setting size and location of controls on the form, we need to use point objects, so we'll create a local helper function ❷ to simplify things.

We need to load both the Windows Forms assembly ❸ and the Drawing assembly ❹ so we can create an instance of the point class. Although the classes defined in the forms library refer to the classes in the Drawing library, PowerShell will only find types in the explicitly loaded assemblies.

As in the previous example, we create the top-level form and set the caption, but this time, we're also setting the size of the form.

Next we create the label ❺, setting both the size and the location. We also set the `Anchor` property to `top`; this tells the layout manager to keep the label control "anchored" to the top of the form control. No matter what the size of the control is, the label will always stay the same distance from the top of the form.

Then we create the OK button ❻, setting the caption and location. Again, we're using the `Anchor` property to tell the layout manager to maintain the button's position relative to the bottom and left edges of the form when resizing the form. We also defined the click handler scriptblock. This sets the `DialogResult` property to "OK". When the form is closed, this is the value that will be returned from the call to `ShowDialog()`.

Finally, we defined the Cancel button ❼, this time anchoring it to the lower right side of the form and adding a click handler that will cause `ShowDialog()` to return "Cancel" when the form is closed.

The last step is to add all of the controls to the form and call `ShowDialog()` ❽. As before, the window may be hidden on your desktop when it appears.

There are a couple things to note about this example. The first is that figuring out the size and location for each control is annoying. Calculation or a lot of trial and error is needed. This is what the Form editor in an IDE such as Visual Studio takes care of for you. If you look at the code, the form editor generates mostly property assignments.

The second thing is a lot of code is almost identical. The definition for each of the buttons is the same except for the label and the anchor position. Again, this is something that the form editor takes care of for you. Unfortunately, there is no form editor available for PowerShell at the time of this writing. Fortunately, we have a high-level scripting language we can use to build a library of functions to simplify this. And we'll also look at using smarter layout managers that do more of the work for you. In the next section, we'll introduce a WinForms library that addresses a number of these issues.

11.3.4 Example: A WinForms library

There are a lot of elements in building a Windows Forms application that are repeated over and over. If you're working in an environment such as Visual Studio, the environment takes care of generating the boilerplate code. But if you're building a form using Notepad, you need to be a bit more clever to avoid unnecessary work. Let's build a library of WinForms convenience functions that can be dot-sourced into a script. We'll call this library `winform.ps1`. If this file is placed somewhere in your path then you can use it by including the line

```
. winform
```

at the beginning of your script. The code for this helper library is shown in listing 11.12.

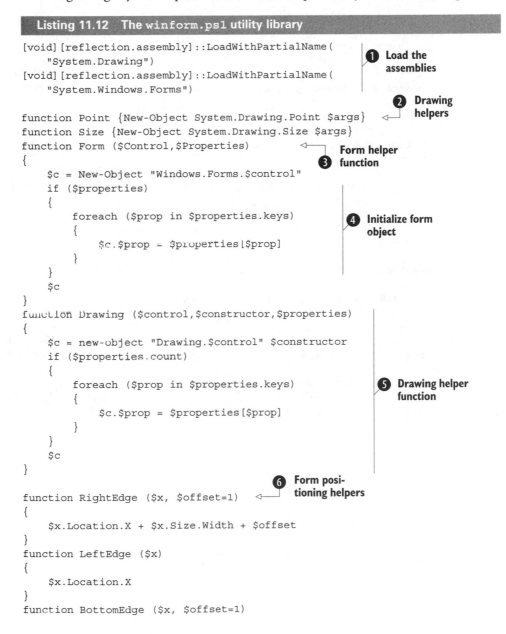

Listing 11.12 The `winform.ps1` utility library

```
[void][reflection.assembly]::LoadWithPartialName(          ❶ Load the
    "System.Drawing")                                         assemblies
[void][reflection.assembly]::LoadWithPartialName(
    "System.Windows.Forms")

                                                           ❷ Drawing
                                                             helpers
function Point {New-Object System.Drawing.Point $args}  <┘
function Size {New-Object System.Drawing.Size $args}
function Form ($Control,$Properties)                     <┐  Form helper
{                                                        ❸  function
    $c = New-Object "Windows.Forms.$control"
    if ($properties)
    {
        foreach ($prop in $properties.keys)            ❹ Initialize form
        {                                                object
            $c.$prop = $properties[$prop]
        }
    }
    $c
}
function Drawing ($control,$constructor,$properties)
{
    $c = new-object "Drawing.$control" $constructor
    if ($properties.count)
    {
        foreach ($prop in $properties.keys)
        {                                              ❺ Drawing helper
            $c.$prop = $properties[$prop]                function
        }
    }
    $c
}
                                                       ❻ Form posi-
function RightEdge ($x, $offset=1)                  <┘   tioning helpers
{
    $x.Location.X + $x.Size.Width + $offset
}
function LeftEdge ($x)
{
    $x.Location.X
}
function BottomEdge ($x, $offset=1)
```

```
{
    $x.Location.Y + $x.Size.Height + $offset
}
function TopEdge ($x) {
    $x.Location.Y
}
```

❼ **MessageBox helper function**

```
function Message ( ◄──┘
$string,
$title='PowerShell Message')
{
    [windows.forms.messagebox]::Show($string, $title)
}
```

❽ **MenuStrip helper function**

```
function New-Menustrip ($Form, [scriptblock] $Menu) ◄──┘
{
    $ms = Form MenuStrip
    [void]$ms.Items.AddRange((&$menu))
    $form.MainMenuStrip = $ms
    $ms
}
```

❾ **Menu helper function**

```
function New-Menu($Name, [scriptblock] $Items) ◄──┘
{
    $menu = Form ToolStripMenuItem @{Text = $name}
    [void] $menu.DropDownItems.AddRange((&$items))
    $menu
}
```

❿ **MenuItem helper function**

```
function New-MenuItem($Name, $Action) ◄──┘
{
    $item = Form ToolStripMenuItem @{Text = $name}
    [void] $item.Add_Click($action)
    $item
}
```

⓫ **Menu Separator helper function**

```
function New-Separator { Form ToolStripSeparator } ◄──┘
```

⓬ **Layout Style helper function**

```
function Style ($RowOrColumn="row",$Percent=-1) ◄──┐
{
    if ($Percent -eq -1)
    {
        $typeArgs = "AutoSize"
    }
    else
    {
        $typeArgs = "Percent",$percent
    }
    New-Object Windows.Forms.${RowOrColumn}Style $typeArgs
}
```

The most important thing a WinForms library should do is make sure that the necessary assemblies are loaded ❶. Note that "loading" the assembly multiple times is harmless.

Next we define some convenience functions ❷ for creating common Drawing objects: point and size. These functions, like many of the helpers, just hide the long type names used to construct the objects.

The function Form ❸ is the function we'll use most often when creating Win-Form objects. It takes as arguments the name of the WinForms class to create and an optional hashtable of properties to create. If the properties hashtable is provided ❹ the function will iterate over the keys in the hashtable, setting the property on the object named by the key to the value associated with that key. This makes object initialization very easy. Drawing ❺ is a similar function for creating and initializing System.Drawing objects.

Next is a series of convenience functions ❻ that can be used to calculate coordinates for a Form object. These are handy when we're explicitly laying out the controls on a form.

The Message function ❼ is a simple utility for popping up a message box.

Next is a series of functions that work together to simplify building menus. The New-MenuStrip function ❽ allows us to create and add a menu strip to a form. Notice that it takes a scriptblock for its second argument. This is the "little-languages" concept mentioned in chapter 8. This function expects that when the scriptblock is executed, it will return a collection of menu objects that the function can add to the menu.

We'll use the New-Menu ❾ function to create these menu objects. This function also takes a scriptblock that should return a collection of MenuItem objects. These MenuItem objects will be added to the current Menu object. Finally, MenuItem objects are created with the New-MenuItem function ❿. This function takes a name and an action in the form of a scriptblock. When this menu item is selected, the action scriptblock will be executed. One more helper function for building menus, the New-Separator function ⓫, is used to add separators between menu items.

The last function in this library is Style ⓬ which is used to produce the row and column style objects used by the layout managers that we'll use later in this chapter.

Although there doesn't seem to be much to this library, it can significantly simplify building a forms applications. In the next section, we'll use it to build a significant application.

11.3.5 Example: A simple calculator

In this section, we'll build our own replacement for the Windows calculator applet. We'll use this exercise to show how the WinForms library can help construct an application. We'll also use this example to introduce the table layout manager. In the process, we'll show how some of PowerShell's features can be used to create flexible application architecture.

At the end of the exercise, we want to build an application that looks like what's shown in Figure 11.5.

It's not as fancy as the calculator that ships with Windows, but it has more functions and, since it's a script, we can add our own custom features when we want to. The basic structure includes a simple File menu with two actions— Clear and Exit. Next there is a text box that will hold the value of the most recent calculation. Finally, there are all of the buttons in the calculator. This is where the table lay out manager is important. We don't want to have to lay out each of these buttons by hand. (Even in an interface builder such as Visual Studio, this would be tedious.) The `TableLayoutPanel` allows us to lay out a grid of controls. It has a `ColumnCount` property that allows us to control the number of

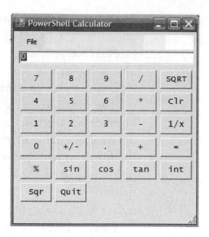

Figure 11.5   What the PowerShell calculator example form looks like. This example uses the WinForm library to construct an extensible graphical calculator application.

columns that are used in laying out the buttons. We'll design the application so that by simply changing this value, we can lay out our buttons in two columns, producing a tall, skinny calculator, or set it to 10 columns, producing a shorter, wider layout. The code is shown in listing 11.13.

Listing 11.13   The PowerShell graphical calculator

```
. winform              <——┐  Load WinForm
                        ❶  library              ❷  Set up
$script:op = ''                              <——┘  functions
$script:doClear = $false
function clr { $result.text = 0 }
[decimal] $script:value = 0
                        ❸  Set up operator
$handleDigit = {       <——┐  scriptblock
    if ($doClear)
    {
        $result.text = 0
        $script:doClear = $false
    }

    $key = $this.text
    $current = $result.Text
    if ($current -match '^0$|NaN|Infinity')
    {
        $result.text = $key
    } else {
        if ($key -ne '.' -or $current -notmatch '\.')
        {
```

```
                            $result.Text += $key
            }
        }
}
                         ❹  Set up Number
$handleOp = {      ←⌐       scriptblock
        $script:value = $result.text
        $script:op = $this.text
        $script:doClear = $true
}
                    ❺  The key/action
                        table
$keys = (       ←⌐
    @{name='7'; action=$handleDigit},
    @{name='8'; action=$handleDigit},
    @{name='9'; action=$handleDigit},
    @{name='/'; action = $handleOp},            ❻  The Sqr
    @{name='SQRT'; action = {          ←⌐          handler
            trap { $resultl.Text = 0; continue }
            $result.Text = [math]::sqrt([decimal] $result.Text)


        }
    },
    @{name='4'; action=$handleDigit},
    @{name='5'; action=$handleDigit},
    @{name='6'; action=$handleDigit},
    @{name='*'; action = $handleOp},
    @{name='Clr'; action = $function:clr},
    @{name='1'; action=$handleDigit},
    @{name='2'; action=$handleDigit},
    @{name='3'; action=$handleDigit},
    @{name=' '; action = $handleOp},
    @{name='1/x'; action = {
            trap { $resultl.Text = 0; continue }
            $val = [decimal] $result.Text
            if ($val -ne 0)
            {
                $result.Text = 1.0 / $val
            }
        }
    },
    @{name='0'; action=$handleDigit},
    @{name='+/-'; action = {
            trap { $resultl.Text = 0; continue }
            $result.Text = - ([decimal] $result.Text)
        }
    },
    @{name='.'; action=$handleDigit},
    @{name='+'; action = $handleOp},            ❼  The "="
    @{name='='; action = {          ←⌐             handler


            $key = $this.text
```

```
                    trap { message "error: $key" "error: $key"; continue }
                    $operand = [decimal] $result.text
                    $result.text = invoke-expression "`$value $op `$operand"
                }
            },
        @{name='%'; action = $handleOp},
        @{name='sin'; action = {
                    trap { $resultl.Text = 0; continue }
                    $result.Text = [math]::sin([decimal] $result.Text)
                }
            },
        @{name='cos'; action = {
                    trap { $resultl.Text = 0; continue }
                    $result.Text = [math]::cos([decimal] $result.Text)
                }
            },
        @{name='tan'; action = {
                    trap { $resultl.Text = 0; continue }
                    $result.Text = [math]::tan([decimal] $result.Text)
                }
            },
        @{name='int'; action = {
                    trap { $resultl.Text = 0; continue }
                    $result.Text = [int] $result.Text
                }
            },
        @{name='Sqr'; action = {
                    $result.Text = [double]$result.Text * [double]$result.text
                }
            },
        @{name='Quit'; action = {$form.Close()}}
)

$columns = 5   ←┘
```

❽ Number of columns

```
$form = Form Form @{
    Text = "PowerShell Calculator"
    TopLevel = $true
    Padding=5
}
```

❾ Top-level layout

```
$table = form TableLayoutPanel @{   ←┘
    ColumnCount = 1
    Dock="fill"
}
$form.controls.add($table)
```

❿ Define menus

```
$menu = new-menustrip $form {   ←┘
    new-menu File {
        new-menuitem "Clear" { clr }
        new-separator
        new-menuitem Quit { $form.Close() }
```

```
        }
    }
    $table.controls.add($menu)

    $cfont = New-Object Drawing.Font          <──  ⑪  Set font
        'Lucida Console',10.0,Regular,Point,0

    $script:result = form TextBox @{          <──┐     Create display
        Dock="fill"                              ⑫  text box
        Font = $cfont
        Text = 0
    }
    $table.Controls.Add($result)

    $buttons = form TableLayoutPanel @{       <──  ⑬  Button
        ColumnCount = $columns                        layout panel
        Dock = "fill"
    }

    foreach ($key in $keys) {                 <──┐  ⑭  Bind key
        $b = form button @{                          actions
            text=$key.name
            font = $cfont;
            size = size 50 30
        }
        $b.add_Click($key.action)
        $buttons.controls.Add($b)
    }
    $table.Controls.Add($buttons)

    $height = ([math]::ceiling($keys.count / $columns)) *  <──┐ ⑮ Set form
    40 + 100                                                    size
    $width = $columns * 58 + 10

    $result.size = size ($width - 10) $result.size.height
    $form.size = size $width $height
    $form.Add_Shown({$form.Activate()})
    [void] $form.ShowDialog()
```

We start our calculator script by loading the forms ❶ library. Next we'll set up some variables and functions ❷ that we'll use later in the script. The clr function will be used for setting the calculator back to zero. The variable $op is used for holding the pending operation. This is the operation that the user has clicked, but it won't be executed until "="or another operation is selected.

The basic logic for handling a number key click ❸ is the same, so we'll build a common scriptblock for it. This scriptblock will incrementally append numbers to the display, resetting it when appropriate.

Pressing one of the operation keys such as + or - is also handed in pretty much the same way for all of the keys, so again we'll define a common scriptblock ❹ to handle it. This scriptblock saves the current calculated value as well as the operation to perform, and then allows the user to enter the next value in the calculation.

The next step is to build a table ❺ that holds all of the actions that will be associated with each key. This table will be used to bind these actions to all of the button controls. It's defined as an array of hashtables. Each hashtable has a member name that specifies the name to put on the key and an action to perform when the key is pressed. This action is implemented by a scriptblock. Most of the keys will call either the `handleDigit` scriptblock or the `handleOp` scriptblock, but some will have their custom scriptblock.

For example, the "Sqr" key implements the square root ❻ function. It uses the static method `[math]::sqrt()` to do the calculation. Since having your calculator throw exceptions is not very friendly, we also add a trap handler to catch and discard any exceptions that might occur when calculating the square root. We'll see this pattern again in some of the other trap handlers. (See chapter 9 for information on handing exceptions with the `trap` statement.)

The scriptblock associated with the "=" key handles executing actual calculation ❼. It builds an expression that will generate the result we want using the `$value` and `$op` variables. This expression is then evaluated using the `Invoke-Expression` cmdlet. (See chapter 13 for cautions about using `Invoke-Expression`.)

Now that we've defined all of the logic for the calculator, let's build the form. Rather than explicitly laying out where all of the controls go, we'll use the table layout manager, which allows us to lay out a series of controls onto a grid. By default, we'll set the number of columns ❽ to 5.

We'll create the top-level `TableLayoutPanel` control ❾ to lay out the menu, display, and button elements.

Now we need to define the menus ❿. Here we're using the menu helper functions from the `winform` library. As mentioned previously, these functions use the "little-language" technique described in chapter 8. The `new-menustrip` function takes a scriptblock which will return a collection of menus to add to the menu strip. Similarly, the `new-menu` function will take a scriptblock that should return a collection of menu items to add to the calling menu. Finally, the `new-menuitem` scriptblock takes a name and scriptblock to use as an action and returns a menu item to the caller.

We'll pick a specific font ⓫ to use for the display and the buttons, and then build the `TextBox` control ⓬ to display the current value.

Finally, we'll create a second `TableLayoutPanel` ⓭ to hold the calculator buttons. We iterate through the table of keys created in step ❺, creating a new button for each entry in the table ⓮. We set attributes on this button control, attach the scriptblock to it, and add it to the table.

The last step is to do the math ⑮ to figure out the best size for the form, set the form, and display it using the ShowDialog() method.

And there you have it, a basic calculator application. In fact, this isn't a very good calculator at all, it doesn't handle order of operations; it doesn't even chain calculations properly or handle the keyboard events. But it does demonstrate a number of useful techniques, both in PowerShell and in WinForms for building graphical applications.

11.3.6   Example: Displaying data

A common activity in user interface programming is displaying collections of data. The Windows Forms framework makes this easy through a feature called *data binding*. Data binding is the ability to tell a control such as a grid to use a collection of objects as the data it should display. The programmer doesn't have to write any code; the control figures everything out by examining the data. PowerShell objects (PSObjects) also support data binding, so we can take the output from a pipeline and use that as the data source for a control. In this section, we'll work through a short script that does exactly this. We'll take the output of the Get-Process cmdlet and display it in a grid on a form. In the process, we'll look at a additional features of the TableLayoutPanel. The resulting form is shown in figure 11.6.

The code that implements this form is shown in listing 11.14.

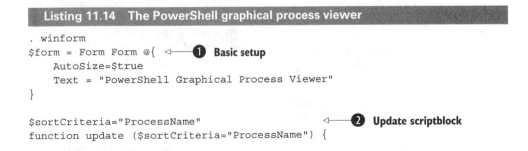

Figure 11.6   What the PowerShell graphics process viewer form looks like. Clicking on any of the buttons will cause the data to be refreshed and sorted based on the property named by the button.

Listing 11.14   The PowerShell graphical process viewer

```
. winform
$form = Form Form @{   ◁───① Basic setup
    AutoSize=$true
    Text = "PowerShell Graphical Process Viewer"
}

$sortCriteria="ProcessName"                          ◁───② Update scriptblock
function update ($sortCriteria="ProcessName") {
```

```
    $grid.DataSource = New-Object Collections.ArrayList `
        (,(gps | sort $sortCriteria |
select name,id,handles,workingset,cpu))
    $grid.CaptionText = "Process Data Sorted by $sortCriteria"
    $status.Text =
        "Last Updated on $(get-date | out-string)" -replace "`n"
}
```

❸ Create layout panel

```
$table = form TableLayoutPanel @{
    columncount=6
    Dock="Fill"
    AutoSizeMode = "GrowOnly"; AutoSize = $true
}
$form.Controls.Add($table)
```

❹ Set styles

```
[void] $table.RowStyles.Add((style))
[void] $table.RowStyles.Add((style -percent 50))
1..3 | %{
    [void] $table.RowStyles.Add((style))
}

1..4 | %{
    [void] $table.ColumnStyles.Add((style column 17))
}
```

❺ Create menus

```
$menu = new-menustrip $form {
    new-menu File {
      new-menuitem "Update" { update }
        new-separator
        new-menuitem "Quit" { $form.Close() }
    }
    new-menu Help {
      new-menuitem "About" {
            message (
                "PowerShell Process Viewer`n`n" +
                "Windows Forms Demo Applet`n" +
                "From Windows PowerShell in Action`n" +
                "Manning Publications Co. 2006"
                )
        }
    }
}
$table.controls.add($menu)
$table.SetColumnSpan($menu, 6)
```

❻ Create grid control

```
$grid = Form DataGrid @{
    Dock="fill"
    CaptionText = "PowerShell Graphical Process Viewer"
}
$table.Controls.Add($grid);
$table.SetColumnSpan($grid, 6)
```

❼ New-button helper

```
function New-Button($label,$action)
```

CHAPTER 11   GETTING FANCY— .NET AND WINFORMS

```
{
    $b = form button @{text=$label; anchor = "left,right" }
    $b.add_Click($action);
    $table.Controls.Add($b);
}
New-Button "Name" {update ProcessName}        <———  Make buttons
New-Button "Id" {update Id}
New-Button "Handles" {update Handles}
New-Button "WorkingSet (WS)" {update WS}
New-Button "CPU" {update cpu}

$status = form label @{
    dock="fill"
    flatstyle="popup"
    borderstyle="fixed3d"
}
$table.Controls.Add($status);
$table.SetColumnSpan($status, 6)

Update                                        <———  Show form
$form.Add_Shown({$form.Activate()})
[void] $form.ShowDialog();
```

We begin the process viewer example with the standard preamble ❶, where we load the winform library and create the top-level form. Next we create the scriptblock ❷ that will be used to update the form when a button is clicked. This is also used to update the form when it is first displayed.

We create a TableLayoutPanel ❸ to lay out all of our controls. We'll use the Style helper function ❹ in the winform library to set up how the form will be resized. We want the grid to occupy most of the form space with the buttons and menus remaining at the top and bottom.

Next we create the menus ❺, add them to the form, and create the actual Data-Grid control ❻ that will be used to display the information.

We're going to have a bunch of buttons at the bottom, so we'll define a helper function New-Button ❼ so we don't have to repeat the code. We use this function to create each of the operation buttons. The last thing to do is run the update script-block to fill the gird with an initial collection of data values and then display the form. And that's the end of the grid example.

11.3.7   Example: Using the GDI+ to do graphics

The last example in this chapter involves actual graphics programming. All of the earlier WinForms examples have depended on the controls to do the drawing. Now we'll look at drawing directly with PowerShell. In the process, we'll see how to use the paint and timer events on a Form object. We'll also touch on some of the more sophisticated graphics feature in .NET.

Graphics programming in Windows (at least in the post XP/Server 2003) world is done using a set of APIs called the *GDI+*. GDI stands for *graphics device interface*. It's the abstraction that Windows uses to hide the details of working with specific graphics hardware. In .NET, this API surfaces through the `System.Drawing` collection of namespaces. The particular example is a script that draws a spiral on a form. This form is shown in figure 11.7.

The script draws a spiral out from the center of the form. It periodically redraws the form, changing the foreground and background colors on each iteration. This redraw is handled by the `Timer` event on the form. Resizing the form will also trigger the `Paint` event to cause the spiral to be redrawn.

The script takes parameters that allow you to specify the opacity (or translucency) of the form, as well as its initial size and the amount of detail used in drawing the form. See listing 11.15.

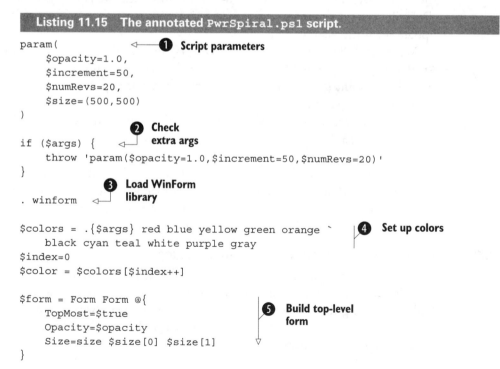

Figure 11.7 Screen capture of the PwrSpiral GDI+ example form. This form is drawn by a PowerShell script. It will redraw itself in a different color every 5 seconds. It can also be started such that it will be displayed as a transparent window.

Listing 11.15 The annotated `PwrSpiral.ps1` script.

```
param(                    ←———❶ Script parameters
    $opacity=1.0,
    $increment=50,
    $numRevs=20,
    $size=(500,500)
)
                     ❷ Check
if ($args) {    ←——┘  extra args
    throw 'param($opacity=1.0,$increment=50,$numRevs=20)'
}
                     ❸ Load WinForm
. winform    ←——┘   library

$colors = .{$args} red blue yellow green orange `    ❹ Set up colors
    black cyan teal white purple gray
$index=0
$color = $colors[$index++]

$form = Form Form @{
    TopMost=$true                    ❺ Build top-level
    Opacity=$opacity                    form
    Size=size $size[0] $size[1]
}
```

```
$myBrush = Drawing SolidBrush $color
$pen =    Drawing pen black @{Width=3}
$rec = Drawing Rectangle 0,0,200,200
```

5 **Build top-level form**

```
function Spiral($grfx)
{
    $cx, $cy =$Form.ClientRectangle.Width,
        $Form.ClientRectangle.Height
    $iNumPoints = $numRevs * 2 * ($cx+$cy)
    $cx = $cx/2
    $cy = $cy/2
    $np = $iNumPoints/$numRevs
    $fAngle = $i*2.0*3.14159265 / $np
    $fScale = 1.0 - $i / $iNumPoints
    $x,$y = ($cx * (1.0 + $fScale * [math]::cos($fAngle))),
            ($cy * (1.0 + $fScale * [math]::Sin($fAngle)))

    for ($i=0; $i -lt $iNumPoints; $i += 50)
    {
        $fAngle = $i*2.0*[math]::pi / $np
        $fScale = 1.0 - $i / $iNumPoints
        $ox,$oy,$x,$y = $x,$y,
            ($cx * (1.0 + $fScale * [math]::cos($fAngle))),
            ($cy * (1.0 + $fScale * [math]::Sin($fAngle)))
        $grfx.DrawLine($pen, $ox, $oy, $x, $y)
    }
}
```

6 **Spiral function**

7 **Initialize values**

8 **Draw spiral**

```
$handler = {
    $rec.width = $form.size.width
    $rec.height = $form.size.height
    $myBrush.Color = $color
    $formGraphics = $form.CreateGraphics()
    $formGraphics.FillRectangle($myBrush, $rec)
    $form.Text = "Color: $color".ToUpper()
    $color = $colors[$index++]
    $index %= $colors.Length

    $pen.Color = $color
    Spiral $formGraphics
    $formGraphics.Dispose()
}
```

9 **Timer event handler**

```
$timer = New-Object system.windows.forms.timer
$timer.interval = 5000
$timer.add_Tick($handler)
$timer.Start()
```

10 **Set up timer event**

```
$Form.add_paint($handler)
```

11 **Add paint handler**

```
$form.Add_Shown({$form.Activate()})
[void] $form.ShowDialog()
```

12 **Show form**

First define the parameters ❶ for the script (remember, the `param` statement always has to be the first executable statement in the script). Opacity of a form is a built-in capability in the GDI+, allowing for some cool visual effects. An opacity of 1 is a solid form. The spiral is drawn using a series of line segments. The more segments there are, the smoother the curve, but the longer it takes to draw. This is controlled by the `$increment` parameter. The `$numRevs` parameter controls the number of revolutions used in drawing the spiral. The spiral will always fill the form, so the higher the number of revolutions, the closer together the curves will be.

Checking `$args` ❷ is a "trick" to check for extra parameters. If there are any extra parameters to the script, an error will be generated.

Of course, we still need to load the basic assemblies and create a form to draw on, so we load the usual `winform` utility library ❸.

We want the spiral to be drawn in a different color on each iteration, so set up a list ❹ of the colors to loop through. The `$index` variable is used to keep track of the last color used.

And now we'll create the objects ❺ we need. We'll create a top-level form, passing in the size and opacity arguments to the script. Then we'll create a couple of drawing objects—a brush to do the drawing and a rectangle to use for drawing the form background.

The `Spiral` function ❻ is the routine that does all of the drawing. It takes a graphics context to draw on and then uses the information about the number of revolutions and the increment to calculate the number of segments to draw.

Once we have all of the basic information—the number of points and the angle of rotation—calculated ❼, we loop ❽, drawing each segment until the spiral is complete. We're using multivariable assignment in the loop to simplify the code and speed things up a bit.

Next we'll create a scriptblock ❾ that we can use as the event handler for triggering drawing the spiral. This handler creates the graphics object for drawing on the form, fills it with the background color, then calls the `Spiral` routine to draw on the graphics object.

With the basic pieces in place, we can now create the timer control ❿ and add it to the form to trigger the redraws. The script sets up the timer control's interval to redraw the form every 5 seconds.

Any activity that triggers the paint ⓫ event will cause the spiral to be redrawn. For example, resizing the form will cause a new paint cycle.

Finally, we show the form ⓬, blocking it from view until it is closed.

This example shows additional uses of the scriptblock as a timer event handler as well as using the `[math]` capabilities to do some fairly complex calculations. It's not a particularly practical application, but it give us the basics of how to write an application that graphs a sequence of values. For example, we could extend the calculator example from earlier in this chapter to do graphics. (We could, but we won't. We'll leave this as a rainy-day exercise for the reader.)

11.4 SUMMARY

Chapter 11 covered a variety of application areas where PowerShell can be applied because of its ability to access classes in the .NET frameworks. When a particular application domain may not have adequate coverage through cmdlets (at least not yet), if there is a .NET API for that area, the odds are good that PowerShell can be used to script it. In the first part of this chapter we covered:

- The basic concepts in .NET and the common language runtime, including the basics of assemblies and types.
- How to load assemblies into the PowerShell session and then how to find the new types once the assemblies have been loaded.
- How to create instances of types, including creating generic collections.
- Some of the problems programmers (particularly C# programmers) may run into when trying to fit their experience onto PowerShell semantics.

The remainder of the chapter was taken up by a series of examples. These examples included network programming in PowerShell. We looked at:

- Retrieving a simple web page in a script.
- Reading and processing an RSS feed.
- Writing a (toy) web server in PowerShell.

Next we looked at a series of examples showing how to do basic WinForms programming in PowerShell. We implemented:

- A simple "my first form"-style example that just displayed a button.
- A slightly more complicated example for building a basic dialog.
- A significantly more complex graphical calculator example.
- An example that used data binding to display a grid of objects in a form.

C H A P T E R   1 2

Windows objects: COM and WMI

A horse! A horse! My kingdom for a horse!

—William Shakespeare
The Life and Death of King Richard III

A horse is a horse of course of course
And no one can talk to a horse, of course
That is, of course, unless the horse is the famous Mister Ed!

—The *Mr. Ed* TV Show

At the end of Shakespeare's *Richard III*, King Richard stands upon a plain, surrounded by foes, crying out for the one thing that he needs to continue on. Sort of like a sysadmin. Okay, perhaps not exactly like that, but at times, we do feel set upon from all sides, crying desperately for something to help us solve our problems. Fortunately, we in the PowerShell world do get our horse. In fact, we get two of them—WMI and COM.

In earlier chapters, we devoted a lot of attention to .NET, the new object model from Microsoft. But there are two older workhorse technologies that are still heavily used on the Windows platform. The first of these is COM, Microsoft's Component Object Model. This is most commonly used as the Windows automation mechanism.

The other major object model is WMI, Windows Management Instrumentation. This is Microsoft's implementation of the Common Instrumentation Model or CIM. CIM is an industry standard created by Microsoft, HP, IBM, and many other computer companies with the intent of coming up with a common set of management abstractions.

We care about these technologies because there are still elements of the system that are accessible only from COM or WMI. Until there is full cmdlet or .NET coverage for everything we need, we'll sometimes find ourselves turning to COM or WMI to complete a task.

In this chapter, we'll cover the important details for accessing these two facilities from PowerShell. We'll look at a number of examples that illustrate how things work and the sorts of tasks that can be accomplished. We'll also look at how we can mix the traditional Windows scripting language VBScript into PowerShell scripts. We'll even see how we can make a horse talk (or at least a parrot).

12.1 WORKING WITH COM IN POWERSHELL

Working with COM requires creating instances of COM objects. As with .NET objects, this is done with the New-Object cmdlet, but this time you have to specify the -ComObject parameter.

The signature of New-Object is different when creating COM objects. See figure 12.1. We can't specify any arguments when constructing the object, and then there's the -strict switch. This switch tells the cmdlet to generate an error if a .NET/COM Interop library is loaded. This is an important feature because of the way object adaptation works in PowerShell. This is complicated, so let's go through it in pieces.

In chapter 3, we talked about how PowerShell adapts different types of objects. COM objects are one of types that are adapted. The form that this adaptation takes, however, is affected by the presence or absence of a COM Interop library. In effect,

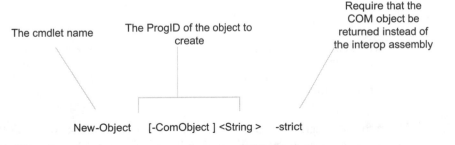

Figure 12.1 New-Object **usage for creating COM objects**

the Interop library is .NET's "adaptation layer" for COM. The PowerShell adapter will project a different view of the COM object depending upon whether there is an Interop library available. For a specific COM object on a specific machine, there may or may not be an Interop library. Consequently, if we write scripts assuming that there is no Interop library and it turns out that there is one, our script may break because the data model is different. By specifying the -strict parameter, we can detect this condition. Once we know what is happening, we can decide whether we want to fail or whether we want to continue, but along a different code path. This is something to keep in mind when writing a script that uses COM that you plan to deploy on other machines. We'll discuss this more later in the chapter.

As far as PowerShell is concerned, COM objects are identified by something called the ProgID. This is a string alias that is provided when the class is registered on the system. This is the most human-friendly way of identifying the object. By convention, the ProgID has the form:

```
<Program>.<Component>.<Version>
```

and, per the MSDN documentation, should be less than 39 characters in length.

AUTHOR'S NOTE While this format is the recommended presentation, there is no real way to enforce it, resulting in some "interesting" interpretations for what each of the elements actually means. Generally, it seems in practice that <Program> is the application suite, toolset, or vendor which installs it; <component> is actually the COM class name; and the version number is normally not used in calls, although it may exist in even a multipart form. Thus, even as wshom.ocx has been extended, it has retained the versioned form WScript.Shell.1, but is almost always used in script as just WScript.Shell; and the XML DOM is exposed as Msxml2.DOMDocument with a .2.6, .4.0, .6.0 suffix and so on, but is always instantiated as Msxml2.DOMDocument.

COM objects are registered in (where else?) the registry. This means that we can use the registry provider to search for ProgIDs from PowerShell. Here's a function we'll call Get-ProgID that will do it:

```
function Get-ProgID
{
    param ($filter = '.')

    $ClsIdPath = "REGISTRY::HKey_Classes_Root\clsid\*\progid"
    dir $ClsIdPath |
        % {if ($_.name -match '\\ProgID$') { $_.GetValue("") }} |
        ? {$_ -match $filter}
}
```

This searches through the registry starting at the classes root, where COM objects are registered for keys whose paths end in "ProgID". From the keys, we retrieve the default property, which contains the name string of the `ProgID`. We check this string against the filter and, it if matches, write it to the output stream. Let's try it out. We want to find the `ProgID` for Internet Explorer.

```
PS (1) > Get-ProgID internetexplorer
InternetExplorer.Application.1
```

And there it is: `InternetExplorer.Application.1`. As described previously, the program is `InternetExplorer` and the component in this case is the actual Internet Explorer application. We can use this same pattern to find the automation interfaces for other applications. Let's look for Microsoft Word.

```
PS (2) > Get-ProgID word.*applica
Word.Application.11
```

We find the `ProgID` for Word 11, which is part of Office 2003. What about non-Microsoft applications? Let's pick an application that we may have installed on our computer. We'll look for the Apple Computer iTunes media player.

```
PS (3) > Get-ProgID itunes.*application
iTunes.Application.1
```

Again, it follows the naming convention.

Now let's look at another way to find `ProgID`s. This can be done through WMI—the subject of the second half of this chapter. Here's the alternative script.

```
function Get-ProgID
{
    param ($filter = '.')

    Get-WMIObject Win32_ProgIDSpecification |
        ? {$_.ProgId -match $filter} |
        select-object ProgID,Description
}
```

Not only is this script simpler, it provides additional information: a description of the `ProgID`. Let's look up Microsoft Word again:

```
PS (6) > (get-progids word.application) | select-object -First 1

ProgID                          Description
------                          -----------
Word.Application.11             Microsoft Word Application
```

This time we get the `ProgID` and its description. The downside to this mechanism is that it only locates a subset of the registered `ProgID`s, so the registry-based script is usually the best approach.

Once you have the `ProdID`, you can use it with `New-Object` to create instances of these objects. In the next few sections, we'll go over examples of the broad range of things you can do with COM objects.

12.1.1 Automating Windows with COM

The first group of examples will be to work with and automate the basic elements of Windows itself. We'll start with automating Windows Explorer, then look at activating a control panel applet, and finally look at automating an application by sending keystrokes to it.

Example: "Exploring" with the Shell.Application class

First we'll work with Windows Explorer (you know—that other Windows shell—the GUI one). The Explorer application exports an automation model that lets you automate some tasks from a script. *Automation model* means that there is a COM object interface that lets an external program manipulate some aspects of an application. For the GUI Shell, this is done through the `Shell.Application` object. Let's explore what this can do. First we create an instance of the object:

```
PS (3) > $shell = new-object -com Shell.Application
```

COM objects, like all other object types in the system, can be examined through `Get-Member`. Let's look at the members on the object we've instantiated:

```
PS (4) > $shell | gm


   TypeName: System.__ComObject#{efd84b2d-4bcf-4298-be25-eb542a5
9fbda}

Name                   MemberType Definition
----                   ---------- ----------
AddToRecent            Method     void AddToRecent (Variant, st...
BrowseForFolder        Method     Folder BrowseForFolder (int, ...
CanStartStopService    Method     Variant CanStartStopService (...
CascadeWindows         Method     void CascadeWindows ()
ControlPanelItem       Method     void ControlPanelItem (string)
EjectPC                Method     void EjectPC ()
Explore                Method     void Explore (Variant)
ExplorerPolicy         Method     Variant ExplorerPolicy (string)
FileRun                Method     void FileRun ()
FindComputer           Method     void FindComputer ()
FindFiles              Method     void FindFiles ()
FindPrinter            Method     void FindPrinter (string, str...
GetSetting             Method     bool GetSetting (int)
GetSystemInformation   Method     Variant GetSystemInformation ...
Help                   Method     void Help ()
IsRestricted           Method     int IsRestricted (string, str...
IsServiceRunning       Method     Variant IsServiceRunning (str...
MinimizeAll            Method     void MinimizeAll ()
NameSpace              Method     Folder NameSpace (Variant)
Open                   Method     void Open (Variant)
RefreshMenu            Method     void RefreshMenu ()
ServiceStart           Method     Variant ServiceStart (string,...
```

```
ServiceStop              Method        Variant ServiceStop (string, ...
SetTime                  Method        void SetTime ()
ShellExecute             Method        void ShellExecute (string, Va...
ShowBrowserBar           Method        Variant ShowBrowserBar (strin...
ShutdownWindows          Method        void ShutdownWindows ()
Suspend                  Method        void Suspend ()
TileHorizontally         Method        void TileHorizontally ()
TileVertically           Method        void TileVertically ()
ToggleDesktop            Method        void ToggleDesktop ()
TrayProperties           Method        void TrayProperties ()
UndoMinimizeALL          Method        void UndoMinimizeALL ()
Windows                  Method        IDispatch Windows ()
WindowsSecurity          Method        void WindowsSecurity ()
Application              Property      IDispatch Application () {get}
Parent                   Property      IDispatch Parent () {get}
```

Woohoo! Jackpot! (At least that's how I felt when I first saw this.) Look at all that stuff! Let's try it out. We'll start with the `Explore()` method, which will launch an Explorer window on the path specified.

```
PS (10) > $shell.Explore("c:\")
PS (11) >
```

At which point you should see something that looks like what's shown in figure 12.2.

The method call started an Explorer window at the root of the C: drive. Now let's look at another example. We'll use the `Windows()` method to get a list of the Explorer windows that are open.

```
PS (16) > ($shell.Windows()).count
13
```

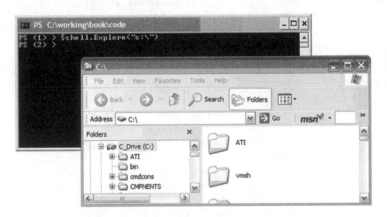

Figure 12.2   Launching the Windows Explorer on C:

Thirteen are open; let's look at the first one. We'll look at the members on this object:

```
PS (17) > $shell.Windows() | gm


    TypeName: System.__ComObject#{d30c1661-cdaf-11d0-8a3e-00
c04fc9e26e}

Name                    MemberType Definition
----                    ---------- ----------
ClientToWindow          Method     void ClientToWindow (int...
ExecWB                  Method     void ExecWB (OLECMDID, O...
GetProperty             Method     Variant GetProperty (str...
GoBack                  Method     void GoBack ()
GoForward               Method     void GoForward ()
GoHome                  Method     void GoHome ()
GoSearch                Method     void GoSearch ()
Navigate                Method     void Navigate (string, V...
Navigate2               Method     void Navigate2 (Variant,...
PutProperty             Method     void PutProperty (string...
QueryStatusWB           Method     OLECMDF QueryStatusWB (O...
Quit                    Method     void Quit ()
Refresh                 Method     void Refresh ()
Refresh2                Method     void Refresh2 (Variant)
ShowBrowserBar          Method     void ShowBrowserBar (Var...
Stop                    Method     void Stop ()
AddressBar              Property   bool AddressBar () {get}...
Application             Property   IDispatch Application ()...
Busy                    Property   bool Busy () {get}
Container               Property   IDispatch Container () {...
Document                Property   IDispatch Document () {g...
FullName                Property   string FullName () {get}
FullScreen              Property   bool FullScreen () {get}...
Height                  Property   int Height () {get} {set}
HWND                    Property   int HWND () {get}
Left                    Property   int Left () {get} {set}
LocationName            Property   string LocationName () {...
LocationURL             Property   string LocationURL () {g...
MenuBar                 Property   bool MenuBar () {get} {s...
Name                    Property   string Name () {get}
Offline                 Property   bool Offline () {get} {s...
Parent                  Property   IDispatch Parent () {get}
Path                    Property   string Path () {get}
ReadyState              Property   tagREADYSTATE ReadyState...
RegisterAsBrowser       Property   bool RegisterAsBrowser (...
RegisterAsDropTarget    Property   bool RegisterAsDropTarge...
Resizable               Property   bool Resizable () {get} ...
Silent                  Property   bool Silent () {get} {set}
StatusBar               Property   bool StatusBar () {get} ...
StatusText              Property   string StatusText () {ge...
TheaterMode             Property   bool TheaterMode () {get...
ToolBar                 Property   int ToolBar () {get} {set}
Top                     Property   int Top () {get} {set}
```

```
TopLevelContainer      Property    bool TopLevelContainer (...
Type                   Property    string Type () {get}
Visible                Property    bool Visible () {get} {s...
Width                  Property    int Width () {get} {set}
```

And again we see lots of tantalizing things to play with. Let's look at the first item:

```
PS (21) > $shell.Windows()[0]
Unable to index into an object of type System.__ComObject.
At line:1 char:18
+ $shell.Windows()[0 <<<< ]
```

We got an error. So what happened here? If you look at the type of the object; you'll see that it's a System.__ComObject, which is the .NET mechanism for accessing COM objects. PowerShell wraps and adapts these objects, but the adaptation is not perfect, and this is one of the places it shows through.

> **AUTHOR'S NOTE** These problems are not strictly PowerShell's fault. There are general interop problems between COM and .NET, and PowerShell inherits these problems since PowerShell uses the .NET mechanism to interoperate with COM. It can also, however, benefit from the solutions. If there is a workaround to an interop problem in .NET, that solution can generally be applied in the PowerShell world as well. And as bugs are fixed in the .NET/COM interop code, they are also automatically fixed in PowerShell.

The PowerShell interpreter doesn't know how to index on these objects. This doesn't mean that you can't do it, however. Instead of simple indexing, you have to use the Item() parameterized property.

> **AUTHOR'S NOTE** A parameterized property is like a method—it takes arguments in parentheses just like a method, but it can also be assigned to like a property. Indexing on a COM collection in PowerShell is done using the Item() parameterized property.

Let's try it again:

```
PS (18) > $shell.Windows().Item(0)

Application         : System.__ComObject
Parent             : System.__ComObject
Container          :
Document           : mshtml.HTMLDocumentClass
TopLevelContainer  : True
Type               : HTML Document
Left               : 354
Top                : 80
Width              : 838
Height             : 489
LocationName       : Windows PowerShell : Casting a scrip
                     tblock to an arbitrary delegate sign
                     ature
```

```
LocationURL            : http://blogs.msdn.com/powershell/arc
                         hive/2006/07/24/Casting_a_scriptbloc
                         k_to_an_arbitrary_delegate_signature
                         .aspx
Busy                   : False
Name                   : Windows Internet Explorer
HWND                   : 591430
FullName               : C:\Program Files\Internet Explorer\i
                         explore.exe
Path                   : C:\Program Files\Internet Explorer\
Visible                : True
StatusBar              : True
StatusText             :
ToolBar                : 1
MenuBar                : True
FullScreen             : False
ReadyState             : 4
Offline                : False
Silent                 : False
RegisterAsBrowser      : False
RegisterAsDropTarget   : True
TheaterMode            : False
AddressBar             : True
Resizable              : True
```

Once again, there are many tantalizing things to play with. For example, there are a couple properties that tell you the title of a window as well as the URL that is being viewed in it. Let's select just those properties.

```
PS (15) > $shell.Windows() |
>> select-object -first 1 locationname,locationurl |
>> fl
>>

LocationName : Windows PowerShell : Casting a scriptblock t
               o an arbitrary delegate signature
LocationURL  : http://blogs.msdn.com/powershell/archive/200
               6/07/24/Casting_a_scriptblock_to_an_arbitrar
               y_delegate_signature.aspx
```

We can see that it's pointing at the PowerShell team blog (purely by accident of course). Now let's do something about all those extras that clutter up our browser windows. Let's get rid of the menu bar. First we'll examine its current state:

```
PS (10) > $shell.Windows().Item(0).MenuBar
True
```

The browser window with the menu bar turned on is shown in figure 12.3.

Let's turn it off by setting the MenuBar property to $false.

```
PS (19) > $shell.Windows().Item(0).MenuBar = $false
```

Figure 12.3
A browser window with the menu bar showing. Notice where the menu bar shows up, as we will hide it later on.

Figure 12.4 shows what the window looks like now. The menu bar is gone and we've reclaimed that space to view our web pages.

Here's another useful set of functions. There are three functions is this set. The first is `Export-Window`, which will grab all of the open window URLs and save then in a script that can be used later on to reopen the windows. We'll save them as a collection of hashtables where the `title` member of the hashtable contains the window title and the `url` member holds the URL for that location. The `Export-Window` function is shown in listing 12.1.

Listing 12.1 The Export-Window function

```
function Export-Window
{
    param($file=(join-path (resolve-path ~) saved-urls.ps1))      ❶ Default
                                                                     path

    $shellApp = new-object -com Shell.Application              ❷ Get the
    $shellApp.Windows() | % {                                      windows
            @"
@{
    title='$($_.LocationName -replace "'","''")'               ❸ Format
    url='$($_.LocationUrl -replace "'","''")'                     hashtable
}
"@

    } | out-file -width 10kb -filepath $file `                 ❹ Write
            -encoding Unicode                                       file
}
```

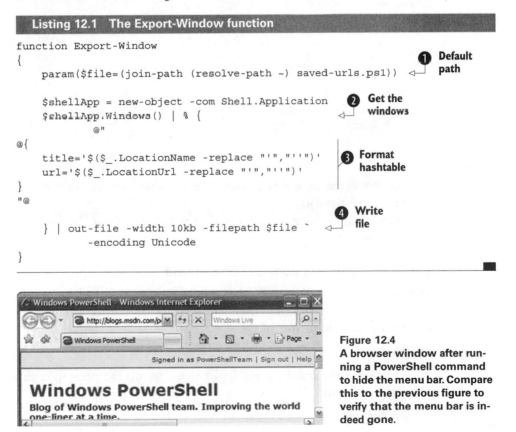

Figure 12.4
A browser window after running a PowerShell command to hide the menu bar. Compare this to the previous figure to verify that the menu bar is indeed gone.

The default place where the data is saved is a file called "saved-urls.ps1" ❶ in our home directory. We'll use the `Shell.Application` object to obtain a list of the windows to save ❷. A here-string is used to format the information in PowerShell hash literal syntax ❸. Note that the `-replace` operator is used to handle embedded single quotes in the either the title or the URL. Finally the text is written out to the file in large blocks encoded as Unicode data ❹.

The next function (see listing 12.2) will reload the saved window descriptions. There is almost nothing to this function—it takes the path to the script created by `Export-Window` and simply executes it.

Listing 12.2 The Import-Window function

```
function Import-Window
{
    param(
        $File=(join-path (resolve-path ~) saved-urls.ps1),
        [switch] $show
    )

    & $file | foreach {
        if ($Show)
        {
            explorer $_.url
        }
        else
        {
            $_
        }
    }
}
```

The script uses the `$show` parameter to decide whether it should reopen the windows or simply emit the data.

Opening and closing windows is all very nice, but what else can we open? We'll look at that next.

Example: Opening control panel items

Here's one more example using the `Shell.Application` class: opening a control panel item. This saves us from having to navigate through all those tedious menus. As before, we need an instance of the `Shell.Application` object.

```
$shell = new-object -com Shell.Application
```

Now let's open the control panel applet that controls the desktop settings. Run the following command

```
$shell.ControlPanelItem("desk.cpl")
```

The "Display Properties" control panel applet will appear on the desktop. Likewise, if we want to run the Add/Remove Programs wizard, we can use the following command

```
$shell.ControlPanelItem("appwiz.cpl")
```

In fact, you can open any of the control panel applets found using

```
dir $env:windir\system32 -recurse -include *.cpl
```

Now let's move on to another COM class used for scripting Windows.

Example: Working with the WScript.Shell class

The WScript.Shell class should be familiar to most VBScript users. It contains a collection of common services useful for writing scripts on Windows. Let's explore this control. First we create an instance to work with:

```
PS (1) > $wshell = new-object -com WScript.Shell
```

Now let's see what it can do using Get-Member:

```
PS (2) > $wshell | Get-Member


   TypeName: System.__ComObject#{41904400-be18-11d3-a28b-00104bd
35090}

Name                      MemberType             Definition
----                      ----------             ----------
AppActivate               Method                 bool AppActiva...
CreateShortcut            Method                 IDispatch Crea...
Exec                      Method                 IWshExec Exec ...
ExpandEnvironmentStrings  Method                 string ExpandE...
LogEvent                  Method                 bool LogEvent ...
Popup                     Method                 int Popup (str...
RegDelete                 Method                 void RegDelete...
RegRead                   Method                 Variant RegRea...
RegWrite                  Method                 void RegWrite ...
Run                       Method                 int Run (strin...
SendKeys                  Method                 void SendKeys ...
Environment               ParameterizedProperty  IWshEnvironmen...
CurrentDirectory          Property               string Current...
SpecialFolders            Property               IWshCollection...
```

The purpose of many of these methods is fairly obvious. For example, to pop up a message box, we can use the Popup method. We enter the following command:

```
PS (24) > $wshell.Popup("Hi there")
1
```

And up pops a message box that looks like what's in figure 12.5.

One nice thing about calling this method: This message box doesn't get lost on your desktop. You'll remember we had that problem with the WinForms message box. Now let's look at something a bit more sophisticated.

Figure 12.5
When you use the `WScript.Shell` object to pop up a message box, it will look like this.

Example: Sending keystrokes to a Windows application

One of the methods on the `WScript.Shell` class is `SendKeys()`. This lets you send keys to an application as if you were typing them yourself. Let's look at how we can use this to automate a Windows GUI application. We'll work with the Windows calculator in this example. First we need an instance of the object. (If you're following along with these examples, you can reuse the same instances. There's no need to keep creating new ones.)

```
$shell = new-object -com WScript.Shell
```

Next we start the calculator. Since PowerShell is a shell, we could enter `calc` on the command line and be done with it. Instead, since we're working with this object, we'll use its `Run()` method to start the application.

```
[void] $shell.Run("calc")
```

Now give the application a second to start, then use the `AppActivate()` method to set the focus on the calculator. Once we're sure it's active, we'll send a sequence of keys to the application, waiting for a second between each operation.

```
start-sleep 1
if ($shell.AppActivate("Calculator"))
{
    "Calculator activated..."
    start-sleep 1
    $shell.SendKeys("10{+}")
    start-sleep 1
    $shell.SendKeys("22")
    start-sleep 1
    $shell.SendKeys("~")
    start-sleep 1
    $shell.SendKeys("*3")
    start-sleep 1
    $shell.SendKeys("~")
    start-sleep 1
    $shell.SendKeys("%{F4}")
}
```

If you run this script, you'll see "10" appear in the result window, followed by 22, then the two are added to give 32, and so on. Finally we send the sequence *<alt><f4>*

to tell the application to close. (This is why we make sure that the calculator is active. Closing the wrong window could be bad.)

AUTHOR'S NOTE If you're interested in this kind of thing, there is a freely available tool called *AutoIT* that many people recommend as being a better approach to this type of activity.

So far, we're still just opening and manipulating windows, so let's move on to some non-shell-related classes.

12.1.2 Networking, applications, and toys

In this section, we'll look at some of the networking classes, some examples of working with Microsoft Office applications, and, finally, an entertaining application that uses the MSAgent class to do some animations. We'll start with the networking class.

Example: Looking up a word using Internet Explorer

In this example, we're going to use Internet Explorer to access a web page through its COM automation object. The goal is to use the *Wiktionary* website to look up the definition of a word. The script takes two parameters—the word to look up and an optional switch to tell the script that we want to make the browser window visible and leave it open during the search. This script is shown in listing 12.3.

Listing 12.3 Get-WordDefinition script

```
param(
    $word = $(throw "You must specify a word to look up."),
    [switch] $visible
)                                                                    Load ❶
                                                              System.Web

[void] [Reflection.Assembly]::LoadWithPartialName("System.Web")  ◁┘

$ie = new-object -com "InternetExplorer.Application"
$ie.Visible = $visible                                   ❷ Navigate to
$ie.Navigate2("http://en.wiktionary.org/wiki/" +    ◁┘     Wiktionary
    [Web.HttpUtility]::UrlEncode($word))

while($ie.ReadyState -ne 4)       ◁┐  Wait until
{                                  ❸  ready
    start-sleep 1
}                                                      Extract ❹
                                                          data
$bodyContent = $ie.Document.getElementById("bodyContent").innerHtml  ◁┘

$showText=$false
$lastWasBlank = $true
$gotResult = $false                         ❺ Process
                                               data
switch -regex ($bodyContent.Split("`n"))  ◁┘
```

```
                {
                '^\<DIV class=infl-table' {
                        $showText = $true
                        continue
                    }
                '^\<DIV|\<hr' {
                        $showText = $false
                    }
                '\[.*edit.*\].*Translations' {
                        $showText = $false
                    }
                {$showText} {
                        $line = $_ -replace '\<[^>]+\>', ' '
                        $line = ($line -replace '[ \t]{2,}', ' ').Trim()

                        if ($line.Length)
                        {
                            $line
                            $gotResult = $true
                            $lineWasBlank = $false
                        }
                        else
                        {
                            if (! $lineWasBlank)
                            {
                                $line
                                $lineWasBlank = $true
                            }
                        }
                    }
                }
        }

        if (! $gotResult)
        {
            "No Answer Found for: $word"
        }

        if (! $visible)
        {
            $ie.Quit()        <──── 6  Close IE
        }
```

We're going to load an additional .NET assembly ❶ because we need to encode our word into a URL to send to the Wiktionary site. Next we get an instance of the Internet Explorer object. Tell IE to navigate to the Wiktionary website and look up the word ❷. This may take a while, so we loop, waiting for the document to be loaded ❸. When the document is ready, we use the Internet Explorer Document object model to extract the information we want out of the document ❹. Even after we've extracted the document, the information we're after still requires a significant amount of work to locate and extract. We do this using the `switch` statement ❺. If there was an answer then we'll display it; if not, we'll give the user an error message.

And finally, if the `visible` flag hasn't been specified, close the browser window ❻.

Let's try looking something up:

```
PS (1) > ./Get-WordDefinition.ps1 factorial

Singular factorial

Plural factorials
factorial ( plural factorials )

( mathematics ) The result of multiplying a given number of
 consecutive integers from 1 to the given number. In equati
ons, it is symbolized by an exclamation mark (!). For examp
le, 5! = 1 * 2 * 3 * 4 * 5 = 120.

[ edit ] Usage notes
" n !" is read as "factorial of n ."

PS (2) >
```

And there we go—the world of critical knowledge at our fingertips!

AUTHOR'S NOTE In practice, this type of script, which is dependent on a website that we don't control, is very fragile. It is extremely dependent on the structure of pages generated by the target website, and these are subject to change at any time. (In fact, this example had to be revised during the production of the book because Encarta, the original target website, did change its format.) If the page structure changes our script will be broken. (A well-structured data source such as the RSS feed, as we'll see in the next example, allows for much more reliable scripts.) This is also not the most efficient way to do this. We could have just used the .NET `WebClient` object instead of firing up the browser. On the other hand, this example does illustrate how you can use a script to automate the browser.

Example: Using the WinHTTP class to retrieve an RSS feed

Now we'll look at using the `WinHTTP` COM object to write a script that accesses an RSS feed. This is similar to what we did with .NET, but illustrates how to use COM to do the same thing. This script will grab the most recent headlines from the popular Digg.com RSS feed, format them as a page of links in HTML, then display this page using the default browser.

First we define a function `Get-ComRSS` that will do the actual network access. This is shown in listing 12.4.

Listing 12.4   Get-ComRSS function

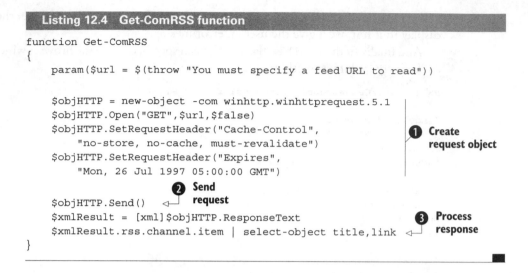

```
function Get-ComRSS
{
    param($url = $(throw "You must specify a feed URL to read"))

    $objHTTP = new-object -com winhttp.winhttprequest.5.1
    $objHTTP.Open("GET",$url,$false)
    $objHTTP.SetRequestHeader("Cache-Control",
        "no-store, no-cache, must-revalidate")
    $objHTTP.SetRequestHeader("Expires",
        "Mon, 26 Jul 1997 05:00:00 GMT")

    $objHTTP.Send()
    $xmlResult = [xml]$objHTTP.ResponseText
    $xmlResult.rss.channel.item | select-object title,link
}
```

❶ Create request object

❷ Send request

❸ Process response

We create the `WinHTTP` request object, specify that we're doing a page GET, then set some headers ❶. These headers tell the channel not to do any caching. Since we want to get the latest and greatest headlines, getting stale cached data would be bad.

Send the request ❷ then get the response text (note we're not checking the result code from the request, which we probably should do). We take the response text, convert it into XML, then extract and return the title and link fields ❸.

Now let's use this function. We'll write a script called `Get-Digg.ps1` that will download the RSS feed from the popular news aggregation site Digg.com, format it as a web page with links to the articles, and then display this page in the browser. We can run this script by typing:

```
PS (1) > ./get-digg
```

After the script runs, the web browser should open up, displaying a page that will look like that shown in figure 12.6.

Not the most exciting document in terms of appearance, but it gets the job done. The script to do this is shown in listing 12.5.

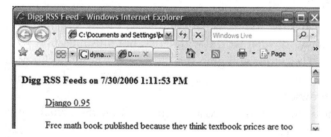

Figure 12.6
Web browser showing the result of running the `Get-Digg` script. This script creates an HTML page with links to the current top stories on Digg.com and then displays this page in the browser.

Listing 12.5 Get-Digg script

```
$url = "http://digg.com/rss/containertechnology.xml"
filter fmtData {                                          ❶ Format
    "<p><a href=`"{0}`">{1}</a></p>" -f $_.link,$_.title      function
}
              ❷ Here-string
                 for page
@"  ⤶
    <html>
      <head>
          <title>Digg RSS Feed</title>
      </head>
      <body>
          <p><b>Digg RSS Feeds on $(get-date)</b></p>
          <ul>
          $(comrss $url | fmtData)
      </body>
    </html>
"@ > $env:temp\digg_rss.htm
                        ❸ Invoke
                           browser
& $env:temp\digg_rss.htm  ⤶
```

First we'll put the URL we're going to fetch into a variable to use later. We'll also create a function ❶ that will format our data with appropriate HTML tags. Each data row will be formatted as an anchor element with the body text as the element title and the HREF as the link. Next we'll build our document. We'll use a single here-string ❷, directed into a temporary file. In the here-string, we'll use string expansion to insert the headline data using the fmtData function. The final step is to invoke this file ❸ using the default browser.

Obviously, a little work with table tags could make it much more attractive. Also, since the main article content was also down-loaded in the HTTP request, it should be possible to embed the content (or at least a synopsis) of the article in the page. This is left as an exercise for the reader.

That's enough networking and web-related stuff for now. In the next example, we'll look at using COM to manipulate Microsoft Office applications.

Example: Using Microsoft Word to do spell-checking

Wouldn't it be great if every environment we worked in had spell-checking like word processors do? With PowerShell and COM, we can get ourselves at least part of the way there. We're going to write a script that will use Microsoft Word to spell-check the contents of the clipboard and then paste them back. We'll call this script Get-Spelling.ps1.

Let's see how it's used. First we start notepad and type some text with errors into it.

```
PS (1) > notepad
```

Next select the text and copy it to the clipboard. This is shown in figure 12.7.

Now we'll run our script

```
PS (2) > Get-Spelling
```

Figure 12.7 Notepad window showing the misspelled text that we will fix using the `Get-Spelling` script.

We'll see the Word spell-check dialog pop up, as shown in figure 12.8.

We go through all of the spelling errors and fix them as appropriate. Once all of the errors are fixed, the dialog will disappear and the pop-up box will be displayed, indicating that the revised text is available in the clipboard. Switch back to the Notepad window and paste the revised text into the window as shown in figure 12.9.

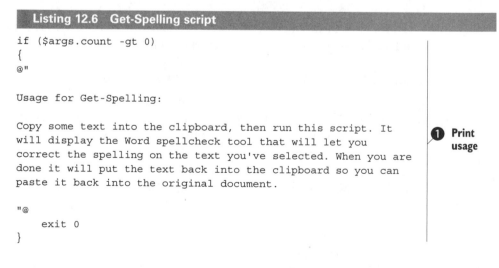

Figures 12.8 and 12.9 On the left is the The Microsoft Word spell checker launched by the Get-Spelling script, showing the misspelled text that was copied from the clipboard. On the right is the Notepad window showing the corrected text.

And we're done. The file in the Notepad window is now correctly spelled. Now that we know how to use this script, let's take a look at the actual code, which is shown in listing 12.6.

Listing 12.6 Get-Spelling script

```
if ($args.count -gt 0)
{
@"

Usage for Get-Spelling:

Copy some text into the clipboard, then run this script. It
will display the Word spellcheck tool that will let you
correct the spelling on the text you've selected. When you are
done it will put the text back into the clipboard so you can
paste it back into the original document.

"@
    exit 0
}
```

❶ Print usage

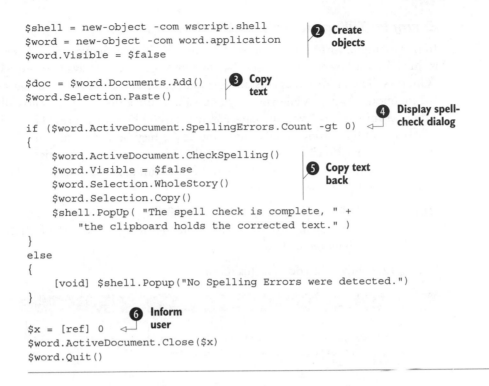

```
$shell = new-object -com wscript.shell        ❷ Create
$word = new-object -com word.application          objects
$word.Visible = $false

$doc = $word.Documents.Add()         ❸ Copy
$word.Selection.Paste()                 text
                                                           ❹ Display spell-
                                                              check dialog
if ($word.ActiveDocument.SpellingErrors.Count -gt 0)  ⟵
{
    $word.ActiveDocument.CheckSpelling()
    $word.Visible = $false                 ❺ Copy text
    $word.Selection.WholeStory()              back
    $word.Selection.Copy()
    $shell.PopUp( "The spell check is complete, " +
        "the clipboard holds the corrected text." )
}
else
{
    [void] $shell.Popup("No Spelling Errors were detected.")
}
                       ❻ Inform
$x = [ref] 0     ⟵       user
$word.ActiveDocument.Close($x)
$word.Quit()
```

Since we're working with only the clipboard, this script takes no arguments, but we'll check $args anyway and write a description of how to use the script to the output stream ❶.

Now we have to create ❷ the objects we're going to use. We want to use the WScript.Shell object from earlier in the chapter to pop up a message box, and, rather obviously, we need to set up the Word automation object for our use. We'll get an instance of that object, make the Word application window itself invisible, and then add a dummy document to hold the text we want to spell-check. Next we copy the contents from the clipboard to the dummy Word document we created ❸ and see whether we need to spell check the text ❹. If we do, we'll present the spell-check dialog; otherwise, we don't need to do anything.

Next, select all of the text and copy it back to clipboard so we can paste it into the original document ❺.

Finally, tell the user we're done and close the application ❻.

With this script, we can "add" spell-checking capabilities to any application that lets us select and copy text.

AUTHOR'S NOTE   Obviously, if Microsoft Word is not your word processor of choice, it should be simple to modify the script to work with any word processor that exports a similar automation model.

Example: Telling stories with Windows agents

In this example, we're going to look at a script that Jeffrey Snover created as a prelude to his talks on PowerShell. It uses the animated agent feature available on Microsoft Windows. The animated agents are cartoon characters that can move and talk, like the infamous clippie. While you may not want a cute animated paperclip calling you a dolt for misspelling "disambiguate", animations do have their uses. This script is an effective tool for getting people's attention at the beginning of a presentation. It also shows how PowerShell can be used in application spaces that you might not expect, such as animations and media. (And besides—it's fun in a "yikes-this-is-a-shell-script-you-must-be-kidding" kind of way.)

AUTHOR'S NOTE The set of characters that are available on any particular computer may vary. Go to http://www.microsoft.com/msagent/ to find more information about the agent feature.

Listing 12.7 shows the code for this script.

Listing 12.7   The Start-Agent script

```
param(
    [DateTime]$StartTime = [datetime]::Now.AddMinutes(10),
    $SessionTitle="Wizzo PowerShell Session",
    $Speaker="Bob"
)
                              ❶ Invoke-Display
function Invoke-Display()  ←      function
{
    Invoke-MSAgent $Message `
        -Character (Get-RandomElement $Characters) `
        -Size $CharacterSize `
        -MoveToX $Random.Next(500) -MoveToY $Random.Next(500) `
        -StartX  $Random.Next(500) -StartY  $Random.Next(500)
    Start-Sleep $SleepTime
}

function Get-RandomElement($Array)
{
    $Array[ $Random.Next( $Array.Count ) ]
}
                         ❷ Initialize
                            variables
$Sleeptime = 20    ←
$CharacterSize = 250
$WiseCracks=(
    "PowerShell Rocks baby",
    # This is misspelled but it has to be to sound correct
    "Hay Hay, My My, the CLI will never die",
    "Powershell is wicked easy to use",
    "Scripting to Infinity and beyond!",
    "Powershell is like, ya know, wicked consistent",
    ("fish heads, fish heads, rolly polly fish heads" +
```

```
         "fish heads, fish heads, eat them up yumm"),
    "We like questions, ask them",
    ("Powershell has direct support for " +
        "WMI, ADO, ADSI, XML, COM, and .NET"),
    "Hush up or I'll replace you with a 2 line Powershell script",
    "PowerShell goes to 11",
    "Dude! This totally rocks!",
    "Manning Books are cool!",
        "triple panic abort"
)
```

❸ Random number generator

```
$Random=New-Object Random    ←┘
```

❹ Get agent files

```
$Path = $(Join-Path $env:windir "msagent\chars\*.acs")    ←┘
$Characters=@(dir $Path |
    foreach {($_.Name.Split("."))[0]})
```

```
while ($True)    ←─── ❺ Main loop
{
    $till = $StartTime - [DateTime]::now
    if ($till.TotalSeconds -le 0)
    {
```

❻ Show start message

```
        $Message = "hay $Speaker, Start the session!!"    ←┘
        $SleepTime = 10
        $CharacterSize = 600
        while ($true)
        {
            Invoke-Display
        }
    }

    $Message = "$SessionTitle will start in $($Till.Minutes) " +
        "minutes and $($till.Seconds) seconds"
    Invoke-Display
```

❼ Show wisecrack

```
    $Message = Get-RandomElement $WiseCracks    ←┘
    Invoke-Display
}
```

❽ Invoke-MSAgent function

```
function Invoke-MSAgent    ←┘
{
    param(
        $Messages="Hello",
        $size=250,
        $CharacterName="Merlin",
        $MoveToX=500,
        $MoveToY=500,
        $StartX=0,
        $StartY=0,
        $Async=$false
    )
```

```
$Random = New-Object System.Random
$CharacterFileName = Join-path $env:windir `
    "msagent\chars\${CharacterName}.acs"
$AgentControl = New-Object -COMObject Agent.Control.2
$AgentControl.Connected=$True
[void]$AgentControl.Characters.Load(
    $CharacterName, $CharacterFileName)

$Character = $AgentControl.Characters.Item($CharacterName)
$AnimationNames = @($Character.AnimationNames)
$Character.width = $Character.height=$Size
$action = $Character.MoveTo($StartX,$StartY)
$action = $Character.Show()
$action = $Character.MoveTo($MoveToX,$MoveToY)

foreach ($Message in @($Messages))
{
    $action = $Character.Speak($Message)
}
$action = $Character.Hide()
if (!$Async)
{
    while ($Character.Visible)
    {
        Start-Sleep -MilliSeconds 250
    }
}
$Character = $Null
$AgentControl.Connected=$False
$AgentControl = $Null
}
```

This script takes three arguments: the time that talk starts (defaulting to 10 minutes from now), the session title, and the presenter's name. The Invoke-Display function ❶ is used to select which animated character to display and where that character should appear on the screen.

Now we'll set up some script variables ❷ that we're going to use. The $Wise-Cracks array holds the set of phrases that the agents will say.

AUTHOR'S NOTE You may notice that this collection of phrases is wrapped in parentheses. This isn't necessary, but it makes the script a little easier to maintain. The error message you get if you forget a comma when adding a new phrase will be cleared if the whole collection is wrapped in parentheses.

Next we'll create an instance of the .NET random number generator ❸. We use this to pick the phrase to display as well as the character to show. The agent characters are found in .ACS files located in the directory shown in the code ❹. We search the directory to get a list of available characters.

Once we have everything set up, we'll loop forever ❺ (or at least until the user hits Control-C), showing characters and wisecracks. Eventually it'll be time to start the talk, at which point we'll show a different message ❻.

When it's time to show a message, we pick a character ❼ and a piece of text to say and display them. The Invoke-MSAgent function ❽ takes care of creating the agent control instance and then animating the character that was chosen.

The main takeaway from this script is that PowerShell is suitable in a wide variety of application domains, including animations and speech. But enough fun. Let's get back to more serious matters!

12.1.3 Using the ScriptControl object

In this section, we'll show you how to use the ScriptControl object from Power-Shell. This may be the most important use of COM when transitioning from traditional Windows scripting (with VBScript) to PowerShell. This control will allow you to embed fragments of VBScript (or JavaScript or any other language that has an ActiveScript engine) into a PowerShell script. This means that you can take and reuse existing VBScript code directly in PowerShell. There's another reason that this is important. Some COM objects work in COM automation languages such as VBScript, but not in .NET environments such as PowerShell. (At least not yet. We're working to fix this in future releases as much as we can.)

Example: Embedding VBScript code in a PowerShell script

We start by using the ScriptControl class to build a VBScript CodeObject. This object makes the VBScript functions defined in the script available to the caller as methods on this code object. The function shown in listing 12.8 returns a code object with two of these methods on it: GetLength(), which returns the length of a string, and Add(), which adds two objects together.

Listing 12.8   Call-VBScript function

```
function Call-VBScript
{
    $sc = New-Object -ComObject ScriptControl
    $sc.Language = 'VBScript'
    $sc.AddCode('
      Function GetLength(ByVal s)
          GetLength = Len(s)
      End Function
      Function Add(ByVal x, ByVal y)
          Add = x + y
      End Function
    ')
    $sc.CodeObject
}
```

Now let's use the function to mix and match some PowerShell with VBScript.

```
PS (1) > $vb = call-vbscript
```

Calling the function gives us an object with the VBScript functions available as methods. First we'll use the GetLength() method to get the length of a string.

```
PS (2) > "Length of 'abcd' is " + $vb.getlength("abcd")
Length of 'abcd' is 4
```

Now we'll use the Add() method, but we'll use it inside a string expansion to illustrate how seamless this all is.

```
PS (3) > "2 + 5 is $($vb.add(2,5))"
2 + 5 is 7
PS (4) >
```

In the string expansion, the VBScript function is called to add the two numbers and return the result. The result is converted to a string and included in the expanded result string. Now let's try the same thing with another ActiveScript language.

Example: Embedding JScript code in a PowerShell script

The script control also supports JScript, Microsoft's implementation of ECMAScript (JavaScript). Listing 12.9 shows the same example, but using JScript this time.

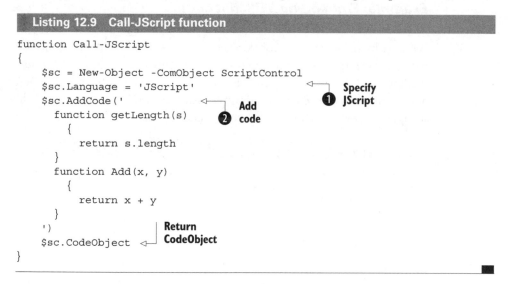

Listing 12.9   Call-JScript function

```
function Call-JScript
{
    $sc = New-Object -ComObject ScriptControl
    $sc.Language = 'JScript'                        ◁─┐ ❶ Specify
    $sc.AddCode('                       ◁─┐ ❷ Add       JScript
      function getLength(s)                  code
        {
          return s.length
        }
      function Add(x, y)
        {
          return x + y
        }
    ')                          ┌ Return
    $sc.CodeObject  ◁───┘ CodeObject
}
```

First we create the script control, this time specifying that the language be JScript ❶.

Then we add the code to define our functions ❷ and finally return the object containing our functions. We call this function to get the code object back.

```
PS (4) > $js = Call-JScript
```

When we run the functions on this object, we get the same results as we got from the VBScript example.

```
PS (5) > "Length of 'abcd' is " + $js.getlength("abcd")
Length of 'abcd' is 4
PS (6) > "2 + 5 is $($js.add(2,5))"
2 + 5 is 7
```

This time, the JScript functions are called to return the results to PowerShell for display.

Example: JScript, VBScript, and PowerShell in one script

Our last example with the ScriptControl mixes everything together. In a one-line "script" (command line), we can mix PowerShell, VBScript, and JScript. In fact, we can have three languages all in one expression.

```
PS (7) > "The answer is " +
>> $js.add($vb.getlength("hello"),2) * 6
>>
The answer is 42
PS (8) >
```

Using COM in PowerShell lets us do amazing things—automating applications, mixing and matching languages, and so on. But there are also issues with COM support, which we cover in the next section.

12.1.4 Issues with COM

Support for COM in the first version of PowerShell is very good but not great. In part, this is due to the fact the .NET's support is for COM is very good but not great either. There are a few problems that you may run into when using COM from PowerShell.

Thread model problems

PowerShell runs in what's called *multi-threaded apartment (MTA)* mode. A lot of COM objects require the calling application to be run in *single-threaded apartment (STA)* mode. The PowerShell COM adapter does a number of tricky things to work around this, and most of the time it works fine. If you run into something that doesn't work, things get a bit tricky. You can work around it, but it involves writing some code in C# or VB.Net to spin up a new STA thread that does the object access and returns the result to the calling thread. Actually doing this is beyond the scope of this book, but will be covered in the companion *Windows PowerShell in Practice* book.

Interop assemblies, wrappers, and typelibs

The other thing that can potentially cause problems has to do with the way the COM object has been wrapped or adapted. There are three possible categories of COM object we may encounter: a COM object that has a .NET interop library, a

COM object that has a type library (commonly called a *typelib*) but no interop assembly, and a COM object which has neither.

In the first category, we can get a COM object that has been wrapped in a .NET *interop wrapper*. This wrapper may introduce changes in the object's interface that affect how we work with that object compared to the raw COM object. For this reason, the `New-Object -com` parameter set has an additional parameter `-strict` that causes a non-terminating error to be written if an interop assembly is loaded. Let's look at some examples. We'll start with creating an instance of the `Word.Application` object we used earlier.

```
PS (23) > $word = new-object -com word.application
```

Now try it again but with the `-strict` parameter.

```
PS (24) > $word = new-object -com word.application -strict
New-Object : The object written to the pipeline is an insta
nce of the type "Microsoft.Office.Interop.Word.ApplicationC
lass" from the component's primary interop assembly. If thi
s type exposes different members than the IDispatch members
, scripts written to work with this object might not work i
f the primary interop assembly is not installed.
At line:1 char:19
+ $word = new-object  <<<< -com word.application -strict
```

We get a detailed error message explaining that the object that was loaded is a wrapped object. Note that this is a non-terminating error message, so the object was still returned. Here's how to use it in a script. We don't want the error message to appear in the output of our script, so we'll redirect it to `$null`. Even when we do this, the `$?` variable, which indicates whether the last command executed was successful, is still set to `$false` so we know that an error occurred.

```
PS (26) > $word = new-object -com word.application `
>>   -strict 2> $null
>>
PS (27) > $?
False
```

A script should check this variable and take alternate action for the wrapped and non-wrapped cases. Now let's take a look at what was returned by `New-Object`.

```
PS (28) > $word.gettype().fullname
Microsoft.Office.Interop.Word.ApplicationClass
```

We can see that's an instance of the interop assembly as we discussed earlier. Now let's take a look at an object for which there is no interop assembly.

```
PS (43) > $shell = new-object -com Shell.Application
PS (44) > $shell | gm


    TypeName: System.__ComObject#{efd84b2d-4bcf-4298-be25-eb
542a59fbda}

Name                    MemberType Definition
----                    ---------- ----------
AddToRecent             Method     void AddToRecent (Varian...
BrowseForFolder         Method     Folder BrowseForFolder (...
:
```

In this case, we see that the type of the object is System.__ComObject followed by the GUID of the registered type library. This type library is what allows us to see the members on the object. What about an object where there is no type library? Let's try it and see. We'll create an instance of the Windows installer.

```
PS (45) > $in = new-object -com WindowsInstaller.Installer
PS (46) > $in | gm


    TypeName: System.__ComObject

Name                    MemberType Definition
----                    ---------- ----------
CreateObjRef            Method     System.Runtime.Remo...
Equals                  Method     System.Boolean Equa...
GetHashCode             Method     System.Int32 GetHas...
GetLifetimeService      Method     System.Object GetLi...
GetType                 Method     System.Type GetType()
InitializeLifetimeService Method   System.Object Initi...
ToString                Method     System.String ToStr...
```

The results here are pretty disappointing. We see that the type is just plain System.__ComObject with little in the way of useful methods and properties on it. So is that it? Can't we do anything with this object? Well there are a couple things we can do, but they're not easy.

The first thing we can do is to use a tool such as tlbimp.exe to generate a *runtime-callable wrapper (RCW)* for the COM class. With this RCW wrapper, we can use the class like any other .NET type, but it means that we have to run the tool and then load an assembly before we can use these objects. Let's look at a more technical but also more portable mechanism.

Using the PowerShell type system to wrap COM objects

The other solution is to use .NET reflection directly to build our own wrapper library. This is an advanced topic and requires a pretty good understanding of `System.Reflection` to accomplish. We'll create a types extension file called `Com-Wrappers.ps1xml`. The following fragment from that file shows how the `InvokeMethod` extension method is defined.

```
<ScriptMethod>
<Name>InvokeMethod</Name>
<Script>
    $name, $methodargs=$args
    [System.__ComObject].invokeMember($name,
      [System.Reflection.BindingFlags]::InvokeMethod,
      $null, $this, @($methodargs))
</Script>
</ScriptMethod>
```

This script method uses the `InvokeMember` method on the type object to invoke a dynamically discovered method. There are similar implementations for getting and setting properties as well. We'll load `ComWrappers.ps1xml` and then examine the `WindowsInstaller` object again.

```
PS (1) > Update-TypeData ./ComWrappers.ps1xml
PS (2) > $in = new-object -com WindowsInstaller.Installer
PS (3) > $in | gm


   TypeName: System.__ComObject

Name                        MemberType   Definition
----                        ----------   ----------
CreateObjRef                Method       System.Runtime.Re...
Equals                      Method       System.Boolean Eq...
GetHashCode                 Method       System.Int32 GetH...
GetLifetimeService          Method       System.Object Get...
GetType                     Method       System.Type GetTy...
InitializeLifetimeService   Method       System.Object Ini...
ToString                    Method       System.String ToS...
GetProperty                 ScriptMethod System.Object Get...
InvokeMethod                ScriptMethod System.Object Inv...
InvokeParamProperty         ScriptMethod System.Object Inv...
SetProperty                 ScriptMethod System.Object Set...
```

We can see the methods we added at the end of the list. Now let's look at how we can use these methods. We'll use the `WindowsIntaller` class to look at an MSI file we'll call "myapplication.msi". The code to do this is shown in listing 12.10.

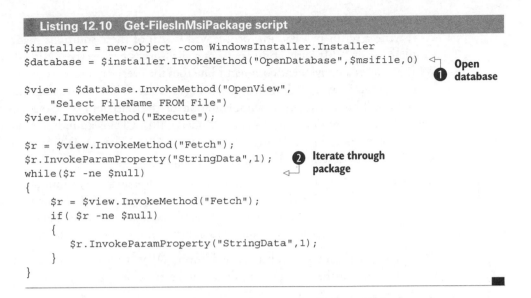

```
$installer = new-object -com WindowsInstaller.Installer
$database = $installer.InvokeMethod("OpenDatabase",$msifile,0)     Open
                                                                    database

$view = $database.InvokeMethod("OpenView",
    "Select FileName FROM File")
$view.InvokeMethod("Execute");

$r = $view.InvokeMethod("Fetch");
$r.InvokeParamProperty("StringData",1);        Iterate through
while($r -ne $null)                             package
{
    $r = $view.InvokeMethod("Fetch");
    if( $r -ne $null)
    {
        $r.InvokeParamProperty("StringData",1);
    }
}
```

We create the object and use the InvokeMethod() call to invoke the OpenData-
Base() installer method ❶, passing it the full path to the MSI file. Next we open a view
on the installer database object to get a list of the files. And finally, we'll iterate ❷
through the contents of the installer package.

> **AUTHOR'S NOTE** As you can see, this is a task not for the faint of heart. If you do run across
> this kind of problem and don't feel comfortable working with reflection,
> chances are good that someone in the PowerShell community has already
> solved this problem, so consulting the community resources may get you
> the answer you need.

At this point, we're going to switch from COM and move on to WMI.

12.2 WORKING WITH WMI IN POWERSHELL

In this section, we'll look at the "other" management object model—WMI. We'll
cover what it is, where it came from, and why you should care. Then we'll look at a
series of examples that show you how to find the information you need and then how
to access it.

12.2.1 Exploring WMI—what is it, and why do you care?

If you do Windows system administration or develop Windows server applications,
WMI should be very familiar. If you're not a Windows administrator chances are good
you've never heard of it, which is too bad. WMI is the best not-so-secret management
technology that Microsoft has—at least for users. Why don't we hear more about it?
Because it has historically suffered from the "one-telephone" syndrome. There is no
point in owning a telephone if no one is listening. Prior to PowerShell, the only way

you could use the information that WMI made available was to write a program in C++, write a script in VBScript, or use WMIC. All of these solutions made even the simplest use of WMI fairly complex from a shell-user's perspective. With PowerShell, WMI becomes a convenient command-line tool for everyday users, as we'll see.

In chapter 1, we mentioned that WMI stands for Windows Management Instrumentation. This is Microsoft's implantation of the Distributed Management Task Force (DMTF) Common Information Model (CIM). CIM is an industry standard for an object model for surfacing management APIs. The DMTF website (http://www.dmtf.org) describes CIM in the following way:

AUTHOR'S NOTE CIM provides a common definition of management information for systems, networks, applications, and services, and allows for vendor extensions. CIM's common definitions enable vendors to exchange semantically rich management information between systems throughout the network.

That's a spiffy if somewhat abstract definition. What it really means is that there are ways of getting at the management data that a service or application makes available

12.2.2 The Get-WmiObject cmdlet

Let's look at how to get at instances of WMI objects. Notice that, unlike .NET or COM objects, we "get" these objects instead of creating them with a "new" verb. This is because WMI is essentially a set of *factories* for strongly typed objects that are organized into namespaces.

AUTHOR'S NOTE These factories are called *WMI providers*. You may remember that PowerShell also has namespace providers for accessing stores such as the filesystem and the registry. WMI providers and PowerShell providers are distinct technologies, although conceptually they're both ways of accessing objects. In fact, there will eventually be a PowerShell provider that will let you access WMI providers as a set of PowerShell drives.

The overall WMI architecture is also rather like a database in that you connect to the WMI service on a particular computer, optionally specifying credentials, and retrieve the objects using a query. Figure 12.10 shows the signature for this cmdlet.

As always, the best way to see what's going on is to look at an example. Here is a quick little PowerShell script that will list the software installed on a computer system. This will return the installed program and the date that it was installed:

```
get-wmiobject -class "win32reg_addremoveprograms" `
    -namespace "root\cimv2" |
    select-object -property Displayname,Installdate
```

To run this against a remote computer, just use the -ComputerName parameter with Get-WmiObject cmdlet (see appendix B for examples).

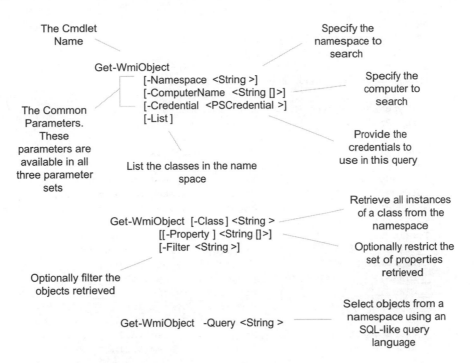

Figure 12.10 The signature for the Get-WmiObject cmdlet

The most important element in this example is the class name, which, in this case, is Win32_AddRemovePrograms. These class definitions are stored in the WMI repository on a computer. You can get a list of the installed classes by using the -list option to Get-WmiObject.

The standard classes that Microsoft provides are well documented. This documentation is available online at: http://msdn.microsoft.com/library/default.asp?url=/library/en-us/wmisdk/wmi/wmi_classes.asp

AUTHOR'S NOTE If you're reading the electronic version of this book, you can just click on the link.

The WMI documentation includes many examples of how to use classes, which is terrific. Not so terrific is that these examples are still mostly written in VBScript. The nice thing is that it's pretty easy to translate the important bits—the actual WMI query—into a form that's usable by PowerShell without a lot of work. We'll go through a detailed example of this later in the chapter.

12.2.3 The WMI object adapter

Let's take a look at what an object returned from WMI looks like We'll look at the Win32_Process class.

```
PS (1) > calc
PS (2) > $g=Get-WmiObject Win32_process `
>> -filter 'Name = "calc.exe"'
>>
PS (3) > $g |gm -membertype "Method,Property"


    TypeName: System.Management.ManagementObject#root\cimv2\
Win32_Process

Name                 MemberType Definition
----                 ---------- ----------
AttachDebugger       Method     System.Management....
GetOwner             Method     System.Management....
GetOwnerSid          Method     System.Management....
SetPriority          Method     System.Management....
Terminate            Method     System.Management....
__CLASS              Property   System.String __CL...
__DERIVATION         Property   System.String[] __...
__DYNASTY            Property   System.String __DY...
__GENUS              Property   System.Int32 __GEN...
__NAMESPACE          Property   System.String __NA...
__PATH               Property   System.String __PA...
__PROPERTY_COUNT     Property   System.Int32 __PRO...
__RELPATH            Property   System.String __RE...
..........
```

Notice that the methods are the WMI methods for that particular WMI object, and not the methods for WMI. If you want those, you can still get them using the PSBase property. (If you remember from chapter 8, PSBase is the way to bypass the type adapter and get at the native capabilities of an object.)

```
PS (7) > $g.psbase |gm -membertype Method

    TypeName: System.Management.Automation.PSMemberSet

Name                 MemberType Definition
----                 ---------- ----------
add_Disposed         Method     System.Void add_Dis...
Clone                Method     System.Object Clone()
CompareTo            Method     System.Boolean Comp...
CopyTo               Method     System.Management.M...
CreateObjRef         Method     System.Runtime.Remo...
Delete               Method     System.Void Delete(...
Dispose              Method     System.Void Dispose()
Equals               Method     System.Boolean Equa...
Get                  Method     System.Void Get(), ...
get_ClassPath        Method     System.Management.M...
..........
```

Now that we know a little bit about WMI objects, let's do something with them. We'll start with a different approach this time. We'll look at converting an existing VBScript example that uses WMI into the equivalent PowerShell script.

12.2.4 WMI shootout—VBScript versus PowerShell

We said earlier that the traditional scripting tool for WMI is VBScript. PowerShell is the new kid on the block. Let's show why PowerShell is "better" than VBScript.

> **AUTHOR'S NOTE** Disclaimer: the example we're going to look at is a bit of a straw man. The deficiencies we're going to address haven't really got much to do with VB-Script. The central issue is to highlight a key difference between a programming language and a shell environment. Shell environments provide automatic facilities for things such as default presentations of data so you don't have to write the same tedious formatting code over and over. (In fact, this kind of thing is so tedious that the `Scriptomatic` tool was created to automatically generate formatting code for ActiveScript languages such as VBScript and JScript.)

Wait a minute. Didn't we just talk about hosting VBScript in PowerShell because PowerShell can't do everything? Correct. When working with COM, there are some things that VBScript can do that PowerShell can't (yet). PowerShell has an edge in that it has simpler access to system resources than VBScript, but where it really wins is in presenting the output of an object. Remember, separating presentation from logic was one of the driving forces that led to PowerShell's creation. A significant amount of code in many VBScripts exists simply to format output. In PowerShell, most of the time this is free—the default output rendering mechanism just works.

A VBScript example

Let's start with a simple VBScript that uses WMI—the kind of thing that the `Scriptomatic` tool generates. We'll get this from Microsoft's ScriptCenter, a repository for all things scripting. ScriptCenter is available at http://www.microsoft.com/technet/scriptcenter/default.mspx and the repository of scripts is available at http://www.microsoft.com/technet/scriptcenter/scripts/default.mspx?mfr=true The script we're going to look at uses WMI to get a list of the codecs installed on your system.

> **AUTHOR'S NOTE** The term *codec* stands for, variously, coder-decoder, compressor/decompressor, or compression/decompression algorithm. A codec is a piece of software that allows you to encode or decode a data stream. The most common use these days is for media formats such as WMA, MP3, and so on. By checking the list of codecs, you can tell whether the system will be able to decode and play a particular file.

The VBScript code to do this is shown in listing 12.11. (This has been simplified somewhat from the original example.)

Listing 12.11 VBScript to list codecs

```
strComputer = "."
Set objWMIService = GetObject("winmgmts:" _
    & "{impersonationLevel=impersonate}!\\" & strComputer _      ❶ WMI
    & "\root\cimv2")                                                preamble
Set colItems = objWMIService.ExecQuery(
    "Select * from Win32_CodecFile") #1


                          ❷ Format
                              data
For Each objItem in colItems    ⬅┘
    Wscript.Echo "Manufacturer: " & objItem.Manufacturer
    Wscript.Echo "Name: " & objItem.Name
    Wscript.Echo "Path: " & objItem.Path
    Wscript.Echo "Version: " & objItem.Version
    Wscript.Echo "Caption: " & objItem.Caption
    Wscript.Echo "Drive: " & objItem.Drive
    Wscript.Echo "Extension: " & objItem.Extension
    Wscript.Echo "File Type: " & objItem.FileType
    Wscript.Echo "Group: " & objItem.Group
    strCreationDate = WMIDateStringToDate(objItem.CreationDate)
    Wscript.Echo "Creation Date: " & strCreationdate
    strInstallDate = WMIDateStringToDate(objItem.InstallDate)
    Wscript.Echo "Install Accessed: " & strInstallDate
    strLastModified = WMIDateStringToDate(objItem.LastModified)
    Wscript.Echo "Last Modified: " & strLastModified
    Wscript.Echo ""
Next

                          ❸ Date helper
                              function
Function WMIDateStringToDate(dtmDate)   ⬅┘
    WMIDateStringToDate = CDate(Mid(dtmDate, 5, 2) & "/" & _
        Mid(dtmDate, 7, 2) & "/" & Left(dtmDate, 4) _
            & " " & Mid (dtmDate, 9, 2) & ":" & _
                Mid(dtmDate, 11, 2) & ":" & Mid(dtmDate, _
                    13, 2))
End Function
```

This script begins with the standard preamble ❶ that you see in most VBScripts that use WMI. It sets up a query against the local WMI provider for this machine.

Next we display the set of fields ❷ we're interested in. This is straightforward but tedious. The code formats and prints each field. One thing to note is how the date fields are handled. WMI uses a string encoding of a date object. To convert this into a date object, we need to use a function. This function ❸ takes the string apart and puts it into a format that the system can convert into a date object.

Now let's look at the PowerShell version.

The PowerShell version

We'll do this in two steps. You may have noticed that the VBScript function to parse the date was a bit complex. Rather than converting it into PowerShell, we'll just reuse it for now through the ScriptControl object we saw earlier. The first version, which is still using the VBScript date converter function, is shown in listing 12.12 (there are much easier ways of doing this, as we'll see later).

Listing 12.12 PowerShell script to list codecs

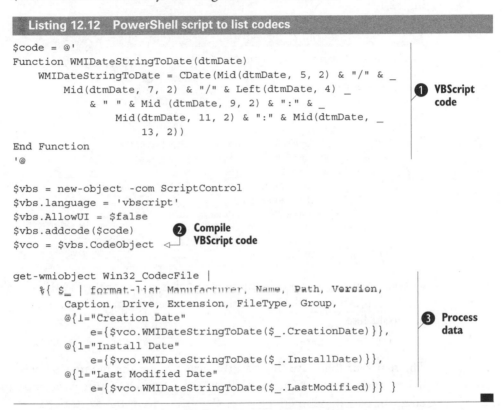

```
$code = @'
Function WMIDateStringToDate(dtmDate)
    WMIDateStringToDate = CDate(Mid(dtmDate, 5, 2) & "/" & _
        Mid(dtmDate, 7, 2) & "/" & Left(dtmDate, 4) _
            & " " & Mid (dtmDate, 9, 2) & ":" & _
                Mid(dtmDate, 11, 2) & ":" & Mid(dtmDate, _
                    13, 2))
End Function
'@


$vbs = new-object -com ScriptControl
$vbs.language = 'vbscript'
$vbs.AllowUI = $false
$vbs.addcode($code)
$vco = $vbs.CodeObject


get-wmiobject Win32_CodecFile |
    %{ $_ | format-list Manufacturer, Name, Path, Version,
        Caption, Drive, Extension, FileType, Group,
        @{l="Creation Date"
            e={$vco.WMIDateStringToDate($_.CreationDate)}},
        @{l="Install Date"
            e={$vco.WMIDateStringToDate($_.InstallDate)}},
        @{l="Last Modified Date"
            e={$vco.WMIDateStringToDate($_.LastModified)}} }
```

1 VBScript code

2 Compile VBScript code

3 Process data

We'll use a here-string to hold the VBScript code **1** for the date converter function. Now use the ScriptControl object to compile it into a CodeObject **2**. We'll use $vco to hold the CodeObject just to make things a bit more convenient. This lets us invoke the method by doing $vco.WMIDateStringToDate().

Next is the PowerShell code to retrieve and print out the data **3**. As you might expect, it's rather shorter than the VBScript code. We use Get-WmiObject to directly get the data and Format-List to format the output. We have to specify the set of fields to display; otherwise we'll just get everything (in fact this shows PowerShell not at its best, since you have to work harder to do less). Also of note is how the date fields are specified. In chapter 8, we showed an example of using this construction with Select-Object. Its use was a bit different there—we were selecting properties so we used the name (n) and expression (e) entries. Now we're using label (l) and expression (e). The *label* specifies the label to use for the field and *expression* is a scriptblock used to calculate the value to display.

Of course, if we're going to work with WMI objects a lot and expect to run into dates on a regular basis, it behooves us to add a PowerShell native date converter to our toolbox. The second version of the script does this. That version is shown in listing 12.13.

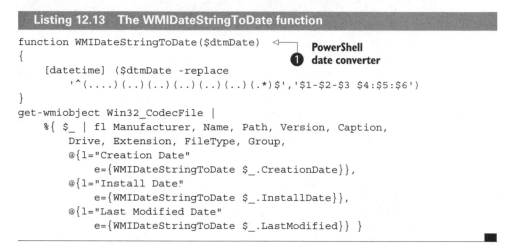

```
Listing 12.13   The WMIDateStringToDate function

function WMIDateStringToDate($dtmDate)        ◁────┐  PowerShell
{                                                   ❶ date converter
    [datetime] ($dtmDate -replace
        '^(....)(..)(..)(..)(..)(..)(.*)$','$1-$2-$3 $4:$5:$6')
}
get-wmiobject Win32_CodecFile |
    %{ $_ | fl Manufacturer, Name, Path, Version, Caption,
        Drive, Extension, FileType, Group,
        @{l="Creation Date"
            e={WMIDateStringToDate $_.CreationDate}},
        @{l="Install Date"
            e={WMIDateStringToDate $_.InstallDate}},
        @{l="Last Modified Date"
            e={WMIDateStringToDate $_.LastModified}} }
```

WMIDateStringToDate is the function that converts the WMI dates ❶. We use regular expressions to do it, since they are so convenient in PowerShell. This date format looks like:

```
20051207090550.505000-480
```

The first four digits are the year; the next two are the month, followed by the day, hours, minutes, and seconds. We'll use the submatch feature with replace to rearrange the date into something that .NET can convert into a [datetime] object. The rest of the script is unchanged.

Now let's look at the progress we've made. The VBScript version of the function was 29 lines long. The first PowerShell version that used the VBScript date function was 25 lines, not much better because of the overhead of using the script control. The final version, however, was only 14 lines—half the size.

When exploring WMI, a baseline VBScript is roughly 6 lines + 1 line per property exposed by the object, merely to show values of all instances. And it won't work for individual values that are arrays (e.g., a network adapter has an array IPAddress property, even if there is only one address in the array). For PowerShell, getting a complete, viewable result from a WMI class collection is always one line of code.

If we'd just consulted our documentations, we'd see that there is a COM class that deals with these dates, saving us a bunch of entertaining but unnecessary hacking about.

```
PS (1) > $d = new-object -com WbemScripting.SWbemDateTime
PS (2) > $d.value = "20051207090550.505000-480"
PS (3) > $d.GetVarDate()
Wednesday, December 07, 2005 9:05:50 AM
```

And there is also a fully functional .NET class that lets us do things like:

```
[Management.ManagementDateTimeConverter]::ToDateTime(
    "20051207090550.505000-480")
```

An interesting observation to take away from this exercise is that script is as long as it is because we didn't want to show everything about the object. In VBScript (and most other non-shell languages), the more you want to show, the more work you need to do. In PowerShell, the output and formatting subsystem takes care of this for us. When we just want to dump all of the fields, the script becomes as simple as:

```
get-wmiobject Win32_CodecFile
```

This is where PowerShell has a significant advantage in terms of "whipupitude" over a more programmer-oriented language such as VBScript. It also means that much of WMI can be accessed with simple interactive commands, making it an everyday tool instead of a programmer-only thing.

12.2.5 The WMI type shortcuts

In early versions of PowerShell, the only way to get a WMI object was to use the Get-Wmiobject command we've been looking at. But WMI is the life's blood of many Windows system administrators. This fact was pointed out politely but loudly to the development team at a Microsoft Management conference. As a consequence, late in the development cycle, additional support for WMI was added in the form of type aliases and conversions. Three new aliases were added: [WMI], [WMICLASS], and [WMISEARCHER].

The [WMISEARCHER] alias is a type accelerator for [System.Management.ManagementObjectSearcher]. This type accelerator allows you to directly cast a string containing a WMI Query Language (WQL) query into a searcher object. Once we have a searcher object, we just have to call its GET() method to retrieve the corresponding data:

```
PS (1) > $qs = 'Select * from Win32_Process ' +
>> 'where Handlecount > 1000'
>>
PS (2) > $s = [WmiSearcher] $qs
PS (3) > $s.Get() | sort handlecount |
>> fl handlecount,__path,name
>>
```

```
handlecount : 1124
__PATH      : \\BRUCEPAY64H\root\cimv2:Win32_Process.Handle
              ="3144"
name        : iexplore.exe

handlecount : 1341
__PATH      : \\BRUCEPAY64H\root\cimv2:Win32_Process.Handle
              ="3380"
name        : OUTLOOK.EXE

handlecount : 1487
__PATH      : \\BRUCEPAY64H\root\cimv2:Win32_Process.Handle
              ="2460"
name        : powershell.exe

handlecount : 1946
__PATH      : \\BRUCEPAY64H\root\cimv2:Win32_Process.Handle
              ="988"
name        : svchost.exe
```

The [WMI] alias is a *type accelerator* or shortcut for the type [System.Manage-
ment.ManagementObject].

> **AUTHOR'S NOTE** The term *type accelerator* is one that we haven't used so far. It's simply a shortcut for a commonly used type in PowerShell, but with special handling when used as a cast that allows for more advanced behavior. The best example is the [xml] type accelerator, which allows you to take a string or array of strings and simply cast it into an XML document. Interestingly enough, this term more or less spontaneously appeared in the PowerShell team vocabulary because its members really "accelerated" solving certain classes of problems.

This type accelerator will cast a string specifying a local or absolute WMI path into a WMI instance and return an object bound to that instance. We'll reuse our previous [WMISEARCHER] code to get the paths for processes with more than 1,000 open handles:

```
PS (1) > $qs = 'Select * from Win32_Process ' +
>> 'where Handlecount > 1000'
>>
PS (2) > $s = [WmiSearcher] $qs
PS (3) > $s.Get() | sort handlecount |
>> fl handlecount,__path,name
>>

handlecount : 1124
__PATH      : \\BRUCEPAY64H\root\cimv2:Win32_Process.Handle
              ="3144"
name        : iexplore.exe
```

```
handlecount : 1341
__PATH      : \\BRUCEPAY64H\root\cimv2:Win32_Process.Handle
              ="3380"
name        : OUTLOOK.EXE

handlecount : 1487
__PATH      : \\BRUCEPAY64H\root\cimv2:Win32_Process.Handle
              ="2460"
name        : powershell.exe

handlecount : 1946
__PATH      : \\BRUCEPAY64H\root\cimv2:Win32_Process.Handle
              ="988"
name        : svchost.exe

PS (4) > $wp = '\\BRUCEPAY64H\root\cimv2:' +
>> 'Win32_Process.Handle="3144"'
>>
PS (5) > $proc = [WMI] $wp
PS (6) > $proc.Name
iexplore.exe
PS (7) > $proc.OSCreationClassName
Win32_OperatingSystem
PS (8) >
```

Finally, the [WMICLASS] alias is a type accelerator for [System.Management.ManagementClass]. This has a string constructor taking a local or absolute WMI path to a WMI class and returning an object bound to that class:

```
PS (9) > $c = [WMICLASS]"root\cimv2:Win32_Process"
PS (10) > $c | fl *

Name              : Win32_Process
__GENUS           : 1
__CLASS           : Win32_Process
__SUPERCLASS      : CIM_Process
__DYNASTY         : CIM_ManagedSystemElement
__RELPATH         : Win32_Process
__PROPERTY_COUNT  : 45
__DERIVATION      : {CIM_Process, CIM_LogicalElement, CIM_Ma
                    nagedSystemElement}
__SERVER          : BRUCEPAY64H
__NAMESPACE       : ROOT\cimv2
__PATH            : \\BRUCEPAY64H\ROOT\cimv2:Win32_Process
```

These type accelerators can simplify working with WMI in PowerShell significantly.

12.2.6   Working with WMI methods

Another important addition to PowerShell's WMI support was the ability to directly invoke WMI class methods. Let's use the [WMICLASS] type accelerator to get an instance of the Win32_Process class definition.

```
PS (1) > $c = [WMICLASS]"root\cimv2:WIn32_Process"
```

And we'll look at the members on this object.

```
PS (2) > $c | gm -type methods


    TypeName: System.Management.ManagementClass#ROOT\cimv2\W
in32_Process

Name                     MemberType   Definition
----                     ----------   ----------
Create                   Method       System.Management.Ma...
ConvertFromDateTime      ScriptMethod System.Object Conver...
ConvertToDateTime        ScriptMethod System.Object Conver...
CreateInstance           ScriptMethod System.Object Create...
Delete                   ScriptMethod System.Object Delete();
GetRelatedClasses        ScriptMethod System.Object GetRel...
GetRelationshipClasses   ScriptMethod System.Object GetRel...
GetType                  ScriptMethod System.Object GetTyp...
Put                      ScriptMethod System.Object Put();
```

We can use the Create() method to start an instance of the Windows calculator application.

```
PS (3) > $proc = $c.Create("calc.exe")
PS (4) > $proc | ft -auto ProcessID, ReturnValue

ProcessID ReturnValue
--------- -----------
     6032           0
```

Let's use Get-Process to verify that the process was created and that its ID matches what was returned. (Of course, the more obvious way is to simply see whether the calculator windows appeared after running the command.)

```
PS (5) > get-process calc | ft -auto name,id

Name Id
---- --
calc 6032
```

Now we'll use a WMI query to retrieve the process object for the calculator process. We create the query and then call the Get() method to retrieve the objects.

```
PS (6) > $query = [WMISEARCHER] `
>>    "SELECT * FROM Win32_Process WHERE Name = 'calc.exe'"
```

```
>>
PS (7) > [object[]] $procs = $query.Get()
```

This method returns a collection of objects, so we check the count and get the name property from the first object in the collection to make sure that we've got what we expected.

```
PS (8) > $procs.count
1
PS (9) > $procs[0].name
calc.exe
```

And, now that we have the necessary object, we can finally call the WMI method to shut down the calculator process.

```
PS (10) > $procs[0].terminate(0)

__GENUS          : 2
__CLASS          : __PARAMETERS
__SUPERCLASS     :
__DYNASTY        : __PARAMETERS
__RELPATH        :
__PROPERTY_COUNT : 1
__DERIVATION     : {}
__SERVER         :
__NAMESPACE      :
__PATH           :
ReturnValue      : 0
```

The calculator window should have vanished from the desktop at this point. We'll use Get-Process one more time to verify that the process is indeed gone.

```
PS (12) > get-process calc
Get-Process : Cannot find a process with the name 'calc'. V
erify the process name and call the cmdlet again.
At line:1 char:12
+ get-process  <<<< calc
PS (13) >
```

This example illustrates that methods on WMI objects work pretty much as expected. The WMI adapter takes care of the details.

12.2.7 Working with WMI events

The last element of WMI we're going to talk about is the WMI event. Unfortunately this doesn't quite work the way we would like it to. One would expect that one could just attach a scriptblock to an event like we did with WinForms in chapter 11. This worked for WinForms because the form does a synchronous callback on the original thread. In WMI (and other event sources in Windows), these events are generated asynchronously, which requires that they run on a new thread. The first release of PowerShell doesn't allow this. What you'd have to do is write a cmdlet that listens to the events and then "forwards" them to PowerShell by writing them into the pipeline. You can, however, handle them synchronously. Let's look at how to do this. We'll look at detecting when a user plugs in a USB device. We start by creating an instance of `Management.EventQuery`. This query describes the events we're interested in being notified about.

```
PS (1) > $query = new-object Management.EventQuery
PS (2) > $query.QueryString =
>> "SELECT * FROM __InstanceCreationEvent WITHIN
>> 10 WHERE Targetinstance ISA 'Win32_PNPEntity' and
>> TargetInstance.DeviceId like '%USBStor%'"
>>
```

Next we create a `ManagementEventWatcher` object from this query object.

```
PS (3) > $watcher = new-object Management.ManagementEventWatcher `
>>> $query
```

And we wait to be notified that an instance of this event has occurred. This will block the script until the event happens.

```
PS (4) > $result = $watcher.WaitForNextEvent()
```

As soon was we plug in (or turn on) a USB device, the event occurs and unblocks the script. The event details are placed into the `$result` variable. Let's take a look and the name and device ID for what was plugged in.

```
PS (5) > $result.TargetInstance | fl name, DeviceId

name      : HP Photosmart 2575 USB Device
DeviceId : USBSTOR\DISK&VEN_HP&PROD_PHOTOSMART_2575&REV_1.0
            0\7&31BC8B2D&0&MY586121MF04B8&0
```

The object in `$result` tells us that the device that was plugged in was an HP Photosmart printer.

12.2.8   Putting modified WMI objects back

There's one last, very important topic we need to cover about using WMI in PowerShell. So far we've looked at getting data and we've looked at calling methods. Now we need to look at putting data back. In other words, how do we go about saving changes we've made to a WMI object back to the repository?

Why is this even a topic, you ask? After all, we don't have to do this with any of the other object types, right? The reason is that the underlying store for a WMI object may be on a remote computer, and incrementally flushing a set of changes over a remote connection is simply too inefficient to use on a large scale.

AUTHOR'S NOTE   It would have been great if incremental updates had worked, since it would make the user experience much simpler. Unfortunately, when we tried it, while it was OK for small demos, it just didn't work in real applications. As Einstein observed, things should be as simple as possible but no simpler.

As a consequence, in PowerShell, WMI objects have a Put() method that must be called before changes made to the local copy of an object are reflected back to the underlying store. Let's look at an example to see how this works. In this example, we're going to use WMI to change the volume name of the C: drive. First we'll get the WMI object for the logical C drive.

```
PS (9) > $disks = Get-WmiObject WIN32_LogicalDisk
```

On this system, the C: drive is the first logical disk:

```
PS (10) > $disks[0]

DeviceID      : C:
DriveType     : 3
ProviderName  :
FreeSpace     : 95329701888
Size          : 241447768064
VolumeName    : C_Drive
```

It currently has the boring name of "C_Drive". Let's give it a rather more dramatic name:

```
PS (11) > $disks[0].VolumeName = "PowerShellRocks"
```

Now verify that the property in the object has actually been changed:

```
PS (12) > $disks[0]

DeviceID      : C:
DriveType     : 3
ProviderName  :
FreeSpace     : 95329701888
Size          : 241447768064
VolumeName    : PowerShellRocks
```

and it has. But has this information actually been updated in the system yet? We can check on this by querying the repository again:

```
PS (13) > (get-wmiobject win32_logicaldisk)[0]

DeviceID      : C:
DriveType     : 3
ProviderName  :
FreeSpace     : 95329603584
Size          : 241447768064
VolumeName    : C_Drive
```

Clearly, while the local object may have been changed, the system itself hasn't been updated. The change remains local to the object we modified. Now let's call the Put() method on the object to flush the changes back to the system.

```
PS (14) > $result = $disks[0].Put()
```

Notice we've save the result of the Put() call. We'll get to that in a second. First let's make sure that the system was property updated.

```
PS (15) >  (Get-WmiObject WIN32_LogicalDisk) [0]

DeviceID.     : C:
DriveType     : 3
ProviderName :
FreeSpace     : 95329579008
Size          : 241447768064
VolumeName    : PowerShellRocks
```

We see that it was. Now let's look at what we got back from the Put() call. Let's look at the type first.

```
PS (16) > $result.GetType().FullName
System.Management.ManagementPath
PS (17) > "$result"
\\localhost\root\cimv2:Win32_LogicalDisk.DeviceID="C:"
```

It's a [Management.ManagementPath] object, which we can then cast back into the corresponding drive object, per the earlier discussion of the WMI type accelerators.

```
PS (18) > $d = [wmi] "$result"
PS (19) > $d

DeviceID      : C:
DriveType     : 3
ProviderName  :
FreeSpace     : 95328575488
Size          : 241447768064
VolumeName    : PowerShellRocks
```

Now we have a new instance of the logical disk object.

This example illustrates the basic approach for using PowerShell to modify system settings through WMI. First we retrieve the object, then make the necessary updates, and finally Put() it back. Because this is an unfortunate but necessary departure from the behavior of the other types of objects, it is important to be aware of it.

This completes our coverage of using WMI from PowerShell. With these basics, it should be possible to adapt existing WMI samples and resources for your work with PowerShell.

AUTHOR'S NOTE Appendix B contains a number of examples showing how to use WMI to perform admin tasks. These examples include a script for checking a set of machines to see whether a particular set of hot fixes have been deployed to those machines.

12.3 SO WHICH OBJECT MODEL SHOULD I CHOOSE?

So far, we've looked at three different technologies—.NET, COM, and WMI. We've also seen that there is significant overlap in what you can do in each model. In fact, one blogger was sufficiently inspired by the plethora of options in PowerShell that he wrote a song called "50 Ways to Kill a Process". While there may not be 50 ways, between cmdlets, .NET, WMI, COM, the ScriptControl, and external commands, there are certainly a lot of choices. So how do we know which one to choose? Here are some guidelines.

Cmdlets should generally be your first choice. They are designed to operate best in the PowerShell environment.

Next, if there is a .NET class available that does what you want, that should be the preferred solution. But keep in mind the limitations that we discussed in chapter 11 concerning paths and such.

If there isn't a .NET class or you need to access the information remotely, use WMI. There is good support for WMI with cmdlets and with the type accelerators.

Finally, if none of the other solutions suits your purpose and there is a COM object available, use COM. Remember, however, you'll need to look out for some of the issues discussed earlier in the chapter.

There is another angle to consider when choosing to use one object model over another. If you're adapting existing code samples, your best option is to use whatever the sample used. If the code sample you're adapting is VBScript then COM and/or WMI will likely be what you use. If you're adapting a piece of C# or VB.Net code then .NET is the usual answer.

In the end, the "best" answer is the one that gets the job done in the shortest time with the least effort. PowerShell is all about pragmatics: maximal return for minimal effort.

> **AUTHOR'S NOTE**   Actually there's one more technology that we haven't really covered but is very important when administering Windows systems: ADSI. ADSI support was added very late in the release cycle for PowerShell V1. It follows the same basic model used for WMI. See section B.8 for more information and examples of how to use this.

12.4 SUMMARY

Chapter 12 covered the world of Windows management objects—WMI and COM. These mechanisms are the kernel of the previous generations for Windows scripting tools such as VBScript and JScript. Pretty much any scripting activity involved using one or both of these object models. As a consequence, PowerShell also supports WMI and COM along with the newer .NET frameworks.

For COM, we covered the following points:

- We introduced the basic elements of COM and showed how to get a list of `ProgIDs`.
- We discussed that PowerShell uses .NET for COM interop, so has the same limitations as .NET.
- As with .NET objects, COM objects can be examined using the `Get-Member` cmdlet.
- PowerShell support for COM collections is incomplete. As a result, they can't be addressed with the usual array notation square brackets. Instead, the `Item()` parameterized property must be called explicitly. For example: if `$windows` contains the desktop window collections returned from a `Shell.Application` COM object, we cannot address the first window as `$windows[0]`. Instead, we use `$windows.Item(0)`.
- Manipulating browser and shell windows.
- Getting a list of open browser windows.
- Using the `WScript.Shell` object to pop up message boxes.
- Sending keystroke sequences to automate a Windows application.
- Using the browser to look up a word in an online resource.
- Using the `WinHTTP` class to do network programming.
- Using MS agents to create an animated presentation, including spoken output.
- Using the ScriptControl to allow a PowerShell script to call functions written in VBScript or JScript.

We also covered some of the issues you might run into using COM from PowerShell and some of the available workarounds.

The second part of this chapter covered the use of WMI, briefly describing what it is and why it matters. We discussed:

- Using the `Get-WmiObject` cmdlet to list available classes or to get a class instance. To get classes on a remote system, add the parameter `-Computer-Name <Computer>` to the command.
- The WMI object adapter and what it does.
- A limited comparison between VBScript and PowerShell when it comes to WMI scripting.
- The type accelerators `[WMI]`, `[WMICLASS]`, and `[WMISEARCHER]` that PowerShell provides for the WMI types and how they can be used.
- How to use WMI methods and events.
- Modifying editable WMI object properties by changing the value and then calling the object's `Put()` method to set the changes.

We ended the chapter with a discussion of the wide variety of ways to accomplish a task through all of these object models and provided a set of guidelines for favoring one solution over another.

At this point, we're done with our discussion of what PowerShell can do and how we can use it. But there's one more vital topic to discuss. By now it should be clear that PowerShell is, in fact, very powerful. It gives you access to nearly all of Windows through one tool. However, this power also has the potential to introduce risk, and so the last, but by no means least, topic to cover is security and PowerShell. This is the subject of the final chapter of this book.

Security, security, security

With great power comes great responsibility.

—Stan Lee, *The Amazing Spiderman*

In this chapter, we'll review security modeling concepts, and then look at the security features in PowerShell. We'll also look at how to write secure scripts in PowerShell. Boring, you say. Do we really need to know this stuff? Yeah, we do. In a connected world, security is incredibly important. A small mistake can have huge consequences. People will talk about a "zone of influence"—the idea that something that happens far away can't impact us. This idea is basically meaningless in a connected world. Anyone anywhere can attack your system just like they were next door. We also have to consider cascading consequences: a useful script that someone posts on his blog may get copied thousands of times. If there is a security flaw in that script it will propagate along with the script; get copied into new scripts, and so on. A small flaw in the original script may now be replicated around the world. Now that we are all appropriately terrified, let us proceed.

When discussing security and PowerShell, there's only one thing to keep in mind. PowerShell executes code. That's what it does—that's all it does. As a consequence, we need to consider how having PowerShell on your system might introduce security risks. Of course, this is not specific to PowerShell. It's true of anything that runs code—Perl, Python, even cmd.exe. Making sure that a system with PowerShell installed is secure is the topic of the first part of this chapter. Once you have PowerShell installed, of course you're going to want to write, deploy, and execute scripts. The latter portion of the chapter covers some approaches to writing secure PowerShell scripts.

13.1 INTRODUCTION TO SECURITY

We'll begin our security discussion with some basic definitions. In this section, we'll look at what security is and what that means. We'll also talk about what it isn't, which can be just as important.

13.1.1 What security is

Computer security is the field devoted to the creation of techniques and technologies that will allow computers to be used in a secure manner. Obvious perhaps, but there are two parts to the story. Secure means that the computer is protected against external danger or loss of valuables (financial, personal, or otherwise). The flip side is that the system has to remain useful. (There is a common joke in the security industry that the only way to make a computer completely secure is to turn it off, disconnect all of the cables, seal it in concrete, and dump it into the middle of the ocean. While this makes for a pretty secure computer, it's not a very useful one.) In approaching security, security requirements must be balanced with utility. If the techniques needed to secure a system are too hard to use, users won't use them, and the system will be unsecured. If they interfere with the basic tasks that need to be performed, they will be disabled or bypassed and the system will be unsecured. Are we getting the picture?

13.1.2 What security is not

Security is not cryptography. This is oddly surprising to many people. Security *uses* cryptography—it's one of the main tools used to secure an environment. They are, however, separate fields. The corollary is that unless you are a cryptographer, you shouldn't write your own cryptography code. It's very hard. And even the experts don't always get it right. And even if it's right today, it may be wrong tomorrow.

> **AUTHOR'S NOTE**   At the time this book was written, the MD5 hash algorithm, which had been considered the gold standard for secure hashes, had been found to be vulnerable.

The PowerShell environment, through .NET and the Windows platform, has access to a variety of cryptographic tools for building secure systems. You should use these tools instead of trying to roll your own. We'll spend a considerable amount of time on some of these tools later in this chapter.

13.1.3 Perception and security

One last thing. Regardless of what computer security is or is not, sometimes it is the perception of security that matters most. Let's take a look at a couple of stories that illustrate this.

The Danom virus

As we have discussed, PowerShell can be used to write scripts. It can be used to create, copy, and modify files. This means that, like any scripting or programming language, it can be used to write viruses, worms, and other malware.

> **AUTHOR'S NOTE**   The term *malware* is short for malicious software and is used to generally describe all of the forms of software (spyware, viruses, and so on) designed to cause damage in a computing environment. This may be the only definition in the security vocabulary that everybody agrees on. Or maybe not.

The fact that PowerShell can be used for this purpose has not gone unnoticed in the malware community.

In August 2005, a virus author created a proof-of-concept virus called Danom (Monad backwards). This virus script was essentially a port of existing virus code to the PowerShell language. This same virus code had previously been written in a variety of other scripting languages. It didn't take advantage of any vulnerability in either the operating system or the language interpreter. It required explicit and significant user action to execute the virus code. In fact, all it really did was demonstrate that PowerShell was a decent scripting language. There wasn't even a delivery vehicle. In other words, there was no way to distribute the malicious code. And with no mechanism to distribute the virus code, the "threat" was purely hypothetical.

This "coding exercise" was noticed by a security researcher who then issued a bulletin about it. This bulletin was picked up, first by the blogs and later by members of the popular press, without really investigating the details of the situation.

> **AUTHOR'S NOTE**   There were notable exceptions to this. For example, Scott Fulton at Tom's Hardware waited until he had the facts and then published a responsible, accurate report on the situation. Thanks Scott!

Because of the work that was going on with the next generation of Windows at the time (the Vista release), the press called this the first Vista virus. The Microsoft security response team members, who are busy analyzing real threats and can't track all of the new projects that are being worked on, responded by saying that it wasn't a Vista virus because PowerShell wasn't in the official list of features for Vista at that time. The press immediately turned this into "PowerShell cancelled due to virus threat". None of this was true, of course, but it made a good headline and lots of people, even inside Microsoft, believed the story.

What was gratifying was how the community responded to all of this coverage. They reviewed the virus code and the security measures that the PowerShell team had designed into the product and saw that Danom presented no significant threat.

> **AUTHOR'S NOTE** Even sites not known for being strong Microsoft supporters responded in a mature, responsible, and supportive way. Thanks to everyone who help get the real story out. Community support is very important to the Power-Shell team, and we really appreciate the help.

With the help of the community and some aggressive blogging, the tide was turned and people realized that there was really nothing there. All returned to normal, at least for a while.

The MSH/Cibyz worm

Almost exactly one year later, in August 2006, the MSH/Cibyz worm was released. This was essentially the Danom code with some updates and bug fixes.

> **AUTHOR'S NOTE** In between the first and second releases, the malware dictionary had been revised, so the second time around, the same code was reclassified as a worm instead of a virus. It's like being at a ball game listening to the guy handing out today's program sheets: "Programs! Programs! Get your programs! You can't tell a worm from a virus without a program!"

This time, there was a delivery vehicle using one of the peer-to-peer networks. The story was picked up by the blogging community initially, but eventually a large security software vendor issued a press release with an inflammatory title. The body of the release, however, essentially said "there's nothing to see here. These aren't the droids you're looking for. Please move along." But it still generated discussion and rumors for about a week.

The moral of the story is that it pays to investigate security alerts rather than just react to headlines. Without being properly informed, it's impossible to plan appropriate action, and planning is the key to establishing a secure environment. Since one of the best tools for planning is security modeling, we'll spend the next couple of sections discussing these techniques.

13.2 SECURITY MODELING

In this section, we'll briefly review some of the theories and concepts that have been developed to help build secure systems. We'll review the concepts of threats, vulnerabilities, and attacks. We'll cover the basics of threat modeling and why it's important. Note that this is an active and rapidly changing area of research. Theories and approaches are postulated, applied, and refuted over very short periods of time. The theoretical material we present in this section may even be obsolete by the time you read this. Still, having an awareness of the approaches that are being developed for building secure systems is always beneficial.

13.2.1 Introduction to threat modeling

Threat modeling is a systematic approach to identifying and categorizing threats to a system. So what does that mean? A *model* is a simplified representation of a system with unnecessary or unimportant details left out. By building a model, we can focus on the details that matter and ignore the ones that don't. Modern computer systems are too complex to address every detail. We have to focus our attention on what matters most.

Let's look at some more definitions. A *threat* to a system is "a potential event that will have unpleasant or undesirable consequences". A *vulnerability* is a weakness in the design or implementation of a system that an attacker may exploit to cause one of these undesirable events. An *attack* is when someone takes advantage of these vulnerabilities to gain some advantage that they are not otherwise permitted to have.

Back to modeling. The point of a model is to have a formal approach for looking at threats and vulnerabilities with the idea of defeating attacks. This is important because we can quite literally spend the rest of eternity trying to guard a system against things that don't matter. If we don't have a way of focusing our efforts, the result will be a solution that will be useless at best.

13.2.2 Classifying threats using the STRIDE model

STRIDE is a well-known threat classification model. STRIDE is an acronym for Spoofing, Tampering, Repudiation, Information Disclosure, and Elevation of Privilege. It's a way to categorize all of the significant threats to a system. Remember—a threat is something the attacker wants to happen, which means it's something we don't want. The idea is that if we model all of the STRIDE threat classifications we have a decent chance of covering the most important areas. Explanations for each of the components of STRIDE are shown in table 13.1.

Table 13.1   The threat classifications in the STRIDE model

Threat Classification	Explanation
Spoofing identity	Spoofing refers to various ways of assuming the identity of another user for the duration of a task.
Tampering with data	Tampering simply means of changing data. Note that this does not imply information disclosure—simple corruption may be all that is achieved.
Repudiation	From an attacker's perspective, repudiation essentially means covering your tracks. A particular act can not be traced and attributed to the committer of the act.
Information Disclosure	Information disclosure is simply allowing unauthorized persons access to sensitive information such as credit card numbers, passwords, and so on.

continued on next page

Table 13.1 The threat classifications in the STRIDE model *(continued)*

Threat Classification	Explanation
Denial of service	A denial of service (or DOS) attack means some form of resource exhaustion takes place. It could be network bandwidth, CPU cycles, or disk space. The problem with DOS attacks is that they are easy to launch anonymously and sometimes it's difficult to tell if it's actually an attack or that $2.99 special that you just announced on your website that's causing a sudden burst of network traffic.
Elevation of Privilege	In elevation of privilege attacks, an unprivileged user or process gains privileged access.

For more information on STRIDE, see *Writing Secure Code* by Michael Howard and David LeBlanc, available from Microsoft Press.

Now that we have a system for understanding and classifying threats, let's look at the remaining pieces we need to build the threat model.

13.2.3 Security basics: Threats, assets, and mitigations

There are three parts to building a security model: threats, assets, and mitigations. We talked about threats at length in the previous section. *Assets* are things that motivate the attacker to launch an attack. These assets may be things that are of direct value, such as credit card numbers or other financial information. They may also be of indirect value, such as code execution. This is an asset because once we have the ability to execute code on a machine, we can use these resources to do things such as send spam or execute distributed denial of service attacks against other targets.

Mitigation is what you're doing to mitigate those threats. The dictionary definition of mitigation is to "to cause to become less harsh or severe". We use this term instead of *prevent* because it may well be that the activity you're mitigating is necessary; for example, the ability to execute code in PowerShell can't be prevented, since that's its purpose. But we want to allow only authorized users to be able to execute approved scripts. The threat of unauthorized script execution is mitigated though a variety of approaches we describe later in this chapter. Now let's look at a few things to keep in mind when securing a system.

Avoid lawn gnome mitigation

There is a tendency, when trying to mitigate problems or otherwise reduce the attack surface of a system, to focus on reducing attacks in a particular area instead of looking at the system as a whole. This approach can add complexity to the system without actually increasing security. This approach is *lawn gnome mitigation*. The story goes like this. We hire a security consultant to secure our home. He drives up to our house, parks, gets out, and stands on the sidewalk looking at the house. After a while, he says that he sees where the vulnerability lies. He goes to the trunk of his car, takes out a ceramic lawn gnome (as illustrated in figure 13.1), and places it on the lawn between

Figure 13.1
A brave and noble Lawn Gnome protecting a home in Kitchener, Ontario, Canada. Hopefully it didn't cost the owner $2,000.

himself and the front door of the house. "I have mitigated the threat," he says. "That will be $2,000 please."

Has our high-priced security consultant actually mitigated a threat? As a matter of fact, he has. A burglar trying to break into the house, who crosses the lawn at that exact spot, will now trip over a lawn gnome. Of course, the burglar could go around it, or come at the house from a different direction. In fact, our house isn't really any safer, and we now have an ugly ceramic statue in the middle of our lawn that we have to mow around.

> **AUTHOR'S NOTE** There is a variation of this approach that is considered legitimate sometimes called "picket-fence" mitigation. A picket fence has holes in it, so we put another one behind it. And if there are still holes then we keep adding fences until there are no more holes. This is equivalent to dumping truckloads of lawn gnomes on our property until the house is surrounded by a 30-foot-high wall of ceramic gnomes. It'll work, but it's not very attractive.

The moral of this story is that, when securing a system, don't add unnecessary or inappropriate checks. We have to look at the system as a whole. This is particularly true when writing code. The more lawn gnomes we add, the more code we add to the system. Each new line of code introduces new possibilities for errors, and these errors can, in turn, become additional vulnerabilities.

Blacklisting/whitelisting

Short and sweet—*blacklisting* is saying who's bad and *whitelisting* is saying who's good. In general, whitelisting is preferred. Assume that the world is bad and we only trust people we know. This is inherently the most secure approach to use with Power-Shell. The number of people we trust to give us scripts to run is much smaller than the number of people we don't trust to run scripts. PowerShell supports the use of script signing to verify the identity of a script publisher and also validate the integrity of a published script. This is discussed at length in section 13.4.

Authentication authorization and roles

Authentication is verifying the identity of the user. *Authorization* is determining whether the user is authorized to perform an action. Finally, *roles* are groupings of activities for which authorization can be granted. By grouping multiple activities into a role, it becomes easier to manage authorization. When users are assigned a particular role, they are automatically authorized to perform all of the activities associated with that role. PowerShell depends primarily on the operating system for authentication and authorization, and currently has no special support for roles, unfortunately. A PowerShell script operates with the capabilities associated with the security token of the user who is running the script. We will see an example later in the chapter where it is possible to run a program from PowerShell as a different user, however.

Input validation

The rule is that we must validate any input received from outside our script. In scripting, this is the second most important rule for writing secure scripts. (The most important rule is "don't run unknown or untrusted scripts".)

Most scripting environments have the ability to dynamically compile and execute code (this is one of the things that makes them dynamic languages). It's tempting to use this capability to simplify our code. Say the user needs to do some arithmetic calculations in her script. In PowerShell, we could just pass this code directly to the Invoke-Expression cmdlet and let it evaluate the expression.

```
PS (1) > $userInput = "2+2"
```

Now we'll use Invoke-Expression to execute the command:

```
PS (2) > invoke-expression $userInput
4
```

Wasn't that easy! But what if the user types the following?

```
PS (3) > $userInput = "2+2; 'Hi there'"
PS (4) > invoke-expression $userInput
4
Hi there
```

It still executed the calculation, but it also executed the code after the semicolon. In this example, it was a harmless statement. But it might have been something like

```
$userInput = "2+2; del -rec -force c:\"
```

If this statement were executed, it would try to delete everything on your C: drive. Which would be bad.

There are other places where you need to do input validation. If the user is supplying a path you should make sure that it's a path that the user actually should have access to. For example:

```
$userInput = "mydata.txt"
get-content $userInput
```

This fragment of script will return the contents of the file "mydata.txt" from the current directory. This is what the script author intended. But because the script is not doing any path checking, the user could have specified a path like

```
$userInput = "..\bob_dobbs\mydata.txt"
```

in which case he might get the contents of another user's file. If instead, the script were written as

```
PS (1) > $userinput = "..\bob_dobbs\mydata.txt"
PS (2) > $safePath = join-path . `
>> (split-path -leaf $userInput)
>>
PS (3) > $safePath
.\mydata.txt
```

Then, despite providing a relative path, users can still only get their own data. Alternatively, we may wish to generate an error message explaining that it's an invalid file name:

```
PS (5) > if (split-path -parent $userInput) {
>> "Invalid file name: $userInput"
>> }
>>
Invalid file name: ..\bob_dobbs\mydata.txt
```

But you need to be careful with this; you may inadvertently leak information about the system through the error message.

AUTHOR'S NOTE People sometimes find it hard to understand why this is an issue. Let's look at an example. Say you're logging into a system. If you enter a user name and password and the system responds with "invalid account" if the user name is wrong and "invalid password" if the password is wrong, the attacker now has a way of finding out whether or not an account name is valid. In a sense, they've now won half the battle.

You need to trade off being friendly to the user with maintaining a secure system. So even in quite simple systems, it's fairly tricky to get this kind of thing right.

Code injection

Code injection is closely related to the input validation. In fact, the first couple examples that we looked at in the input validation section are code injection attacks. When writing PowerShell code, any use of Invoke-Expression is suspect. There are usually other ways of doing the same thing that don't require the use of Invoke-Expression. But there are other ways of injecting code into a PowerShell session. Scripts are the most obvious one. Every time a script is called, the script is loaded, parsed, and executed. Not only must you not execute scripts from unknown sources, you must make sure that no one can tamper with your own scripts. In the next section, we'll go over the features in PowerShell for doing exactly that.

Because PowerShell exists in mixed-language environments, you also need to be careful with other types of code injection attacks. The most common example is SQL injection attacks. This is the classic attack in the Web application world. The basic attack mechanism is the same—unvalidated user input is used to construct an SQL query. This query is then passed to the database and bad things happen. The query is being executed on behalf of the user, so there may be an information disclosure attack. The query may delete data from the database, in which case you're looking at a DOS attack.

Even more common in the PowerShell environment is the use of languages such as VBScript and/or cmd.exe batch scripts. All of these file types represent opportunities for code injection.

At this point, we've covered the basic principles for creating a secure computing environment. Now let's take a look at the features in PowerShell that were designed to support these principles.

13.3 SECURING THE POWERSHELL ENVIRONMENT

The whole point of PowerShell is to execute scripts that automate system management tasks. As a consequence, there is no such thing as an inherently "safe" Power-Shell script. PowerShell has no concept of *sandboxing*; that is, executing in a safe restricted environment. We must treat all PowerShell scripts as if they were executables. Because of this, when PowerShell is installed, it does a number of things to be secure by default. In the next few sections, we'll go over these features.

13.3.1 Secure by default

In this section, we'll go over the elements of the PowerShell installation process that are intended to meet the requirement that it be secure by default. *Secure by default* means that simply installing PowerShell on a system should not introduce any security issues.

The default file association for PowerShell is Notepad

File association is the way Windows figures out what application to launch as the default handler for files having a particular extension. For many scripting languages, the default association launches the interpreter for that language. This has led to many virus outbreaks. With PowerShell, the default file association for the `.ps1` extension is `notepad.exe`. This means that if an attacker does manage to get a script onto your computer and you accidentally double-click on this script, instead of executing the script, it will open up in Notepad, at which point you can review the hacker's code. Or just delete the script.

No remote access to PowerShell

There is no remote access to PowerShell. That is, there is no way for an external user to directly invoke the PowerShell engine. In order to remotely execute PowerShell code, the attacker has to leverage some other mechanism to allow them to access PowerShell.

No execution of scripts by default

PowerShell is installed in such a way that it won't run scripts by default. It can only be used as an interactive command interpreter.

Before scripts can be run, the user has to take explicit action to change the execution policy for PowerShell to allow script execution. In the default configuration, the only way to execute code is if the user manually starts PowerShell and types commands in at the prompt. This is covered in detail in the section 13.3.3.

So PowerShell is secure by default because it doesn't do much of anything. Now let's see how to make it useful by enabling script execution. But first, we'll cover a somewhat more mundane topic. PowerShell uses the PATH environment variable to find commands. This has some security implications, so we'll review those first before we talk abut how to enable scripting.

13.3.2   Managing the command path

A common local attack vector involves the PATH and PATHEXT environment variables. These variables control where commands are found and which files are considered to be executable. The PATHEXT variable lists the extensions of all of the file types that PowerShell will try to execute directly through the `CreateProcess()` API. The PATH variable, of course, controls what directories PowerShell will look in when it searches for external commands. If an attacker can compromise these variables or any of the files or directories that they reference, they can use a Trojan Horse attack—making something dangerous appear harmless.

> **AUTHOR'S NOTE**   OK, who thinks a 20-foot-high wooden horse looks harmless? If you saw a 20-foot wooden horse appear in your driveway, would you say "Oh, look dear, let's bring this giant wooden horse that we've never seen before into our house. Perhaps it will be our pet. I've always wanted a giant wooden horse as a pet!"?

The most important mitigation for this type of attack is to not include the current directory in your command search path. This is the default in PowerShell. This guards against the situation where you `cd` into an untrusted user's directory and then execute what you think is a trusted system command such as `ipconfig.exe`. If we execute commands out of the current directory and the user had placed a Trojan `ipconfig.exe` command in this directory, their command would execute with all of the privileges we have as a user. This is, shall we say, not a good thing. In general, it's best to leave the current path out of `$ENV:PATH`.

There is one other thing to consider in this situation. The `cmd.exe` interpreter does execute out of the current directory so if you run a `.cmd` script from PowerShell in an untrusted directory, there is a risk that the batch file could be compromised by Trojan programs.

13.3.3 Choosing a script execution policy

When PowerShell is installed, script execution is disabled by default. This is controlled by the PowerShell execution policy. PowerShell defines four execution policies: Restricted, AllSigned, RemoteSigned, and Unrestricted. The details of these policies are shown in table 13.2.

Table 13.2 Descriptions of the four execution policies

Policy	Description
Restricted	This is the default execution policy on installation. When this policy is in effect, script execution is disabled. PowerShell itself is not disabled. It may still be used as an interactive command interpreter. While this is the most secure policy, it severely impacts our ability to use PowerShell for automation.
AllSigned	When the execution policy is AllSigned, scripts can be executed, but they must be Authenticode-signed before they will run. When running a signed script, you will be asked if you want to trust the signer of the script. Section 13.4 covers the details of script signing. This is still a secure policy setting, but it makes script development difficult. In an environment where scripts will be deployed rather than created, this is the best policy.
RemoteSigned	RemoteSigned requires that all scripts that are downloaded from a remote location must be Authenticode-signed before they can be executed. Note that this depends on the application doing the download to mark the script as coming from a remote location. Not all applications may do this. Anything downloaded by Internet Explorer 6.0 or above, Outlook, or Outlook Express will be properly marked. This is the minimum recommended execution policy setting. It is the best policy setting for script development.
Unrestricted	When the execution policy is unrestricted, PowerShell will run any script. It will still prompt the user when it encounters a script that has been downloaded however. This is the least secure setting. It is not recommend that you use this setting, but it may be necessary in some developer scenarios where RemoteSigned is still too restrictive.

The execution policy is controlled by a registry key. Two cmdlets, `Get-Execution-Policy` and `Set-ExecutionPolicy`, can be used to change this key. First we'll take a look at where the information is stored in the registry.

Finding the current script execution policy

We'll use the registry provider to find out the current execution policy setting. First we need to cd into the area of the registry containing the PowerShell configuration.

```
PS (1) > cd hklm:\software\microsoft\PowerShell
PS (2) > cd "$($host.version.major)\ShellIDs\$ShellID"
```

Now we'll use the `Get-ItemProperty` cmdlet to access the `ExecutionPolicy` property.

```
PS (3) > Get-ItemProperty. ExecutionPolicy

PSPath           : Microsoft.PowerShell.Core\Registry::HKEY_LOCAL
                   _MACHINE\software\microsoft\PowerShell\1\Shell
                   Ids\Microsoft.PowerShell
PSParentPath     : Microsoft.PowerShell.Core\Registry::HKEY_LOCAL
                   _MACHINE\software\microsoft\PowerShell\1\Shell
                   Ids
PSChildName      : Microsoft.PowerShell
PSDrive          : HKLM
PSProvider       : Microsoft.PowerShell.Core\Registry
ExecutionPolicy  : Restricted
```

Changing the execution policy

Now let's use Set-ExecutionPolicy to change the policy to RemoteSigned.

```
PS (4) > Set-ExecutionPolicy RemoteSigned
```

And again use Get-ItemProperty to verify that the value has been changed.

```
PS (5) > Get-ItemProperty. ExecutionPolicy

PSPath           : Microsoft.PowerShell.Core\Registry::HKEY_LOCAL
                   _MACHINE\software\microsoft\PowerShell\1\Shell
                   Ids\Microsoft.PowerShell
PSParentPath     : Microsoft.PowerShell.Core\Registry::HKEY_LOCAL
                   _MACHINE\software\microsoft\PowerShell\1\Shell
                   Ids
PSChildName      : Microsoft.PowerShell
PSDrive          : HKLM
PSProvider       : Microsoft.PowerShell.Core\Registry
ExecutionPolicy  : RemoteSigned
```

Of course, it's much easier to check it with Get-ExecutionPolicy:

```
PS (6) > Get-ExecutionPolicy
RemoteSigned
```

So why did we bother looking at the registry? Because it's always useful to know how things work and where they're stored. It may be that you're in a situation where you need to enable (or disable) script execution and aren't able to use an interactive PowerShell session to do it.

Remember, execution policy depends heavily on the signing infrastructure to determine whether or not a script should be run. In the next section, we'll review the overall script signing architecture in Windows and look at how to sign scripts in PowerShell.

13.4   SIGNING SCRIPTS

Signing a script is the process of adding extra information that identifies the publisher of the script in a secure way. By *secure way*, we mean that it is done in such a way that you can verify:

- that the script really was signed by the correct person.
- that the contents of the script haven't been changed in any way since it was signed.

13.4.1   How public key encryption and one-way hashing work

Script signing is accomplished using two technologies: *public key encryption* and *one-way hashes*. Public key encryption is important because it uses two keys: a private key for encrypting information and a second public key for decrypting the data encrypted with the private key. The other technology we need is a one-way hash function. This is a type of function where it's easy to calculate the output for any input, but is very hard to recover the input if you have only the output. These hash functions also need to be collision resistant. In other words, it should be highly unlikely that two inputs produce the same output. Here's how these technologies are used to verify the authenticity and integrity of the script.

- First the script author (or publisher) calculates a one-way hash of the contents of the script using a secure hashing algorithm.
- This hash is then encrypted with the publisher's private key and attached to the script in the form of a comment block.
- The script is then delivered to the consumer who is going to run the script.
- Before the script is run, PowerShell removes the signature block, and then calculates its own one-way hash of the document using the same algorithm as the publisher.
- Using the publisher's public decryption key, PowerShell decrypts the hash contained in the signature comment block.
- Finally, it compares the hash it calculated against the one that was recovered from the signature block. If they match, the script was created by the owner of the private key and hasn't been tampered with. If they don't match, the script is rejected. It's either not legitimately signed by the publisher or it has been tampered with.

There is one small thing that we've skipped in this discussion. How do we get the right public key to decrypt the signature in the first place? Calling up the publisher on the telephone every time we run the script is not going to work. This is where signing authorities and certificates come in. First we'll look the role of a signing authority in creating certificates. Then we'll talk about how we can create our own self-signed certificates. This is a two stage process: creating a local signing authority and then using that authority to issue a certificate.

13.4.2   Signing authorities and certificates

Making all of this signing stuff work requires a way of getting the public key associated with a signer's identity. This is done using the signing certificate. A certificate is a piece of data that uses a digital signature to bind together a public key and an identity. But wait! If it's signed then aren't we back we started? Now we need to get a public key to verify who we should get the public key from. Yikes. This is where signing authorities come in. These are well-known, trusted third-party organizations from which authors can purchase signing certificates. When someone wants to be able to sign scripts, they contact a signing authority to purchase a certificate. The signing authority then verifies the identity of the party requesting the certificate. Once this is done, the signer receives the private key and can now start signing documents. Part of the signature includes the user's identity, which will be verified using the public key of the certificate that you look up at the signing authority. This is called the chain of trust.

All of this machinery is part of what's called a *Public Key Infrastructure* or PKI. In fact, there are a number of additional pieces necessary to make it all work. One of these pieces is the local certificate store. This store is used as a local cache for certificates. If we had to establish a network connection to the signing authority every time we wanted to do something, it wouldn't work very well. Also, we wouldn't be able to work when we weren't connected to a network. By caching the certificates locally, we can avoid these problems. (There are other intermediate tiers in the trust chain, and some other details such as expiry and revocation that we're not going to cover here because they are well documented elsewhere. MSDN has a good discussion of this material, for example.)

So do we need to contact a signing authority before we can safely run scripts? This is the topic of the next section on self-signed certificates.

Self-signed certificates

So what does the average person do if she wants to sign scripts but doesn't want to invest time and money getting a certificate from a signing authority? The answer is that we can use self-signed certificates. This is a certificate we create for ourselves where the computer itself becomes the signing authority. Obtaining this type of certificate doesn't have the issues associated with a public signing authority. It's free and easy to get, however other computers won't trust our computer as a valid authority and so won't run scripts that we sign with this certificate.

AUTHOR'S NOTE   If you create a self-signed certificate, be sure to enable strong private-key protection on your certificate. This will prevent other programs from signing scripts on your behalf. We'll see how to do this later in the chapter.

This sounds somewhat less that useful, but it allows us to control what scripts can be run on our computer. In the next section, we'll see how to create a self-signed certificate.

13.4.3 Creating a self-signed certificate

To create a self-signed certificate, we'll use the `MakeCert.exe` program. This utility is included as part of the Microsoft .NET Framework SDK and the Microsoft Platform SDK. These can be freely downloaded from Microsoft if you don't already have them. Even if they are installed on the computer, we may have to modify the setting of `$ENV:PATH` so it includes the directory that contains these commands. You can use `Get-Command` to see whether `makecert.exe` is installed and where it is located.

```
PS (1) > get-command makecert.exe | fl

Name            : makecert.exe
CommandType     : Application
Definition      : C:\Program Files\Microsoft Visual Studio 8\SDK
                  \v2.0\Bin\makecert.exe
Extension       : .exe
Path            : C:\Program Files\Microsoft Visual Studio 8\SDK
                  \v2.0\Bin\makecert.exe
FileVersionInfo : File:            C:\Program Files\Microsoft V
                  isual Studio 8\SDK\v2.0\Bin\makecert.exe
                  InternalName:    MAKECERT.EXE
                  OriginalFilename: MAKECERT.EXE
                  FileVersion:     5.131.3790.0 (srv03_rtm.0303
                  24-2048)
                  FileDescription: ECM MakeCert
                  Product:         Microsoftr Windowsr Operatin
                  g System
                  ProductVersion:  5.131.3790.0
                  Debug:           False
                  Patched:         False
                  PreRelease:      False
                  PrivateBuild:    False
                  SpecialBuild:    False
                  Language:        English (United States)
```

We can see that it's installed in the Visual Studio SDK directory (this doesn't mean you have to run out and buy Visual Studio, by the way. The free SDK is all you need). This is a fairly complex command with a lot of options. We're going to get set up for signing in two steps—creating a local certificate authority and using that authority to create a signing certificate.

Creating a local certificate authority

First, we're going to run the following command to create a local certificate authority for our computer. Let's run the command.

```
PS (2) > makecert -n "CN=PowerShell Local Certificate Root" `
>> -a sha1 -eku 1.3.6.1.5.5.7.3.3 -r -sv root.pvk root.cer `
>> -ss Root -sr localMachine
>>
Succeeded
```

Figure 13.2 What you see when you run `makecert` to create the self-signing authority.

When we run this command, a dialog box will appear, asking us to establish our identity by entering a password for this signing authority. This is shown in figure 13.2.

So what did this command actually do? We've instructed the command to create a self-signed certificate that will be used for code-signing purposes. We want this certificate placed in the root certificate store on the local machine. We've also said that we want to use SHA-1 (Secure Hash Algorithm, version 1) for hashing the document. Table 13.3 has further explanation for each of the parameters we've specified to the command.

Table 13.3 `MakeCert` parameters used to create a self-signing authority

MakeCert parameter	Description
-r	Instruct the utility to create a self-signed certificate.
-n "CN=PowerShell Local Certificate Root"	This allows us to specify the X.500 name to use for the certificate subject. We're going to use "CN= PowerShell Local Certificate Root".
-a sha1	This selects the algorithm used to generate the signature hash. It can be either "md5" or "sha1". The default is "md5" but this is no longer considered robust so we'll choose "sha1" instead.
-eku 1.3.6.1.5.5.7.3.3	Inserts a set of comma-separated Enhanced Key Usage (eku) object identifiers (or OIDs) into the certificate. In our case, the enhanced use we want is for code signing. That is, we want to create a key for the particular purpose of signing executable files.
-sv root.pvk	Specify the name of the file where the private key is to be written. In this example, a file called root.pvk will be created in the current directory.
-ss Root	Subject's certificate store name that stores the output certificate.
-sr localMachine	Specify whether the certificate is to be created in the current user's store or the local machine store. The default is CurrentUser, but we want this certificate to be machine-wide so we specify LocalMachine.

Creating the signing certificate

Now that we've created a signing authority, we need to give ourselves a signing certificate. Again, we can also do this with `MakeCert.exe` by running the following command:

```
PS (3) > makecert -pe -n "CN=PowerShell User" -ss MY -a sha1 `
>> -eku 1.3.6.1.5.5.7.3.3 -iv root.pvk -ic root.cer
>>
Succeeded
PS (4) >
```

This will create a certificate file in `root.cer` using the private key stored in `root.pvk` file. Table 13.4 explains the options we're using in this command.

Table 13.4   MakeCert parameters used to create a code-signing certificate

MakeCert parameter	Description
-pe	Marks the generated private key as exportable. This allows the private key to be included in the certificate.
-n "CN=PowerShell User"	Specifies the X.500 name for the signer.
-ss MY	Specifies the subject's certificate store name that stores the output certificate.
-a sha1	As before, specifies the hash algorithm to use.
-eku 1.3.6.1.5.5.7.3.3	Specifies that we want code-signing certificates.
-iv root.pvk	Specifies where the certificate issuer's .pvk private key file is. (We created this file in the previous step).
-ic root.cer	Specifies the issuer's certificate file should be written.

Let's check out what we've created. Let's look at for files named "root" in the current directory:

```
PS (10) > dir root.*

    Directory: Microsoft.PowerShell.Core\FileSystem::C:\working\

Mode                LastWriteTime     Length Name
----                -------------     ------ ----
-a---          8/12/2006   6:32 PM       591 root.cer
-a---          8/12/2006   6:32 PM       636 root.pvk
```

In the first step, we create the file root.pvk—the private key—for our signing authority. In the second step, we create the certificate file root.cer that we need for signing. However, the more important question is whether or not we created the certificate in the certificate store. We can verify this using the Certificate snap-in in MMC. Figure 13.3 shows what this looks like.

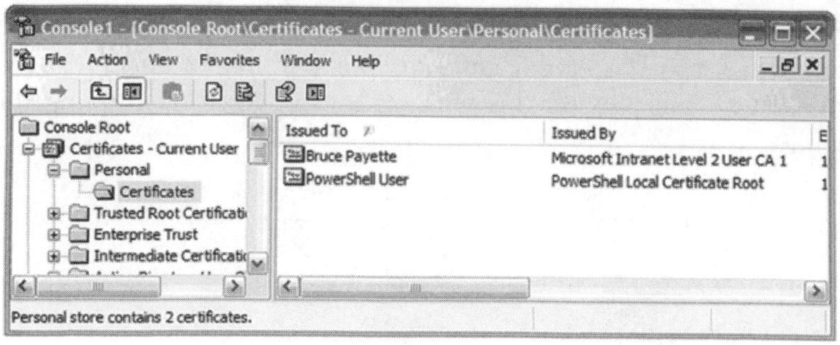

Figure 13.3   Verifying that the certificates have been created from the Certificates snap-in.

Of course, this is PowerShell, so there must be a way to verify this from the command line. We can do this using the PowerShell certificate provider by typing the following command:

```
PS (13) > dir cert:\CurrentUser\My -codesigning | fl

Subject       : CN=PowerShell User
Issuer        : CN=PowerShell Local Certificate Root
Thumbprint    : 145F9E3BF835CDA7DC21BD07BDB26B7FCFEA0687
FriendlyName  :
NotBefore     : 8/12/2006 6:34:31 PM
NotAfter      : 12/31/2039 3:59:59 PM
Extensions    : {System.Security.Cryptography.Oid, System.Securit
                y.Cryptography.Oid}
```

If the certificate was created, the output shows us the thumbprint of the certificate, which contains authentication data for "PowerShell User". Now we have everything set up! We've established a signing authority and issued ourselves a certificate. Now let's move on and sign some scripts.

13.4.4   Using a certificate to sign a script

Now that we have a self-signed certificate, we can sign scripts. In this section, we'll go through the steps to do this. We'll also look at how to change the script execution policy to verify that our scripts are signed properly.

Setting up a test script

First, let's create an unsigned script that we can use for testing purposes:

```
PS (16) > '"Hello there"' > test-script.ps1
```

Now, assuming that our execution policy is currently set to something like `Remote-Signed` that lets us run local scripts, let's run `test-script.ps1`.

```
PS (17) > ./test-script.ps1
Hello there
```

Now change the execution policy to `AllSigned` and verify that we can't run unsigned scripts any longer. We'll use `Set-ExecutionPolicy`:

```
PS (18) > Set-ExecutionPolicy AllSigned
```

Now when we try to run the script, it will fail.

```
PS (19) > ./test-script.ps1
File C:\Temp\test-script.ps1 cannot be loaded. The file C:\Temp\
test-script.ps1 is not digitally signed. The script will not exe
cute on the system. Please see "get-help about_signing" for more
 details..
At line:1 char:17
+ ./test-script.ps1 <<<<
```

The error message tells us that the script is not signed and suggests a help topic that will explain what's going on. Now let's sign the script.

Signing the test script

First we need to get a certificate object to use to sign the script. We use the Power-Shell certificate provider to do this.

```
PS (20) > $cert = @(Get-ChildItem cert:\CurrentUser\My `
>> -codesigning)[0]
>>
PS (21) > $cert


    Directory: Microsoft.PowerShell.Security\Certificate::Curren
    tUser\My


Thumbprint                                Subject
----------                                -------
145F9E3BF835CDA7DC21BD07BDB26B7FCFEA0687  CN=PowerShell User
```

This shows that we have a certificate object in `$cert`. Now we'll use the `Set-AuthenticodeSignature` (remember, Tab-completion works on cmdlet names) cmdlet to sign this file:

```
PS (22) > Set-AuthenticodeSignature test-script.ps1 $cert


    Directory: C:\Temp


SignerCertificate                         Status   Path
-----------------                         ------   ----
145F9E3BF835CDA7DC21BD07BDB26B7FCFEA0687  Valid    test-sc...
```

This cmdlet returns the signature information for the signed file. Now let's try to run it.

```
PS (23) > ./test-script
```

```
Do you want to run software from this untrusted publisher?
File C:\Temp\test-script.ps1 is published by CN=PowerShell User
and is not trusted on your system. Only run scripts from trusted
```

```
    publishers.
    [V] Never run   [D] Do not run   [R] Run once   [A] Always run
    [?] Help(default is "D"): a
    Hello there
```

Notice that we are prompted to confirm that this signing authority should be trusted. Assuming we trust ourselves, we answer that we should always trust the signing authority we created. Now let's run this script again.

```
PS (24) > ./test-script
Hello there
```

This time, we didn't get prompted, since we've told the system that this certificate should always be trusted.

So what exactly happened to the script? It used to be one line long. Let's look at the beginning of the script. We'll use the `Select-Object` cmdlet to get the first 10 lines of the file:

```
PS (25) > gc test-script.ps1 | Select-Object -first 10
"Hello there"

# SIG # Begin signature block
# MIIEMwYJKoZIhvcNAQcCoIIEJDCCBCACAQExCzAJBgUrDgMCGgUAMGkGCisGAQQB
# gjcCAQSgWzBZMDQGCisGAQQBgjcCAR4wJgIDAQAABBAfzDtgWUsITrck0sYpfvNR
# AgEAAgEAAgEAAgEAAgEAMCEwCQYFKw4DAhoFAAQU0O2MiFZBx/X1iLwTml3Dg6o3
# iOygggI9MIICOTCCAaagAwIBAgIQ0QlVf5hB+oZM3DApkhHZMTAJBgUrDgMCHQUA
# MCwxKjAoBgNVBAMTIVBvd2VyU2hlbGwgTG9jYWwgQ2VydGlmaWNhdGUgUm9vdDAe
# Fw0wNjA4MTMwMTM0MzFaFw0zOTEyMzEyMzU5NTlaMBoxGDAWBgNVBAMTD1Bvd2Vy
# U2hlbGwgVXNlcjCBnzANBgkqhkiG9w0BAQEFAAOBjQAwgYkCgYEAtB75pWZTD5Jo
```

How long is the file? Let's check:

```
PS (26) > (gc test-script.ps1).count
27
```

Signing the file increased the size from one line to 27. As you can see, signing a file adds a lot of ugly comments to the end of the file. We can use the `Get-Authenti-codeSignature` to retrieve the signature information from the file:

```
PS (28) > Get-AuthenticodeSignature test-script.ps1 | fl

SignerCertificate      : [Subject]
                           CN=PowerShell User

                         [Issuer]
                           CN=PowerShell Local Certificate Root

                         [Serial Number]
                           D109557F9841FA864CDC30299211D931

                         [Not Before]
                           8/12/2006 6:34:31 PM
```

```
                            [Not After]
                             12/31/2039 3:59:59 PM

                            [Thumbprint]
                             145F9E3BF835CDA7DC21BD07BDB26B7FCFEA0
                            687

TimeStamperCertificate :
Status                  : Valid
StatusMessage           : Signature verified.
Path                    : C:\Temp\test-script.ps1
```

Among other things, this shows you who signed the file (PowerShell User) and who issued the certificate (PowerShell Local Certificate Root), both of which we've just created. Now let's see what happens if we tamper with this file.

Testing the integrity of the script

We'll use an editor and duplicate the "Hello there" line in the script.

```
PS (29) > notepad test-script.ps1
```

So the file now looks like:

```
PS (30) > gc test-script.ps1 | Select-Object -first 10
"Hello there"
"Hello there"

# SIG # Begin signature block
# MIIEMwYJKoZIhvcNAQcCoIIEJDCCBCACAQExCzAJBgUrDgMCGgUAMGkGCisGAQQB
# gjcCAQSgWzBZMDQGCisGAQQBgjcCAR4wJgIDAQAABBAfzDtgWUsITrck0sYpfvNR
# AgEAAgEAAgEAAgEAAgEAMCEwCQYFKw4DAhoFAAQU0O2MiFZBx/X1iLwTml3Dg6o3
# iOygggI9MIICOTCCAaagAwIBAgIQ0QlVf5hB+oZM3DApkhHZMTAJBgUrDgMCHQUA
# MCwxKjAoBgNVBAMTIVBvd2VyU2hlbGwgTG9jYWwgQ2VydGlmaWNhdGUgUm9vdDAe
# Fw0wNjA4MTMwMTM0MzFaFw0zOTEyMzEyMzU5NTlaMBoxGDAWBgNVBAMTD1Bvd2Vy
```

We try to run the modified file:

```
PS (31) > ./test-script
File C:\Temp\test-script.ps1 cannot be loaded. The contents of f
ile C:\Temp\test-script.ps1 may have been tampered because the h
ash of the file does not match the hash stored in the digital si
gnature. The script will not execute on the system. Please see "
get-help about_signing" for more details..
At line:1 char:13
+ ./test-script <<<<
```

It fails with an error telling us that the file has been tampered with. This shows how signing is used to verify the integrity of the script. Now let's look at the last topic we've going to cover on signing scripts.

13.4.5 Enabling strong private key protection for your certificate

When we create a private certificate on our computer, it's possible that malicious programs might be able to access the certificate and sign scripts on your behalf. This would then allow the malicious program to create Trojan scripts that appear to be legitimately signed.

To address this vulnerability, we'll use the Certificate Manager tool (Certmgr.exe), another utility included in the .NET SDK and the Microsoft Platform SDK. It's also included with Internet Explorer 5.0 and later.

The Certificate Manager enables us to export the signing certificate to a .pfx file. Once we have the PFX available, we can use it to sign a document, but we'll have to interactively provide a password as part of the signing process. This interactive step prevents a malicious program from quietly signing scripts. A user has to provide the password.

In this section, we'll go over the steps necessary to export a certificate, and then we'll use the exported file to re-sign the file we tampered with in section 13.4.3.

Exporting the certificate

Exporting a certificate using the Certificate Manager is a straightforward task. We'll take the certificate we created in the previous sections and export it to a file called "mycert.pfx".

Step 1 Start Certmgr.exe and select the certificate to export

First we start the certificate manager (which is a graphical tool). This will result in a window opening on our desktop that looks something like what is shown in figure 13.4

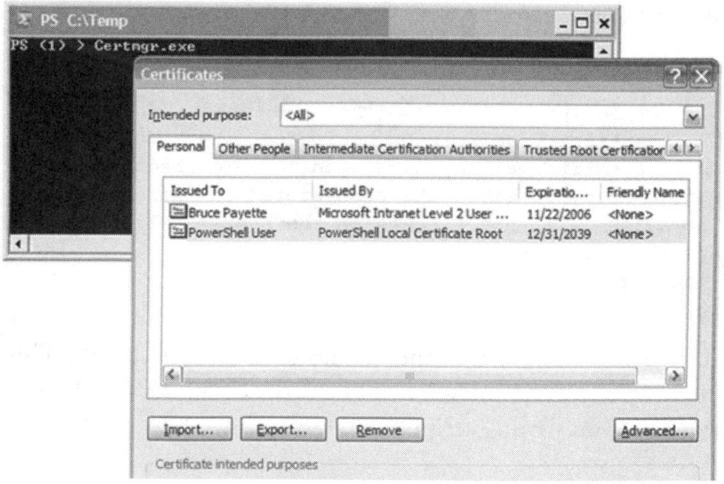

Figure 13.4 Launching the Certificate Manager tool

Figure 13.5   Launching the Certificate Export Wizard

The Certificate Manager window will display one or more certificates. Select the certificate we created in section 13.4.2. This will be the one issued by the "PowerShell Local Certificate Root". When you have selected the certificate, click Export to start the Certificate Export Wizard. Now you should see something that looks like what is shown in figure 13.5.

Click Next. This will take you to a dialog with two option buttons. Select the "Yes, export the private key" option and click on Next.

Step 2   Specify the file format and password

The next step in the wizard will ask you to specify the export file format. Select the "Personal Information Exchange" option. Be sure the "Enable strong protection" box is checked (this should be the default).

At this point, the system will ask you to enter a password to use to protect the key you are exporting, as shown in figure 13.6.

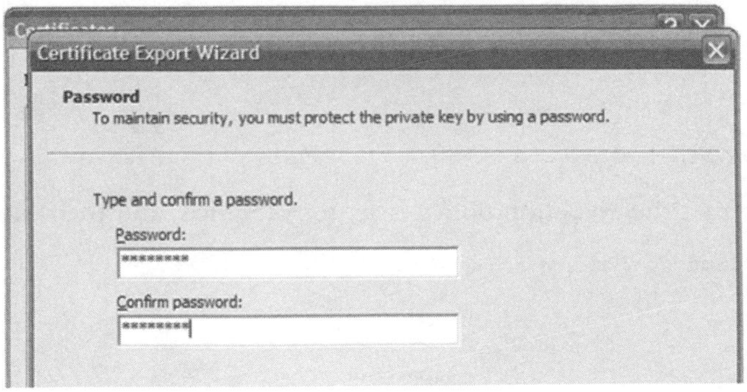

Figure 13.6
In this figure, we see the dialog to set the password used to secure the private key.

Choose a password you can remember, enter it twice and click Next.

Step 3 Specify the name for the pfx file

Now we enter the name of the file we want to create with a .pfx extensions. We'll call it "mycert.pfx". We click Next, verify the information, and click Finish. The export is done.

Step 4 Verify that the pfx file was created

Now we'll verify that the file was created. Enter the following command:

```
PS (1) > Certmgr.exe
CertMgr Succeeded
PS (2) > dir *.pfx


    Directory: Microsoft.PowerShell.Core\FileSystem::C:\Temp


Mode                LastWriteTime     Length Name
----                -------------     ------ ----
-a---          8/13/2006   5:38 PM      1768 mycert.pfx
```

And there it is: "mycert.pfx" as requested.

Using the pfx file to sign a file

Now we can use this file to get a signing certificate by using the Get-PfxCertificate cmdlet.

```
PS (3) > $cert = Get-PfxCertificate mycert.pfx
Enter password: ********

PS (4) > $cert

Thumbprint                                Subject
----------                                -------
145F9E3BF835CDA7DC21BD07BDB26B7FCFEA0687  CN=PowerShell User
```

Let's use this certificate object to re-sign the file we tampered with earlier:

```
PS (5) > Set-AuthenticodeSignature test-script.ps1 $cert


    Directory: C:\Temp

SignerCertificate                         Status    Path
-----------------                         ------    ----
145F9E3BF835CDA7DC21BD07BDB26B7FCFEA0687  Valid     test-sc...
```

Next, make sure that the execution policy is set to AllSigned, and then run the script.

```
PS (6) > Set-ExecutionPolicy allsigned
PS (7) > ./test-script.ps1
Hello there
Hello there
PS (8) >
```

The script runs properly. There is no prompt because we've already told the system that we trust this signing authority.

This is the end of our discussion of signing as well as the overall discussion on securing PowerShell installations. In the next (and final) part of this chapter, we're going to shift our focus away from securing PowerShell and over to writing secure PowerShell scripts.

13.5   WRITING SECURE SCRIPTS

As we've seen, the PowerShell team has been very careful in designing the various security features in the PowerShell runtime.

> **AUTHOR'S NOTE**   In fact, we (the PowerShell team) have been described as obsessive in our security focus. Here's a quote from Microsoft security guru Michael Howard:
>
> *I want folks to realize that the PowerShell guys are very, VERY savvy when it comes to security. In fact, they are borderline anal. Actually, they're not borderline at all.*

In the end, however, the whole point of PowerShell is to allow people to create and run scripts that will automate system administration tasks. As a consequence, vulnerable or badly written scripts could inadvertently lead to substantial damage to the system. All the security features in the world can't defend us from badly written scripts, so we're going to look at some of the techniques we can use to make our code more robust.

13.5.1   Using the SecureString class

At some point, we'll want to write a script that acquires passwords or other sensitive data such as credit card numbers. PowerShell, through .NET, provides a number of features for dealing with sensitive data in a secure way. In this section, we're going to discuss how to use those features to write scripts that can deal with sensitive information.

Most of the sensitive data we'll be dealing with will be in the form of strings. When a string is created in .NET, the runtime retains that string in memory so it can efficiently reuse it. Even after we are done with the data, the string will remain in memory until it is finally cleaned up by the garbage collector. So what's the big deal—if an attacker can access the process's memory, we're already compromised, right? That's true if the information only stays in memory; however, there are a number of ways that it could end up being persisted to the disk. For one thing, Windows uses virtual memory. This means that blocks of memory are periodically paged to disk. Once it's on the disk, it potentially becomes available to applications that can do raw accesses to the disk. Now, this may require the attacker to steal your hard disk and use forensic tools to analyze it but it is possible and has happened before. Similarly, using hibernate on a laptop will write an image of memory to the disk. Finally, the string could wind up on the disk due to a crash dump, where an image of the computer's memory is dumped to the disk during a system crash.

So how can we avoid these problems? When writing .NET programs, the way to safely work with strings containing sensitive data is to use the System.Security.SecureString class. This type is a container for text data that the .NET runtime stores in memory in an encrypted form. The most common way to get secure strings is using the Get-Credential cmdlet or the [System.Management.Automation.PSCredential] type. This type also forms the basis for writing secure scripts in PowerShell using the SecureString cmdlets, which we'll look at next.

Creating a SecureString object

When we write a script or function that requires sensitive data such as passwords, the best practice is to designate that password parameter as a SecureString in order to help keep passwords confidential. Let's look at a how we can create a secure string. The simplest way to do this is to use the -AsSecureString parameter on the Read-Host cmdlet.

```
PS (1) > read-host -AsSecureString -prompt "Password"
Password: ********
System.Security.SecureString
```

Let's take a look at the members on the SecureString object using the Get-Member cmdlet.

```
PS (2) > $ss = read-host -AsSecureString -prompt "Password"
Password: ********
PS (3) > $ss | gm


    TypeName: System.Security.SecureString

Name           MemberType Definition
----           ---------- ----------
AppendChar     Method     System.Void AppendChar(Char c)
Clear          Method     System.Void Clear()
Copy           Method     System.Security.SecureString Copy()
Dispose        Method     System.Void Dispose()
Equals         Method     System.Boolean Equals(Object obj)
get_Length     Method     System.Int32 get_Length()
GetHashCode    Method     System.Int32 GetHashCode()
GetType        Method     System.Type GetType()
InsertAt       Method     System.Void InsertAt(Int32 index, Cha...
IsReadOnly     Method     System.Boolean IsReadOnly()
MakeReadOnly   Method     System.Void MakeReadOnly()
RemoveAt       Method     System.Void RemoveAt(Int32 index)
SetAt          Method     System.Void SetAt(Int32 index, Char c)
ToString       Method     System.String ToString()
Length         Property   System.Int32 Length {get;}
```

The only way we can convert a string to a secure string is by appending one character at a time. Let's append another character to the string.

```
PS (4) > $ss.AppendChar("1")
```

Here's a way to make a secure string out of a normal one. First, we create an instance of the secure string class:

```
PS (9) > $ss = new-object System.Security.SecureString
```

Then we send each character to the Foreach cmdlet and append it to that secure string. Normally strings in PowerShell don't stream by default, but if you explicitly get an enumerator, it is possible to stream a string one character at a time.

```
PS (10) > "Hello there".GetEnumerator() | % {$ss.AppendChar($_)}
```

Now let's look at the results.

```
PS (11) > $ss
System.Security.SecureString
```

Not very interesting, is it? But that's the point. It's secure—there's no easy way to get the data back. We'll take one final precaution. We don't want our secure string tampered with, so we'll make it read-only.

```
PS (12) > $ss.MakeReadOnly()
PS (13) > $ss.IsReadOnly()
True
```

Now if we try to modify it, we'll get an error.

```
PS (14) > $ss.AppendChar('!')
Exception calling "AppendChar" with "1" argument(s): "Instance i
s read-only."
At line:1 char:15
+ $ss.AppendChar( <<<< '!')
```

Marking a secure string read-only once it's complete is generally considered to be a best practice.

The SecureString cmdlets

Manually building secure strings is obviously a bit tedious, so PowerShell has two cmdlets for working with secure strings: ConvertTo-SecureString and ConvertFrom-SecureString. These cmdlets allow you to write data to disk in a reasonably secure fashion.

By default, the SecureString cmdlets uses the Windows Data Protection API (DPAPI) when they convert your SecureString to and from a plain text representation. The Data Protection API is the standard way on the Microsoft Windows platform for programs to protect sensitive data. The encryption key that the DPAPI uses is based on Windows logon credentials. This means that we don't have to specify a key to encrypt or decrypt data—the system will generate one for us automatically based on the logon credentials. Of course, this means that we can only decrypt our own data using this mechanism. If there is a need to export or share encrypted data across multiple machines or with additional users then we have to create and manage a key for these purposes.

However, there are many instances when you may want to automatically provide the `SecureString` input to a cmdlet, rather than have the host prompt you for it. In these situations, the ideal solution is to import a previously exported `Secure-String` from disk (using `ConvertTo-SecureString`). This retains the confidentiality of your data and still allows you to automate the input.

If the data is highly dynamic (for example, coming from a CSV file) then the best approach is to do something like:

```
$secureString = ConvertTo-SecureString "Kinda Secret" `
    -AsPlainText -Force
```

The cmdlet requires the `-Force` parameter to ensure we acknowledge the fact that PowerShell cannot protect plain text data, even after you've put it in a `SecureString`.

13.5.2 Working with credentials

To do any sort of administrative work on a computer, at some point we're going to need to get the credentials of the user account authorized to do the work. Obviously, it is bad practice to put passwords in scripts, so you should always prompt for passwords or credentials. In PowerShell, this is done through the `Get-Credential` cmdlet as shown in figure 13.7.

Running the `Get-Credential` cmdlet will return a credential object that you can then use for operations that require a password. Of course, to do this, you need to store the credential object in a variable as shown:

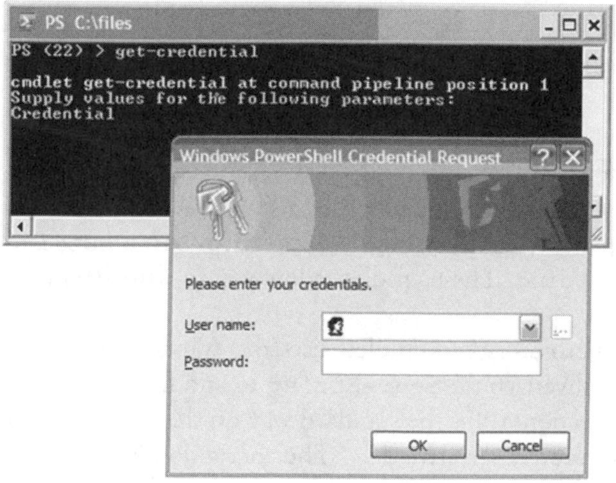

Figure 13.7
When you use the `Get-Credential` cmdlet, it will pop up a dialog that looks like this.

```
PS (2) > $cred = get-credential

cmdlet get-credential at command pipeline position 1
Supply values for the following parameters:
Credential
```

Now let's display this credential object:

```
PS (3) > $cred

UserName                                            Password
--------                                            --------
mymachine\myuserid                  System.Security.SecureString
```

The domain and user name are stored as a regular string, but the password has been stored as an instance of the type `System.Security.SecureString`. As discussed previously, this allows the credential object to remain in memory without presenting a significant security risk.

Now let's look at an example where we want to use the credential object. Let's write a script that will start a process using different credentials. This works approximately like the `runas.exe` command. We're going to use this function to launch the Local User Administration dialog. When we run the script, we'll see something that looks like what is shown in figure 13.8.

In this example, we're entering the user name and password for a user that hasn't logged in yet, so we'll get an error:

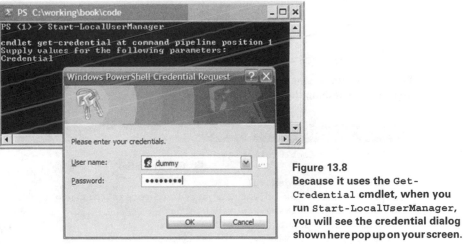

Figure 13.8
Because it uses the Get-Credential cmdlet, when you run Start-LocalUserManager, you will see the credential dialog shown here pop up on your screen.

```
PS (1) > Start-LocalUserManager

cmdlet get-credential at command pipeline position 1
Supply values for the following parameters:
Credential
Exception calling "Start" with "1" argument(s): "The user's pass
word must be changed before logging on the first time"
At line:12 char:36
+ [System.Diagnostics.Process]::Start( <<<< $StartInfo)
PS (2) >
```

Now we'll try it again, but this time with a valid user account. The results are shown in figure 13.9. The source for this function is shown in listing 13.1.

Figure 13.9   When you start the Local User Manger snap-in in MMC, you'll see something that looks like this.

Listing 13.1   The Start-LocalUserManager Function

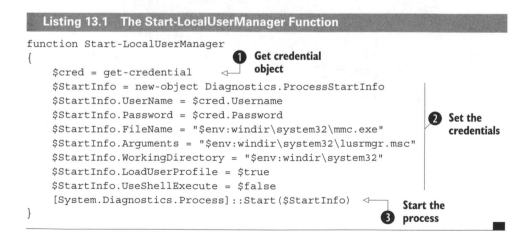

```
function Start-LocalUserManager
{                                              ❶ Get credential
    $cred = get-credential          ◁─┘           object
    $StartInfo = new-object Diagnostics.ProcessStartInfo
    $StartInfo.UserName = $cred.Username
    $StartInfo.Password = $cred.Password
    $StartInfo.FileName = "$env:windir\system32\mmc.exe"          ❷ Set the
    $StartInfo.Arguments = "$env:windir\system32\lusrmgr.msc"        credentials
    $StartInfo.WorkingDirectory = "$env:windir\system32"
    $StartInfo.LoadUserProfile = $true
    $StartInfo.UseShellExecute = $false
    [System.Diagnostics.Process]::Start($StartInfo)   ◁─┐ Start the
}                                                    ❸ process
```

CHAPTER 13   SECURITY, SECURITY, SECURITY

Since the function will prompt for credentials, we don't need to give it any arguments. The first thing we do in function is to call `Get-Credential` ❶ to get the credential information that we want the process to run with. Then we create a `ProcessStartInfo` object that we will use to set the various properties ❷ we want the process to have when it starts. The most important of these in this example are the `UserName` and `Password` properties. The `Process` object will safely decrypt the `Password SecureString` using the DPAPI when creating the process. Next we set the program we want to run—the Microsoft Management Console (`mmc.exe`)—and give it the path to the MMC console file that will load the local user admin MMC snap-in. We're running as a particular user, so we want the user profile to be run and we don't want to use `ShellExecute` to launch the process because then we wouldn't be able to pass the credentials to the underlying `CreateProcess()` call. Once we've finished setting all of the properties on the `ProcessStartInfo` object, we call the static `Start()` method ❸ on `[System.Diagnostics.Process]` to start the process running.

13.5.3 Avoiding Invoke-Expression

At the beginning of this chapter, we talked about the risks around using the `Invoke-Expression` cmdlet and code injection attacks in general. If we can avoid using this cmdlet, it's a good idea for two reasons: first, not using it makes our code less vulnerable, and second, `Invoke-Expression` has performance consequences because it requires that the expression be recompiled every time it gets called. In most circumstances, it's possible to rewrite our code using scriptblocks instead of `Invoke Expression`.

In this section, we'll work through a real example were we take a piece of script code using `Invoke-Expression` and rewrite it to use scriptblocks.

The original wheres script

The idea behind this script was to come up with a version of the `Where-Object` cmdlet that had a simpler syntax. The function was created by one of the developers on the PowerShell team. Instead of typing a command line that looked like:

```
PS (3) > dir | where {$_.extension -eq ".ps1"}

    Directory: Microsoft.PowerShell.Core\FileSystem::C:\Temp

Mode            LastWriteTime        Length Name
----            -------------        ------ ----
-a---      8/13/2006   5:44 PM         3250 test-script.ps1
```

He wanted to simply type:

```
PS (1) > dir | wheres extension eq .ps1

    Directory: Microsoft.PowerShell.Core\FileSystem::C:\Temp
```

```
Mode                LastWriteTime        Length Name
----                -------------        ------ ----
-a---          8/13/2006   5:44 PM         3250 test-script.ps1
```

There's certainly a lot less punctuation in the second command line, so it seems a worthy goal. The original version of the command is show in listing 13.2.

Listing 13.2 The original wheres function

```
function wheres($property, $operator, $matchText)    ◁─────  The function
{                                                          ❶ definition
    begin {
        $expression = "`$_.$property -$operator `"$matchText`""    ◁─
    }                                                              Set up the
    process {                                                      expression ❷
        if( invoke-expression $expression)    ◁──────  Evaluate the
        {                                          ❸ expression
            $_
        }
    }
}
```

This function takes three parameters ❶—the property on the inbound pipeline object to check, the operation to perform, and the value to check against. In the begin clause of the function, we precalculate as much of the expression as possible, expanding the property name and the operator into $expression ❷. This gets rid of the string expansion step that would otherwise be performed for each pipeline object. Finally, in the process clause of the function, Invoke-Expression is used to evaluate the expression ❸ for the current pipeline object and emit the object if it matches.

This is a straightforward implementation of the function, but there is one worrisome aspect. Executing a command such as the following is fine

```
dir | wheres mode match d
```

but something like

```
dir | wheres extension eq '.ps1"; write-host hi; "'
```

will both interfere with the results we expect and execute the extra code "write-host hi". If the extra code were something like "del –force –rec c:\" then it would be more than merely annoying.

Of course, the author of this script would never do anything like this. But someone else who is just using the script might think it's actually safe to pass untrusted arguments to it. After all, looking at it from the outside, there are no obvious code injection vulnerabilities. It appears to accept a simple operator, nothing more. This is why we need to be cautious with this kind of script—because of the cascading consequences problem we discussed at the beginning of the chapter. This script appears on a blog, gets copied into someone else's application, which gets copied into a third individual's web application, and now this script that was never intended to be used with untrusted input is being used for exactly that in a network-facing application. Not a good situation. Let's see what we can do to make it more robust and also run faster at the same time.

A safer, faster wheres script

The problem with the old script was that it used `Invoke-Expression` to evaluate an expression at runtime. We want to use scriptblocks to be a bit more static in our approach. The solution is shown in listing 13.3.

Listing 13.3 The safe wheres function

```
function wheres
{
    begin {
        if ($args.count -ne 3)        ❶ Validate
        {                                arguments
            throw "wheres: syntax <prop> <op> <val>"
        }
        $prop,$op,$y= $args          ❷ Bind the operator
        $op_fn = $(                      function         ❸ Switch on the
            switch ($op)                                     operator string
            {
                eq       {{$x.$prop -eq $y}; break}  ❹ Function
                ne       {{$x.$prop -ne $y}; break}     implementing EQ
                gt       {{$x.$prop -gt $y}; break}
                ge       {{$x.$prop -ge $y}; break}
                lt       {{$x.$prop -lt $y}; break}
                le       {{$x.$prop -le $y}; break}
                like     {{$x.$prop -like $y}; break}
                notlike  {{$x.$prop -notlike $y}; break}
                match    {{$x.$prop -match $y}; break}
                notmatch {{$x.$prop -notmatch $y}; break}  ❺ Error on unknown
                default {                                      operator
                    throw "wh: operator '$op' is not defined"
                }
            }
        )
    }                                 ❻ Invoke operator
    process { $x=$_; if( . $op_fn) { $x }}    function
}
```

In this version of the function, we begin by validating the number of arguments ❶ and reporting an error if there isn't the correct number. We want to place a scriptblock in the variable `$op_fn` ❷, which we will use to implement the processing for that operator. We use a `switch` statement ❸ to select the right scriptblock to return. There is one scriptblock for each operator; for example, the eq operator is shown in ❹. If the operator isn't one of the ones we're chosen to implement, we'll throw an error ❺.

Once we've selected the scriptblock, we'll invoke it ❻ once for each inbound pipeline object. Notice that we don't pass any arguments to the scriptblock. Dynamic scoping allows the scriptblock to pick up the arguments from the enclosing scope.

This second implementation is clearly more complex; however, it does more error checking, is more robust in general, and has no code injection vulnerabilities. It is also significantly faster than the `Invoke-Expression` version. (It also makes a good illustration of the use of scriptblocks.)

There are many more examples where we can replace `Invoke-Expression` with scriptblocks, but in the end, the approach is basically the same—decide whether we really need to generate code at runtime or whether we can just select from a set of precompiled alternatives. If the set of alternatives is large, you may want to use a hashtable instead of a `switch` statement, but the principle remains the same.

This brings us to the end of our discussion of security and PowerShell. Securing systems and writing secure code can be a subtle, twisty, and arcane topic. It can also be alternately completely fascinating or as dull as toast.

13.6 SUMMARY

Let's review what we covered in this chapter. We began with a rant (sorry—discussion) on security and threat modeling. We covered:

- What security is: mechanisms for operating a computer without the risk of danger or loss.
- That security is not equivalent to cryptography and its related technologies (although these tools are used to build a secure system).
- Basic threat modeling and the STRIDE approach.
- Definitions for the elements of a threat model: *vulnerability*, *threat*, *asset*, and *mitigation*.

In the next section, we covered securing the PowerShell installation itself. This included discussions of how PowerShell is secure by default. As installed, PS limits its attack surface by:

- Having no default file association; this prevents use of attachment invocation or point-and-click social engineering attacks.
- Exposing no remote access method, forcing a hopeful attacker to depend on other tools.
- Having a default execution policy of Restricted, which prevents any scripts from running.
- Not including the current directory in the command search path, preventing working directory exploits.

- Additional issues around managing the execution path.
- Execution policy—what it is and how you can examine the current EP using `Get-ExecutionPolicy`. To allow signed scripts to run, use `Set-ExecutionPolicy AllSigned`, and to allow any local scripts to run—the loosest reasonable policy—use `Set-ExecutionPolicy RemoteSigned`.
- Script signing: how it works and how to set up certificates, keys, and so on.

The final part of the chapter covered technologies and techniques we can use for making our scripts more robust. The topics we covered included:

- That we should always store sensitive information in memory using the .NET `SecureString` class and that we can read data as a secure string from the keyboard using the `Read-Host` cmdlet.
- Working with credentials and using the `Get-Credential` cmdlet.
- Approaches for avoiding the use of `Invoke-Expression` in scripts.

Computer security is a complex, evolving field. It is obviously important to keep abreast of the latest tools and techniques, as well as monitor the current crop of threats and exploits. However, while thinking though a problem can be facilitated by tools and models, it cannot be replaced by them. In the end, there is no replacement for common sense.

Comparing PowerShell to other languages

Most people will come to PowerShell with experience using other languages or shells, so in this appendix we'll compare PowerShell to a number of common shells and languages people may know. We'll spend most of our time on cmd.exe (the traditional Windows shell) and the UNIX shells. We'll also look at a variety of issues that Perl, VBScript, and C# programmers may encounter. Along the way, we'll introduce a number of handy techniques that will be of interest to the general PowerShell user.

AUTHOR'S NOTE These sections are not strictly feature-by-feature comparisons. Rather, they are sets of hints and tips that I have gathered over the years based on questions that people have asked. They represent the most common stumbling blocks and questions that new users seem to have. Of course, it's impossible to capture every problem in an appendix. The community, through blogs and newsgroups, is a tremendous resource for assisting new users in becoming successful with PowerShell.

A.1   POWERSHELL AND CMD.EXE

The most commonly used shell on Windows today is cmd.exe. Let's look at some of the things a cmd.exe user might need to know in order to use PowerShell successfully.

A.1.1   Basic navigation and file operations

PowerShell provides a set of default aliases so the basic command names that a cmd.exe user knows are also available in PowerShell. We can do basic operations such as `dir`, `copy`, and `sort`, and they will do more or less what we expect. It becomes more complex when we start to specify options to these commands, because PowerShell uses a different option syntax. Commands are also *factored* quite differently in PowerShell. By factored, we mean how the functionality is distributed across the various commands. Cmd.exe has a small number of commands with a lot of functionality in each command. Unfortunately, these commands are hard to compose together. PowerShell has a somewhat larger set of commands with fewer options that are designed to be composed. For example, the PowerShell equivalent of `dir` doesn't have a sort option; you use the `sort` command instead. In the following set of tables, we'll present some of the most common command patterns that cmd.exe users encounter. Table A.1 shows the basic navigation commands in cmd.exe and their equivalent in PowerShell. We mentioned earlier that the commands in PowerShell are aliases. In the table, there are sometimes second examples in italics. These second examples are the unaliased versions of the commands. For example, "dir" is an alias for "Get-ChildItem".

Table A.1   Basic navigation operations in cmd.exe and PowerShell

Operation description	cmd.exe syntax	PowerShell
Get a listing of the current directory	dir	dir *Get-ChildItem*
Get a listing of all of the files matching a particular pattern	dir *.txt	dir *.text *Get-ChildItem *.txt*
Get a listing of all of the files in all of the subdirectories of the current directory.	dir /s	dir –rec *Get-ChildItem –rec*
List all text files in all subdirectories	dir /s *.txt	dir –rec –filter *.txt *Get-ChildItem –rec –filter *.txt*
Sort files in order by last write time	dir /o:-d	dir | sort –desc LastWriteTime
Set the current working directory to a particular location	cd c:\windows	cd c:\windows *Set-Location c:\windows*

Copying, moving, and deleting files are also common operations. Table A.2 covers a set of common scenarios comparing the cmd.exe commands against their PowerShell equivalents.

Table A.2 Basic file operations in cmd.exe and PowerShell

Operation description	cmd.exe syntax	PowerShell
Copy a file to the screen	type file.txt	type file.txt *Get-Content file.txt*
Copy a file	copy f1.txt f1.txt	copy f1.txt f2.txt *Copy-Item f1.txt f2.txt*
Copy several files	copy f1.txt,f2.txt,f3.txt c:\	copy f1.txt,f2.txt,f3.txt c:\
Concatenate several files	copy f1.txt+f2.txt+f3.txt f4.txt	type f1,txt,t2,txt,f3.txt > f4.txt
Delete a file	del file.txt	del file.txt *Remove-Item file.txt*
Delete all text files in the current directory	del *.txt	del *.txt *Remove-Item *.txt*
Delete all text files in all subdirectories of the current directory.	del /s *.txt	del –rec *.txt *Remove-Item –rec *.txt*

Another common way to do file operations is using the redirection operators. Of course, PowerShell supports the pipe operator (|). It also supports the same set of redirection operators (>, >>, 2>, 2>&1) that are in cmd.exe, but it does not support input redirection. Instead, we have to use the Get-Content command (or its alias type).

In the next section, we'll look at some of the syntactic features of each environment that are used for scripting.

A.1.2   Variables and substitution

In cmd.exe, environment variables are enclosed in percent (%) signs and are set using the set command, as shown in the following example.

```
C:\>set a=3

C:\>echo a is %a%
a is 3
```

In PowerShell, variables are indicated with a dollar sign ($) in front of the variable. No special command is required to set a variable's value—simple assignment is enough. Here's the previous example using PowerShell syntax.

```
PS (1) > $a = 3
PS (2) > echo a is $a
a is 3
```

There is another thing that should be noted about variables. PowerShell supports different kinds of variables; for the most part, cmd.exe variables are environment variables. This means that these variables are automatically exported to child processes when cmd.exe creates a process. On the other hand, in PowerShell, environment variables are stored in a separate namespace ENV:. To set an environment variable in PowerShell, we do

```
$env:envVariable = "Hello"
```

The next thing to discuss is how to perform calculations. The set command in cmd.exe is used to do arithmetic calculations. Here's what a calculation looks like cmd.exe:

```
C:\>set /a sum=33/9
3
C:\>echo sum is %sum%
sum is 3
```

Again, PowerShell requires no special syntax. To do a calculation, you simply write the expressions as shown in the next few examples.

```
PS (1) > $a = 2 + 4
PS (2) > $a
6
PS (3) > $b = $a /3 -[math]::sqrt(9)
PS (4) > $b
-1
PS (5) > [math]::sin( [math]::pi * 33 )
4.88487288813344E-16
PS (6) >
```

Because PowerShell is build on top of .NET, it has the full mathematical capabilities that languages such as C# and VB have, including floating point and access to transcendental functions.

Finally, in cmd.exe, there are a variety of string operations that can be done as a side effect of expanding a variable. In PowerShell, these types of operations are done with expressions and operators. For example, if you want a variable containing a file name "myscript.txt" and you want to change it to be "myscript.ps1", you would do it with the -replace operator:

```
PS (1) > $file = "myscript.txt"
PS (2) > $file -replace '.txt$','.ps1'
myscript.ps1
```

This just displayed the changed string. Now let's update the variable itself.

```
PS (3) > $file = $file -replace '.txt$','.ps1'
```

And now we'll verify that it has been changed.

```
PS (4) > $file
myscript.ps1
```

Using operators to update variable values is not as concise as the variable expansion notation that cmd.exe uses, but it is consistent with the rest of PowerShell instead of being a special-case feature that only applies to variable expansion.

A.1.3   Running commands

Now let's look at differences in how commands are run in the two environments. In PowerShell, we don't have to use a command to echo something to the screen. A string on the command line is directly output.

```
PS (3) > "a is $a"
a is 3
```

On the other hand, we also need to be able to run commands where the names have spaces in them. This is done with the PowerShell call operator "&". To run a command with a space in the name, we do:

```
& "command with space in name.exe"
```

Another difference between the environments is how scripts are run. Normally with cmd.exe, when you run a script, any changes that that script makes affect your current shell session. This has led to a common practice where bat files are used to set up the environment. The "vcvars.bat" file that is part of Visual Studio is a good example of this. When we run the file, it updates the path and sets all of the variables that are necessary for use to use the Visual Studio command-line tools. (In section A.1.7, we'll talk about how to use this type of batch file.)

This is not the default behavior in PowerShell. By default, when a script is run, it runs in its own scope so that any nonglobal variables that are created are cleaned up when the script exits. To use a PowerShell script to modify our environment, we need to "dot" it. In other words, we put a dot and a space in front of the script to run. This is described in detail in chapter 7.

In cmd.exe, when we want to create a local scope for variables, we use the set-local/endlocal keywords. PowerShell has the equivalent ability, again using the ampersand notation. Here's what it looks like:

```
PS (1) > $a = 3
PS (2) > $a
3
PS (3) > & { $a = 22; $a }
22
PS (4) > $a
3
```

In this example, in the outer scope, we set the value of $a to 3 and then display it. Then we use the & operator and braces to create an nested scope. In this nested scope, we define a new value for $a 22 then display this new value. Once we exit the local scope, we again display the value of $a, which is the original value of 3.

A.1.4   Differences in syntax

The PowerShell syntax is obviously quite different from cmd.exe, but beyond basic syntax, there are some significant differences in the way commands are processed. One thing that a lot of people coming from cmd.exe find annoying is that in cmd.exe, you don't have to put spaces between built-in commands and their arguments. This means that you can issue commands like the following:

```
C:\>cd\windows

C:\WINDOWS>cd..

C:\>dir\files\a.txt
 Volume in drive C is C_Drive
 Volume Serial Number is F070-3264

 Directory of C:\files

04/25/2006  10:55 PM                   98 a.txt
               1 File(s)               98 bytes
               0 Dir(s)   94,158,913,536 bytes free
```

and they work just fine. However, in PowerShell they will result in errors:

```
PS (1) > cd\windows
The term 'cd\windows' is not recognized as a cmdlet, functi
on, operable program, or script file. Verify the term and t
ry again.
At line:1 char:10
+ cd\windows <<<<
PS (2) > cd..
The term 'cd..' is not recognized as a cmdlet, function, op
erable program, or script file. Verify the term and try aga
in.
At line:1 char:4
+ cd.. <<<<
```

Commands can be used this way in cmd.exe because it treats its built-in commands as special cases and doesn't require spaces to separate the commands from the arguments. PowerShell doesn't have any special built-in commands—all commands are treated the same. This allows for greater consistency in PowerShell and, down the road, greater extensibility. But that doesn't help all of the people who have cd.. or cd\ burned into their "finger-memory". For people who find it to be a real problem, it's possible to define functions to work around the difficulty. Let's define a couple of these functions as an example:

```
PS (1) > function cd.. { cd .. }
PS (2) > function cd\ { cd \ }
```

Now we'll try them out. First we cd into the root of the filesystem, then into the filesystem, and finally back to the root.

```
PS (3) > cd\
PS (4) > cd windows
PS (5) > cd..
```

This works around some of the problems, but it doesn't fix everything. We still had to put a space between "cd" and "windows". Even so, many people do find this approach useful. If we want to make these functions available every time we start PowerShell, we can put them in our personal profile, which is named by the variable $PROFILE. Run

```
notepad $profile
```

Add the definitions you want to have available and then save the file. The next time you start PowerShell, the functions you've defined in the profile will be available.

A.1.5 Searching text: findstr and Select-String

A common command for searching through files from cmd.exe is `findstr.exe`. (Note that since it's an external command, it will also work just fine from PowerShell.) PowerShell has a similar command, `Select-String`. So why have a new cmdlet when the old executable already works? There are a couple reasons. First, the `Select-String` cmdlet returns objects that include the matching text, the number of the line that matched, and the name of the file as separate fields, making it easier to process the output. Secondly, it uses the .NET regular expression library, which is much more powerful than the patterns `findstr` can handle.

If we look at the help for `findstr`, we'll see that it actually has a lot of operations that aren't built into `Select-String`. This is because PowerShell uses a composition model. Instead of building a large but fixed set of operations into one command, there are more small composable commands. For example, to search all of the C# files in all of the subdirectories with `findstr`, the command is

```
findstr /s Main *.cs
```

With `Select-String`, we'd pipe the output of `dir` into the command

```
dir -rec -filter *.cs | select-string main
```

A.1.6 For loop equivalents

Iteration (that is, operating over collections of things) is done in cmd.exe with the `for` statement. This is a powerful flow control statement, but it's also rather complex. Again, PowerShell has several simpler mechanisms for doing the same thing using pipelines. Table A.3 shows a number of simple examples comparing a cmd.exe `for` statement with the equivalent PowerShell construct.

Table A.3 Examples of iteration in cmd.exe and PowerShell

Description	cmd.exe	PowerShell
Iterate over files	for %f in (*) do echo %f	dir | ? {! $_.PSIsContainer} \| % {$_ }
Iterate over directories	for /d %f in (*) do echo %f	dir | ? { $_.PSIsContainer} \| % {$_ }
Iterate over the numbers from 1 to 9 by twos	for /l %i in (1,2,10) do (@echo %i)	for ($i=1; $i -lt 10; $i+=2) { $i }

Now let's look at a somewhat more complex example. As well as iterating over files, the cmd.exe `for` statement can be used to parse files. Listing A.1 shows a `for` command that will extract and print the first three tokens from a data file.

Listing A.1 Tokenization using cmd.exe `for` statement

```
for /f "tokens=1-3" %a in (c:\temp\data.txt) do (
@echo a is %a b is %b c is %c)
```

The corresponding command in PowerShell is shown in listing A.2.

Listing A.2 Tokenization using PowerShell

```
type c:\temp\data.txt |%{ $a,$b,$c,$d = [regex]::split($_,' +');
"a is $a b is $b c is $c" }
```

The `for` statement is monolithic—there's no way to use the tokenizing capability of the `for` statement separate from the `for` statement. In PowerShell, all of the operations (reading the file, tokenizing, and so on) are done with separate components. The `[regex]::Split()` method can be used anywhere because it's not part of any particular statement.

A.1.7 Batch files and subroutines

In cmd.exe, subroutines are invoked with the `goto` statement and also use a `goto` to return to the calling location. A cmd.exe procedure is invoked using the `call` statement. PowerShell, on the other hand, has first-class functions including named parameters, optionally typed parameters, and recursion. PowerShell scripts are also callable as commands, and again recursion and named parameters are permitted. PowerShell does not have a `goto` statement, but labels can be used with the PowerShell loop statements.

Also note that there are no differences in behavior between code typed on the command line and code executed out of a function or script in PowerShell. The syntax and semantics are the same everywhere.

One of the most common uses for cmd.exe batch files is to set up environment variables. As mentioned previously, if Visual Studio is installed, there will be a batch file called "vcvarsall.bat" installed along with the product that is used to set up the environment variables in cmd.exe to do development work. It's also possible to use these batch files from PowerShell by executing them, dumping the changes that have been made to the environment, then importing those changes back into the PowerShell environment. This sounds complicated, but turns out to be quite simple. First we'll define the batch command we want to run in a variable called `$cmd`.

```
PS (1) > $cmd =
>> '"C:\Program Files\Microsoft Visual Studio 8\VC\vcvarsall.bat"' +
```

```
>> ' & set'
>>
```

Next, we'll invoke the command, piping the output into the % command.

```
PS (2) > cmd /c $cmd |%{
>> $p,$v = $_.split('='); set-item -path env:$p -value $v }
>>
```

In the body of the block, the incoming command is split into name ($n) and value
($v) pieces. These pieces are then passed to Set-Item to set the values of corre-
sponding environment variables. Now let's check the result of what we've done.

```
PS (3) > ls env:v*

Name                         Value
----                         -----
VS80COMNTOOLS                C:\Program Files\Microsoft Visual...
VSINSTALLDIR                 C:\Program Files\Microsoft Visual...
VCINSTALLDIR                 C:\Program Files\Microsoft Visual...
```

We can see that the variables have been set properly. Let's generalize this into a function that can work with any batch file. Listing A.3 shows the source for this Get-
BatchFile function.

Listing A.3   Get-BatchFile example

```
function Get-BatchFile ($file)
{
    $cmd = "`"$file`" & set"
    cmd /c $cmd | Foreach-Object {
        $p,$v = $_.split('=')
        Set-Item -path env:$p -value $v
    }
}
```

This function does the same thing as the commands we typed in. The only difference
is that we're using the full cmdlet names instead of the % alias for Foreach-Object,
and the batch file to run is passed in as an argument. (By the way, it's a recommended
practice to use the full command names in scripts rather than the aliases. The person
who's reading our scripts in the future will appreciate our efforts.)

A.1.8   Setting the prompt

One of the most common questions people moving to PowerShell ask is how can I
customize my prompt? In cmd.exe, this is done by setting the PROMPT variable. The
typical setting for PROMPT is

```
C:\files>set prompt
PROMPT=$P$G
```

In PowerShell, the prompt is controlled by the `prompt` function. This is a function that should return a single string. The equivalent of "PG" is

```
PS (31) > function prompt {"$PWD> "}
C:\files>
```

The nice thing about `prompt` being a function in PowerShell is that it can do anything. For example, if you wanted to display the day of the week as your prompt, we could do:

```
C:\files> function prompt { "$((get-date).DayOfWeek)> " }
Monday>
```

We redefine the function and now we see what day it is. Here's something else we can do: the problem with displaying the path in the prompt is that it can get quite long. As a consequence, many people prefer to show it in the window title. This can be done using a function like what is shown in listing A.4:

Listing A.4 Prompt function example

```
function prompt {
    $host.ui.rawui.WindowTitle = "PS $pwd"
    "PS > "
}
```

The result of this prompt definition is shown in figure A.1. The string "PS > " is still displayed as the actual prompt, but the function also sets the window title. These examples produce results as shown in figure A.1.

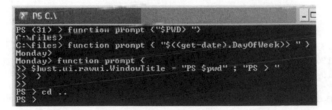

**Figure A.1
Setting in the prompt
in PowerShell**

Because the prompt is a function, it can do pretty much anything log commands, play sounds, print quotes, and so on.

A.1.9 Using doskey in PowerShell

The `doskey` tool lets us define *keyboard macros* in a console window. What do we mean by this? Doskey macros are processed by the console subsystem—the part of the Windows operating system that handles rendering the console window and reading from the keyboard. When a console program does a `Readline()` call, the console subsystem checks to see whether any macros are available for that program. If there are, it does the macro substitution on the string before they are returned to the user. So why do we care? Because it means that we can also use doskey macros in PowerShell. Here's an example that shows how to use the `doskey` utility from PowerShell. First we'll take a look to see whether there are any macros defined for PowerShell initially.

```
PS (2) > doskey /macros:powershell.exe
```

Nothing is returned so, obviously, there are currently no `doskey` macros for PowerShell. Notice that we have to specify the full name of the executable file. The default is cmd.exe, so to make our doskey commands apply to PowerShell we always have to specify the name "powershell.exe". Now let's define a macro:

```
PS (3) > doskey /exename=powershell.exe `
>>   ddir = dir `$* `| ? `{ '$_.PSIsContainer' `}
>>
```

This requires a fair bit of quoting to make sure that the arguments get passed through to `doskey` properly. If you want to define a number of macros, it's probably easiest to define them using the `doskey /file` option. Now let's make sure that the macro was defined properly. Remember, the text will be substituted on the command line, so the resulting command line has to be syntactically correct.

```
PS (4) > doskey /macros:powershell.exe
ddir=dir $* | ? { $_.PSIsContainer }
```

It looks fine. Notice the use of `$*` in the macros. When `doskey` macro substitution is done, `$*` will be replaced by any arguments to the macro. Now let's try it.

```
PS (5) > ddir


    Directory: Microsoft.PowerShell.Core\FileSystem::C:\files


Mode            LastWriteTime        Length Name
----            -------------        ------ ----
d----      8/19/2006   2:35 PM              d1
d----      8/19/2006   2:36 PM              d2
d----      8/19/2006   2:35 PM              d3
```

It displays only the directories in the current directory. Let's give it the option `-rec` and see what happens.

```
PS (6) > ddir -rec


    Directory: Microsoft.PowerShell.Core\FileSystem::C:\files


Mode            LastWriteTime        Length Name
----            -------------        ------ ----
d----      8/19/2006   2:35 PM              d1
d----      8/19/2006   2:36 PM              d2
d----      8/19/2006   2:35 PM              d3
```

```
Directory: Microsoft.PowerShell.Core\FileSystem::C:\files\d2


Mode                LastWriteTime     Length Name
----                -------------     ------ ----
d----         8/19/2006   2:36 PM            dd1
d----         8/19/2006   2:36 PM            dd2
```

This time, we get all of the directories including subdirectories. doskey also lets you look at the console command history. Let's try it. Again we have to specify the full executable name.

```
PS (7) > doskey /exename=powershell.exe /h
cd c:\files
doskey /macros:powershell.exe
doskey /exename=powershell.exe `
 ddir = dir `$* `| ? `{ '$_.PSIsContainer' `}
doskey /macros:powershell.exe
ddir
ddir -rec
doskey /exename=powershell.exe /h
```

This shows us all of the commands we've typed. But PowerShell also maintains a history of all of the commands that it executed. Since these commands are recorded after the doskey substitutions, it should have the expanded commands instead of what you actually typed.

```
PS (8) > get-history

  Id CommandLine
  -- -----------
   1 cd c:\files
   2 doskey /macros:powershell.exe
   3 doskey /exename=powershell.exe `...
   4 doskey /macros:powershell.exe
   5 dir  | ? { $_.PSIsContainer }
   6 dir -rec | ? { $_.PSIsContainer }
   7 doskey /exename=powershell.exe /h
```

Notice the commands with IDs 5 and 6. These are the expanded commands that correspond to the typed commands "ddir" and "ddir –rec". This is a way you can see what the macro expansion actually did.

doskey is another tool that you can use to help ease your transition from cmd.exe to PowerShell. It let's you define parameterized macros that can expand simple strings into more complex PowerShell expressions.

A.1.10   Using cmd.exe from PowerShell.

The final topic is how we can use cmd.exe from PowerShell. In particular, how can we use our existing scripts? The answer is that, for the most part, you can just use them. If PowerShell sees a file with a .cmd file extension, it will simply run it. The part that doesn't work comes in with all of the configuration scripts that people use. These are scripts that set a number of variables and then exit. They won't work when run from PowerShell because the cmd.exe process that's created to run them will exit when the batch file has completed, discarding any changes.

We can also run any of the cmd built-ins from PowerShell using "cmd /c". Here's an example of using cmd.exe `for` command from PowerShell:

```
PS (1) > cmd /c 'for %f in (*) do @echo %f'
a.txt
b.txt
c.txt
d.txt
```

Now let's use the cmd.exe `for` command to generate a set of files that we'll then process using the PowerShell `foreach` statement. Here's what this looks like:

```
PS (2) > foreach ($f in cmd /c 'for %f in (*) do @echo %f')
>> { $f.ToUpper() }
>>
A.TXT
B.TXT
C.TXT
D.TXT
```

From this, we can see that, as we're learning to use PowerShell, we don't have to abandon all of the hard-won knowledge we've accumulated with cmd.exe scripting over the years. We can mix and match as we see fit.

A.2 POWERSHELL AND UNIX SHELLS

In this section, we'll look at examples where we compare PowerShell to the UNIX shells, in particular the Bourne shell family (sh, ksh, bash, and so on). While inspired by these shells, PowerShell is very different from the UNIX shells. The most obvious difference is that PowerShell uses objects as the basic model of interaction instead of strings. Second, the list of "built-in" commands is both larger and user extensible. There is no difference between the built-in commands and user-created extension cmdlets. This model is necessitated by and a consequence of the decision to use objects. The out-of-process extension model used by traditional shells is simply impractical for an object-based shell. Even using XML as an intermediate representation is impractical due to the cost of serializing and deserializing each object.

Instead of doing a feature-by-feature comparison between PowerShell and the UNIX shells, the approach we'll use in this section is to work through a set of illustrative examples of each.

A.2.1 Example: Stopping all processes

To stop all processes that begin with the letter "p" on a UNIX system, we would have to type the following shell command line:

```
$ ps -e | grep " p" | awk '{ print $1 }' | xargs kill
```

The ps command retrieves a list of processes and sends the output text to grep. The grep command searches the string for processes whose names begin with "p". The output of grep is, in turn, sent to the awk command, which selects the first column in the input text (which is in the process ID) and then passes those to the xargs command. The xargs command then executes the kill command for each process it receives as input. Beyond the complexity of the number of stages that need to be executed, this command is also fragile. The problem is that the ps command behaves differently on different systems (and sometimes on different versions of the same system). For example, the -e flag on ps may not be present, or if the processed command is not in column 1 of the output, this command-line procedure will fail.

Now let's look at the equivalent command in PowerShell. The corresponding command is both simpler and more understandable.

```
PS (1) > get-process p* | stop-process
```

This command line simply says "get the processes whose names start with 'p' and stop them". The Get-Process cmdlet takes an argument that matches the process name; the objects returned by Get-Process are passed directly to the Stop-Process cmdlet, which acts on those objects by stopping them. Now let's look at a more sophisticated example.

A.2.2 Example: Stopping a filtered list of processes

Let's tackle a more complex task: "find the processes that use more than 10MB of memory and kill them". The UNIX commands to do this are:

```
$ ps -el | awk '{ if ( $6 > (1024*10)) { print $3 } }' |
grep -v PID | xargs kill
```

The success of this command line relies on the user knowing that the ps -el command will return the size of the process in kilobytes (KB) in column 6 and that the PID of the process is in column 3. It also requires that the first row in the output of ps be removed..

Now let's look at the corresponding PowerShell commands. Again, the command is shorter and simpler.

```
PS (2) > get-process | where { $_.VS -gt 10M } | stop-process
```

Here we can see that the commands act against objects rather than against text. There is no issue with determining the column that contains the size of the process, or which column contains the ProcessID. The memory size may be referred to logically, by its name. The Where cmdlet can inspect the incoming object directly and refer to its properties. The comparison of the value for that property is direct and understandable.

A.2.3   Example: Calculating the size of a directory

In this example, we want to calculate the number of bytes in the files in a directory. We'll iterate over the files, getting the length and adding it to a variable, and then print the variable. First, we'll look at the UNIX shell code.

```
$ tot=0; for file in $( ls )
> do
>     set -- $( ls -log $file  )
>     echo $3
>     (( tot = $tot + $3 ))
> done; echo $tot
```

This example uses the set shell command that creates numbered variables for each whitespace-separated element in the line rather than the awk command as in earlier examples. If the awk command were used, it would be possible to reduce the steps to the following:

```
$ ls -l | awk '{ tot += $5; print tot; }' | tail -1
```

This reduces the complexity of what we typed, but requires that we know both the shell language and also how to script in awk, which has its own complete language.

The PowerShell loop is similar; each file in the directory is needed, but it is far simpler, as the information about the file is already retrieved as part of the file information object.

```
PS(3) > get-childitem | measure-object -Property length
```

The Measure-Object cmdlet interacts with objects, and if it is provided with a property from the object, it will sum the values of that property. Because the property length represents the length of the file, the Measure-Object cmdlet is able to act directly on the object by referring to the property name rather than "knowing" that the length of the file is in column 3 or column 5.

A.2.4   Example: Working with dynamic values

Many objects provided by the system are not static but dynamic. This means that after an object is acquired, it's not necessary to reacquire the object at a later time because the data in the object is continually updated as the conditions of the system change. Conversely, any changes we make to these objects are reflected immediately in the system. We call these *live objects*.

As an example, suppose one wanted to collect the amount of processor time that a process used over time. In the traditional UNIX model, the ps command would need to be run repeatedly, the appropriate column in the output would need to be found, and then the subtraction would need to be done. With a shell that is able to access live process objects, we only have to get the process object once and, since this object is continually updated by the system, we can keep rereading the same property. The following examples illustrate the differences, where the memory size of an application is checked in 10-second intervals and the differences are output. First the UNIX shell script to do this:

```
$ while [ true ]
do
    msize1=$(ps -el|grep application|grep -v grep|awk '{ print $6}')
    sleep 10
    msize2=$(ps -el|grep application|grep -v grep|awk '{print $6}')
    expr $msize2 - $msize1
    msize1=$msize2
done
```

Now the same example in PowerShell:

```
PS> $app = get-process application
PS> while ( $true ) {
>> $msize1 = $app.VS
>> start-sleep 10
>> $app.VS - $msize1
>> }
```

Again, the PowerShell script is quite a bit simpler and more easily understood.

A.2.5 Example: Monitoring the life of a process

It is even more difficult to determine whether a specific process is no longer running. In this case, the UNIX user must collect the list of processes and compare them to another list.

```
$ processToWatch=$( ps -e | grep application | awk '{ print $1 }'
$ while [ true ]
> do
>     sleep 10
>     processToCheck=$(ps -e |grep application |awk '{print $1}' )
>     if [ -z "$processToCheck" -or \
>        "$processToWatch" != "$processToCheck" ]
>     then
>        echo "Process application is not running"
>        return
>     fi
> done
```

In PowerShell it looks like:

```
PS (1) > $processToWatch = get-process application
PS (2) > $processToWatch.WaitForExit()
```

As is seen in this example, the PowerShell user need only collect the object and then just wait to be notified that the object has exited.

A.2.6 Example: Checking for prerelease binaries

Suppose we want to determine which processes were compiled as prerelease code. This information is not kept in the standard UNIX executable, so we would need a set of specialized utilities to add this information to the binary and then another set of utilities to collect this information. These utilities do not exist; it is not possible to accomplish this task. This information is, however, part of the standard Windows executable file format. Here's how we can use PowerShell to find out which of the running processes on the system are marked as prerelease binaries.

```
PS (1) > get-process | where {
>> $_.mainmodule.FileVersioninfo.isPreRelease}
>>
Handles  NPM(K)   PM(K)   WS(K) VS(M)  CPU(s)     Id ProcessName
-------  ------   -----   ----- -----  ------     -- -----------
    643      88    1024    1544    15   14.06   1700 AdtAgent
    453      15   25280    7268   199   91.70   3952 devenv
```

In this example, we're using a cascade of properties. The appropriate property from the process object (MainModule) is inspected, the property FileVersionInfo is referenced (a property of MainModule), and the value of the property IsPreRelease is used to filter the results. If IsPreRelease is true, the objects that are output by the Get-Process cmdlet are output.

A.2.7   Example: Uppercasing a string

The availability of methods on objects creates an explosion of possibilities. For example, if we want to change the case of a string from lowercase to uppercase, we would do the following in a UNIX shell.

```
$ echo "this is a string" | tr [:lower:] [:upper:]
```

or

```
$ echo "this is a string" | tr '[a-z]' '[A-Z]'
```

Now let's see what this looks like in PowerShell:

```
PS (1) > "this is a string".ToUpper()
```

Here we can use the ToUpper() method on the string object instead of having to use external commands such as tr to do the mapping.

A.2.8   Example: Inserting text into a string

Now let's look at another example using methods. Suppose we want the string "ABC" to be inserted after the first character in the word "string", so we have the result "sABCtring". Here's how to do it with the UNIX shell, which requires using the sed command.

```
$ echo "string" | sed "s|\(.\)\(.*\)|\1ABC\2|"
```

We could use the same approach—regular expressions—in PowerShell, which looks like:

```
PS (1) > "string" -replace '(.)(.*)','$1ABC$2'
sABCtring
```

or we could simply use the insert method on the string object to accomplish the same thing, but much more directly:

```
PS (2) > "string".Insert(1,"ABC")
sABCtring
```

While both examples require specific knowledge, using the Insert() method is more intuitive than using the regular expressions.

A.3   POWERSHELL AND PERL

If you can figure out Perl, PowerShell should be a breeze. There are, however, a couple things Perl programmers need to be aware of. The first two also apply to most other programming languages as well:

- Functions in PowerShell are invoked like commands.
- The result of a statement is not voided by default.

These two items are discussed more in the section on C# and in chapter 7 on functions and scripts.

There are a couple things that are very Perl-specific, however. Where Perl uses different sigils for different types of variables ($ for scalar, @ for array, and % for hashtables), PowerShell uses only the dollar sign for all types of variables. In fact, because it's based on .NET, PowerShell has to deal with many more data types than Perl does, so it's not possible to use sigils for each type.

Another significant difference for Perl users is that arrays are passed to functions by reference automatically. If you have a variable containing three objects and you pass it to a function, it will be passed as a single argument containing a reference to the array. Let's look at an example to illustrate this. First we'll define a function that takes three arguments:

```
PS (3) > function foo ($a,$b,$c) { "a=$a`nb=$b`nc=$c" }
```

Next we invoke it with the arguments 1, 2, and 3.

```
PS (4) > foo 1 2 3
a=1
b=2
c=3
```

Each argument is printed as expected. Now let's define an array containing 1,2,3 and pass that array to the function:

```
PS (5) > $a = 1,2,3
PS (6) > foo $a
a=1 2 3
b=
c=
```

This time, the three values all end up in $a because the array is passed by reference as a single argument instead of the elements being distributed across the arguments.

Finally a common question that Perl users ask is if PowerShell has the equivalent of the Perl `map` operation. The answer is yes—approximately. The `Foreach-Object` cmdlet (or its alias `%`) is essentially the equivalent of Perl's `map`. The Perl `map` operation looks like:

```
map <BLOCK> <LIST>
```

and the PowerShell equivalent is

```
<LIST> | foreach <BLOCK>
```

In practice, the `Foreach-Object` cmdlet is more powerful than `map` because it also allows initialization and completion blocks:

```
$list | foreach {begin code…} {process code…} {end code…}
```

And of course, because it is a pipelined operation, it is more easily composable than the `map` operator. For example, here's a way to find out what cmdlets have no alias that takes advantage of nested pipelines with `begin` and `end` blocks:

```
gal | %{$ac = @{}} {$ac[$_.definition] = $true} {
    gcm | ?{! $ac[$_.name]}}
```

This example initializes a hashtable in $ac in the `begin` clause, then for each alias returned by `gal`, it adds the definition as the hashtable key and sets its value to true. Finally, in the `end` clause it uses the `where-object` cmdlet (whose alias is `?`) to filter the output of `gcm` so only commands that don't have entries in the hashtable are emitted.

A.4   POWERSHELL AND C#

PowerShell is syntactically quite similar to C#. For example, the flow-control statements are mostly the same in PowerShell as they are in C# (except that PowerShell is not case-sensitive). There are, however, a number of common problems that C# users encounter when they start using PowerShell. These problems stem from the fact that PowerShell has shell-like parsing and semantics. These issues are documented at some length in chapter 11, but we'll reiterate them here in a condensed form.

A.4.1   Calling functions and commands

PowerShell functions are commands and are invoked like commands, not like methods. This means that if you have a function called `my-function` that takes three arguments, it will be invoked like:

```
my-command 1 2 3
```

not

```
my-command(1,2,3)
```

The latter example is actually invoking the command with a single argument that is an array of three values, not three separate arguments.

A.4.2 Calling methods

Methods are invoked in PowerShell as they are in C# except that *spaces are not permitted* between the name of a method call and the opening parenthesis of the arguments. Therefore the expression

```
$data.method($a1, $a2)
```

is valid but

```
$data.method ($a1, $a2)
```

will result in a syntax error. Similarly, spaces are not permitted around the period (.) between the expression and the method name. These restrictions are needed because of the way PowerShell parses expressions and how it parses command parameters. Because command parameters are separated by spaces, allowing spaces in method calls can lead to confusion. Chapter 2 discusses this topic in much greater detail.

A.4.3 Returning values

PowerShell supports multiple *implicit* returns from a function. By *implicit*, we mean that values are simply emitted from a function without using the `return` statement. The following function

```
function foo { 13 }
```

will return the number 13, and the function

```
function bar ( 10; 11; 12 }
```

will return three values: 10, 11, and 12. While this seems odd in a programming language, it makes perfect sense in a shell (remember, it's named Power*Shell* for a reason). In fact, this characteristic can greatly simplify our code because we don't need to explicitly accumulate the data when we want to return a collection from a function. The system will take care of that for us.

A corollary is that, by default, the return value of a statement is not voided. This means that if we call a method that returns a value we aren't going to use, we have to explicitly discard it, either by casting it to `[void]` or redirecting output to `$null`. For example, adding a value to an `ArrayList` returns a number indicating the number of elements in the collection. See chapter 7 for the full details of the behavior of PowerShell functions.

A.4.4 Variables and scoping

Unlike most programming languages, PowerShell is dynamically scoped. This means that the variables in the calling function are visible in the called function. Variables come into existence on first assignment and vanish when they go out of scope. You can use scope modifiers to explicitly change variables in other scopes if necessary.

While PowerShell does not require variables to be typed, it is possible to add type constraints to them. The semantics, however, are not quite the same as in C#. In PowerShell, a type-constrained variable will accept any value that can be converted to the constraining type rather than strictly requiring that the value be of the same type or a subtype.

A.5　POWERSHELL AND VBSCRIPT

If cmd.exe is the traditional shell on Windows, VBScript has become the standard scripting tool on Windows. Let's look at some things a VBScript user should know when working with PowerShell.

PowerShell shares very little syntax with VBScript, which is mostly due to the verbosity of that syntax. Because the primary mode of use of PowerShell is as an interactive shell, we chose the more concise C-style syntax. (The fact that the two languages are so different may actually help the VBScript user, as they are less likely to get mixed up between PowerShell and VBScript.)

> **AUTHOR'S NOTE** Most of the issues that were discussed in section A.4 also apply to VBScript (and, indeed, most other programming languages). This section contains material that is more specific to VBScript.

Since management scripting in VBScript is mostly about working with COM and WMI objects, the most important thing for a VBScript user to know about are the equivalents to `CreateObject()` for creating COM objects and `GetObject()` for getting instances of WMI objects. The way to create a COM object in PowerShell is with the `New-Object` command as in:

```
$ie = New-Object -com InternetExplorer.Application
```

And the way to get a WMI object is with the `Get-WmiObject` cmdlet:

```
$tz = Get-WMIObject win32_timezone
```

Chapter 12 covers these subjects in detail. That chapter also includes a comparison of the same script written in VBScript and in PowerShell.

While these are the most important operational details for a VBScript user, there are a number of other points that are useful to know:

- Variables always begin with a "$" like $a.
- Method invocations must always include the parentheses in the method name, since it is possible for an object to have a property named `SomeName` and a method `SomeName()`.
- Attempting to read nonexistent object properties does not cause an error.
- There is no "Set" keyword for setting object properties.

- PowerShell strings can be delimited with either single or double quotes. Inside double quotes, escape sequences and variable references are expanded. See chapter 3 for details on how this works and how to use it.

- PowerShell uses quite different comparison operators: -lt instead of "<" for less-than, -gt instead of ">" for greater-than, and so on. See chapter 4 for the details on PowerShell operators. PowerShell comparisons are also case-insensitive by default.

- Arrays are indexed using square brackets instead of parentheses. Assigning to an element in an array looks like:

```
$a[2] = "Hello"
```

- The plus (+) operator is used for concatenating strings and arrays. The type of the left-hand argument controls the type of the conversion. See chapter 7 for details.

- The PowerShell syntax is very C-like in that statement blocks are delimited with braces "{" and "}" instead of keywords. For example, in PowerShell we would write

```
if ($false -neq $true)  { "false is not true "}
```

instead of

```
If (False <> True) Then
    MsgBox "false is not true"
End If
```

- Multiple statements on one line are separated with the semicolon ";" instead of the colon as in VBScript.

- Like in VBScript, if a statement is syntactically complete at the end of the line, no line termination is needed. However, if a PowerShell statement is not complete, it may be spread across several lines without explicit continuation. If a continuation character is needed, continuation is specified by a single backtick "`" at the end of the line. Note that backtick (`) is not the same character as single-quote (').

- While PowerShell doesn't have the exact equivalent of option explicit. which requires a variable to be declared before it can be used, it does have a feature that requires that variables be *initialized* before they are used. This is turned on with the following command:

```
set-psdebug -strict
```

- Any expression that returns a value in a function will become part of the return value of the function. There is no need to assign to the function name. There is also a return statement in PowerShell that is only needed if you want to change the flow of control in the function and return early. For example, in VBScript, we might write

```
Function GetHello
    GetHello = "Hello"
End Function
```

- The PowerShell equivalent is simply

```
function Get-Hello { "Hello" }
```

- The closest equivalent to the VB on error construct is the PowerShell trap statement, which is covered in chapter 9.

Even with all of these differences, sometimes it's surprisingly easy to translate a VBScript into a PowerShell script. This is because, in many cases, we're working with the same set of WMI or COM objects. Of course, some other things are done quite differently—string manipulation being a prime example. Take a look at the examples in section 12.2.4 to see an example of a small VBScript translated into a PowerShell script

Also, even when the translations are simple, they rarely take advantage of the features that PowerShell has for creating more concise scripts.

Lastly, by using the ScriptControl COM object, it's possible to include fragments of VBScript code in a PowerShell script.

Admin examples

Although this book is not intended to be a solutions cookbook, it's always handy to have a few domain-specific examples. This section contains a number of short examples showing how common administration tasks might be accomplished with PowerShell.

B.1 GETTING ACTIVE DIRECTORY DOMAIN INFORMATION

The following script will list the active directory information for a list of computers. If no computer names are provided, it shows the domain information for this computer. You can optionally specify a set of properties to return.

To display the domain information for the current host:

```
Get-DomainInfo
```

or

```
Get-DomainInfo .
```

To display the domain information for a set of machines:

```
Get-DomainInfo machine1, machine2, machine3
```

To get the domain information for a list of machines stored in a text file:

```
Get-Content machines.txt | Get-DomainInfo
```

To list only the domain name and domain controller name for the current machine:

```
Get-DomainInfo -Properties DomainName, DomainControllerName
```

The code for this script is shown in listing B.1

Listing B.1   Get-DomainInfo script

```
param(
    [string[]] $ComputerNames = @(),
    [string[]] $Properties = @()
)

$ComputerNames += @($input)

if (! $ComputerNames)
{
    $ComputerNames = "."
}

if ($Properties.Length -eq 0)
{
    Get-WmiObject -Class Win32_NTDomain `         ❶ Retrieve
        -ComputerName $ComputerNames                 information
}
else
{
    Get-WmiObject -Class Win32_NTDomain `
        -ComputerName $ComputerNames |            ❷ Extract
            select-object $properties                 properties
}
```

The script uses the Get-WmiObject cmdlet ❶ to retrieve the information from a set of machines and return it. If the option list of properties is specified then the Select-Object cmdlet ❷ is used to extract those properties from the result set.

B.2   LISTING INSTALLED SOFTWARE FEATURES

This script will display a list of the software features installed on a set of computers. You can optionally specify a list of properties to return (by default, all properties are returned). To show all of the properties for the current computer, simply run

```
Get-SoftwareFeatures
```

To get the software features from a list of computers, you can either pass them on the command line

```
Get-SoftwareFeatures machine1, machine2, machine2
```

or input them from the pipeline

```
get-content machines.txt | Get-SoftwareFeatures
```

You can also specify a subset of the properties to display. For example, to display only the vendor and caption fields, you would do

APPENDIX B: ADMIN EXAMPLES

```
Get-SoftwareFeatures -properties Vendor, Caption
```

The listing for this script is shown in listing B.2.

Listing B.2   Get-SoftwareFeatures.ps1 script

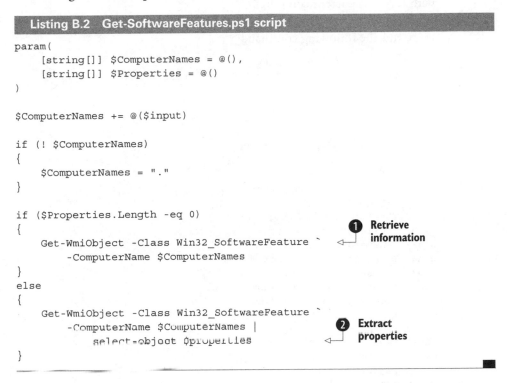

```
param(
    [string[]] $ComputerNames = @(),
    [string[]] $Properties = @()
)

$ComputerNames += @($input)

if (! $ComputerNames)
{
    $ComputerNames = "."
}

if ($Properties.Length -eq 0)
{
    Get-WmiObject -Class Win32_SoftwareFeature `
        -ComputerName $ComputerNames
}
else
{
    Get-WmiObject -Class Win32_SoftwareFeature `
        -ComputerName $ComputerNames |
            select-object $properties
}
```

❶ Retrieve information

❷ Extract properties

As in the previous example, Get-WmiObject is used to retrieve the data ❶ and optionally filter it ❷.

B.3   RETRIEVING TERMINAL SERVER PROPERTIES

Terminal server properties can also be retrieved using simple WMI queries. For example, to list the terminal server service properties on the current machine, use the following command:

```
get-wmiobject -class Win32_TerminalService -computername .
```

To list the terminal services accounts, we can use the Win32_TSAccount object as follows

```
get-wmiobject -class Win32_TSAccount -computername . |
    select AccountName, PermisionsAllowed
```

To get the terminal services remote control setting from a computer, you can do:

```
get-wmiobject  Win32_TSRemoteControlSetting |
select-object TerminalName, LevelOfControl
```

Note that in this example, we used the fact that the `Class` parameter is positional so we didn't have to specify -class. We also used the default value for `ComputerName` with "."—the current computer.

To see a list of all of the WMI classes that can be used for managing terminal services, run the following command:

```
PS (1) > get-wmiobject -list |
>> where {$_.name -like "win32_ts*"} | select name
>>

Name
----
Win32_TSNetworkAdapterSettingError
Win32_TSRemoteControlSettingError
Win32_TSEnvironmentSettingError
Win32_TSSessionDirectoryError
Win32_TSLogonSettingError
Win32_TSPermissionsSettingError
Win32_TSClientSettingError
Win32_TSGeneralSettingError
Win32_TSSessionSettingError
Win32_TSSessionDirectory
Win32_TSRemoteControlSetting
Win32_TSNetworkAdapterSetting
Win32_TSAccount
Win32_TSGeneralSetting
Win32_TSPermissionsSetting
Win32_TSClientSetting
Win32_TSEnvironmentSetting
Win32_TSNetworkAdapterListSetting
Win32_TSLogonSetting
Win32_TSSessionSetting
Win32_TSSessionDirectorySetting
```

This command searches all of the WMI classes looking for ones that have names starting with the sequence "Win32_ts".

B.4   LIST HOT FIXES INSTALLED ON A MACHINE

The following script will list the hot fixes installed on a list of computers. If no computer names are provided, it shows the hot fix information for this computer. We can optionally specify a set of properties to return. To get a list of all hot fixes installed on the current computer displaying all properties, do

```
Get-HotFixes
```

If you only want to see certain properties:

```
Get-HotFixes -prop ServicePackInEffect,Description
```

The listing for this script is shown in listing B.3.

```
param(
    [string[]] $ComputerNames = @(),
    [string[]] $Properties = @()
)

$ComputerNames += @($input)

if (! $ComputerNames)
{
    $ComputerNames = "."
}

if ($Properties.Length -eq 0)
{
    Get-WmiObject -Class Win32_QuickFixEngineering `
        -ComputerName $ComputerNames
}
else
{
    Get-WmiObject -Class Win32_QuickFixEngineering `
        -ComputerName $ComputerNames |
            select-object $properties
}
```

At this point, we can see that there is a pretty consistent solution for all of these examples. Once we know the WMI class for a particular feature, the pattern for getting information about that feature is basically the same. PowerShell makes it easy to use WMI on the command line to retrieve information about the system once you know the class name.

B.5   FINDING MACHINES MISSING A HOT FIX

Let's build on the script we wrote in the previous example to accomplish a more specific task. We want to write a new script that will search computers for missing hot fixes. Here's what we want the output to look like

```
PS (1) > ./Get-MachinesMissingHotfix.ps1 -computer . `
>> -hotfix KB902841,KB902842,KB902843,KB902844
>>

Name                              Value
----                              -----
name                              .
missing                           {KB902842, KB902843, KB902844}
```

This result of the command shows that three of the four hot fixes aren't installed on the current machine.

AUTHOR'S NOTE
Some of these hot fix identifiers are fictitious so we can see some failures. So don't be worried if you cannot find them in the knowledge base.

Notice that the output retains structure. Instead of emitting strings, we're going to emit hashtables so they can more easily be used in further processing such as building update packages for distribution. And of course, since we want to be able to check a list of machines, the script can either take the list on the command line or read it from input stream as shown in the next example.

```
PS (2) > Get-Content machines.txt|./Get-MachinesMissingHotfix.ps1 `
>> -hotfix KB902841,KB902842,KB902843,KB902844
>>

Name                           Value
----                           -----
name                           machine1
missing                        {KB902842, KB902843, KB902844}
name                           machine4
missing                        {KB902842, KB902843, KB902844}
name                           machine5
missing                        {KB902841,KB902842, KB902843, KB902844}
```

The file "machines.txt" contains a list of machine names "machine1" through "machine5" to check. In the output, we see that machines 2 and 3 are up to date—they don't show up in the output. Machines 1 and 4 are missing three hot fixes and machine 5 is missing all four.

This script is shown in listing B.4.

Listing B.4   Get-MachinesMissingHotfix.ps1 script

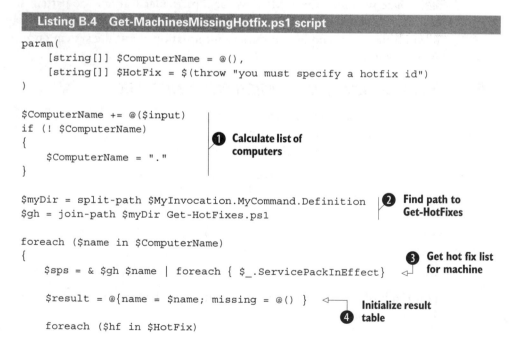

```
param(
    [string[]] $ComputerName = @(),
    [string[]] $HotFix = $(throw "you must specify a hotfix id")
)

$ComputerName += @($input)
if (! $ComputerName)                         ❶ Calculate list of
{                                              computers
    $ComputerName = "."
}

$myDir = split-path $MyInvocation.MyCommand.Definition   ❷ Find path to
$gh = join-path $myDir Get-HotFixes.ps1                     Get-HotFixes

foreach ($name in $ComputerName)
{                                                          ❸ Get hot fix list
    $sps = & $gh $name | foreach { $_.ServicePackInEffect}    for machine

    $result = @{name = $name; missing = @() }   ❹ Initialize result
                                                    table
    foreach ($hf in $HotFix)
```

```
{
    if ($sps -notcontains $hf)
    {
        $result.missing += $hf
    }
}
if ($result.missing.length -gt 0)
{
    $result
}
}
```

⑤ Add missing hot fixes

⑥ Emit result

This script takes two parameters—the list of computer names to check and the list of hot fixes to check for. If no computer names are specified, the script defaults to checking the current computer. We can specify names of computers to check both on the command line and in the input stream. We'll catenate these two lists together ❶.

We're going to require that the Get-HotFixes script be in the same directory as this script. Given that's the case, we can figure out the path to the Get-HotFixes script by getting the path ❷ to the current script, which is available in $MyInvocation, and then use this to build up the path to the Get-Hotfixes script. (This is a generally useful technique to keep in mind when you're writing other scripts.)

Once we have the path to the Get-HotFixes command, we use it to get the list of hot fixes ❸, but we want only the ServicePackInEffect field, so we'll use the foreach cmdlet to extract just this property.

We initialize the variable $result to be a hashtable object with the current machine name and set the list of missing hot fixes to be an empty array ❹. Note that we may not return this object if there are no missing hot fixes. We'll check that by seeing whether the length of the missing member in that hashtable is 0.

Now loop over the list of hot fixes, checking each hot fix to see whether it's in the list installed on the target machine. If the list of installed hot fixes doesn't contain the current hot fix identifier, append that identifier to the missing array ❺ in the result hashtable.

Finally, if, after checking all of the hot fixes, the missing array in the hashtable is still of length zero, this machine has all of the hot fixes installed. If the array is non-zero then emit the $result object ❻.

B.6   WORKING WITH THE EVENT LOG

A major source of information for admins is the event log. PowerShell has exactly one cmdlet for dealing with the event log: Get-EventLog. The syntax for this cmdlet is shown in figure B.1.

To get a list of the existing event logs, use the -list parameter. This returns a collection of objects of type System.Diagnostics.EventLog. Once we have these objects, we can then do pretty much anything we want on the associated log.

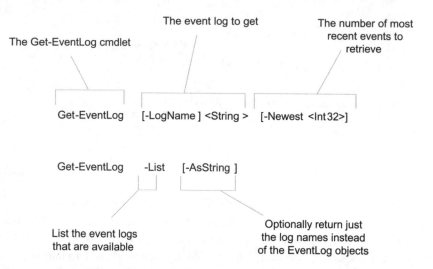

Figure B.1 Get-EventLog is the cmdlet we use to retrieve events from the event log. The syntax for this command is shown here. You can get either a list of existing event logs or the contents of a specific event log.

```
PS (1) > get-eventlog -list

  Max(K) Retain OverflowAction      Entries Name
  ------ ------ --------------      ------- ----
     512      7 OverwriteOlder           48 ACEEventLog
     512      7 OverwriteOlder        2,895 Application
     512      7 OverwriteOlder            0 Internet E...
  15,360      0 OverwriteAsNeeded        80 PowerShell
     512      7 OverwriteOlder            1 Security
     512      7 OverwriteOlder        2,105 System
```

In the output from this example, we can see that there are a number of logs available on this system.

B.6.1 Getting a specific EventLog object

Let's get the log object for the PowerShell event log (see chapter 9 for information on errors and events in PowerShell).

```
PS (1) > $log = get-eventlog -list |
>> ? { $_.logdisplayname -like "Pow*" }
>>
```

And verify that we got the right log:

```
PS (2) > $log.LogDisplayName
PowerShell
```

Now let's look at the five newest events in the log.

```
PS (3) > get-eventlog $log.LogDisplayName -newest 5

Index Time          Type Source             EventID Mess
                                                     age
----- ----          ---- ------             ------- ----
  128 Sep 14 22:52  Info PowerShell             400 T...
  127 Sep 14 22:52  Info PowerShell             600 T...
  126 Sep 14 22:52  Info PowerShell             600 T...
  125 Sep 14 22:52  Info PowerShell             600 T...
  124 Sep 14 22:52  Info PowerShell             600 T...
```

But what about the log itself? For example, let's look at the maximum log size.

```
PS (4) > $log.MaximumKilobytes
64
```

The log on this computer is currently set to 64K. Now let's double it.

```
PS (7) > $log.MaximumKilobytes *= 2
PS (8) > $log.MaximumKilobytes
128
```

As we can see, this type of manipulation is quite simple.

B.6.2   The event log as a live object

One important characteristic of the EventLog object is that it is a *live* object. This means that once we get the object, we can continue to check it for updates to see what's changed. For example, we take a look at the PowerShell log in $log.

```
PS (9) > $log

  Max(K) Retain OverflowAction        Entries Name
  ------ ------ --------------        ------- ----
     128      0 OverwriteAsNeeded          40 PowerShell
```

Currently it shows that there are 40 entries in the log. Now we'll start some additional instances of PowerShell which will create additional entries in this log. We'll pass in the exit command so each new instance immediately exits.

```
PS (10) > powershell exit
PS (11) > powershell exit
PS (12) > powershell exit
```

Now we'll check the log again

```
PS (13) > $log

  Max(K) Retain OverflowAction        Entries Name
  ------ ------ --------------        ------- ----
     128      0 OverwriteAsNeeded          88 PowerShell
```

and we see that the log has been updated with the new entries. Now let's clear the log. We'll do this is a separate instance of PowerShell to further illustrate the live nature of the `EventLog` object. Here's the command to do this:

```
PS (14) > powershell {
>> (get-eventlog -list |
>> ?{$_.LogDisplayName -like "Pow*"}).Clear()
>> }
>>
```

This command passes a scriptblock to a new PowerShell process. This scriptblock contains code to get the PowerShell `EventLog` object and then call the `Clear()` method on it. When the child process finishes running the command and exits, we'll again check the count in the current log:

```
PS (15) > $log

   Max(K) Retain OverflowAction       Entries Name
   ------ ------ --------------       ------- ----
      128      0 OverwriteAsNeeded          8 PowerShell
```

And we see that the log has been cleared.

B.6.3 Getting remote event logs

One feature that is conspicuously missing from the `Get-EventLog` cmdlet is the ability to access the event logs on other machines. Fortunately, this is easy to work around by constructing the `EventLog` objects directly. For example, to access the event log on a machine named "test1", we can use the following command.

```
PS (1) > $pslog = new-object System.Diagnostics.EventLog (
>>     "PowerShell", "test1")
>>
```

Now that we have an instance of the `EventLog` object, we can access the entries in that log as we did for the local logs. For example, to see the first six entries in the log, we can do:

```
PS (2) > $pslog.Entries[0..5]

Index Time          Type Source            EventID Mess
                                                   age
----- ----          ---- ------            ------- ----
    1 Sep 16 17:18  Info PowerShell            601 T...
    2 Sep 16 17:18  Info PowerShell            601 T...
    3 Sep 16 17:18  Info PowerShell            601 T...
    4 Sep 16 17:18  Info PowerShell            601 T...
    5 Sep 16 17:18  Info PowerShell            601 T...
    6 Sep 16 17:18  Info PowerShell            601 T...
```

Now let's get the last six entries from the log using the `select` command. These are the most recent entries in the log.

```
PS (3) > $pslog.Entries | select -last 6

Index Time          Type Source             EventID Mess
                                                     age
----- ----          ---- ------             ------- ----
   54 Sep 16 21:49  Info PowerShell             601 T...
   55 Sep 16 21:49  Info PowerShell             601 T...
   56 Sep 16 21:49  Info PowerShell             601 T...
   57 Sep 16 21:49  Info PowerShell             601 T...
   58 Sep 16 21:49  Info PowerShell             601 T...
   59 Sep 16 21:49  Info PowerShell             403 T...
```

These examples show that, even though there isn't cmdlet support for a particular feature, using the .NET classes is frequently not much more difficult.

B.6.4 Saving event logs

We can use PowerShell's Export-CliXML cmdlet to save the event log in a form that we can easily rehydrate for future processing. This is shown in the next example.

```
PS (4) > $pslog.Entries | export-clixml c:\temp\pslog.clixml
```

Now let's retrieve the data. Again, the command is very simple.

```
PS (5) > $data = import-clixml C:\temp\pslog.clixml
```

Let's compare the original to the recovered data. Here are the entries from the live log:

```
PS (6) > $pslog.Entries[0..3] |
>> ft -auto Index,Time,EventID,Message
>>

Index Time EventID Message
----- ---- ------- -------
    1          601 The description for Event ID '601' in...
    2          601 The description for Event ID '601' in...
    3          601 The description for Event ID '601' in...
    4          601 The description for Event ID '601' in...
```

And here are the entries from the rehydrated data:

```
PS (7) > $data[0..3] |
>> ft -auto Index,Time,EventID,Message
>>

Index Time EventID Message
----- ---- ------- -------
    1          601 The description for Event ID '601' in...
    2          601 The description for Event ID '601' in...
    3          601 The description for Event ID '601' in...
    4          601 The description for Event ID '601' in...
```

So the contents are more or less identical. Of course, the rehydrated data has one significant difference: It's no longer a live object. It has no methods, and changing any of the properties will have no effect on the system.

B.6.5 Writing events

The other major thing that's missing from the PowerShell event log support is the ability to write events. Again, we can work around this by using the .NET classes. In the following example, we'll add some events to the PowerShell event log. First we need to create an event source:

```
PS (1) > [System.Diagnostics.EventLog]::CreateEventSource(
>>     "me", "PowerShell")
>>
```

Next, we'll get the PowerShell event log on this machine:

```
PS (2) > $pslog = new-object System.Diagnostics.EventLog (
>>     "PowerShell", ".")
>>
```

And set it the event source for this object to match the event source we just created.

```
PS (2) > $pslog.Source="me"
```

Now we can use this object to write a log entry by calling the `WriteEntry()` method.

```
PS (4) > $pslog.WriteEntry("Hi")
```

Finally, we'll verify that the event has been written to the log.

```
PS (5) > $pslog.Entries | select -last 8

Index Time              Type Source          EventID Mess
                                                     age
----- ----              ---- ------          ------- ----
    2 Sep 16 17:18      Info PowerShell          601 T...
    3 Sep 16 17:18      Info PowerShell          601 T...
    4 Sep 16 17:18      Info PowerShell          601 T...
    5 Sep 16 17:18      Info PowerShell          601 T...
    6 Sep 16 17:18      Info PowerShell          601 T...
    7 Sep 16 17:18      Info PowerShell          601 T...
    8 Sep 16 17:18      Info PowerShell          403 T...
    9 Sep 16 17:30      Info me                    0 Hi
```

And we see that our event has been added to the log.

B.7 WORKING WITH EXISTING UTILITY COMMANDS

Let's look at how to we can take the text output from an existing utility program and convert it into a form that is more usable in PowerShell. In this example, we'll process the output of the task scheduler utility "schtasks.exe". First let's take a look at what the output of this command looks like:

```
PS (1) > schtasks

TaskName                               Next Run Time
  Status
===================================== =======================
= ===============
AppleSoftwareUpdate                    12:45:00, 9/30/2006

MP Scheduled Scan                      02:06:00, 9/26/2006
```

This output is a stream of text that we want to turn into objects so we can do things such as sort it. We want the converted output of this command to look like:

```
PS (2) > get-sched

TaskName         NextRunTime         Status
--------         -----------         ------
AppleSoftwareUpd... 9/30/2006 12:45:...
MP Scheduled Sca... 9/26/2006 2:06:0...
```

I'll admit formatting limitations in this example don't make it look very attractive. The more interesting part is that we can then sort the data by NextRunTime by simply doing:

```
PS (3) > get-sched | sort NextRunTime

TaskName         NextRunTime         Status
--------         ---------- .        ------
MP Scheduled Sca... 9/26/2006 2:06:0...
AppleSoftwareUpd... 9/30/2006 12:45:...
```

The source for this script is shown in listing B.5. This script is a good illustration of how to bring the old world of string-based utilities into the new PowerShell world of objects.

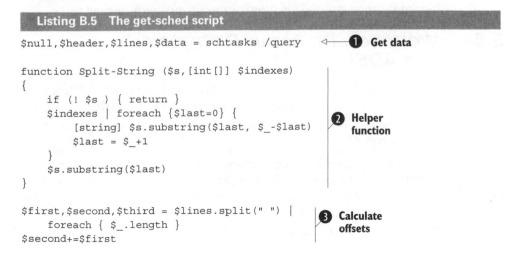

Listing B.5   The get-sched script

```
$null,$header,$lines,$data = schtasks /query      ◁──❶ Get data

function Split-String ($s,[int[]] $indexes)
{
    if (! $s ) { return }
    $indexes | foreach {$last=0} {                    ❷ Helper
        [string] $s.substring($last, $_-$last)          function
        $last = $_+1
    }
    $s.substring($last)
}

$first,$second,$third = $lines.split(" ") |          ❸ Calculate
    foreach { $_.length }                                offsets
$second+=$first
```

```
$h1,$h2,$h3 = split-string $header $first, $second |        ➍  Get property
    foreach { $_ -replace " " }                                   names

$data | foreach {                                            ➎  Split up
    $v1, [datetime] $v2, $v3 = split-string $_ $first, $second ◁┘  data

    new-object psobject |                                    ➏  Build
        add-member -pass -mem NoteProperty $h1 $v1 |             objects
        add-member -pass -mem NoteProperty $h2 $v2 |
        add-member -pass -mem NoteProperty $h3 $v3
}
```

Get the data from the command ➊. As we saw earlier, this data has the format:
empty line, followed by a line of headers, followed by underlines separating the header
from the data and finally the data. We use multiple assignment to separate each of the
sections into its own variable (assigning to null just discards the data). This leaves the
collection of data records in $data.

Next we define a helper function ➋ that will split strings into chunks at specific
offsets. We'll use that to split apart the data records.

Now we'll figure out how wide the fields are by parsing the underlining ➌. We'll
split the underlining string on spaces, then get the length of each of these strings and
use those lengths as offsets to split the data into fields.

Next we want to reformat the headers ➍ so we can use them as the names of the
properties in the objects we're going to build. We'll do this by splitting the header line
up and then removing the spaces from the names.

Finally, turn the data lines into objects with properties. Split each line of data into
three chunks using the offsets we calculated ➎, and then construct a synthetic object
and attach note properties ➏ using the header names above. We also know the second field is a DateTime object, so we'll throw in a cast so it's a strongly typed object
instead of just a string. This allows for more intelligent sorting.

B.8 WORKING WITH ACTIVE DIRECTORY AND ADSI

Active Directory (AD), which was introduced with Windows 2000, is the cornerstone
of Windows enterprise management. It's a hierarchical database that is used to manage all kinds of enterprise data. In this example, we'll look at how PowerShell can be
used to script AD.

AUTHOR'S NOTE All of the examples shown in this section were done using ADAM—Active
Directory Application Mode—a free download from Microsoft.com.
ADAM is a standalone Active Directory implementation that doesn't require
Windows Server to run. It can be installed on a computer running Windows
XP. It's a great tool for learning about Active Directory.

As with WMI, the keys to PowerShell's AD support are the ADSI (Active Directory Service Interface) object adapter and the [ADSI] type shortcut. For the purpose of these examples, we've set up an Active Directory installation for a fictitious company "Fabrikam.com".

AUTHOR'S NOTE	Although the first version of PowerShell does include features that make ADSI easier to work with than in other environments, it's still not ideal. The best solution would be to have an AD provider that would let us navigate Active Directory in much the same way as we navigate the filesystem or the registry. Unfortunately, as the PowerShell architect is fond of saying, "to ship is too choose". There's always a next version.

B.8.1 Accessing the Active Directory service

Here's how we can access the Fabrikam AD service. We take the LDAP (Lightweight Directory Access Protocol) URL for the service and cast it into an ADSI object.

```
PS (1) > $domain = [ADSI] `
>>    "LDAP://localhost:389/dc=NA,dc=fabrikam,dc=com"
>>
```

Now that we've connected to the Active Directory service, we want to create a new organizational unit for the human resources (HR) department. We can use the Create() method on the object in $domain to do this.

```
PS (2) > $newOU = $domain.Create("OrganizationalUnit", "ou=HR")
PS (3) > $newOU.SetInfo()
```

Once we've created the object, we need to call SetInfo() to cause the server to be updated.

B.8.2 Adding a user

To retrieve the object that represents the organizational unit we just created, again we use an [ADSI] cast, but this time we include the element "ou=HR" in the URL.

```
PS (5) > $ou = [ADSI] `
>>    "LDAP://localhost:389/ou=HR,dc=NA,dc=fabrikam,dc=com"
>>
```

Now we want to create a user object in this department. We'll use the Create() method on the object in $ou to create a new "user" object that has the CN (common name) "Dogbert".

```
PS (6) > $newUser = $ou.Create("user", "cn=Dogbert")
```

And we also want to set some properties on this user, so we use the Put() method on the user object to do this. (The set of properties we can set is defined by the AD schema for the user object.)

```
PS (7) > $newUser.Put("title", "HR Consultant")
PS (8) > $newUser.Put("employeeID", 1)
```

```
PS (9) > $newUser.Put("description", "Dog")
PS (10) > $newUser.SetInfo()
```

We set the `title`, `employeeID`, and `description` properties for this user and then call `SetInfo()` to update the server when we're done.

As one might expect, to retrieve this user object again, we use a URL with the path element "cn=Dogbert" added to it.

```
PS (12) > $user = [ADSI] ("LDAP://localhost:389/" +
>>   "cn=Dogbert,ou=HR,dc=NA,dc=fabrikam,dc=com")
>>
```

We should verify that the properties have been set, so let's display them:

```
PS (13) > $user.title
HR Consultant
PS (14) > $user.Description
Dog
```

B.8.3 Adding a group of users

Now let's see how we can create a bunch of users all at once. We'll define a set of data objects where the object contains a `name` property that will be used to name the employee and additional properties to set for the user. In this example, we'll define this data as an array of hashtables:

```
PS (15) > $data =
>> @{
>>   Name="Catbert"
>>   Title="HR Boss"
>>   EmployeeID=2
>>   Description = "Cat"
>> },
>> @{
>>   Name="Birdbert"
>>   Title="HR Flunky 1"
>>   EmployeeID=3
>>   Description = "Bird"
>> },
>> @{
>>   Name="Mousebert"
>>   Title="HR Flunky 2"
>>   EmployeeID=4
>>   Description = "Mouse"
>> },
>> @{
>>   Name="Fishbert"
>>   Title="HR Flunky 3"
>>   EmployeeID=5
>>   Description = "Fish"
>> }
>>
```

Now let's write a function to process this data and add these users to Active Directory. We'll call this function New-Employee. This function takes two arguments—the list of employee objects to create and, optionally, the organizational unit to create them in. This defaults to the OU we created.

```
PS (16) > function New-Employee (
>>      $employees =
>>          $(throw "You must specify at least one employee to add"),
>>      [ADSI] $ou =
>>          "LDAP://localhost:389/ou=HR,dc=NA,dc=fabrikam,dc=com"
>> )
>> {
>>      foreach ($record in $employees)
>>      {
>>          $newUser = $ou.Create("user", "cn=$($record.Name)")
>>          $newUser.Put("title", $record.Title)
>>          $newUser.Put("employeeID", $record.employeeID)
>>          $newUser.Put("description", $record.Description)
>>          $newUser.SetInfo()
>>      }
>> }
>>
```

This function iterates over the list of employees, creating each one, then setting the properties, and writing the object back to the server.

This function doesn't care what type of objects are in $employees (or even if it's a collection). The only thing that matters is that the objects have the correct set of properties. This means that instead of using a hashtable, you could use an XML object or the result of using the Import-Csv cmdlet.

AUTHOR'S NOTE Using Import-Csv is particularly interesting because it means that you can use a spreadsheet application to enter the data for your users, export the spreadsheet to a CSV file, and run a simple command like

```
New-Employee (Import-Csv usersToCreate.csv)
```

to import all of the users from that spreadsheet into AD.

We'll also write another function Get-Employee that can be used to retrieve employees from an OU. This function allows wildcards to be used when matching the employee name. It's also optional, and all employees will be returned by default. Again, we'll default the OU to be "ou=HR".

```
PS (17) > function Get-Employee (
>>      [string] $name='*',
>>      [adsi] $ou =
>>          "LDAP://localhost:389/ou=HR,dc=NA,dc=fabrikam,dc=com"
>> )
>> {
>>      [void] $ou.psbase
```

```
>>         $ou.psbase.Children | where { $_.name -like $name}
>>
>> }
>>
```

Now let's try out these functions. First we'll use New-Employee to populate the OU with user objects.

```
PS (18) > New-Employee $data
```

Then we'll use Get-Employee to retrieve the users. We'll display the name, title, and homePhone properties for each user.

```
PS (19) > Get-Employee | Format-Table name,title,homePhone
```

```
name                    title                   homePhone
----                    -----                   ---------
{Birdbert}              {HR Flunky 1}           {}
{Catbert}               {HR Boss}               {}
{Dogbert}               {HR Consultant}         {}
{Fishbert}              {HR Flunky 3}           {}
{Mousebert}             {HR Flunky 2}           {}
```

This shows all of the users and their titles. Since we didn't set the home phone number property when we created the users, that field shows up as empty.

Of course, this raises the question—how can we update the user properties after we've created the users?

B.8.4   Updating user properties

We'll create another function to do this called Set-EmployeeProperty. This function will take a list of employees and a hashtable containing a set of properties to apply to each employee. As always, we'll default the OU to be "HR".

```
PS (20) > function Set-EmployeeProperty (
>>      $employees =
>>      $(throw "You must specify at least one employee"),
>>      [hashtable] $properties =
>>        $(throw "You muset specify some properties"),
>>      [ADSI] $ou =
>>        "LDAP://localhost:389/ou=HR,dc=NA,dc=fabrikam,dc=com"
>> )
>> {
>>      foreach ($employee in $employees)
>>      {
>>      if ($employee -isnot [ADSI])
>>      {
>>            $employee = get-employee $employee $ou
>>        }
>>
>>        foreach ($property in $properties.Keys)
>>        {
>>            $employee.Put($property, $properties[$property])
```

```
>>         }
>>         $employee.SetInfo()
>>     }
>> }
>>
```

Unlike the New-Employee function, this time we're requiring the properties object be a hashtable because we're going to use the Keys property to get the list of properties to set on the user object. (This is similar to the Form function that we saw back in chapter 11.) We're also using the Get-Employee function to retrieve the user objects to set.

Now let's use this function to set the title and homePhone properties on two of the users in this OU.

```
PS (21) > Set-EmployeeProperty dogbert,fishbert @{
>>     title="Supreme Commander"
>>     homePhone = "5551212"
>> }
>>
```

And verify the changes using the Get-Employee function.

```
PS (22) > Get-Employee | ft name,title,homePhone

name                    title                   homePhone
----                    -----                   --------
{Birdbert}              {HR Flunky 1}           {}
{Catbert}               {HR Boss}               {}
{Dogbert}               {Supreme Commander}     {5551212}
{Fishbert}              {Supreme Commander}     {5551212}
{Mousebert}             {HR Flunky 2}           {}
```

We can see that the titles for the specified objects have been updated and the phone numbers for those users are now set.

B.8.5   Removing users

The last thing to do is figure out how to remove a user. Again, we'll write a function to do this called Remove-Employee.

```
PS (23) > function Remove-Employee (
>>     $employees =
>>         $(throw "You must specify at least one employee"),
>>     [ADSI] $ou =
>>         "LDAP://localhost:389/ou=HR,dc=NA,dc=fabrikam,dc=com"
>> )
>> {
>>     foreach ($employee in $employees)
>>     {
>>     if ($employee -isnot [ADSI])
>>     {
>>             $employee = get-employee $employee $ou
```

```
>>          }
>>
>>      [void] $employee.psbase
>>          $employee.psbase.DeleteTree()
>>      }
>> }
>>
```

Now use it remove a couple of users:

```
PS (24) > remove-employee fishbert,mousebert
```

And verify that they have been removed.

```
PS (25) > get-employee

distinguishedName
-----------------
{CN=Birdbert,OU=HR,DC=NA,DC=fabrikam,DC=com}
{CN=Catbert,OU=HR,DC=NA,DC=fabrikam,DC=com}
{CN=Dogbert,OU=HR,DC=NA,DC=fabrikam,DC=com}
```

As we can see, with very little effort, it's possible to significantly automate tasks involving Active Directory by using PowerShell.

B.9   JOINING TWO SETS OF DATA

PowerShell cmdlets return collections of data. In many ways, these collections are like "data tables". Sometimes we need to combine fields from two collections to produce a new object that includes properties from objects from each of the collections. In effect, what we need to do is execute a "join" across the two datasets.

A real-world scenario where this occurred was a customer who needed to export a list of mailbox users from an Exchange server to a CSV file, but also needed to merge in some additional data about each user that was stored in a separate CSV file.

While PowerShell V1 doesn't have built-in tools to do this, it's easy to do using hashtables. Here's the basic solution. Get the first set of data into a hashtable indexed by the "primary key" property. Then traverse the second set, adding in the additional properties extracted from the hashtable. (Or create new objects and add properties from both sets.)

Here's an example showing how to do this. It merges properties from collections of Process and ServiceController objects into a single object, and then exports the joined result as a CSV file:

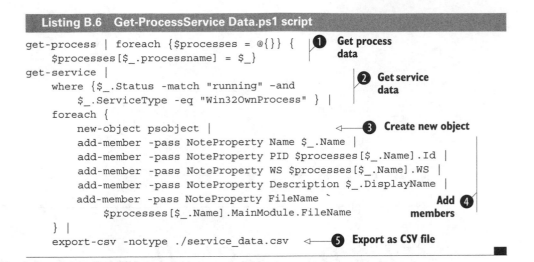

Listing B.6   Get-ProcessService Data.ps1 script

```
get-process | foreach {$processes = @{}} {          ❶ Get process
    $processes[$_.processname] = $_}                    data
get-service |
    where {$_.Status -match "running" -and          ❷ Get service
        $_.ServiceType -eq "Win32OwnProcess" } |        data
    foreach {
        new-object psobject |                       ◄──❸ Create new object
        add-member -pass NoteProperty Name $_.Name |
        add-member -pass NoteProperty PID $processes[$_.Name].Id |
        add-member -pass NoteProperty WS $processes[$_.Name].WS |
        add-member -pass NoteProperty Description $_.DisplayName |
        add-member -pass NoteProperty FileName `        Add ❹
            $processes[$_.Name].MainModule.FileName     members
    } |
    export-csv -notype ./service_data.csv   ◄──❺ Export as CSV file
```

Get all of the process data ❶ into a hashtable indexed by process name. Then get the `ServiceController` objects for all of the services ❷ that are running in their own processes. Build up a new object ❸, extracting fields from service objects and, using the service name to index into the process data hashtable, add the additional information from the process objects ❹, then export this information to a CSV file ❺. Note that the -notype parameter is used with the Export-Csv command—the synthetic object doesn't really have a type, so there's no point in including that information.

We can see that this is actually a simple example, and by simply replacing the data sources (the cmdlets) and the keys (the names of the properties), this technique can be used to do an arbitrary join between tow collections of data.

The PowerShell grammar

One way to learn a new language is to look at its grammar. This appendix presents the PowerShell grammar annotated with notes and examples to help explain what's happening.

PowerShell is parsed using an augmented recursive descent parser. The augmentations are needed to deal with some of the complexities in tokenizing the PowerShell language. This topic is discussed in more detail in chapter 2.

The complete parser is composed of a set of parsing rules and tokenizing rules. These parsing and tokenization rules are what we're covering in this appendix. These rules can be separated into five layers:

1 Statement list: the rules for parsing a basic statement list and a statement block.
2 Statements: various kinds of statements in the language.

3 Expressions

4 Values

5 Tokenizer rules

In the following sections, we'll expand on each of these topics.

C.1 STATEMENT LIST

```
<statementBlockRule> =
  '{' <statementListRule> '}'

<statementListRule> =
  <statementRule> [ <statementSeparatorToken> <statementRule> ]*
```

C.2 STATEMENT

```
<statementRule> =
  <ifStatementRule> |
  <switchStatementRule> |
  <foreachStatementRule> |
  <forWhileStatementRule> |
  <doWhileStatementRule> |
  <functionDeclarationRule> |
  <parameterDeclarationRule> |
  <flowControlStatementRule> |
  <trapStatementRule> |
  <finallyStatementRule> |
  <pipelineRule>
```

C.2.1 Pipeline

```
<pipelineRule> =
  <assignmentStatement> | <firstPipelineElement> [ '|' <cmdletCall> ]*

<assignmentStatementRule> =
  <lvalueExpression> <AssignmentOperatorToken> <pipelineRule>

<lvalueExpression> =
  <lvalue> [? |? <lvalue>]*

<lvalue> =
  <simpleLvalue> <propertyOrArrayReferenceOperator>*

<simpleLvalue> =
  <AttributeSpecificationToken>* <variableToken>

<firstPipelineElement> =
  <expressionRule> | <cmdletCall>

<cmdletCall> =
  [ '&' | '.' | <empty> ] [ <name> | <expressionRule> ]
    [ <parameterToken> | <parameterArgumentToken> |
      <postfixOperatorRule> | <redirectionRule> ]*

<redirectionRule> =
  <redirectionOperatorToken> <propertyOrArrayReferenceRule>
```

Notes:

Here are examples showing what pipelines may look like:

```
get-childitem -recurse -filter *.ps1 | sort name
(2+3),3,4 | sort

& "c:\a path\with spaces.ps1" | % { $_.length }
get-childitem | sort-object > c:/tmp/junk.txt
```

This rule also handles parsing assignment expressions to allow things such as

```
$a = dir | sort length
```

to parse properly.

C.2.2 The if statement

```
<ifStatementRule> =
  'if' '(' <pipelineRule> ')' <statementBlockRule>  [
  'elseif' '(' <pipelineRule> ')' <statementBlockRule> ]*
  [ 'else' <statementBlockRule> ]{0|1}
```

Notes:

The `if` statement is the basic conditional in Powershell. An example of an `if` statement is

```
if ($x -gt 100)
{
    "x is greater than 100"
}
elseif ($x -gt 50)
{
    "x is greater than 50"
}
else
{
    "x is less than 50"
}
```

In the PowerShell `if` statement, braces are required around the bodies of the statements even when the body is a single line. Also, the `elseif` token is a single word with no spaces. An `if` statement may return one or more values when used in a subexpression. For example:

```
$a = $( if  ( $x -gt 100  ) { 100 } else { $x } )
```

will constrain the value of $x assigned to $a to be no larger than 100.

C.2.3 The switch statement

```
<switchStatementRule> =
  'switch' ['-regex' | '-wildcard' | '-exact' ]{0 |1}
    ['-casesensitive']{0|1}
    ['-file' <propertyOrArrayReferenceRule> |
       '(' <pipelineRule> ')' ]
     '{' [
      ['default' | <ParameterArgumentToken> |
        <propertyOrArrayReferenceRule> | <statementBlockRule> ]
      <statementBlockRule> ]+ '}'
```

Notes:

The switch statement allows you to select alternatives based on a set of clauses. It combines features of both the conditional and looping constructs. An example of a switch statement looks like

```
switch -regex -casesensitive (get-childitem | sort length)
{
    "^5" {"length for $_ started with 5" ; continue}
    { $_.length > 20000 } {"length of $_ is greater than 20000"}
    default {"Didn't match anything else..."}
}
```

There can only be one default clause in a switch statement

C.2.4 The foreach statement

```
<foreachStatementRule> =
  <LoopLabelToken>{0 |1} 'foreach' '(' <variableToken>
    'in' <pipelineRule> ')' <statementBlockRule>
```

Notes:

The foreach statement loops over an enumerable collection. An example of a foreach statement is:

```
foreach ($i in get-childitem | sort-object length)
{
    $i
    $sum += $i.length
}
```

Also note that there is a Foreach-Object cmdlet that can be used to process objects one element at a time. While this cmdlet is similar to the foreach statement, it is not part of the language.

C.2.5 The for and while statements

```
<forWhileStatementRule> =
  <LoopLabelToken>{0 |1} 'while' '(' <pipelineRule> ')'
    <statementBlockRule> |
 <LoopLabelToken>{0 |1} 'for' '(' <pipelineRule>{0 |1} ';'
    <pipelineRule>{0 |1} ';' <pipelineRule>{0 |1} ')'
      <statementBlockRule>
```

Notes:

A while statement looks like

```
while ($i -lt 100)
{
    echo i is $i
    $i += 1
}
```

A `for` statement looks like

```
for ($i=0; $i -lt 10; $i += 1)
{
    echo i is $i
}
```

C.2.6   The do/while and do/until statements

```
<doWhileStatementRule> =
  <LoopLabelToken>{0 |1} 'do' <statementBlockRule> ['while' | 'until']
    '('<pipelineRule> ')'
```

Notes:

Here is an example of a do/while statement:

```
do
{
    write-host $i
    $i += 1
} while ($i -lt 100)
```

And an example of a do/until statement:

```
do
{
    write-host $i
    $i += 1
} until ($i -ge 100)
```

C.2.7   The trap statement

```
<trapStatementRule> =
  'trap' <AttributeSpecificationToken>{0 |1} <statementBlockRule>
```

Notes:

A `trap` statement looks like

```
trap { ... }
```

or

```
trap [system.nullreferenceexception] { ... }
```

A `trap` statement is scoped to the statement list that contains it. See chapter 9.

C.2.8   The finally statement

```
<finallyStatementRule> =
  'finally' <statementBlockRule>
```

Notes:

A `finally` statement looks like

```
finally { ... }
```

This statement is not implemented in version 1 of PowerShell and will result in a not-implemented compile-time error.

C.2.9 Flow control statements

```
<flowControlStatementRule> =
  ['break' | 'continue']
    [<propertyNameToken> | <propertyOrArrayReferenceRule>]{0 |1} |
    'return' <pipelineRule>
```

Notes:
Flow control statements alter the normal flow of execution in PowerShell. Here are examples of what flow control statements look like:

```
break
break label
break $labelArray[2].name
return
return 13
return get-content | sort | pick-object -head 10
```

C.2.10 Function declarations

```
<functionDeclarationRule> =
  <FunctionDeclarationToken> <ParameterArgumentToken>
    [ '(' <parameterDeclarationExpressionRule> ')' ]
      <cmdletBodyRule>

<cmdletBodyRule> =
  '{' [ '(' <parameterDeclarationExpressionRule> ')' ] (
    [ 'begin' <statementBlock> |
      'process' <statementBlock> |
      'end' <statementBlock> ]* |
      <statementList> '}'
```

Notes:
Function declarations in PowerShell take a variety of forms, from a simple function with an implicit argument collection to a full cmdlet specification. A function definition in its simplest form looks like

```
function foo { ... }
```

or

```
function foo ($a1, $a2) { ... }
```

A function that acts like a full cmdlet looks like

```
function foo ($a1, $a2) { begin { … } process { … } end { … } }
```

Parameters can alternatively be specified using the `param` statement:

```
function foo ($a1, $a2) { begin { … } process { … } end { … } }
```

Finally, a filter may be specified as

```
filter foo  ( $a1, $a2 ) { … }
```

which is equivalent to

```
function ( $a1, $a2) { process { … } }
```

In all cases, the parameter specification is optional.

C.2.11   Parameter declarations

```
<parameterDeclarationRule> =
  <ParameterDeclarationToken> '('
    <parameterDeclarationExpressionRule> ')'

<parameterDeclarationExpressionRule> =
  <parameterWithIntializer>
    [ <CommaToken> <parameterWithIntializer> ]*

<parameterWithIntializer> =
  <simpleLvalue> [ '='  <expressionRule> ]
```

Notes:

This rule captures the parameter declaration notation in PowerShell. Parameter declarations allow for option type qualifiers and initializers to be specified for each parameter. Multiple type qualifiers can be specified to allow for more complex argument transformations. Argument initializers can contain subexpressions, allowing for arbitrary initialization including pipelines. Parameter declarations look like:

```
param ($x, $y)
param ([int] $a, $b = 13)
param ([int][char] $a = "x",
    [System.IO.FileInfo[]] $files = $(dir *.ps1 | sort length))
```

C.3   EXPRESSION

```
<expressionRule> = <logicalExpressionRule>

<logicalExpressionRule> =
  <bitwiseExpressionRule>
    [<LogicalOperatorToken> <bitwiseExpressionRule>]*

<bitwiseExpressionRule> =
<comparisonExpressionRule> [<BitwiseOperatorToken>
  comparisonExpressionRule>]*

<comparisonExpressionRule> =
  <addExpressionRule>
    [ <ComparisonOperatorToken> <addExpressionRule> ]*

<addExpressionRule> =
 <multiplyExpressionRule>
```

```
       [ <AdditionOperatorToken> <multiplyExpressionRule> ]*

  <multiplyExpressionRule> =
    <formatExpressionRule>
      [ <MultiplyOperatorToken> <formatExpressionRule> ]

  <formatExpressionRule> =
    <rangeExpressionRule>
      [ <FormatOperatorToken> <rangeExpressionRule> ]*

  <rangeExpressionRule> =
    <arrayLiteralRule> [ <RangeOperatorToken> <arrayLiteralRule> ]*

  <arrayLiteralRule> =
    <postfixOperatorRule> [ <CommaToken> <postfixOperatorRule> ]*

  <postfixOperatorRule> =
    <lvalueExpression> <PrePostfixOperatorToken> |
    <propertyOrArrayReferenceRule>

  <propertyOrArrayReferenceRule> =
    <valueRule> <propertyOrArrayReferenceOperator>*

  <propertyOrArrayReferenceOperator> =
    '[' <expressionRule> ']' ] |
    '.' [ <PropertyNameToken> <parseCallRule>{0|1} | valueRule> ]

  <parseCallRule> = '(' <arrayLiteralRule> ')'
```

C.4   VALUE

```
  <valueRule> =
    '(' <assignmentStatementRule> ')' |
    '$(' <statementListRule> ')' |
    '@(' <statementListRule> ')' |
    <cmdletBodyRule> |
    '@{' <hashLiteralRule> '}' |
    <unaryOperatorToken> <propertyOrArrayReferenceRule> |
    <AttributeSpecificationToken> <propertyOrArrayReferenceRule> |
    <AttributeSpecificationToken> |
    <PrePostfixOperatorToken> <lvalue> |
    <NumberToken> |
    <LiteralStringToken> |
    <ExpandableStringToken> |
    <variableToken>

  <hashLiteralRule> =
    <keyExpression> '=' <pipelineRule> [ <statementSeparatorToken>
      <hashLiteralRule> ]*
```

Notes:

The `valueRule` is used to process simple values where a simple value may actually include things such as hash literals or scriptblocks. This rule also handles the processing of subexpressions.

C.5 TOKENIZER RULES

```
<ComparisonOperatorToken> =
    "-eq"  |  "-ne"  |  "-ge"  |  "-gt"  |  "-lt"  |  "-le"  |
    "-ieq"  |  "-ine"  |  "-ige"  |  "-igt"  |  "-ilt"  |  "-ile"  |
    "-ceq"  |  "-cne"  |  "-cge"  |  "-cgt"  |  "-clt"  |  "-cle"  |
    "-like"  |  "-notlike"  |  "-match"  |  "-notmatch"  |
    "-ilike"  |  "-inotlike"  |  "-imatch"  |  "-inotmatch"  |
    "-clike"  |  "-cnotlike"  |  "-cmatch"  |  "-cnotmatch"  |
    "-contains"  |  "-notcontains"  |
    "-icontains"  |  "-inotcontains"  |
    "-ccontains"  |  "-cnotcontains"  |
    "-isnot"  |  "-is"  |  "-as"  |
    "-replace"  |  "-ireplace"  |  "-creplace"

<AssignmentOperatorToken> = "="  |  "+="  |  "-="  |  "*="  |  "/="  |  "%="

<LogicalOperatorToken> = "-and"  |  "-or"

<BitwiseOperatorToken> = "-band"  |  "-bor"

<RedirectionOperatorToken> =
    "2>&1"  |  ">>"  |  ">"  |  "<<"  |  "<"  |  ">|"  |  "2>"  |  "2>>"  |  "1>>"

<FunctionDeclarationToken> = "function"  |  "filter"
```

An expandable string does variable expansion inside them.

```
<ExpandableStringToken> =   ".*"
```

A constant string doesn't do expansions; also escape sequences are not processed.

```
<StringToken> = '.*'
```

Variables look like $a123 or ${abcd} - escaping is required to embed { or } in a variable name.

```
<VariableToken> = \$[:alnum:]+  |  \${.+}
```

The `ParameterToken` rule is used to match cmdlet parameters such as `-foo` or `-boolProp: <value>`. Note that this rule will also match `--foobar`, so this rule has to be checked before the `--token` rule.

```
<ParameterToken> = -[:letter:]+[:]{0 |1}

<CallArguementSeparatorToken> = '  |'

<CommaToken> = '  |'
```

```
<MinusMinusToken> = '--'

<RangeOperatorToken> = '..'
```

Tokenizing numbers is affected by what character follows them, subject to the parsing mode.

```
<NumberToken> = C# number pattern...

<ReferenceOperatorToken> = "." | "::" | "["
```

The following token rule is used to parse command argument tokens. It is only active after reading the command name itself. The goal is to allow any character in a command argument other than statement delimiters (newline, semicolon, or close brace), expression delimiters (close parenthesis, the pipe sysmbol), or whitespace. It's a variation of a string token (escaping works), but the token is delimited by any of a set of characters. The regular expression shown does not accurately capture the full details of how this works.

```
<ParameterArgumentToken> = [^-($0-9].*[^ \t]

<UnaryOperatorToken> = "!" | "-not" | "+" | "-" | "-bnot" | <attributeSpeci-
ficationToken>

<FormatOperatorToken> = '-f'

<LoopLabelToken> = [:letter:][:alnum:]*:

<ParameterToken> = "param"

<PrePostfixOperatorToken> = '++' | <MinusMinusToken>

<MultiplyOperatorToken> = '*' | '/' | '%'

<AdditionOperatorToken> = '+' | '-' | emDash | enDash | horizontalBar
```

The attribute specification looks like [int] or [system.int32] and will also eventually allow the full range of PowerShell metadata.

```
<AttributeSpecificationToken> = \[..*\]
```

The following tokens make up the end-of-line token class. The tokens && and || are not parsed but will result in a not-implemented error in version 1 of PowerShell.

```
<StatementSeparatorToken> = ';' | '&&' | '||' | <end-of-line>
```

A cmdlet name can be any sequence of characters terminated by whitespace that doesn't start with the one of the following characters. This basically matches a cmdlet that could be a native mode cmdlet or an executable name: foo/bar, foo/bar.exe, foo\bar.exe, foo.bar.exe, c:\foo\bar, and so on are all valid.

```
<CmdletNameToken> = [^$0-9(@"'][^ \t]*
```

index

organizational unit, Active
Directory 515
origin 0 352
original 92
original type definition 342
origin-zero 72
out-default 52
outer scope 267, 269
OuterXml property 337
Out-File cmdlet 53, 140,
313, 318
synopsis 141
Out-Host cmdlet 53
Outlook Express 451
Out-Null cmdlet 52
output and formatting subsystem, v.s. VBScript 429
output message 263
output objects 263
output redirection 138
formatting 139
merging error and
output 139
output stream 253, 313, 411
Out-String cmdlet 53
overriding a method 233
overwriting output 141

P

PadLeft() method 316
page, displaying 408
param keyword 208, 213
param statement 208, 219, 390
parameter binder 47–48, 288
algorithm 289
steps 288
trace category 287
parameter processing 188
ParameterArgumentToken,
PowerShell grammar 529
parameterDeclarationExpres-
sionRule, PowerShell
grammar 526
parameterDeclarationRule,
PowerShell grammar 526

parameterized macros,
doskey 487
parameterized property,
definition 399
ParameterizedProperty 225
parameters 31, 45
ParameterToken, PowerShell
grammar 528–529
parameterWithIntializer, Power-
Shell grammar 526
parent scope 282
parentheses 119, 135
Parse() 84
parseCallRule, PowerShell
grammar 527
parsing 25, 37, 257, 512
modes 42, 183
process 311
partial cmdlet names 16
partial name 347
pass by reference 493
passed 179
–passthru parameter 226
password 466, 468
Password property,
ProcessStartInfo 471
PATH environment
variable 450
path parameter 289, 313
PATHEXT environment
variable 450
patience, practice, and
experimentation 311
pattern matching 114, 161, 165
operators 107
peer-to-peer networks 443
Perl 9, 26, 108, 180
security 441
vs PowerShell 493
Personal Information Exchange,
Certificate Export
Wizard 463
PHP 26
physical path 308
Pi 78

pipe operator 478
pipeline 45, 71, 148, 150, 199
pipeline object 288–289
pipelineRule, PowerShell
grammar 521
PKI. *See* Public Key Infrastructure
plus-equals 73
point class 238
polymorphic 89
behavior 145, 185
definition 72, 88
Popup method,
WScript.Shell 403
port number 364
positional parameters 183, 189,
288, 290
PositionMessage member 255
POSIX 9, 27
postfix operators 118
postfixOperatorRule, PowerShell
grammar 527
PowerShell
as a management tool 252
basic navigation
commands 477
basic structure 54
blog 364
call operator & 480
community 421
errors 255
event log 291, 294
grammar 149
help files 330
help text files 300
installation directory
319, 334
interpreter 283, 304
language, extending 238
path 308
provider 307
provider infrastructure 144
runtime 247
scripts 260
SDK 356